D1595540

Hispanic Periodicals in the United States, Origins to 1960

Recovering the U. S. Hispanic Literary Heritage

Board of Editorial Advisors

Hispanic Periodicals in the United States, Origins to 1960

A Brief History and Comprehensive Bibliography

Nicolás Kanellos
with
Helvetia Martell

Recovering the U.S. Hispanic Literary Heritage

Arte Público Press
Houston, Texas
2000

Printing and publication of this book is made possible through a grant from the A.H. Belo Foundation. Compilation of the bibliography was made possible through grants from the Ford Foundation and the Meadows Foundation. Research for this volume as well as for the overall Recovering the U.S. Hispanic Literary Heritage project has been made possible by support from the Rockefeller Foundation.

Recovering the past, creating the future

Arte Público Press
University of Houston
Houston, Texas 77204-2174

Cover design by James F. Brisson

Text design by Cynthia Alvarez and Lisa Alexander

Library of Congress Cataloging-in-Publication Data

Kanellos, Nicolás.
  Hispanic periodicals in the United States, origins to 1960: a brief history and comprehensive bibliography/by Nicolás Kanellos and Helvetia Martell.
        p.   cm.
  Includes bibliographical references and index.
  ISBN 1-55885-253-0 (cloth:alk. paper)
  1. Hispanic American periodicals—Bibliography—Union lists.
  2. Hispanic American newspapers—Bibliography—Union lists.
  3. Hispanic Americans—Periodicals—Bibliography—Union lists.
  4. Catalogs, Union—United States. I. Martell, Helvetia
  II. Title.
  Z6953.5.S66K36 1998
  (PN4885.S75)
  015.73'034'08968—dc21   98-28341
                                                                                            CIP

All photographs and other illustrations in this volume are from archives of the Recovering the U.S. Hispanic Literary Heritage program at the University of Houston, with the following exceptions: Photographs of Carlos Velasco and of *El Tucsonense* staff are courtesy of the Arizona Historical Society; photograph of man buying *La Prensa* at newsstand is courtesy of the Center for Puerto Rican Studies Library, Hunter College, City University of New York.

0 1 2 3 4 5 6 7 8   10 9 8 7 6 5 4 3 2 1

Contents

A Brief History of Hispanic Periodicals in the United States

by Nicolás Kanellos

A Comprehensive Bibliography of Hispanic Periodicals in the United States

by Nicolás Kanellos and Helvetia Martell

ILLUSTRATIONS

To the A. H. Belo Foundation Board,

especially Drs. Arturo Madrid and Judith Cravens,

who know that the Spanish-language media will continue to endure

and even flourish in our communities.

For the Kanellos clan: Mima and Pop, Charley, Maria, Laura and always Georgie.

For the Pérez clan: Doña Emma, Cristelia,

Yolanda, Joe Robert, Emma, Sonja and always José.

For Miguel José Pérez Kanellos.

—NK

A mi mamá Beatriz Martell-Ruiz y a mi querido hijo.

—HM

A Brief History of Hispanic Periodicals in the United States

by Nicolás Kanellos

The Spanish introduced the first printing press into the Americas in 1533, just fourteen years after having landed in what is now Mexico. It is remarkable that this introduction took place only forty-seven years after Columbus's first voyage to this hemisphere and just seventy-nine years after the invention of movable type. "It is surprising to find that in less than one hundred years such excellent printing was done in Mexico," stated one noted historian of printing.[1]

The tradition of the book, literacy and printing flourished in New Spain early on in colonial days. By the mid-sixteenth century, seven printers were operating in Mexico City, issuing everything from contracts and religious books to public notices and literary works. Among the first books printed were catechisms, religious works, grammars of the indigenous languages, dictionaries and some technical and scientific volumes. It was in Mexico City that the first news sheets (*hojas volantes*) and the first newspapers in the Americas were published. As early as 1541, a news sheet was issued, reporting on the devastation caused by an earthquake in Guatemala.[2]

The first periodical was the *Mercurio Volante*, founded in 1693 by the famous mathematician, scientist and humanist of the University of Mexico, Carlos de Sigüenza y Góngora, more than a decade before the Boston *News-Letter* of 1704.[3] On January 1, 1722, *La Gaceta de México* (The Mexico Gazette), the first true newspaper appeared; shortly thereafter, others appeared in Guatemala, Lima, Buenos Aires and elsewhere.[4] Journalism in the Americas thus began in Mexico, when it was joined politically to the area from South Carolina south to the Florida peninsula and west to the California coast as part of the Spanish Empire.

The actual introduction of written culture into lands that would later become part of the continental United States occurred early on as well, when in 1513, explorer Juan Ponce de León searched for the land of Bimini in Florida. Because Ponce de León recorded his travels in diaries, his voyage of exploration represents the first introduction of a written language into what later became the mainland United States. From that point on, the history of literacy, books and writing in what became the United States was developed by Spanish, mestizo and mulatto missionaries, soldiers and settlers. From then on, there are civil, military and ecclesiastical records in what eventually became the South and Southwest of the United States. Of course, this was followed by the importation of books, the translation of books to the indigenous languages, the penning of original historical and creative writing, later the use of the printing press and still later the publication of newspapers. But as Spanish settlement advanced in the Floridas and the northern frontier of New Spain (later the Southwest of the United States), printing and publishing were not allowed to take root as they did in central New Spain, perhaps because the population was too sparse to support a press and/or because mission and governmental authorities rigidly controlled the importation and circulation of printed matter in their efforts to indoctrinate the Native Americans while fending off competition for lands from the French and the British.

Gaceta de Texas

Not until the late eighteenth century was a Spanish government press in operation in Louisiana, about the same time that Spanish-language documents and books began to be printed in Philadelphia and New York. The first Spanish-language newspapers in the United States were published in 1808 and 1809 in New Orleans: *El Misisipí* and *El Mensagero Luisianés*, respectively. The first newspapers published in what may be considered the Southwest were *La Gaceta de Texas* (The Texas Gazette) and *El*

Mexicano, both published in Nacogdoches, Texas, but they were actually printed in Natchitoches, Louisiana, in 1813 (Gutiérrez, 37). These were followed by the first Spanish-language newspaper in Florida, *El Telégrafo de las Floridas* (1817); the first in the Northeast, *El Habanero* (1824); and numerous others in Louisiana, Texas and the Northeast (see the Chronological Index). However, the first presses were not introduced into California and New Mexico until 1834, during the period of Mexican national rule. Despite the late start in Arizona, California, Colorado and New Mexico, however, Spanish-language newspapers were in full bloom in the Southwest by the 1870s and continued to flourish in the Northeast. From that time to the present, the Spanish-language newspaper has been a mainstay in Hispanic communities throughout the United States, preserving and advancing Hispanic culture and maintaining its relationship with the larger Spanish-speaking world.

Throughout the last two centuries, Hispanic communities from coast to coast have supported newspapers of varying sizes and missions, from the eight-page weekly printed in Spanish or bilingually to the highly entrepreneurial large-city daily published completely in Spanish. The periodicals have run the gamut from religious bulletins to international trade and scientific journals, as both the domestic and the international Hispanic readership have always been important targets for United States business and intellectual interests.

Since the founding of *El Misisipí* in 1808, U. S. Spanish-language newspapers have had to serve functions hardly ever envisioned in Mexico City, Madrid or Havana. The Hispanic press has primarily informed the community about current affairs and politics and advertised local businesses and products. Additionally, however, most of the newspapers, if not functioning as bulwarks of immigrant culture, have protected the language, culture and rights of an ethnic minority within a larger culture that was in the best of times unconcerned with the Hispanic ethnic enclaves and in the worst of times openly hostile. As an *immigrant* press, news of the homeland and its relationship with the United States was of primary concern; as a *minority* press, the protection of civil rights and the monitoring of the community's economic, educational and cultural development came to the fore. In both roles, it was always incumbent on the press to exemplify the best writing in the Spanish language, to uphold high cultural and moral values and to maintain and preserve Hispanic culture. This mission often extended to the protection and preservation of Catholicism within the larger cultural environment of Protestantism. Quite often, too, Hispanic-owned newspapers took on the role of contestation, offering alternative views and reports challenging those published in the English-language press, especially as concerned their own communities and homelands.

While the few scholars who have researched and written on the Spanish-language press have pointed out the contestatory nature of the U. S. Hispanic press throughout its history, few have identified a third characteristic in its development: that of a *press in exile*. In fact, many of the newspapers founded during the last two centuries were established by political refugees who took advantage of the U. S. tradition of a free press to offer their compatriots (here and in their homelands) uncensored news and political commentary—even if their sheets had to be smuggled on and off ships and passed surreptitiously hand-to-hand back home. In many cases, the exile press was also engaged in political fund-raising, community organizing and revolutionary plots to overthrow the homeland regime. Often, the exile press became an immigrant and ethnic minority press as their communities became more settled in the United States and/or the return to the homeland was no longer feasible or of particular interest.

It is difficult to classify this or that newspaper as being exclusively an immigrant or exile or minority enterprise, however. Hispanic communities in the United States have been segmented among ethnic, nationality, class and religious lines almost from the beginning. And even the newspapers that sprang up in provincial New Mexico in the late nineteenth century were often divided by allegiances to particular political parties. While small weeklies could serve the specific interests of one subgroup or another, larger weeklies and the dailies often had to appeal to many varying and conflicting interests. A newspaper such as San Antonio's *La Prensa* often simultaneously represented Mexican exile as well as Mexican-American interests in the period before the Great Depression. In the late nineteenth and early twentieth centuries, New York's *Las Novedades* served the interests of all Spanish-speaking groups, including the Spanish, Cubans and Puerto Ricans—even while Cuba and Puerto Rico were waging wars of independence from Spain. In the bibliography that follows, the newspapers are self-described as anarchist, socialist, Democratic, Republican, union-affiliated, defending Mexican or Cuban or Spanish interests, promoting a pan-Hispanism, upholding Catholic or Baptist or Methodist or Presbyterian values, or as dedicated to the overthrow of fascism in Spain or dictatorships in specific American republics. They are as dead serious as the Brothers Flores-Magón's anarcho-syndicalist *Regeneración* (part of the conspiracy for revolution in Mexico) and as humorous and irreverent as P. Viola's *El Fandango* and Daniel Venegas' *El Malcriado*, 1920s satirical weeklies identified with the working classes in San Antonio and Los Angeles, respectively.

Beyond the news and advertising, the newspapers were community leadership institutions, often serving as forums for intellectuals, writers and politicians, and often spearheading political and social movements— not only in local communities but also among like-minded souls around the United States. Such was the case with Cuban and Puerto Rican revolutionary periodicals in New York, Philadelphia, Tampa, Key West, New Orleans and elsewhere, which made concerted and orchestrated efforts to further the independence movement against Spain.

The local Spanish-language newspaper assumed an importance parallel to that of the church and the mutualist society in providing leadership, solidifying the community, protecting it and furthering its cultural survival. Not always for commercial viability and financial profit, the newspapers often assumed roles associated with patriotism, mutualism, political organizing and religion. They sponsored patriotic and cultural celebrations, organized the community for social and political action (spearheading the founding of Spanish-language schools, community clinics, relief funds for victims of wars, floods and other natural disasters, and so forth). They battled segregation and discrimination not only through their editorials and news coverage, but through real-life organizing and the pursuit of civil rights through courts, consular offices and government agencies.

Finally, newspapers have always functioned as purveyors of education, culture and entertainment. During the nineteenth and the first half of the twentieth centuries, they were the primary publishers of creative literature in the Spanish language, including poetry, literary prose, serialized novels and even plays. The newspapers provided this fare as a function of cultural preservation and elevating the level of education of the community. Often work was drawn from local writers as well as reprinted from the works of the greatest writers of the Hispanic world, from the classical Cervantes to the modernist Rubén Darío. The editors, almost to a person, believed ardently in the power of literacy to uplift and improve the lot of Hispanics. They fought for education, schooling and knowledge and converted their newspapers into compendiums that offered the best examples of writing in the vernacular; the widest variety of information on scientific, historical and cultural topics; analysis of social and political issues; an interminable stream of wisdom literature (epigrams, proverbs and exemplary anecdotes); and entertainment—not only literary fare but endless jokes, humorous anecdotes and miscellany used as filler.

The impact of this publishing movement throughout this century should not be underestimated. Considerable economic resources were concentrated in this effort, and it involved the cooperation of thousands of intellectuals, creative writers, and political and business figures. The press helped to shape the fundamental identities and ethos of U. S. Hispanic communities as they developed. The language, the values, the relationship of the community to the larger society and to the lands of origin, the sex roles, the education of children, the responsibilities of the citizen and/or the immigrant—all of these were prescribed and reinforced daily in the pages of Hispanic newspapers published from San Diego to New York, from the nineteenth century at least until World War II.

The Press In Exile

An exile press is one that utilizes the vantage point and the protection of foreign soil to issue messages unwelcome to authorities in the homeland. The United States, having established itself as the first political democracy in the western hemisphere, has served since its independence from the British Empire as a refuge for other expatriates. The important tenets in the U. S. Constitution guaranteeing freedom of speech and of the press ensured that editors who could afford paper and printing would see their work in print, ready to be distributed to whichever communities, domestic and foreign, they could reach. But the *raison d'etre* of the exile press has always been influencing life and politics in the homeland—even if that goal is moved forward only by distributing publications to expatriate communities. These efforts—to provide information and opinion about the homeland, to change or solidify opinion about politics and policy in the *patria*, to assist in raising funds to overthrow the current regime—although mostly discussed within the confines of U. S. communities, nevertheless maintain a foreign point of reference. A purely immigrant or an ethnic press, on the other hand, is more oriented to the needs of immigrants and/or citizens in the United States: to assisting immigrants in adjusting to the new social environment here, understanding or affecting policy here, providing information on the homeland and/or securing and furthering rights and responsibilities here.[5]

To study the Hispanic exile press in the United States is to examine great moments in the political history of the Hispanic world: the Napoleonic intervention in Spain, the struggles of the Spanish-American colonies for independence, the French intervention in Mexico, the Spanish-American War, the Mexican Revolution, the Spanish Civil War, the Cuban Revolution, the recent civil wars in Central America and the numerous struggles in Latin America to wrest democracy from dictators and foreign interventions, including incursions by the United States. The very act of U. S. partisanship in the internal politics of the Latin American republics often drew the expatriate stream to these shores. All of these struggles contributed thousands of political refugees to the United States over time, not only because of the traditions of democracy and freedom of expression here, but also because through expansion and Hispanic immigration, the United States became home to large communities of Spanish-speakers. Thus, the refugees found societies where they could conduct business and eke out a livelihood while they hoped for and abetted change in the lands that would someday welcome them home.

The flip side of the coin of freedom in exile is the repression that existed in the homelands that forced intellectuals and writers out. The historical record is rife with prison terms served, tortures suffered and the names of writers, journalists, publishers and editors executed over the last two centuries in Spanish America. At home, many newspaper editors devised ingenious stratagems for hiding presses and hiding the identity of the writers while smuggling issues to readers in secret societies and the privacy of their homes. In Cuba, books and newspapers often stated on their title pages and mastheads that they were published in New Orleans, attempting to throw off the censor and the repressive Spanish authorities.[6]

The first newspapers printed in exile were the bilingual *La Gaceta de Texas* and *El Mexicano*,[7] printed in 1813 in the safety of U. S. territory just across the border from New Spain in Natchitoches, Louisiana (just across the Sabine River from Nacogdoches, Texas). Actually written and typeset in Texas by its publishers William Shaler and José Alvarez de Toledo y Dubois, but printed in Louisiana, both papers were part of the independence movement set in motion by Miguel de Hidalgo y Costilla in central Mexico and taken up by José Bernardo Gutiérrez de Lara in Texas. The insurgency in Texas was violently quashed by Spanish royalist troops; we know of no other pro-Mexican independence newspapers published in Texas.

The Cuban and Puerto Rican Exile Press

The longest-lasting independence movement in the hemisphere was that of Spain's Caribbean colonies: Cuba and Puerto Rico. One of Cuba's first and most illustrious exiles was the philosopher-priest Félix Varela, who founded *El Habanero* in Philadelphia in 1824. Subtitled "papel político, científico y literario" (political, scientific and literary paper), *El Habanero* openly militated for Cuban independence. Varela was one of many intellectuals within the expatriate communities in Philadelphia and New York who for some twenty years had been translating the U. S. Constitution and the works of Paine and Jefferson and smuggling them into Latin America in books printed in Spanish by early American printers.

Félix Varela (1788-1853)

Varela, however, set the precedent for Cubans and Puerto Ricans of printing and publishing in exile and having their works circulating in their home islands. In fact, Varela's books on philosophy and education (many of which were published abroad) were said to be the only "best sellers" in Cuba, and Varela himself the most popular author in Cuba in the first third of the nineteenth century—despite there being in effect a "conspiracy of silence," in which his name could never even be brought up in public on the island (Fornet, 73–4).

That Varela would launch *El Habanero* in 1824 and other Cubans and Puerto Ricans would continue the exile press in New York's *El Mensajero Semanal* and *El Mercurio de Nueva York* (both established in 1828) with scores of exile newspapers to follow in New Orleans, Tampa, Philadelphia and New York, is remarkable, given the scant tradition of newspaper publishing on these islands under rigid Spanish control. Licenses to publish had to be obtained directly from the Spanish crown, and materials were subject to review by both state and religious authorities. In 1810, the Spanish *cortes* (legislative body) created the Junta Suprema de Censura (Supreme Censorship Commission), and in 1820 the *cortes* passed the *Ley de Imprenta* (Law of the Printing Press), which severely restricted printing and publishing.[8] As revolutionary fervor rose and ebbed in Cuba and Puerto Rico, so too did censorship, repression and persecution of the press, with dissident intellectuals often suffering imprisonment, exile or death by garroting.[9]

For the most part, the expatriate journalists and writers founded and wrote for Spanish- language or bilingual publications. Some of their politically oriented newspapers were bilingual because they aspired to influencing Anglo-American public opinion and U. S. government policy regarding Cuba and Puerto Rico. Very few exiled intellectuals found work in the strictly English-language press except as translators. One notable exception was Miguel Teurbe Tolón, who in the 1850s worked as an editor for Latin American affairs on the New York *Herald*.[10] Teurbe Tolón had been an editor of Cuba's *La Guirnalda*, where he also launched his literary career as a poet. In the United States, besides working for the *Herald*, he published poems and commentary in both Spanish- and English-language periodicals, and translated into Spanish Paine's *Common Sense* and Emma Willard's *History of the United States*. Montes-Huidobro believes Teurbe Tolón to be one of the most important pioneers of Hispanic journalism in the United States (Montes-Huidobro, 135). But it is not only as a journalist that Teurbe Tolón must be remembered. He is one of the founders of the literature of Hispanic exile, not only because of the exile theme in the many poems he published, but also because he was seen as a leader of the literary exile. His work figures most prominently in the first anthology of exile literature ever published in the United States, *El laúd del desterrado* (1856), issued a year after his death. Since the writings of Varela and Teurbe Tolón and their colleagues, exile literature has been a continuing current in Hispanic letters of the United States.

Cuba's first newspaper, *El Papel Periódico*, was founded in Havana in 1790. The first book ever printed in Cuba had appeared a scant twenty-nine years earlier (Fornet, 12, 36). Puerto Rico's first newspaper, *La Gaceta de Puerto Rico*, did not appear until 1806, the same year as the introduction of the printing press to the island. In the world of literature and journalism, the creative and publishing activity of Cubans and Puerto Ricans overseas often rivaled the productivity at home, and many of the leading writers and intellectuals of both islands produced a substantial corpus in the freedom of exile rather than under repressive Spanish colonial rule. Some of the most important Cuban and Puerto Rican literary, journalistic and patriotic figures followed Varela's example—writing, publishing and militating from Philadelphia, New York, Tampa, Key West and New Orleans until the outbreak of the Spanish-American War in 1898. All of them wrote for or published newspapers: José María Heredia, José Antonio Saco, Cirilo Villaverde, Francisco "Pachín" Marín, Lola Rodríguez de Tió and, most importantly, José Martí.

The extent of commitment by literary figures to the exile and revolutionary press can be gauged by the example of Cirilo Villaverde, a seminal founder of Cuban literature now remembered for his novel *Cecilia Valdés* (1839), which critic William Luis considers "the most important novel written in nineteenth-century Cuba and perhaps one of the most important works in Latin America during that period."[11] Despite his growing celebrity in Cuba as a man of letters, Villaverde left the island for New York in 1849, after escaping from imprisonment for his political activities; he remained in the United States until his death in 1894, working as a revolutionary journalist—"a man of action," as he put it, rather than a man engaging in the vanity of letters.[12] Villaverde devoted himself almost exclusively to the revolutionary cause by writing for various exile newspapers; for him the revolutionary battle was to be found in the struggle to influence public opinion. One can only guess what clandestine political activities he engaged in.

Beginning in 1852, Villaverde began working for New York's *La Verdad* (The Truth, 1848-185-?), but before leaving Cuba he had already been sending dispatches and had helped to smuggle this banned newspaper into the country. In 1853, he and Manuel Antonio Marino began publishing their own bilingual, *El Independiente: Organo de la democracia cubana* (The Independent: Organ of Cuban Democracy), in New Orleans. Villaverde was an editor and also wrote anonymously for New York's *La Voz de la América: Organo político de las repúblicas hispano-americanas y de las Antillas españolas* (The Voice of America: Political Organ of the Spanish American Republics and the Spanish Antilles, 1865-7), *La Ilustración Americana* (The American Enlightenment, 1866-70) and for Narciso Villaverde's monthly *El Espejo* (1873-93?),[13] among other papers. Villaverde's political ideology was most reflected in the important filibustering organ *La Verdad*, which promoted U. S. annexation of Cuba. (Later he supported independence for Cuba.) *La Verdad* was created by a junta of Cuban exiles called the Club de Habana (Havana Club), who raised $10,000 for its founding, and by U. S. expansionists such as John O'Sullivan and Moses Beach, editor of the New York *Sun*, at which facilities *La Verdad* was actually printed. The bilingual *La Verdad*'s mission was to lobby the U.S. public as well as Cubans for the annexation of Cuba, but the newspaper also supported Manifest Destiny and U. S. filibustering expeditions in Latin America in addition to Cuban annexation as part of the effort to create another slave state for the South. *La Verdad* called for the U. S. purchase of Cuba from Spain, and, in fact, in 1848 President James K. Polk did tender an offer of $100 million to Spain for the island.

Issues of race and slavery were central to the Cuban independence movement and were interrelated with the politics of race in the United States. One of the more interesting revolutionary newspapers was *El Mulato* (The Mulato, 1854–?), which was published in New York before the U. S. Civil War and had as its mission uniting the Cuban revolutionary movement with the movement to abolish slavery. Founded by Carlos de Colins, Lorenzo Alló and Juan Clemente Zenea, it sounded a contrary note to the Cuban annexationist movement and its papers. The reaction among the Creole elite leaders of the annexationist movement was bitter. Editorials attacked *El Mulato* and mass meetings were called to condemn the newspaper for promoting social unrest.[14]

Proudly proclaiming the paper's Afro-Cuban identity, *El Mulato* editor Carlos de Colins challenged the leadership of the revolution to consider Cuba's Africans (he did not permit the euphemism "colored classes") as worthy of freedom, just as their country was worthy of liberty. De Colins' barbs in the April 17, 1854 issue were aimed directly at *La Verdad*: "La verdad, no es verdad si los verdaderos y lejítimos principios se confunden por el egoísmo y se contrarian por el temor: verdad por verdad y *en avant* y á los que no la conocen *go ahead*." (The truth is not the truth if truthful and legitimate principles are muddled because of selfishness and are countered out of fear: truth for truth's sake and *en avant*, and to those who do not know it *go ahead*.) In the April 25 issue, De Colins attacked *La Verdad*'s support of filibustering:

> When *The Filibuster* let it be known that *La Verdad* was no longer a defender of our rights, it was perhaps based on the fact that it was being published by an enemy of our cause, that's why we feel repugnance upon

seeing that one of the organs of the revolution is in the hands of a royalist, a satellite of despotism.[15]

Another editorial, in the April 17 issue, expressed admiration for the liberties and stability existing in the United States. De Colins sounded a note frequently repeated by Hispanic editorialists from New York to Los Angeles: fear that U. S. expansionism—in this case forcibly freeing and then annexing Cuba—would result in cultural annihilation: "¿O esperan poseerla por sus propios esfuerzos para llevar á ella su idioma, usos, costumbres y especulaciones?" (Or do they [the United States] expect to possess her [Cuba] through their own force in order to extend to her their language, behavior, customs and business?)

But the greatest fear of the publishers of *El Mulato* was that Cuba would be bought or otherwise annexed and that Cuban free blacks and mulattoes would be enslaved forever as in the southern states of the Union. The irony of *El Mulato* enjoying the freedom of the press and the other freedoms for which the United States was famous was not lost on the editors, who were combating manumission:

> In the land of the *free*, liberty enslaves, torments, oppresses, punishes, wounds and burns some people like us . . . Oh, Humanity! Where have you gone? Could it be that in the land of Washington you have decided to look for a better home in regions where liberty is truly cultivated and where men are firm and there are legitimate guarantees? While the downtrodden suffers tremendous whip lashes, he looks in vain without finding a beneficent hand to detain the barbarous strokes, he then raises his arms and his eyes to the heavens exclaiming, "Is there no freedom, great God, on Earth! Those men who invoke her [liberty], offend her with lies and they injure with cruelty."
>
> The institutions that typify democracy are opposed by their own promoters . . . vulnerable to study, they are also stained by ambition and vile profit. The people with coin lack all generous instinct. (17 June 1854)[16]

The early political perspective on race and culture evident in these editorials would rarely be duplicated in U. S. Hispanic journalism until the 1920s, in the writings of such journalists and *cronistas* as New York's Alberto O'Farrill and Jesús Colón, writing for *Gráfico*.

Partially as a result of the ideas presented in *El Mulato* and *La Voz de*

América (The Voice of America, 1865–67?), as well as in the Cuban political clubs in New York and Florida during the 1850s and 1860s, efforts were
made to expand the revolution to include all sectors of Cuban society and
to unite the separatist and abolitionist movements. A leading newspaper
in this trend was *La Voz de América*, under Cuban editor Juan Manuel
Macías and Puerto Rican editor José Bassora. Theirs was a growing trend to
challenge the elites and democratize the revolution. They stated that *La
Voz de América*

> has tried and succeeded in raising the spirit of the PEOPLE, and has final-
> ly ensured that the REVOLUTION no longer represents the egotistical
> aspirations of the aristocratic slaveholders [*eslavócratas*], but is an osten-
> sible manifestation of the desires of the PEOPLE in general. [The revolu-
> tion requires the incorporation of the] ignorant, the peasant, the cigar-
> maker, the freedman, the slave, the real PEOPLE. (30 September 1866)[17]

La Voz de América editorially urged the inclusion of slaves not only in
the revolutionary ranks but in the concept of Cuban nationality. It also
actively cultivated a following among the tobacco workers. According to
Poyo,

> Few before the 1860s had seriously considered such a strategy, but many
> now believed that the mass of slaves could provide the numbers neces-
> sary to defeat the Spanish militarily. The North American Civil War had
> demonstrated that disruption did not lead inevitably to slave uprisings.
> Indeed, slaves and free people of color helped when given the opportu-
> nity. This was an important psychological breakthrough that opened the
> door for a political nationalism (as opposed to just a cultural nationalism)
> that many had feared to promote. (Poyo, 16)

Back on the island, the rebel cause had made significant advances.
When the Republican government drafted its constitution in 1869, it
declared all Cubans free. This landmark decision had repercussions
throughout the U. S. expatriate colonies and was promoted by the official
newspaper of the Republican government, *La Revolución* (The
Revolution), published in New York from 1869 to 1876. *La Revolución* had
begun publishing one year after the outbreak of the Ten Years' War, the
most significant armed rebellion of Cuban nationalists against Spain up to
that time.

With the end of the American Civil War, annexation of Cuba as a slave state was moot. At the same time, Cuban immigration to the United States increased greatly as hostilities on the island intensified with the Ten Years' War. The tobacco industry in Florida and New York expanded dramatically. The Cubans now immigrating were mostly tobacco workers, highly unionized and politicized; they became a financial and organizational base for the final phase of the Cuban revolution—and for the publication of important revolutionary and labor newspapers (see the section titled "The Immigrant Press," below), such as Key West's *El Yara* (1878–?), named after the battle where Cuban independence was proclaimed. Founded after the signing of the Pact of Zanjón concluded the Ten Years' War, *El Yara* kept the independence movement alive. Both Cuban and Puerto Rican expatriates gradually intensified their efforts against Spain and became even more militant. Mirroring this militancy was New York's *El Pueblo,* published in the mid-1870s, which proclaimed, "Republicanos radicales, proclamamos y exigimos del tirano el reconocimiento de nuestra República para que inmediatamente pueda sucederse la paz." (Radical Republicans, we proclaim and exhort from the tyrant the recognition of our republic, so that peace will follow immediately [23 October 1875]). As long as peace was not achieved, *El Pueblo* regularly called for the U. S. Cuban community to donate money for war material:

> Our brothers who are fighting on the fields of Cuba remind us that it is very just that those of us who reside in foreign lands be indefatigable in developing funds to acquire war materials in sufficient amounts and to send them . . . The Cuban expatriate community is the richest that has been registered in history; because of the amounts of cash that it has, because of the immense value that its industry represents. The proverbial generosity and largesse of the Cubans cannot at all be doubted . . . (29 September 1875)[18]

El Pueblo had a rival in New York: *La Revolución de Cuba,* also published in the mid-1870s, which went to great lengths to prove that it was more radical than *El Pueblo* and the other political sheets: "Es el periódico mas radical, a pesar de que su Director es un hombre pobre sin otra riqueza que su trabajo y su patriotismo, sin otra aspiración que el cumplimiento de su deber patriótico" ([*El Pueblo*] is the most radical newspaper, despite its director [Rafael Lanza] being a poor man without any other riches than his work and his patriotism, without any other aspiration than the achievement of his patriotic duty [29 January 1876]). As indicated by his protestation, Lanza was probably from the working class and demonstrated that perspective in his opposition to the Creole elites.

The period after the American Civil War was characterized by infighting in the Cuban separatist movement between Creole elites (supporting annexation) and workers and intellectuals (supporting complete independence and self-determination for the island). Race was still an important divisive factor that highlighted the hypocrisy of the elite pursuit of democracy. Such factionalism—whether caused by divisions of philosophy, race or class—mired support for the revolution from within the United States. But eventually a clear leader emerged who worked assiduously to bring all of the diverse factions together, including the expatriate Creoles and Afro-Cubans, the elite New York intellectuals and the unionized tobacco workers in Tampa and Key West. Most importantly, this man united their efforts with those of the revolutionary forces fighting on the island.

José Martí (1853-1895)

He was José Martí, the consummate man of arms and letters. Through tireless organizational efforts in New York, Tampa, Key West and New Orleans, through fund-raising and lobbying of the tobacco workers distrustful of the Creole elites, through penning and delivering eloquent political speeches and publishing a variety of essays in Spanish and English, Martí embodied Villaverde's hoped-for "man of action" while at the same time becoming a pioneer of Spanish-American literary Modernism. Martí invested his freedom and his life in the cause, ultimately losing the latter on a Cuban battlefield in 1895. Before his death, however, Martí was a key fig-

La Patria

ure in the revolutionary press movement, especially in New York where he was the founder of the important newspaper of the last phase of the revolution: *La Patria* (1892-19?).

Martí's experience as a revolutionary journalist dated back to his youth in Cuba, where he had been imprisoned for ideas contained in an essay and in a play he had published in the newspaper *La Patria Libre*. He later was sent to study in Spain, where he obtained his law degree and published a political pamphlet, *El presidio político en Cuba* (Political Imprisonment in Cuba) (Trujillo, 107). In 1873, Martí moved to Mexico, where he edited *Revista Universal* (Universal Review); in 1877 he served as a professor in Guatemala and edited the official state newspaper there. In 1879, he returned to Cuba and was promptly exiled to Spain. From 1880 on, he began the first of his various residencies in New York. In Caracas in 1881, Martí founded and edited the *Revista Venezolana*, which only lasted for two numbers, and then he promptly returned to New York. In the grand metropolis, Martí maintained an active life as a writer, publishing books of poetry and numerous essays and speeches. The most curious of his publishing feats was the founding and editing of *La Edad de Oro* in 1889, a monthly magazine for children[19]—he had earlier published a book of verse, *Ismaelillo* (1881?), written for his son.

In all his organizing and countering of annexationist impulses with demands for independence and self-determination, Martí warned of the imperialist tendencies of the United States.[20] He did not live to see his fears become reality: the United States declared war on Spain, and, after signing the peace with Spain unilaterally, forced a constitution on the Republic of Cuba that depended on U. S. intervention, as called for in the Platt Amendment.

One of Martí's greatest virtues was his ability to bring the various classes and factions together in the revolutionary cause; this virtue included extending open arms to Puerto Rican intellectuals to unite their efforts with those of the Cubans. The earliest participation of Puerto Ricans in the revolutionary journalistic efforts in the United States had been the founding of *La Voz de la América* in 1865 by José J. Bassora (with Cuban Juan Manuel Macía).[21] From that point on, important Puerto Rican intellectuals and revolutionaries had often joined their Cuban brethren in New York in the late nineteenth century to plot the overthrow of Spanish colonialism.[22] This exodus of Puerto Rican intellectuals was hastened in 1868 after the failed Lares Rebellion (Fitzpatrick, 304). Among those in New York were such important nationalist philosophers and creative writers as Eugenio María de Hostos, Ramón Emeterio Betances, Lola Rodríguez de Tió and Luis Muñoz Rivera—all leading figures in the independence movement, and all contributing to exile publications. Muñoz Rivera, founder of the successful *La Democracia* on the island, later founded *The Puerto Rican Herald* in Washington, D. C., an English-language newspaper aimed at influencing U. S. policy towards the newly acquired colony.

These intellectuals joined an expatriate community in supporting revolutionary clubs and book and newspaper publication. In clubs such as Las Dos Antillas (The Two Antilles), co-founded by the Afro-Puerto Rican bibliographer Arturo Alfonso Schomberg, they delivered eloquent speeches that would be printed in the newspapers circulated throughout the exile communities and smuggled into Puerto Rico. From her home in New York, an important convener of this group was the thrice-exiled Doña Lola Rodríguez de Tió,[23] whose nationalistic verse not only appeared frequently in newspapers but also became enshrined as the national anthem for Puerto Rico.

In addition to these illustrious philosophers, essayists and poets, there were two craftsmen whose work was essential to the cause of revolutionary journalism: typesetters Francisco Gonzalo "Pachín" Marín and Sotero Figueroa.[24] In 1891, Marín brought his revolutionary newspaper *El Postillón* to New York from Puerto Rico, where it had been suppressed by the Spanish authorities. His exile had taken him to Santo Domingo, Haiti, Curazao, Venezuela, Jamaica, Martinique and Colombia. He was expelled from Venezuela in 1890 for attacking its president, Anueza Palacio, briefly returned to Puerto Rico, and from there went on to New York. In addition to his newspaper, he published from his print shop books and broadsides

Sotero Figueroa

for the Cuban and Puerto Rican expatriate communities. His shop became a meeting place for intellectuals, literary figures and political leaders. He also published two volumes of his original verse that are foundational for Puerto Rican letters: *Romances* and *En la arena*.[25] Like Martí, Marín died in battle on Cuban soil, in 1897.

Out of his print shop Imprenta América, Sotero Figueroa not only produced revolutionary newspapers and other publications, he also served as president of the Club Borinquen. Sotero Figueroa printed the newspaper *El Porvenir* (The Future) for publisher/editor Enrique Trujillo and *Borinquen*, a bimonthly newspaper (issued by the Puerto Rican section of Cuban Revolutionary Party) founded in 1898 and edited by Robert H. Todd (Fitzpatrick, 304). More importantly, Figueroa worked closely with José Martí on his publishing projects and provided the printing for one of the most important organs of the revolutionary movement, New York's *La Patria*, founded by Martí as the official organ of the Cuban Revolutionary Party in which Martí published essays and speeches (Fornet, 178). In addition, Figueroa's Imprenta América probably prepared the books issued for *La Patria*'s publishing house, Ediciones de *La Patria*, as well as works for the book-publishing arm of *El Porvernir*, which issued, beginning in 1890, the monumental five-volume biographical dictionary *Album de "El Porvenir"*.[26]

The Mexican Exile Press

While Cubans and Puerto Rican patriots had to endure passage by ship and customs authorities to enter the United States, the Mexican exile press was relatively easy to establish: Expatriate revolutionaries simply crossed a border and installed themselves in long-standing Mexican-origin communities of the Southwest. The relatively open border had served to protect numerous *personae non grata* on both sides of the dividing line for decades. The Mexican expatriate revolutionary press movement was begun around 1885, when the Porfirio Díaz regime in Mexico became so repressive that scores of publishers and editors went or were forced into exile. Publishers such as Adolfo Carrillo, who had opposed Díaz with his *El Correo del Lunes* (The Monday Mail), relocated all along the border, hoping to smuggle their papers back into Mexico. Carrillo settled in San Francisco, where he established *La República* (The Republic, 1885) and General Ignacio Martínez went into exile in Brownsville to launch *El Mundo* in 1885 and organize insurgent groups from there.[27] An assassin's bullet terminated Martínez's activities in 1891. Paulino Martínez (no rela-

Ricardo Flores Magón

tion) established his *El Monitor Democrático* in San Antonio in 1888 and his *La Voz de Juárez* and *El Chinaco*, both in Laredo in 1889 and 1890, respectively.[28]

By 1900, the most important Mexican revolutionary journalist and ideologue, Ricardo Flores Magón, launched his newspaper *Regeneración* (Regeneration) in Mexico City and was promptly suppressed.[29] Flores Magón was jailed four times in Mexico for his radical journalism; following a sentence of eight months (in which the judge prohibited his reading and writing while in jail), Flores Magón went into U. S. exile; in fact, the Mexican government, backed by its supreme court, had prohibited the publication of any newspaper by Flores Magón (Argudín, 110). In 1904, he began publishing *Regeneración* in San Antonio,[30] then in Saint Louis in 1905 and in Canada in 1906; in 1907, he founded *Revolución* in Los Angeles, and once again in 1908 revived *Regeneración* there. Throughout these years, Ricardo and his brothers (Enrique and Jesús) employed any and every subterfuge possible to smuggle the newspapers from the United States into Mexico, even stuffing them into cans or wrapping them in other newspapers sent to San Luis Potosí, where they were then distributed to sympathizers throughout the country (Argudín, 110).

Along with his brothers, Ricardo Flores Magón emerged as a leader of
the movement to overthrow the Díaz regime, founding the Liberal
Reformist Association in 1901. Flores Magón's approach differed in that he
wedded his ideas about revolution in Mexico to the struggle of working
people in the United States, and this difference in part accounted for the
newspaper's popularity among Mexican and Mexican-American laborers
engaged in unionizing efforts in the United States:

> *Regeneración*'s view was that the Mexicans, in their struggle against
> political tyranny and exploitive capitalism, were leading the way for the
> liberation of the working-class Mexicans in the United States. Magón used
> *Regeneración* to publicize rallies and labor conferences in Los Angeles
> and elsewhere; the constant theme was the alliance of the Mexicans,
> Chicano and Anglo-American working class.[31]

Pursued by Díaz's agents[32] in San Antonio, Ricardo and Enrique moved to
St. Louis, where they established the Partido Liberal Mexicano (Mexican
Liberal Party), dedicated to proletarian social justice in its provision of an
ideological base for the revolutionaries. They established a chain of chapters across the Southwest that spread their ideology, largely through meetings, fund-raising events, and the publication of newspapers, pamphlets
and books. By the time he moved to Los Angeles in 1907 to publish
Revolución, Flores Magón was openly embracing anarchism and losing
many of his Mexican and Mexican-American followers, who rejected his
extremism.[33]

Flores Magón and *Regeneración* were considered radical by the U. S.
government, which during World War I was attempting to suppress radical
politics within its borders. The weapon used by the U. S. government
against the radical foreign language press was implementation by the post
office of the Trading with the Enemy Act[34] and the 1917 Espionage Act; the
post office denied second-class mailing privileges to some radical newspapers on the grounds that the government would not function as "an agent
in the circulation of printed matter which it regards as injurious to the
people" and it otherwise refused its services to persons engaged in enemy
propaganda.[35] *Regeneración* was targeted, and Flores Magón indicted, on
the basis of a manifesto to anarchists and laborers of the world published
in the March 16, 1918 edition.[36] The manifesto supposedly contained false
statements, interfered with U. S. military operations, incited disloyalty and

mutiny, interfered with enlistment and recruiting, and violated the provisions of the Espionage Act; in addition, no English translation had been filed with the U. S. Post Office.[37] In 1918, Ricardo Flores Magón was arrested by federal authorities for breaking the neutrality laws; he was found guilty and sentenced to twenty years in federal prison.[38] He died in Leavenworth in 1922 of mysterious causes, some of his friends and correspondents alleging that he had been denied treatment[39] for heart ailments and diabetes.[40]

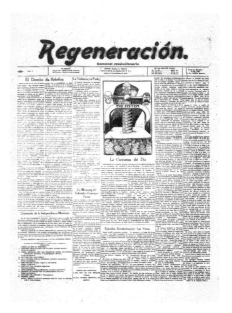

Regeneración

According to Griswold del Castillo, "Of all the border papers, *Regeneración* was undoubtedly the most influential in Mexico, at least in terms of affecting social change in Mexico. Many reforms suggested by Magón in the pages of the paper were later incorporated into the Mexican constitution of 1917" (43). Numerous Spanish-language periodicals in the Southwest echoed the ideas of Flores Magón and were affiliated with the Partido Liberal Mexicano (PLM), including *La Bandera Roja, El Demócrata, La Democracia, Humanidad, 1810, El Liberal, Punto Rojo* and *La Reforma Social,* all of which were located along the border from the Rio Grande Valley in South Texas to Douglas, Arizona. In addition to *Regeneración* and *Revolución* in Los Angeles, *Libertad y Trabajo* was another PLM newspaper.

Among the most interesting writers were those articulating labor and gender issues[41] as part of the social change to be implemented with the triumph of the revolution. Notable among the early writers and editors associated with the PML and Flores Magón was schoolteacher Sara Estela Ramírez, who emigrated from Mexico in 1898 to teach in Mexican schools in Laredo, Texas. Her passionate and eloquent speeches and poetry, performed at meetings of laborers and community people, spread the ideas of labor organizing and revolutionary social reform in Mexico. Ramírez wrote for two important Mexican immigrant newspapers, *La Crónica* and *El*

Demócrata Fronterizo. In 1901 she began editing and publishing her own newspaper *La Corregidora* (named after the heroine who furthered the Mexican independence movement from Spain almost a century earlier), which she printed in Mexico City, Laredo and San Antonio.[42] In 1910, Ramírez founded a short-lived literary magazine, *Aurora*; she died that same year of a long-standing illness (Hernández Tovar, 29). During the pre-revolutionary years, Ramírez also wrote for Juana Gutiérrez de Mendoza's newspaper *Vésper: Justicia y Libertad* (Dawn: Justice and Liberty), said to have had a weekly circulation of 8,000.[43] Ramírez joined with Gutiérrez de Mendoza and other women revolutionaries in founding *Regeneración y Concordia* (Regeneration and Concordance), an organization to further "the betterment of conditions for Indians and the proletariat, elevation of the economic as well as moral and intellectual status of women, and unification of all revolutionary forces" (Hernández Tovar, 13). Ramírez was one of a cadre of women activists engaged in the revolutionary struggle, quite often utilizing the press to further their ideas.

According to Lomas, the following periodicals under the direction of women not only furthered the revolutionary cause but articulated gender issues: Teresa Villarreal's *El Obrero* (The Worker, 1909), Isidra T. de Cárdenas' *La Voz de la Mujer* (The Woman's Voice, 1907) and Blanca de Moncaleano's *Pluma Roja* (Red Pen, 1913–1915).[44] Gómez-Quiñones adds *La Mujer Moderna* (The Modern Woman) to the list; it was published by Teresa and Andrea Villarreal in San Antonio in affiliation with the feminist Club Liberal "Leona Vicario," established for educational and PLM fund-raising purposes (Gómez-Quiñones, *Sembradores*, 36).

While each of these publications directly opposed the Díaz regime and were influenced by the Brothers Flores Magón and the PLM, only *Pluma Roja* placed the emancipation of women at the center of its agenda. Lomas (300) further states that the clear model of feminist militancy was the Guanajuato, Mexico, newspaper *Vésper* (Dawn), edited by Juana Belén Gutiérrez de Mendoza, in which Sara Estela Ramírez had previously collaborated. The language of both *Vésper* and the women's newspapers north of the border has been characterized as *viril* (virile) and *estilo en pantalones* (wearing pants, i.e., manly),[45] which can clearly be seen in this passionate expression of the revolutionary mission of *La Voz de la Mujer*: "Hoy el dilema es otro: tomar lo que se necesita, ¡libertad! Y ésta sólo se conquista con rebeldías. ¡Hay que ser rebeldes! Primero morir, antes que consentir que nuestros hijos lleven el estigma de la esclavitud. A nosotras, madres y esposas, hermanas o hijas, toca encausar este dilema" (28 July 1907) [Today the dilemma is another: to take what is needed, liberty! Liberty can be conquered only through rebellion. It is up to us, mothers and wives, sisters and daughters, to confront this dilemma (Cited in and translated by Lomas, 302).] Lomas has shown that although *La Voz de la Mujer* exhorted women to become active in the public sphere, its purpose ultimately was to benefit the state and thus was limited within the constraints of nationalism. However, *La Voz de la Mujer* was innovative, consistently representing a collective and decisive voice for women in print, where they had not often appeared as leaders, intellectuals and revolutionaries. Not only was the title of the newspaper a collective expression, most of the editorials and commentaries were unsigned, and were simply written in the first person plural, *we*: "nosotras."[46]

La Voz de la Mujer

Pluma Roja was founded in Los Angeles and edited by Blanca de Moncaleano, an anarchist from Colombia who had been drawn (with her husband, Juan Francisco Moncaleano, another revolutionary journalist) to Mexico to support Flores Magón's cause. After the Moncaleanos were expelled from Mexico in 1912 by President Francisco Madero, Blanca founded her newspaper, which positioned women's liberation as central to any social change. In Lomas' words, "the need to recode the position of women in society was at the center of the struggle for social, political and economic freedom, and was an integral part of the ideal of anarchism. For *Pluma Roja*, unquestioned patriarchal authority, upheld by religion and the state, was the target of the red pen" (305). The anarchist program proposed by *Pluma Roja* called for full emancipation of women from three oppressors: the state, religion and capital. Editor Blanca de Moncaleano addressed both women and men to participate in the re-making of society, and she was severely critical of any men in the revolutionary movement not conscious of their own suppression and enslavement of women (Lomas, 306): "Engolfados los hombres en su supuesta superioridad, fatuos por su ignorancia, han creído que sin la ayuda de la mujer, pueden llegar a la meta de la emancipación humana" (*Pluma Roja*, 27 June 1915: 1) [Lost in the supposition of their superiority, stupefied by their ignorance, men have believed that, without the assistance of women, they can reach the goal of human emancipation]. At this juncture in history, it is hard to assess the effect of such writing and these newspapers on Mexican women of the Southwest; in Mexico, however, the Revolution did serve as a catalyst for the women's movement.

The Mexican exile press flourished into the 1930s, with weekly newspapers siding with one faction or another. By no means was this press as liberal as the exile press prior to the outbreak of the Revolution. What sprang up was an exile press founded largely by conservatives dislodged by the socialist revolution; they came to established Mexican-American communities, many with resources in hand, and became businesspeople and entrepreneurs. Some founded newspapers to serve the rapidly expanding community of economic refugees, and their newspapers eventually became the backbone of an *immigrant* rather than *exile* press, as their entrepreneurial spirit overtook their political commitment to change in the homeland. Others founded political papers as part of their commitment to restoring the peace and prosperity as they knew it in Mexico prior to the upheaval; some publishers were overt politicians and ideologues, as had been the revolutionaries who were their precursors in exile.

El Paso's political newspapers were as divided as those throughout the Southwest: *México Libre* supported Victoriano Huerta, while *La Patria* and *El Correo del Bravo* were partisans of Venustiano Carranza (see Griswold del Castillo, 43). With the Cristero War (1926–1929), resulting from government persecution of the Church (arising from the anticlerical tenets of the 1917 Mexican constitution), a fresh batch of political refugees founded newspapers to attack the Mexican government and to serve the needs of the exiled religious community. During the build-up of conflict between church and state in Mexico, such periodicals as *La Guadalupana: Revista Mensual Católica* (The Guadalupan: Catholic Monthly Magazine, 1922) and *El Renacimiento: Semanario Católico* (The Renascence: Catholic Weekly, 1923) were founded in El Paso, and *La Esperanza* (Hope, 1924) in Los Angeles. The weekly *El Amigo del Hogar*

(Friend of the Home, 1925) was founded by the Círculo de Obreros Católicos San José in Indiana Harbor, Indiana, but its pages were not limited to issues of religious persecution and exile, extending to general news, literature and culture. It also defended the local community by such actions as leading a battle to desegregate local movie houses.[47] In truth, the influence of the Cristero refugees was felt in many newspapers, not just in specialized publications; the already conservative counter-revolutionary papers naturally focused on religious persecution in Mexico and atrocities committed by the government.

Other Exile Press Movements

The next wave of Hispanic political refugees to reach U. S. shores came from across the Atlantic: those fleeing Spanish fascism. Hispanic communities across the United States embraced the refugees and sympathized with their cause; many Cuban, Mexican and Puerto Rican organizations had fund-raisers for the Republican cause during the Spanish Civil War. Expatriates were fast to establish their own exile press.Their efforts hit fertile soil in Depression-era communities that were already hotbeds for union and socialist organizing. Manhattan and Brooklyn were the centers of Hispanic anti-fascist fervor and contributed *España Libre* (Free Spain, 1939-1977), *España Nueva* (New Spain, 1923-1942), *España Republicana* (Republican Spain, 1931-1935), *Frente Popular* (Popular Front, 1937-1939) and *La Liberación* (The Liberation, 1946-1949). Many Hispanic labor and socialist organizations, in which Spanish immigrant workers were prominent, published newspapers supporting the Republican cause: the long-running anarchist paper *Cultura Proletaria* (Proletarian Culture, 1910-1959), *El Obrero* (The Worker, 1931-1932) and *Vida Obrera* (Worker Life, 1930-1932).[48] The Hispanic labor press in Tampa, Chicago and the Southwest also felt solidarity with the Spanish expatriates, supporting the Republican cause in their pages and raising funds for refugees and victims of the Spanish Civil War.

Exiles and political refugees have continued to make up an important segment of Hispanic immigrants to the United States. With the Cuban Revolution, along with U. S. involvement during the Cold War in the civil wars of Central America and Chile, large-scale immigration of political refugees has continued to the present day. Beginning in 1959, a new wave of refugees from the Cuban Revolution established a widespread exile press as well as a more informal network of hundreds of newsletters. Chileans, Salvadorans, Nicaraguans and other Latin American expatriates have all issued political newspapers and magazines in recent years. As the Hispanic population of the United States continues to grow (it is estimated to reach one-third of the total population by 2030), and as the economy of the United States becomes more internationally integrated through agreements such as the North American Free Trade Agreement, U. S. culture will likely become even more directly linked to the internal politics of Latin America. The culture of Hispanic exile will continue to be part of the overall culture of the United States into the foreseeable future; the United States will continue to be a base from which political refugees will use the press—and, today, electronic media such as Radio Martí—to express their opposition to governments in their homelands.

But more than that, Hispanic political refugees have always represented an important immigration trend in the development of Hispanic communities within the United States. Their knowledge and perspectives live on in Hispanic culture today; the refugees did not always return to the homeland. Many of them and their children intermarried here with other Hispanic natives and immigrants; many of them and their children eventually blended into the grand community that is recognizable today as a national ethnic minority. The children of the political refugees who founded Indiana Harbor's *El Amigo del Hogar* in 1925 began publishing *The Latin Times* (1956-), a bilingual ethnic minority newspaper in the post-World War II period. The tobacco workers who so fervently supported the Cuban revolutionary movement through publications, such as *El Yara*, eventually became United States citizens and are the basis for today's ethnic minority communities in Tampa and Key West, where they support such newspapers as the still trilingually published *La Gaceta*.

The Immigrant Press

Scholars of the press have confused ethnicity with immigrant status when studying the press of Hispanic groups in the United States. For instance, Sally M. Miller, in her *The Ethnic Press in the United States: An Historical Analysis and Handbook*, makes it clear that for her the "ethnic" press was established and sustained by immigrants from the eighteenth century on, but flourished at the end of the nineteenth century, when the greatest number of immigrants arrived in the United States.[49] In fact, this

identification of ethnicity with immigrant status does not function well at
all for the Hispanic press, and may not function either for studying the
press of African Americans, Native Americans and other groups who have
been incorporated into the United States or whose second, third and
fourth generations maintain a press. Many Hispanic newspapers, especially in the Southwest, were not related to immigration in the nineteenth century, but were created by and for long-standing native residents. Then, too,
much of the periodical production of Hispanics since the nineteenth century has been created and sustained by second, third and fourth generations. Language, too, is an issue that is not as clear cut as Miller would have
it. Many of the nineteenth-century periodicals of Hispanics were Spanish-
English bilingual. There were even some that were Spanish-French bilingual and Spanish-Italian; and a notable Tampa newspaper, *La Gaceta*, has
been trilingual (English-Spanish-Italian) since its founding in 1922. From
World War II to the present, many Hispanic periodicals have appeared solely in English.

The Wynars, in their *Encyclopedic Directory of Ethnic Newspapers
and Periodicals in the United States*, make no distinction between exile,
immigrant, foreign language or ethnic- minority press, preferring to group
all of these various sociological and linguistic designations together under
the general rubric of "ethnic press," and insisting that there is a qualitative
difference between the "immigrant" and "ethnic" designations.[50] Their definition is: "The *American* ethnic press may be defined as consisting of
newspapers and periodicals published either in English, in non-English or
bilingually, published by ethnic organizations or individuals in the United
States, and specifically aimed at an ethnic readership. The contents of such
publications are primarily designed to satisfy the needs and interests common to persons of a particular ethnic group or community" (15). I would
apply the Wynar definition (below) of the function of the ethnic press, not
to the *exile* press at all, but to Hispanic *immigrant* and ethnic- minority
newspapers:

> . . . the principal agent by which the identity, cohesiveness and structure
> of the ethnic community are preserved and perpetuated. It is by provid-
> ing the sense of shared identity and common consciousness that the eth-
> nic press serves as the cementing element within the community. The
> function of the press, as one of the major educational agents within the
> ethnic community, evolves from that of a primarily immigrant society to

that of an established native American ethnic community. While the community still remains in its immigrant stage, the press primarily serves as the major tool of adjustment. By printing American news, describing the American way of life, and interpreting the conditions, customs, laws, and mores of the new society, the immigrant press eases the process of adjustment and consequently hastens the assimilative process. While the immigrant press acts as an agent of assimilation, at the same time it also functions as a force that retards assimilation. This latter role, the slowing of the assimilative process, results from the press's tendency to preserve the ethnic culture and identity by encouraging language retention, stimulating a continued interest in the country of origin, and sustaining involvement in ethnic community affairs within the host country. (18)

I believe it is best to differentiate between an immigrant press and an ethnic or ethnic-minority press. As can be seen above, the Wynars make them subcategories of the "ethnic" press: immigrant and native American ethnic presses. Since the mid-nineteenth century, Hispanic immigrants have created periodicals serving their enclaves in their native language, maintaining a connection with the homeland while helping the immigrants to adjust to a new society and culture here. The Hispanic immigrant press shares many of the distinctions that Park identified in 1922 in a study on the immigrant press as a whole.[51] Included among these distinctions were: (1) the predominant use of the language of the homeland, (2) serving a population united by that language, irrespective of national origin, and (3) the need to interpret events from a particular racial or nationalist point of view, and furthering nationalism (9–13). Park also noted that immigrants read more in the United States than in their lands of origin, for a variety of reasons: The press there was not available or it was restricted, "there is more going on or they need to know" and "news is a kind of urgent information that men use in making adjustments to a new environment, in changing old habits, and in forming new opinions" (9). He further states, "The very helplessness of the immigrant . . . is a measure of the novelty of the American environment and the immigrant's lack of adjustment to it" (9). To summarize, then, the immigrant press serves a population in transition from the land of origin to the United States by providing news and interpretation to orient them and facilitate adjustment to the new society, while maintaining the link with the old society. Underlying Park's distinctions and those of other students of immigration are the concepts of the American Dream and the Melting Pot: that the immigrants came to find a better life, implicitly a better culture, and that soon they or their descendants would become Americans and there would no longer be a need for this type of press. In fact, Park's study was implemented as part of a more generalized study on how to Americanize immigrants. For Park, the immigrant press was a transitory phenomenon, one that would disappear as the group became assimilated into the melting pot of U. S. society. The attitude of not assimilating or melting, in fact, has characterized the Hispanic immigrant press from the nineteenth century to the present. The advice in 1880 of Corpus Christi's *El Horizonte* (The Horizon, 1879–80) to its Mexican and Spanish readership was typical of many of the Mexican immigrant papers: in essence, Do not become citizens of the United States because there is so much prejudice and persecution here that you will never enjoy the benefits of that citizenship, while you will lose those benefits in your homeland:

> Mexicans, known as such or having renounced the title, are always treated unjustly and negatively by judges, citizens, the powerful, and in general all of the children of this nation.
>
> Therefore, if no improvement will be achieved, and we are all convinced of that, why should we renounce the title of children of the Republic of Mexico . . . we shall always be foreigners in the United States and they will always consider us as such?[52]

Although Park's analysis is somewhat dated, it resulted from a closer, more ethnically broader and generally more thorough study than most of subsequent studies. I agree with many of Park's observations on the functions of the immigrant press, but I would add that the defense of the community was also an important function of the press. Hispanic newspapers were especially sensitive to racism and abuse of immigrant rights. Almost all of the Hispanic immigrant newspapers announced their service in protection of the community in mastheads and/or in editorials, and some of them followed up on this commitment in leading campaigns to desegregate schools, movie houses and other facilities or to construct their alternative institutions for the Hispanic community's use. Contrary to Park's prognosis for the ethnic identity of immigrants, the history of Hispanic groups in the United States has shown an unmeltable ethnicity. Immigration from Spanish-speaking countries has been almost a steady flow from the founding of the United States to the present, and there seems no end to the phenomenon in the foreseeable future. The immigrant newspapers of individual Hispanic groups do, however, seem to give way over time to newspapers serving more than one Hispanic nationality; and the children of this readership may consume English-language or bilingual periodicals that serve ethnic-minority interests rather than immigrant ones. Thus, today, while many immigrants may read New York's *El Diario–La Prensa* or Los Angeles' *La Opinión*, subsequent generations of Hispanics may subscribe to a variety of English-language Hispanic magazines, such as *Hispanic* or *Latina*.

The *immigrant* press is not to be confused with the *native* Hispanic press, to be addressed in the next section. The native Hispanic press developed first in the Southwest in the mid-nineteenth century and later in most Hispanic communities, and has served a readership predominantly of U. S. citizens. This press was cognizant of the racial, ethnic and/or minority status of its readers within U. S. society and culture. The ethnic-minority press may make use of Spanish or English; it may include immigrants in its readership and among its interests; it may cover news and commentary of various "homelands," such as Cuba, Mexico, Puerto Rico or Spain; but its fundamental reason for existence and its point of reference is its audience's life and conditions *in the United States*. Unlike the immigrant press, it does not have one foot in the homeland.

Important Immigrant Newspapers

What follows immediately is a brief survey of newspapers serving newly arrived communities of Hispanic immigrants. Of course, the diverse and often conflicting missions of Hispanic newspapers were (and are) not always clear-cut. In fact, Hispanic newspapers, especially large dailies such as San Antonio's *La Prensa,* Los Angeles' *La Opinión,* New York's *La Prensa* and *El Diario de Nueva York* served diverse publics of exiles, immigrants and U. S. minority citizens. But their largest readership was— and, for those that still exist, continues to be—Spanish-speaking immigrants. Furthermore, while a newspaper may have been founded to serve an immigrant or exile group, as the community evolved, so too may have the newspaper from an immigrant journal into an ethnic-minority newspaper. *El Amigo del Hogar* was founded in Indiana Harbor, Indiana, in 1925 by religious and political refugees, but soon was taking on many of the responsibilities of a typical immigrant newspaper and even fought civil rights battles with local businesses and authorities. It ceased publication during the Depression and was reincarnated in 1956 by the same family of printer-publishers, the Figueroas, as *The Latin Times*. Since its establishment, the weekly has been a predominantly English-language newspaper designed to provide an alternative news source, relevant to the concerns of the Mexican-American and the growing Puerto Rican communities of East Chicago. *The Latin Times* has always served as a watchdog over local politics and as a defender of the civil rights of Hispanics.

With these distinctions in mind, then, the following are some of the more important immigrant newspapers.

While *El Mercurio de Nueva York* (1829–1830) and *El Mensagero Semanal de Nueva York* (1828–1831) may have served immigrant populations and functioned somewhat as described above, it was not until much later, when larger Hispanic immigrant communities began to form, that more characteristic immigrant newspapers were founded. Among these, I would include San Francisco's *Sud Americano* (1855), *El Eco del Pacífico* (1856),

El Nuevo Mundo (San Francisco)

La Voz de Méjico (1862) and *El Nuevo Mundo* (1864),[53] which served a burgeoning community of immigrants from northern Mexico and from throughout the Hispanic world, as far away as Chile, all drawn to the Bay Area during the Gold Rush and collateral industrial and commercial development. From the 1850s through the 1870s, San Francisco supported the largest, longest-running and most financially successful Spanish-language newspapers in the United States.

In fact, San Francisco was able to support two daily Spanish-language newspapers during this period: *El Eco del Pacífico* and *El Tecolote* (1875–1879). And the ownership and editorship of many of these papers was made up of immigrants from Spain, Chile, Colombia and Mexico.[54] The largest of these was *El Eco del Pacífico*, which had grown out of a Spanish-language page of the French-language newspaper *L'Echo du*

Pacifique and had become independent in 1856 under the editorship of José Marcos Mugarrieta (Goff, 64). San Francisco's Spanish-language newspapers covered news of the homeland, which varied from coverage of Spain and Chile to Central America and Mexico, and generally assisted the immigrants in adjusting to the new environment. Very closely reported on was the French Intervention in Mexico, with various of the newspapers supporting fund raising events for the war effort and aid for widows and orphans, in addition to working with the local Junta Patriótica Mexicana, even printing *in toto* the long speeches made at the Junta's meetings. The newspapers reported on discrimination and persecution of Hispanic miners and generally saw the defense of the Hispanic *colonia* to be a priority, denouncing abuse of Hispanic immigrants and natives. Hispanic readers in the Southwest were acutely aware of racial issues in the United States, and sided with the North during the Civil War, which also was extensively covered in the newspapers.

While San Francisco's Hispanic population was the state's largest in the nineteenth century, it was Los Angeles that received the largest number of Mexican immigrants with the massive exodus of refugees from the Revolution of 1910. It was thus Los Angeles in the twentieth century that, along with San Antonio and New York, supported some of the most important Spanish-language daily newspapers, periodicals that began as immigrant newspapers. Between 1910 and 1924, some half million Mexican immigrants settled in the United States; Los Angeles and San Antonio were their settlements of choice. Into these two cities an entrepreneurial class of refugees came with cultural and financial capital sufficient to establish businesses of all types to serve the rapidly growing Mexican enclaves; they constructed everything from tortilla factories to Hispanic theaters and movie houses, and through their cultural leadership in mutual aid societies, the churches, theaters and newspapers, they were able to reinforce an nationalistic ideology that ensured the solidarity and insularity of their community, or market, if you will. In addition to being home to important existing Mexican communities, Los Angeles and San Antonio were chosen by the new economic and political refugees because both cities were undergoing rapid industrialization and modernization, and work and opportunities were available. Los Angeles and San Antonio were also good bases for recruitment of agricultural and railroad workers. The flood of Mexican workers into both cities spurred the founding of numerous Spanish-language newspapers from 1911 until the Depression; each of these two cities supported more Spanish-language newspapers during this period than any other city in the United States.

El Heraldo de México, founded in Los Angeles in 1915 by owner Juan de Heras and publisher Cesar F. Marburg, has been called a "people's newspaper"[55] because of its focus on and importance to the Mexican immigrant worker in Los Angeles. It often proclaimed its working-class identity, as well as its promotion of Mexican nationalism; through its publishing house it issued the first novel narrated from the perspective of a "Chicano," i.e., a Mexican-working class immigrant: Daniel Venegas' *Las aventuras de Don Chipote o Cuando los pericos mamen*.[56] The most popular Mexican newspaper at this time, its circulation extended beyond 4,000 (Chacón, 50). As Chacón has stated,

> *El Heraldo* was the common man's newspaper, a mass press for the growing Spanish-reading population that had recently trekked across from Mexico. *El Heraldo* claimed that it was the "Defender of the Mexicans in the United States" and expressed appreciation to the Chicano working class, who were its chief subscribers. The focus of the newspaper was local, national and international in scope. However, news coverage was oriented to events in Mexico and the United States, particularly in California, that were of interest to Chicanos. Other news pertaining to U. S. developments, unless it directly affected the lives of the Spanish speaking of the Southwest, was minimal (50).

Like many other Hispanic immigrant newspapers, *El Heraldo de México* devoted the largest proportion of its coverage to news of the homeland, followed by news directly affecting the immigrants in the United States, followed by news and advertisements that would be of interest to working-class immigrants. Chacón found that among the social roles played by *El Heraldo de México*, the most important was the defense of the Mexican immigrant, by publishing editorials and devoting considerable space to combating discrimination and the exploitation of immigrant labor; it particularly brought attention to the role played by labor contractors and American employers in mistreating the immigrant workers (62). *El Heraldo de México* even went a step further in 1919 by attempting to organize Mexican laborers into an association, the Liga Protectiva Mexicana de California, to protect their rights and further their interests (62).

El Heraldo de México was in no way an exception in considering the defense of its community to be one of its most important missions. In fact, both the immigrant and the ethnic-minority press shared this mission and proudly announced it often on mastheads, in editorials and in prospectuses. The defense of the Hispanic community within the larger society, perceived as alien and hostile, was a mission shared by such newspapers throughout the Southwest, the Midwest, Florida and the Northeast. This prospectus for New York's *Gráfico* (32 July 1937), safeguarding the rights of Spanish speakers in Harlem, echoed the same sentiments of prospectuses and editorials in Los Angeles, San Antonio, Laredo and Tampa:

> We want to make this weekly publication an efficient instrument dedicated to the defense of the Spanish speaking population of Harlem and a vehicle for mutual understanding and comprehension between the two main racial groups living in this section.
>
> We do not expect financial compensation. The cooperation given to GRAFICO will not be used for individual aggrandizement. Ours is amateur and disinterested journalism.
>
> We feel the immediate necessity of taking up important issues pertaining to our common defense . . .

This defense of the Mexican immigrant community was primary even in a Midwestern Spanish-language newspaper like *El Cosmopolita* (The Cosmopolitan, 1914-1919), despite its being owned by Jack Danciger, an Anglo-American businessman intent on selling alcoholic beverages and other products imported from Mexico to the Mexican colony in Kansas City.[57] While Danciger was principally interested in protecting and furthering his business interests on both sides of the border, even to the extent of forging extensive relations with the Constitutionalist government of Venustiano Carranza, the priorities of his Mexican editors lay in providing the vast array of information that the Spanish-speaking immigrants needed to survive in Kansas City—such as housing and employment information—as well as defending them from discrimination and exploitation.

The newspaper protested against segregation, racial prejudice, police harassment and brutality, injustice in the judicial system and mistreatment in the work place. Unlike other commercial newspapers, such as San Antonio's *La Prensa*, Kansas City's *El Cosmopolita* consistently supported the Mexican Revolution and railed against United States interventionism, although the paper also supported Woodrow Wilson, who had been responsible for the sending U. S. troops into Mexico (Smith, 80-2). All of these stances may have reflected Danciger's own political alliances and business interests—there is even some suggestion that the Carranza administration may have partially funded *El Cosmopolita* (Smith, 74)— rather than the Kansas City Mexican colony's being any more liberal than San Antonio's, for example. But, as Kansas City was a railroad center, as well as a labor market for the Midwest, its Mexican immigrant community probably consisted of a higher percentage of laborers and did not attract as many political refugees and Mexican bourgeoisie as did El Paso, Los Angeles and San Antonio. Consequently, Danciger's political stances may have been reflected by the Mexican working class in the city. *El Cosmopolita* tried to maintain a balance between protecting the rights and interests of its community and urging the community to better itself, especially through education (Smith, 77); and while the newspaper did promote Mexican and Hispanic culture, and pride in these, it does not appear that the editors and writers were as fervent in promoting these as their counterparts in the newspapers of the Southwest.

For the Mexican immigrant communities in the Southwest, defense of the civil and human rights also extended to protecting Mexican immigrants from the influence of Anglo-American culture and Protestantism. The publishers, editorialists and columnists were almost unanimous in developing and promoting the idea of a "México de afuera"—a Mexican colony existing outside of Mexico, in which it was the duty of the individual to maintain the Spanish language, keep the Catholic faith and insulate their children from what community leaders perceived as the low moral standards practiced by Anglo-Americans.

In the canon of "México de afuera," the highest niches in the pantheon, in fact, were reserved for preserving the Spanish language and preserving the Mexican culture and Catholicism. Mexican Catholicism in the United States was further reinforced when the Cristero War produced a flood of refugees, including the Church hierarchy, into the U. S. Southwest. Basic to the belief system of this culture in "exile" was the return to Mexico when the hostilities of the Revolution were over and the chaos had subsided to a point that order was reestablished in its pre-Revolutionary form. Mexican national culture was to be preserved while in exile in the midst of iniquitous Anglo Protestants, whose culture was aggressively degrading even while discriminating against Hispanics. The ideology was most expressed and disseminated by cultural elites, many of whom were the political and religious refugees from the Revolution. They represented the most conservative segment of Mexican society; in the United States, their cultural and business entrepreneurship exerted leadership in all phases of life in the *colonia* and solidified a conservative substratum for Mexican-American culture for decades to come. And these educated political refugees often played a key role in publishing. The "México de afuera" ideology was markedly nationalistic and militated to preserve Mexican identity in the United States. In a philosophical, cultural and biological sense, the ideology ensured the preservation of the group in an environment where Hispanic women were in short supply and seen as subject to pursuit by Anglo-American males, where the English language and more liberal or progressive Anglo-American customs and values were overwhelming and where discrimination and abuse against Mexicans occurred.

Park noted that the immigrant press of all groups tends to be highly nationalistic:

> The nationalistic tendencies of the immigrants find their natural expression and strongest stimulus in the national societies, the Church, and the foreign-language press—the institutions most closely connected with the preservation of the racial languages. In these, the immigrant feels the home ties more strongly; they keep him in touch with the political struggle at home and even give him opportunities to take part in it. Both consciously and unconsciously they might be expected to center the immigrants interests and activities in Europe and so keep him apart from American life. (50-1)

Park further makes clear that, as seen through their press of late nineteenth- and early twentieth-centuries, immigrants did not come to the United States to assimilate its culture:

> But foreign-language institutions and agencies, the Church and the press and the nationalist societies, have sought not merely to protect against assimilation those immigrants who were here temporarily, but to protect among those who would remain permanently in the United States the traditions and language of the home country. At least, some of the leaders among the immigrant peoples have thought of the United States as a region to be colonized by Europeans, where each language group would maintain its own language and culture, using English as a *lingua franca* and means of communication among the different nationalities. (60)

Inherent in the ideology of "México de afuera" as it was expressed by many cultural elites was an upper-class and bourgeois mentality that ironically tended to resent association with the Mexican immigrant working class. To them, the poor *braceros* and former *peons* were an uneducated mass whose ignorant habits only gave Anglo-Americans the wrong impression of Mexican and Hispanic culture. To such self-exiled elites, many Mexican Americans and other Hispanics long residing within the United States were little better than Anglos themselves, having abandoned their language and many cultural traits in exchange for the almighty dollar. It was, therefore, important that *la gente de bien*, this educated and refined class, grasp the leadership of the community, down to the grass roots, if need be, in the holy crusade of preserving Hispanic identity in the face of the Anglo onslaught.

Among the most powerful of the political, business and intellectual figures in the Mexican immigrant community was Ignacio E. Lozano, founder and operator of the two most powerful and well distributed daily newspapers: San Antonio's *La Prensa,* founded in 1913, and Los Angeles' *La Opinión*, founded in 1926 and still publishing today. Lozano, from a successful business family in northern Mexico, relocated to San Antonio in 1908 with his mother and sister in search of business opportunities; there he opened a bookstore and gradually learned the newspaper business through on-the-job experiences while working first for San Antonio's *El Noticiero* and later for *El Imparcial de Texas* (di Stefano, 99–103). With the business training and experience that he received in Mexico, Lozano was able to contribute professionalism and business acumen to Hispanic journalism in the United States, resulting in his successfully publishing two of the longest-running Spanish-language daily papers. His sound journalistic policies and emphasis on professionalism were reflected in his hiring of well-trained journalists, starting at the top with his appointment of Teodoro Torres, the "Father of Mexican Journalism," to edit *La Prensa*.

The ideas of Torres and Lozano reached thousands not only in San Antonio but throughout the Southwest, Midwest and northern Mexico through a vast distribution system that included newsstand sales, home delivery and mail. *La Prensa* also set up a network of correspondents in the United States who were able to report on current events and cultural activities of Mexican communities as far away as Chicago, Detroit and New York. When around 1920 Obregón's presidency effected more liberal stances toward the expatriate community, *La Prensa* began to circulate freely in northern Mexico, gaining a large readership from Piedras Negras west to Ciudad Juárez; Lozano was even able to travel to Mexico City and meet with the president himself.[58] Unlike the publishers of many other Hispanic immigrant newspapers, Lozano also set about serving the long-standing Mexican-American population in San Antonio and the Southwest. In his business and marketing acumen, he sought to reach broader segments and all classes, in part by not being overtly political or partisan of any political faction in Mexico and by recognizing the importance of the Mexicans who had long resided in the United States. He and his staff sought to bring Mexican Americans within the "México de afuera" ideology. Nemesio García Naranjo summarized the importance of Lozano's vision regarding both the Mexican Americans and "México de afuera" in the founding and running of a newspaper in what García Naranjo viewed as the culturally impoverished environment of San Antonio:

> Unable to find direction in a directionless environment, Ignacio E. Lozano made the indisputably correct decision of basing his work on the Mexicans that had resided for many years outside of the national territory. They were humble and barely educated people, but in spite of having existed far from Mexican soil, had preserved intact the traditions and customs of our ancestors. Without going into detailed analysis, they felt that there was something that does not sink in a shipwreck, that is not shaken by earthquakes nor burned in fires, and that immutable and eternal something is the soul of the Fatherland, which is always there to uplift the fallen, forgive the sinful, console the children who because they are absent cannot take refuge in their mother's lap.
>
> That's why, while I appealed to expatriates, Lozano united with that simple crowd he liked to call the "México de afuera" which had nothing to do with our political and social convulsions. Because he united with a permanent public, Lozano had given *La Prensa* a solid base that, at that time, was unmovable.[59]

Bruce-Novoa has commented that Mexican Americans themselves felt very Mexican and that *La Prensa* gave them an opportunity to see themselves as still part of that nationality:

> I would venture to suggest that a good percentage of the native population of central and south Texas, even some who had never been in Mexico, wanted to be Mexican and considered themselves Mexican, perhaps because the Anglo Americans kept telling them they were exactly that. For these people Lozano provided a vehicle through which they could play out their illusion in a way previous Spanish-language newspa-

pers had not made possible and that English-language publications could never do.[60]

Bruce-Novoa has also offered an alternative reading of the "México de afuera" ideology, suggesting that the Mexican expatriates began to see themselves—and perhaps the Mexican Americans—as more authentically "Mexican" than those people who had remained in the country during and after the Revolution:

> *La Prensa*, molded and controlled by men who were continually living the trauma of exile, reflected the disenchantment, especially in the first two decades of its existence. It was not until the mid-1930s that a general amnesty was declared for exiles by the president of Mexico Lázaro Cárdenas; so until then many of the editors and writers who had fled were not welcomed back in Mexico. And when exiles cannot return, they dedicate themselves to justifying their existence in a dual manner: they manipulate the image and significance of their residence outside their country by discrediting what the homeland has become; and two, they set about proving that they are the authentic bearers of the true tradition of the homeland and even of the ideals of the attempted revolution. Thus, they must declare the revolution a failure, at least temporarily, because only they have remained faithful to the true patriotic ideals. Eventually this exercise in self-justification leads to the claim that the homeland has actually moved with the exiles, that they have managed to bring it with them in some reduced form, and that if the opportunity should arise, they can take it back to replant it in the original garden of Eden. This explains how the Lozano group dared call themselves "El México de Afuera," a term coined by one of the editors. (153)

In fact, many of the expatriates and their families never moved back to Mexico, and their children became United States citizens and the newspaper continued to serve them and their children until the early 1960s. *La Prensa* was able to evolve with the community into ethnic minority status and provide ideological and political analysis for the post-war Mexican American civil rights movement. According to Rubén Munguía, a printer, publisher and writer himself associated with the newspaper,

> *La Prensa*, a conservative paper, can well lay claim to having awakened, even if this was not its goal, the liberal thinking of men such as Alonso Perales, Florencio Flores, M. C. González, Mauro Machado, Ben Garza from

Corpus Christi, Santiago Tafolla, Eleuterio Escobar, Jacob Rodríguez, Charles Albidress, Johnny Solís, Raúl A. Cortez, Joe Olivares, Rubén Lozano, and thousands of Garcías, López', Martínez', etc. who no longer sought to return to the old country. They finally realized that they belonged here, and they organized vibrant, aggressive organizations such as the Knights of America, the Sons of America and LULAC to ensure for the new citizen, the Mexican American, his right to life, liberty and the pursuit of happiness.

The results of their labor were slow coming but in the 1950s great changes took place and the children of *La Prensa*'s early readers began to flex their muscles . . .[61]

Unfortunately, *La Prensa* did not survive long enough to see the Chicano Movement of the 1960s, the civil rights movement that promoted a cultural nationalism of its own. *La Prensa* suffered a slow death beginning in 1957, when it reverted to a weekly and then was sold repeatedly to various interests until it shut down forever in 1963. Unlike Los Angeles, where *La Opinión* still thrives today,[62] San Antonio did not continue to attract a steady or large enough stream of immigrants to sustain the newspaper as the children of the immigrants became English-dominant. Munguía has eloquently characterized *La Prensa*'s demise:

As more of our Mexican group became fluent in English and became qualified to enter into the mainstream, participate in our politics, compete efficiently in the markets and shops, less became our dependency on *La Prensa* which, like an old grandmother, was tolerated, pampered and loved. As her influence became weaker and weaker, she reluctantly lost her hold on our people and gave way to progress and passed on to the world of bittersweet memories. (135)

But in her day *La Prensa* was indeed influential. Lozano and many of his prominent writers and editorialists became leaders of Mexican/Mexican-American communities in the United States. Businessmen such as Lozano captured an isolated and specialized market. They shaped and cultivated their market for cultural products and print media as efficiently as others sold material goods and Mexican foods and delivered specialized services to the community of immigrants. The Mexican community truly benefitted in that the entrepreneurs and businessmen did provide needed goods, information and services that were often denied by the larger society through official and open segregation. And, of course, writers, artists and intellectuals provided both high and popular culture and entertainment in a language not offered by Anglo-American society: Spanish-language books and periodicals, silent films with Spanish-dialog frames and Spanish-language drama and vaudeville, among other entertainment and popular art forms.

The *Cronistas*

Many talented writers from Mexico, Spain and Latin America earned their living as reporters, columnists and critics in the editorial offices of *La Prensa*, *La Opinión* and *El Heraldo de México*. Included among these were Miguel Arce, Adalberto Elías González, Esteban Escalante, Gabriel Navarro and Daniel Venegas. They and many others used the newspapers as a stable source of employment and as a base from which they launched their books or wrote plays and revues for the theater flourishing in Los Angeles and San Antonio. Editorialists such as Nemesio García Naranjo and other political exiles also used the newspapers as a base from which to pursue their political agendas through organizing, speech-making and agitation. García Naranjo, who Lozano recruited for *La Prensa* in 1920 after his *Revista Mexicana* had failed, provided *La Prensa* with that all-important link to the Patria through his intelligent and consistent editorials, both signed and unsigned, that helped to form opinion on the political evolution in Mexico; García Naranjo also married Lozano's sister and became a very strong contributor to the family business, including the publishing house. Various newspaper companies, in fact, established publishing houses—as did both Lozano papers and *El Heraldo de México*—and they marketed the books of authors on their staffs as well as those of many others. The Casa Editorial Lozano advertised its books in the family's two newspapers to be sold via direct mail and in the Lozano bookstore in San Antonio; *El Heraldo de México* also operated a bookstore, in Los Angeles. In addition to the publishing houses owned by the large dailies, in the same cities and in smaller population centers there were many other newspapers publishing books.

The largest and most productive publishing houses resided in San Antonio. Leading the list was the Casa Editorial Lozano, owned by Ignacio E. Lozano, publisher of *La Opinión* and *La Prensa*. Issuing and distributing hundreds of titles per year, it was the largest publishing establishment owned by an Hispanic in the United States. Another was the Viola Novelty Company, owned by P. Viola and associated with his two satirical weekly newspapers, *El Vacilón* (The Joker) and *El Fandango* (The Fandango), which were active from 1916 through at least 1927. The Whitt Company, run by descendants of an English officer who had remained in Mexico after his tour of duty during the French Intervention, still exists today, but only as a printing establishment. Another was the Librería Española, which today only survives as a bookstore. These houses produced everything from religious books to political propaganda, from how-to books (such as Ignacio E. Lozano's *El Secretario Perfecto* [The Perfect Secretary]) to novels and poetry. Many of the novels produced by these houses were part of the genre known as "novels of the Mexican Revolution"; the stories were set within the context of the Revolution in Mexico, often before its outbreak and subsequent chaos, and often commented on historical events and personalities, especially from a conservative or reactionary perspective. As mentioned in the above section on the exile press, much of the counter-revolution was directed from the U. S. Southwest.[63]

While novels were an important expression of the ideology of exile and nationalism, another genre was more traditionally identified with Hispanic newspapers and became essential in forming and reinforcing community attitudes. It was the *crónica*, or chronicle, a short, weekly column that humorously and satirically commented on current topics and social habits in the local community. Rife with local color and inspired by oral lore of the immigrants, it owed its origins to Joseph Addison and Richard Steele in England and arrived in Spain via France. The leading *costumbristas* (chroniclers of customs) in Spain were Ramón de Mesonero Romanos and José Mariano de Larra; *costumbristas* and *cronistas* existed in Mexico since the writings of Joaquín Fernández de Lizardi.[64] In Mexico, the *crónica* was cultivated extensively and evolved further[65] in helping to define and develop Mexican identity over the course of the nineteenth century:

> From the beginning of the nineteenth century to almost our time, the role of the *crónica* was that of verifying or consecrating change and social habits and describing daily life, elevating it to the level of the idiosyncratic (without which Mexicans would be, for example, Paraguayans). In the transition from a colonial mentality to one of independence ... a small collective, unsure of its accomplishments, unsure of its nationalism, saw in the

crónica the shining (ideal) mirror of its transformations and fixations.

To write is to populate. Over a long period of time, the inexhaustive details provided by the *cronistas* served a central purpose: to contribute to the forging of nationhood, describing it and, as much as possible, moralizing for it. The writers of the nineteenth century wrote *crónicas* to document and, what is more important, promote a life style, one that repeated the customs of the authentic civic rituals. The *cronistas* are powerful nationalists because they desire independence and the greatness of the country as a whole . . . or because they wished for an identity that would help them, individualize them, liberate them and eliminate the anxiety and their greatest fear: being the privileged witnesses of things of no importance, of narrating the process of formation of this society which no one was observing. It is necessary to strengthen the Nation, investing pride in her and describing her local and regional pride, representing in literature the most ostensibly "Mexican" ways of living and emphasizing their disdain for imitation of the French and nostalgia for the Hispanic.[66]

In the Southwest, it came to serve purposes never imagined in Mexico or Spain. From Los Angeles to San Antonio and even up to Chicago, Mexican moralists assumed pseudonyms (as was the tradition in the *crónica*) and, from this masked perspective, commented satirically in the first person as witnesses to the customs and behavior of the colony whose very existence was seen as threatened by the dominant Anglo-Saxon culture. The *cronistas* were very influenced by popular jokes, folk anecdotes and vernacular speech, and in general their columns mirrored the surrounding social environment. It was the *cronista*'s job to fan the flames of nationalism and to enforce the ideology of "México de afuera." He had to battle the influence of Anglo-Saxon immorality and Protestantism and to protect against the erosion of the Spanish language and Mexican culture with equally religious fervor. But this was always done not through direct preaching but through sly humor and a burlesque of fictional characters in the community who represented general ignorance or admiringly adopted Anglo ways as superior to those of Hispanics.

Using such pseudonyms as El Malcriado (The Brat—Daniel Venegas), Kaskabel (Rattlesnake—Benjamín Padilla),[67] Loreley (María Luisa Garza), Az.T.K. (The Aztec)[68] and Chicote (The Whip), the *cronistas* tried to whip their community into conformity, poking fun at common folks who mixed Spanish and English (contaminating the purity of Cervantes's beautiful language) and were overly impressed with Yankee ingenuity and technology.

These writers portrayed the two ways of life as being in direct conflict, down to the food consumed, the clothes worn and the furniture placed in the home. The worst transgressors in adopting these ways were labeled *agringados*[69] and *renegados*, that is, gringoized and renegades (originally, the term *renegade* referred to those who denied Christ). And Mexican Americans, who were seen as traitors beyond hope, were similarly brand-

ed in addition to being called *pocho*, the derogatory term refering to an individual of Mexican origin but no longer Mexican.

Among the cultural elites who disseminated the ideology of "México de afuera" was one political refugee who became immensely influential through publishing a newspaper and writing a widely syndicated column. Julio G. Arce was a newspaper publisher from Guadalajara who took up exile in San Francisco, vowing never to return to Mexico owing to his disillusionment with the Revolution. Born in 1870 to an eminent physician in Guadalajara, Arce dedicated himself

Julio G. Arce

to journalism by founding a newspaper when he was only fourteen: *El Hijo del Progreso* (The Child of Progress).[70] After the failure of this venture and while studying for a degree in Pharmacy (no doubt following his father's wishes), Arce returned to journalism and founded the very successful newspaper *El Amigo del Pueblo* (The People's Friend), in which he assumed the pseudonym of "Krichoff" to pen *crónicas*. After this venture and becoming a practicing pharmacist, Arce continued to write for a number of newspapers, including Mazatlán's *El Correo de la Tarde* (The Evening Courier), in which he first used "Jorge Ulica," the pen name that would become famous throughout the Mexican immigrant community of the U. S. Southwest (Rodríguez, 11). It was in Culiacán, Sinaloa, that Arce developed a professional career in journalism, became a professor of Spanish, co-founded his first magazine and was appointed and elected to various political offices. Arce later credited all of the political positions and even his university chair to his pro-government journalistic stances.[71] In Culiacán in 1901, Arce also founded the city's first daily newspaper printed on the first mechanical press in the area, *Mefistófeles* (Mephistopheles), the name he would give to his newspaper in San Francisco. When the Maderist revolution arrived in Sinaloa, Arce used his latest newspaper, *El Diario del Pacífico* (The Pacific Daily), to attack it. In 1911, he had to pack up his family and abandon his home and belongings to escape to Guadalajara in fear of violent reprisals as revolutionary forces arrived in triumph. In Guadalajara, he started a new newspaper, *El Diario del Occidente* (The Western Daily), and attempted to protect the free press from persecution by the revolutionaries. In 1915, Arce was imprisoned for two months by the Carranza army and, when liberated by fellow journalists, he and his family took the next boat into exile in San Francisco (Rodríguez, 14).

In San Francisco, Arce first worked as a laborer for the American Can Company, but soon became associated with *La Crónica* (The Chronicle), an immigrant newspaper published by Spaniard J. C. Castro; the newspaper shortly thereafter was bought by Mexican and Guatemalan business people who appointed Arce director. When the newspaper was once again sold after Arce had professionalized it and made it a financial success, Arce left it and founded his own *Mefistófeles*. To partially underwrite the cost of publication of his new periodical, Arce requested funds from the government of President Venustiano Carranza, supposedly to offset the propaganda put out by enemies of the Revolution writing in other U. S. Spanish-language newspapers; in fact, it seems that *Mefistófeles* did, indeed receive funding of $50 per month (later upped to $60 monthly) from Carranza.[72] Two years later, he ended this paper and returned to *La Crónica,* which was now named *Hispano América*; in 1919, he bought the newspaper outright, and as its sole publisher and owner, transformed it into the most important Hispanic newspaper in the Bay Area (Rodríguez, 16). Like *La Prensa*'s Igancio E. Lozano, Arce took pride in the independent, non-political nature of his newspaper and his service to the immigrant/expatriate community: "sin ligas ni compromisos con nadie, juzgando imparcialmente personalidades y sucesos, desarrollando el programa que forma la base y el principio en que descansan nuestras actividades periodísticas: por la Patria y por la Raza"[73] (without ties or indebtedness to anyone, impartially judging personalities and events, while developing the program that is the basis and principle on which our journalism rests: for our Homeland and for our People). In this, Arce celebrated the spirit of immigrant journalism. Indeed, his newspaper delivered news of the homeland while informing the immigrant community about news and the culture of the host country; he sought to ease the separation from the old and the adjustment to the new. The newspaper continued publishing until 1934, eight years after Arce's death.

As editor and publisher of *Hispano América*, Arce took up the pseudonym of "Jorge Ulica" once again and launched a weekly column that eventually would become the most syndicated *crónica* in the Southwest because of its ability to reflect the life in the Mexican immigrant community of the urban Southwest: "Crónicas Diabólicas" (Diabolical Chronicles). As was the convention in such local-color columns, his pseudonymous alter ego would report weekly on his own adventures and observations in the local community. Through this simple artifice, he satirized humorously the errant customs that were becoming all too common in the *colonia*, such as Mexicans remembering their heritage only during the celebration of Mexican Independence Day, or Mexicans calling themselves Spaniards to assume greater social prestige and avoid the barbs of discrimination. By and large, Ulica assumed the elite perch of satirist observing the human comedy as a self-elected conscience for the Mexican immigrant community. As a purveyor of the ideology of "México de afuera," like many other elites, he revealed his upper class and bourgeois resentment of the working-class Mexican immigrants who, on the one hand, were fascinated by Yankee technology, know-how and economic power, and on the other hand were poor, ignorant representatives of Mexican national culture, all of which he clearly and forcefully illustrated in his *crónicas*. Ulica's particular talents lay in caricature, in emulating the colloquialisms and popular culture of the working-class immigrant while satirizing the culture conflict and misunderstanding encountered by the greenhorn immigrants from the provinces in Mexico. And while his message was rarely subtle, his language and imagery were so richly reflective of common immigrant humor and folk anecdote that they are worthy of study as literature, a literature that arises directly out of the immigrant experience and its folklore.

By far, Ulica's favorite and probably most popular target was the poor Mexican woman who had emigrated from the interior provinces, such as the imaginary "Palos Bonchis" in his story "Por No Hablar English" (Because of Not Speaking English)—in other words, the sticks, as in "Bunch of Sticks." The poor, uneducated female consistently bore the brunt of Ulica's attempts to stem the tide of acculturation and support the survival of the Hispanic family and its culture in an alien environment.[74] In his story "Inacia y Mengildo" (rural-sounding proper names which are truncated in common rural dialect), Ulica warned Mexican men not to bring their wives to the United States, for:

> If married men don't want to become less happy . . . they should not come
> with their companions to the United States. Because things are going very
> poorly here, as the masculine gender is losing in giant steps its "sacred pre-
> rogatives and inalienable rights"... it sickens my soul to see unfortunate
> husbands subjected to a dog's life, to a dog's future and a tragic end.[75]

After this introduction lightly satirizing the U. S. Bill of Rights, Ulica goes on to narrate the apocryphal tale of a Mexican immigrant woman who defenestrated her husband and was acquitted by the courts. Ulica has her testifying in court, in the most provincial and uneducated Spanish, that she was frustrated because her husband was "encevelizado" (uncivilized) and "impropio" (an Anglicism meaning *improper*). According to her testimony, Mengilda went to all lengths to dress and eat stylishly, according to U. S. customs, but her husband resisted tooth and nail. He committed such sins as taking his shoes off on arriving home and going barefoot, and refusing to get his hair cut in "ese rape aristocrático que se usa por acá" (that very aristocratic shaved style that is used here). For food, he would consume only "cosas inominiosas" ("ignominious things"—mispronounced as a sign of her using big words ineffectually to put on airs). Included in the "ini- minius" were such "low-class" Mexican foods as *chicharrones, chorizos, sopes, tostadas, frijoles, menudo y pozole*. It was just impossible to get him to eat clam chowder, bacon, liver and onions, beef stew or hot dogs— supposedly high-class American fare.

It turns out that Inacio came home one Saturday with his fingernails so unkempt (he was a working stiff, after all) that his wife insisted on hir- ing a girl to give him a manicure. When he locked himself in his room and refused to cooperate, Mengilda became enraged and tossed him out the window and then threw a monkey wrench at him, splitting his skull. The poor man expired on the street below. After an eloquent defense by her lawyer, who insists that Mengilda is just a poor foreigner struggling to better herself and become cultured in the United States, Ulica shows Mengilda being exonerated by unanimous jury decision.

After this, narrator Ulica breaks in to emphasize to the reader that this is just one of a legion of incidents that happen every day in the United States, and that as soon as pretty compatriot women arrive, they find out that they are the bosses here, and their husbands must remain shy of heart, short on words and with still hands (meaning that they cannot beat their wives anymore). That is why, Ulica concludes, it is common to see the husband carrying the baby in public, along with packages from the store and grocery bags, ambling along—sad, meditative, crestfallen, depressed—as if fearing possible sentencing to San Quentin or execution for rebelling against his wife.

It seems that no matter where Ulica turns, he encounters the deflated remains of once proud and independent Mexican men. A general of the Mexican Revolution, now a waiter in a third-rate restaurant, bemoans his fate to Ulica:

> In this country women do as they damn well please. My wife, who used to be so obedient, so faithful and such a little mouse in Ojinaga, has become "fireworks" here. She does not heed me, she locks herself up with male friends to play bridge and who knows what else, and when I call her on it, she curses me out. Back home, I could knock her teeth out for less, but here, if you do that, they hang you in San Quentin.[76]

In "Arriba las Faldas" (Up with the Skirts), after affirming that women wear the pants in this country, Ulica attests that, contrary to what happens in Mexico, after dinner here, it is the wife who tells the husband, "Hijito, voy al cine; lava los platos, acuesta los niños y dale un limón al W.C. Después, si tú quieres, te acuestas". (Baby, I'm going to the movies; so wash the plates, put the children to sleep and clean the bathroom. After that, you can go to bed, if you want to" (146). In "Como Hacer Surprise Parties" (How to Give a Surprise Party), Doña Lola Flores is another uneducated denizen of the *colonia* who is enamored of everything American. She, too, attempts to adopt all of the customs here and rid herself of the trappings of the homeland. Doña Lola Flores and her daughters go to the extreme of changing their names: she from Dolores Flores to Pains Flowers; her daughters Esperanza and Eva to Hope and Ivy; she changes her husband's from Ambrosio to Hungrious Flowers; even their dog Violeta has been re-baptized "Vay-o-let."

One of the customs most attractive to Ms. Pains Flowers is that of the surprise party, and so she plots with her daughters to throw herself one on Pain's saint's day; they prepare even for the exact minute when everyone should surprise her yelling, "Olé, Hurrah, Hello!" So the mother, daughters and their Anglo boyfriends spend the whole day decorating, making sandwiches and punch, when finally the ignorant oaf Hungrious shows up full of moonshine. However, he is lucid enough to inform her that there is no reason to party, because it is not her saint's day. When she replies that it is Viernes de Dolores—Saint Dolores' Friday—Hungrious reminds her that she is Mrs. Pains Flowers now, not Dolores—and there are no saints' days on U.S. calendars! The episode ends with Pains dragging Hungrious into the bathroom to give him a sound beating.

If these women are anxious to shuck off their Hispanic culture, their loyalty to the mother tongue is even more suspect, as Ulica ably demonstrates in the letters he receives at the newspaper from the likes of Mrs. Pellejón, who has changed her name to "Skinnyhon." The letter is replete with Anglicisms, malapropisms, regionalisms, poor grammar, misspellings, etc. (see p. 154). And when it comes to the entry of women into the workplace, more specifically the office domain of men, Ulica outdoes himself. In "La Estenógrafa," he is not only scandalized but titillated by the Mexican-American flapper whom he employs as a stenographer. Ulica relates that he had the misfortune of employing Miss Pink, a comely young lady who not only has Anglicized her last name (Rosa), but insists that she is "Spanish." Despite her having graduated from "grammar school," "high school" and "Spanish class," Miss Pink makes horribly embarrassing typing errors. However, the main problem is that even after Miss Pink has found out that Ulica is married, she compromises his modesty. She removes her hose in front of him and changes out of her street shoes, leaving hose and shoes in back of his chair. She tells him that she hopes he is not like her other bosses, who liked to pick up the stockings and smell and kiss them. Eventually, Ulica becomes so intrigued that he does just that—one of the few examples of self-deprecating humor to be found in Arce's *crónicas*. When Ulica confronts the steno about her typing errors, she quits, complaining that he is the worst boss she has ever had, because the married Ulica never invited her to a show or to dinner. And that tells you exactly what Ulica and his cohorts thought about the morality of women in the workplace.

It is in another of Ulica's *crónicas*, "Repatriación Gratuita" (Free

Repatriation), that it becomes evident that one of the main motives for these efforts to control and isolate Mexican/Hispanic women is the fear of exogamy. In this outrageous story, Ulica creates Mrs. Blackberry, a Mexican woman who has just married an Anglo after divorcing her Mexican husband because he refused to wash his face with gasoline in order to whiten it. "Lo dejé por prieto, por viejo y porque no tenía olor en los dientes como los 'americanos fines.'" (I left him because he was dark, old and his teeth didn't smell nice like those refined Americans.) In this anecdote, greater freedom for women, higher aspirations through association with the "white race" and American materialism all come together to entice the vain and ambitious Mexican woman to abandon both her ethnic culture and her husband.

While Ulica was without a doubt expressing a bourgeois sensibility in censuring Mexican women for adopting supposed Anglo-American customs and especially identifying the flapper as the most representative figure in this acculturation, his point of view was by no means exclusive to his social class. Another immigrant journalist and creative writer, who identified himself as a working-class Mexican immigrant, Daniel Venegas, expressed similar views in his satirical weekly newspaper *El Malcriado* (The Brat), and in his picaresque novel of immigration *Las aventuras de Don Chipote o cuando los pericos mamen* (The Adventures of Don Chipote, or When Parakeets Suckle Their Young). In Venegas' humor-filled novel, he displays little sympathy for women, depicting them almost exclusively as prostitutes, gold-digging flappers and vaudeville actresses of low morality. The one exception is Don Chipote's wife, who typically represents home and hearth and the nuclear family; she has no name of her own, other than Doña Chipota, an extension of her husband's identity. Doña Chipota serves to restore order; she brings the novel to its resolution by rescuing her errant husband who has been beguiled by the incarnation of Gringo corruption of Mexican femininity: the flapper. The message of the novel, by the way, is that Mexicans should not be deceived by the glitter of the United States, for Mexicans will never become rich in the United States as long as parakeets do not suckle their young; Mexicans serve only as beasts of burden in the States and as lambs to be fleeced by both corrupt institutions and individuals.

It is even more ironic that Venegas, who so identified with the working-class immigrant, would not make common cause with working-class women. This is amply seen in *El Malcriado*, which he single-handedly wrote, illustrated and typeset. In the April 17, 1927, edition, Venegas drew a caricature of a poor waitress with her toe protruding from her *huarache* and satirized such waitresses' delivering food orders up and down Main Street of Los Angeles in dirty, broken-down shoes, smelling up the sidewalk to the extent of overcoming the fragrance of the food on their trays. On the front page of the same issue, Venegas drew a scene of two flirtatious Mexican flappers getting their hair bobbed in a men's barber shop under the headline of "¡Cómo Gozan los Barberos Rapando las Guapetonas! Se Pasan los Días Enteros Papachando a las Pelonas." (The Barberos Love to Cut the Hair of these Beauties! They Spend the Entire Day Caressing Flappers.) Beneath the cartoon, Venegas placed the following satirical verse:

> To get their hair done two flappers
> went to the barber Don Simón
> That night both chickees were going out
> to party and have a good time.
>
> "Please finish me in a hurry,"
> said Julieta while her neck was shaved,
> "And then Enriqueta's turn will come,
> and I'll give you both a kiss."
>
> The barber then worked so fast
> that he did Juliet before a minute passed,
> but he wasn't given what was promised to him
> not even after finishing with Enriqueta.[77]

Mexican immigrants were not the only Latinos to agonize over the dangers of assimilation, cultural annihilation and exogamy. Hispanic immigrant newspapers in New York—catering to a diverse community of Cubans, Puerto Ricans, Dominicans, Spanish and others—also utilized the *crónicas* in a similar fashion. But the ideas expressed in these *crónicas* and their host newspapers did not coalesce into as strong an ideology as the "México de afuera"; in fact, *Gráfico*, like many other Hispanic papers of New York, promoted a pan-Hispanism that united the Hispanics in the metropolis with all of Latin America. Nationalism could not develop as strongly in an environment of such diverse Hispanic ethnicity. According to the mission statement in its first issue, one of *Gráfico*'s main objectives was to bring the diverse Hispanic immigrants together as brothers:

> The constant growth of the Spanish and Spanish American colony has led
> us to publish this weekly that comes to participate in the defense of all
> those who make up the grand Hispanic family. We shall make an effort to
> further than greatest advancement and well being of us, who far from our
> beloved homelands, must join together on foreign soil under only one
> banner: that of brotherhood.[78]

But standing on their Hispanic cultural background, the predominantly
male journalists and *cronistas* quite often did attempt to influence the
community in tightening the reins on Hispanic women. New York's
Gráfico (Illustrated, 1926–1931),

Gráfico

published by a consortium of
tobacco workers, writers and theatrical artists, was first edited by
Alberto O'Farrill, an Afro-Cuban
actor and playwright very popular
for depicting the stereotyped
Cuban farce role of Negrito
(Blackie) in blackface. In addition
to editing *Gráfico*, he served as its
chief cartoonist and also as a frequent *cronista* who signed his
column as "Ofa," the name of the
first-person mulatto narrator
whose main preoccupation is
finding work and keeping life and
limb together. Almost every issue
during the first year of publication of *Gráfico* displayed an
O'Farrill cartoon that satirized
American flappers. But more than satire and censure, the cartoons make
apparent the sexual attraction that Latino men felt for these women of
supposedly looser morals than Latin women. Almost all are displayed with
flesh peeking out of lingerie or from under their short dresses. At least
two of the cartoons have purposefully ambiguous legends with titillating
double entendres. In one (3 July 1927), a flapper is reclined in an unlady-

like position on an overstuffed chair, holding a basket of flowers in her lap; the legend reads, "Lector ¿No te da el olor?" (Reader, doesn't the smell hit you?) In another (27 March 1927), a flapper is raising the skirt of her dress while a man with a cigarette lighter is reclining at her feet and in front of a parked car. The legend reads, "Buscando el Fallo" (Looking for the Problem). But the man's wandering eyes clearly reveal an intentional titillation.

O'Farrill published a series of signed and unsigned columns in *Gráfico*. It was in the "Pegas Suaves" (Easy Jobs) *crónicas* that he signed "Ofa" where he developed the running story of the

Alberto O'Farrill

mulatto immigrant trying to survive in the big city. In the unsigned ones, O'Farrill poked fun at local customs, which more often than not dealt with the relationship of *viejos verdes* (dirty old men), machos and flappers. On the page above the unsigned ones, he usually placed a cartoon illustration of the *crónica* below. Again, flappers were a frequent preoccupation in these whimsical pieces. In "El Misterio de Washinbay" (Mystery on Washingbay, 5 June 1927), O'Farrill depicts three American flappers who abandon their customary Broadway cabarets in an attempt to attract publicity and rich husbands by establishing a three-woman colony of abstention and deprivation in a rural location. In "El Emboque" (The Maw, 8 May 1927), O'Farrill goes at length to describe how Latin men position themselves strategically at the street-level entrance to the subway, to ogle the flappers as they descend to their trains: "contemplando las líneas curvas que más derecho entran por su vista" (observing the curves that went straight into their view). The sight of two flappers, who the narrator compares to merchant ships, is so enticing that even the *Gráfico* photographer who supposedly provided the above illustration, could not steady his hands, he was so filled with jealousy of the two oglers. O'Farrill states that the custom has become so popular that its has become a true plague and closes the column with a warning that the police have on occasion used their blackjacks on oglers.

A much more serious note on the subject of Hispanic women adapting the American flapper dress and personality was sounded by Jesús Colón, one of the most important Hispanic columnists and intellectuals in the New York Hispanic community for more than fifty years. Colón also began his career as a *cronista* in *Gráfico* and other Spanish-language newspapers in the area. Over the years, he would write for Puerto Rico's labor union newspaper *Justicia* (Justice) in the 1920s, and later New York's *Gráfico* (1926-1931), *Pueblos Hispanos* (1943-1944, Hispanic Peoples), *Liberación* (1946-1949, Liberation), *The Daily Worker* (1924-1958), among various others. A cigar worker who was an autodidact and one of the most politicized members of the community of cultural workers and union organizers, Colón made the transition to writing in English and in the mid-1950s became the first Puerto Rican columnist for *The Daily Worker*, the newspaper published by the Communist Party of America.[79] Colón was a progressive thinker and even penned feminist essays long before such thinking became politically correct. However, upon assuming the convention of *cronista* and taking on the moralistic persona of his pseudonym "Miquis Tiquis,"[80] which he used in *Gráfico* in 1927 and 1928, Colón joined his colleagues in attacking Hispanic women for assuming flapper customs:

> Reader, if you would like to see the caricature of a flapper, you only have to look at a Latina who aspires to be one. The Yanqui flapper always makes sure that her ensemble of exaggerations looks chic, as they say in German (*sic*). They also possess that divine jewel of finely imitated frigidity. That disdainful arching of their eyes that upon crossing their legs almost from . . . to . . . it seems not important to them that they are being watched. *Seeming frigidity, that's the phrase.* That Latin *would-be flapper* likes to be looked at, and to attract attention paints her face into a mask. Two poorly placed splashes of rouge on the cheeks and four really noticeable piles of lipstick on the lips. They criticize new fads; then they adopt them, to the extreme of exaggeration.[81]

Colón's further preoccupation with the flapper is also seen in the following poem which he published in *Gráfico*:

The Flapper

Like a chole girl who would be a New Yorker,
the "flapper" agitates the air with her affectatious struts.
Her dress, a futurist version of the latest style,
is a thousandfold suggestive with its divine silk.

That men should look her over as she walks
is her supreme desire. If someone should mention marriage,
her answer is a loud laugh that cuts
the most sublime illusion. Assassinating laugh!

Expert queen of the latest dangerous dance jump,
make-up streaked, superficial, fickle girl,
like a liberated slave entering a new life.

In contrast, they make me remember my grandmother,
who as she sewed told me of flying giants,
in a voice as shaky as a lost prayer.[82]

In summary, the graphic and written records of community moralists and satirists not only amply illustrate the nationalistic attitudes promoted by these immigrant newspapers,[83] but also how those attitudes pressed readers to conform to old gender roles and resist the social change that the new American host culture was making imminent. The pressure placed on women in this conflict of cultural roles and mores was probably greater than what was ever felt in the homeland, given the greater competition for Latinas perceived to exist here because of their scarcity in the immigrant community and because of the perceptibly greater freedoms that women enjoyed in the United States. While the Roaring Twenties saw the liberalization of women's roles and their entrance into the workplace, it was also the period of massive immigration of very conservative segments of the Mexican population. Their first reaction was not to liberalize but to resist the liberal influence by tightening men's control over women.

Hispanic male writers on the East Coast, while not as severe as the Mexican writers in the Southwest, also censured women for Americanizing and, perhaps less moralistically, allowed themselves to be titillated, and openly displayed this behavior in their cartoons and columns. Of course, in both groups, the Mexicans in the Southwest and the Latinos in the

Buying *La Prensa* at a New York newsstand.

Northeast, Hispanic women were seen as the center of the family and the key to survival of the group, the culture and the language. However, it was men doing the seeing, and they controlled the media: publishing houses, newspapers, theaters, etc. It was these very men who saw themselves as the self-appointed conscience of the community in the *crónicas* that were so popular in the immigrant communities.

In 1913, José Campubrí founded *La Prensa* in New York City to serve the community of mostly Spanish and Cuban immigrants in and around Manhattan's 14th Street; little did he know then that *La Prensa* would become the nation's longest-running Spanish-language daily newspaper (in 1962 it merged with *El Diario de Nueva York*). One of the main reasons for its longevity is that *La Prensa* was able to adapt to the new Spanish-speaking nationalities that immigrated to the city, especially the Puerto Ricans who migrated from their island *en masse* during and after World War II and came to form the largest Hispanic group in the city. *La Prensa* at first featured a daily column, "Informaciones de Puerto Rico," but over the years Puerto Rican interest and staff grew steadily until becoming the dominant ethnic interest in the paper; by the 1980s, one million Puerto Ricans were residing in New York.

In 1948, *El Diario de Nueva York* was founded by Dominican immigrant Porfirio Domenici, specifically appealing to the Puerto Rican community and giving *La Prensa* competition for this growing readership. In 1958, *La Prensa* hired its first Puerto Rican editor, Francisco Cardona; he had served as a press secretary for Governor Luis Muñoz Marín of Puerto Rico. Cardona reshaped the paper, converting it to a tabloid and involving it more in the Puerto Rican community of the city (Fitzpatrick, 306–7). In the 1950s, the new owner, Fortune Pope, a prominent Italian businessman and publisher of the daily *Il Progreso*, founded an important Spanish-language radio station, WHOM-FM and AM, and hired from *El Diario de Nueva York* the popular Puerto Rican newspaperman José Lumén Román, who under the auspices of *La Prensa* had founded the Spanish American News Agency to provide news to the press about the Hispanic community; he also conducted many investigative campaigns for *La Prensa* (Fitzpatrick, 307).

Then, too, during the 1950s and into the 1960s, *La Prensa* had on its staff the *grand dame* of Puerto Rican journalism, Luisa Quintero, who in her column took up all the causes of the Puerto Rican community and covered its issues, culture and religious life with loving concern. At one point, Quintero played a crucial role in rallying the Puerto Rican community to its first victory at the state level: pressuring Governor Nelson Rockefeller to commute the death sentence to life imprisonment of Salvador (The Capeman) Agrón, who otherwise would have been the youngest person to ever be executed in the electric chair. "For a generation Luisa Quintero's influence was outstanding. No one has emerged to take her place" (Fitzpatrick, 309).

Using the slogan of "Champion of the Puerto Ricans," *El Diario de Nueva York* was targeted at the Puerto Rican community from the first, despite its having been founded by a Dominican with considerable Venezuelan backing. Publisher Domenici hired as its first editor Vicente Gegel Polanco, a well known journalist and political figure from Puerto Rico; in 1952, he replaced Gegel with José Dávila Ricci, a journalist associated with Governor Luis Múñoz Marín (Fitzpatrick, 307). In 1954, Dávila was replaced by Stanley Ross, a news correspondent with years of experience in Latin America. Over the years, *El Diario de Nueva York* conducted many campaigns and programs on behalf of the Puerto Rican community. It published an exposé of the abuse and inhuman conditions in Puerto Rican migrant farm labor camps on the east coast of the United States, as well as an exposé of labor racketeering and phantom labor unions that were bleeding funds from poor Puerto Ricans. *El Diario* opened and operated a center to receive and follow up on grievances brought by Hispanics about housing conditions, employment, union activities, consumer fraud and other issues. The paper often published these grievances in the newspapers as a means of applying pressure to resolve the problems. Young lawyers began gathering at *El Diario*'s grievance center and rendering free assistance to the poor. Community leaders claim that both programs inspired the city government to open a consumer fraud division and legal aid centers (Fitzpatrick, 308).

Like San Antonio's *La Prensa* and Los Angeles' *La Opinión*, both *El Diario de Nueva York* and *La Prensa* were fundamentally business enterprises, rendering services to the Hispanic community, tailoring the news and commentary to the major Hispanic groups residing in the city. As such, they did not get directly involved in politics, but echoed the general mood of their community. Both newspapers favored Governor Luis Muñoz Marín and the commonwealth status of the island; they opposed Fidel Castro and Dominican dictator Rafael Trujillo. They operated as typical immigrant newspapers even while a large number of readers, the Puerto Ricans, were citizens of the United States.

In 1962, O. Roy Chalk, owner of *El Diario de Nueva York*, purchased *La Prensa* and merged the two journals. From the 1970s to the present, the Hispanic ethnic balance in the city and metropolitan area has shifted repeatedly, with the immigration of Cuban refugees, then Central Americans, and always a steady flow of Dominicans, who today form the largest Hispanic group in the city. Following its well tested formulas, *El Diario-La Prensa* has repeatedly adjusted its focus to embrace the new groups and reflect their concerns and interests.

In 1981, the Gannett newspaper corporation bought *El Diario-La Prensa*; in 1989, it was sold to El Diario Associates, Inc., a corporation founded by Peter Davidson, a former Morgan Stanley specialist in the newspaper industry. In 1990, the Times Mirror Corporation purchased a fifty percent interest in *La Opinión* (San Antonio's *La Prensa* had ceased to exist in 1963). In 1976, the *Miami Herald* founded *El Miami Herald*; in 1987 this Spanish-language daily was transformed into the new and improved *El Nuevo Herald*. Both the Spanish- and the English- language dailies are owned by the Knight-Ridder newspaper chain.[84] Thus today, the three major Hispanic dailies are owned and controlled by American (non-Hispanic) multimedia corporations; how this has affected their relation to Hispanic immigrants has not as yet been assessed. There are, however, other smaller dailies which in varying degrees remain independent.

The Labor Press

Both immigrant and native Hispanic workers have engaged in the founding and building of unions throughout their history as industrial and farm workers in the United States. Since the nineteenth century, Hispanic workers have been embraced on a large scale by industry in the United

States—at times, as a means of undermining labor organizing here. This fact makes their labor press mostly a phenomenon of *immigrant* life. There are notable exceptions to this tendency, such as California's *El Malcriado* (1964–1975), a farm-worker newspaper founded by the United Farm Workers under César Chávez; the UFW was made up mainly of Mexican-American workers. But historically, the Hispanic labor unions and their periodicals were created by and for Latinos working in specific industries—often ones associated with their native cultures or old-country backgrounds: cigar rolling, agricultural work, ranching, copper mining and fruit harvesting. In more contemporary times, Hispanics have been leaders in organizing other trades and industries, such the steel mills, needle trades, hospitals and manufacturing.[85]

One of the first, largest and most significant industries to rely almost exclusively on Hispanic labor was the cigar manufacturing industry based in Key West, Tampa, New York and San Antonio, among other locations. In 1886, the first transfer of a whole industry from Latin America to the United States began when Spanish and Cuban entrepreneurs acquired Florida swampland near Tampa and built a cigar-producing town, Ybor City. In 1880, the population of Tampa itself was only 721; a decade later the combined population of Tampa and Ybor City was 5,500, and that number tripled by 1900. The first of the entrepreneurs to establish their cigar factories, Vicente Martínez Ybor and Ignacio Haya, hoped to attract a docile workforce (unlike the labor union activists in Cuba), avoid U. S. import tariffs and get closer to their markets in the United States. Also, the Cuban wars for independence were raging and continually disrupting business. Martínez Ybor, Spanish by birth, had immigrated to Cuba when he was fourteen; after working in the cigar trade in Key West and New York, he settled on Tampa and built the world's largest cigar factory there. The industry in Ybor City grew to ten factories by 1895 and became the principal cigar-producing area in the United States, at a time when cigar-smoking was at a peak. By 1900, there were about 150 cigar factories in West Tampa and Ybor City, producing more than 111 million cigars annually.[86]

Not only were the cigar company owners wrong about escaping the labor unrest endemic to the industry in Cuba, the greater freedom of expression afforded on U. S. soil allowed the cigar workers to organize more openly and to publish their periodicals more extensively. In 1899, the cigar workers organized their first large strike in Ybor City. They struck again in 1901, 1910, 1920 and 1931 (Mormino, 40-5). The cigar workers ultimately formed the strongest unions of any Hispanic workers in the history of the United States.

Workers in the cigar crafts in Cuba and Puerto Rico had traditionally been more politicized because of the high level of informal education obtained through the institution of the *lector*: a person selected and paid by the workers to read to them throughout their laborious and boring work day. The *lectores* would read extensively from world literature, as well as from national authors and, of course, newspapers and magazines. The importance of the *lector* institution was summarized by Fornet:

> The proletariat encountered in the reading—or "the desire to hear reading," as an editorialist for *El Siglo* (The Century) put it—the most democratic and efficient means of acculturation that existed at the time. Oral transmission, effected in their own work place during working hours, was the ideal mechanism for satisfying the intellectual needs of a class that had emerged wanting books, but not having the resources, the time and in many cases the schooling to read them. The Reading was the first attempt at extending books to the masses for solely educational and recreational reasons. Among the privileged classes, the book had always been a sumptuous object and, ultimately, an instrument of domination or lucre; the proletariat converted it into an instrument of self-education, using it only to advance itself ideologically and culturally.[87] (185-6)

During the nineteenth century in Cuba, the institution was repeatedly repressed, as cigar workers became part of the vanguard for Cuban independence from Spain. In Key West and Tampa, the cigar workers publicized the independence movement in their publications and theatrical performances, and the cigar workers became the most important sector in raising funds for the revolutionary movement. It was in fact in these communities that Cuban nationalism became much advanced, that the revolutionary ideology escaped the workshop and permeated all social activities in the clubs, theaters and mutualist societies. It became the basis for an alliance of the manual workers with the cultural workers (intellectuals such as José Martí); and these intellectuals, writers and journalist began to write especially for this intellectually and politically aware society of artisans (Fornet, 192). After the Spanish-American War, many cigar workers in New York, Tampa and Key West became socialists and anarchists, and were also supporters of the Puerto Rican nationalist movement, pushing for Puerto

Rico's independence from the United States.

The roots of the Cuban-American labor press are to be found in Cuba in this tobacco workers' tradition. *La Aurora*, the first workers' newspaper in Cuba, was founded by tobacco worker-poet Saturnino Martínez in 1865, and was closely identified with the *lector* tradition; in addition to publishing news of interests to workers, the newspaper pioneered schools for workers, encouraged workers to use libraries and vigilantly protected the *lector* tradition (Fornet, 138-40). Following in this tradition, the Cuban tobacco workers in Florida established the first labor newspaper, *La Federación* (The Federation, 1899-?), as the official organ of the union of tobacco workers in Tampa. Before that, their interest in organizing and in anarchism had been addressed by their local newspapers, *El Esclavo* (The Slave, 1894) and *La Voz del Esclavo* (The Voice of the Slave, 1900).[88] Other important union newspapers from the Tampa area were *Boletín Obrero* (Worker Bulletin, 1903-?), *El Federal* (The Federal, 1902-03), *La Defensa* (The Defense, 1916-?), *El Internacional* (The International, 1904-?) and *Vocero de la Unión de Tabaqueros* (Voice of the Tobacco Workers' Unions, 1941-?).

In New York, Hispanic laborers, mostly Spanish and Cuban cigar workers, built a labor and radical press on the base of a revolutionary press that already existed there (see the "Press in Exile," above). At the end of the nineteenth century, New York received a large influx of Spanish working-class immigrants, just as it did other southern Europeans; they joined their fellow Spanish-speakers in Harlem, on 14th Street and in Brooklyn, and participated in raising working-class consciousness through such newspapers as *El Despertar* (The Awakening, 1891-1912), *Cultura Proletaria* (Proletarian Culture, 1910-59) and *Brazo y Cerebro* (Brawn and Brains, 1912), which were primarily anarchist periodicals with articles written by some of the most noted anarchists of the day, including Federico Urales and Anselmo Lorenzo (Chabrán, 157). *Cultura Proletaria* became the longest-lasting anarchist periodical published in Spanish in the United States. Edited by the noted Spanish anarchist author Pedro Esteves and published by Spanish workers, over the years the paper passed into the hands of Cubans and Puerto Ricans as the composition of the workforce changed. According to Chabrán, Puerto Ricans early on established their own labor and radical press in such organs as *La Mísera* (The Miserable One, 1901), *Unión Obrera* (Worker Union, 1902) and, much later, *Vida Obrera* (Worker Life, 1930- 32).

Cultural Magazines

While union and workers' periodicals served the organizational and cultural interests of a highly politicized segment of the immigrant working-class and intellectual population, Hispanic elites felt the need to reproduce the cultural refinement that was a product of their education and breeding in the homeland. Whether to remain connected to the cultural accomplishments of the greater international Hispanic community or to fill a void that existed in exile, whether political or intellectual, a number of high-quality periodicals were established in the Northeast and Southwest. Some of them, such as the New York monthlies *El Ateneo: Repertorio Ilustrado de Arte, Ciencia y Literartura* (The Athenaeum: Illustrated Repertoire of Arts, Science and Literature, 1874-77) and *El Americano* (The American, 1892-?), retained the newspaper format, but published primarily literature and commentary, as well as illustrations. Others looked much like the mainstream cultural magazines being published at the turn of the century, such as *Harper's Magazine* and *Cosmopolitan*. What was most distinctive about them was that they placed the Hispanic immigrant community of the United States on the international cultural map, for they drew their selections from essayists, fiction writers and poets from Spain and Spanish America as well as from the United States. Pan-Hispanism and hemispheric integration, in fact, formed the basis of *El Ateneo's* and *El Americano's* ideological stance. And they both had a circulation overseas as well as in the United States. *El Ateneo*—which claimed a circulation and agents in Mexico, Central and South America, the West Indies, California, New Mexico and cities within the United States—made a special appeal to American manufacturers to advertise within its pages as a way to reach the Spanish-speaking world; it also promised to supply information for advertisers on the markets in Spanish America, according to its own advertisement published in English in the January, 1877 edition of this Spanish-language magazine. While these magazines were celebrating the art and culture of the Americas, *Ambas Américas: Revista de Educación, Bibliografía y Agricultura* (Both Americas: Educational, Bibliographic and Agricultural Magazine, 1867-68), a short-lived quarterly published in New York, set a task for itself of informing the people and institutions in Central and South America of the educational, scientific and agricultural advances in the United States so that they would be emulated in the Spanish American countries.

El Americano's masthead read "periódico mensual de literatura, comercio, artes, ciencia, noticias y anuncios" (monthly periodical of literature, commerce, arts, science, news and announcements); however, its guiding principal was hemispheric integration, that is, the identification and promotion of the culture and identity of the Americas, that "¡Todos somos americanos!" (We are all Americans!):

> In favor of the unification of the Americas, whose children, without distinction of origin nor religion, should not recognize nor sustain any other doctrine than that of free men, that of solid unity, indivisible, like an Egyptian monolith, a giant shield extending its protection over all of the reaches of the Americas, from the Boreal regions of Cape Barrow to the latitudes of Cape Horn. (June, 1893)[89]

El Americano was for the Monroe Doctrine, but very much in favor of immigration from the rest of the world to further the progress in all fields to make of the Americas the most prosperous and enlightened continents in the world:

> We maintain the principle of the Monroe Doctrine, that the Americas belong to their children, and to those who with the sincere honor of the citizen who aspires to dignify his moral existence by living in the free communities of the American world, comes from other parts of the planet and applies his shoulders to the wheel of progress that unifies and makes nations great; who comes to make common cause with all of the ambitions, with all of the noble efforts of the masses, in the development of all of the activities of life in the broad spheres of the sciences, arts, industries and commerce, whose motors, running on the heat of manifold ideas stimulated by glory, grow into titanic-sized enterprises to the surprise of the Old World. (June, 1893)[90]

In opposition to Europe, the Old World, *El Americano* believed in democracy and the American Dream: the freedoms and opportunities available in the New World would allow men from all over the planet to prosper:

> The Americas, triumphant, gives the example for the world to follow, opening its doors to those who are buried in the degradation of vassalage, and offering the generous protection of its institutions that makes equal all men of good faith. (June, 1893)[91]

In referring to South America, a November 1, 1893, editorial exclaimed:

> Ah, how much we cherish that sweet hope of the fusion of the nations of this continent, because they, while preserving their autonomy, will be unified in industry, commerce, riches, production, consumption and in the glory of having arrived at the goal of prosperity by applying their exclusive spirit and their own conviction.[92]

To involve its readership in its cause, *El Americano* sponsored essay contests, offering a gold medal for the best article written on developing the friendship and commerce between Latin America and the United States (August 1892). Published by American businessman Lincoln Valentine, owner of the Valentine Brothers Produce Exchange, who invested his money in the cause of hemispheric integration, *El Americano* afforded the services of an outstanding editor, Cuban poet Enrique Nattes and some of the leading writers from throughout the hemisphere. The magazine aspired to publish in the heart of the United States the greatest Latin American voices at the precise moment when the United States was forging its leadership of the world in science, technology and freedom, explained its inaugural issue in June, 1892. It was Valentine who chose for the newspaper as well as his own life the theme of "Todos somos americanos." And in its first number, *El Americano*'s prospectus promised that this magazine, unlike others, would always have enough financial resources to continue its mission:

> We soulfully commit ourselves to the enterprise, after having in place the necessary resources so that in a short while we can avoid being forced to search for support in pursuing the ideal that we cherish, which is sustaining here a cultured, illustrated, patriotic periodical that will be the genuine expression of the ideas, sentiments, aspirations, advances and abilities of our American race. (June, 1892)[93]

And, indeed, those financial resources did not derive from produce alone, for Valentine Brothers was invested in diverse businesses in Latin America, including the construction of the inter-oceanic railroad in Honduras (*El Americano*, September, 1892).

From a similarly internationalist perspective, the most important illustrated Hispanic magazine, *La Revista Ilustrada de Nueva York* (The Illustrated Revue, 1882-?) aspired to be an Hispanic *Harper's*:

In this genre it has succeeded admirably in creating, in Spanish, the genuine type of magazine: it is no more nor less our own *Harper's Magazine*. Its illustrations complete and perfect the readings, that, thanks to them, acquire artistic representation, —and they are so fine and well executed that by themselves and independently from the themes they illustrate constitute additional works of art.[94]

Publisher Elías de Losada explained on the front page of the January 1893 issue that the magazine was meant to be a complement to daily newspapers; it would select the most important world events for commentary. Yet it was evident from the outset that *La Revista Ilustrada de Nueva York* would give clear preference to the publication of literature from some of the most renowned living writers of the Hispanic world. This was made additionally clear in the same issue as the editor spoke of upcoming projects:

We shall dedicate special attention to literary matters, that so much seduce our people of vivid imagination and passionate temperament, and therefore we shall offer short novels, which can fit in one issue, ingenious and pleasant stories, original or translated, but by force written by the most distinguished writers; literary criticism, that should contribute to the formation of good taste; poetic compositions by the most renowned lyric poets of Spain and Spanish America, and in general all that will tend to make this section a specialty markedly favored by all of our subscribers.[95]

Among the best-known writers who sent works to be published in *La Revista Ilustrada de Nueva York*, including works for exclusive publication, were the international leader of Modernism Rubén Darío and many of his followers, such as Mexicans Salvador Díaz Mirón and Manuel Gutiérrez Nájera; among the Spaniards were Gaspar Núñez de Arce, Benito Pérez Galdós, Juan Valera and Emilia Pardo Bazán. To attract such distinguished collaborators, editor-owner Elías de Losada had to spend handsomely[96] and, consequently, had to charge subscribers high enough prices to sustain the operation—three dollars in U. S. currency—placing the magazine beyond the reach of the Hispanic working class. (Of course, the magazine was targeted to the middle and upper classes of educated Hispanics.) Literally all of the countries of Spanish America were represented, as were expatriate writers residing in New York, such as Cubans Antonio and Francisco Sellén, José María Heredia and José Martí.[97] And the dissemination of the magazine was equally international, as it was distributed by a network of agents throughout the Caribbean, Central and South America and even as far east as the Philippines. (Chamberlin and Shulman, 5)

According to Chamberlin and Shulman, *La Revista Ilustrada de Nueva York* saw itself as thoroughly modern and progressive and identified highly with American technology, industrial and scientific advancement:

> Service in the cause of civilization and progress constituted its ideological base. The editors' Spencerian positivistic philosophy—evolution towards progress achieved in social systems characterized by order and stability—led them to eulogize North American life in which progress, order, liberty, and technical advancement stood in such marked contrast to Latin America's. (8)

Part of this progressive attitude was seen as the magazine's special appeal to women, not only covering their issues but including subjects that were seen as feminine: fashions and sentimental prose and poetry. In particular, the magazine posited an intellectual and thinking life for women, where stereotype and conventional thought posited none at all for Hispanic American women:

> More than once we have read with indignation in foreign newspapers that the women of our America live separated from intellectual life, that they vegetate in ignorance and are consumed by sterile mysticism. We shall oppose those observations with practical truth, and it will be shown that Hispanic American women know how to present themselves to the world, in order to take their place with dignity and pride among the legions who live in thought and spirit and enlighten humanity with their knowledge.[98]

Despite this apparently progressive attitude, there were few women who contributed stories, poems or essays to the magazine; the most represented was Peruvian Amalia Puga, who had twenty-three items published from 1890 to 1892. Among these was her essay "La Literatura en la Mujer" (The Literature in Women), which was her inaugural speech upon being elected to the Lima Ateneo, a society of intellectuals and writers, much like an academy; it was published in the third issue of 1892. Puga's contributions to the magazine were among the most successful, for they gave rise to a steady flow of correspondence and to writers from Ecuador, Peru and elsewhere sending in poems in her honor.[99] More than women writing themselves, however, there were numerous essays written by men about women's issues or in honor of specific women writers and intellectuals. It seems, on the whole, that there was more a recognition of women as a market than as creators and thinkers to be included in the pages of the magazine. The most renowned female contributor to the magazine was Spaniard Emilia Pardo Bazán, who had four items published between 1891 and 1892; but notably absent were many other women intellectuals of the Americas, some of whom, such as Lola Rodríguez de Tió, were publishing in New York's *El Americano*.

Like so many of the newspapers and other cultural magazines, *La Revista Ilustrada de Nueva York* was a promoter and defender of what it identified as Hispanic values. Despite its generally positive stance on American civilization and the wonders of its science and technology and the stability of its government, the magazine called for pan-Hispanic unity in resisting U. S. expansionism during a time characterized by American filibustering and interventionism: "En presencia de la [raza] anglosajona, que por superioridad industrial nos menosprecia, y por cálculo nos espía en cada una de nuestras lamentables caídas, españoles de España y América deben aparecer unidos, siquiera sea en terreno literario, mantener sus tradiciones, perseguir sus propios ideales . . ." (In the presence of the Anglo-Saxon [people], who because of their industrial superiority disparage us, and who purposefully spy on each of our lamentable failures, we Spanish of Spain and the Americas must unify, even if it is only on literary terrain, we must maintain our traditions, pursue our own ideals . . . [December, 1891]) Thus, despite its elitism, *La Revista Ilustrada de Nueva York* had to protect Hispanic language, culture and values from a perceived onslaught of American imperialism; on an international, pan-Hispanic scale, this too was reminiscent of the nationalism of immigrant newspapers and the preoccupations of both workers and elites.

New York thus launched and supported a number of fine illustrated magazines at the end of the century. Most were the product of American and Latin American business ties and depended on a network of elite Hispanic business people and intellectuals. This was nowhere more obvious than when in 1892 the New York Press Club invited editor Enrique Nattes to establish an Hispanic American branch of the club—precisely at the time when the club was entering a fund-raising campaign to construct a new building—and to enlist the services of their wives in putting on a fund-raising fair. Elected to the leadership of the Hispanic section were the Mexican consul, Dr. Juan N. Navarro, to the presidency; Nicanor Bolet Peraza, director of *Las Tres Américas*, as first vice president; Cuban printer-publisher Nestor Ponce de León as treasurer; publisher Lincoln Valentine as secretary; and to the executive board (*vocales*) Enrique Trujillo, director of *El Porvenir*, and Fernando Valentine, editor of *Medical News*.

Over the years in New York, pan-Hispanism and the need to promote Hispanic culture led to the founding of numerous cultural magazines, many of which clearly catered to the educated tastes of the Hispanic middle class and bourgeoisie, and especially to women engaged in cultural and philanthropic endeavors. One notable example, *Artes y Letras*,[100] was founded in 1933 by Josefina (Pepina) Silva de Cintrón in association with the Grupo Cultural Cervantes (Cervantes Cultural Group), constituted mainly of Puerto Rican amateur actors and writers. Silva de Cintrón was a feminist and cultural advocate who was a member of the Unión de Mujeres Americanas (American Women's Union). Under her directorship, *Artes y Letras* succeeded as a monthly cultural magazine with an international readership for a number of years. Its distribution extended to Central and South America, the Caribbean and even the Canary Islands. In its pages were poems, essays and short stories of the leading figures of contemporary literature of Puerto Rico: Isabel Cuchí Coll, Luis Palés Matos, Ferdinand Cestero, Carmen Alicia Cadilla, Martha Lomar, Concha Meléndez, Carmelina Vizacarrondo and Enrique Laguerre. The number of women published was notable and furthered the mission of editors, Pedro Caballero and Pedro Juan Labarthe, to reach a feminine readership. Caballero was a well-traveled high school teacher and novelist who placed Puerto Rican letters within the framework of the best of Latin American literature by including collaborations from such distinguished writers as Chilean Nobel laureate Gabriela Mistral, Cuban Jorge Mañach, Peruvian José Santos Chocano and Argentine Alfonsina Storni. Labarthe, a novelist, stressed pan-Hispanism in his works as well as in *Artes y Letras*.

One of the finest magazines in the Southwest was *La Revista Mexicana* (The Mexican Review), which catered directly to political and religious refugees of the Mexican Revolution. Founded in San Antonio in 1915 by exiled columnist and intellectual Nemesio García Naranjo, *La Revista Mexicana* lasted until 1920; its financial base eroded as many exiles returned to their homeland when the new, more tolerant, government began to welcome them back. Despite a failed attempt to sell stocks in the operation, García Naranjo was ultimately forced to sell his press and equipment in 1920 and make the transition to writing for *La Prensa* (García Naranjo, 199-301). *La Revista Mexicana* had ascended in popularity and subscription base through 1917 by offering a varied fare of excellent cultural commentary and literature, along with García Naranjo's hard-hitting editorials on the Mexican government and on U. S. policy towards Mexico. Never a political periodical, *La Revista Mexicana* sought to offer Mexican expatriates the type of intellectual and artistic stimulation the educated class had enjoyed in Mexico before the Revolution. Nevertheless, García Naranjo's editorial commentary did attract attention from the American authorities, and he was harassed, spied upon and finally accused of breaking the neutrality laws (much like Ricardo Flores Magón, mentioned earlier). García Naranjo was tried, found guilty and forced to pay a $500 fine by the Federal Court in Laredo (García Naranjo, 353-67). As evidence to force García Naranjo to plead guilty (which he ultimately did), the prosecutor ordered the translation of all of the editorials García Naranjo had published criticizing President Woodrow Wilson, General John Pershing and U. S. Secretary of State Bryan (García Naranjo, 366). Ironically, this trial led to the rehabilitation of his intellectual leadership in Mexico. His writings for *La Prensa* were soon in demand for syndication by newspapers throughout Mexico; this was the beginning of his road back to the homeland as an eloquent orator and writer.

As García Naranjo states in his memoirs (159), the weekly *La Revista Mexicana* served to console the Mexican expatriates and offer them hope; but more than that, it was in itself an example and symbol that all had not been destroyed, that "aún hay patria" (there is still a homeland), even if only within the magazine's pages. The news and editorial commentary, which covered politics and culture in both countries, was entirely written by García Naranjo and Ricardo Gómez Robelo. Articles and other matter were provided by a staff that included humorist-poet Guillermo Aguirre y Fierro and caricaturist Mariano Martínez Vizuet. All of these worked for modest wages. Nothing was paid to the volunteer accountant Arnulfo Botello and the regular columnists and creative writers: *cronista* Alfonso G. Anaya (alias Tiberio), Manuel Músquiz Blanco, famed Mexican journalist Teodoro Torres, Celedonio Junco de la Vega, Emilio Rabasa, Victoriano Salado Alvarez, Pepe Rebollar, Francisco Sentíes and Federico García y Alba, among others (García Naranjo, 224).

In addition, *La Revista Mexicana* published *crónicas*, other columns and commentary from contributors as far away as Havana, South America and New York, as well as from *throughout interior Mexico. With these distinguished offerings, García Naranjo took pride in claiming that never before had a periodical in Texas published such quality writing (García Naranjo, 225). While in this sense *La Revista Mexicana* brought an international framework to its offerings, its vision was never as cosmopolitan nor as pan-Hispanic as the magazines and newspapers of New York. Nowhere in the periodicals of the Southwest was that pan-Hispanic vision represented, perhaps because the communities in the Southwest at that point were not as ethnically heterogeneous, perhaps because the communities in the Southwest were not as tied to the rest of Spanish America and Spain through trade and commerce as was the port city of New York.

While clearly the central concern of *La Revista Mexicana* was to serve the Mexican expatriate community by printing and interpreting news of the homeland and of the U. S. that affected it, the magazine also sought to preserve an elite sense of culture and good taste. It accomplished this in large part by publishing the best writing in Spanish that could be afforded outside the homeland. *La Revista Mexicana* also projected an enlightened, patriotic attitude about Mexican Americans, and included them in its spiritual community—even if not among the writers. This was evident in the stances taken by the magazine against racism and discrimination, voiced in editorials protesting Texas Ranger abuses against Mexican Americans, as well as through referring to the historical record of how the lands of Texas Mexicans had been stolen by Anglo-Americans (García Naranjo, 209). According to García Naranjo, Mexican Americans were tenacious patriots, worthy of being considered Mexicans in the truest sense—an idea reminiscent of Ignacio E. Lozano's interpretation of "México de afuera":

> The Fatherland lives. The United States should remember that more than two-thirds of a century ago the treaties of Guadalupe were signed, and nevertheless, the Mexicans who live in Texas and New Mexico, Arizona and California have not become Americanized. Our people are persistent and, amidst their conflicts and divisions, they have preserved intact their identity and character. And such a country made up of a people which does not mix so easily with other peoples, which does not blend with the other races, which preserves its traditions and perpetuates its legends,

which, in one word, continues to increase the marvelous force of its genius, cannot be dominated through occupation by two or three military bases, not even through the total assimilation of its territory.

Mexico, therefore, will not lose its national identity, even should it be defeated in war. Our vitality, like Poland's and Ireland's, like Armenia's and Belgium's, is even out of reach of total disaster.[101]

Thus, unlike the criticism of the *cronistas* who attacked the Mexican American's adoption of *gringo* customs and language, García Naranjo extended his vision of Mexican nationality and his ideology of "México de afuera" to the native Mexican-origin population of the Southwest: The very existence of this identifiable population within the United States was a testament to the endurance and persistence of Mexican culture. If Mexican Americans could preserve their identity—not even having the benefits of education and acculturation in the homeland—then so, too, could the immigrants.

Trade, Scientific and Technological Journals

The commercial and trade relationship between the United States and Latin America has been an important motive for communications in both directions since the beginnings of Spanish-language periodical publication in the United States. Over the course of nearly two centuries, various industries, scientific groups and trade associations have published and exported journals to readers in Latin America, not only keeping them abreast of the latest findings in science and technology but also cultivating them as a market for products and ideas. This process has also been seconded by the publication of books in Spanish with similar motive for export.

In serving as a center for the dissemination of ideas and products to Latin America, the United States has always been abetted and promoted by Hispanics residing within this country; over time, many of these ventures seem to have been supported and maintained by both non-Hispanic and Hispanic immigrant businesspersons. Forerunners of the trade journals were various of the commercial newspapers published in New Orleans in the early nineteenth century, such as *El Telégrafo* (The Telegraph), founded in 1825 by the Spanish-Cuban Manuel Ariza and the French-Dominican Francois Delaup; in its pages there was a heavy representation of commercial news, price quotations, maritime notices and advertisements, and its distribution included subscribers in Cuba, Mexico, St. Augustine and Pensacola, in addition to Louisiana.[102]

The first Spanish-language or bilingual technical journal seems to have been published in the other important port for Latin American trade: New York. It was there that in 1845 *Scientific American* began publishing an export edition in Spanish, which lasted until 1908. This was followed in 1862 by the trade journal *Boletín de Noticias y Precios Corrientes* (The Bulletin of News and Current Prices), issued by Charles B. Richardson & Co. every sailing day of the steamer for Havana and Panama, for distribution in Cuba, Mexico, Panama and South America; the year of its founding it had a name change to *El Continental* (The Continental) and continued for an as yet undetermined period. Other specialized trade journals began publishing in the 1870s, such as New York's *El Boletín Comercial* (The Commercial Bulletin, 1871-?) of the Inter-American Commission on Tropical Tuna; the quarterly *Circular del Joyero* (Jeweler's Circular, 1874-?) issued by D. H. Hopkinson; the monthly *Revista Agrícola Industrial* (Agricultural Industrial Review, 1877-1880?); and *El Comercio* (Commerce, 1870s), a monthly journal dedicated to advancing commerce, manufacturing and finance in the United States and Spanish America. On this solid base was built a tradition that extends to Spanish and bilingual trade and technical publishing today.[103]

One of the most important developments in trade, technical and professional journalism was the founding and centering of inter-American cooperation in the United States. Since the late nineteenth century, Washington, D. C. has been the most important city for the meeting of the official representatives of the governments of the Americas, and since then, this type of publishing has characterized that capital city. From 1893 to 1911, the Bureau of the American Republics in Washington, D. C. published its *Bulletin* in English with portions and/or sections in Spanish, Portuguese and French. Beginning in 1911, the foreign language sections grew into separate editions; the Spanish-language edition was now entitled *Boletín de la Unión Panamericana*, to reflect the founding of the Pan American Union (PAU). With the metamorphosis of the PAU into the Organization for American States in 1948, the OAS began publishing a plethora of Spanish-language professional and technical journals relating to everything from demography to sanitation, in addition to the widely popular *Americas* magazine, which it has published since 1949.

The Native Hispanic Press

Various scholars have concluded that the ethnic press in the United States functions in a dynamic manner to define and redefine the new and evolving objectives which they hold in common with their respective ethnic communities:

> It is by identifying these common concerns that the ethnic press preserves the cohesiveness and identity of the community as it undergoes various changes within its internal structure. Since most members of this ethnic community are no longer viewed as immigrants, the new concerns are centered not on adjustment problems, but rather on the need to preserve the ethnic identity and community within the larger social order and to establish a socioeconomic and political power base that will assure the community's existence. A few examples of such new interests are the protesting of discriminatory practices within various social institutions; the election of political figures who are sensitive and responsive to the specific ethnic needs; the improvement of the socioeconomic status of the ethnic community; preservation of the ethnic heritage and language within a constantly changing society, etc.
>
> By educating the ethnic readership in these common concerns, the press assures the continuation of the ethnic society. Thus, while on the one hand it promotes the full and equal participation of the ethnic community within the larger order, at the same time it encourages retention of the distinctiveness that differentiates the community from the dominant society. In general, the existence of this ethnic press is assured as long as its readers' needs remain unfulfilled within the framework of the existing social institutions and as long as their concerns are not voiced in the pages of the dominant press media. (Wynar, 18-19)

This analysis by the Wynars still very much relies on the premise that the ethnic press evolves from an immigrant press. I accept their analysis of the function of the press, but I must add that there is a substantial and qualitative difference between building on a base of European or even Asian immigration and developing out of the experience of colonialism and racial oppression. Hispanics were subjected to more than a century of "racialization"[104] through such doctrines as Manifest Destiny and the Spanish Black Legend (the propaganda campaign that Spaniards were too cruel and backward to rightly govern the Americas); they were subsequently conquered and/or incorporated into the United States through territorial purchase and then treated as colonial subjects, as were the Mexicans of the Southwest, the Hispanics in Florida and Louisiana, the Panamanians in the Canal Zone and in Panama itself, and the Puerto Ricans in the Caribbean. In many ways Cubans and Dominicans also developed as if under United States colonial rule during the twentieth century. The subsequent migration and immigration of these peoples to the United States was directly related to the administration of their homelands by the United States. Their immigration and subsequent cultural perspective on life in the United States have been substantially different from that of the "classical" immigrant groups. And the Hispanic native or ethnic minority perspective has specifically manifested itself in the political realm and the attitude towards civil and political rights.

Many of the Hispanic newspapers which developed in the Southwest after the Mexican War ended in 1848 laid the basis for the development of Hispanics throughout the United States seeing themselves as an ethnic minority. While the origins of their journalistic endeavors date well before the all-important signing of the peace treaty between the United States and Mexico, it was the immediate conversion to colonial status of the Mexican population in the newly acquired territories of California, New Mexico, and Texas that made of their journalistic efforts a sounding board for their rights first as colonials and later as "racialized" citizens of the United States.

While the printing press was not introduced to California and New Mexico until 1834, the society there, as in Texas, was sufficiently literate to sustain a wide range of printing and publishing once the press had been allowed.[105] Newspaper publication in the Southwest of what became the United States originated, it will be recalled, in 1813 with the publication of Texas' *La Gaceta de Texas* and *El Mexicano*, papers published to support Mexico's independence movement. In 1834 and 1835, almost contemporary with the introduction of the press to California and New Mexico, Spanish-language newspapers began to appear in these northern provinces of Mexico: Santa Fe's *El Crepúsculo de la Libertad* (The Dawn of Liberty, 1834)[106] and Taos' *El Crepúsculo* (Dawn, 1835–?). (There is some indication that a bilingual English-Spanish newspaper may have been published in San Antonio, Texas, during the 1820s, but no extant copies have been found.)[107] Prior to the Mexican War, these newspapers were published in New Mexico: *La Verdad* (The Truth, 1844–45) and its successor, *El Payo de Nuevo México* (The New Mexico Countryman, 1845).

Beginning with the American presence during the outbreak of the Mexican War in 1846, various newspapers began publishing in English and bilingually in English and Spanish in California and New Mexico; numerous English-language newspapers had been publishing in Texas for Anglo-Texan communities since just before the proclamation of the Texas Republic in 1836, with newspapers in Stephen F. Austin's colonies dating back to as early as 1824 (Wallace, 74). From California to Texas the norm among many of these first Anglo-owned newspapers was to publish in English and Spanish. In New Mexico, publishing only in Spanish or bilingually was a necessity for the Anglo owners of the newspapers because the vast majority of the inhabitants of the territory were Spanish speakers. In California, newspapers received a subsidy from the state as well as from some cities for printing laws in Spanish, as the state constitution required laws to be issued in both languages.[108] One can envision how this initial motivation developed into a profitable enterprise once the Spanish-language market was identified and cultivated. Indeed, the Spanish-language section of Los Angeles' *Star* grew into *La Estrella de Los Angeles* and then a separate newspaper: *El Clamor Público* (The Public Clamor, 1855–59). From San Francisco's *The Californian* (1846–48), the first Anglo-American newspaper in Alta California, to New Mexico's *Santa Fe Republican* (1847–?), to Brownsville's *La Bandera* (184?) and to *The Corpus Christi Star* (1848–?), the Anglo-established press was a bilingual institution. In this introduction of the Anglo-American press into the newly acquired territories, what ruled was translation of the English-language news into Spanish, but, according to Stratton, only about twelve percent of the journalists employed by these newspapers were Hispanics.[109] Gutiérrez has seen this imbalance and the predomination of Anglo ownership and administration of the press as typical of the colonial condition of Hispanics in the Southwest:

> The conquering group establishes media for the conquered group, but then controls the media by restricting employment opportunities, establishing a dual labor market, controlling the context of the news, and delivering even that news a week later to members of the conquered group. A more concise description of neo or internal colonial control of the press could not be more clear. (Gutiérrez, 39)

Even Spanish-language newspapers that were published independently by

Hispanics were often dependent on the Anglo business community and the economic and political power structures for their existence. Many of the Hispanic publishers, drawn from the elite classes, were able to survive in business by working within the system, not attacking it in the name of ethnic or civil rights.[110] In fact, many Spanish-language newspapers maintained links to their English-language counterparts and to the Anglo establishment. Los Angeles' *La Crónica* (The Chronicle, 1872–92), in fact, advertised itself as the city's "official" newspaper, principally because it held a city printing contract. Still other Spanish-language newspapers from California to Texas were affiliated to the political parties and published only around election time to support party platforms and candidates in the Hispanic communities. All of this leads Gutiérrez to conclude that "the lines of dependency, coupled with the content of the newspapers, would seem to indicate that attempts were made to harness the Spanish-language press and utilize it as an instrument of social control" (41).

In any case, the Anglo-American migration from the East did bring advanced technology and equipment to the region. This resulted in printing presses coming into Hispanic hands as never before, and more and more Spanish-language newspapers were subsequently founded to serve the native Hispanic population of the Southwest. And when the railroad reached the territories, dramatic changes occurred as a consequence of greater access to machinery and technology as well as the better means of distribution. The last third of the century, thus, saw an explosion of independent Spanish-language publishing by Hispanics.

New Mexico

Because it drew comparably fewer Anglo settlers and entrepreneurs than California and Texas and because of its proportionally greater Hispanic population—only in New Mexico did Hispanics maintain a demographic superiority in the late nineteenth and early twentieth centuries— New Mexico was the territory that first developed a widespread independent native Hispanic press. Not only did more Hispanics live there, but they lived in a more compact area and with comparably less competition and violence from Anglo newcomers.

The *Nuevomexicanos* were able to hold onto more lands, property and institutions than did the Hispanics of California and Texas. Control of their own newspapers became essential in the development of

Nuevomexicano identity and self-determination in the face of adjusting to a new culture during the territorial period.

Nuevomexicanos were living under a double-edged sword in this period. On the one hand, they wanted to control their own destiny and preserve their own language and culture (while enjoying the benefits and rights of the advanced civilization that the United States had to offer through statehood). On the other hand, the *Nuevomexicanos* immediately became aware of the dangers of Anglo-American cultural, economic and political encroachment. According to Meléndez, many of the intellectual leaders, especially newspaper publishers, believed that the native population would advance, learn to protect itself and merit statehood through education; they saw the newspapers as key to the education and advancement of the natives as well as to the protection of their civil and property rights.[111] *Nuevomexicanos* felt the urgency of empowering themselves in the new system—and/or retaining some of the power they had under Mexico—while Washington was delaying statehood for more than fifty years, in expectation, most historians agree, of Anglos achieving a numerical and voting superiority in the territory.[112]

In the decade following the arrival of the railroad in 1879, native Hispanic journalism increased dramatically in the New Mexico territory, and, according to Meléndez (26), a true flowering of *Nuevomexicano* periodicals followed in the 1890s, when some thirty-five Spanish- language newspapers were being published. The result was that English-language and bilingual newspapers were left to serve a mostly English-speaking elite, while Spanish-language papers served the majority of the inhabitants. By 1900, every settlement along the Rio Grande corridor had Spanish-language newspapers, and the activity extended into southern Colorado and to El Paso, Texas. The most populous cities supported the greatest activity: Las Cruces, Albuquerque, Santa Fe and Las Vegas (Meléndez, 28). From 1879 to 1912 (the year New Mexico was admitted as a state of the Union), more than ninety Spanish-language newspapers were published in New Mexico (Meléndez, 29). By 1891, native Hispanic journalism had become so widespread and intense that a newspaper association was founded, La Prensa Asociada Hispano-Americana, to set up a network of correspondents, to share resources and to facilitate reprinting items from each member newspaper in a type of informal syndication. Thus, in a few short decades, a corps of the native inhabitants of what had been a backwater province under Mexico had been transformed into intellectuals and activists by utilizing the published word through print and transportation technology; they took the lead in ushering their community into the twentieth century and statehood.

How and why did this occur? Meléndez posits the political exigency of preserving their language, culture and civil rights: "The 'communications circuit' used by local journalists functioned, on the one hand, as counterhegemonic discourse that subverted assaults on *Mexicano* culture, and on the other, as a way to channel the power of literacy to change society" (30). The new technology that *Nuevomexicanos* adopted did not represent fundamental cultural change; rather it empowered cultural expression that was long-held and deeply rooted. As Meyer puts it, "The Spanish-language press, as a bridge between tradition and modernity and as an advocate of its people in Hispanic New Mexico, served as a counter discourse contesting the Anglo myth of the frontier and claiming a space for otherness in American society. In its pages one finds the multivocal reality of neomexicano cultural identity that resists monolithic definition." [113]

Just as important as the technology and communications introduced into New Mexico was the empowering effect of formal institutions of education in the territory. Meléndez (45) and others credit the Catholic Church for establishing schools within the territory, not only at the primary levels, but more importantly at the college level to train the Hispanic leadership in New Mexico: Many of the Hispanic newspaper owners and editors were, in fact, trained in parochial schools and had graduated from one of the three Catholic colleges: St. Michael's College (Colegio de San Miguel), in Santa Fe, and Lorreto Academy and the Jesuit College of Las Vegas. Among the pioneers of Catholic education in the territory was Reverend Donato M. Gasparri, an Italian Jesuit who headed the New Mexico-Colorado Mission; he founded the Catholic press in New Mexico and was the first editor of the all-important and long-lasting *La Revista Católica* (The Catholic Magazine, 1875–1962), which he issued from the Jesuit College that he founded in Las Vegas. According to Meléndez:

> The most durable journalistic achievement of the Jesuits at Las Vegas was the establishment of the Jesuit newspaper *La Revista Católica. La Revista* offered *Nuevomexicano* youth and the *Mexicano* community of Las Vegas and the rest of New Mexico unheard possibilities for voicing positions on secular and religious issues. For the first time, journalism became a realistic aspiration for the region's youth. (53)

Meléndez goes on to specify that, in addition to their high-quality education in New Mexico and the "States" and their access to print technology, the young professionals entering journalism in the 1880s and 1890s also carried with them "a sense of mission and urgency fostered by the social, racial and political contentions of their age":

> Educated in the classics, inspired in the power of the press, seasoned in the copy room, they were driven by the imperative to raise their voices in opposition to suppression of their culture and language, and as they did so, this generation began to assert its civic, cultural, and human rights as never before. They also began to realize and sense that cultural political ascendancy was not only desirable, but achievable as well. The ascendancy they struggled to promote and propagate argued for the creation of institutions and vehicles of cultural empowerment heretofore unseen in New Mexico. (58)

In his book, Meléndez amply documents how the *Nuevomexicano* journalists set about constructing what they saw as a "national" culture for themselves, which consisted of using and preserving the Spanish language, formulating their own version of history and their own literature, all of which would ensure their self-confident and proud entrance as a state of the Union. From within the group of newspaper publishers and editors, in fact, sprung a cohesive and identifiable corps of native creative writers, historians and publishers who were elaborating a native and indigenous intellectual tradition which is the basis of much of the intellectual and literary work of Mexican Americans today. In addition, the young journalists quite often went on to become leaders in New Mexico trade, commerce, education and politics—a legacy still felt today. The development of the New Mexican Hispanic press, thus, followed a very different pattern from that of New York's Hispanic press, which received publishers, writers and journalists trained abroad and who saw themselves as exiles or immigrants.

The cultural nationalism of the native New Mexican journalists arose from the necessity to defend their community from the cultural, economic and political "outsiders." Their newspapers were to provide "la defensa de nuestro pueblo y nuestro país" (the defense of our people and our homeland) and the newspaper was the armament for that defense, according to editor Manuel C. de Baca (*El Sol de Mayo*, 31 March 1892); or "buscar preferentemente el mejoramiento y adelanto del pueblo hispano-amer-

El Nuevo Mundo (Albuquerque)   *La Voz del Pueblo*

icano" (preferably seek the improvement and progress of the Hispanic American people), according to *El Nuevo Mundo* (The New World, 8 May 1897). And, in keeping with their community leadership, their defense of cultural and civil rights was often issued in front-page editorials that made it clear that *Nuevomexicanos* had to assume a posture of defense to survive, and that part and parcel of the defense was the furthering of education and cultural solidarity. Typical of these editorials were the many printed by Enrique H. Salazar, founding editor of *La Voz del Pueblo* (The Voice of the People, 1889–1924) and later *El Independiente* (The Independent, 1894–?), in which he blamed the social decline of *Nuevomexicanos* on Anglo-American domination and racism. Salazar clearly envisioned a battle of cultures and rights:

> Our periodical . . . will continue its watch to protect the interests, honor and advancement of all of the segments of our great territory. The well-being of the people of New Mexico and principally of the native population will be at every instance the powerful motive that will impel with great vigor our efforts in the publication of our weekly. We are the foot soldiers of the community, guarding its rights.[114]

On the Hispanic newspapers as a vehicle for furthering the education of *Nuevomexicanos*, *El Nuevo Mundo* (5 June 1897) argued that the papers

defend their rights, and try to educate them and always, always at the risk
of personal danger are promoting justice and progress for the masses. . . .
Take, therefore, all of the Spanish newspapers and their children will be
able to learn more than in voluminous textbooks. . . . The people should
convince themselves that the newspaper is the best medium for public
education; learn in them to defend their rights and not give in to any foreign element.[115]

In keeping with the inter-cultural conflict of the times, the battle was not
just rhetorical, as vigilante and grass-roots militancy sprang up to counter
Anglo-American encroachment. Some newspapers even came out in favor
of some of the militant resistance movements despite their acts of violence
and their operation outside of the law. Such was the case when editor Félix
Martínez took over the helm of *La Voz del Pueblo*. Martínez openly sup-
ported the two most widespread populist movements, the vigilante Gorras
Blancas (White Caps) and the populist Partido del Pueblo Unido (United
People's Party), which opposed Anglo encroachment on the natives' lands,
bias in the legal system and a dual pay system for Anglos and Mexicans.[116]
Martínez had to pay a high cost for his stance: he was forced to leave Las
Vegas and relocate to El Paso, Texas, where he published the *El Paso Daily
News* and founded the *El Paso Times-Herald* (Meléndez, 83).

To combat the American myth of civilizing the West, i.e., subduing the
barbarous and racially inferior Indians and Mexicans, the *Nuevomexicano*
journalists began elaborating a myth of their own, that of the glorious
introduction of European civilization and its institutions by the Spanish
during the colonial period. Prior achievement legitimized their claims to
land as well as to the protection and preservation of their language and
culture:

> The 'glorious' deeds of the Spanish colonial enterprise... provided the
> *periodiquero* generation with a powerful master narrative to counter
> Anglo-American pretensions to primacy in the region. Essentialist in this
> regard, the emphasis on the colonial narratives overshadowed the com-
> plexities of social and class formation in New Mexico tied to its *mestizo,
> genízaro*, and Indian past. As it was, nineteenth century historicism attrib-
> uted great history to the actions of great men, and following this line of rea-
> soning, the monumental stature of the colonial epic was proof that Anglo-
> American achievement paled in comparison to that of "los bizarros con-
> quistadores" (the gallant conquistadors) of a bygone age. (Meléndez, 108-9)

But in their sally to battle the Anglo myth with their own, the *Nuevomexicanos* devalued their own mixed racial history, their mestizo and Indian past, as well as the contributions of the indigenous peoples of the Southwest. It was not enough to praise the accomplishments of the Aztecs and Mayas; there was no recognition of the Pueblos, Comanches, Apaches, etc., some of whose blood also ran in the *hispanos'* veins. But they distanced themselves from their mixed- blood heritage and their historical, even present, association with Indians. Nowhere in Mexico either at that time was Comanche or Apache blood recognized as part of the making of the Mexican identity. And New Mexicans were not alone in the construction of this myth of pure Spanish origin; the Californios themselves had also constructed a fantasy heritage highlighting their Spanish roots and their supposedly once pastoral existence.

In elevating the accomplishments of their forebears, the *Nuevomexicanos* also attacked East-Coast writers of history and their followers in the English-language territorial press:

> To the dissatisfaction of all the people we frequently see articles slanderous of the Neo-Mexicans in the eastern newspapers, denouncing us as a race without honor, virtue or manners . . . The people surely want to know who the authors of such infamous calumny and libel are. We shall say it. They are that class of persons who are without honor, scruples or conscience, and some of them live among us and generally show us their teeth with a superficial smile on their lips . . .[117]

In fact, *La Voz del Pueblo* made the combating of the slanderous eastern press a specific part of its mission of promoting the admission of New Mexico as a state of the Union:

> Our principal task will exert as much as possible our humble efforts in acquiring admission of New Mexico as a sovereign state of the American Union. Our pen will always, and on every occasion, without any fear, be ready to combat any calumny hurled at the good name and honor of the people of New Mexico. On account of our request for justice from the sovereign United States Congress in pursuing our admission to the confederation of states, we have been denigrated by most of the eastern press: without reason, without cause and without need. (2 February 1889)[118]

The *Nuevomexicano* editorialists were able to turn the tables on Anglo-American settlers and businessmen by claiming their own higher breeding and Catholic religion over the alleged low morality, vicious opportunism and hypocrisy of Protestant interlopers and adventurers. In the construction of their history, the editors included historical and biographical materials regularly, even in weekly columns, covering the full gamut of Hispanic history, from the exploration and colonization of Mexico, including what became the U. S. Southwest, to the life histories of important historical figures such as Miguel de Hidalgo y Costilla, Simón Bolívar and José San Martín. And the *Nuevomexicanos* went beyond the greats of the epic of Spanish American independence to document, through biographies in their newspapers, the contributions of their forebears and even *contemporaries* in New Mexico and the Southwest.

> *Neo-Mexicano* biographical profiles emerge in the print discourse of *Neo-Mexicano* newspapers as an extremely important field of representation that registers *nativo* civic participation in the affairs of their society. These texts, which at their core are self-reflective, celebrate in unabashed and laudatory terms the lives of those whom the community selects as worthy of emulation; thus, one result is the authentication of positive self-representation in the face of hegemonic effacement. (Meléndez, 113)

Likewise, the interest that the *Nuevomexicano* editors registered in literature was not confined to past glories. In publishing thousands of poems, short stories and other literary pieces, not only did they provide living examples of fine writing in the Spanish language—and thus assist in the maintenance of language and culture—but they also gave evidence that *Nuevomexicano* culture was not the unrefined and uneducated morass that the Eastern press made it out to be. Literary representation became the best and most elevated means of self-representation and creation of self-esteem in the face of Anglo disparagement, and so the editors fostered the creation of a "national" literature for the *Nuevomexicanos*. In so doing, texts from the entire Hispanic world were reprinted in the New Mexico newspapers as inspiration and models for the local community. And the incipient canon was not limited to the written word. The editors collected and printed thousands of items of oral lore, from proverbs to songs and folk tales. More than that, the editors respected the work of local bards, composers and even illiterate poets and included them within their literary canon. In this oral tradition lay the bedrock of *Nuevomexicano* heritage: the knowledge and educational practices that had allowed the citizenry to take on an identity as a society when it made up a lonely outpost on the frontier of three imperial powers: Spain, Mexico and the United States.

One institution stands out in its furthering of the literary goals of the *Nuevomexicanos*: the *Revista Ilustrada* (Illustrated Review), which Camilo Padilla founded in El Paso, Texas, in 1907 and continued to publish in Santa Fe, New Mexico, from 1917 to 1931—specifically for the dissemination of Mexican-American literature and art. *Revista Ilustrada* was ahead of its time in identifying and furthering an Hispanic ethnic minority culture in the United States. Unlike New York's *Revista Ilustrada*, which envisioned an international, pan-Hispanic readership, New Mexico's situated itself squarely in the home ("magazine del hogar"—magazine for the home), although taking efforts to connect the culture of New Mexico and the Southwest to that of Mexico and the greater Hispanic world. In addition to publishing poetry, stories and history, often graphically illustrated, the magazine offered space to *Nuevomexicano* intellectuals to ponder the fate of their culture. Among the collaborators were such notables as *Nuevomexicano* historian Benjamin M. Read, poet and novelist Eusebio Chacón and linguist and professor Aurelio M. Espinosa. Padilla also included the works of some of the outstanding Spanish American literary figures of the time and advertised books of European and Latin American literature in Spanish that could be bought directly from the magazine, including works by Cervantes, Dumas, Fernández de Lizardi, Hugo, Jorge Isaacs and Verne; also appearing on the lists were works of regional and folk literature. After 1925, Padilla's cultural work went far beyond the pages of the magazine to the founding and administration of El Centro de Cultura in Santa Fe, a center for cultural, literary and social events, but foremost a place for native art and culture practice. Another activity brought Padilla's nativist concerns directly into the political realm: He was one of the organizers of a third party, El Club Político Independiente (The Independent Political Club), to represent the concerns of the native *Nuevomexicanos* (Meléndez, 198).

As Meléndez asserts, the promotion of literature and history by these editors and writers demonstrates that as early as the late nineteenth century *Nuevomexicanos* saw themselves as a national minority of the United States. This idea was furthered by the region-wide Hispanic-American Press Association, by the exchanges with newspapers in Texas and

California, by the awareness of region-wide dispossession and proletarization of the Mexican-origin population. They had recognized the value of their own local history, folklore and literature and had elevated it to print. They simply needed to preserve an identity within the bounds of a pervasive Anglo-American national culture.

Meléndez (199) states that Camilo Padilla's death in 1933 brings to a close this most dynamic period in New Mexico Hispanic publishing; statehood achieved, the forces of cultural homogenization in the United States and the demographic ascendancy of the Anglo-American population made it increasingly difficult to sustain Spanish-language publishing in New Mexico (by the time of statehood, Anglos had achieved numerical parity):

> By the 1930s the social authority to determine what was suitable and appropriate learning for both native and nonnative peoples in New Mexico . . . had passed into the hands of a growing community of recently emigrated Anglo-American educators, authors, historians, ethnographers, editors, and a sundry group of cultural do-gooders, who, for all their love of Southwestern subjects, remained tied to the print culture of the eastern United States, that is to say, they operated as agents of a "circuit of communications" that privileged Euro-American observations and ideas over those of regional and ethnic communities. This change in the social validation of learning meant that English would become the prerequisite for the publication of anything resembling "high literacy." (201)

The Public Education Law of 1894 made English the language of instruction in public schools, and after statehood, public education further accelerated the displacement of Spanish as a public language. The Depression likewise took its toll on an industry that was competing with larger periodical entities for shrinking advertising dollars as well as subscription support. In 1958, *El Nuevo Mexicano*, the last remaining of the Spanish-language newspapers founded in the 1890s, ceased publication.

California

With the influx of Anglo-Americans occasioned by the Gold Rush and statehood in 1850, the native Hispanic population of California was quickly converted to minority status.[119] Post-Civil War migration further increased the arrival of Anglos, as did the building of the railroads, the breaking up of the Californio ranches and the conversion of the economy to capitalism. Californios and Hispanicized Indians were displaced from farms and ranches and were assimilated into the new economy as laborers on the railroads, in mines and in the fields.

Almost as soon as newspaper ownership came into the hands of the native Hispanic population of California, an ethnic minority consciousness began to develop.[120] When Francisco P. Ramírez took the Spanish section from the *Los Angeles Star* and founded a separate newspaper, *El Clamor Público* (The Public Clamor, 1855-59), he created a landmark in awareness that Hispanics in California were being treated as a race apart from the Euro-Americans. Even the wealthy Californios who had collaborated in the Yankee takeover saw their wealth and power diminish under statehood. In addition to covering California and U. S. news, *El Clamor Público* also maintained contact with the Hispanic world outside California and attempted to present an image of refinement and education that demonstrated the high level of civilization achieved throughout Hispanism; this, in part, was a defensive reaction to the negative propaganda of Manifest Destiny.

Francisco P. Ramírez

El Clamor Público depended on a subsidy from the city of Los Angeles and had strong ties to the Anglo-American business community in the city; in addition, it was aligned with the Republican Party. Ramírez and his paper were also staunch supporters of learning English;[121] not only was it important for business, but also for protecting Californios' rights. These pro-business, pro-English and pro-Republican Party stances did not conflict with editor Francisco P. Ramírez's assuming an editorial stance in defense of the native population: "Hemos puesto nuestro mayor conato en servir como órgano del sentimiento general de la raza española para manifestar las injurias atroces de que han sido victimas en este pais en donde nacieron y en el cual ahora se ven en un estado inferior la mas infeliz de sus perseguidores" (14 June 1856: It has been our intent to serve as an organ for the general perspective of the Spanish race as a means of manifesting the atrocious injuries of which they have been victims in this country where they were born and in which they now live in a state inferior to the poorest of their persecutors).

Only seventeen years old when he took the helm of *El Clamor Público*, Ramírez was from the outset a partisan of Mexicans' learning the English language, of California statehood and of the United States Constitution; however, his indignation grew as the civil and property rights of Californios were not protected by the Constitution that he loved so much. He became a consistent and assiduous critic, attempting to inspire Hispanics to unite in their own defense and to spur the authorities to protect the Hispanic residents of California. In his August 28, 1855, editorial "Inquisición" (Inquisition), Ramírez decried the vigilantism of the Americans who had come to displace the native population and the penchant of some for lynching Mexicans:

> The authorities of a country should care for the security of its citizens, and it is incumbent upon them to judge and punish the criminal; but the infuriated mob has no right to take the life of a man without finding out if he has committed the crime of which he is accused. . . . Since 1849, there has existed an animosity between Mexicans and Americans, so foreign to a magnanimous and free people to such an extent that these [Americans] have wished with all their heart that all of the Mexicans had just one neck so that it could be cut off all at once. They [the Mexicans] have suffered many injustices, and they have especially been mistreated and abused with impunity in the mines. If a Mexican has the misfortune to place a suit in a court of this state, he is sure to lose it. It is impossible to negate this assertion because we know this has befallen many unfortunates in spite of the efforts they have made to obtain their rights and impartial justice.[122]

By reprinting news and editorials from around the state, Ramírez was instrumental in building a consciousness that injustice and oppression was not an isolated and local phenomenon. Ramírez emphasized the role of the Spanish-language press in building this consciousness. In his editorial "El Periodismo en California" (Journalism in California), Ramírez reprinted D. J. Jofre's editorial from San Francisco's *El Eco del Pacífico* (The Pacific

Echo, 1856–?) which emphasized the role of the press in protecting *la raza* in California:

> Nowhere is the need for a Spanish-language newspaper more evident than in the state of California, . . . as Americans and as individuals of the noble Spanish race to which we belong, we believed it our duty . . . to raise our powerful voice with the armaments of reason, in order to denounce before the supreme court of public opinion the abuses and injury that have been and continue to be with frequency inflicted upon the individuals of our race; we believed it our duty to construct a permanent shield in the service of our Spanish countries as an alert against all of the illegal advances in the past and present towards absorbing them, outrageously taking them by surprise to extermination and death, and annihilating the nationalities of the invaded peoples. . . . All of the individuals of the diverse Spanish nationalities in California, in honor of our race, should protect it [the Spanish-language press] . . .[123]

What is especially notable about this stance—which was presumably held by Ramírez as well, for he states that Jofre's editorial "contiene mucha verdad y sano juicio" (has much truth and sane judgment)—is its placing of the oppression of Hispanic peoples in California within the larger context of U. S. territorial expansion in the hemisphere.

It was thanks to *El Clamor Público* on April 26, 1856, that the eloquent speeches made by leader Pablo de la Guerra before the state legislature on behalf the Californios' land grants were shared with the Spanish-speaking public:

> [The Californios] are the conquered who lay prostrate before the conqueror and ask for his protection in the enjoyment of the little which their fortune has left them. They are the ones who had been sold like sheep—those who were abandoned and sold by Mexico. They do not understand the language which is now spoken in their own country. They have no voice in this Senate, except such as I am now weakly speaking on their behalf . . . I have seen old men of sixty and seventy years of age weeping like children because they have been cast out of their ancestral home. They have been humiliated and insulted. They have been refused the privilege of taking water from their own wells. They have been refused the privilege of cutting their own firewood. And yet those individuals who have committed these abuses have come here looking for protection, and surprisingly the Senate sympathizes with them. You

Senators do not listen to the complaints of the Spanish citizens. You do not sufficiently appreciate their land titles and the just right to their possessions.[124]

Ramírez became more bitter as time progressed, at times calling democracy a "lynchocracy" and advising Hispanics to abandon California; in 1859, he took his own advice and closed *El Clamor Público* down. Ramírez emigrated to Ures, Sonora, Mexico, where he directed the official state newspaper, *La Estrella de Occidente* (The Western Star), and served as director of printing for the state. However, he returned to California in 1862 (Gutiérrez, 41). In January of 1865, Ramírez became the director of San Francisco's *El Nuevo Mundo*, where he adjusted his vision to that of a promoter of pan-Hispanism for its mostly immigrant readership (*El Nuevo Mundo*, 6 January 1865). In 1872, Ramírez became part of the staff of Los Angeles' *La Crónica* (The Chronicle, 1872–92), but was forced to resign. On August 14, 1880, Santa Barbara's *La Gaceta* (The Gazette, 1879–81) reported that he had been working in Los Angeles as a lawyer for some eight years and was considered one of the best writers in California; it also supported him in his current run for the state legislature on the Republican ticket, even though the paper was certain that he would be defeated. In 1881, Ramírez fled Los Angeles after being charged with fraud, and returned to Sonora (*La Gaceta*, 26 March 1881). He lived out his years in Baja California, it is presumed (Gómez-Quiñones, 218).

The editorials of Francisco P. Ramírez certainly form a basis for the development of an Hispanic ethnic minority consciousness in the United States; his influence in disseminating that point of view in the native population cannot be underestimated: "The very force of occupation brought the first notions of Mexican American nationalism and resistance in the nineteenth century—predating the Chicano Movement by about one hundred years. It was Francisco P. Ramírez, through his Los Angeles Spanish weekly *El Clamor Público*, who proposed the term *La Raza* to denote Mexican Californians." [125]

Historians have also seen him as a pioneer in the struggle for civil rights of Mexican Americans and Hispanics in the United States:

El Clamor Público was a public defender speaking out against unfair administration, the manipulation of juries, corrupt practices, and prejudiced application of the law. It also sought to inform and instruct the

Mexican people on civics as well as the basics of statue and emigration law. . . . Ramírez loudly and frequently stated that though life had been poorer, matters were a lot better off before 1848, and he used a phrase that would be heard again, *this land is our land.* (Gómez-Quiñones, 218)

In summary, Ramírez seems to have been the first Mexican-American journalist of the West and Southwest to consistently use the press to establish a nativist perspective and to pursue civil rights for his people.

In many ways, Los Angeles' *La Crónica*, on which Ramírez worked for a while, became a successor to *El Clamor Público*. The major investor in *La Crónica* was Antonio Coronel, a major figure among Californios, a business and political leader who had served in the militia, and an administrator of missions and a judge during the Mexican period. During the American period, he was elected a councilman, a county assessor and even mayor; when he founded *La Crónica* in 1872, he had just finished a four-year term as state treasurer (Gómez-Quiñones, 233–4).

Coronel was a devout believer in democracy and majority rule; however, he was more involved in the struggle to stem the tide of dispossession of Californio land and culture. His activism toward preservation of the Spanish language was formalized in 1856, when he unsuccessfully petitioned the Los Angeles school board for bilingual education. He continued to insist on the utility of the Spanish language in the public sphere, based on its importance in business, commerce and public service. His support of *La Crónica* must be seen as part of his commitment to the language and culture of California-native Hispanics. *La Crónica*, like Coronel himself and the majority of Mexican Americans in the Southwest at this time, was Republican in orientation.

As former citizens of Mexico, where slavery had been abolished since 1821, many Hispanics sympathized with the Union and the Republican Party during the Civil War; in addition, many of them were of mixed Indo-Afro-Hispanic heritage. Their "race" was continuously under attack; even Antonio Coronel had been the subject of racial slurs from Democratic opponents in the mayoral race of 1856. Throughout its issues, *La Crónica* not only defended Mexican Americans against racism but waged a battle for cultural preservation. And preserving the Spanish language, again, was at the heart of preserving the culture. In its February 24, 1877 issue, for instance, *La Crónica* bemoaned the trend of Mexican Americans losing their ability to speak Spanish and specifically called upon the Spanish-language press to take on the defense of Spanish as part of its community mission. *La Crónica,* as holder of the concession for printing public notices in Spanish for the city government, had a certain stake in this regard.

In the three decades after statehood was established, however, *El Clamor Público, La Crónica* and most of the other Spanish-language newspapers of California insisted on integration into the American education and political system and promoted learning the English language for survival. In doing so, they created a firm basis for the development of not only of an ethnic-minority identity but also *biculturation* (Treviño, 23–24), that is, a bicultural way of life for Mexican Americans—precisely what many Hispanics advocate today in the United States.

In California as elsewhere in the Southwest, the mass of economic and political refugees fleeing the Mexican Revolution overwhelmed the native populations. The large immigrant daily newspapers, such as *El Heraldo de México, La Prensa* and *La Opinión,* focused most of their attention on the expatriate communities, even while intending to accommodate Hispanic native issues and culture, as was Ignacio E. Lozano's desire. As a result, nativist interest became incorporated or subsumed in the immigrant press, hindering the development of a separate Hispanic nativist press, especially in the big cities. Nevertheless, as the community matured and made the transition toward a Mexican-American or U. S. Hispanic culture, those same immigrant newspapers also became more oriented to their communities as being more than just immigrants who were temporary residents. By the time of World War II, more Hispanic periodicals were published in English rather than Spanish or bilingually, and a new second generation saw itself as a citizenry—a view reflected in their pages. These new publications and this new consciousness existed side-by-side with immigrant and exile publications.

In California, one such periodical was *The Mexican Voice* (1938–44), a publication of a YMCA-initiated youth program, the Mexican American Movement (MAM). As Arturo Rosales explains,

> They were a new generation who had either been born in the U. S. or had been very young upon arriving from Mexico. Increasingly, more young people graduated from high school, giving them greater expectations in the larger society than those held by their parents. They could not identify with the symbolism perpetuated in the previous decades by immigrant leaders. Instead, they leaned more towards Americanization. (Rosales, 99)

Rosales sees the MAM as the quintessential Mexican youth organization in that it promoted citizenry, upward mobility through education and active participation in civil and cultural activities on the larger national scene, i.e., outside the barrio (99). If Mexicans were poor and represented mostly the laboring classes, it was because they lacked educational achievement, something that could be remedied in this land of opportunity and access. Through *The Mexican Voice*, editors and writers promoted these values and attempted to counter stereotypes of their people, even while at times expressing negative beliefs themselves about Mexican and Hispanic lack of ambition. While the youth group publishing *The Mexican Voice* was hesitant to acknowledge racism as a factor hindering success, it did promote pride in the pre-Colombian background and in Mexican *mestizaje*. The often-reiterated purpose of the magazine was to promote "Pride in Our Race"; this it accomplished by publishing brief biographies of high-achieving Mexican Americans in southern California. In an article titled "Are We Proud of Being Mexican?" published in 1938 (the individual issues then were not dated or numbered), Manuel de la Raza (probably a pseudonym for editor Félix Gutiérrez, Jr.) wrote of the advantages of *mestizaje*, bilingualism and a U. S. upbringing:

> The Mexican Youth in the United States is, indeed, a very fortunate person. Why? Where else in one country do you have two cultures and civilizations of the highest that have been developed and come together to form into one? Mexican Youth comes from a background of the highest type Aztec and Spanish cultures, and now is living in a country whose standard of life is one of the highest and where there are the best opportunities for success. Take the best of our background, and the best of the present one we are now living under, and we will have something that cannot be equaled culturally . . . . When this rich background has been tempered with the fires of the Anglo-Saxon understanding and enlightenment, you will have something that is the envy of all.

On Americanization and entitlement, Manuel de la Raza claimed a heritage in the Southwest, a typical nativist perspective:

> Still our paper sticks for Americanism. If you desire to remain here, if your future is here, you must become a citizen, an American; you can't be a "man without a country." Be proud of your background nevertheless. Our people settled this country, California, New Mexico, Arizona and Texas —

maybe not our people directly by family ties, but still our people. What has the borderline between Mexico and the United States to classify these people as different?

Numerous *Mexican Voice* editorials and articles were written by women, in which they announced that they stood equally with men. In one, "A Challenge to the American Girl of Mexican Parentage," Dora Ibáñez echoed aspirations for girls similar to those of Manuel de la Raza for boys: education and achievement. While respecting home-making and motherhood, Ibáñez also exhorted her readers to become professional women:

> My little college aspirant, will you please look far into the future, and once a professional woman, won't you honor your profession or career by your intelligence, alertness, thoroughness, tact and understanding of mankind so that it will be said of you: "Her success is an immediate result of the blend of her rich Aztec culture and the best this country has given her." (Christmas, 1938)

Another MAM leader, Consuelo Espinosa, in "The Constitution and the Fourteenth Amendment," drew parallels between the war the U. S. was fighting to preserve democracy and the lack of democracy here because of discrimination and segregation:

> I am not afraid to say that some parents teach their children not to talk or play with a Negro or a Mexican. This is un-Christian and un-American. We say that we have to teach the youth of Germany the way of Democracy. Let me tell you, Americans, we still have a great job ahead of us, especially against the same racial prejudice.

These ideas were not far from those expressed by the Mexican-American civil rights organizations such as LULAC (League of United Latin American Citizens) and their publications, nor from those expressed during the Chicano Movement of the 1960s. In fact, these and other similar English-language periodicals formed a vital link to the attitudes that would produce the Chicano Movement and its politically committed newspapers, magazines and scholarly journals in the 1960s and 1970s. In California, the founding of *El Malcriado* in 1965 as the organ of the United Farm Workers Organizing Committee was one signal of the beginning of the Chicano civil-rights movement. The founding of *Con Safos*, a literary magazine, in

The staff and headquarters of *El Tusconense.*

Los Angeles in 1968 presaged a grass-roots Chicano literary movement, and the publication of the quarterly *El Grito*, also in 1968, by two University of California-Berkeley professors, initiated an academic and scholarly movement which continues to this date.

Arizona

Two Arizona newspapers were noteworthy for developing a sense of Americanism among the Mexicano-origin population within the United States: Tucson's *El Fronterizo* (1878–1914) and *El Tucsonense* (1915–57). Founded by Carlos Velasco, an immigrant businessman from Sonora, Mexico, *El Fronterizo* covered news from both sides of the Arizona-Sonora border and developed a sense of regionalism, catering to the needs of the area's mining communities as well as to the Tucson business community. It was progressive and promoted modernization of the region and pacification of the local Indian tribes—often in virulently genocidal terms. But more than anything, Velasco, who had been a senator and superior court judge in Sonora,[126] advocated participation in the political system:

> The *raza* because of its respectable numbers in Arizona, could well partake of the greatest amount of guarantees, if they had their just represen-

tation in the more important public posts. But in a very injurious manner it seems that, with a few honorable exceptions, the *raza* has resigned itself to licking the chain which binds it to the controlling powers of those who would take advantage of their ignorance and disunity, those who do not return the service rendered, nor judge them worthy of any kind of consideration. (Quoted and translated in Gómez-Quiñones, 268, from *El Fronterizo* 18 November 1880)

Like most Mexican-American newspapers in the Southwest, *El Fronterizo* was aligned with the Republican Party; however, it would customarily endorse Democratic candidates if they were Hispanic.

What made *El Fronterizo* a particularly notable milestone in the development of a Mexican-American ethnic minority conscience was that its editorials and stories mirrored the civil rights agenda of the Alianza Hispano Americana (The Hispanic American Alliance), the longest lived Mexican American civil rights organization, not coincidentally also founded by Carlos Velasco. According to Gómez-Quiñones, "*El Fronterizo* published perhaps the clearest and strongest advocacy for Mexican electoral and civil rights of any southwestern newspaper in the 1870s" (268). Velasco campaigned tirelessly against discrimination throughout the Southwest and suffered "enmity, poverty and insult in defending the people of his race."[127]

Carlos Velasco

Although Velasco was a prime mover in the Alianza and the founder of *El Fronterizo,* it was Ramón Soto, a rancher whose lineage went back to the Spanish colonists of the area, who best articulated the ethnic minority ideology that would solidify the community. And he did it with three essays published in *El Fronterizo* in July 1892. Soto called for Mexicans in Arizona to unite and set aside their differences to vote as a bloc for Mexican candidates. He sounded the call that exercising their rights could combat the disenfranchisement that came from considering themselves foreigners:

> All of us in general believe that this country is the exclusive property of the Americans, any one of whom arriving from New York, San Francisco or Chicago has the right to be sheriff, judge, councilman, legislator, constable or whatever he wants . . . . Such an American can be Swiss, Italian, Portuguese or whatever. Always, in the final analysis, he is an American. And ourselves? Are we not American by adoption or birth? Of course we are. And as sons of this country, being born here, do we not have an equal or greater right to formulate and maintain the laws of this land that witnessed our birth than naturalized citizens of European origin? Yes. Nevertheless the contrary occurs. Why? Because of the indifference with which we view the politics of this country. Erroneously possessing a patriotic feeling for our racial origins, our interests are here yet our souls remain in Mexico. This is a grave error, because we are American citizens . . .[128]

Sheridan believes that Soto's essays and speeches were very influential in getting the Mexican-American community to realize once and for all that its destiny was truly within the United States and that it had to concentrate on bettering the conditions of Mexicans here; he even purposefully referred to the community not as the "Mexican colony" but as the "Hispanic *American* colony" to bring the community into the mainstream of life in the United States, much as European immigrant groups had been doing in their newly adopted country (Sheridan, 110). Then, too, there was the realization that Spaniards and Cubans in the Northeast, and Chileans and other Hispanics in northern California, were faced with similar dilemmas and would eventually make the same transition.

El Fronterizo was followed by *El Tucsonense*, published by conservative businessman Francisco Moreno. It set the tone in the area for most of the twentieth century. Ostensibly dedicated to promoting the Mexican-American middle class and furthering its business interests, *El Tucsonense* navigated the turbulent waters of merging the interests of the native population with those of the ever-growing waves of economic and political refugees coming to Tucson as a result of the Mexican Revolution. While battling against segregation and the general treatment of Mexicans as second-class citizens, the newspaper also railed against the liberal-radical factions of the revolution in Mexico and took up the cause of the Cristeros. *El Tucsonense* lasted until 1957, the very eve of the Chicano Movement.

Texas

After Texas achieved statehood, a few Texas Mexican newspapers from 1850s on assumed activist roles, such as San Antonio's *El Bejaraño* (The Bejar County, 1855-?), whose masthead proclaimed "dedicado a los intereses de la población México-Tejana" (dedicated to the interests of the Texas Mexican population). While clearly helping to define the interests of the native Mexican population and taking the lead on such issues as teaching Spanish in the public schools (1 February 1855) and defending the rights of Mexican American teamsters to do business (13 February and 5 March 1855), *El Bejareño* never assumed the aggressiveness that Francisco P. Ramírez's *El Clamor Público* had in California.

Towards the end of the century there were a number of newspapers in Texas that represented Tejano issues and culture. *El Regidor* (The Regent, 1888-1916), founded in San Antonio by Pablo Cruz, was such a journal. In 1901, Cruz took on the cause of an unjustly accused and condemned Tejano, Gregorio Cortez—not only in the pages of the paper, but out in the community, raising funds for this man who soon would be elevated to legendary hero status by the Tejano folk. Through Cruz's efforts, Anglo lawyers were hired for Cortez's defense, and through appeals and various changes of venue to avoid local prejudices, Cortez was eventually found innocent of murdering a sheriff.[129]

An important figure in establishing a Texas Mexican identity and fighting for Tejano rights was the militant journalist Catarino E. Garza. Born on the border in 1859 and raised in and around Brownsville, Garza was educated in both the United States and Mexico and worked in newspapers in Laredo, Eagle Pass, Corpus Christi and San Antonio. In the Brownsville-Eagle Pass area, he became involved in local politics and published two newspapers, *El Comercio Mexicano* (Mexican Commerce, 1886-?) and *El Libre Pensador* (The Free Thinker, 1890-?), which "criticized the violence, usurpation, and manipulation suffered by Mexican Americans" (Gómez-Quiñones, 291). Beginning in 1888, when he confronted U. S. Customs agents for killing two Mexican prisoners, Garza became more militant and struck out at authorities on both sides of the border, including the representatives of dictator Porfirio Díaz, with a band of followers that included farmers, laborers and former Texas separatists. A special force of Texas Rangers eventually broke up his force of raiders and Garza fled in 1892 to New Orleans, and from there to Cuba and Panama, where he was reportedly killed fighting on behalf of Panamanian independence from Colombia (Meier and Rivera, 144). Garza's extra-legal exploits were followed in detail in the Spanish-language newspapers of the Southwest and helped to coalesce feelings about exploitation and dispossession among the Mexican-American population. This process was also abetted by the reprinting of Garza's articles in newspapers throughout the Southwest.

La Crónica

One of the most influential newspapers along the border was Laredo's *La Crónica* (The Chronicle, 1909–?), written and published by Nicasio Idar and his eight children. Nicasio Idar had been a railroad worker and one of the organizers of a union of Mexican railroad workers in Texas: La Alianza Suprema de Ferrocarrileros Mexicanos (Griswold, 44). As a publisher, his working-class and union background was not left behind. He and his family took the forefront in representing the rights of Texas Mexicans and through the pages of *La Crónica* and a magazine, *La Revista de Laredo*, they promoted the defense of the native Mexican population and their civic and political projects. Idar was in the vanguard of establishing Mexican schools in Texas as an alternative to segregated schools. His daughter Jovita Idar was at the forefront of women's issues and collaborated in a number of women's periodicals. One of his sons also went off to Colorado to help in organizing miners. *La Crónica* decried everything from racism to negative stereotypes in traveling tent theaters; it also criticized factionalism and bloodshed in revolutionary Mexico. Idar saw the Revolution as an opportunity for Texas Mexicans and Mexican immigrants to unite and reconquer their homelands and enjoy greater freedom (*La*

Crónica, 24 December 1910). According to Griswold (46), "His view was that the revolution should motivate Chicanos to organize and unite their communities so as to fight for civil and economic rights."

In building the identity of Mexican Americans, *La Crónica* was opposed to the more internationalist and radical efforts of *Regeneración* and the Brothers Flores Magón. However, Idar headed up a political movement of his own: El Primer Congreso Mexicanista (The First Mexicanist Congress). Held from September 14 to 20 in Laredo, the congress's main purpose was to bring about and promote unification among all Mexicans in Texas as a way to battle injustice. According to Gómez-Quiñones (315-16),

> Such action was to be premised on a consensus that would arise from addressing the following questions: (1) Mexican civic consciousness, that is "nationalism" in the community; (2) trade union organizing; social and education discrimination; (4) the role of the Republic of Mexico's consular offices and relations with consuls; (5) the necessity of community-supported schools to promote Spanish-language and Mexican cultural instruction by Mexican teachers; (6) strategies and tactics to protect Mexican lives and economic interests in Texas; and (7) the importance of women's issues and organizations for improving the situation of "La Raza." In part a civil rights agenda, the program was a combination of questions or themes as well as organizing and advocacy priorities that took into account cultural, economic and political aspects.

The congress, which had attracted some four hundred delegates from organizations throughout the state, concluded with the founding of La Gran Liga Mexicanista (The Great Mexicanist League), an association of organizations that promoted the nationalist ethos of "Por la raza y para la raza" (by the people and for the people); "education and ethnic pride were viewed as a means to strengthen the community" (Gómez-Quiñones, 317). The congress also founded the women's association of the movement, the Liga Femenil Mexicana (League of Mexican Women), in which Jovita Idar took a leadership role.

Another newspaper that served the Tejano community was San Antonio's *El Imparcial de Texas* (The Texas Imparcial, 1908-24), which while developing out of the native population found new readers with the large influx of refugees from the Mexican Revolution. Founded by a druggist from the border, Francisco A. Chapa, who had been educated at Tulane

University in New Orleans and settled in San Antonio in 1890, *El Imparcial de Texas* was strictly a business venture of a man who had gained the reputation in both Anglo and Mexican communities of being a progressive man of science, interested in education; he was so widely respected that he was elected treasurer of the board of education and a member of the Business Men's Club. Chapa, nevertheless, had a political commitment to the Mexican-American population, and used his newspaper to promote electoral activism, as well as to celebrate Mexican-American contributions to the World War I effort at a time when Mexican-American loyalty was in question among some Anglos. Chapa was called upon by Anglo politicians to get the Mexican-American vote behind them, and became a man of considerable power and influence (Rosales, 91).

One of Chapa's most historically valuable contributions may have been his hiring of Ignacio E. Lozano as business manager for the newspaper; that experience solidified Lozano's interest in the native population and later led Lozano to include it within the scope of his *La Prensa*. In working for Chapa, Lozano went beyond the business side of the operation and began writing editorials and news items. By 1911, Lozano was the main force behind *El Imparcial de Texas* (di Stefano, 104-5). Ultimately, Lozano broke with *El Imparcial*, possibly because it served primarily Mexican Americans, and Lozano saw the need for a grander, more professional newspaper that would encompass the large *immigrant* community, as well as the natives. The daily newspapers that were founded in the major urban centers of the Southwest by Mexican immigrant publishers soon displaced many native Mexican-American efforts, although the natives' issues and perspectives were also assimilated and represented in many of these papers, much as they were in *La Prensa*. In smaller towns and cities, nativist efforts were able to survive into the post-World War II era and the open recognition of a Mexican

El Imparcial de Texas

American identity.

While immigrant newspapers dominated the large urban centers, nativist papers continued to develop in the small cities and towns. One such newspaper was Santiago G. Guzmán's *El Defensor del Pueblo* (The People's Defender, 1930), which promoted a Mexican-American identity and supported the nascent League of United Latin American Citizens (LULAC). Located in Edinburg, in impoverished south Texas, *El Defensor del Pueblo* became a watchdog over local politics, with a particular eye to political corruption and the disenfranchisement of Mexican Americans. However, the greatest concern of Guzmán and his paper was the development of a Mexican-American conscience and the assumption of the responsibilities of citizenship and voting as a way to vouchsafe the liberties and rights authorized by the U. S. Constitution. He envisioned his paper as a guardian of those rights and as a beacon for guiding Mexican Americans in combating racism and shucking off their sense of inferiority:

> And this solemn objective is primarily to make known to the white man that we bronze-skinned people are not inferior in any way and that it is a solemn lie what a certain history textbook of Texas used in public schools to oppress us, says, "that we don't know how to govern ourselves, much less elect our own governors" . . . In the future, the Latin American instructed in civics and ambitious for progress and well being, then, I say, there will be a new era for our race, now capable of decisively influencing the destiny of the collective as a racial entity, and they will not deny us political rights and social equality without them threatening us nor our fearing individual punishment, not when faced with violence, not even with dictatorships. (8 April 1930)[130]

Implicit in his call was the idea of a national voting bloc of Latinos, and on the local level a reversal of the political structure in south Texas, where a white minority held all of the positions of power. It was not beyond *El Defensor del Pueblo*, however, to forge alliances with Anglos in order to improve political prospects. *El Defensor del Pueblo*, in fact, became a staunch supporter of the Pro-Good Government League, which became a political party in south Texas, in an attempt to break the hold the Democratic party had on all elected positions in the region. The Anglo- and Mexican-American party promised to put an end to the abuse and intimidation of Mexican Americans during elections and to clean up political corruption (24 October 1930). The Pro-Good Government Party went down in defeat, but Guzmán did not give up.

The greatest opportunity for political organizing, he now believed, was in the founding and developing of LULAC. Guzmán and his newspaper spared no space in expressing confidence in the nascent civil-rights organization, which has survived to this day. As an organizer of LULAC, Guzmán saw that what afflicted Mexican Americans could not be resolved by party politics; it called for a much broader and unifying force of Mexican Americans: "Es necesario que nos comprendamos y nos unamos, nuestros problemas no son de un partido, son problemas que afectan a nuestra raza y hay que luchar unidos" [It is necessary that we understand each other and we unite, our problems are not about one political party, they are problems that affect our race and we must fight in unity (12 December 1930)]. And one of the first projects that LULAC and *El Defensor del Pueblo* took on was a campaign to see that all Mexican Americans in Hidalgo County paid their poll tax as a first step toward voting; payment was considered dues for belonging to LULAC (23 January 1931). To be a member of LULAC, the individual also had to be a Latin American born in the United States or a naturalized citizen.

Mexican Americans were successful in electing various representatives to the Edinburg school board on April 4, 1931, which caused a furious reaction among Anglo citizens. Guzmán proudly urged his readers to organize further in pursuit of even greater gains for the benefit of their children:

> Fellow citizens of our race! Let us walk toward the dawning of greater understanding and better representation and our children will bless their memory of us for their inheritance of our own inbred civilization. So that the hate that we traditionally bear on our backs will be converted in the future into eternal peace, when the sun of justice finally shines with greater appreciation for our people and will warm up their homes.... Let us extend our powerful unity and inscribe it in the sacred book of the struggle for the liberty, equality and fraternity of Latin American people. (10 April 1931)[131]

In Texas, the process of Mexican Americanization—that is, establishing a firm identity as a U. S. ethnic minority—gave rise to two important, national civil rights organizations, both of which still exist today: LULAC and the American GI Forum. Founded in 1929, LULAC at first was made up mostly of middle-class Mexican Americans, and it early on targeted segregation and unfairness in the judicial system as primary concerns. It also fought the federal government's "non-white" classification of Mexicans as discriminatory. Its main periodical—various local chapters had their own newsletters—was *LULAC News* (1931–1979), published monthly in English and Spanish for national distribution. A running account of LULAC battles was covered in the *News*. For example, in 1946 the *News* covered LULAC's campaign against discrimination in restaurants and bars, the denial of low-cost federal housing to Mexican-American GIs who had just "finished helping this country defeat countries . . . who would impose upon the world a superior culture . . . [We demand] social, political and economic equality and the opportunity to practice that equality . . . not as a favor, but as a delegated right guaranteed by our Constitution and as a reward for our faithful service" (quoted in Rosales, 96). *LULAC News* sought to use the outstanding service rendered during World War II by Mexican Americans—they were the most highly decorated and casualty-ridden of any American group—as a wedge to pry open more opportunities and win greater protection from discrimination.

When a funeral director in Three Rivers, Texas, refused to bury in a city cemetery a Mexican American soldier, Félix Longoria, killed in the Pacific theater, the American GI Forum was born. A former medical officer, Dr. Héctor García Pérez, and a civil-rights lawyer, Gus García, took on the battle. They succeeded in having Longoria buried at Arlington National Cemetery, and in the process created the new organization, which at first fought for the civil rights of veterans alone, but later enlarged its focus. The Forum became actively involved in electoral politics and was responsible for creating a voting bloc within the Democratic Party, one which experts believe was partly responsible for winning the 1960 presidential election for John F. Kennedy. The American GI Forum published its *The Forumeer* to keep the membership abreast of politics and the regional and national civil-rights campaigns. In addition, various of its state chapters, such as the California one, published their own magazines and newsletters.

LULAC News and *The Forumeer* were predecessors of the hundreds of Chicano Movement publications issued in the 1960s and early 1970s. They kept the populace informed of the civil rights struggle and provided a ideological framework from which to consider social and political progress. All of these publications reenforced the position of Mexican Americans as citizens of the United States to the rights and benefits of American society. At their root, they were patriotically American, exhibiting great faith in the U. S. Constitution, Congress and the judicial system to remedy discrimination and injustice. On the cultural front, such periodicals as *The Mexican Voice* and literary publication in the newspapers were mirrored by such Chicano Movement-era grass-roots magazines as San Antonio's *El Magazín* and *Caracol.* Today they are succeeded by such general news and culture magazines as *Texas Hispanic.*

New York

Since the late nineteenth century, New York has served as the principal port of entry for immigrants from Europe and the Caribbean. It has harbored and nurtured a culture of immigration through a social service and educational infrastructure developed for accommodating immigrants and facilitating their integration into the U. S. economy and overall culture. Within this general framework, numerous immigrant newspapers flourished, in part to facilitate this transition. In some of those newspapers, the awareness of their communities' evolution towards citizenship status or American naturalization is reflected, and the demand for the rights of citizenship become more pronounced. Even *Gráfico*, which in most respects was a typical immigrant newspaper, began to recognize the American citizenship of its readers (mostly Puerto Ricans and Cubans residing in East Harlem) in order to demand rights guaranteed under the Constitution. In the following English-language editorial, the editors balked at being considered foreigners in the United States and the subjects of discrimination:

> The great majority of our detractors forget that the citizens residing in the Harlem vicinity enjoy the prerogatives and privileges that American citizenship brings. We are almost all originally from Puerto Rico and the rest of us are naturalized citizens. Whosoever has identified himself with the history of this country knows that when we speak of foreigners we are talking about ourselves, because that is what the inhabitants of this young nation are. The United States is a young nation and we believe that the melting pot of peoples that it constitutes clearly indicates that its components belong to all of the cultures and all of the nations of the world. Thus, we are making fools of ourselves when we try to categorize anyone here as a foreigner.

Many of the individuals who attempt to knock down our co-citizens in this locale were no better than them before learning the customs and ways of this country. One has to be blind not to see in any of those individuals who call themselves complete citizens the fringes of their old country and their old customs . . . .

We, of course, do not participate in this intransigent hate and we are not going to wave the battle flag of animosities and prejudices that would further feed hate and serve no other purpose . . . .

The recent clashes between the inhabitants of the barrio and some authorities who have also lowered themselves to the common and ignorant judgment about our colony have obligated us to take up the forum ready to brave the consequences implied in our just and reasonable defense. (August 7, 1927)

La Defensa

And while the editors of *Gráfico* often made comparisons of their community with that of other immigrant groups, it is obvious from the above editorial (as well as other *Gráfico* articles) that some differences existed; because of the Jones Act of 1917, Puerto Ricans did not have to take steps to become citizens—it was automatic. And, with the advent of the Depression, New York did not experience the massive repatriation of Hispanics that occurred in the Southwest. Instead, hard economic times on the island brought even more Puerto Ricans to the city, a trend that would intensify during World War II as northeastern industries experienced labor shortages and recruited heavily in Puerto Rico. The massive influx of Puerto Ricans during and just after the war further intensified the community's identity as a native American citizenry. And their local newspapers appealed to them as citizens to organize politically and vote. In 1941, a new newspaper, *La Defensa* (The Defense) appeared in East Harlem specifically to further the interests of the Hispanics of the area who were there to *stay* ("no somos aves de paso"—we are not here as temporary birds):

> Considering that this publication comes from the heart of our humble Harlem barrio; from the center of the most abject poverty; where vice and pain inexorably battle each other over the squalid victims of ignorance, racial prejudice and the present defective system of political economy, we cannot help but dedicate this weekly newspaper to the defense of our legitimate rights as citizens and justify the principle that the free press is the most effective defender of human rights and the strongest guaranty and the correct functioning of justice.
>
> In spite of all the evils—real or imaginary—that have been attributed to our barrio, the majority of its residents are of complete moral solvency, lovers of order and possessors of all of the essential attributes for accomplishing the duties of good citizens; therefore, one of the main objectives of LA DEFENSA is to prove the fact that in the barrio there exist individuals capable of bringing to bear their intelligence and force of will on the historic scene of civic events relating to our Hispanic collective. It is not because of this that we shall limit ourselves from condemning with all of our energy the evils which in reality do exist and which are the cause of our collective denigration.
>
> It is time that we realize that we are not temporary birds; that we are here to stay and that it is necessary to prepare the road for those who will follow us. (23 April 1941)[132]

Even earlier, in 1927, a league had been formed in New York to increase the power of the city's Hispanic community through unification of its diverse organizations. Among the very specific goals of the Liga Puertorriqueña e Hispana (The Puerto Rican and Hispanic League) were representing the community to the "authorities," working for the economic and social betterment of Puerto Ricans and propagating the vote among Puerto Ricans.[133] That same year the Liga founded a periodical, *Boletín Official de la Liga Puertorriqueña e Hispana* (The Official Bulletin of the...), to keep its member organizations and their constituents informed of community concerns. However, the *Boletín* evolved into much more than a newsletter, functioning more like a community newspaper, including essays and cultural items as well as news items in its pages.

Supported at first mainly by the Puerto Rican Brotherhood, a mutualist organization, the *Boletín*'s goals included providing information and education as well as promoting suffrage among Puerto Ricans; however, partisan politics was frowned upon (although it was open knowledge that most Hispanics were Democrats).[134] The *Boletín* began publishing bi-weekly with the idea of someday becoming a daily newspaper (See 15 January 1928), and included on its staff many names prominent in New York Hispanic journalism, such as Jesús Colón, Isabel O'Neill and J. Dávila Semprit. While cultural items were front and center in the early years, later in its run under the directorship of Jesús Colón, coverage of working-class issues and ideology became more emphasized.[135] The *Boletín* never evolved into a daily; throughout its history it was plagued by internal dis-

cord over political stances and factionalism (see the editorial for the
1 May 1932 issue). However, the
bi-weekly was influential in raising
the level of awareness of Puerto
Ricans as an electorate and
emphasizing their need to associate and form political coalitions
with other Hispanic groups for
mutual political and economic
betterment.

Pueblos Hispanos

*Pueblos Hispanos: Seminario
Progresista* (Hispanic Peoples:
Progressive Weekly, 1943–1944)
was through its director, Juan
Antonio Corretjer, affiliated with
both the Puerto Rican Nationalist
Party and the Communist Party of
America.[136] *Pueblos Hispanos*
was a nativist Puerto Rican news-
paper that, even while encouraging political involvement in the Democratic Party and openly endorsing candidates for office—including the reelection of FDR through front-page editorials—promoted Puerto Rican independence from within the context of "liberation movements" in Europe and Latin America.[137] As its name indicated, *Pueblos Hispanos* promoted pan-Hispanism and a future integration of Latin American countries. Edited by the important Puerto Rican poet and delegate to the Communist Party of America, Juan Antonio Corretjer, the newspaper promoted social-ist causes around the globe, ran weekly columns on politics and culture in the Soviet Union as well as on socialist movements in Peru, Ecuador, Brazil,

Mexico, Central America and elsewhere, and covered Puerto Rican politics on the island and in New York in detail. *Pueblos Hispanos* was a devout enemy of fascism everywhere and supported the U. S. war effort and FDR, and especially applauded Roosevelt's liberal policies regarding the United States colony of Puerto Rico.

In each issue, *Pueblos Hispanos* ran the same list of nine points enunciating its mission:

THE REASONS FOR PUEBLOS HISPANOS
Because the VICTORY needs:

1. . . . the unification of all of the Hispanic colonies in the United States to vanquish Nazi fascism, united with all of the democratic forces.
2. . . . so that the rights of all Hispanic minorities in the United States be defended—Puerto Ricans, Filipinos, Mexicans, etc.
3. . . . the immediate independence of the Puerto Rican nation.
4. . . . to combat the prejudice against Hispanics because of their race or creed, and the disintegration of prejudices against other minorities.
5. . . . the tenacious battle against Spanish Falangist enemy as an inte gral part of the Fifth Column of the Axis operating in the Americas, and to help and promote the unity of all Spaniards on behalf of democratic freedoms in Spain.
6. . . . the freeing of all political prisoners in the world.
7. . . . improved relations among the Americas through the spreading of the Hispanic cultures.
8. . . . making the independence of the Philippines a fact recognized by law.
9. . . . labor union unity throughout the Americas. (25 March 1944)[138]

Within this broad context, *Pueblos Hispanos* issued a continuing stream of poetry, short stories, essays and commentary, in original and reprinted form, by some of the leading writers of the Hispanic world, past and present, including Federico García Lorca, Antonio Machado, Pablo Neruda, Nicolás Guillén, Gabriela Mistral, Alejandro Tapia y Rivera and Juan Ramón Jiménez, among many others. *Pueblos Hispanos* was a veritable anthology of the poetry and writings of Corretjer, poet Clemente Soto Vélez and Jesús Colón. In addition, the paper's administrator, Consuelo Lee Tapia, created a space in the newspaper for the analysis and advancement of Hispanic feminism, often commenting on news and culture from a feminist perspective and writing biographies of outstanding Puerto Rican women throughout history. The four principal members of the editorial team were all members of the Communist Party, with Consuelo Lee Tapia, the granddaughter of the important Puerto Rican literary figure Alejandro Tapia y Rivera, being the most militant. Puerto Rico's leading woman poet, Julia de Burgos, was a frequent contributor to the newspaper, providing poetry and commentary.

Julia de Burgos

It is a paradox that while *Pueblos Hispanos* was most concerned with safeguarding the civil rights and promoting the political participation of Puerto Ricans in New York and national politics, it was at the same time advocating the island's separation from the United States. But this confidence in America's safeguards on freedom of the press, freedom of expression and freedom of assembly for even dissenting political parties only underlines the degree of confidence that the editors and community felt in their status as U.S. citizens. They were exercising their rights fully and openly, assuming stances otherwise unheard of in immigrant newspapers.

The career of *cronista* Jesús Colón is illustrative of the evolution of newspapers from immigrant to ethnic minority consciousness in this century. Colón was born in Cayey, Puerto Rico, in 1901, shortly after the island became a colony of the United States, and he stowed away on a ship to New York in 1917, the year U. S. citizenship was granted to Puerto Ricans. Originally from the tobacco growing and manufacturing region of Puerto Rico, where he had already labored among the cigar rollers, he was able to attend the Central Grammar School in San Juan, where he edited the school newspaper, *Adelante* (Forward). Upon his arrival in New York City, he became involved in numerous community and labor organizations, as

El Diario de Nueva York: Before the U.S. House Committee on Un-American Activities, newspaper columnist Jesús Colón is identified as a "Red leader" for his Communist Party activities in New York's Puerto Rican and Hispanic communities.

well as the Puerto Rican Socialist Party, and dedicated himself assiduously to reading and learning as much as he could. After graduating from the Boys' High Evening School in Brooklyn, Colón became the quintessential autodidact and strove to exercise his learning through journalism and commentary in Spanish-language newspapers. Through the course of his career, it is estimated that he produced more than four hundred published items in some thirty newspapers and periodicals.[139] He also served as an officer for numerous community organizations and even ran for Controller of the City of New York on the Communist Party ticket.

Coming from a modest background and having been socialized among tobacco workers and union organizers, Colón became the voice of the working class, and his trajectory through labor and Hispanic community newspapers was consistent in its ideological focus, although he did at first assume the guise required by the conventions of Spanish-language *cronista.* As best can be gleaned from the incomplete historical record, Colón began his formal journalistic career in 1923 as a correspondent for Puerto Rico's *Justicia* (Justice), the official newspaper of the Federación Libre de Trabajadores (Free Federation of Workers). His writings appeared consistently in *Gráfico*, beginning in 1927 under his own name and the pseudonyms Miquis Tiquis and Pericles Espada.

In his signed articles, Colón takes on the persona of a serious intellectual commentator on social and political matters. As Pericles Espada, he assumes the persona of the lover giving advice to his beloved, who personified the island of Puerto Rico; thus the words of love are analysis of

Puerto Rico's relationship to the United States. As Miquis Tiquis, however, Colón adopts the convention of the *cronista* as satirist and critic of the customs of his immigrant community, displaying an aloof and often harshly negative view of the uneducated and unruly Hispanic working-class of New York, a stance comparable to the bourgeois Jorge Ulica's in San Francisco: Not only does Colón criticize what is pernicious in the barrio, he also takes jabs at Hispanics wishing to assimilate. As we have noted earlier, he even censured Latina flappers, as did *cronistas* Ulica and Venegas. In all, Colón's writings in *Gráfico* were the typical fare of immigrant journalism,[140] chronicling in Spanish the adaptation of the Hispanic newcomers to the city, but still very much concerned about politics and society in the homeland.

It is difficult to discern if Colón wrote for other Spanish-language newspapers between 1928 and 1943 because at this stage in his career he wrote under pseudonyms. In 1933, Colón became a member of the Communist Party of America. He next surfaced as a weekly columnist in *Pueblos Hispanos* in 1943, at which point he had already made the transition to defender of the rights of Hispanics in the barrio and of the working class in general. In his column "Lo que el pueblo me dice" (What the people tell me), Colón directed his words mostly to the Puerto Rican community and was very concerned about the preservation of its identity and nationhood (3 July 1943). He suggested such projects symbolic of an ethnic minority conscience as the placing of a statue in the Puerto Rican barrio of East Harlem—simultaneously a symbol of Puerto Rican permanence in the city and a monument to the memory of the homeland (14 August 1943). And most importantly, he exhorted Puerto Ricans to register and vote, especially for politicians such as the favored Congressman Vito Marcantonio, who protected Social Security and other important programs for the working class and had even pushed for Puerto Rican independence (4 September 1943).

Beginning in 1955, Colón wrote a regular column in English, "As I See It from Here," for *The Daily Worker*, through which he introduced the culture and concerns of Puerto Ricans and Hispanic workers to the Communist Party membership. Colón thus became the first Hispanic columnist to make the transition to the English-language press. From 1955 through May 18, 1974, (the date of his last article in *The Daily World*), Colón became the interpreter of the Hispanic world and Latin America for the readership of the Communist Party newspapers in the United States.

He also provided consistent ethnic minority and racial minority perspectives on news events and public issues of every sort. But it was only in his later publications in English that he at times wrote as a black man about racial prejudice; in his earlier Spanish-language *crónicas* in *Gráfico*, his racial identity was not discernible. In his mature persona of black working-class Puerto Rican, as well as in his indomitable spirit and combativeness—he was denounced by McCarthy-era politicians and ran for political office in New York City on the Communist Party ticket—he foreshadowed the literary stance of the Nuyorican writers of the 1970s and was adopted as a model and muse by them. As a result of his evolution from immigrant writer to that of an Hispanic minority voice, the bulk of Colón's work was published in English through newspapers that nurtured his political and social analysis. His was a humane and caring voice that spoke for the Hispanic urban working class in simple, direct, man-in-the-street language that emphasized his membership in their class. According to Acosta-Belén and Sánchez Korrol,

> As a whole, Colón's writings offer an incisive view of U. S. society. He admires the democratic foundations upon which this nation was built, but recognizes the betrayal of those principles by a capitalist system of accumulation that perpetuates profound inequalities, exploits the workers and works against their well-being while keeping power and privilege in the hands of a wealthy few. In his sketch "The Head of the Statue of Liberty," he perceives and poignantly captures the "credibility gap" between what the statue symbolizes and the struggles for freedom and justice that Puerto Ricans and other minority groups must confront in U. S. society. (25)

Like many Hispanics before him, Colón developed from a rather naive and unschooled immigrant in the big city, into a defender of his community's civil and human rights, and then into an ethnic minority leader clamoring for the realization of the dream envisioned by the Founding Fathers in the U. S. Constitution.

Conclusion

This has been a brief historical survey of Hispanic periodicals published in the United States before 1960. Of necessity, it has been selective in studying certain typical and trend-setting examples of newspapers and magazines, without providing a complete history of any one periodical and by glossing over some entire groups of periodicals that bear further, careful and detailed study—such as religious publications and trade and scientific journals. The general purpose has been to further the understanding of the three main manifestations of periodical publication, which in turn reflect the nature of Hispanic culture in the United States: *exile, immigration and nativism.* These manifestations are to be understood as operating simultaneously in a dynamic environment of mutual influence and interrelationship, as exiles, immigrants and Hispanic citizens of the United States often live in the same area, work in the same factories or fields and send their children to the same schools. Furthermore, both Hispanic exile and immigrant communities, in time, evolve into native communities, that is, a national ethnic minority that we call Hispanic or Latino today. Hispanic publications reflect these processes and dynamic relationships.

The study of the history of Hispanic periodicals is an oblique manner of studying the socio-historical evolution of Hispanic peoples within the United States and their pursuit of self-expression and self-definition as a people within the cultural and geographic borders of a multicultural nation. A major purpose for the publication of periodicals among Hispanics has been the defense of civil and cultural rights. Even immigrants brought north of the border or to these shores from overseas as a result of U. S. economic or political dominance sought the opportunities for freedom and economic advancement without wholly abandoning their language and culture.

The legacy today of this diverse background of news publication, interpretation and the self-imaging by editors and writers is a rich print culture in both English and Spanish. This legacy continues to accommodate the expression of both economic and political refugees and seeks to continue to define the place of Hispanics in not only the national context but the hemispheric one as well. Thus, in Chicago, Los Angeles, Miami and New York, Spanish-language daily newspapers still thrive in helping immigrants make the transition to a new society. There still appear underground and not-so-clandestine revolutionary sheets fomenting rebellions in Latin America. But the last twenty years have also seen the appearance of highly commercial, glossy and slick, English-language magazines for nationwide distribution among Latinos, such as *Hispanic*, *Latina* and *Hispanic Business*, and many others for regional audiences, such as *Texas Hispanic* and *Latin N.Y.* This is in addition to all of the Spanish-language versions of American news and illustrated magazines such as *People*, *Cosmopolitan*, *Reader's Digest* and numerous others, which originally may have been export editions but today have developed a large domestic circulation.

The Hispanic periodical is here to stay, even if in the wired twenty-first century it reaches its audience online. In the new global economy and the integrated hemisphere, we can also look forward to more Spanish-language journalism emanating from the United States to the rest of the Hispanic world, precisely because the existing historical basis has already supported such development in the media of today. The transmission and distribution of news and programming from the Spanish-speaking Americas to the United States has been a reality for thirty years and will continue to be part of the U.S. media mix. It may be the Spanish language, and the media infrastructure that transmits it, that makes the greatest strides towards integrating this hemisphere overall. Hispanic population growth in and outside of the United States as well as the economic and political development of the Spanish-speaking Americas will result in further growth of Spanish-language print and electronic media.

Works Cited

Almaguer, Tomás. *Racial Fault Lines: The Historical Origins of White Supremacy in California* (Berkeley: University of California Press), 1994.

Aponte Alsina, María. "Culture and Identity: Periodical Literature in Puerto Rican Archives." Ms. report to the Recovering the U.S. Hispanic Literary Heritage Project, University of Houston, 1994.

Arce, Julio G. (Jorge Ulica). "Treinta años de galeras . . . periodísticas, 1881-1911." Manuscript, Chicano Studies Collection, University of California-Berkeley, s.d.

Argudín, Yolanda. *Historia del periodismo en México desde el Virreinato hasta nuestros días*. Mexico City: Panorama Editorial, 1997.

Artigas, Miguel, and Pedro Sáinz Rodríguez. *Epistolario de Valera y Menéndez Pelayo, 1877-1905*. Madrid: Espasa-Calpe, 1946.

Babín, María Teresa. *Panorama de la cultura puertorriqueña*. New York: Las Américas Publishing Company, 1958.

Bruce-Novoa. "*La Prensa* and the Chicano Community." *The Americas* 17/3-4 (Winter 1989):150-56.

Calcagno, Francisco. *Diccionario biográfico cubano*. New York: Imprenta y Librería de N. Ponce de León, 1878.

Carrasco Puente, Rafael. *La prensa en México: Datos históricos*. Mexico City: Universidad Nacional Autónoma de México, 1962.

Castañeda, Carlos E. *The Beginning of Printing in America*. Austin: University of Texas Latin American García Library, s.d.

Chabrán, Rafael. "Spaniards," *The Immigrant Labor Press in North America, 1840s-1970s*. Ed. Dirk Hoerder. (Westport, Conn.: Greenwood Press, 1987): 151-190.

Chacón, Ramón D. "The Chicano Immigrant Press in Los Angeles: The Case of 'El Heraldo de México,' 1916-1920." *Journalism History* 4.2 (Summer, 1977): 48-50, 62-4.

Chamberlin, Vernon A. "La colaboración de Juan Valera en *La Revista Ilustrada de Nueva York*." *Hispanófila* 53 (January 1975): 1-13.

Chamberlin, Vernon A., and Ivan A. Shulman, eds. *La Revista Ilustrada de Nueva York: History, Anthology, and Index of Literary Selections*. Columbia: University of Missouri Press, 1976.

Cockroft, James D. *Intellectual Pioneers of the Mexican Revolution, 1900-1913*. Austin: University of Texas Press, 1968.

Colón, Jesús. *A Puerto Rican in New York and Other Sketches*. 2nd edition New York: International Publishers, 1982.

————. *The Way It Was and Other Writings*. Eds. Edna Acosta-Belén and Virginia Sánchez Korrol. Houston: Arte Público Press, 1993.

————. *Tiquis Miquis*. Ed. Edwin Padilla. Houston: Arte Público Press, in press.

Figueroa, Sotero. *La verdad de la historia*. San Juan: Instituto de Cultura Puertorriqueña, 1977.

Fincher, E.B. *Spanish Americans as a Political Factor in New Mexico, 1912-1950*. New York: Arno Press, 1974.

Fitzpatrick, Joseph P. "The Puerto Rican Press." *The Ethnic Press in the United States: An Historical Analysis and Handbook*. Ed. Sally M. Miller. (Westport, Conn.: Greenwood Press, 1987): 303-14.

Flores, Juan. *Divided Borders*. Houston: Arte Público Press, 1993.

Florida Department of State. *Florida Cuban Heritage Trail*. Tallahassee: Florida Department of State, Division of Historical Resources, 1995.

Fornet, Ambrosio. *El libro en Cuba*. Havana: Editorial Letras Cubanas, 1994.

Gallegos, Bernardo P. *Literacy, Education, and Society in New Mexico, 1693-1821*. Albuquerque: University of New Mexico Press, 1992.

García Naranjo, Nemesio. *Memorias de Nemesio García Naranjo*. 9 Vols. Monterrey, Mexico:Talleres de "El Porvenir," s.d.

Goff, Victoria. "Spanish-Language Newspapers in California." *Outsiders in 19th-Century Press History: Multicultural Perspectives*. Ed. Frankie Hutton and Barbara Straus Reed. (Bowling Green, Ohio: Bowling Green State University Popular Press, 1995): 55-70.

Gómez-Quiñones, Juan. *Roots of Chicano Politics, 1600-1940*. Albuquerque: University of New Mexico Press, 1994.

———. *Sembradores, Ricardo Flores Magón y El Partido Liberal Mexicano:A Eulogy and Critique*. Los Angeles: UCLA Chicano Studies Research Center Publications, 1977.

González Ramírez, Manuel, ed. *Epistolario y textos de Ricardo Flores Magón*. México: Fondo de Cultura Económica 1964.

Griswold del Castillo, Richard. "The Mexican Revolution and the Spanish-Language Press in the Borderlands." *Journalism History* 4.2 (Summer 1977): 42-7.

Gutiérrez, Félix. "Spanish-Language Media in America: Background, Resources, History." *Journalism History* 4:2 (Summer, 1977): 34-41, 65-67.

Gutiérrez-Witt, Laura. "Cultural Continuity in the Face of Change: Hispanic Printers in Texas." *Recovering the U.S. Hispanic Literary Heritage*. Vol. II. Eds. Erlinda Gonzales Berry and Chuck Tatum (Houston: Arte Público Press, 1996): 260-78.

Henderson, Ann L., and Gary R. Mormino. *Spanish Pathways in Florida*. Sarasota: Pineapple Press, 1991.

Hernández, Eleuteria. "La representación de la mujer mexicana en los EE.UU. en las *Crónicas Diabólicas* de Jorge Ulica." *Mester* 12/2 (Fall, 1993): 31-38.

Hernández Tovar, Inés. *Sara Estela Ramírez: The Early Twentieth Century Texas-Mexican Poet*. Houston: University of Houston Dissertation, 1984.

History of the Southwest, Vol. 1. Chicago: The Lewis Publishing Co., 1907.

Horgan, Henry. *The Doctrina Breve*. New York: United States Catholic Historical Society, 1928.

Horn, Calvin. *New Mexico's Troubled Years: The Story of the Early Territorial Governors*. Albuquerque: Horn and Wallace, 1963.

Jamieson, Stuart. *Labor Unionism in American Agriculture*. New York:Arno Press, 1976.

Kanellos, Nicolás, with Pérez, Cristelia. *Chronology of Hispanic American History*. Detroit: Gale Research Inc., 1995.

Kanellos, Nicolás. "Un relato de Azteca (Bromeando)." *Revista Chicano-Riqueña* 1/1 (1973): 5-8.

———. "Brief History/Overview of Spanish-language Newspapers in the United States." *Recovering the U.S. Hispanic Literary Heritage*. Vol. I. Eds. Ramón Gutiérrez and Genaro Padilla (Houston:Arte Público Press, 1993): 107-28.

Kushner, Sam. *Long Road to Delano:A Century of Farmworkers' Struggle*. New York: International Publishers, 1975.

Langham, Thomas C. *Border Trials: Ricardo Flores Magón and the Mexican Liberals*. El Paso:Texas Western Press, 1981.

Larson, Robert W. *New Mexico's Quest for Statehood*. Albuquerque: University of New Mexico Press, 1968.

El laúd del desterrado. Ed. Matías Montes-Huidobro. Houston:Arte Público Press, 1995.

Lazo, Rodrigo. "A Man of Action: Cirilo Villaverde as American Revolutionary Journalist." *Recovering the U.S. Hispanic Literary Heritage*, Vol. III. Eds. María Herrera-Sobek and Virginia Sánchez Korrol (Houston: Arte Público Press, 1999).

Leitman, Spencer. "Exile and Union in Indiana Harbor." *Revista Chicano-Riqueña* 2/1 (Winter1974): 50-7.

Limón, José. "*Agringado* Joking in Texas Mexican Society," *Perspectives in Mexican American Studies* 1 (1988): 109-28.

Lomas, Clara. "Resistencia cultural o apropriación ideológica: Visión de los años 20 en los cuadros costumbristas de Jorge Ulica." *Revista Chicano-Riqueña* 6/4 (Otoño

1978): 44-49.

————. "The Articulation of Gender in the Mexican Borderlands, 1900-1915." *Recovering the U.S. Hispanic Literary Heritage*. Eds. Ramón Gutiérrez and Genaro Padilla. (Houston: Arte Público Press, 1993): 293-308.

Luis, William. "*Cecilia Valdés*: The Emergence of an Antislavery Novel," *Afro-Hispanic Review* 3.2 (1984): 15-19.

Luna Lawhn, Juanita. "Victorian Attitudes Affecting the Mexican Woman Writing in *La Prensa* during the 1900s and the Chicana of the 1980s." *Missions in Conflict: Essays on United States-Mexican Relations and Chicano Culture*. Ed. Juan Bruce-Novoa (Tübingen, Germany: Narr, 1986): 65-71.

Lutrell, Estelle. *Newspapers and Periodicals of Arizona, 1859-1911*. Tucson: University of Arizona Press, 1950.

MacCurdy, Raymond R. *A History and Bibliography of Spanish-Language News-papers and Magazines in Louisiana, 1808-1949*. Albuquerque: University of New Mexico Press, 1951.

MacLachlan, Colin M. *Anarchism and the Mexican Revolution. The Political Trials of Ricardo Flores Magón in the United States*. Berkeley: University of California Press, 1991.

McWilliams, Carey. *North from Mexico: The Spanish-Speaking People of the United States*. Philadelphia: Lippincott, 1949.

Medeiros, Francine. "*La Opinión*, A Mexican Exile Newspaper: A Content Analysis of Its First Years, 1926-1929." *Aztlán* 11.1 (Spring, 1980): 65-87.

Meléndez, Gabriel. *So All Is Not Lost: The Poetics of Print in Nuevo mexicano Communities, 1834-1958*. Albuquerque: University of New Mexico Press, 1997.

Mendieta Alatorre, María de los Angeles. *Carmen Serdán*. Mexico City: Centro de Estudios Históricos de Puebla, 1971.

Meyer, Doris. *Speaking for Themselves: Neomexicano Cultural Identity and the Spanish-Language Press, 1880-1920*. Albuquerque: University of New Mexico Press, 1996.

Miller, Sally M., ed. *The Ethnic Press in the United States: An Historical Analysis and Handbook*. Westport, Conn.: Greenwood Press, 1987.

Monsiváis, Carlos. *A ustedes les consta: Antología de la crónica en México*. Mexico City: Ediciones Era, 1980.

Munguía, Rubén. "*La Prensa*: Memories of a Boy . . . Sixty Years Later." *The Americas Review, 17≠3-4* (Fall-Winter, 1989): 130-35.

Neri, Michel C. "A Journalistic Portrait of the Spanish-Speaking People of California, 1868-1925." *Historical Society of Southern California Quarterly* 55 (Summer 1973): 193- 208.

Ochoa Campos, Moisés. *Reseña historica del periodismo mexicano*. Mexico City: Editorial Porrúa, 1968.

Padilla, Benjamín. *Un puñado de artículos: filosofía barata*. 2da edición. Barcelona: Casa Editorial Maucci, s.d.

Park, Robert E. *The Immigrant Press and Its Control*. New York: Harper & Brothers, 1922.

Pérez, Emma. "'A la Mujer': A Critique of the Partido Liberal Mexicano's Gender Ideology." *Between Borders: Essays on Mexicana/Chicana History*. Ed. Adelaida R. Del Castillo (Encino, Calif.: Floricanto, 1990): 459-82.

Pitt, Leonard. *The Decline of the Californios: A Social History of the Spanish-Speaking Californians, 1846-1890*. Berkeley: University of California Press, 1966.

Poyo, Gerald E. *"With All, and for the good of All." The Emergence of Popular Nationalism in the Cuban Communities of the United States, 1848-1898*. Durham: Duke University Press, 1989.

Rice, William B. *The Los Angeles Star, 1851-1864*. Berkeley: University of California Press, 1951.

Richmond, Douglas W. *Venustiano Carranza's Nationalist Struggle, 1893-1920*. Lincoln: University of Nebraska Press, 1983.

Ríos-McMillan, Nora. "A Biography of a Man and His Newspaper." *The Americas Review* 17:3-4 (Fall-Winter, 1989): 136-49.

Rodríguez, Emilio Jorge. "Apuntes sobre la visión del emigrante en la narrativa puertorriqueña." *Primer seminario sobre la situación de las comunidades negra, chicana, cubana, india y puertorriqueña en Estados Unidos.* Havana: Editora Política, 1984. pp. 445-85.

Rodríguez, Juan. "Jorge Ulica y Carlo de Medina: escritores de la Bahía de San Francisco." *La palabra* 2/1 (primavera, 1980): 25-47.

———. *Crónicas diabólicas de "Jorge Ulica"/Julio B.Arce.* San Diego: Maize Press, 1982.

Rodríguez Fraticelli, Carlos. "Pedro Albizu Campos: Strategies of Struggle and Strategic Struggles." *Centro* (Center for Puerto Rican Studies, Hunter College) 4/1 (1992): 24-33.

Rosales, F. Arturo. *Chicano! The History of the Mexican American Civil Rights Movement.* Houston: Arte Público Press, 1996.

Rosario, Rubén del, Esther Melón de Díaz and Edgar Martínez Masdeu. *Breve enciclopedia de la cultura puertorriqueña.* San Juan: Editorial Cordillera, 1976.

Sánchez Korrol, Virginia. *From Colonia to Community: The History of Puerto Ricans in New York City, 1917-1948.* Westport, Conn.: Greenwood Press, 1983.

Serrano Cabo, Tomás. *Crónicas: Alianza Hispano Americana.* Tucson: Alianza Hispano Americana, 1929.

Sheridan, Thomas E. *Los Tucsonenses: The Mexican Community in Tucson, 1854-1941.* Tucson: University of Arizona Press, 1986.

Smith, Michael M. "The Mexican Immigrant Press beyond the Borderlands: The Case of *El Cosmopolita*, 1914-1919." *Great Plains Quarterly* 10 (Spring 1990): 71-85.

Stefano, Onofre di. "'Venimos a Luchar': A Brief History of *La Prensa's* Founding," *Aztlán* 16.1-2 (1985): 95-118.

Stratton, Porter A. *The Territorial Press of New Mexico, 1834-1912.* Albuquerque: University of New Mexico Press, 1969.

Subervi, Federico. "Media." *The Hispanic American Almanac.* Ed. Nicolás Kanellos. 2nd edition. (Detroit: Gale Research Inc., 1997): 681-88.

Treviño, Roberto. *Becoming Mexican American: The Spanish-Language Press and Biculturation of California Elites, 1852-1870.* Palo Alto, Calif.: Stanford University History Department Working Paper Series No. 27, 1989.

Trujillo, E. *Album de "El Porvenir."* Vols. 1-5. NY: Imprenta de "El Porvenir," 1890.

A Twentieth-Century History of Southwest Texas (Vol. I and II). Chicago: Lewis Publishing, 1970.

Velasco Valdés, Miguel. *Historia del periodismo mexicano (apuntes).* Mexico City: Librería de Manuel Porrúa, s.d.

Venegas, Daniel. *Las aventuras de Don Chipote, o cuando los pericos mamen.* Ed. Nicolás Kanellos. Houston: Arte Público Press, 1999.

Wagner, Henry R. "New Mexico Spanish Press." *New Mexico Historical Review.* 12/1 (January, 1937): 1-40.

Wallace, John Melton. *Gaceta to Gazette: A Check List of Texas Newspapers, 1812-1846.* Austin: University of Texas Department of Journalism Development Program, 1966.

Wynar, Lubomyr R. and Anna T. *Encyclopedic Directory of Ethnic Newspapers and Periodicals in the United States.* 2nd edition. Littleton, Colorado: Libraries Unlimited Inc., 1976.

Zamora, Emilio. "Sara Estela Ramírez: Una Rosa Roja en el Movimiento." *Mexican Women in the United States: Struggles Past and Present.* Ed. Magdalena Mora and Adelaida R. del Castillo (Los Angeles: University of California Chicano Studies Research Publications, 1980): 163-78.

Zanetti, Susana. *Costumbristas de América Latina: Antología.* Buenos Aires, 1973.

Notes

1. See Henry Horgan, "The Oldest American Book," introduction to *The Doctrina Breve* (New York: The United States Catholic Historical Society, 1928) and Carlos E. Castañeda, "The Beginning of Printing in America" (Austin: University of Texas Latin American García Library).

2. The first *hoja volante* was published by printer Juan Pablos in 1541: *Relación del espantable terremoto que ahora nuevamente ha acontecido en las Indias en una ciudad llamada Guatemala...* For a facsimile of this news sheet, reporting on an earthquake in Guatemala, see Rafael Carrasco Puente, *La prensa en México: Datos históricos* (Mexico City: Universidad Nacional Autónoma de México, 1962), p. 19.

3. See Félix Gutiérrez, "Spanish-Language Media in America: Background, Resources, History," *Journalism History* 4:2 (Summer, 1977), p. 37.

4. For a facsimile of the front page of this newspaper, see Rafael Carrasco Puente, *La prensa en México*, p. 31. Before *La gaceta de México* appeared there were various other "gazettes" that appeared, in 1666, 1667, 1668, 1671, 1673 and 1682, but they all lacked periodicity. The first regular periodical documented is truly *La gaceta de México* (Carrasco Puente, p. 35).

5. Francine Medeiros, in *"La Opinión*, A Mexican Exile Newspaper: A Content Analysis of Its First Years, 1926-1929," *Aztlán* 11.1 (Spring, 1980): 65-87, fails to understand this distinction and incorrectly classifies *La Opinión* as an "exile" newspaper on the basis that 73 percent of the newspaper's editorials during these first of its long years of publication were devoted to issues internal to Mexico. *La Opinión*, just as its parent newspaper, San Antonio's *La Prensa*, were sophisticated business enterprises administered by a consummate entrepreneur, Ignacio Lozano, who knew precisely how to cater to the Mexican immigrant population; at no time did either newspaper throw full support to any one faction of the Revolution nor did they as a matter of policy meddle in politics in Mexico or the United States. For a biography of the founder and his business acumen—as well as to correct some of the errors in the Medeiros article—see Onofre di Stefano, "'Venimos a Luchar': A Brief History of *La Prensa's* Founding," *Aztlán* 16.1-2 (1985): 95-118.

6. Ambrosio Fornet, *El libro en Cuba* (Havana: Editorial Letras Cubanas, 1994), p. 31.

7. These were possibly the same newspaper with a title change. See Laura Gutiérrez-Witt, "Cultural Continuity in the Face of Change: Hispanic Printers in Texas," *Recovering the U. S. Hispanic Literary Heritage*, Vol. II. Eds. Erlinda Gonzales-Berry and Chuck Tatum (Houston: Arte Público Press, 1996): 278.

8. See Nicolás Kanellos with Cristelia Pérez, *Chronology of Hispanic American History* (Detroit: Gale Research Inc., 1995), p. 68.

9. Such was the fate suffered by Eduardo Facciolo for clandestinely publishing the revolutionary newspaper *La Voz del Pueblo Cubano* in 1852. The interesting story of how Facciolo transported and hid his press from the authorities and was ultimately discovered is related by Fornet, pp. 32-4. Juan Clemente Zenea, another journalist and literary figure associated with *La Voz del Pueblo Cubano* who went into exile in New York to escape persecution, continued his revolutionary journalism for *La Revolución* newspaper there and, on returning to Cuba with a Spanish government pass to conduct interviews of political figures, was arrested and executed by a Spanish firing squad in 1871. See *El laúd del desterrado*. Ed. Matías Montes-Huidobro (Houston: Arte Público Press, 1995), p. 163.

10. See Matías Montes-Huidobro's brief biography of Teurbe Tolón in *El laúd del desterrado*, pp. 134-46.

11. *"Cecilia Valdés*: The Emergence of an Antislavery Novel," *Afro-Hispanic Review* 3.2 (1984), p. 15.

12. See Rodrigo Lazo, "A Man of Action: Cirilo Villaverde as a American Revolutionary Journalist," in *Recovering the U. S. Hispanic Literary Heritage*, Vol. III. Eds. María Herrera- Sobek and Virginia Sánchez Korrol (Arte Público Press, 1999) for a study of Villaverde's complete trajectory as a revolutionary journalist in the United States.

13. See Francisco Calcagno, *Diccionario biográfico cubano* (NY: Imprenta y Librería de N. Ponce de León, 1878), pp. 687-89, for a brief biography of Villaverde.

14. See Gerald E. Poyo, *"With All, and for the good of All." The Emergence of Popular Nationalism in the Cuban Communities of the United States, 1848-1898* (Durham: Duke University Press, 1989), p. 17, for a detailed discussion of the *El Mulato* controversy. Poyo's landmark study of the development of Cuban identity was accomplished through the first detailed analysis in history of the role of the Cuban expatriate newspapers in the formation of political ideology and nationalism by an Hispanic group. His book is a real-life demonstration of the value of preserving and studying the Hispanic press.

15. Cuando *El Filibustero* dió a entender que *La Verdad* no era ya la defensora de nuestros derechos, se apoyaba tal vez en que era redactada por un enemigo de nuestra causa, en fin, hemos visto con repugnancia que uno de los órganos de la revolución estuviese en manos de un *realista*, de un satélite del despotismo.

16. En el país de los *libres*, la libertad esclaviza, atormenta, oprime, castiga, hiere y quema á algunos de nuestros semejantes . . . ¡Humanidad! ¿a dónde habeis ido? Será que enojada en la tierra libre de Washington, habeis resuelto buscar mejor morada en tras rejiones, donde la libertad tenga su verdadero culto y los hombres firmes y lejítimas garantías? Mientras el desvalido sufre tremendos azotes, busca en vano, sin encontrar la mano benéfica que detenga tan bárbaros golpes, levanta entónces los brazos y eleva su vista al cielo esclamando: "¡ya no hay libertad, gran Dios, en la tierra: los hombres que la invocan, la ofenden con la mentira, la injurian con la crueldad".

Instituciones que se reputan como el tipo de la democracia son contrariadas por sus propios promulgadores . . . vulneradas con estudio, tambien son manchadas por la ambicion y el vil interés. —Los jenios metalizados carecen de todo instinto jeneroso.

17. Quoted and translated in Poyo, p. 16.

18. Nuestros hermanos que combaten en los campos de Cuba nos recuerdan, que es justísimo que los que estamos en tierra extranjera seamos infatigables en la creación de fondos para adquirir y remitirles elementos de guerra en cantidad suficiente . . . la emigración cubana es la emigración más rica que registra la historia; ya por el monto de capitales efectivos con que cuenta, ya por el inmenso caudal que representa su industria. No puede ponerse nada en duda la proverbial generosidad y largeza de los cubanos . . .

19. This emphasis on Hispanic children in the United States was not new or unusual, given that entire Hispanic communities were now developing on the East Coast. Over the course of the nineteenth century more and more textbooks for Spanish-speaking children were being published, and the all-important printer-book-seller-publisher Nestor Ponce de León even founded in 1873 a periodical to assist Hispanic families in the education for their children: *El Educador Popular.* Ponce de León was *the* most important publisher of books and pamphlets advancing the revolutionary cause. A man of letters and historian himself, Ponce de León had edited liberal magazines and newspapers in Cuba before becoming persecuted and going into political exile in New York. Almost immediately on arriving on these shores, he wrote and published a book in English, *The Book of Blood*, denouncing Spain's bloody rule over Cuba. See Calcagno, pp. 519- 20.

20. Poyo, p. 61, has summarized Martí's stance toward the United States: "But Martí did not reject Cuba's annexation to the United States only because of what he considered its unnatural implications for Cuban national identity or because of his contempt for North American racism. He also did not share the annexationists' glowing assess-

ment of North American life. A man of high ideals, the Cuban publicist did not believe that the United States could offer the Cuban people a great deal. His own vision of Cuba's future could never be achieved as part of what he considered to be an increasingly decadent North American society. During his many years in the United States, Martí had observed the nation in all its complexities. While he had originally admired many aspects of North American life, by the late 1880s he had concluded that many aspects of its negative internal political and socioeconomic characteristics and its increasingly aggressive international posture would probably dominate its future."

21. According to Joseph P. Fitzpatrick, "The Puerto Rican Press," *The Ethnic Press in the United States*, p. 304, *La Voz* had branches in New York, Philadelphia and New Orleans.

22. See Juan Flores, "Puerto Rican Literature in the United States: Stages and Perspectives," *Divided Borders* (Houston: Arte Público Press, 1993): 142-53.

23. Rodríguez de Tió arrived in New York in 1895 and left in 1899, the third of her exiles; the first and second were in Venezuela (1877-80) and Cuba (1889-95). After the Spanish American War, Rodríguez de Tió spent out the rest of her life in a quasi-independent Cuba, preferring not to live in Puerto Rico, which had become a colony of the United States. See Rubén del Rosario, Esther Melón de Díaz and Edgar Martínez Masdeu, *Breve enciclopedia de la cultura puertorriqueña* (San Juan: Editorial Cordillera, 1976): 393-95.

24. For the periodical writings of Sotero Figueroa, see Sotero Figueroa, *La verdad de la historia* (San Juan: Instituto de Cultura Puertorriqueña, 1977). Carlos Ripoll's introduction, pp. 5-9, includes interesting data on Sotero's activity in New York.

25. See María Teresa Babín, *Panorama de la cultura puertorriqueña* (New York: Las Américas Publishing Company, 1958), 329-33, for an evaluation of his poetry. Also see Emilio Jorge Rodríguez, "Apuntes sobre la visión del emigrante en la narrativa puertorriqueña," *Primer seminario sobre la situación de las comunidades negra, chicana, cubana, india y puertorriqueña en Estados Unidos* (Havana: Editora Política, 1984): 445-85.

26. See E. Trujillo, *Album de "El Porvenir"* Vols. 1-5 (New York: Imprenta de "El Porvenir," 1890).

27. See Yolanda Argudín, *Historia del periodismo en México desde el Virreinato hasta nuestros días* (Mexico City: Panorama Editorial, 1997), pp. 94-95.

28. For more on both revolutionaries, see Juan Gómez-Quiñones, *Roots of Chicano Politics, 1600-1940* (Albuquerque: University of New Mexico Press, 1994), pp. 290-1.

29. Prior to launching *Regeneración*, Flores Magón had founded *El Demócrata* (The Democrat), a student newspaper, in Mexico in 1893, and before coming to the United States, he also took over the editorship of the famous anti-Díaz newspaper *El hijo del Ahuizote* (Son of the Nutria) in 1903, which was closed down by the government and restarted various times by Flores Magón as the "Grandson of . . ." and "Great Grandson of . . .," according to Manuel González Ramírez, ed., *Epistolario y textos de Ricardo Flores Magón* (México: Fondo de Cultura Económica 1964), pp. 8-9.

30. According to Argudín, p. 111, *Regeneración* was at this point printing and distributing 30,000 copies.

31. See Richard Griswold del Castillo, "The Mexican Revolution and the Spanish-Language Press in the Borderlands," *Journalism History* 4.2 (Summer 1977), p. 46. Also see Juan Gómez- Quiñones, *Sembradores, Ricardo Flores Magón y El Partido Liberal Mexicano: A Eulogy and Critique* (Los Angeles: UCLA Chicano Studies Research Center Publications, 1977).

32. Mexican government agents, indeed, pursued the Brothers Flores Magón and others on American soil, at times even with the complicity of U. S. authorities. And in Mexico itself, reprisals were often brutal, if not fatal. Suppression of the press was most

intense during the regimes of dictators Antonio López de Santa Anna and Porfirio Díaz. For a detailed account of the form that this suppression took, see Miguel Velasco Valdés, *Historia del periodismo mexicano (apuntes)* (Mexico City: Librería de Manuel Porrúa, s.d.), pp. 113-18.

33. See James D. Cockroft, *Intellectual Pioneers of the Mexican Revolution, 1900-1913* (Austin: University of Texas Press, 1968) and Juan Gómez-Quiñones, *Roots of Chicano Politics, 1600-1940* (Albuquerque: University of New Mexico Press, 1994).

34. Section 19 of the Trading with the Enemy Act required newspapers publishing in foreign languages to file a translation of all items that mentioned the United States government or the conduct of the war. See Robert E. Park, *The Immigrant Press and Its Control* (New York: Harper & Brothers, 1922), p. 440.

35. See Park, pp. 412-47, for a lengthy discussion of press censorship and suppression under these circumstances; in 1922, Park did not really consider these acts to be suppressive: "The files of the [Post Office] Department at Washington contain the records of hundreds of hearings in which immigrant newspapers were given an opportunity to answer the complaints against them. These records show that the most searching examination was made of the character and contents of the papers complained of. They show that the number of foreign papers actually denied the services of the Post Office Department were very small, probably not more than ten. A number of newspaper offices were, to be sure, raided at different times by the Department of Justice, but no papers were suppressed by the Post Office Department" (p. 441). In addition to *Regeneración*, Park gives some indication that New York's *Cultura Obrera* was another targeted Spanish-language newspaper (p. 246). Thomas C. Langham, *Border Trials: Ricardo Flores Magón and the Mexican Liberals* (El Paso: Texas Western Press, 1981), p. 55, notes that the Post Office also revoked the second-class mailing privileges of New York's Spanish newspaper *Voluntad* (Will Power) in 1916 for political reasons.

36. Actually, the *Regeneración* offices had been raided earlier, on June 14, 1911, and Flores Magón and other PLM members were arrested by U. S. federal authorities, following a PLM led insurgency in Baja California. Raising the bail and freeing the PLM members became a *cause célébre* for radicals in the United States. On June 22, 1912, Flores Magón and the other PLM members were convicted of conspiracy to organize armed expeditions from the United States territory against a friendly nation. The "Los Angeles 13" were sentenced to twenty-three months of imprisonment. See Gómez-Quiñones, *Sembradores*, pp. 46-50.

37. Colin M. MacLachlan, *Anarchism and the Mexican Revolution. The Political Trials of Ricardo Flores Magón in the United States* (Berkeley: University of California Press, 1991), pp. 80-92, goes into great detail of the actual indictment and trial of Flores Magón.

38. Actually, Flores Magón had been sentenced to various other terms in the United States before serving his last in Leavenworth: two months in St. Louis in 1905; thirty-six months, beginning in 1907; thirty-three months in Los Angeles in 1911; two months at Leavenworth in 1916. (González Ramírez, 8)

39. See the letters reproduced in Juan Gómez-Quiñones, *Sembradores*, pp. 154-5.

40. Velasco Valdés, p. 156, lists the following as examples of revolutionary journalists whom U. S. authorities suppressed in compliance with the wishes of the Díaz regime: Jesús, Enrique and Ricardo Flores Magón, Antonio Villarreal, Santiago R. de la Vega, Inocencio Arreola, los hermanos Sarabia, Librado Rivera and Aarón López Manzano.

41. Emma Pérez, "'A la Mujer': A Critique of the Partido Liberal Mexicano's Gender Ideology," *Between Borders: Essays on Mexicana/Chicana History*. Ed. Adelaida R. Del Castillo (Encino, Calif.: Floricanto, 1990): 459-82, states that *Regeneración* and the PLM did help to politicize Mexican women, but it was not truly to analyze and address their

issues as women at all, only to serve the nationalist cause of the revolution.

42. See Emilio Zamora, "Sara Estela Ramírez: Una Rosa Roja en el Movimiento," *Mexican Women in the United States: Struggles Past and Present*. Ed. Magdalena Mora and Adelaida R. del Castillo (Los Angeles: University of California Chicano Studies Research Publications, 1980): 163-78.

43. Inés Hernández Tovar, *Sara Estela Ramírez: The Early Twentieth Century Texas-Mexican Poet* (Houston: University of Houston Dissertation, 1984), p. 12.

44. Clara Lomas, "The Articulation of Gender in the Mexican Borderlands, 1900-1915," *Recovering the U. S. Hispanic Literary Heritage*. Eds. Ramón Gutiérrez and Genaro Padilla (Houston: Arte Público Press, 1993): 293-308.

45. María de los Angeles Mendieta Alatorre, *Carmen Serdán* (Mexico City: Centro de Estudios Históricos de Puebla, 1971), p. 33.

46. Lomas, 304, has found a letter that indicates that men may have been using women's voices in *La Voz de la Mujer* or they may have been writing down what the women's staff dictated or commented upon instead of women appropriating the right to write and publish, and she further states that, "This may explain why the narrative voices in *La Voz de la Mujer* are not at all different from those of the male precursors of the revolution, why the newspaper lacks an analysis of women's condition and why attempts are made therein to develop women's sense of state nationalism."

47. See Spencer Leitman, "Exile and Union in Indiana Harbor," *Revista Chicano-Riqueña* 2/1 (Winter 1974): 50-7.

48. For further description of newspapers, see Rafael Chabrán, "Spaniards," *The Immigrant Labor Press in North America, 1840s -1970s*, ed. Dirk Hoerder. (Westport, CN: Greenwood Press, 1987): 151-190.

49. See her "Introduction," pp. xi-xxii, in which she also states that for the most part she refers to the foreign-language press (p. xii).

50. Lubomyr R. and Anna T. Wynar, in *Encyclopedic Directory of Ethnic Newspapers and Periodicals in the United States* 2nd edition (Littleton, Co.: Libraries Unlimited Inc., 1976), pp. 14-15, include an extensive discussion of terminology, which there is no reason to reproduce here. Suffice it to say that, in general, I agree with their use of the term "ethnic" as all-inclusive, but insist that my study of the subcategories of "exile," "immigrant" and "ethnic minority" is necessary and revelatory, especially of the experience of the Hispanic press. Furthermore, the Wynars treat the African American, Native American and Hispanic presses solely as ethnic press without their special functioning as the expression of oppressed racial minorities. In my study, I insist on the relevance of race, ethnicity and minority status in studying these press manifestations.

51. I refer to the 1970 edition issued by Greenwood Press of Westport, Connecticut, of Robert E. *Park, The Immigrant Press and Its Control* (New York: Harper & Brothers Publishers, 1922).

52. "Los mejicanos, bien lo sean o hayan renegado de este título, son siempre tratados con injusticia y prevención, por los jueces, los ciudadanos, los pudientes, y en general todos los hijos de esta nación.

Por consiguiente, si no se ha de lograr ningún mejoramiento, y de ello estamos todos convencidos, ¿a qué renegar del título de hijos de la República de Méjico ... permaneceremos extranjeros en los Estados Unidos y como tal nos consideran siempre?" (24 March 1880)

In fact, *El Horizonte* repeatedly ran editorials protesting the unequal treatment of Mexicans in court, lynchings and the non-admission of Mexican children to the Corpus Christi schools, despite the school system counting the children as students in order to receive funding for them from the state. The struggle for civil rights, furthermore, led *El Horizonte*, as well as numerous other immigrant institutions to support the creation of mutual aid societies, and *El Horizonte* wholeheartedly exhorted its readership to associate with the Sociedad Mutualista Benito Juárez founded in Brownsville in

1879: "Los mejicanos en Corpus hemos sido siempre considerados como seres indig-
nos aun del título de extrangeros: se han pisoteado nuestros derechos; nos han negado
hasta las ínfimas garantías a que es creedor un ciudadano, y hemos sido en fin miser-
ables parias, sin porvenir . . . De hoy . . . respetarán nuestros derechos y no seremos el
objeto de su ludibrio y escarnio" (6 December 1879). (We Mexicans in Corpus have
always been considered unworthy of even the title of foreigner: they have stepped all
over our rights; they have denied us even the few guaranties owed to a citizen and we
have been, in short, miserable pariahs, without a future . . . From today . . . they will
respect our rights and we shall not be the object of their jokes and insult.)

53. I obviously disagree with Victoria Goff, in "Spanish-Language Newspapers in
California," *Outsiders in 19th-Century Press History: Multicultural Perspectives*, ed.
Frankie Hutton and Barbara Straus Reed (Bowling Green, OH: Bowling Green State
University Popular Press, 1995): 55-70, when she states that "California's Hispanic press
has never truly been an immigrant press, making it unique among the immigrant/eth-
nic press in the United States" (55). As I stated above in my text, it does not matter that
some of the readers were native Californians; the majority of the readers were immigrants, and before their arrival in California, in fact, there was no native Spanish-language press. It is true that there developed, beginning with the Spanish-language sections of the *Californian* (1846) and *The California Star* (1847) an Hispanic ethnic
minority press, but this press existed side-by-side with the immigrant press. In my text,
I shall later trace the development of the Hispanic ethnic-minority press in California.

54. According to Goff, p. 56, the editors of *La Crónica*, of *El Eco de la Raza
Latina* and of *El Joven* were Spanish; the editor of *La Voz del Nuevo Mundo* was
Chilean and of *El Tecolote* was Colombian.

55. See Ramón D. Chacón, "The Chicano Immigrant Press in Los Angeles: The Case
of 'El Heraldo de México,' 1916-1920," *Journalism History* 4.2 (Summer, 1977): 48-50, 62-
4.

56. See the recent edition, introduced by Nicolás Kanellos (Houston: Arte Público
Press, 1999).

57. See Michael M. Smith, "The Mexican Immigrant Press beyond the Borderlands:
The Case of *El Cosmopolita*, 1914-1919," *Great Plains Quarterly* 10 (Spring 1990): 71-
85, for a complete history of *El Cosmopolita*.

58. See Nemesio García Naranjo, *Memorias de Nemesio García Naranjo*, Vol. 8
(Monterrey, Mexico: Talleres de "El Porvenir," s.d.), p. 341.

59. No pudiendo encontrar orientaciones en un medio desorientado, Ignacio E.
Lozano tuvo el acierto indiscutible de fincar su obra en los mexicanos que llevaban
muchos años de residir fuera del territorio nacional. Eran gentes humildes y de escasa
cultura, pero que no obstante de haber pasado su existencia lejos del suelo de México,
conservaban intactas sus costumbres y las tradiciones de nuestros antepasados. Sin
hacer trabajosos análisis sentían, que hay algo que no se hunde en los naufragios, que
no vacila ni cae en los terremotos, que no se carboniza en los incendios, y ese algo
inmutable y eterno, es el alma de la Patria, siempre lista a levantar a los caídos, a per-
donar a los pecadores, a consolar a los hijos que por encontrarse ausentes, no se
pueden refugiar en su regazo maternal.

Así pues, mientras yo me dirigía a los desterrados, Lozano se vinculó con ese con-
glomerado sencillo que le gustaba llamar "México de afuera" y que nada tenía que ver
con nuestras convulsiones políticas y sociales. . . . Lozano, al vincularse con un público
permanente, le había dado a "La Prensa" unos cimientos que en aquel tiempo, eran
inconmovibles. (318-319)

60. Bruce-Novoa, "*La Prensa* and the Chicano Community," *The Americas Review*
17/3-4 (Winter 1989), p. 151. Bruce-Novoa's article appears in a special issue dedicated almost entirely to *La Prensa* and represents thus the major source for the study of
this important newspaper.

Notes

61. Rubén Munguía, "*La Prensa*: Memories of a Boy … Sixty Years Later," in *The Americas Review* special issue dedicated to *La Prensa*, op. cit., p.132.

62. Ignacio E. Lozano, Jr., publisher of *La Opinión*, still sees the purpose of his newspaper in the terms that could apply to his father's *La Prensa* and *La Opinión*: "The paper is put out by Hispanics for Hispanics. The Spanish-speaking community is a long way from entering the American mainstream. We cover things not covered by the mainstream press, such as columns devoted to legal advice for Hispanics, where to go for public services and generally how the system works." Quoted in Nora Ríos-McMillan, "A Biography of a Man and His Newspaper," *The Americas Review*, op. cit., p. 141.

63. Typical of these polemical works that often attacked the Revolution and particular political leaders, thus making up a good core of exile literature, were Miguel Bolaños Cacho's *Sembradores de viento* (1828, Sowers of Wind), Brigido Caro's *Plutarco Elías Calles: Dictador Bolchevique de México* (1924, Plutarco Elías Calles: Bolshevik Dictator of Mexico) and Lázaro Gutiérrez de Lara's *Los bribones rebeldes* (1932, The Rebel Rogues). Many were the authors of this very popular genre—Miguel Arce, Conrado Espinosa, *La Opinión*'s editorialist Alfredo González, Esteban Maqueos Castellanos, Manuel Mateos, Ramón Puente and *La Prensa*'s editorialist Teodoro Torres—but the most famous of all has become Mariano Azuela, author of the masterpiece that has become one of the foundations of modern Mexican literature, *Los de abajo* (The Underdogs), which was first published in 1915 in El Paso's newspaper *El Paso del Norte* (The Northern Pass) and was later issued as a book by the same newspaper.

64. For an evolution of *costumbrista* writing, see Susana Zanetti, *Costumbristas de América Latina: Antología* (Buenos Aires, 1973), pp. 8-10.

65. For a history and anthology of the *crónica* in Mexico, see Carlos Monsiváis, *A ustedes les consta: Antología de la crónica en México* (Mexico City: Ediciones Era, 1980).

66. De principios del siglo XIX hasta casi nuestros días, a la crónica mexicana se le encomienda verificar o consagrar cambios y maneras sociales y describir lo cotidiano elevándolo al rango de lo idiosincrático (aquello sin lo cual los mexicanos serían, por ejemplo, paraguayos). En el tránsito de la mentalidad colonial a la independiente… una colectividad pequeña, insegura de sus logros, incierta en su nacionalismo, ve en la crónica el espejo refulgente (ideal) de sus transformaciones y fijaciones.

Escribir es poblar. Durante un periodo prolongado el detallismo exhaustivo de los cronistas sirve a un propósito central: contribuir a la forja de la nación, describiéndola y, si se puede, moralizándola. Los escritores del siglo XIX van a la crónica a documentar y, lo que les importa más, promover un estilo de vida, aquel que va a la reiteración de las costumbres el verdadero ritual cívico. Los cronistas son nacionalistas acérrimos porque desean la independencia y la grandeza de una colectividad …o porque anhelan el sello de identidad que los ampare, los singularice, los despoje de sujeciones y elimine sus ansiedades y su terror más profundo: ser testigos privilegiados de lo que no tiene ninguna importancia, narrar el proceso formativo de esta sociedad que nadie contemple. Se necesita fortalecer a la Nación infundiéndole y aclarándole sus orgullos locales y regionales, recreando literariamente las formas de vida más ostensiblemente "mexicanas" y subrayando el desdén por la imitación de lo francés y la nostalgia servil de lo hispánico. (Carlos Monsiváis, pp. 26-7.)

67. Originally a journalist from Guadalajara, after his return to Mexico Padilla published a collection of his *crónicas* which included many of those published and syndicated in the United States: *Un puñado de artículos: filosofía barata*. 2nda edición. (Barcelona: Casa Editorial Maucci, s.d.)

68. A few studies of these *cronistas* have appeared sporadically, but as yet there have been no definitive studies nor have their texts been collected. See Clara Lomas, "Resistencia cultural o apropiación ideológica: Visión de los años 20 en los cuadros

costumbristas de Jorge Ulica," *Revista Chicano-Riqueña* 6/4 (otoño, 1978): 44-49; Juan Rodríguez, "Jorge Ulica y Carlo de Medina: escritores de la Bahía de San Francisco," *La palabra* 2/1 (primavera, 1980): 25-47; Juan Rodríguez, *Crónicas diabólicas de "Jorge Ulica"/Julio B. Arce* (San Diego: Maize Press, 1982); Nicolás Kanellos, "Un relato de Azteca (Bromeando)," *Revista Chicano-Riqueña* 1/1 (1973): 5-8; Nicolás Kanellos, "Brief History/Overview of Spanish-language Newspapers in the United States," *Recovering the U. S. Hispanic Literary Heritage* Vol. I, pp. 107-28.

69. See José Limón, "*Agringado* Joking in Texas Mexican Society," *Perspectives in Mexican American Studies* 1 (1988):109-28, for a definition and study of usage of *agringado*. The conflict of cultures and perceived abandonment of Mexican nationality was already a common topic in the nineteenth century; it especially took on racial overtones when a Mexican or Mexican American whose skin color was dark seemed to be passing for an Anglo-American in the eyes of Mexican commentators. For instance, the Editor of El Paso's *El Monitor* (The Monitor), on August 13, 1897, chastised *agringados* for not donating money to the celebration of Mexican Independence Day in El Paso: "A esos *agringados* que niegan ser mexicanos, por el solo hecho de haber nacido en los Estados Unidos, les preguntamos, ¿qué sangre corre por sus venas? Acaso perteneséis a la raza sajona y sois trigueños por el hecho de haber nacido en la Frontera! ¡Qué barabaridad!" (We want to ask those *agringados* who deny they are Mexicans based on the sole reason that they were born in the United States: What blood flows in your veins? Is it possible that you belong to the Saxon race and that you are dark just because you were born on the Border?)

70. This and other biographical information is provided by Juan Rodríguez, "Julio G. Arce: vida y obra," *Crónicas diabólicas (1916-1926) de "Jorge Ulica"/Julio G. Arce*, ed. Juan Rodríguez (San Diego: Maize Press, 1982): 9-21.

71. See Jorge Ulica, "Treinta años de galeras . . . periodísticas, 1881-1911," manuscript in the Chicano Studies Collection, University of California-Berkeley, cited in Rodríguez, p. 12.

72. See the files of Mexican Consul in San Francisco De Negri, Secretaría de Relaciones Exteriores, 23-21-156, which detail the correspondence between Arce, the consul De Negri and head of the Secretariat of Foreign Relations Cándido Aguilar. It seems that this underwriting of Mexican immigrant newspapers in the United States by the government and various political factions in Mexico was not rare. On Carranza's policy of underwriting newspapers abroad, see Douglas W. Richmond, *Venustiano Carranza's Nationalist Struggle, 1893-1920* (Lincoln: University of Nebraska Press, 1983), p. 190. In addition to *Mefistófeles*, Carranza may have invested in *Gale's Magazine*, Kansas City's *El Cosmopolita* (1914-1919), New York's *El Gráfico* (1916-1918) and its parent Columbus Publishing Company, headed by Modesto C. Rolland, who also formed the Latin American News Association with Carranza.

73. Proclaimed in an unsigned article, "Hoy cumple *Hispano América* once años de vida activa," on the anniversary of *Hispano América*, 18 April 1925.

74. Eleuteria Hernández, in her article "La representación de la mujer mexicana en los EE.UU. en las *Crónicas Diabólicas* de Jorge Ulica," *Mester* 12/2 (Fall, 1993): 31-38, has rightly attributed Ulica's attack on Mexican women to an attempt to preserve the family in an alien environment (34), but she attributes this attack primarily to Ulica's desire to stem the feminist advances made by women in both the United States and Mexico. While I agree that Ulica is certainly anti-feminist, I would add that his fears of cultural annihilation led him to place that burden on women as the center of the family, as I explain below in my essay. And making poor, uneducated women the target for his barbs in no way served as a direct and clear reaction to the feminist movements alluded to in Hernández's otherwise incisive article.

75. Si los hombres quieren ser menos felices ... no deben venir, con sus consortes, a los Estados Unidos. Porque aquí andan las cosas muy mal y el género masculi-

no va perdiendo, a pasos agigantados ... "sus sagradas prerrogativas y sus inalienables derechos".... me duele en el alma ver a los pobres "maridos" sujetos a una perra vida, a un porvenir parecido y a un fin trágico. (p. 89)

76. ... en este país las mujeres hacen lo que les da la real gana. La mía, que era tan obediente, tan fiel y tan mosquita muerta en Ojinaga, aquí se ha vuelto "de cohetería", no me hace caso, se encierra con sus amigos a jugar "bridge" y no sé qué cosas más, y, cuando reclamo, me echa de la mamá. En mi tierra, podía haberle tumbado los dientes a manazos; pero aquí, si hace eso, lo cuelgan en San Cuintín. (p. 145)

77. Al arreglarse la coca dos pelonas
fueron al "Barber Shop" de Don Simon,
Pues iban esa noche las gallonas
a darle vuelo y duro al vacilón.

—Acabe pronto en mi,— decia Julieta,
Mientras le razuraban el pescuezo,
Para que suba luego Enriqueta;
Y acabando a las dos le doy un beso.

Trabajó el peluquero
Que acabo en un momento.
Mas no le dieron de lo prometido,
Ni despues que acabo con Enriqueta.

78. El constante aumento de la colonia española e iberoamericana nos ha impelido a editar este semanario que viene a cooperar a la defensa de todos los que forman la gran familia hispana. Haremos una labor tendente a buscar la mayor compenetración y bienestar de los que ausentes de la patria amada debemos en suelo extraño agruparnos bajo una sola bandera: la de la fraternidad. (27 February 1927)

79. Two collections of his English-language columns have been published: Jesús Colón, *A Puerto Rican in New York and Other Sketches*, 2nd edition (New York: International Publishers, 1982) and Jesús Colón, *The Way It Was and Other Writings*, Eds. Edna Acosta-Belén and Virginia Sánchez Korrol (Houston:Arte Público Press, 1993). See the Acosta Belén and Sánchez Korrol "Introduction" for a biography of Colón, pp. 13-30.

80. With this pseudonym, a Caribbean-Spanish phrase originating with the Latin *mihi* and *tibi*, Colón was indicating that these were intimate conversations "between you and me," from one Latino to another.

81. Si quieres ver lector la caricatura de una flapper no tienes nada más que mirar a una latina que aspira a serlo. La flapper yanqui siempre busca que su conjunto de exageraciones tenga una apariencia chic, como se dice en alemán. Además poseen esa divina joya de la frialdad bien imitada. Ese arquear desdeñoso de ojos que al cruzar las piernas casi desde ... desde ... parecen no importarle que las miren. *Seeming frigidity, that's the phrase.* La *would be flapper* latina le gusta que la miren y para conseguirlo se pinta como una mascarita. Dos chapotas mal puestas en cada buche y cuatro bien pronunciadas montañas de rouge en los labios. Critican primero los nuevos fads; después los adaptan, llevándolo hasta la exageración. (*Gráfico* 25 September 1927)

82. La Flapper

Como una niña Chole que fuera neoyorquina,
rasga el aire la "flapper" contoneándose toda.
Su traje, un futurísimo de la última moda,
hace mil sugerencias con seda divina.

Que la miren los hombres mientras ella camina

es su supremo anhelo. Si hay quien le hable de boda,
contesta con alguna carcajada que poda
la ilusión más sublime. ¡Carcajada asesina!

Reina experta del último salto mortal bailable,
niña pintarrajeada, superficial, variable,
como el liberto esclavo al probar nueva vida.

Por contraste me hacen recordar a mi abuela,
que hilando me contaba del gigante que vuela,
con su voz temblorosa cual plegaria perdida.
(*Gráfico* 25 September 1927)

83. Juanita Luna Lawhn, "Victorian Attitudes Affecting the Mexican Woman Writing in *La Prensa* during the 1900's and the Chicana of the 1980's," *Missions in Conflict: Essays on United States-Mexican Relations and Chicano Culture*, ed. Juan Bruce Novoa (Tübingen, Germany: Narr, 1986): 65-71, has provided examples of how San Antonio's *La Prensa* reinforced traditional gender roles and "never encouraged the Mexican woman to seek professional careers or to attempt self-realization anywhere other than inside the home or in occupations that were stereotypically acceptable for women"(65).

84. See Federico Subervi, "Media," *The Hispanic American Almanac*, ed. Nicolás Kanellos. 2nd edition (Detroit: Gale Research Inc., 1997), pp. 681-88, for complete information on current Hispanic newspapers.

85. See Tomás Almaguer, *Racial Fault Lines*, pp. 183-203; McWilliams, *North from Mexico*, p. 190; Kushner, *Long Road to Delano: A Century of Farmworkers' Struggle*, pp. 20-21; F. Arturo Rosales, *Chicano!*, p. 117; Jamieson, *Labor Unionism in American Agriculture*, pp. 76-77.

86. See Henderson and Mormino, *Spanish Pathways in Florida*, p. 40-45, 262; Florida Department of State, *Florida Cuban Heritage Trail*, p. 34.

87. El proletariado halló con la Lectura —con "la afición a oír leer", como la llamaba un editorialista de *El Siglo*— la forma más democrática y eficaz de difusión cultural que hubo en su época. La transmisión oral, realizada en el mismo taller durante las horas laborables, era el mecanismo idóneo para satisfacer las necesidades intelectuales de una clase que había surgido pidiendo libros, pero que carecía de recursos, de tiempo y en muchos casos de escolaridad para leerlos. La Lectura fue el primer intento de hacer "llegar" el libro a las masas con un propósito exclusivamente educativo y recreativo. Entre las clases privilegiadas el libro había sido siempre un objeto suntuario y en última instancia un instrumento de dominio o de lucro; el proletariado lo convirtió en un instrumento autodidáctico, empleándolo con el único fin de superarse ideológicamente y culturalmente. (Fornet, 185-6)

88. See Rafael Chabrán, "Spaniards," *The Immigrant Labor Press in North America, 1840s-1970s: An Annotated Bibliography*. Ed. Dirk Hoerder (Westport, Conn.: Greenwood Press, 1987), p. 157.

89. . . . en favor de la unificación de América, cuyos hijos, sin distinción de origen ni sectas, no deben conocer ni sustentar otro dogma que el dogma de los hombres libres, el de la unidad sólida, indivisible, como un monolito egipcio, atalaya gigantesco extendiendo sus brazos protectores por todos los ámbitos de América, desde las regiones boreales del Cabo Barrow, hasta las latitudes del Cabo de Hornos.

90. Nosotros sustentamos el principio dogmático de Monroe, que América es de sus hijos, y de aquéllos que con sincera honradez del ciudadano que aspira a la dignificación de su existencia moral en las comunidades libres del mundo americano, viene de otros confines del planeta y pone sus hombros al carro del progreso que unifi-

ca y engrandece a los pueblos; que viene a ser causa común con todas las ambiciones, con todos los esfuerzos nobles de las masas, para el desarrollo de todas las actividades de la vida en las esferas amplias de las ciencias, de las artes, de las industrias y del comercio, cuyos motores, al calor de las ideas multiplicadas por el estímulo de la gloria, desenvuelven las empresas titánicas que asombran el viejo mundo.

91. América, triunfante, da el ejemplo al viejo mundo, abre sus puertas a los que viven sumidos en la degradación del vasallaje, y les brinda generoso abrigo bajo el amparo de instituciones que hacen iguales a los hombres de buena voluntad.

92. Ah! con cuanta fruición acariciamos la halagüeña esperanza de la fusión de las naciones de este continente, porque ellas, conservando su autonomía, tendrán la unidad en la industria, en el comercio, en la riqueza, en la producción, en el consumo y en la gloria de haber llegado a la meta de su prosperidad por ministerio de su exclusivo aliento y de su propia convicción.

93. ... acometemos con ánimo resuelto la empresa, después de haber puesto los medios necesarios para no vernos a poco obligados a defendernos en pos del ideal que acariciamos, que es de mantener aquí un periódico culto, ilustrado, patriota, que sea la expresión genuina de las ideas, sentimientos, aspiraciones, adelantos y aptitudes de nuestra amada raza americana.

94. En este género ella realiza admirablemente, en español, el tipo genuino del *magazín*: es ni más ni menos, el *Harper's Magazine* nuestro. Sus grabados completan y perfeccionan las impresiones de lectura, que, gracias á ellos, adquiere representación artística, —y son tan finos y tan bien ejecutados que por sí solos é independientemente del motivo que ilustran, constituyen otros tantos trabajos de arte. In "La Revista Ilustrada de Nueva York," *Revista de Costa Rica* 1 (3 January 1892): 142-51, reproduced in *La Revista Ilustrada de Nueva York* (March 1892): 168-69.

95. Consagraremos particular atención a los asuntos literarios, que tanto seducen a nuestros pueblos de imaginación lozana y de temperamento apasionado, y así daremos novelas de pequeñas dimensiones, que puedan caber en un sólo número; cuentos ingeniosos y amenos, ya orginales y traducidos, pero que sean de los más distinguidos escritores; críticas literarias, que contribuyan á formar el buen gusto; producciones poéticas de los más renombrados líricos de España y de América, y en general todo cuanto tienda á hacer de esta sección una especialidad que acojan siempre con marcada predilección todos nuestros abonados.

96. Juan Valera, for one, collaborated in the magazine because of the high fees paid to famous authors. See *Epistolario de Valera y Menéndez Pelayo, 1877-1905*, eds. Miguel Artigas y Pedro Sáinz Rodríguez (Madrid: Espasa-Calpe, 1946), p. 434. Similarly, newspapers such as New York's *Las Novedades* paid well to obtain exclusive writings from such famed Spanish cultural and literary critics as Leopoldo Alas. See the special issue of *Cuadernos americanos* 13-14 (June, 1994), titled "Los artículos de Leopoldo Alas 'Clarín' en 'Las Novedades' Nueva York, 1894-1897," introduction by Adolfo Sotelo Vásquez. Also see Vernon A. Chamberlin, "La colaboración de Juan Valera en *La Revista Ilustrada de Nueva York*," *Hispanófila* 53 (January 1975): 1-13.

97. For an index of authors and contributions, see *La Revista Ilustrada de Nueva York: History, Anthology and Index of Literary Selections*, Eds. Vernon A. Chamberlin and Ivan A. Shulman (Columbia, MO: University of Missouri Press, 1976): 194-212.

98. "Más de una vez hemos leído con indignación en periódicos extranjeros, que la mujer de nuestra América vive apartada del todo de la vida intelectual, que en la ignorancia vegeta y en el estéril misticismo se consume. A tales aseveraciones vamos nosotros á oponer la verdad práctica, y ya se verá cómo saben presentarse ante el mundo las americanas, para figurar digna y altivamente en la escogida legión de los que viven del pensamiento y del espíritu y van alumbrando la humanidad con sus luces." In Román Mayorga Rivas, "La mujer hispano-americana y *La Revista Ilustrada de Nueva York*" (February, 1980).

99. See Chamberlin and Shulman, p. 35, for her brief biography; Puga later married the editor Elías Losada and bore him children during their brief life together before his death. She returned to Lima and literary celebrity, publishing a number of novels, books of poetry and short fiction.

100. For a complete analysis of the *Artes y Letras*, see María Aponte Alsina, "Culture and Identity: Periodical Literature in Puerto Rican Archives," a report to the Recovering the U. S. Hispanic Literary Heritage Project, University of Houston, 1994, pp. 17-20.

101. Y la Patria vive. Los Estados Unidos debieran tener presente que hace más de dos tercios de siglo se firmaron los tratados de Guadalupe, y sin embargo, aún no se han americanizado los mexicanos que viven en Texas y Nuevo México, Arizona y California. Nuestra raza es persistente y en medio de sus odios y divisiones, conserva inalterables su homogeneidad y carácter. Y un país así, que no se confunde fácilmente con los demás pueblos, que no se fusiona sino excepcionalmente con las otras razas, que conserva sus tradiciones y perpetúa sus leyendas, que, en una palabra, mantiene siempre creciente la fuerza maravillosa de su genio, no se domina con la ocupación de tres o cuatro plazas militares, ni aun con la absorción total de su territorio.

México, por consiguiente, no perderá su nacionalidad, aun cuando llegare a ser vencido. Nuestra vitalidad, como la de Polonia e Irlanda, como la de Armenia y Bélgica está por encima del desastre mismo. (García Naranjo, 195-6)

102. See Raymond MacCurdy, pp. 12-22, for further information.

103. It is also interesting to note that at least one cultural periodical grew out of a trade journal. When Panamanian Elías de Lozada assumed the directorship of the Spanish section of the firm of Thurber-Whyland in New York, he also became the editor of its trade journal, *Thurber-Whyland and Company's Spanish Review*. Losada eventually obtained exclusive rights to the review, in 1885 re-baptized it *La Revista Mercantil y de Precios Corrientes del Mercado de Nueva York* and in 1886 reorganized it into the cultural review studied in the text: *La Revista Ilustrada de Nueva York*. (Chamberlin and Shulman, 10)

104. See Tomás Almaguer, *Racial Fault Lines*, p. 3, for the definition and use of this term and the remainder of his book for details on how Mexicans became racialized.

105. See Bernardo P. Gallegos, *Literacy, Education, and Society in New Mexico, 1693-1821* (Albuquerque: University of New Mexico Press, 1992). According to Gallegos' study, roughly one-third of New Mexican society was literate in the early nineteenth century (p. 53).

106. Henry R. Wagner, "New Mexico Spanish Press," *New Mexico Historical Review* 12/1 (January, 1937), pp. 2-3, presents an in-depth discussion about the founding of both *El Crepúsculo de la Libertad* in Santa Fe and the *El Crepúsculo*, another newspaper published in Taos by the important historical figure Father Antonio José Martínez. Also see Gutiérrez, p. 38.

107. A prospectus dated April 9, 1823, announced that an American printer named Ashbridge would be issuing the *Texas Courier* or *Correo de Texas* every Wednesday morning beginning April 16 in English and Spanish editions. Stephen F. Austin expressed joy in a letter dated May 20, 1823, at hearing of the newspaper, but documents attest that, if any issues were ever published, the newspaper would have ceased by July, because that is when Ashbridge's press was shipped to Monterrey, Mexico, following its sale on June 13, 1823. Another newspaper for which no copies have been found is the *Mexican Advocate,* published in Nacogdoches in 1829; it may have been a bilingual English-Spanish newspaper. See John Melton Wallace, *Gaceta to Gazette: A Check List of Texas Newspapers, 1812-1846* (Austin: University of Texas Department of Journalism Development Program, 1966), pp. 42, 64 .

108. See William B. Rice, *The Los Angeles Star, 1851-1864* (Berkeley: University of

California Press, 1951), pp. 17-24.

109. See Porter A. Stratton, *The Territorial Press of New Mexico, 1834-1912* (Albuquerque: University of New Mexico Press, 1969), p. 12.

110. Gutiérrez, p. 39, points out how the Tubac *Arizonian* (3 November 1859) praised the "educated Mexicans" who were "American in sentiment and feeling and they, with the leading Americans, control the masses," and how Tucson's *El Fronterizo* (The Frontier Journal, 11 May 1879) reprinted an article from the *Arizona Citizen* complimenting the Spanish-language newspaper for being "the organ of the good Mexicans."

111. See Gabriel Meléndez, *So All Is Not Lost: The Poetics of Print in Nuevomexicano Communities, 1834-1958* (Albuquerque: University of New Mexico Press, 1997), pp. 24-5. Meléndez's history is the most thorough and deeply interpretive study ever performed on any segment of Hispanic print culture in the United States. In addition to providing a model of the type of study that must be conducted for California, Texas and elsewhere, *So All Is Not Lost* provides in-depth documentation and analysis of the development of Hispanic newspapers in New Mexico.

112. See Juan Gómez-Quiñones, *Roots of Chicano Power, 1600-1900* (Albuquerque: University of New Mexico Press, 1994), pp. 323-8. Also, see E. B. Fincher, *Spanish Americans as a Political Factor in New Mexico, 1912-1950* (New York: Arno Press, 1974); Calvin Horn, *New Mexico's Troubled Years: The Story of the Early Territorial Governors* (Albuquerque: Horn and Wallace, 1963); Robert W. Larson, *New Mexico's Quest for Statehood* (Albuquerque: University of New Mexico Press, 1968).

113. Doris Meyer, *Speaking for Themselves: Neomexicano Cultural Identity and the Spanish-Language Press, 1880-1920* (Albuquerque: University of New Mexico Press, 1996), p. 110. Meyer's book presents an excellent in-depth study of the poetry published in the *Nuevomexicano* newspapers as an indication of *Nuevomexicano* identity formation.

114. Nuestro periódico . . . velará continuamente por los intereses, honor y adelanto de todas las secciones de nuestro gran Territorio. El bienestar del pueblo Neo-Mexicano y principalmente del pueblo nativo, será en toda ocasión el podersoso móvil que impulsará nuestros esfuerzos a mayor energía en la publicación de nuestro semanario. Somos soldados del pueblo que velamos por sus derechos . . . (*La Voz del Pueblo*, 7 June 1890)

115. . . . defienden sus derechos, que procura educarlos y que siempre por siempre con el peligro personal están abogando por la justicia y el progreso de las masas populares. . . . Tomen, pues, todos los periódicos españoles en los que sus niños podrán aprender más que en los grandes libros de texto. . . . Convénzase el pueblo que el periódico es el mejor de los medios para la educación popular; aprenda en ellos a defender sus derechos para no abatirse ante ningún elemento extranjero.

116. According to Gómez-Quiñones, *Roots of Chicano Power*, p. 282, *El Sol de Mayo* was founded by the Republican Party precisely to counteract the popularity of *La Voz del Pueblo* and its backing of the populist movements.

117. Al desagrado de todo el pueblo frecuentemente vemos artículos calumniosos en contra de los Neo-Mexicanos en los periódicos del Oriente, denunciándonos como una raza sin honor, sin virtud y sin delicadeza . . . Acaso el pueblo quiere saber quienes son los autores de esas infames calumnias y libelos. Nosotros lo diremos. Son aquella clase de personas que no tienen honor, escrúpulo ni conciencia y algunos de ellos viven entre nosotros y por lo general nos muestran los dientes y una sonrisa superficial en sus labios . . . (*El Solo de Mayo*, 1 May 1891)

118. Nuestra tarea principal se concentrará en cuanto puedan servir nuestros débiles esfuerzos en conseguir para Nuevo México su admisión como estado soberano de la Unión Americana. Nuestra pluma siempre, y en toda ocasión, sin temor ninguno, estará lista para rechazar cualquiera calumnia arrojada en contra del buen nombre y el

honor del pueblo de Nuevo México. A causa de pedir justicia en exigir nuestra admisión a la confederación de estados ante el soberano Congreso de los Estados Unidos, hemos sido denigrados por la mayor parte de la prensa del oriente: sin razón, sin causa y sin necesidad.

119. The standard text describing this process is Leonard Pitt's *The Decline of the Californios: A Social History of the Spanish-Speaking Californians, 1846-1890* (Berkeley: University of California Press, 1966).

120. Michel C. Neri, "A Journalistic Portrait of the Spanish-Speaking People of California, 1868-1925," *Historical Society of Southern California Quarterly* 55 (Summer 1973): 193-208, chooses the year 1868 as the turning point in Mexican American cultural identity in California.

121. Roberto Treviño, in his "Becoming Mexican American: The Spanish-Language Press and the Biculturation of Californio Elites, 1852-1870" (Stanford: Stanford University History Department Working Paper Series No. 27, 1989), pp. 8-13, examines at length the stance on English-Spanish language issue taken by the California Hispanic newspapers.

122. Este proceder por parte del pueblo Americano ha llenado de indignación a todos los descendientes de la raza Española. Las autoridades de un país deben mirar por la seguridad de sus ciudadanos, y a ellas les incumbe juzgar y castigar al criminal; pero el populacho enfurecido no tiene derecho de quitar la vida a un hombre sin estar cerciorados que ha cometido el crimen que se le imputa.... Desde el año de 1849 ha existido cierta animosidad entre los Mexicanos y Americanos, tan agena de un pueblo magnánimo y libre; de manera que estos han deseado con todo corazón que los Mexicanos todos no tuvieran mas que un solo pesquezo para cortárselo. Han sufrido muchas injusticias, y principalmente en las minas han sido abusados y maltratados impugnemente. Si un Mexicano tiene por desgracia un pleito en las cortes de este Estado está seguro de perderlo. Es imposible negar esta aserción porqué conocemos a muchos infelices que así les ha sucedido apesar de los esfuerzos que han hecho para obtener sus derechos y justicia imparcial. [When Ramírez refers to "raza Española" in the first line, he is not using the term *raza* in its tradition Spanish-language denotation of "people," but in the Anglo-American sense of *race*; he has internalized and now applied the English-language concept of race as a biological, not cultural, classification of people.]

123. En ninguna parte es tan evidente la necesidad de un periódico en español como en California, ... como americanos y como individuos de la noble raza española a que pertenecemos creímos de nuestro deber ... alzar nuestra poderosa voz con las armas de la razón, para denunciar ante el supremo tribunal de la opinión pública las injusticias, los atropellamientos y los ultrajes de que han sido y continuan con demasi-ada frecuencia siendo víctimas los individuos de nuestra raza; creímos de nuestro deber constituirnos en un atalaya constante que sirviera a nuestros países españoles de alerta contra todos esos avances ilegales con que se ha pretendido y se pretende absorverlos, llevando a ellos del modo mas inaudito y escandaloso al esterminio y la muerte, y aniquilando las nacionalidades de los pueblos invadidos.... Todos los indi-viduos de las diversas nacionalidades españolas que hay en California, por honor a nuestra raza, deben protegerla [la prensa en español] ...

124. [Los Californios] Son los conquistados postrados ante el conquistador pidi-endole su proteccion en el goce de lo poco que su mala suerte les ha dejado. Son los que han sido vendidos como carneros—son los que fueron abandonados y vendidos por México. No entienden el idioma prevalente de su tierra natal. Son extrangeros en su propio país. No tienen ninguna voz en este Senado, exceptuando la que ahora tan débilmente está hablando a su favor. He visto llorar como niños a ancianos de sesenta y setenta años de edad, porque habían sido arrojados del hogar de sus padres. Han sido humillados e insultados. Se les ha rehusado el privlegio de sacar agua de sus propios

pozos. Se les ha rehusado el privilegio de cortar su propia leña. Y todavía los individuos que han cometido estos ultrajes han venido aquí a buscar protección, y para mi mayor admiración el Senado simpatiza con ellos. Vosotros, Senadores, no oís las quejas de la clase Española. Vosotros no considerais suficientemente la equidad de sus títulos y los justos derechos de sus posesiones.

125. F. Arturo Rosales, *Chicano!*, p. 18. Rosales explores the complete history of Mexican-American civil rights with particular attention to expression in the Spanish-language newspapers.

126. See Estelle Lutrell, *Newspapers and Periodicals of Arizona, 1859-1911* (Tucson: University of Arizona Press, 1950), p. 100.

127. Quoted from Tomás Serrano Cabo, Velasco's biographer, in *Crónicas: Alianza Hispano Americana* (Tucson: Alianza Hispano Americana, 1929), pp. 278-9, and translated and cited in Thomas E. Sheridan, *Los Tucsonenses: The Mexican Community in Tucson, 1854-1941* (Tucson: University of Arizona Press, 1986), p. 103.

128. Translated by Sheridan, pp. 109-10, from *El Tucsonense* 9 July 1892.

129. See ——, *History of the Southwest*, Vol. I (Chicago: The Lewis Publishing Co., 1907), pp. 438-9.

130. ...y esta solemne finalidad es primeramente, dar a conocer al blanco, que nosotros los bronceados, nada tenemos de inferioridad y que es una solemne mentira lo que dice cierta historia de Texas y que sirve de texto en las escuelas públicas, para aprobio (sic.) nuestro "aquello de que no sabemos gobernarnos, mucho menos nombrar nuestros gobernantes."

Entonces el Latino Americano, instruido en civismo, por su ambición al progreso y al bienestar, entonces, digo, habrá una nueva era para nuestra raza, capaz de influir decisivamente, en los destinos de la colectividad como entidad racial y ni se nos negarán los derechos políticos y la igualdad social, sin que nos arredren ni ofusquemos ante las penas individuales, ante los atropellos, ni ante las dictaduras.

131. Conciudadanos de nuestra raza! unámonos, caminemos hacia el oriente de un mejor entendimiento y una mayor representación y leguemos a nuestros hijos que bendicerán nuestra memoria, nuestra ingénita y propia civilización. Que los odios que ahora cargamos en nuestras espaldas por herencia tradicional, se convertirán mañana, en eterna quietud, cuando el sol de la justicia de los tiempos tenga mayor aprecio hacia los nuestros y caliente apaciblemente sus hogares. . . . Extendamos nuestra fuerza unida para dejarla escrita en el libro sagrado de la lucha por la libertad, igualdad y fraternidad de la raza latinoamericana.

132. Considerando que esta publicación sale a la luz en el corazón de nuestra humilde barriada de Harlem; en medio de la más abyecta miseria; donde inexorables, el vicio y el dolor se disputan las escuálidas víctimas de la ignorancia, los prejuicios de raza y de los defectos del presente sistema de economía política, no podemos menos que consagrar este semanario a la defensa de nuestros legítimos derechos de ciudadanos y, justificar el principio de una prensa libre es el más eficaz defensor de los derechos humanos y las más firme garantía del recto funcionamiento de la justicia.

A pesar de los muchos males—reales o imaginarios—que se le atribuyen a nuestra barriada, una gran parte de sus residentes son de completa solvencia moral, amantes del orden y en posesión de todos los atributos esenciales al cumplimiento de los deberes de los buenos ciudadanos; así pues, uno de los fines fundamentales de LA DEFENSA, es comprobar el hecho, que existen en la barriada individuos capaces para actuar e influir con su inteligencia y fuerza de voluntad en el escenario histórico de los acontecimientos cívicos de toda nuestra colectividad hispana. No por esto, dejaremos de condenar con todas las fuerzas de nuestras energías los males que en realidad existen y que son la causa de la denigración colectiva.

Ya es tiempo de que nos demos cuenta que no somos aves de paso; que estamos aquí para quedarnos y que es necesario preparar el camino para los que han de seguirnos.

133. See Virginia Sánchez Korrol, *From Colonia to Community: The History of Puerto Ricans in New York City, 1917-1948* (Westport, Conn.: Greenwood Press, 1983), p. 153, who in her study charts the development of a national minority consciousness among Puerto Ricans.

134. See Sánchez Korrol, p. 153, for a complete list of the goals of the Liga.

135. For a complete analysis of the *Boletín*, see María Aponte Alsina, "Culture and Identity: Periodical Literature in Puerto Rican Archives," pp. 12-15.

136. See Carlos Rodríguez Fraticelli, "Pedro Albizu Campos: Strategies of Struggle and Strategic Struggles," *Centro* (Center for Puerto Rican Studies, Hunter College) 4/1 (1992), pp.XX, for details on the founding of *Pueblos Hispanos*.

137. This stance of combining Puerto Rican nationalist discourse and goals while affirming civil rights and participation in U. S. electoral politics was not unique to *Pueblos Hispanos*. It was shared by a number of predecessors, including *Alma Boricua* (Puerto Rican Soul), which was founded in 1934 and had a readership in Manhattan and Brooklyn.

138. EL PORQUE DE PUEBLOS HISPANOS
Porque la VICTORIA necesita:

1. . . . la unificación de todas las colonias hispanas en los Estados Unidos para la derrota del Nazi-fascismo, en unidad con todas las fuerzas democráticas.
2. . . . que se defiendan todos los derechos de las minorías hispanas en los Estados Unidos—puertorriqueños, filipinos, mexicanos, etc.
3. . . . la inmediata independencia de la nación puertorriqueña.
4. . . . combatir el prejuicio contra los hispanos por su raza o credo, y la difusión de prejuicios contra otras minorías.
5. . . . la lucha tenaz contra la enemiga Falange Española como parte integrante de la Quinta Columna del Eje operando en las Américas, y ayudar e impulsar la unidad de todos los españoles por las libertades democráticas en España.
6. . . . la liberación de todo preso político en el mundo.
7. . . . mejores relaciones entre las Américas mediante la difusión de las culturas hispánicas.
8. . . . la instauración de hecho de la independencia de Filipinas y reconocida en derecho.
9. . . . la unidad sindical en las Américas.

139. See Edna Acosta-Belén and Virginia Sánchez Korrol, "The World of Jesús Colón," in Jesús Colón, *The Way It Was and Other Writings* (Houston: Arte Público Press, 1993), p. 20. This is an introductory essay to their collection of twenty-six English-language columns published by Colón. The edition includes a bibliography of Colón's writings.

140. See Edwin Padilla's Introduction to his edition of Colón's early writings in Jesús Colón, *Miquis Tiquis* (Houston: Arte Público Press, in press).

About the Bibliography

Objectives

Identifying, locating, and making accessible the publications of a people whose intellectual production was ignored by most institutions responsible for bibliographic control (publication, preservation, and access) are very large and at times frustrating tasks. Nevertheless, we took on the compilation of this bibliography as part of Recovering the U. S. Hispanic Literary Heritage to support reconstituting the documentary legacy of Hispanics in the United States. The present bibliography offers a list of periodical publications whose pages have survived in some form, or whose existence is remembered only through bibliographic documentation, because to date no vestiges of the original serial have been recovered.

Our list contains some 1,700 records, of which only some 900 titles are accessible in one form or another. All of those serials that are missing bear the annotation "No extant issues located." In all cases we have noted the sources of our information.

The criteria used for inclusion of records in this list were: (1) all known serials published in the Spanish language in the United States; and (2) all known serials published in the United States, whether in English or bilingually (Spanish-English), that were produced by or that served U.S. Hispanic communities.

Sources

The titles included were located in various electronic and print sources, as well as through direct contact with individuals and by research in various institutions. In some cases, the Recovery Project itself discovered the serials, microfilmed them, and is now making them universally accessible for the first time since the publications' demise. The electronic sources most relied upon were the public catalogs of the Library of Congress (LOCIS-LOC), WorldCat (the OCLC Online Union Catalog), and catalogs of individual libraries. Titles found in the Library of Congress or OCLC catalogs are identified in our text as being "In OCLC system" or "In LOCIS system." For any title that can be found only in print catalogs, and for which we found no repository, we have reproduced the catalog entry as cited in the particular source and identified it as "No extant issues located." In the cases where the titles are not found in OCLC or LOCIS, but an institutional repository has been identified, the name of the holding institution has been included. Owing to a lack of time and resources, it was impossible to physically examine all the extant publications when preparing the entries or verifying their existence and availability. To make accessible the results of our project in as timely a manner as possible, we unfortunately had to sacrifice this more arduous task. However, we were able to examine hundreds of newspapers and are now (in a separate project) digitizing the literature contained within as many of them as possible. However, because it was not possible to bring each serial in-house, we have been unable to verify data on a number of the titles (nor have we always been able to resolve discrepancies that frequently appear in sources).

Organization

The entries are arranged alphabetically by title. When the identity of a publication varies, we have made the necessary cross-references to facilitate its identification. When titles begin with an article, the title is placed in alphabetical order according to the next word after the article, except in the case where the article itself is part of the place name, such as in "El Paso," in which case the article itself is alphabetized.

Indexes

Our bibliography includes three indexes: one geographical, one chronological, and a general name and subject index. The geographical index is arranged alphabetically by state and then city. When the city of publication is unknown, the title appears at the end of the state list, under the "Unknown" category. If the state of publication is unknown, the title appears at the end of the entire list. The chronological index is arranged by the beginning year of publication. When the exact date is not known, the year of the earliest number available is used.

Bibliographic Information

Each entry contains information on the title, place of publication, publisher, and dates of publication. When these data do not appear in the serial itself, external sources have been used to provide the information. Because not all of the issues of these publications have survived, and because even the publications often do not provide clear bibliographic information, determining actual dates of origin and demise has been an arduous task. When the dates cannot be verified, we substitute for the missing dates a lower-case "u." In these cases, furthermore, we include in the entry note the date corresponding to the specific number or issue that the reader may use to locate the publication within a more specific framework of dates. Any approximate date offered is always accompanied by a question mark: "(?)." A dash immediately after the beginning date indicates that the serial is still publishing, or that we do not know of its demise. For some titles we have included, in addition to the bibliographic data, brief information on its history of publication; where possible, we have included the source of this information.

Our bibliography does not pretend to be exhaustive, nor is it definitive. We hope that by making the results of our research available, other titles not on our list will surface, and that some of our "non-extant" titles will also come to light. We invite our readers to provide us with additional information, sources, and titles.

Helvetia Martell
Washington, D.C.

Sources Cited

Batista Villarreal, Teresita, Josefina García Carranza, and Miguelina Aponte. *Catálogo de publicaciones periódicas cubanas de los siglos XVIII y XIX*. Havana: Biblioteca Nacional José Martí, Departamento de Colección Cubana, 1965.

Brigham, Clarence S. *History and Bibliography of American Newspapers*: 1690-1820. Worcester, Mass.: American Antiquarian Society, 1947.

Carrasco Puente, Rafael. *La prensa en México: Datos históricos*. México, D.F.: Universidad Nacional Autónoma de México, 1962.

Chabrán, Rafael and Richard Chabrán. "The Spanish Language and Latino Press of the United States: Newspapers and Periodicals." In *Handbook of Hispanic Cultures in the United States: Literature and Art*. Edited and introduced by Francisco Lomelí. Houston: Arte Público Press, 1993, pp. 360-383.

Chabrán, Rafael. "Spaniards." In Hoerder, Dirk. *The Immigrant Labor Press, 1840-1970: An Annotated Bibliography*. Westport, Conn.: Greenwood, 1987.

Chamberlin, Vernon A. and Ivan A. Schulman. *La Revista Ilustrada de Nueva York*: History, Anthology, and Index of Literary Selections. Columbia: University of Missouri Press, 1976.

Colón, Jesús. *The Way It Was and Other Writings*. Edited by Edna Acosta-Belén and Virginia Sánchez Korrol. Houston: Arte Público Press, 1993.

Common Council for American Unity. *Foreign Language Publications in the United States*. New York: Common Council for American Unity, 1954.

Ezell, Camp. *Historical Story of Bee County, Texas*. Beeville, Texas: Beeville Pub. Co. [1973].

Fox, Louis Hewitt. *New York City Newspapers, 1820-1850: A Bibliography*. Chicago: University of Chicago Press, 1928.

Franco, Jesús. *El alma de la raza: Narraciones históricas de episodios y vida de los mexicanos residentes en los Estados Unidos de Norte América*. El Paso: Compañía Editora "La Patria" [1920].

Gómez-Quiñones, Juan. *Sembradores Ricardo Flores Magón y el Partido Liberal Mexicano: A Eulogy and Critique*. Los Angeles: Chicano Studies Center, University of California, 1973.

Gregory, Winifred, ed. *American Newspapers, 1821-1936: A Union List of Files Available in the United States and Canada*. New York: H.W. Wilson Co., 1937.

Grove, Pearce S. *New Mexico Newspapers: A Comprehensive Guide to Bibliographical Entries and Locations*. Albuquerque: University of New Mexico Press, 1975.

Gutiérrez, Félix. "Spanish-Language Media in America." *Journalism History* 4:2 (Summer 1977), pp. 34-41.

Historical Records Survey Texas. *Texas Newspapers, 1813-1939: A Union List of Newspaper Files Available in Offices of Publishers, Libraries, and a Number of Private Collections.* Houston: San Jacinto Museum of History Association, 1941.

Ireland, Sandra L. Jones. *Ethnic Periodicals in Contemporary America: An Annotated Guide.* New York: Greenwood Press, 1990.

Kanellos, Nicolás. "A Socio-Historic Study of Hispanic Newspapers in the United States." *In Recovering the U. S. Hispanic Literary Heritage.* Edited by Ramón Gutiérrez and Genaro Padilla. Houston: Arte Público Press, 1993, pp. 107-128.

Kemble, Edward Cleveland. *A History of California Newspapers, 1846-1858.* Los Gatos, Calif.: Talisman Press, 1962.

Keniston, Hayward. *Periodicals in American Libraries for the Study of the Hispanic Languages and Literatures.* New York: Hispanic Society of America, 1927.

Leal, Luis. "The Spanish-Language Press: Function and Use." *The Americas Review* 17 (Winter 1989): 161-168.

LOCIS (Library of Congress Information System). Contains millions of records held by the Library of Congress and other institutions throughout the nation located in a variety of databases. Available via telnet: <ftp://locis.loc.gov>.

Lomas, Clara. "The Articulation of Gender in the Mexican Borderlands, 1900-1915." *In Recovering the U. S. Hispanic Literary Heritage.* Edited by Ramón Gutiérrez and Genaro Padilla. Houston: Arte Público Press, 1993, pp. 293-308.

Lutrell, Estelle. *Newspapers and Periodicals of Arizona, 1859-1911.* Tucson: University of Arizona, 1950.

MacCurdy, Raymond R. *A History and Bibliography of Spanish Language Newspapers and Magazines in Louisiana, 1808-1949.* Albuquerque: University of New Mexico Press, 1951.

"Más de cuatrocientos periódicos en español se han editado en Estados Unidos." La Prensa (San Antonio), 13 Feb. 1938.

Meier, Matt S. and Feliciano Rivera. *The Chicanos: A History of Mexican Americans.* New York: Hill and Wang, 1972.

Meléndez, A. Gabriel (Anthony Gabriel). *So All Is Not Lost: The Poetics of Print in Nuevomexicano Communities, 1834-1968.* Albuquerque: University of New Mexico Press, 1997.

Miguélez, Armando. "Index of Spanish-Language Newspapers in the U. S. Southwest. Lista copilada de los periódicos en español en Arizona de la Arizona Historical Society y las noticias en los mismos sobre los canjes con otras publicaciones." Manuscript deposited in the collection of Recovering the U.S. Hispanic Literary Heritage project, University of Houston.

Miller, John W. *Indiana Newspaper Bibliography: Historical Accounts of All Indiana*

Bibliography

Bibliography

Newspapers Published from 1804 to 1980 and Locational Information for All Available Copies, Both Original and Microfilm. Indianapolis: Indiana Historical Society, 1982.

N. W. Ayer & Son's American Newspaper Annual. Philadelphia: N.W. Ayer & Son, 1880-1909.

N. W. Ayer & Son's Directory of Newspapers and Periodicals. Philadelphia: N.W. Ayer & Son, 1930-1969.

N. W. Ayer & Son's American Newspaper Annual and Directory. Philadelphia: N. W. Ayer & Son, 1910-1929.

Newspapers in Microform: United States, 1948-1972. Washington, D.C.: Library of Congress.

OCLC-First Search. Online database that contains bibliographic data of library holdings in the United States and the world.

Oehlerts, Donald E. *Guide to Colorado Newspapers, 1859-1963.* Denver: Biographical Center for Research, Rocky Mountain Region, 1964.

Peraza Sarausa, Fermén. *Directorio de revistas y periódicos de Cuba.* Gainesville, Fla., 1963.

Pino, Frank. *Mexican Americans: A Research Bibliography.* East Lansing: Latin American Studies Center, Michigan State University, 1974.

Poyo, Gerald Eugene. *With All and for the Good of All: The Emergence of Popular Nationalism in the Cuban Communities of the United States, 1848-1898.* Durham, N.C.: Duke University Press, 1989.

Richmond, Douglas W. *Venustiano Carranzas' Nationalist Struggle, 1893-1920.* Lincoln: University of Nebraska Press, 1983.

Ríos-C., Herminio. "Toward a True Chicano Bibliography: Part II." *El Grito* 5: 4 (Summer, 1972), 384-7.

Ríos-C., Herminio and Guadalupe Castillo. "Toward a True Chicano Bibliography: Mexican-American Newspapers: 1848-1942." *El Grito* 3:4 (Summer, 1970), 172-4.

Rowell's American Newspaper Directory. New York: Printers' Ink, 1869-1908. 40 vols.

Sax, Antimaco. *Los mexicanos en el destierro.* San Antonio, Texas: International Printing, 1916.

Sheridan, Thomas E. *Los Tucsonenses: The Mexican Community in Tucson, 1854-1941.* Tucson: University of Arizona Press, 1986.

Smith, Michael M. "The Mexican Immigrant Press Beyond the Borderlands: The Case of El Cosmopolita." *Great Plains Quarterly 10* (Spring 1990): 71-85.

Somoza, Oscar U. and Armando Miguélez. *Literatura de la Revolución Mexicana en el exilio:*

fuentes para su estudio. Mexico, D.F.: Universidad Nacional Autónoma de México, 1997.
State Historical Society of Wisconsin Library. *Hispanic Americans in the United States: A Union List of Periodicals and Newspapers Held by the Library of the State Historical Society of Winsconsin and the Libraries of the University of Wisconsin-Madison*. Compiled by Neil E. Strache and James P. Danky. Madison: State Historical Society of Wisconsin Library, 1979.

Trujillo, Enrique. *Album del Porvenir*. New York: Imprenta de "El Provenir," 1890. 5 vols.

Union of International Associations. *Directory of Periodicals Published by International Organizations (Repertoire des periodiques publiés par les organizations internationales non gouvernmentales)*. 2nd ed. Brussels: Union of International Associations, 1959.

Villegas de Magnón, Leonor. *The Rebel*. Edited and introduced by Clara Lomas. Houston: Arte Público Press, 1994.

Wallace, John Melton. *Gaceta to Gazette: A Checklist of Texas Newspapers, 1813-1846*. Austin: University of Texas Dept. of Journalism Development Program, 1966.

Willging, Eugene Paul and Herta Hatzfeld. *Catholic Serials of the Nineteenth Century in the United States*. Washington, D. C.: Catholic University of America Press, 1959-1968.

Wright, William C. and Paul A. Stellhorn, eds. *Directory of New Jersey Newspapers, 1765-1970*. Trenton: New Jersey Historical Commission, 1977.

Wyllys, Rufus Kay. Arizona: *The History of the Frontier State*. Phoenix: Hobson & Herr, 1950.

Zamora, Emilio. "Sara Estela Ramírez: Una rosa roja en el movimiento." *In Mexican Women in the Unites States: Strugles Past and Present*. Edited by Magdalena Mora and Adelaida R. del Castillo. Los Angeles: Chicano Studies Research Center Publications, University of California, 1980.

Bibliography of Periodicals

ABC. Chicago: Armando Almonte, 19uu–19uu.
  Weekly.
  Año 9, no. 534 dated 13 abr. 1946. In Spanish. In OCLC system.
L'Abeille. Nouvelle-Orleans: F. Delaup, 1827-1830.
  In French, English and Spanish. Spanish section titled "La Abeja". English title: *Bee.* In OCLC system.
Abeja (New Orleans, Louisiana). *See* L'Abeille.
La Abeja. San Luis, Col.: J.R. Valdez, 1901-19uu.
  Mentioned in Somoza, *Literatura de la Revolución Mexicana...*, p. 236. On the same page Somoza cites this title as *La Abeja del Valle.* No extant issues located.
El Abogado Cristiano. Albuquerque, N. M.: Thomas Harwood, 1uuu-1903.
  Monthly.
  Año 22, núm. 1 dated enero de 1902. Continues *Abogado Cristiano Neo-Mexicano* (Socorro, N. M., 1893). Continued by *El Abogado Cristiano Neo-Mexicano* (Albuquerque, N. M., 1904). Variant title: *New Mexico Christian Advocate.* In Spanish and English. In OCLC system.
El Abogado Cristiano Fronterizo. Laredo, Tex., 1880-1uuu.
  Mentioned in *El Fronterizo* (Tucson) Mar. 14, 1880, cf. Somoza, *Literatura de la Revolución Mexicana...*, p. 249. No extant issues located.
El Abogado Cristiano Hispano-Americano. Albuquerque, N. M.: Rev. Thomas Harwood, 1907-1908.
  Monthly.
  Began with año 27, no. 2 dated feb. de 1907. Ceased with año 28, núm. 3 dated marzo de 1908. Continues *El Abogado Cristiano Neo-Mexicano* (Albuquerque, N. M., 1904). Continued by *El Abogado Cristiano* (Albuquerque, N. M.: 1917). In Spanish and English. In OCLC system.
El Abogado Cristiano Neo-Mexicano. Albuquerque, N. M.: Rev. Thomas Harwood, 1904-1907.
  Monthly.
  Began with año 24, núm. 1 dated enero de 1904; ceased with año 27, núm. 1 dated enero de 1906. Continues *El Abogado Cristiano* (Albuquerque, N. M., 1902). Continued by *El Abogado Cristiano Hispano-Americano.* Variant title: *New Mexico Christian Advocate.* In Spanish and English. In OCLC system.
El Abogado Cristiano Neo-Mexicano. Socorro, N. M.: [Rev. Thos. Harwood], 1893-1uuu.
  Monthly.
  Began with tomo 9, núm. 1 dated enero 2 de 1893. Published in Albuquerque, N. M. on Nov. 1893. Continues *Metodista.* Continued by *El Abogado Cristiano* (Albuquerque, N. M., 1902). In Spanish and English. In OCLC system.
El Abogado del Estado de Nuevo México. Santa Fe, N. M., 1889-1uuu.
  Mentioned in Somoza, *Literatura de la Revolución Mexicana...*, p. 242. No extant issues located.
Acción. Fullerton, California: Francisco Moreno, 19uu-19uu.
  Weekly.
  Listed in Common Council for American Unity, *Foreign Language Publications in the United States: Newspaper Lists.* In Spanish. No extant issues located.
Acción. Kingsville, Tex.: [s.n.], 1931-193u.
  Semimonthly, 1931-Apr. 1932; monthly, May 1932.
  Continued by *El Eco* (Kingsville, Texas). In Spanish. In OCLC system.
Acción Cívica. New York, 1928-19uu.
  Monthly.

"Organo de la Unión Cívica Venezolana". In Spanish. In OCLC system.

The Acorn. Las Vegas, N. M.: Ancheta & Mess, 1873-1875.

> Weekly.

> Began publication c. Oct. 5, 1873; ceased Aug. 1875, cf. Grove, Pearce S., *New Mexico Newspapers.* Vol. 2, no. 6 dated May 25, 1875. Includes a Spanish-language section variously titled "La Beliota", "La Bellota", or "La Buliota". Variant title: *The Las Vegas Acorn.* In OCLC system.

Actualidad. El Paso, Tex.: Federación de Sociedades Latinamericanas, 1936?-19uu.

> Vol. 1, no. 4 dated dic. 11, 1936. Organo Oficial de La Federación. In Spanish. In OCLC system.

La Actualidad. San Bernardino, California: Rev. John Caballería, 1895-1902.

> Weekly.

> Listed in: Willging, Eugene Paul and Herta Hatzfeld, *Catholic Serials of the Nineteenth Century in the United States.* In Spanish. No extant issues located.

Actualidades. Rio Grande, Texas, 1914-1930.

> Weekly, irregular.

> Director: Agapito Cepeda. Listed in: Ríos-C., Herminio, "Toward a True Chicano Bibliography: Part II," p. 46. Also listed in: "Más de cuatrocientos periódicos en español se han editado en Estados Unidos". In Spanish. No extant issues located.

Actualidades Médicas. Rutherford, N.J., 1929-1932. In Spanish. In OCLC system.

El Adelante. Brownsville, Texas, 1908-1913.

> Weekly.

> Año IV dated sept. 22, 1910. Director and editor: Hilario Borjas. Repository: University of Texas, Brownsville, Texas.

Adelante. San Antonio, Texas, 1916-1920.

> Monthly.

> Listed in "Más de cuatrocientos periódicos en español se han editado en Estados Unidos", and Ríos-C., Herminio, "Toward a True Chicano Bibliography: Part II," p. 47. In Spanish. No extant issues located.

Adelante. Santa Fe, N. M.: Allison-James School, Board of National

> Missions, Presbyterian Church, USA, 19uu-19uu. Vol. 3, no. 4 dated 1941. In Spanish. In OCLC system.

Adelanto Bienestar Cultura. Chicago, Illinois: Adelanto Bienestar Cultura Pub. Co., 1936-1950?

> Weekly.

> Listed in *N. W. Ayer & Son's Directory of Newspapers and Periodicals,* 1945, p. 204. In Spanish. No extant issues located.

El Agente Comercial y Minero. El Paso, Tex.: A. N. Daguerre, 1900-1900.

> Monthly.

> Absorbed by *International Industrial Record,* as a separately numbered Spanish section on January 1901. In Spanish. In OCLC system.

El Agricultor Mexicano. San Antonio, Texas, 1918-1919.

> Monthly.

> Listed in "Más de cuatrocientos periódicos en español se han editado en Estados Unidos". In Spanish. No extant issues located.

El Agricultor Moderno. Bernalillo, Nuevo México: G. García, 19uu-19uu.

> Weekly.

> T. 2, no. 4 dated 23 de marzo de 1916. In Spanish and English. In OCLC system.

Agricultura de las Américas. Overland Park, Kan. [etc.]: Intertec Pub. Corp. [etc.], 1952-.

> Monthly.

> In Spanish. In OCLC sytem.

El Aguacero. Los Angeles, Calif., 1878-1uuu.

> Weekly.

Vol. 1, no. 4 dated marzo 24 de 1878. Editor: R. R. Gonzales. In OCLC system.

Ahora. Bakersfield, Calif.: Ahora, 1957-.

Monthly.

"La revista exclusiva para el condado de Kern". In English and Spanish. In OCLC system.

Ahora. El Paso, Tex.: Casa Bautista de Publicaciones; Nashville, Tenn.: Baptist Sunday School Board, 19uu-.

Quarterly.

T. 41, no. 4 dated Jan.-Mar., 1982. "Para intermedios". In Spanish. In OCLC system.

Ahora. Nueva York: Ahora Publishing Co., 19uu-19uu.

Weekly.

Vol. 1, no. 14 dated junio 12, 1950. In OCLC system.

Aki Nueva York. New York, N.Y.: Ecos, Inc., 1955-19uu.

Weekly.

No. 6 dated marzo 26, 1955. Editor and publisher: Enrique Ungría. Repository: The Center for Puerto Rican Studies at Hunter College.

El Alacrán. Los Angeles, California, 1924-19uu.

Weekly.

Director: Guz Aguila; Editor: Rafael Trejo. Listed in "Más de cuatrocientos periódicos en español se han editado en Estados Unidos", and Ríos-C., Herminio, "Toward a True Chicano Bibliography: Part II," p. 40. No extant issues located.

Alba de Nueva York. New York, N.Y.: O.C.A. Enterprises, 1954-19uu.

Weekly.

Vol. 1, no. 3 dated 20 de marzo de 1954. "Revista hispana para el mundo hispano". Director: Emil Acedo Mayore. Repository: Center for Puerto Rican Studies at Hunter College.

Alba Roja. McQueenley, Tex., 1912-19uu.

Listed in Miguélez, Armando, "Index of Spanish-Language Newspapers in the U. S. Southwest." Miguélez indicates that is mentioned in *Regeneración,* 11-v, 1912. No extant issues located.

Alba Roja. San Francisco, Calif.: Práxedis Guerrero, 1uuu-1uuu.

Listed in Miguélez, Armando, "Index of Spanish-Language Newspapers in the U. S. Southwest." No extant issues located.

Albores Seráficos. El Paso, [Tex.]: Roger Bacon College, Franciscan Fathers [1930-19uu].

Quarterly.

"Revista de ensayos varios por los estudiantes del coristado de la Prov. del Sto. Evang. de México". In Spanish. In OCLC system.

El Album de los Niños (New York; Mexico). *See* **La Enseñanza: Revista Americana de Instrucción y Recreo, Dedicada a la Juventud.**

Albuquerque. Las Vegas, New Mexico, 1913-19uu.

Bi-weekly.

Listed in Ríos-C., Herminio, "Toward a True Chicano Bibliography: Part II," p. 44. In Spanish and English. No extant issues located.

Albuquerque Bandera Americana (Albuquerque, New Mexico) *See* **La Bandera Americana.**

Albuquerque Mirror. Albuquerque, N. M., 1879-1uuu.

Weekly.

"Moved from Bernalillo, Sandoval County, and assumed the title *Albuquerque Mirror,* July 26, 1879; moved back to Bernalillo, Sandoval County, and assumed the title *Bernalillo Native,* October 25, 1879," cf. Grove, Pearce S., *New Mexico Newspapers.* In English and Spanish. No extant issues located.

The Albuquerque Press. Albuquerque, N. M.: M.A. Upson, 1867-1867.

Weekly.

Began with Jan. 16, 1867 issue; ceased in 1867, cf. Gregory, Winifred, ed., *American Newspapers, 1821-1936.* No. 211 dated Feb. 9, 1867. Continues *New Mexico Press.*

Continued by *Semi-weekly Review.* Variant titles: *Prensa de Albuquerque, The Albuquerque Weekly Press.* In English and Spanish. In OCLC system.

The Albuquerque Review. Albuquerque, New Mexico: William M'Guiness, 1876-1880.
Weekly.
Continues *The Republican Review.* Continued by *Albuquerque Weekly Review.* Variant title: *La Revista Albuquerque.* In Spanish and English. In OCLC system.

The Albuquerque Weekly Press *See* **The Albuquerque Press.**

El Alcarán. Tucson, Arizona: E. Medina, 1879-1uuu.
Listed in Lutrell, Estelle, *Newspapers and Periodicals of Arizona, 1859-1911,* p. 56.
Mentioned in *Daily Star* (Arizona), Oct. 10, 1879. In Spanish. No extant issues located.

El Aldeano. Uribeño, Tex.: Clemente G. Gonzales, 1906?-19uu.
Weekly.
Began in 1906? Año 2 num. 45 dated Sept. 27, 1908. In Spanish. In OCLC system.

Al Día. Tucson, Ariz., 1920-1uuu.
Semanario de la Alianza Hispano Americana. Mentioned in Somoza, *Literatura de la Revolución Mexicana...,* p. 228. No extant issues located.

La Alegría. Tampa, Fla., 1901?-19uu.
Monthly.
Año XL, no. 1 dated sept. 20, 1940. "Organo oficial del Centro Asturiano". Repository: University of South Florida, Tampa.

Alfa. Kinsgville, Tex.: [Unión Femenil del Presbiterio México-Texano], 19uu-1958.
Monthly.
Published by Presbyterian Pan-American School, Oct. 1956-1958. Año 8, no. 7 dated oct. 15 de 1932. "Organo presbiteriano de las mujeres latino-americanas en Texas". Continued by *Alfa y Omega* (Laredo, Texas). In OCLC system.

Alfa. Laredo, Texas, 19uu-19uu.
Vol. XXIX, núm. 66 dated octubre 1956. "Organo Presbiteriano de las Mujeres Latinoamericanas en Texas". Printed by Presbyterian Pan-American School, (Kingsville, Texas). Continues *Alfa* (Kingsville, Texas). Continued by *Alfa y Omega* (Kingsville, Texas). Repository: University of California (Berkeley).

Alfa y Omega. [Kingsville?, Texas; San Benito?, Texas], 1958-.
"Las iglesias presbiterianas latino americanas del Sínodo de Texas". Continues *Alfa* (Kingsville, Texas, 1932). In OCLC system.

Alhambra. New York, N.Y.: Alhambra Press, 1929-1930.
In English and Spanish. In OCLC system.

La Alianza. Los Angeles, California: Ultima Hora Pub. Co., 1926?-19uu.
Monthly.
Editor: Salvador Gonzalo Becerra. Listed in *N.W. Ayer & Son's Directory of Newspapers and Periodicals,* 1935, p. 84. Also listed in Ríos-C., Herminio, "Toward a True Chicano Bibliography: Part II," p. 40, and in "Más de cuatrocientos periódicos en español se han editado en Estados Unidos". The last two sources indicate starting date of 1927. In Spanish. No extant issues located.

Alianza. Phoenix, Arizona: Alianza Hispano-Americana Pub., 1909-19uu.
Monthly.
Listed in *N.W. Ayer & Son's Directory of Newspapers and Periodicals,* 1954. In Spanish. No extant issues located.

La Alianza. Tucson, Arizona: Carlos H. Tully, 1889?-19uu.
Weekly.
T. 2, no. 57 dated agosto 23 de 1900. In Spanish. In OCLC system.

Alianza. Tucson: Alianza Magazine, 1907-19uu.
Issued 1907-May 1961 by the Alianza Hispano-Americana; Dec. 1961 by Alianza, a fraternal organization. "Alianza Magazine is the official publication of the Alianza, a fraternal insurance society." Director and publisher: José Jordi (as of March 1907), cf. "Más

de cuatrocientos periódicos en español se han editado en Estados Unidos". In OCLC system.

Alma. San Diego, Tex.: Servando Cárdenas, 1938-1941.
Mentioned in Villanueva, Chicanos. & p. 252.

Alma Azul. Mercedes, Tex.: Servando Cárdenas, 1927-19uu.
Mentioned in Somoza, *Literatura de la Revolución Mexicana. . .,* p. 250. No extant issues located.

Alma Boricua. New York, N.Y., 1934-1935?
Repositories: Center for Puerto Rican Studies at Hunter College (New York), and Colección Puertorriqueña, University of Puerto Rico, Río Piedras Campus.

Alma Latina. Miami, Ariz.l 1932-19uu.
Mentioned in *El Tucsonense,* Nov. 10, 1932, p. 3; cf. Somoza, *Literatura de la Revolución Mexicana...,* p. 225. No extant issues located.

Alma Latina. New York, 1916-.
"Edición continental de *El Demócrata* de la Ciudad de México". In OCLC system.

Alma Latina: for the Interest of the Latin-American Children. San Antonio, Texas: LULAC, 1932-19uu.
Irregular.
In English and Spanish. Repository: Bancroft Library (University of California, Berkeley).

Alta California. San Francisco, Calif., 1878-1880?
Listed in Miguélez, Armando, "Index of Spanish-Language Newspapers in the U. S. Southwest." No extant issues located.

Ambas Américas: Revista de Educación, Bibliografía y Agricultura. Nueva York: Imprenta de Hallet y Breen, 1867-1868.
Quarterly.
"Bajo los auspicios de D. [Domingo] F. [Faustino] Sarmiento." Published by J. M. Macías (nov. 1867-jul. 1868). In Spanish. In OCLC system.

América. New York: The Americas Company, 1908–1922.
From 1908 to 1911, subtitle was *Revista mensual ilustrada.*
From 1911 to 1918 published as *América e Industrias Americanas.*

La América Científica, Industrial, Agrícola y Ganadera. Nueva York: Munn, 1890-1909.
In LOCIS system.

América Clínica: Revista de Diagnóstico y Terapéutica. New York: Pan American Publishing Co., 1941?-1964.
Published with the collaboration of the New York Academy of Medicine. In OCLC system.

América Comercial. Philadelphia, Pennsylvania: Commercial Museum, 19uu-19uu.
Monthly.
Listed in Common Council for American Unity, *Foreign Language Publications in the United States: Newspaper Lists.* In Spanish. No extant issues located.

América Continental. Nueva York, N.Y.: Carlos G. Chamizo, 1956-19uu.
No. 5 dated April 1956. "El Magazine de 23 países". In Spanish. Repository: Center for Puerto Rican Studies at Hunter College.

La América Futura. New York, N.Y.: Castillo Pub. Co., 1917-1921?
Monthly.
Listed in *N.W.Ayer & Son's American Newspaper Annual and Directory,* 1920, p. 653; also in "Más de cuatrocientos periódicos en español se han editado en Estados Unidos". This last source indicates publication dates of 1920-1921. In Spanish. No extant issues located.

América Ilustrada. New York: J. L. Delgado Borges, 187u?-1uuu.
In Spanish. In OCLC system.

La América: Periódico Quincenal Ilustrado. Nueva York: Hallet & Breen, 1871-1uuu.
Weekly.

In Spanish. In OCLC system.

América Unida. Nueva Orleans: José Ortiz Monasterio, 1943-19uu.
>Monthly.

>Editor: Rafael J. Urruela. In Spanish. In OCLC system.

American Flag. Sonora, Tuolumne County, Calif.: D. O. McCarthy, 1861?-1864?
>Weekly.

>Vol. 3, no. 4 dated Dec. 24, 1863. Continued by *Weekly American Flag*. Variant title: *La Bandera*. In English and Spanish. In OCLC system.

American Junior Red Cross News. Spanish edition. Washington, D.C.:
The American National Red Cross, 19uu-19uu.
>Monthly.

>Listed in Common Council for American Unity, *Foreign Language Publications in the United States: Newspaper Lists,* p. 2. No extant issues located.

Americana. New York, N.Y.: Ultramar Publications, Inc., 1947-19uu.
>Monthly; quarterly.

>Directora: Tranza de Gamez Losada. In Spanish. In OCLC system.

El Americano. New Orleans, Louisiana: Latin American Publishing Co., 1uuu-1905.
>Tri-monthly.

>Editor: César Zumeta, cf. MacCurdy, Raymond R. *A History and Bibliography of Spanish-Language Newspapers and Magazines in Louisiana, 1808-1949,* p. 34. In Spanish. No extant issues located.

El Americano. Nueva York, 1892-1uuu.
>Monthly.

>"Periódico mensual de literatura, comercio, artes, ciencias, noticias y anuncios". In Spanish. In OCLC system.

Americanos. New Orleans, La.: Inter-American Information Service, 1957-1958.
In Spanish. In OCLC system.

Americans All. Gary, Indiana: Nicolo Accomando, 1924-19uu.
>Monthly.

>Listed in *N. W. Ayer & Son's American Newspaper Annual and Directory,* 1926, p. 20. In Spanish, English and Italian. No extant issues located.

Las Américas. New York, N.Y.: Las Americas Publishing Co., 1940-1944.
>Monthly (except July and August).

>Suspended with vol. 4, no. 7. Editor: Gaetano Massa. In Spanish. In OCLC system.

Las Américas. San Francisco, Calif.: Las Americas Pub. Co., 1914-19uu.
>Irregular.

In Spanish and English. In OCLC system.

The Americas. Washington, D. C.: Academy of American Franciscan History, 1944-.
>Quarterly.

In OCLC system.

Américas. Edición en español. Washington, D. C.: Organization of American States, General Secretariat, 1949-.
>Ten issues a year; monthly (nov./dic. 1979-.); bimonthly (enero-feb. 1983-.)

>Vols. for Mar. 1949- issued by: Pan American Union; May-June 1983- by: General Secretariat of the Organization of American States. Other editions: *Americas* (Portuguese), *Americas* (English). Continues in part *Bulletin of the Pan American Union.* In OCLC system.

Las Américas: Organo Oficial de la All Americas Association. New York, N.Y.: All Americas Pub. Co. 1914-.
>Monthly.

In Spanish. In OCLC system.

Amigo de los Hombres. Bee County, Texas: I. R. Rodríguez, 189u-1uuu.
>Listed in Ezell, Camp. *Historical Story of Bee County, Texas,* p. 52. No extant issues

located.

El Amigo de los Niños. Nampa, Ind.: Pacific Press Pub. Association, 19uu-.
Bimonthly.
Año 37, num. 6 dated Nov.-Dec. 1984. In Spanish. In OCLC system.

El Amigo de los Niños. Nueva York, 18uu-18uu.
Monthly.
Director: A. Sellén. Listed in Batista Villareal, Teresita. *Catálogo de Publicaciones periódicas cubanas...*, p. 19. This source indicates that the Biblioteca Nacional José Martí in Havana holds some issues of this title.

El Amigo del Hogar. Indiana Harbor, Ind.: Figueroa Print. Co., 1925-193u.
Weekly.
Organo del Círculo de Obreros Católicos "San José." Began with July 26, 1925 issue? Año 1, no. 17 dated nov. 22 de 1925. Ceased in the early 1930s, cf. Miller, John W. *Indiana Newspaper Bibliography.* Published for "the working Catholics of the Mexican Colony," cf. Miller, John W. *Indiana Newspaper Bibliography.* Variant title: *Friend of the Home.* In Spanish. In OCLC system.

El Amigo del Hogar. Redlands, Calif.: A. G. Lerma, 1906-19uu.
Semimonthly.
Año 1, no 4 dated 1 de jun. de 1906. In Spanish and English. In OCLC system.

El Amigo del País. Santa Fe, N. M.: José Chaves & Co., 1853-1uuu.
Weekly.
Vol. 1, no. 9 dated 10 de enero, 1854. In Spanish and English. In OCLC system.

El Amigo del Pueblo. Los Angeles, Calif.: J. E. González, 1861-1uuu.
Weekly.
Vol. 1, no. 3 dated nov. 30 de 1861. In Spanish. In OCLC system.

El Amigo del Pueblo. Ratón, Nuevo México: Arellano y Escobar, 189u-1uuu.
Weekly.
T. 1, no. 4 dated enero 8 de 1896. In Spanish. In OCLC system.

Amigo del Pueblo. San Antonio, Texas, 1908-1917?
Weekly.
Director: Ascensión Lozano. Listed in Ríos-C., Herminio, "Toward a True Chicano Bibliography: Part II," p. 47; also listed in "Más de cuatrocientos periódicos en español se han editado en Estados Unidos". In Spanish. No extant issues located.

El Amigo del Pueblo. Tucson, Ariz.: Carlos Tully, 1882-1uuu.
Mentioned in Arizona Enterprise, Oct. 14, 1882; and in *Epitaph,* Oct. 22, 1882. cf. Somoza, *Literatura de la Revolución Mexicana...*, p. 228. No extant issues located.

Anales de la Organización de los Estados Americanos. Washington, D. C.:
Departamento de Información Pública, 1949-1958.
Semiannual, 1958; quarterly, 1949-1957.
In Spanish. Also issued in English, French and Portuguese. In OCLC system.

El Anciano. East Las Vegas, N. M., 1889-1890; 1898-1899.
Weekly.
Published in Mora from 1890 to 1898, cf., Groves, Pearce S., *New Mexico Newspapers,* p. 395. In Spanish. No extant issues located.

El Anciano. Mora, N. M., 1890-1uuu.
Mentioned in Somoza, *Literatura de la Revolución Mexicana...*, p. 241. No extant issues located.

El Anciano. Trinidad, Colo.: Alej. M. Darley, 1882-1uuu.
Biweekly, weekly.
Año 1, num. 2 dated Mayo, 1882. In Spanish. "Trasladado en 1889 a La Junta, Colo. En 1890 apareció en East Las Vegas, Nuevo México. Trasladado en 1895 a More, Nuevo México", cf. "Más de cuatrocientos periódicos en español se han editado en Estados Unidos". In OCLC system.

El Ancon. Santa Fe, N. M., 1844-1845.
Weekly.
Listed in Grove, Pearce S., *New Mexico Newspapers*, p. 438. In Spanish. No extant issues located.

El Angel del Hogar. Tucson, Ariz., 1uuu-1uuu.
Listed in Miguélez, Armando, "Index of Spanish-Language Newspapers in the U. S. Southwest." Miguélez indicates the title is mentioned in *El Tucsonense;* no dates for this source are given. No extant issues located.

Anglo-Spanish Merchant. San Francisco, California, 1880?-1883?
Semi-monthly.
Started August 14, 1880?, cf. Gregory, Winifred, ed., *American Newspapers, 1821-1936*, p. 50. In Spanish and English. Repository: Bancroft Library (University of California at Berkeley).

Angostura. La Luz, N. M., 1900-1902.
Weekly.
Listed in Grove, Pearce S., *New Mexico Newspapers*, p. 320. In English and Spanish. No extant issues located.

Antena: Spanish News. Denver, Colo.: Virgilio Aguirre, 1947-19uu.
Semimonthly.
In Spanish and English. In OCLC system.

El Antifascista. Los Angeles, Calif.: Alfonso Córdoba, 193u-1943?
Semimonthly.
Año 3, no. 31 dated Feb. 15, 1938. "A speaking-trumpet of the anti-fascists on the Pacific coast and western U. S." In Spanish. In OCLC system.

La Antorcha. Tucson, Ariz.: D. Velasco and F. T. Dávila, 1876-1uuu.
Mentioned in *Tucson Daily Citizen,* Oct. 7, 1876, p. 2; cf. Somoza, *Literatura de la Revolución Mexicana...*, p. 228. No extant issues located.

El Anunciador. New York, N.Y.: Export Publishing Co., 1885-1911.
Monthly.
Listed in *Rowell's American Newspaper Directory,* 1907, p. 798. Also listed in "Más de cuatrocientos periódicos en español se han editado en Estados Unidos". In Spanish. No extant issues located.

El Anunciador. New York, N.Y.: El Anunciador Pub. Co., 193u-19uu.
Weekly.
Año 1, no. 20 dated 3 de diciembre de 1938. "New York's Latin-American weekly newspaper." In Spanish. In OCLC system.

El Anunciador. Trinidad, Colo.: La Compañía Publicista de "El Anunciador", 1904-19uu.
Weekly.
Editor: P. J. Martínez, cf. *Rowell's American Newspaper Directory,* 1907, p. 105. Continues *Anunciador & Sherman's Review.* In Spanish and English. In OCLC system.

Anunciador de N. Méjico. Las Vegas, N. M., 1871?-1878.
Weekly.
Variant title: *Anunciador de Nuevo Méjico.* In Spanish. In OCLC system.

Anunciador de Trinidad (Trinidad, Colorado, 1882) *See* **Trinidad Weekly Advertiser.**

El Anunciador del Pacífico. San Francisco, California, 1896-1uuu.
Monthly.
Listed in "Más de cuatrocientos periódicos en español se han editado en Estados Unidos". In Spanish. No extant issues located.

El Anunciador Hispano-Americano. New York, N.Y.: James D. Cudlipp, 1879-1880?
Monthly.
Cited in "Más de cuatrocientos periódicos en español se han editado en Estados Unidos"; also cited in *Rowell's American Newspaper Directory,* 1880. In Spanish. No

extant issues located.

Apachito. St. Johns, Arizona, 1905-1907.

Irregular.

Listed in "Más de cuatrocientos periódicos en español se han editado en Estados Unidos". In Spanish. No extant issues located.

Apretavis. San Francisco, Calif., 1915-19uu.

Listed in Miguélez, Armando, "Index of Spanish-Language Newspapers in the U. S. Southwest." Miguélez indicates the paper is mentioned in *La Crónica,* no dates for this source are given. No extant issues located.

The Argus. Holbrook, Ariz.: A.F. Banta, 1895–1900.

Issue of Dec. 12, 1895 included a Spanish-Language supplement titled "El Argos", which later became a column. In OCLC system.

Ariel: Revista de Hechos e Ideas. Los Angeles, Calif.: Ariel, 1939-19uu.

Monthly.

"Director literario y artístico: Félix Martín Ibáñez". Deals with Spaniard's antifascist cause. In Spanish. In OCLC system.

Aristo. Los Angeles, California: Aristo Pub. Co., 19uu-194u.

Weekly.

Vol. 8, no. 13 dated 24 de marzo de 1945. "Dedicated to the unity and intregration of the Spanish." Continues *Aristo News.* In Spanish and English. In OCLC system.

Arizona. Tucson, Ariz.: Carmen Cecilia Beltrán, 1943-1950.

Mentioned in Somoza, *Literatura de la Revolución Mexicana. . .,* p. 228. No extant issues located.

Arqueología Americana. Washington, D. C.: La Unión Panamericana, 1926-.

In Spanish. In OCLC system.

The Arrow-Pioneer. Wagon Mound, N. M.: Herderson & Hartigan, 188u-1888.

Weekly.

Vol. 3, no. 15 Feb. 11, 1888. Formed by the union of *La Flecha* (Wagon Mound, N. M.) and *Mora County Pioneer* (Watrous, N. M.: 1887). Continued by *Gallup Gleaner* (Gallup, N. M.: 1888). Variant title: *Flecha-Explorador.* In English and Spanish, cf. Grove, Pearce S., *New Mexico Newspapers,* p. 300. In OCLC system.

Arroz. New Orleans, Louisiana: Fort Pipes, 1947-19uu.

Monthly.

"Spanish edition of the *Rice Journal,"* cf. MacCurdy, Raymond R. *A History and Bibliography of Spanish-Language Newspapers and Magazines in Louisiana, 1808-1949,* p. 34. No extant issues located.

El Arte Tipográfico. [Nueva York]: [National Paper & Type Company], 1904-1922.

Continued by *El Arte Tipográfico y el Escritorio.* In Spanish. In OCLC system.

El Arte Tipográfico. Philadelphia: North American Pub. Co. [etc.], 1927-197u.

Quarterly.

Publication suspended from 1933 to Sept. 1937, and Apr. 1942. In Spanish. In OCLC system.

El Arte Tipográfico y el Escritorio. [Nueva York: National Paper & Type Company], 1922-1927.

Quarterly, July 1926-; monthly, Aug. 1922-May 1926.

Absorbed *El Escritorio* in Aug. 1922. Continues *El Arte Tipográfico.* In Spanish. In OCLC system.

Artes y Letras. New York, 1933-1939?

Monthly.

In Spanish. In OCLC system.

Artistas Hispanos. New York, N.Y., 1948-19uu.

Trimestral.

Director and administrator: Isabel Cuchi Coll. Repository: Center for Puerto Rican

Studies at Hunter College, CUNY.

Asociación Interamericana de Ingeniería Sanitaria: Organo Oficial. [Washington], 1947-1950.

Superseded by *Ingeniería Sanitaria* in 1953, cf. *Union of International Associations, Directory of Periodicals Published by International Organizations.* In Spanish, Portuguese and English. In OCLC system.

Astro. Miami, 1960-19uu.

Organo de la Sección Obrera del Movimiento Revolucionario 30 de noviembre. Director: Rafael Hernández Dalmás, cf. Peraza Sarausa, Fermín, *Directorio de Revistas y Periódicos de Cuba*, p. 26. No extant issues located.

El Astur. Tampa, Fla., 1926?-19uu.

Weekly.

"Official organ of the Centro Austuriano." Director: A. Leiva. In Spanish. Repository: University of South Florida, Tampa.

La Atalaya. Brooklyn, New York: Watchtower Bible and Tract Society, 19uu-19uu.

Monthly.

Listed in Common Council for American Unity, *Foreign Language Publications in the United States: Newspaper Lists.* No extant issues located.

El Atalaya. El Paso, Tex.; C. Juárez, Chih. [México]: Casa Bautista de Publicaciones, 19uu-1925.

Weekly.

Continued by *Atalaya Bautista* (El Paso, Tex.: 1926). In Spanish. In OCLC system.

El Atalaya Bautista. El Paso, Tex.; C. Juárez, Chih. [México]: Casa Bautista de Publicaciones, 1926-.

Weekly, Jan. 1926-June 1927. Monthly, July 1927-.

Began with t. 12, no. 1 dated enero 7 1926. Issue for Dec. 23, 1926 misdated Dec. 23, 1923. Continues *El Atalaya* (El Paso, Tex.). In Spanish. In OCLC system.

El Atalaya Bautista: Semanario Evangélico Bautista. El Paso, Tex.: Casa Bautista de Publicaciones, 191u-19uu.

Weekly.

T. 5, no. 1 dated enero 2 de 1919. Continues *El Mensajero Bautista.* Continued by *El Atalaya* (El Paso, Tex.). In OCLC system.

El Ateneo: Repertorio Ilustrado de Arte, Ciencia y Literatura. New York, N.Y., 1874-1877.

Monthly.

Editor: Juan I. [Ignacio] de Armas, cf. "Más de cuatrocientos periódicos en español se han editado en Estados Unidos". In Spanish. In OCLC system.

Ateneo: Revista Cultural. New York, N.Y., 1934-19uu.

Vol. 1 no. 2 dated abril 1934. "Organo del Ateneo Hispano de Nueva York." Repository: Center for Puerto Rican Studies at Hunter College.

El Átomo. Nogales, Ariz., 1892-1uuu.

Mentioned in *El Fronterizo* (Tuscon) ago. 23, 1892, p. 3; cf. Somoza, *Literatura de la Revolución Mexicana...*, p. 225. No extant issues located.

Atrevido. East Las Vegas, N. M., 1887-1uuu.

Weekly.

Listed in Grove, Pearce S., *New Mexico Newspapers*, p. 395. In Spanish. No extant issues located.

La Aurora. Albuquerque, New Mexico, 1928-19uu.

Weekly.

Listed in Ríos-C., Herminio, "Toward a True Chicano Bibliography: Part II," p. 42. Also listed in "Más de cuatrocientos periódicos en español se han editado en Estados Unidos". In Spanish. No extant issues located

La Aurora. Antonito, Colorado: John G. Jeantex, 1911-1924.

Weekly, irregular.

Vol. 6, no. 14 dated dic. 7 de 1918. "Semanario de variedades e inforación general; órgano del pueblo hispano-americano". Published by Beatriz J. de Córdova, Sept. 1918. Listed in "Más de cuatrocientos periódicos en español se han editado en Estados Unidos". In Spanish. Repository: Center for Research Libraries.

La Aurora. Boston [Mass.]: Printed by S. N. Dickinson & Co., 1845-18uu.
> Weekly.
> "A newspaper devoted to politics and literature." Editor: Estevan P. Andrews. In Spanish and English. In OCLC system.

La Aurora. East Las Vegas, Nuevo México: [Sínodo de Nuevo México], 1uuu-19uu.
> Weekly to 1902; semimonthly, 1903-1914; monthly, 1915-.
> Vol. 1, no. 52 dated Dec.1, 1900. Imprint varies; published in Albuquerque after 1904. Text in Spanish and English. Issued by the Synod of New Mexico; published after January 1915 by ' ꞏ naul High School. In OCLC system.

Aurora. Laredo, Texas. ꞏara Estela Ramírez, 190u-19uu.
> Mentioned in Zamora, Emilio. "Sara Estela Ramírez: una rosa roja en el movimiento". In *Mexican Women in the United States: Struggles Past and Present.* No extant issues located.

Aurora. Las Vegas, N. M., 1900-19uu.
> Mentioned in Somoza, *Literatura de la Revolución Mexicana...*, p. 244. No extant issues located.

Aurora. New York, N.Y.: Aurora, 1922?-19uu.
> Semimonthly.
> Vol. 1, no. 14 dated abr. 10 de 1923. "Revista quincenal sociológica". In Spanish. In OCLC system.

La Aurora. San Francisco, Calif.: W. Picoaga Durán, 1940-19uu.
> Repository: Bancroft Library, University of California (Berkeley)

La Aurora. Santa Fe, N. M.: I. L. Chaves, U. Chacón, & R.L. Baca, 1884-1884.
> Weekly.
> In Spanish. In OCLC system.

El Automóvil Americano. New York, N.Y.: Business Publishers InternationalCorp., 19uu-19uu.
> Monthly.
> Listed in Common Council for American Unity, *Foreign Language Publications in the United States: Newspaper Lists,* p. 5. In Spanish. No extant issues located.

El Avance Criollo. Miami, Fla.: M. Menéndez, 1960-1962.
> In Spanish. Variant title: *Avance Exilio.* In OCLC system.

Avance Exilio (Miami, Florida). *See* El Avance Criollo.

L'Avenir du Peuple. [New Orleans, La.] 1840-1841.
> Daily, Oct. 25, 1840-; three times a week, Aug. 7, 1840-Oct. 11, 1840.
> In French and Spanish. In French, Spanish and English Oct. 25, 1840. Published with an additional masthead in Spanish: "El Por-venir del Pueblo," Sept. 13, 1840-Oct. 11, 1840; "El Por-venir, Oct. 25, 1840." Published with an additional masthead in English: "The Future," Oct., 25, 1840. Subtitle varies. In OCLC system.

El Avisador Cubano. New York, N.Y., 1885-1888.
> Poyo indicates Enrique Trujillo was the publisher of this periodical, cf. Poyo, *With All and for the Good of All,* p. 174. In Spanish. The Archivo Nacional de Cuba, Havana holds some issues.

El Avisador Hispano Americano. Nueva York, 1888?-1889?
> Weekly.
> "Comercio, industrias, noticias, ciencias, variedades." In Spanish. Ran 1888-1889?, cf. Poyo, Gerald Eugene, *With All and for the Good of All,* p. 174. In OCLC system.

La Avispa. Del Rio, Texas, 1930-19uu.
> Irregular.

Director: A. Gutiérez. Listed in "Más de cuatrocientos periódicos en español se han editado en Estados Unidos". Also listed in Ríos-C., Herminio, "Toward a True Chicano Bibliography: Part II," p. 45. In Spanish. No extant issues located.

Avispa de Nueva Orleans. [New Orleans, La.]: Tomás Cocco, 1843?-18uu.
Triweekly.
Año segundo, no. 9 dated 18 enero 1844. In Spanish. In OCLC system.

Las Avispas. New York, 1896?-1uuu.
Director: Justo de Lara (2da. época). Repository: Biblioteca, Universidad de la Habana, Cuba.

El Azote. El Paso, Tex: El Grupo de Caballeros [etc.], 192u-19uu.
Weekly.
"Publicado por un Grupo de Caballeros Católicos Amantes de la Verdad." Año 10, no. 5 dated sept. 17 de 1922. In Spanish. In OCLC system.

El Azteca. El Paso, Tex., 1922-19uu.
Repository: Bancroft Library (University of California, Berkeley). Mentioned in Somoza, *Literatura de la Revolución Mexicana...*, p. 248.

El Azteca. Tucson, Ariz.: Club Azteca, 1925-19uu.
Listed in Miguélez, Armando, "Index of Spanish-Language Newspapers in the U. S. Southwest." No extant issues located.

Azucena. San Francisco, Calif.: P. Fijols, 1907-1916?
Listed in Miguélez, Armando, "Index of Spanish-Language Newspapers in the U. S. Southwest." No extant issues located.

The Azusa News. Azusa, Los Angeles County, South California: Geo. Bentley & T. A. Grant, 188u-1890.
Weekly.
4th year, no. 9 dated Mar. 2, 1889. In English and Spanish. In OCLC system.

Azusa Valley News. Azusa, Los Angeles County, California: George Bentley Co., 1885?-1894?
Weekly; semiweekly.
Includes section called "Glendora Echo." Absorbed *Glendora Echo.* Variant title: *Azusa News.* In Spanish and English. In OCLC system.

El Badajo. San Antonio, Tex.: Aguirre Fierro, 191u?-19uu.
Mentioned in Sax, Antimaco, *Los mexicanos en el destierro,* p. 56. No extant issues located.

Baja California. San Diego, Cal.: S. G. Vázquez, 1918?-19uu.
Vol. 1, núm. 6 dated dic. 24 de 1918. In Spanish. In OCLC system.

La Bandera (Albuquerque, New Mexico) *See* La Bandera Americana.

La Bandera. Brownsville, Tex.: John Tabor, 1848?-1863?
Weekly.
Began in 1848?, cf. Gregory, Winifred, ed., *American Newspapers, 1821-1936.* Ceased in 1863?, cf. *Newspapers in Microform, 1948-1983.* Vol. 15, no. 16 dated July 31, 1862. Variant title: *Fort Brown Flag* (Sept. 4-25, 1863). In Spanish and English. In OCLC system.

La Bandera (Sonora, Tuolumne County, California) *See* American Flag.

La Bandera Americana. Albuquerque, Nuevo México: M. Salazar y Otero, 1895-1938.
Weekly.
T. 5, no. 2 dated 18 de mayo de 1895. Absorbed *Nuevo Mundo* (Albuquerque, N. M.) in July 1901, cf. Grove, Pearce S., *New Mexico Newspapers.* Issues for May 1895-July 1901 continue the volume numbering of *Sol de Mayo* (Las Vegas, N. M.: 1894). Issues for Aug. 3, 1901-Dec. 16, 1938 called v. 1-43. Continues *Sol de Mayo* (Las Vegas, N. M.: 1894). Variant titles: *Albuquerque Bandera Americana, La Bandera,* cf. Grove, p. 31. In Spanish. In OCLC system.

Bandera de la Unión. Albuquerque, N. M., 1863-1uuu.
Weekly.

Listed in Grove, Pearce S., *New Mexico Newspapers*, p. 32. In Spanish. No extant issues located.

La Bandera Mexicana. San Francisco, [Calif.]: López del Castillo y Fierro, 1863-1uuu. Triweekly.
In Spanish. In OCLC system.

La Bandera Roja. El Paso, Texas, 190u-19uu.
Linked to the Partido Liberal Mexicano, social and political news, and anti-Díaz protest, cf. Lomas, Clara. "The Articulation of Gender in the Mexican Borderlands, 1900-1915." In Spanish. No extant issues located.

Banner. Springs, New Mexico, 1890-1uuu.
Listed in "Más de cuatrocientos periódicos en español se han editado en Estados Unidos". In Spanish and English. No extant issues located.

El Barbareno. Santa Barbara, Calif.: Mesick & Selover, 1895-1uuu.
Weekly.
"Devoted to literature, especially California literature, local history, clean local news, and the resources of this peerless section." Absorbed by *El Barbareno* (Santa Barbara, Calif.). In OCLC system.

El Bautista Mexicano. Dallas, Texas: Mexican Baptist Convention, Baptist General Convention of Texas, Language Missions Section, 1936-.
In Spanish. In OCLC system.

El Bautista Mexicano. San Antonio, Texas: Convención Bautista Mexicana de Texas, 193u?-19uu.
Monthly.
In Spanish. "Organo oficial de la Convención Bautista Mexicana de Texas". In OCLC system.

Bee (New Orleans, Louisiana) *See* **L'Abeille.**

El Bejareño. San Antonio: Debray y Lewis, 1855-18uu.
Bi-weekly (irregular), 1855; weekly (irregular), 1856-.
"Dedicado a los intereses de la población Méjico-Tejana". In Spanish. In OCLC system.

Belen News. Belen, N.M.: Hispano American Pub Co., 19uu–1947.
In OCLC system.

Beliota (Las Vegas, New Mexico). *See* **The Acorn.**
Bellota (Las Vegas, New Mexico). *See* **The Acorn.**

Bernalillo Condado Demócrata. Albuquerque, N. M.: Las Comitivas Democráticas, 18uu-1uuu.
In Spanish and English. English edition: *Bernalillo County Democrat.* In OCLC system.

Bernalillo Mirror. Bernalillo, N. M., 1878-1879.
Weekly.
"Includes a companion paper: *El Espejo del Valle de Taos. Taos Valley Mirror* moved from Taos, Taos County, and assumed the title *Bernalillo Mirror,* October 1898; moved to Albuquerque, Bernalillo County, and assumed the title *Albuquerque Mirror,* July 26, 1879," cf. Groves, Pearce S., *New Mexico Newspapers*, p. 373. Variant title: *El Espejo del Valle de Taos.* In English and Spanish. No extant issues located.

Bernalillo Native. Bernalillo, New Mexico: Chacón & Perea, 18uu-1uuu.
Weekly.
Listed in *Rowell's American Newspaper Directory,* 1880, p. 531. In Spanish. No extant issues located.

Bernalillo News. Bernalillo, N. M., 1880-1882.
Weekly.
"Moved to Jemez and assumed the title *Jemez Hot Springs Guide,* June 1882," cf. Grove, Pearce S., *New Mexico Newspapers,* p. 373. In English and Spanish. No extant issues located.

The Bernalillo Times. Bernalillo, N. M.: Vida L. Randall, 1929-1971.
 Weekly.
 Vol. 1, no. 48 dated June 20, 1930. In English and Spanish, 1930-1942; predominantly Spanish, 1942-1957; predominantly English, 1957-1971. Other editions: *Independent of Valencia County; Independiente and the New Mexico Independent* (Albuquerque, N. M.: 1933); *Independiente* (Albuquerque, N. M.) *Independiente and the New Mexico Independent* (Albuquerque, N. M.: 1939); *Independiente of Bernalillo County.* Continued by *Sandoval County Times-Independent.* In OCLC system.
Bibliografía Hispanoamericana. [New York: Instituto de las Españas en los Estados Unidos, 1934-1937].
 Issued also as a section of *Revista Hispánica Moderna,* Oct. 1934-July 1937, and again in Oct. 1937-. In Spanish. In OCLC system.
Biblioteca Hispánica. New York [etc.]: Hispanic Society of America [etc.], 1900-1921.
 In Spanish. In OCLC system.
El Bien Público. Brownsville, Tex.: León A. Y Obregón and Catarino Garza, 1879-1uuu.
 "Organo de la Sociedad Mutualista Benito Juárez". Mentioned in Somoza, *Literatura de la Revolución Mexicana...,* p. 246. No extant issues located.
El Bien Público. Rio Grande, Texas: Jesús T. Recio, 1892-1900.
 Bi-weekly.
 Paper began in Camargo, Mexico in 1875 as a weekly, then moved to Texas and became biweekly. The paper "editó la novela de Heriberto Frías *Tomochic* y las *Memorias de un Estudiante* de Alejandro Villaseñor", cf. "Más de cuatrocientos periódicos en español se han editado en Estados Unidos." In Spanish. No extant issues located.
El Bien Público. Tampa, Florida, 1920-19uu.
 Irregular.
 In 1928, the paper published a special issue titled "El bien público: a la memoria del Doctor José Ramón Avellanal". Listed in "Más de cuatrocientos periódicos en español se han editado en Estados Unidos." In Spanish. No extant issues located.
El Bien Público. Taos, Nuevo México: El Bien Público, 1910-1912?
 Weekly.
 Continued by *Taos Recorder and El Bien Público.* In Spanish. In OCLC system.
Blanco y Negro. Tucson, Ariz.: Gustavo Solano, 1921?-19uu.
 Listed in Miguélez, Armando, "Index of Spanish-Language Newspapers in the U. S. Southwest." Miguélez indicates that vol. 2 dated jul. 23, 1921 is in Special Collections, University of Arizona, Tucson.
El Boletín. Bakersfield: El Boletín, 1958-19uu.
 Biweekly, (Aug. 10, 1958-Aug. 22, 1958); three numbers a month, (July 10, 1958-July 30, 1958)
 "Noticias de la colonia". In English and Spanish. In OCLC system.
Boletín. New York: Casa de las Españas, Columbia University, 1931-1934.
 Superseded by *Revista Hispánica Moderna.* Includes music. In Spanish. In OCLC system.
El Boletín. Santa Barbara, Calif., 1892-1uuu.
 Mentioned in *El Fronterizo,* Jul. 23, 1892, p. 3; cf. Somoza, *Literatura de la Revolución Mexicana...,* p. 235. No extant issues located.
El Boletín. Santa Fe, N. M.: New Mexico State Penitentiany, 19uu-19uu.
 Monthly.
 Vol. 6, no. 3 dated nov. 1945. In OCLC system.
Boletín. Tampa, Florida: Comité Consultivo Conjunto, 1941-19uu.
 In OCLC system.
Boletín. Washington, D. C.: Ateneo Americano de Washington, 1949-19uu.
 In Spanish. In OCLC system.

Boletín. Washington, D. C.: Panamerican Sanitary Union, 1922-.
Monthly.
Articles chiefly in Spanish, some in English, some Portuguese, some in French. Summaries in Spanish, English, Portuguese and French. Variant titles: *Bulletin of the Pan American Sanitary Bureau, Boletín Panamericano de Sanidad* (May 1922-June 1923). In OCLC system.
Boletín. Washington, D. C.: United Nations Relief and Rehabilitation Administration; Administración de las Naciones Unidas para el Socorro y la Rehabilitación, 1946-1946. Began with no. 12 dated 15 de marzo de 1946, ceased with no. 19 dated 15 de nov. de 1946. Continues *Carta Quincenal de la UNRRA*. In Spanish. In OCLC system.
Boletín Agrícola y Ganadero del Condado del San Miguel. East Las Vegas, N. M.: Cámara Agrícola y de Ganadería, 1918-191u.
Monthly.
T. 1, no. 2 dated mayo 1918. In Spanish. In OCLC system.
Boletín Católico Checoslovaco. New York, N.Y.: Boletín Católico Checoslovaco, 1941-1946.
Monthly
In Spanish. In OCLC system.
Boletín Checoslovaco. New York [etc.]: Servicio de Información del Gobierno Checoslovaco [etc.], 19uu-.
Monthly, ([Aug.]-Oct./Nov. 1942); biweekly, Dec. 1942- Jun. 1946.
In Spanish. In OCLC system.
El Boletín Comercial. New York, 1871-1uuu.
Repository: Archivo Nacional de Cuba, Havana
Boletín: Comisión Interamericana del Atún Tropical (La Jolla, California) *See* **Bulletin: Inter-American Tropical Tuna Commission.**
Boletín de Anuncios. Las Vegas, New Mexico, 1877?-1uuu.
Weekly.
Repository: University of California (Berkeley).
Boletín de Artes Visuales. Washington, D. C.: Secretaría General de la Organización de los Estados Americanos, 1957-1969.
Semi-annual.
In Spanish. In OCLC system.
Boletín de Ciencia y Tecnología. Washington, D. C.: Oficina de Ciencia y Tecnología, Departamento de Asuntos Culturales, Unión Panamericana, 1950-1950.
In Spanish. In OCLC system.
Boletín de El Internacional. Tampa, Fla.: Labor Temple, 1936-1937.
Weekly.
"Organo local de las Uniones de la Internacional de Tabaqueros." Printer: Solís Print Co. Continued by *El Internacional.* (1937) In English and Spanish. In OCLC system.
Boletín de Información. New York, N.Y.: Sociedades Hispanas Confederadas de Ayuda a España, 1938-19uu.
Weekly.
"Informes, noticias y convocatorias del Servicio Semanal de Sociedades Hispanas Confederadas de Ayuda a España" In Spanish. In OCLC system.
Boletín de Información Vial. Washington, D. C.: Confederación Panamericana de Educación Vial, 1928-19uu.
In Spanish. In OCLC system.
Boletín de la Campaña (Las Vegas, New Mexico). *See* **Campaign Bulletin.**
El Boletín de la Liga Puertorriqueña e Hispana. New York, N.Y., 1928-1933?
Proprietor: A. R. Hernández. Repository: Center for Puerto Rican Studies at Hunter College, CUNY.
Boletín de la Oficina Internacional de las Repúblicas Americanas. Washington, D. C.:

IBAR, 1908-1910.
Began with tomo 27 dated jul.-sept. 1908, ended with t. 31 dated sept. 1910. In Spanish. Also issued in an English edition. Separated from *Bulletin of the International Bureau of the American Republics;* Continued by *Boletín de la Unión Panamericana* [Secciones: española, portuguesa, francesa]. In OCLC system.

Boletín de la Oficina Sanitaria Panamericana. [Washington]: Oficina Sanitaria Panamericana, 1923-.
Monthly.
T. 2, no. 7 dated jul. 1923. Continues *Boletín de la Oficina Sanitaria Panamericana.* English edition, 1966-1973: *Bulletin of the Pan American Health Organization.* In Spanish and English. In OCLC system.

El Boletín de la Revolución. New York, N.Y., 1868-1869.
Listed in Poyo, Gerald Eugene, *With All and for the Good of All,* p. 174. In Spanish. Repository: Archivo Nacional de Cuba, Havana.

Boletín de la Semana Devota. Tucson, Ariz.: P. Carmelo Corbella, 1922-1923.
Mentioned in Somoza, *Literatura de la Revolución Mexicana...,* p. 228. No extant issues located.

Boletín de la Unión Panamericana. Washington, D. C., 1911-.
From Oct. 1893 to June 1908 the monthly *Bulletin of the Bureau of the American Republics* was published in English, with portions in Spanish, Portuguese and French. From July 1908 to June 1911, it was issued with one section in English and another in Spanish, Portuguese and French. Starting on July 1911 the foreign language sections have been published in separate editions. In OCLC system.

Boletín de la Unión Panamericana. Washington, D. C., 1910-1911.
Began with vol. 31 oct. 1910; ceased with v. 32 jun. 1911. "Boletín de la Oficina Internacional de las Repúblicas Americanas." Split into *Boletín de la Unión Panamericana, Boletím da Unión Pan-Americana,* and *Bulletin de l'Union Panaméricaine.* In Spanish. In OCLC system.

Boletín de las Naciones Unidas. [New York: United Nations Dept. of Public Information], 1948-1953.
Frequency varies.
Issued by Departamento de Información Pública de las Naciones Unidas. In Spanish. In OCLC system.

Boletín de Música y Artes Visuales. Washington, D. C.: Departamento de Asuntos Culturales, Unión Panamericana, 1952-1956.
Continued in part by *Boletín de Artes Visuales.* Continued in part by *Boletín Interamericano de Música.* In Spanish. In OCLC system.

Boletín de Noticias y Precios Corrientes. Nueva York [New York, N.Y.]: Chas. B. Richardson y Cía., 1862-1862.
Irregular.
Vol. 1, no. 1 dated enero 11 de 1862. Published on the sailing day of the steamer to Havana and Panama for circulation in the U. S., Cuba, Mexico, and the South America. Continued by *Continental* (New York, N.Y.). In Spanish. In OCLC system.

Boletín de Sigma Delta Pi: Revista de Cultura Hispano-Americano. Berkeley, Calif.: Sigma Delta Pi, 1934-1934.
In Spanish. In OCLC system.

Boletín del Agricultor. Wilmington, Del.: Depto. de Relaciones Exteriores, E.I. du Dupont de Nemours & Co., 19uu-1954.
In Spanish. In OCLC system.

Boletín del Comité de Defensa. Tampa, Fla., 1938-19uu.
In Spanish. In OCLC system.

Boletín Educación Social del Trabajador. Washington, D. C.: Consejo Interamericano Económico y Social, 1954-.

In Spanish. In OCLC system.

Boletín en Español. Nueva York, [i.e. New York, N.Y.]: Dotación de Carnegie para la Paz Internacional, División de Cambio y Educación, 1943-.
In Spanish. In OCLC system.

Boletín Estraordinario. Brownsville, Tex.: Imprenta de Ambros y Segura, 1865-18uu.
Irregular.
In Spanish. In OCLC system.

El Boletín Fronterizo Comercial. Laredo, Tex., 1930-19uu.
Listed in Miguélez, Armando, "Index of Spanish-Language Newspapers in the U. S. Southwest." No extant issues located.

Boletín Interamericano de Música. Washington, D. C.: Organización de los Estados Americanos, 1957-1973.
Quarterly, bimonthly.
Continues in part *Boletín de Música y Artes Visuales.* In Spanish. In OCLC system.

Boletín Latino Americano del CIO. New York, N. Y.: Committee on Latin American Affairs, CIO, 19uu-19uu.
Quarterly.
Listed in Common Council for American Unity, *Foreign Language Publications in the United States: Newspaper Lists,* p. 5. In Spanish. No extant issues located.

Boletín Linotypico. Brooklyn, New York: Mergenthaler Linotype Company, 19uu-19uu.
Quarterly.
Listed in Common Council for American Unity, *Foreign Language Publications in the United States: Newspaper Lists,* p. 5. No extant issues located.

Boletín Mexicano. San Antonio, Texas: Junta Patriótica, 1926-19uu.
Listed in Ríos-C., Herminio, "Toward a True Chicano Bibliography: Part II" and "Más de cuatrocientos periódicos en español se han editado en Estados Unidos". The official organ of the Junta Patriótica. In Spanish. No extant issues located.

Boletín "New History." New York, N.Y.: New History, 1934-19uu.
Quarterly.
In Spanish. In OCLC system.

Boletín Obrero. Tampa, Florida: Centro Obrero, 1903-190u.
Continues *El Federal* (1902-1903), Continued by *El Internacional* (1904).
In Spanish. In OCLC system.

Boletín Oficial: Club Cubano Inter Americano, Inc. New York, N.Y.: Club Cubano Inter Americano, Comisión de Prensa y Propaganda, 194u-19uu.
Monthly.
"Organo oficial del Club Cubano Inter-Americano Incorporated". In Spanish. Repository: Recovering the U. S. Hispanic Literary Heritage Project.

El Boletín Popular. Santa Fe, New Mexico: José Segura, 1885-1908.
Weekly.
T. 1, no. 25 dated abr. 1, 1886. Absorbed by *Eagle* (Santa Fe, N. M.). In Spanish. In OCLC system.

El Boletín Popular. Taos, Nuevo México: Cía. Publicista de El Boletín Popular, 1919-19uu.
Weekly.
Vol. 1, no. 50 dated 31 de marzo, 1920. In Spanish. In OCLC system.

Boletín: Puerto Rico Agricultural Experiment Station. Washington, D. C., 1902-19uu.
In Spanish. In OCLC system.

Boletín Semanal Informativo del Consejo Revolucionario Cubano. Coral Gables, Fla., 1960.
Director: Angel del Cerro, cf. Peraza Sarausa, Fermín, *Directorio de Revistas y Periódicos de Cuba,* p. 27. No extant issues located.

The Border. Tucson, Ariz., 1907-19uu.
Mentioned in Raat, Dirk, *Revoltosos,* p. 59 & p. 228.

The Borderer. Las Cruces, N. M.: N. V. Bennett & A. C. Abacock, 1871-1875.
> Weekly.
> In English and Spanish, cf. Grove, Pearce, *New Mexico Newspapers,* p. 143. A companion Spanish-language newspaper published Sept. 30, 1874-Sept. 1875 titled *El Fronterizo.* In OCLC system.

El Boricua. Nueva York, N. Y: El Boricua Publishing Corp., 194u-19uu.
> Año 1, no. 10 dated 23 de junio de 1948. "Portavoz de la colonia puertorriqueña en Nueva York." Editor and director: Rosendo Marcano. In Spanish. Repository: Center for Puerto Rican Studies at Hunter College, CUNY.

Borinquen: Organo de la Sección Puerto Rico del Partido Revolucionario Cubano. New York, 1898-1uuu.
> Monthly.
> Edited by Robert H. Todd. Listed in Batista Villareal, Teresita, *Catálogo de Publicaciones periódicas cubanas...,* p. 125. This source indicates that the Biblioteca Nacional José Martí in Havana holds some issues of this title.

La Boz del Pueblo. New York, N. Y.: The Nessin Press, 1915-1919.
> Weekly.
> Continues *Progreso* (New York, N. Y.: 1915). Continued by *Epoka de Nu York.* Variant title: *La Bos del Pueblo.* In Ladino and English. In OCLC system.

Brazo y Cerebro. New York, N. Y.: Juan Martínez, ed., 1912-1914.
> Listed in Chabrán, Rafael and Richard Chabrán, "The Spanish-Language and Latino Press of the United States: Newspapers and Periodicals," p. 369. In Spanish. No extant issues located.

Brooklyn Colonia Latina. Brooklyn, N. Y.: Colonia Latina, 1938-19uu.
> Issued by the Social Mutuo-Cooperativo. In Spanish. In OCLC system.

Brújula. New York, 1940-19uu.
> Repository: Erasmo Vando Collection, Hunter College, CUNY.

La Buena Noticia. El Paso, Texas, 19uu-19uu.
> Listed in Chabrán, Rafael and Richard Chabrán, "The Spanish-Language and Latino Press of the United States: Newspapers and Periodicals," p. 373. In Spanish. No extant issues located.

La Buena Prensa: Organo del Comité de la Asociación del Mismo Nombre. El Paso, Tex.: El Comité, 1923-19uu.
> Weekly.
> T. 1, no. 2 dated 15 de sept. de 1923. In Spanish. In OCLC system.

Buliota (Las Vegas, New Mexico). *See* **The Acorn.**

Bulletin: Inter-American Tropical Tuna Commission = Boletín: Comisión Interamericana del Atún Tropical. La Jolla, Calif.: The Commission, 1954-.
> Irregular.
> In English and Spanish. In OCLC system.

Bulletin of the Pan American Union. Washington D. C.: The Union, 1910-1948.
> In OCLC system.

El Cable: Periódico Universal de Noticias. New York, 18uu-1878.
> Edited by Robert H. Todd. Listed in Batista Villareal, Teresita, *Catálogo de Publicaciones periódicas cubanas. . .,* p. 126. This source indicates that the Biblioteca Nacional José Martí in Havana holds some issues of this title.

La Cachiporra. Las Vegas, Nuevo México, 1888-18uu.
> T. 1, no. 1 dated oct. 19, 1888. In Spanish and English. In OCLC system.

La Cachiporrita. Las Vegas, Nuevo México: Comisión Central Republicana de la Condado de San Miguel, 1890-189u.
> Irregular.
> Vol. 1, no. 2 dated 8 de oct. de 1890. In Spanish and English. In OCLC system.

El Cafetal. New York: El Cafetal Journal Co., 1903-19uu.

Monthly.
"Revista Oficial Mensual Dedicada Exclusivamente a la Industria Cafetera en Todos sus Ramos". In Spanish. In OCLC system.

La Calavera. Brownsville, Tex., 19uu-19uu.
Issue for nov. 1, 1934 deposited in Special Collections, University of Texas, Brownsville.

Calaveras. McAllen, Texas, 1917-19uu.
Director: Lorenzo Yáñez, Jr, Colaborador: José Díaz. Listed in Ríos-C., Herminio, "Toward a True Chicano Bibliography: Part II," p. 46. Also listed in "Más de cuatrocientos periódicos en español se han editado en Estados Unidos". No extant issues located.

California Moderna. San Franciso, California, 1905-19uu.
Monthly.
Listed in "Más de cuatrocientos periódicos en español se han editado en Estados Unidos." In Spanish. No extant issues located.

The California Star. Yerba Buena [i.e. San Francisco, Calif.]: Samuel Bannan, 1847-1848.
Weekly.
Editors: E. P. Jones, 1847; Edward C. Kemble, 1847-1848. Yerba Buena later became known as San Francisco. Merged with *Californian* (Monterey, Calif.: 1846) to form *California Star & Californian.* In English and Spanish. In OCLC system.

Californian. San Francisco, Calif., 1846-1848.
In English and Spanish. In OCLC system.

Campaign Bulletin. Las Vegas, New Mexico: T. Romero & W. G. Koogler, 1880-18uu.
Weekly.
Issue number 6 has a companion paper entitled *Boletín de la Campaña.* First issues in Spanish and English. In OCLC system.

El Campeón. Tucson, Ariz.: Francisco Hevia del Puerto, 1918-19uu.
Listed in Miguélez, Armando, "Index of Spanish-Language Newspapers in the U. S. Southwest." Miguélez indicates the newspaper is mentioned in *El Tucsonense,* 17-VI, 1922. No extant issues located.

El Campo Internacional. New York, N.Y.: American International Publishers, Inc., 1920-19uu.
Monthly.
In Spanish. In OCLC system.

Cancionero Fílmico. Los Angeles, Calif.: Armando del Moral, 1952-19uu.
Mentioned in Somoza, *Literatura de la Revolución Mexicana. . .,* p. 231. No extant issues located.

El Capitán. Capitan, N. M.: Capitan Printing Co., 1900-1900.
Weekly.
"A journal devoted to the interests of Lincoln County." Merged with: *Capitan Miner,* to form *Capitan Progress.* In English and Spanish, cf. Grove, Pearce S., *New Mexico Newspapers,* p. 247. In OCLC system.

Cara al Sol. New York, N.Y.: Peninsular News Service, 1938-194u.
Weekly.
Editors: Javier Gaytán de Ayala and Ricardo Mendoza. In Spanish. In OCLC system.

El Caribe. Brooklyn, N.Y., 1923-19uu.
Weekly.
Año 1, no. 2 dated Sept. 8, 1923. Administrator: José J. Meléndez; director: Joaquín Colón López. Repository: Center for Puerto Rican Studies at Hunter College, CUNY.

El Carnicero Mexicano. Eagle Pass, Tex.: Catarino Garza, 1886-1uuu.
Mentioned in Somoza, *Literatura de la Revolución Mexicana. . .,* p. 247. No extant issues located.

Carta Informativa Americana. New York, [N.Y.]: Business Publishers International

Corporation, 1941-1943.
    Semimonthly.
    In Spanish. English edition: *American News Letter.* Published also in Portuguese. In OCLC system.
Carta Quincenal de la UNRRA. Washington, EE. UU.: Administración de las Naciones Unidas para el Socorro y la Rehabilitación, 1945-1945.
    Biweekly.
    Began with no. 2 dated 15 de jul. de 1945, ceased with no. 11 dated 1 de dic. de 1945. Continues *Informativo Quincenal de la UNRRA.* Continued by *Boletín* (United Nations Relief and Rehabilitation Administration). In Spanish. In OCLC system.
Carteles de América: Revista Quincenal Ilustrada. Segunda Etapa. New York, 1960-.
    Biweekly.
    Directors: Diego González Alonso and Eduardo A. Esponosa. "1a. etapa, Habana, 1920-jul. 1960, en que fueron confiscados sus talleres por el gobierno comunista," cf. Peraza Sarausa, Fermín, *Directorio de Revistas y Periódicos de Cuba,* p. 28.
Cascabeles. New York, N.Y., 1934-19uu.
    "Revista mensual cultural-literaria". Repository: The Center for Puerto Rican Studies at Hunter College.
Catholic Banner. Las Cruces, N. M., 1912?-1914?
    Weekly.
    Listed in Grove, Pearce S., *New Mexico Newspapers,* p.144. In English and Spanish. No extant issues located.
The Catholic Expositor. New York, N.Y.: J.D Smith, 1844-1844.
    Monthly.
    Edited by Rev. Félix Varela, D. D. and Rev. Constantine Pise, D. D. Continues *Catholic Expositor and Literary Magazine* (New York, N.Y., 1841-1844). In OCLC system.
El Católico de Nuevo México. [Las Vegas, N. M.], 18uu-1uuu.
    Bimonthly.
    "Periódico inglés y castellano, publicado en esta ciudad, bajo la dirección de los Reverendos Padres, M.I. Grom y T.P. O'Keefe, cuyos nombres aparecen como editores del mismo", cf. *El Independiente,* 9 jun., 1984. No extant issues located.
    Católico del Sudoeste (Santa Fe, New Mexico). *See* Southwestern Catholic.
El Cazador. Brownsville, Texas: Ramiro de Lara, 1896-1uuu.
    Bi-weekly.
    Listed in "Más de cuatrocientos periódicos en español se han editado en Estados Unidos". In Spanish. No extant issues located.
El Centenario. Douglas, Arizona: Enríquez Bermúdez, 1906-19uu.
    "Circulated among Mexican workers in the Arizona cooper mines," cf. Meier, Matt S. and Feliciano Rivera, *The Chicanos: A History of Mexican Americans,* p. 120. In Spanish. No extant issues located.
El Centinela. Brownsville, Tex.: Eduin B. Escarboro, 1849-1uuu.
    Weekly.
    In Spanish. In OCLC system.
El Centinela. Chicago, Ill.: El Centinela Publishing Co., 1959-.
    Monthly.
    "Al servicio de la colonia hispana". In Spanish. In OCLC system.
El Centinela. El Paso, Texas, 1887-1uuu.
    Irregular.
    Listed in "Más de cuatrocientos periódicos en español se han editado en Estados Unidos". In Spanish. No extant issues located.
El Centinela. Hidalgo, Texas, 1899-1901.
    Irregular.
    Administrator: W. Schunion. Listed in "Más de cuatrocientos periódicos en español se

han editado en Estados Unidos". In Spanish. No extant issues located.

Centinela. Key West, Florida: Francisco Gonzales, 1907-1915.
Semi-weekly.
Listed in *N.W.Ayer & Son's American Newspaper Annual and Directory,* 1915, p. 137. In Spanish. No extant issues located.

Centinela del Río Grande. Brownsville, Tex.: J. R. Palmer & E. B. Scarborough, 1850-18uu.
Weekly.
Tom. 1, no. 11 dated mar. 13 1850. June 26, 1861 is published with *The Río Grande Sentinel.* In Spanish and English. In OCLC system.

Centro América. San Francisco, Ca.: José Rodríguez Cerva, 1921-19uu.
Weekly.
In Spanish and English. In OCLC system.

Centro de Valle. Mercedes, Texas: A. Acosta, 1927-1929?
Weekly.
Director: A. Acosta, editor: F.S. de Acosta. Listed in "Más de cuatrocientos periódicos en español se han editado en Estados Unidos". Also listed in Ríos-C., Herminio, "Toward a True Chicano Bibliography: Part II," p. 46. In Spanish. No extant issues located.

Challenge. Denver, Colorado: Rocky Mountain Foundation for a Free Press, Inc., 1946-19uu.
Weekly.
In English and Spanish. In OCLC system.

Chantecler. Tucson, Ariz.: Francisco M. Robredo, 1928-19uu.
Listed in Miguélez, Armando, "Index of Spanish-Language Newspapers in the U. S. Southwest." Miguélez indicates that the Special Collections, University of Arizona, Tucson, holds issue of 25-II-1928.

Charlatán. New Brunswick, New Jersey: Rutgers Univ., 1951-19uu.
Listed in Wright, William C., and Paul A. Stellhorn, eds., *Directory of New Jersey Newspapers, 1765-1970,* p. 139. In Spanish. No extant issues located.

Chieftain-El Defensor (Socorro, New Mexico). *See* **El Defensor Chieftain.**

Chilean Gazette. Washington, D. C.: Chilean Embassy, 1942-19uu.
Numbers 1-9 published in New York by Anibal Jara, Chilean Consul General. In Spanish. In OCLC system.

Chiltipiquin. San Antonio, Texas: Guillermo Aguirre & Fierro, 1914-1915.
Weekly.
Listed in Ríos-C., Herminio, "Toward a True Chicano Bibliography: Part II," p. 47. Also listed in "Más de cuatrocientos periódicos en español se han editado en Estados Unidos". In Spanish. No extant issues located.

El Chinaco. Laredo, Texas: Paulino Martínez, 1890-1892.
Weekly.
Listed in *Rowell's American Newspaper Directory,* 1896, p. 339 with starting publication dated of 1891. Also listed in: "Más de cuatrocientos periódicos en español se han editado en Estados Unidos", with publication dates of 1890-1892. In Spanish. No extant issues located.

El Chismoso. Tucson, Ariz., 1931-19uu.
"Lo menciona Jose Castelán en su poesía publicada en *El Tucsonense,* Jul. 16, 1931, p. 4"; cf. Somoza, *Literatura de la Revolución Mexicana...,* p. 229. No extant issues located.

La Chispa. Chicago, Illinois, 1931-19uu.
Editor: J. Espinoza. Also listed in Chabrán, Rafael and Richard Chabrán, "The Spanish Language and Latino Press of the United States: Newspapers and Periodicals," p. 372. In Spanish. No extant issues located.

La Chispa. Tucson, Ariz., 1uuu-1uuu.
Listed in Miguélez, Armando, "Index of Spanish-Language Newspapers in the U. S. Southwest." Miguélez indicates that the Newspaper is mentioned in *El Tucsonense,* no dates for this source are given. No extant issues located.

El Christiano Latino-Americano (Brownsville,Texas). *See* **The Latin-American Christian.**

The Chronicle. Las Vegas, New Mexico: Chronicle Pub. Co., 18uu-1uuu.
>Weekly.
>Vol. 4, no. 32 dated Nov. 29, 1884. In English with Spanish section called "Crónica." In OCLC system.

The Chronicle. Las Vegas, New Mexico: Louis Hommel, 1886-1886.
>Weekly; semi-weekly.
>A Mexican American publication. Published daily during the election, Oct 13-Nov 1, 1886. Publication suspended June 24-July 31, 1886. Place varies: Cabra Springs. Spanish section called "La Crónica." Repository: Bancroff Library (University of California, Berkeley).

Ciencia Interamericana. Washington, D. C.: División de Fomento Científico, Departamento de Asuntos Culturales, Unión Panamericana, 1960-19uu.
>In Spanish. In OCLC system.

Ciencia y Tecnología. Washington, D. C.: Sección de Ciencia y Tecnología, Unión Panamericana, 1960-19uu.
>In Spanish. In OCLC system.

Ciencias Sociales: Notas e Información. Departamento de Asuntos Culturales, Oficina de Ciencias Sociales, Union Panamericana, 1950-1956.
>In Spanish. In OCLC system.

Cine-Gráfica (Los Angeles, California). *See* **La Novela Cine-Gráfica.**

Cine Mundial. New York, N.Y.: Chalmers Pub. Co.; F. G. Ortega, ed., 1918-19uu.
>Monthly.
>Listed in "Más de cuatrocientos periódicos en español se han editado en Estados Unidos".Also listed in *N.W.Ayer & Son's American Newspaper Annual and Directory,* 1929, p. 730. In Spanish. No extant issues located.

Cine Variedades. New York, N.Y., 1953-19uu.
>Año 1, no. 14 dated julio 1953. Subtitle varies. In Spanish. Repository:The Center for Puerto Rican Studies at Hunter College.

Cinefonia. Los Angeles, California, 1930-1931.
>Monthly.
>Directors: Luis Alver V., José Octavio Cano.Administrator: Louis Rich, listed in "Más de cuatrocientos periódicos en español se han editado en Estados Unidos". In Spanish. No extant issues located.

Cinelandia. Hollywood, Calif.: Spanish-American Publishing Co., 1926-.
>Monthly.
>Variant title: *Cinelandia y Films.* In Spanish. In OCLC system.

Cinema. Los Angeles, Calif., 1935-19uu.
>In OCLC system.

Circular del Joyero. New York, N.Y.: D. H. Hopkinson, 1874-1uuu.
>Quarterly.
>Listed in *Rowell's American Newspaper Directory,* 1875, p. 158. In Spanish. No extant issues located.

City News. Santa Fe, N. M., 1874-1876.
>Semiweekly.
>Listed in Grove, Pearce S., *New Mexico Newspapers,* p.442. In English and Spanish. No extant issues located.

City Terrace Comet. Los Angeles, California: Dolores Sánchez, 1950-1991.
>Weekly.
>Community newspaper. Editor, Rose Soto; publisher, Dolores Sánchez, cf. *Gale Directory of Publications and Broadcast Media,* 1995, p. 156. In Spanish and English. No extant issues located.

El Ciudadano. El Paso,Tex.: Francisco A. Alvarez, 1892-1uuu.

Weekly.

In Spanish. In OCLC system.

El Cable: Periódico Universal de Noticias. New York, 18uu-1878.

Edited by Robert H. Todd. Listed in Batista Villareal, Teresita, *Catálogo de Publicaciones periódicas cubanas...*, p. 126. This source indicates that the Biblioteca Nacional José Martí in La Havana holds some issues of this title.

El Clamor Público. Los Angeles, Calif.: Francisco P. Ramírez, 1855-1859.

Weekly.

Editors: José E. González and Francisco P. Ramírez. "Evolved out of the Spanish section of *The Los Angeles Star,*" cf. Chabrán, Rafael and Richard Chabrán, "The Spanish-Language and Latino Press of the United States: Newspapers and Periodicals," p. 367. In Spanish. In OCLC system.

Claridades. San Antonio, Tex.: Santiago R. de la Vega, 1915-19uu.

Semanario de caricaturas, cf. Miguélez, Armando, "Index of Spanish-Language Newspapers in the U. S. Southwest." No extant issues located.

El Clarín (Walsenburg, Colorado). *See* **The Clarion.**

El Clarín Americano. Walsenburg, Colorado, 1919-1920.

Listed in Oehlerts, Donald E., *Guide to Colorado Newspapers,* p. 79. In Spanish. No extant issues located.

El Clarín del Norte. El Paso, Tex.: El Clarín del Norte, 19uu-19uu.

Weekly.

Vol. 3, no. 91 dated 8 de oct. de 1905. In Spanish. In OCLC system.

El Clarín Disperso. Jerome, Ariz.: Rivera Domínquez, 1916-19uu.

Listed in Miguélez, Armando, "Index of Spanish-Language Newspapers in the U. S. Southwest." No extant issues located.

El Clarín Mejicano. Santa Fe, Nuevo Méjico, 1873-18uu.

Weekly.

In Spanish. In OCLC system.

El Clarín Mexicano. Las Vegas, Nuevo México: Comisión Central del Partido del Pueblo Unido, 189u-1uuu.

In Spanish. In OCLC system.

The Clarion. Walsenburg, Colo.: Earl Gault, 19uu-19uu.

Vol. 12, no. 5 dated Mar. 6, 1945. Additional masthead in Spanish: *El Clarín.* In English and Spanish. In OCLC system.

El Coadjutor. Laredo, Texas, 1890-1uuu.

Irregular.

Listed in "Más de cuatrocientos periódicos en español se han editado en Estados Unidos." In Spanish. No extant issues located.

El Cobrador. Las Cruces, New Mexico, 1899-1uuu.

Irregular.

Listed in "Más de cuatrocientos periódicos en español se han editado en Estados Unidos". In Spanish. No extant issues located.

Colfax County Reporter. Ratón, N. M.: Clarence Smith, 18uu-19uu.

Weekly.

Vol. 45, no. 38 dated feb. 26, 1943. "An independent democratic newspaper." In English and Spanish, cf. Grove, Pearce S., *New Mexico Newspapers,* p. 105. In OCLC system.

La Colonia Mexicana. Laredo, Tex.: Justo Cárdenas, 1885?-1uuu.

Semiweekly.

Vol. 3, no. 273 dated Aug. 24, 1889. "Periódico independiente, político, literario y de avisos". In Spanish. In OCLC system.

Colonia Mexicana. Los Angeles, Calif.: Manuel Guerrero, 1924-19uu.

Mentioned in *El Tucsonense,* ago. 8, 1924; cf. Somoza, *Literatura de la Revolución*

Mexicana..., p. 231. No extant issues located.

La Colonia Mexicana. Tucson, Arizona: [Carlos] Tully, 1883-1884?
> Weekly.
> Founded by Tully. He also founded *Las Dos Repúblicas, La Alianza, La Voz,* cf. Chabrán, Rafael and Richard Chabrán, "The Spanish-Language and Latino Press of the United States: Newspapers and Periodicals," p. 366. Listed in Gregory, Winifred, ed., *American Newspapers, 1821-1936.* In Spanish. No extant issues located.

El Coloradeño. Pueblo, Colo.: Martínez y Luceros, 19uu-19uu.
> Weekly.
> T. 2, no. 1 dated jul. 3, 1920. In Spanish. In OCLC system.

The Colorado Clarion. Denver, Colo.: Rubén C. Valdez, 1953-19uu.
> Weekly.
> In Spanish and English. In OCLC system.

The Colorado Pioneer. Trinidad, Colorado: Urbano Chacón, 1875-1878?
> Weekly.
> Spanish edition: *Explorador, 1876.* Rowell lists a newspaper with the same date called *Trinidad Pioneer* (Trinidad, Co., 1875). In English and Spanish. In OCLC system.

El Combate. Albuquerque, N. M.: José Escobar, 1892-1919?
> Weekly.
> In Spanish. In OCLC system.

El Combate. El Paso, Tex., 1915-19uu.
> Repository: Bancroft Library (University of California, Berkeley). Mentioned in Somoza, *Literatura de la Revolución Mexicana...*, p. 248.

El Combate. Socorro, Nuevo México: José Escobar, 18uu-18uu.
> Weekly.
> T. 1, no. 3 dated Jan. 8, 1898. In Spanish. In OCLC system.

El Combate. Tucson, Ariz.: Santiago F. Rivera, 1916-19uu.
> Mentioned in *El Tucsonense,* Nov. 17, 1922; cf. Somoza, *Literatura de la Revolución Mexicana...*, p. 228. No extant issues located.

El Combate. Wagon Mound, Nuevo Méjico: Diego A. Chacón, 1902-1918.
> Weekly.
> Continues *Sol de Mayo* (Las Vegas, N. M.: 1900). Absorbed by *Wagon Mound Pantagraph.* Issued jointly with *Mora County Sentinel,* Jan. 6, 1911-May 19, 1911. "Periódico dedicado a los intereses del pueblo de Nuevo México". Variant title: *Mora County Sentinel and El Combate,* May 26-June 2, 1911. In Spanish and English. In OCLC system.

El Comerciante y Agricultor. New Orleans, Louisiana: Union Publishing Co., 1897-1uuu.
> Monthly.
> Listed in *Rowell's American Newspaper Directory,* 1902, p. 374. In Spanish and English. No extant issues located.

El Comercio. Brownsville, Texas, 1901-19uu.
> Irregular.
> Listed in "Más de cuatrocientos periódicos en español se han editado en Estados Unidos". In Spanish. No extant issues located.

El Comercio. Los Angeles, California: El Comercio Publishing Company, 19uu-19uu.
> Weekly.
> Listed in Common Council for American Unity, *Foreign Language Publications in the United States: Newspaper Lists.* In Spanish. No extant issues located.

El Comercio. Nueva York, [N. Y.]: A. K. Phillips & Co., 187u-1uuu.
> Monthly.
> Vol. 2, no. 2 dated nov. 15 de 1875. "Periódico independiente, dedicado a los intereses comerciales, fabriles y financieros de los Estados Unidos y la América española". In Spanish. In OCLC system.

El Comercio. San Acacio, N. M.: A. R. Córdova, 1901-19uu.
Biweekly.
T. 1, no. 21 dated jul. 11, 1901. "Derechos iguales para todos, especiales, para ninguno". In Spanish. In OCLC system.
El Comercio. San Francisco, Calif., 1uuu-1uuu.
"Consulado mexicano en tiempo de Porfirio Díaz", cf. Miguélez, Armando, "Index of Spanish-Language Newspapers in the U. S. Southwest." No extant issues located.
El Comercio. Tampa, Fla.: Commercial Pub. Co; 1941-19uu.
Weekly.
Editor: J. C. Otero. In Spanish. In OCLC system.
El Comercio del Valle. St. Louis, Mo.: John F. Cahill, 1876-1890?
Monthly.
"Dedicado a los intereses comerciales y manufactureros del Valle Misisipi". "Organo de los comerciantes continentales y [sic] isleños de ambas Américas". Published until 1890, cf. Chabrán, Rafael and Richard Chabrán, "The Spanish-Language and Latino Press of the United States: Newspapers and Periodicals." In Spanish with some English. In OCLC system.
El Comercio Ilustrado. San Francisco, California: A. P. Alvarey, 1894?-1906.
Monthly.
Listed in *Rowell's American Newspaper Directory,* 1902. In "Más de cuatrocientos periódicos en español se han editado en Estados Unidos", title is listed as *El Comercio,* with publication dates of 1895-1906. In Spanish. No extant issues located.
Comercio Interamericano. Washington, D. C.: Pan American Union, 1946-1953.
Monthly.
In Spanish. In OCLC system.
El Comercio Mexicano . Corpus Christi, Tex.: Catarino Garza, 1888-1uuu.
Mentioned in Somoza, *Literatura de la Revolución Mexicana. . .,* p. 247. No extant issues located.
El Comercio Mexicano. Eagle Pass, Texas: Catarino E. Garza, 1886-1uuu.
Weekly.
According to "Memoirs of Catarino E. Garza," manuscript by Garza held at the library of the University of Texas at Austin, he established this newspaper in Eagle Pass with first issue dated June 20, 1886. He indicates that Adolfo Duclós Salinas was a co-writer, and that the paper existed for a number of years. Listed in "Más de cuatrocientos periódicos en español se han editado en Estados Unidos". In Spanish. No extant issues located.
La Cometa. Folsom, Nuevo México: Manuel B. Sisneros, 19uu-19uu.
Weekly.
Vol. 1, no. 21 dated mar. 9, 1912. In Spanish and English. In OCLC system.
El Cometa. Nueva York, 1855-1uuu.
In Spanish. An inventory list from the Archivo Nacional de Cuba, Havana, indicates the paper is a successor of *El Papagayo,* edited by José Mesa and directed by Miguel Teurbe Tolón. The inventory list is in the collection of the Recovering the U. S. Hispanic Literary Heritage project.
El Cometa. Raton, N. M., 1910-19uu.
Mentioned in Somoza, *Literatura de la Revolución Mexicana. . .,* p. 242. No extant issues located.
El Cometa. Wagon Mound, N. M., 1985-1uuu.
Mentioned in *El Clamor Público,* Aug. 7, 1855; cf. Somoza, *Literatura de la Revolución Mexicana...,* p. 245. No extant issues located.
El Compañero. Springfield, Michigan: Gospel Publishing House, 19uu-19uu.
Quarterly.
Listed in Common Council for American Unity, *Foreign Language Publications in the*

United States: Newspaper Lists, p. 4. No extant issues located.

Compendio Médico. New York, N.Y.: Merck Sharp & Dohme International, 19uu-.
Quarterly.
Año 29, no. 86 dated marzo 1960. In Spanish. In OCLC system.

El Comprador Hispano-Americano. New York, N.Y.: A. S. Baker & Co., 1888?-1902?
Monthly.
Listed in *Rowell's American Newspaper Directory,* 1896, with starting date of 1888, also listed in "Más de cuatrocientos periódicos en español se han editado en Estados Unidos". No extant issues located.

Concarajícara. New York, 1897?-1uuu.
Repository: Archivo Nacional de Cuba, Havana.

Conquista Juvenil. Kansas City, Mo.: Junta Internacional de Publicaciones de la Iglesia del Nazareno, 1955-.
In Spanish. In OCLC system.

Conquistadores. Edición de Alumnos. El Paso, Tex.: Casa Bautista de Publicaciones; Nashville, Tenn.: Baptist Sunday School Board, 19uu-.
Quartely.
T. 55, no. 1 dated enero-feb.-marzo 1982. In Spanish. In OCLC system.

Conquistadores. Edición de Maestros. Nashville, Tenn.: Baptist Sunday School Board; El Paso, Tex.: Casa Bautista de Publicaciones, 19uu-.
T. 55, no. 1 dated enero-feb. 1982. In Spanish. In OCLC system.

El Consejero. McAllen, Tex.: La Imprenta P & R, 1958, 19uu.
Monthly.
Editors: Wayne Partain and Glenn Rogers. In OCLC system.

La Contienda: Radical Cubano. Tampa, Fla.,: 1897-1898.
Editor: Eligio Carbonell. Redactor: Néstor Leonello Carbonell. Listed in Batista Villareal, Teresita, *Catálogo de Publicaciones periódicas cubanas...*, p. 129. This source indicates that the Biblioteca Nacional José Martí in La Havana holds some issues of this title.

El Continental. El Paso, Tex.: World-News, 1926?-19uu.
Daily (except Saturday).
Vol. 10, no. 157 dated 12 de dic. de 1934. "Diario independiente para los mexicanos." In Spanish. In OCLC system.

El Continental. New York, 191u?-19uu.
Monthly.
Directors: Manuel J. Sierra, Héctor and Horacio Casasús, Rodrigo de Llano, and Carlos Serrano; cf. Sax, Antimaco, *Los mexicanos en el destierro,* p. 57. No extant issues located.

El Continental. Nueva York [N.Y.]: Charles B. Richardson y Cía., 1862-186u.
Weekly.
Vol. 2 no. 1 dated 1 de agosto de 1862. Published on the sailing day of the steamer for Havana and Panama, for circulation in the United States, Cuba, México, and South America. Continues *Boletín de Noticias y Precios Corrientes* (New York, N.Y.). In Spanish. In OCLC system.

La Constitución. El Paso, Tex.: Emilio Valenzuela and José Luis Velasco, 191u?-19uu.
Mentioned in Sax, Antimaco, *Los mexicanos en el destierro,* p. 56. No extant issues located.

The Corpus Christi Ranchero. Santa Margarita, Tex.: H.A. Maltby, 1863-1864.
Weekly.
In OCLC system.

The Corpus Christi Star = Estrella de Corpus Christi. Corpus Christi, Texas: John H. Peoples, 1848-1uuu.
Weekly.
In English and Spanish. In OCLC system.

La Corregidora. Laredo, Texas: Sara Estela Ramírez, 190u-19uu.

Mentioned in Zamora, Emilio. "Sara Estela Ramírez: una rosa roja en el movimiento". No extant issues located.

El Correo. Douglas, Arizona: Correo Pub. Co.; C.G. Scriano, ed., 1906-19uu.

Weekly

Listed in "Mas de cuatrocientos periódicos en español se han editado en Estados Unidos", and *N. W. Ayer & Son's American Newspaper Annual,* 1906. No extant issues located.

El Correo. San Antonio, Tex.: J. Zúñiga y A. Lewis, 1858-18uu.

Weekly.

In Spanish. In OCLC system.

El Correo. Tucson, Ariz.: Amado Cota-Robles, 1922-19uu.

Listed in Miguélez, Armando, "Index of Spanish-Language Newspapers in the U. S. Southwest." No extant issues located.

El Correo de Santa Fe. Santa Fe, N. M., 1869-1uuu.

Mentioned in Somoza, *Literatura de la Revolución Mexicana. . .*, p. 242. No extant issues located.

El Correo de Tucson. Tucson, Ariz., 1921-19uu.

Cited in *El Tucsonense,* ago. 13, 1921; cf. Somoza, *Literatura de la Revolución Mexicana...*, p. 228. No extant issues located.

Correo Americano de Medicina y Cirugía. New York, 1923-1924.

In OCLC system.

El Correo Americano y Diario Exportación. New York, N.Y., 18uu-1897.

Monthly.

V. 33, no. 1 dated 1896. Spanish edition of *American Mail and Export Journal.* Absorbed by *American Exporter.* In Spanish. In OCLC system.

El Correo Atlántico: Periódico Polígloto, Comercial, Político y Literario.

New Orleans, Louisiana, 1836.

Weekly.

Published in Mexico City, Mexico in 1835, cf. *A History and Bibliography of Spanish-language Newspapers and Magazines in Louisiana, 1808-1949.* In Spanish. In OCLC system.

El Correo de América. New York, N.Y.: Manuel Vélez, 1897-1uuu.

Semi-monthly.

Listed in "Más de cuatrocientos periódicos en español se han editado en Estados Unidos". In Spanish. Repository: Archivo Nacional de Cuba, Havana.

El Correo de América. Tucson, Ariz.: Luis G. Montejano, 1918-19uu.

Listed in Miguélez, Armando, "Index of Spanish-Language Newspapers in the U. S. Southwest." Miguélez indicates the paper is mentioned in *El Tucsonense,* 17-VI, 1922. No extant issues located.

El Correo de Cuba. New Orleans, Louisiana: C. J. Elizaldi, ed., 1898-1uuu.

Weekly.

Listed in MacCurdy, Raymond R., *A History and Bibliography of Spanish-Language Newspapers and Magazines in Louisiana, 1808-1949.* In Spanish. No extant issues located.

El Correo de la Virgen. San Juan, Hidalgo County, Texas: Shrine of Our Lady Of San Juan, 195u-.

Año 2 núm. 101 dated 18 de abril de 1954. Repository: University of Texas-Pan American.

El Correo de Laredo. Laredo, Tex., 1891-1uuu.

Daily (except Monday and holidays), July 1891-Jan. 1892, triweekly, Feb. 1892-1894, semiweekly, 1894.

"Diario imparcial y de noticias". Editor: Justo Cárdenas, 1891. In Spanish. In OCLC system.

El Correo de México. Chicago, Illinois, 1922-19uu.

Listed in Chabrán, Rafael and Richard Chabrán, "The Spanish-Language and Latino Press of the United States: Newspapers and Periodicals," p. 37. In Spanish. No extant issues located.

El Correo de México. Los Angeles, Calif.: Juan de Heras, 1915-19uu.

Listed in Miguélez, Armando, "Index of Spanish-Language Newspapers in the U. S. Southwest." Miguélez indicates the paper is mentioned in *La Crónica,* San Francisco, 25-IX-1915, c.2. No extant issues located.

El Correo de Nueva York. Nueva York, N.Y.: L. Lameda Díaz, 18uu-1uuu.

Weekly.

No. 33 dated mayo 7 de 1874. Editor: Lisandro Lameda Díaz, 1874. In Spanish. In OCLC system. Also, the Archivo Nacional de Cuba in Havana, holds some issues for years 1873, 1874 and 1875.

Correo de Santa Fe (Santa Fe, New Mexico). *See* **The Santa Fe Daily Post.**

El Correo de Ultramar. San Francisco, Calif., 18uu-1uuu.

Listed in Miguélez, Armando, "Index of Spanish-Language Newspapers in the U. S. Southwest." Miguélez indicates "Se vendía en la librería Louis Gregoire, San Francisco, en 1878." No extant issues located.

El Correo del Bravo. El Paso, Tex.: Darío M. González, 191u-19uu.

Daily.

Época 1, t. 1, no. 85 dated 13 de marzo de 1913. In OCLC system.

El Correo del Río Grande. Brownsville, Texas: E. P. Claudon & Co., 1866?-1uuu.

Daily (except Monday).

Vol. 1, no. 284 dated Jan. 3, 1867. Continues *Courrier du Rio-Grande.* In Spanish and English. In OCLC system.

El Correo del Valle. St. Louis, Missouri, 1880-1886.

Monthly.

Reappeared in 1887 under the name *El Comercio del Valle* until 1890, cf. Chabrán, Rafael and Richard Chabrán, "The Spanish-Language and Latino Press of the United States: Newspapers and Periodicals." In Spanish. No extant issues located.

El Correo Hispano-Americano. New York, N.Y.: Western & Co., 1868-1uuu.

Monthly.

"Devoted to commerce, agriculture, mining," cf. *Rowell's American Newspaper Directory,* 1869. No extant issues located.

El Correo Mexicano. Bakersfield, California, 1913-19uu.

Irregular.

Listed in Ríos-C., Herminio, "Toward a True Chicano Bibliography: Part II," 1972, p. 40, and "Más de cuatrocientos periódicos en español se han editado en Estados Unidos". In Spanish. No extant issues located.

El Correo Mexicano. Douglas, Arizona, 1916-19uu.

Irregular.

Listed in Ríos-C., Herminio, "Toward a True Chicano Bibliography: Part II" and "Más de cuatrocientos periódicos en español se han editado en Estados Unidos". In Spanish. No extant issues located.

El Correo Mexicano. Los Angeles, Calif.: T. Campos, 1907-19uu.

Weekly.

Vol. 11, no. 497 dated oct. 18 de 1917. "Semanario dedicado exclusivamente a la defensa del pueblo mexicano". In Spanish. In OCLC system.

El Correo Mexicano. San Antonio, Texas: J. Zuniga and A. Lewis, 1890-1914.

Weekly.

Supported U. S. cause in Spanish-American War of 1898. Listed in *Rowell's American Newspaper Directory,* 1902. Also listed in "Más de cuatrocientos periódicos en español se han editado en Estados Unidos", with publication dates of 1898-1914. In

Spanish. Repository: University of New Mexico.

Correo Mexicano: El Diario de la Raza. Chicago, Illinois: Francisco Huerta, 1926-19uu.
Daily.
In Spanish. In OCLC system.

El Correo Universal. Los Angeles, California, 1881-1uuu.
Bi-weekly.
Listed in "Más de cuatrocientos periódicos en español se han editado en Estados Unidos". In Spanish. No extant issues located.

La Correspondencia. San Francisco, California, 1885-1887?
Weekly.
Listed in Gregory, Winifred, ed., *American Newspapers, 1821-1936,* p. 52. In Spanish. Repository: Bancroft Library (University of California, Berkeley).

Corriere del Popolo. Gary, Indiana: Nicolo Accomando, 1920-1927.
"Changed its title to *Americans All* and printed editions in English, Spanish and Italian," cf. Miller, John W., *Indiana Newspaper Bibliography: Historical Accounts For All Indiana Newspapers Published From 1804-1980...,* p.228-229. No extant issues located.

Cosas. Nueva York, [N.Y.]: Fernando García, 1931-19uu.
Editor: Fernando García. In Spanish with some text in English. Repository: Center for Puerto Rican Studies at Hunter College.

El Cosmopolita. Alice, Tex., 19uu-19uu. Vol. 7, no. 42 dated May 27, 1912.
Director: Eulalio Velázquez. In Spanish. In OCLC system.

El Cosmopolita. Clayton, Nuevo México: Félix D. Valdez, 191u-19uu.
Weekly.
Año 1, no. 2 dated 9 de oct. 1919. In Spanish and English. In OCLC system.

El Cosmopolita. Kansas City, Mo.; Kansas City, Kansas: Cosmopolita Pub. Co., 1914-1919.
Weekly.
Published in Kansas City, Mo. Oct. 1, 1914 - Nov. 15, 1919. In OCLC system.

Costilla County Free Press. San Luis, Colorado: Alfonso J. LaCombe, 1948-.
Weekly.
Continues *El Demócrata del Condado de Costilla.* In English and Spanish. In OCLC system.

Le Courier. Chicago, Illinois, 1895-1uuu.
Listed in "Más de cuatrocientos periódicos en español se han editado en Estados Unidos". In Spanish and French. No extant issues located.

El Crepúsculo. San Francisco, Calif., 1873-1874.
Repository: Bancroft Library (University of California, Berkeley) has issue of March 28, 1874; cf. Somoza, *Literatura de la Revolución Mexicana...,* p. 234.

El Crepúsculo. Taos, New Mexico, 1948-1955.
Weekly.
"Founded by Padre Martínez in 1835." "Sucessor to the Taoseño Valley News, and La Revista de Taos." In OCLC system.

El Crepúsculo de la Libertad. Santa Fe, New Mexico, 1834-183u.
Weekly.
Mentioned in Gutiérrez, "Spanish-language media in America," p. 34. In Spanish and English. No extant issues located.

El Crepúsculo de la Libertad. Taos, New Mexico: Edward C. Cabot, 1955-1960.
Weekly.
Vol. 7, no. 24 dated June 16, 1955. Includes Spanish section: "Sección español." Continues *Crepúsculo* (Taos, N. M.). Absorbed by *Taos News.* In Spanish and English. In OCLC system.

La Crisis. Los Angeles, Calif., 1930-19uu.
Listed in Miguélez, Armando, "Index of Spanish-Language Newspapers in the U. S.

Southwest." No extant issues located.

El Crisol. Nueva York, N.Y.: El Crisol Co. Pub., 1945-19uu.

Weekly.

Año 5, no. 22 dated 28 de mayo de 1949. "Director-Gerente: José A. Quintero". Repository: Center for Puerto Rican Studies at Hunter College, CUNY.

El Cromo. Río Grande, Texas, 1891-1uuu.

Semi-monthly.

Directors: Antonio García del Formel, Pedro Maldonado. Listed in "Más de cuatrocientos periódicos en español se han editado en Estados Unidos". In Spanish. No extant issues located.

La Crónica. Calexico, California, 1924-1934.

Weekly.

Directors: Isaac Aceves, José S. Castillo & José Gou. Listed in Ríos-C., Herminio, "Toward a True Chicano Bibliography: Part II," and "Más de cuatrocientos periódicos en español se han editado en Estados Unidos". No extant issues located.

La Crónica. Laredo, Tex.: [Idar e Hijos], 1909-19uu.

Weekly.

2.a época, t. 1, no. 52 dated 1 de enero de 1910. "Periódico semanal independiente". In Spanish. In OCLC system.

La Crónica. Logan, New Mexico, 1907-19uu.

Irregular.

Listed in "Más de cuatrocientos periódicos en español se han editado en Estados Unidos". In Spanish. No extant issues located.

La Crónica. Los Angeles, California: Teodoli & Co., 1872-1892?

Weekly, May 4, 1872-Jan. 25, 1873; semi-weekly, Feb. 1, 1873-; weekly, 1883-.

Ceased with July 27, 1892 issue? "Only Spanish newspaper in Southern California." In Spanish and English. In OCLC system.

La Crónica. Mora, New Mexico, 1889-1uuu.

Irregular.

Listed in "Más de cuatrocientos periódicos en español se han editado en Estados Unidos". In Spanish. No extant issues located.

La Crónica. New York, [N.Y.]: A. X. San Martín, 1848-1867.

Semiweekly; triweekly, 1848-1853.

Año 1, no. 28 dated 27 de enero de 1849. Began in Nov. 1848, cf. Willging, Eugene Paul and Herta Hatzfeld, *Catholic Serials of the Nineteenth Century in the United States.* Ceased in May 1867, cf. Gregory, Winifred, ed., *American Newspapers, 1821-1936.* Editor: M. de la Peña, 1862-1863. Continued by *Cronista.* In Spanish. In OCLC system.

La Crónica. Nueva York, [N.Y.]: Marcial Rivera, 1949?-19uu.

Weekly.

Año 1, no. 19 dated enero 14, 1950. Repository: Center for Puerto Rican Studies at Hunter College. In Spanish.

La Crónica. San Francisco: [J. Jofre & J.T. de Lafuente], 185u-1uuu.

Triweekly.

Vol. 1, no. 53 dated 15 de dic. de 1854. "Organo de la población española en California". In Spanish. In OCLC system.

La Crónica. San Francisco, Ca.: J. C. Castro, 1914-1917.

Weekly.

Continued by *Hispano América* (San Francisco, Calif.). In Spanish. In OCLC system.

La Crónica de Mora. Mora, Nuevo México: Louis Hommel, 1889-1890.

Weekly.

Continued by *El Demócrata de Mora.* Variant title: *Mora Chronicle.* In English and Spanish. In OCLC system.

La Crónica de Valencia. Las Cruces, New Mexico, 1890-1895.

Irregular.

Listed in "Más de cuatrocientos periódicos en español se han editado en Estados Unidos". Also listed in Grove, Pearce S., *New Mexico Newspapers,* p. 581. In Spanish. No extant issues located.

La Crónica del Río Colorado (La Cinta, New Mexico). *See* **La Crónica del Río Colorado** (San Lorenzo, New Mexico).

La Crónica del Río Colorado. San Hilario, N. M.: Dorsett Hermanos, 1882-1884.
Weekly.

Began publication with año 2, no. 46 dated Nov. 11 de 1882. Ceased Sept. 26, 1884, cf. Groves, Pearce S., *New Mexico Newspapers.* A companion newspaper was titled *Red River Chronicle* (San Hilario, N. M.). Continues *Crónica del Río Colorado* (San Lorenzo, N. M.). In Spanish. In OCLC system.

La Crónica del Río Colorado. San Lorenzo, N. M.: Dorsett Hermanos, 1880-1882.
Weekly.

Began publication c. Aug. 21, 1880, cf. Grove, Pearce S., *New Mexico Newspapers.* Published in La Cinta around June 26, 1880-August 14, 1880, cf. Grove, p. 393. A companion newspaper was titled *Red River Chronicle* (San Lorenzo, N. M.). Continues *Crónica del Río Colorado* (La Cinta, N.M). Continued by *Crónica del Río Colorado* (San Hilario, N. M.). In Spanish. In OCLC system.

La Crónica Mexicana. Bakersfield, California, 1895-1uuu.
Irregular.

Listed in "Más de cuatrocientos periódicos en español se han editado en Estados Unidos". In Spanish. No extant issues located.

El Cronista. Los Angeles, California: Cronista Pub. Co., 1906-19uu.
Irregular.

Editor: F. S. Manje. Listed in "Más de cuatrocientos periódicos en español se han editado en Estados Unidos", and *N. W. Ayer & Son's American Newspaper Annual,* 1906. In Spanish. No extant issues located.

El Cronista. Nogales, Arizona, 1894-1uuu.

Listed in "Más de cuatrocientos periódicos en español se han editado en Estados Unidos". In Spanish. No extant issues located.

El Cronista. Nueva York: José Ferrer de Couto, 1867-1877.
Semiweekly.

Editor: José Ferrer de Couto, 1876. Continues *La Crónica* (New York, N.Y.), 1848-1867. In Spanish. In OCLC system.

El Cronista. San Francisco, Calif.: El Cronista, 1884-1uuu.
Weekly; Semiweekly.

In Spanish. In OCLC system.

El Cronista Americano. New York, 1888-18uu.
Mentioned in Chamberlin, p. 3. No extant issues located.

El Cronista del Valle. Brownsville, Tex., 1917-19uu.
Daily (except Monday); irregular, Sept. 1927; weekly, irregular, Oct. 1927-.
2a época, t. 6, no. 183 dated 8 de oct. de 1924. In Spanish. In OCLC system.

El Cronista Mexicano. Merced, Calif., 1894-1uuu.
Mentioned in *El Fronterizo* (Tucson), March 10, 1894, p. 3; cf. Somoza, *Literatura de la Revolución Mexicana...,* p. 233. No extant issues located.

El Cronista Mexicano. San Antonio, Texas: León A. Obregón & Co., 1891?-1901.
Weekly; bi-weekly.

Editor: T. del Valle; Director: Alberto F. Martínez. Listed in "Más de cuatrocientos periódicos en español se han editado en Estados Unidos", and *Rowell's American Newspaper Directory,* 1896. No extant issues located.

Las Cruces Citizen. Las Cruces, New Mexico: H. & E. Gruver [etc.], 1902-1968.
Weekly.

Absorbed by *Las Cruces Sun-News*. Listed in Gregory, Winifred, ed., *American Newspapers, 1821-1936;* and "Más de cuatrocientos periódicos en español se han editado en Estados Unidos". These sources indicate the periodical was in English and Spanish during the early years. In OCLC system.

Las Cruces Daily News. Las Cruces, New Mexico: James Kibbee, 1889-1889.
> Daily.
> Vol. 1, no. 31 dated mar. 5, 1889. Continued by *Daily News* (Las Cruces, N. M.: 1889). In English. In OCLC system.

Las Cruces Daily Times. Las Cruces, New Mexico: Valdez & MacDonald, 1889-1uuu.
> Daily.
> Old series, v. 8, no. 17 dated May 4, 1889. In English and Spanish. In OCLC system.

Cuba. New York, N. Y.: Cuba Pub. Co., 189u-1uuu.
> Weekly.
> Año 2, no. 3 dated enero 15 de 1898. In OCLC system.

Cuba. New York City: Cuban Chamber of Commerce in the United States, 1932-19uu.
> Monthly.
> Vol. 4, no. 12 dated Dec. 1932. "A monthly review of Cuba trade and economics." Continues *Journal,* Cuban Chamber of Commerce in the United States, Journal. In OCLC system.

Cuba. Tampa, Florida: José G. Rivero, Pub., 1893-1899.
> Weekly, tri-weekly.
> Año 1 núm. 25 dated 9 de septiembre de 1893. Director: R. Rivero y Rivero. Listed in "Más de cuatrocientos periódicos en español se han editado en Estados Unidos" and *Rowell's American Newspaper Directory,* 1896. In Spanish. Repository: Tony Pizzo Collection University of South Florida, Tampa, and Archivo Nacional de Cuba, Havana.

Cuba Libre. Miami, Fla, 1959-19uu.
> Directores: Rafael Guas Indán y José Ignacio Acosta, cf. Peraza Sarausa, Fermín, *Directorio de Revistas y Periódicos de Cuba.* No extant issues located.

Cuba Libre. New York, 1895?-1uuu.
> Repository: Archivo Nacional de Cuba, Havana.

Cuba Libre. Washington, 1898-1uuu.
> Weekly.
> Editor: Wilburton Benham. In English. Listed in Batista Villareal, Teresita, *Catálogo de Publicaciones periódicas cubanas...,* p. 132. This source indicates that the Biblioteca Nacional José Martí in La Havana holds some issues of this title.

Cuba Sugar Manual. *See* **Manual Azucarero de Cuba = Cuba Sugar Manual.**

Cuba y América. New York: Manuel Montero, 1897-1898.
> Weekly.
> "Política, intereses generales y variedades; crítica, sátira, ilustraciones y caricaturas". In LOCIS system.

Cuba y Puerto Rico. New York, 1897-18uu.
> Director: Gerardo Forrest. Listed in Batista Villareal, Teresita, *Catálogo de Publicaciones periódicas cubanas...,* p. 132. This source indicates that the Biblioteca Nacional José Martí in La Havana holds some issues of this title.

Cuban News. Miami, Fla.:, Cuban Pub. Co., 1935–1935?
> In OCLC system.

Cuban Herald. Tampa, Florida, 1902-19uu.
> Listed in Batista Villareal, Teresita, *Catálogo de Publicaciones periódicas cubanas...,* p. 151. This source indicates that the Biblioteca Nacional José Martí in La Havana holds some issues of this title.

El Cubano. Key West, Florida: Pedro Pequeño and Néstor Carbonell, 1890-1892.
> Daily.
> Mentioned in Poyo, *For All and for the Good of All...,* p. 87. Also listed in "Más de cua-

trocientos periódicos en español se han editado en Estados Unidos". In Spanish. No extant issues located.

El Cubano. New York?, 1889?-1uuu.
Repository:Archivo Nacional de Cuba, Havana.

El Cubano. Nueva York, 1852-1854.
Redactor: Miguel Teurbe Tolón. Listed in Batista Villareal, Teresita, *Catálogo de Publicaciones periódicas cubanas...*, p. 132. This source indicates that the Biblioteca Nacional José Martí in Havana holds some issues of this title.

El Cubano. Tampa, Ybor City, Florida, 191u?-19uu.
Pizzo Colletion at University of South Florida, Tampa, holds a "Suplemento" to this newspaper dated sept. 9 de 1916. No other extant issues located.

La Cucaracha. Tucson, Ariz., 1925-19uu.
Mentioned in Sheridan, *Los Tucsonenses*, p. 203. No extant issues located.

Cultura. Stevens Point, Wisconsin: Worzalla Pub. Co., 1925-19uu.
Monthly.
Adolfo Terres, editor. Listed in *N. W. Ayer & Son's American Newspaper Annual and Directory,* 1928. In Spanish. No extant issues located.

Cultura Hispánica. New York, N.Y.: F. Mayans, 1926-19uu.
Monthly.
Listed in *N. W. Ayer & Son's American Newspaper Annual and Directory,* 1927. In Spanish. No extant issues located.

Cultura Obrera. New York, N.Y.: Cultura Obrera, 19uu-19uu.
Vol. 6, no. 260 dated 22 June 1918. Issues for Sept. 1924-, called *Nueva época.* "Educación, Organización, Emancipación". "Periódico obrero, de doctrina y de combate". In Spanish. In OCLC system.

Cultura Proletaria: Periódico de Ideas, Doctrina y Combate. Nueva York: Cultura Proletaria, 1927-1953.
Weekly, 1927-July 16, 1932; irregular, July 30, 1932-.
In Spanish. In OCLC system.

Cumbres. Victoria, Tex.: Servando Cárdenas, 1939-1941.
Mentioned in Somoza, *Literatura de la Revolución Mexicana...*, p. 252. No extant issues located.

El Curioso. Brooklyn, N.Y., 1934-19uu.
Weekly.
Año 1, no. 14 dated julio 28 de 1934. "Semanario satírico, jocoso y comercial". Director: Crescencio Gómez; editor: Guillermo C. Peña. In OCLC system.

The Daily Chronicle. Las Vegas, N.M:
[Chronicle Pub. Co.], 1884–18uu.
Spanish section titled "La Crónica de las Vegas". In OCLC system.

Daily Gazette (Las Vegas, New Mexico). *See* **Las Vegas Daily Gazette.**

Daily Guide. Eagle Pass, Texas: Jas. O. Boehmer, 1917-1939.
Daily (except Sunday).
Continues *Eagle Pass News-Guide;* Absorbed *Quemado Valley Sun.* Continued by *International News Guide.* Variant titles: *Eagle Pass Daily Guide.* In English and Spanish. In OCLC system.

The Daily New Mexican. Santa Fe, N. M.: Manderfield & Tucker, 1868-1881.
Daily.
Spanish section: *Nuevo Mejicano Diario,* July 9, 1868-Dec. 29, 1877. Weekly eds: *Nuevo Mejicano* (Santa Fe, N. M.: 1863), and *Weekly New Mexican,* Oct. 27, 1868-Aug. 16, 1880. Continued by *Santa Fe Daily New Mexican* (Santa Fe, N. M.: 1881). In English and Spanish. In OCLC system.

The Daily Ranchero and Republican. Brownsville, Texas: J. S. Mansur & Co., 1859-1879?
Daily.

Continues *Daily Ranchero* (Matamoros, México). In English and Spanish. In OCLC system.

Daily Reporter. Tucson, Ariz.: Carmen Cecilia Beltrán, 1950-19uu.

Mentioned in Somoza, *Literatura de la Revolución Mexicana...*, p. 229. No extant issues located.

The Daily Times. Las Cruces, New Mexico: Marcial Valdez and E. Gándara, 1893-1uuu.

Daily.

Vol. 1, no. 2 dated Jan. 10, 1893. Includes a Spanish section entitled "El Tiempo: Diario de Las Cruces, N. M." Variant title: *El Tiempo.* In English and Spanish. In OCLC system.

Daily Times (El Paso, Texas, 1886-1889). *See* **The El Paso Times.**

Dallas Americano. Dallas, Tex.: Ochoa Newspaper, 195u-19uu.

Weekly.

Vol. 5, no. 32 dated January 1, 1958. In English and Spanish. In OCLC system.

De Baca County News (Santa Rosa, New Mexico). *See* **The Santa Rosa News.**

El Debate. New York, N.Y.: Frank Mayans, 1929?-1932.

Weekly.

Listed in "Más de cuatrocientos periódicos en español se han editado en Estados Unidos", with publication dates of 1931 to 1932. Also listed in *N.W. Ayer & Son's Directory of Newspapers and Periodicals,* 1932, with starting publication date of 1929. In Spanish. No extant issues located.

El Deber. New York, 1894-18uu.

Weekly.

Director: Gumersindo Rivas. In 1896 was in its 2nd epoch. Listed in Batista Villareal, Teresita, *Catálogo de Publicaciones periódicas cubanas...*, p. 135. This source indicates that the Biblioteca Nacional José Martí in La Havana holds some issues of this title.

Defender of the People (Socorro, N. M.). *See* **El Defensor del Pueblo** (Socorro, N. M.).

La Defensa. Chicago, Illinois, 1933-19uu.

Editor: José de Mora. Cited in Chabrán, Rafael and Richard Chabrán, "The Spanish-Language and Latino Press of the United States: Newspapers and Periodicals," p. 372. In Spanish. No extant issues located.

La Defensa. Nueva York: José Cintrón, 1941-19uu.

Weekly.

Director: Juan J. Blasini, sub-director: Juan Emmanuelli, administrator: Jack P. Saladaña. Repository: Erasmo Vando Collection, Hunter College, CUNY.

La Defensa. San Antonio, Texas, 1917?-1921.

Weekly.

Listed in Ríos-C., Herminio, "Toward a True Chicano Bibliography: Part II," p. 47, with a starting date of 1917. Also listed in "Más de cuatrocientos periódicos en español se han editado en Estados Unidos", with starting date of 1920. In Spanish. No extant issues located.

La Defensa. Tampa, Florida, 1916-19uu.

Irregular.

Director: Manuel de Jesús Parrilla. Associated with La Sociedad de Torcedores de Tampa, the cigar workers union also known as La Resistencia, cf. Chabrán, Rafael and Richard Chabrán, "The Spanish-Language and Latino Press of the United States: Newspapers and Periodicals," p. 370. In Spanish. In OCLC system.

La Defensa del Ideal Católico Mexicano. Chicago, Illinois. 1uuu-1uuu.

Listed in Chabrán, Rafael and Richard Chabrán, "The Spanish-Language and Latino Press of the United States: Newspapers and Periodicals," p. 373. In Spanish. No extant issues located.

Defensa Obrera. Chicago, Illinois: Comité General de Defensa de los Trabajadores Industriales del Mundo, 1918-19uu.

In Spanish and English. In OCLC system.

El Defensor. Edinburg, Tex.: El Defensor Pub. Co., 1929-1932.

Weekly.

Official organ of the League of United Latin American Citizens (LULAC), Sept. 1931- ; of Latin American Citizens Association of Hidalgo County, Texas, Oct. 1931-. In English and Spanish. In OCLC system.

El Defensor. El Paso, Tex.: Sociedad de los Caballeros del Progeso, 1894-1uuu.

Weekly.

T. 1, no. 2 dated sept. 24 de 1894. Organo Oficial de la Sociedad de los Caballeros del Progreso. In Spanish. In OCLC system.

El Defensor. Socorro, New Mexico: A. D. Morgan, 1950-1959.

Weekly.

Began with Vol. 46, no. 2398 dated May 26, 1950; ceased with vol. 60, no. 43 dated Oct. 28, 1959. Continues *El Defensor del Pueblo* (Socorro, N. M.). Merged with *Socorro Chieftain* (Socorro, N. M.): 1902) to form *El Defensor Chieftain*. Includes a Spanish-language section. In OCLC system.

El Defensor. Tucson, Ariz.: Nicolette, 1uuu-1uuu.

Listed in Miguélez, Armando, "Index of Spanish-Language Newspapers in the U. S. Southwest." Miguélez indicates the paper is mentioned in *El Tucsonense;* no dates are given for this source. No extant issues located.

El Defensor Chieftain. Socorro (N. M.): Jeanette and Lucien File, 1959-.

Semi-weekly (1966); weekly.

Began with Vol. 93, no. 161 dated Nov. 3, 1959-. Formed by the union of *Socorro Chieftain* (Socorro, N. M.: 1902) and *Defensor* (Socorro, N. M.). Variant titles: *Defensor-Socorro Chieftain,* Nov. 10, 1959 and *Chieftain-El Defensor,* Nov. 3, 1959. In OCLC system.

El Defensor del Obrero. Laredo, Tex., 1906-19uu.

Weekly.

In OCLC system.

Defensor del Pueblo. Albuquerque, N. M., 1891-1uuu.

Mentioned in Somoza, *Literatura de la Revolución Mexicana. . .,* p. 237. No extant issues located.

Defensor del Pueblo. Clayton, N. M., 1902-19uu.

In English and Spanish. Mentioned in Somoza, *Literatura de la Revolución Mexicana...,* p. 240. No extant issues located.

Defensor del Pueblo. El Paso, Tex.: Manuel Sarabia, 1906-19uu.

Mentioned in Somoza, *Literatura de la Revolución Mexicana. . .,* p. 248. No extant issues located.

El Defensor del Pueblo. La Mesilla, N. M.: Pedro García de la Lama, 1890-1892.

Weekly.

Published in La Mesilla, July 26-Dec. 20, 1890; in Las Cruces, Jan. 3-May 30, 1891; in Albuquerque, June 27, 1891-May 28, 1892. In Spanish. In OCLC system.

El Defensor del Pueblo. Laredo, Texas, 19uu-19uu.

Cited in Chabrán, Rafael and Richard Chabrán, "The Spanish-Language and Latino Press of the United States: Newspapers and Periodicals," p. 368. In Spanish. No extant issues located.

El Defensor del Pueblo. San Luis, Colorado, 1909-1914.

Weekly, irregular.

Listed in Oehlerts, Donald E., *Guide to Colorado Newspapers, 1859-1963,* p. 23, and "Más de cuatrocientos periódicos en español se han editado en Estados Unidos". No extant issues located.

El Defensor del Pueblo. Socorro, Nuevo México: [Torres Hermanos] 1904-1950.

Weekly.

Includes section in English:"The Defender of the People," Sept. 2, 1938-June 23, 1939. Continued by *Defensor* (Socorro, N. M.). In Spanish. In OCLC system.

El Defensor del Pueblo. Tucson, Ariz., 1904-19uu.

Mentioned in Sheridan, *Los Tucsonenses*, p. 203. No extant issues located.

El Defensor Popular. Denver, Colorado, 1924-1925.

Weekly.

Listed in Oehlerts, Donald E., *Guide to Colorado Newspapers, 1859-1963*, p. 48. In Spanish. No extant issues located.

Defensor-Socorro Chieftain (Socorro, New Mexico). *See* **El Defensor Chieftain.**

Delta. New York: Resp Log. Simb. Benito Juárez, 1937-19uu.

Irregular.

"Revista cultural masónico social." "Organo de la Respetable Logia Simb. Benito Juárez". In Spanish. In OCLC system.

La Democracia. El Paso, Tex.: W. Tovar y Bueno, 190u-19uu.

Weekly.

Vol. 1, no. 7 dated enero 14 de 1906. In OCLC system.

The Democrat and Ranchero. Brownsville, Tex., 1879-1880?

Semiweekly.

Vol. 6, no. 70 dated Sept. 27, 1879. Redactor: León A. Obregón. Formed by the union of *Weekly Ranchero* and *Río Grande Democrat.* Absorbed *Ranchero* (Brownsville, Tex.: 1866); Absorbed *Democrat* (Brownsville, Tex.). Pages 3 and 4 are in Spanish. In OCLC system.

El Demócrata. Albuquerque, N. M., 1878.

Mentioned in Somoza, *Literatura de la Revolución Mexicana...*, p. 238. Repository: Arizona State Department of Libraries and Archives.

El Demócrata. Albuquerque, New Mexico, 1931-19uu.

Irregular.

Listed in "Más de cuatrocientos periódicos en español se han editado en Estados Unidos". In Spanish. No extant issues located.

El Demócrata. Austin, Tex.: Enrique Muñoz, Jr., 1944-19uu.

Weekly.

In Spanish. In OCLC system.

El Demócrata. Brownsville, Tex., 1875?-18uu.

Semiweekly.

Tomo 4, no. 43 dated marzo 3, 1878. English ed.: *The Democrat.* In Spanish. In OCLC system.

Demócrata. Douglas, Arizona: C. G. Soriano, 1uuu-1uuu.

Weekly.

Listed in *N. W. Ayer & Son's American Newspaper Annual,* 1906, p. 1117. In Spanish. No extant issues located.

El Demócrata. La Mesilla, Nuevo México.: Benito Baca, 187u-18uu.

Weekly.

In Spanish. In OCLC system.

El Demócrata. Laredo, Texas, 1900-1918.

Weekly.

Suffered various interruptions. Listed in "Más de cuatrocientos periódicos en español se han editado en Estados Unidos". In Spanish. No extant issues located.

El Demócrata. Las Cruces, Nuevo México: Pedro G. de la Lama, 1894-1894.

Weekly.

In Spanish. In OCLC system.

El Demócrata. Las Vegas, New Mexico, 1895-1uuu.

Irregular.

Listed in "Más de cuatrocientos periódicos en español se han editado en Estados

Unidos". In Spanish. No extant issues located.

El Demócrata. Los Angeles, Calif.: Imp. del "Herald," 1882-1882?
Semiweekly.
Editor: Juan de Toro. In Spanish. In OCLC system.

El Demócrata. Nueva York, N.Y., 1870-1870.
Daily (except Sunday).
Began with Año 1, no. 89 dated 29 de agosto de 1870. Ceased with año 1, no. 185 dated 20 de dec. de 1870. Published in an English edition called *Democrat* (New York, N.Y.: 1868). Continues *Démocrata de Nueva York.* In Spanish. In OCLC system.

El Demócrata. Phoenix, Ariz.: Pedro G. de la Lama, 1898-19uu.
Weekly, 1898-Jan. 24, 1900; daily, Aug. 31, 1900.
T. 1, num. 2 dated feb. 12 de 1898. In Spanish. In OCLC system.

El Demócrata. San Diego, Tex.: F.G. Ramírez, 19uu-.
Weekly.
Vol. 5, no. 39 dated Apr. 18, 1941. In Spanish. In OCLC system.

El Demócrata. San Francisco, Calif.: Editorial Panamericano, 19uu-1952.
Weekly, July 7, 1949-Aug 25, 1949; biweekly, Mar. 15, 1951-Nov. 30, 1952.
Vol. 2, no. 26 dated 7 de jul. de 1949. In OCLC system.

El Demócrata. San Ygnacio, Tex.: Prof. A. Reina y García, 1915-19uu.
Weekly.
In Spanish. In OCLC system.

El Demócrata = The Democrat. Santa Fe, N. M.: Miguel E. Pino, 1857-18uu.
Weekly before elections, biweekly after elections.
In Spanish and English. In OCLC system.

Demócrata and La Aurora. Albuquerque, New Mexico: Daniel Jeantet, 1911-19uu.
Weekly.
Listed in *N.W. Ayer & Son's Directory of Newspapers and Periodicals,* 1934, p. 579. In Spanish. No extant issues located.

El Demócrata de Mora. Mora, New Mexico: Hosmer Bros., 1888-1889.
Weekly.
Continued by *Crónica de Mora.* Variant title: *Mora Democrat.* In English and Spanish. In OCLC system.

El Demócrata de Nueva York. Nueva York, N.Y., 1870-1870.
Daily (except Sunday).
Began with vol. 1, no. 40 dated junio 27, 1870; ceased with v. 1, no. 88 dated agosto 24, 1870. Continues *New York Democrat* (New York, N. Y.: 1870). Continued by *Demócrata* (New York, N. Y.) Also published in an English edition. In Spanish and English. In OCLC system.

El Demócrata del Condado de Costilla. San Luis, Colo.: Frank LaCome, 1923-1939?
Weekly.
Vol. 1, no. 24 dated Sept. 1, 1923. Published as *Costilla County Democrat,* Apr.-Oct. 1939. Continued by *Costilla County Free Press.* In English and Spanish. In OCLC system.

El Demócrata Fronterizo. Laredo, Texas: J. Cardenas, 1896?-1920?
Weekly, Dec. 8, 1917-May 12, 1919; daily (except Sunday), May 19, 1919-.
Began in 1896?; ceased in 1920?, cf. Gregory, Winifred, ed., *American Newspapers, 1821-1936.* Vol. 8, no. 382 dated ene. 7, 1904. In Spanish. In OCLC system.

El Demócrata Independiente. Las Cruces, New Mexico, 1897-1902.
Weekly.
English title: *Independent-Democrat.* Some issues in English and Spanish. In OCLC system.

El Democrático. Douglas, Arizona: Ignacio Araiza, 1906-19uu.
Weekly.

Editor: Lázaro Puente. Listed in Lutrell, Estelle, *Newspapers and Periodicals of Arizona, 1859- 1911,* p. 19. Lutrell indicates the title is listed in *N. W. Ayer & Son's,* 1906; however, this publication only lists *El Demócrata,* same place, same year. In Spanish. No extant issues located.

El Demófilo. Alice, Tex., 19uu-19uu.

Mentioned in Franco, Jesús, *El alma de la raza: narraciones históricas de episodios y vida de los mexicanos residentes en los Estados Unidos de Norte América,* p. 111. No extant issues located.

Despertad. Brooklyn, N.Y.: Watchtower Bible and Tract Society, 19uu-19uu.

Semi-monthly.

Listed in Common Council for American Unity, *Foreign Language Publications in the United States: Newspaper Lists,* p. 5. In Spanish. No extant issues located.

El Despertar. New York; New Jersey: J. C. Campos, 1891-1902.

One of the earliest anarchist papers in the U. S.; contained articles "by many noted Spanish anarchists such as Anselmo Lorenzo and Federico Urales," cf. Chabrán, Rafael and Richard Chabrán, "The Spanish-Language and Latino Press of the United States: Newspapers and Periodicals," p. 369. In Spanish. No extant issues located.

El Día. El Paso, Tex.: Roberto Enríquez, 191u-19uu.

Daily.

Año 1, no. 151 dated 18 de feb. de 1919. In Spanish. In OCLC system.

El Día. Nogales, Ariz.: Brígido Caro, 1915-1920.

Listed in Miguélez, Armando, "Index of Spanish-Language Newspapers in the U. S. Southwest." No extant issues located.

La Diana. New York, N.Y., 1923?-19uu.

Repository: Bancroft Library (University of California, Berkeley).

El Diario. El Paso, Texas, 1905-19uu.

Daily.

Directors: Rafael and Elfego Ronquillo. Listed in "Más de cuatrocientos periódicos en español se han editado en Estados Unidos". In Spanish. No extant issues located.

Diario Cubano. New York, N.Y., 1870-1uuu.

Daily (except Monday).

Director: Rafael M. Merchán. In Spanish. In OCLC system.

Diario de El Paso. El Paso, Texas: Gabriel López Arce, 1924-1928.

Daily.

Director: Nicolás D. Mateo. Listed in "Más de cuatrocientos periódicos en español se han editado en Estados Unidos". In Spanish. No extant issues located.

El Diario de la Frontera. Brownsville, Texas, 1912-1913; 1915-19uu.

Daily.

Editor: Luciano Mascorro, Jr.; Administrator: Vicente F. Tamayo. Listed in "Más de cuatrocientos periódicos en español se han editado en Estados Unidos". In Spanish. Repository: Special Collections, University of Texas, Brownsville, Texas.

Diario de las Novedades. Nueva York, N.Y., 1909-19uu.

Daily (except Sunday & holidays).

Weekly edition: *Novedades* (New York, N.Y.). In English and Spanish. In OCLC system.

El Diario de Nueva York = New York's Spanish Daily. Brooklyn, Nueva York [i.e. New York]: El Diario Publishing Co., 1948-1963.

Daily (except Sunday), 15 de sept. de 1948-9 de abr. de 1949; daily; 10 de abr. de 1949-2 de jun. de 1951; daily (except Sunday), 3 de jun. de 1951-7 de abr. de 1963. Published in New York, N.Y., 1962-1963. Merged with *La Prensa* to form *Diario de Nueva York—La Prensa.* In Spanish. In OCLC system.

Diario de Nueva York (New York, N.Y.). *See* **El Imparcial de Nueva York.**

El Diario de Tampa. Ybor City, Tampa, Fla., 1908-19uu.

Año 1, núm. 6 dated junio 6 de 1908. "Periódico político independiente." Repository:

Recovering the U. S. Hispanic Literary Heritage Project.

El Diario Español. New York, N.Y., 1925-19uu.

Sephardi newspaper. Mentioned in *El Tucsonense,* 21 nov., 1925; cf. Somoza, *Literatura de la Revolución Mexicana...*, p. 245. No extant issues located.

Diario Las Américas. Miami, Fla.: Américas Pub. Co., 1953-.

Daily (except Monday).

Vol.1, no. 121 dated Nov. 26, 1953. In Spanish. In OCLC system.

Diógenes. McAllen, Texas: Lorenzo Yáñez & Adrián Tapia, 1921-1933?

Weekly.

Listed in "Más de cuatrocientos periódicos en español se han editado en Estados Unidos". In Spanish. No extant issues located.

El Dios Momo. Tucson, Ariz.: José Castelán, 1918-19uu.

Mentioned in *El Tucsonense,* 24 jul., 1918, p. 3; cf. Somoza, *Literatura de la Revolución Mexicana...*, p.229. No extant issues located.

El Diputado. Laredo, Tex.: López Montalvo Hermanos, 1882?-1uuu.

Weekly.

Año 2, no. 91 dated dic. 22, 1884. In Spanish. In OCLC system.

La Doctrina de Martí. New York, N.Y., 1896-1898.

Vol. 1, Number 1 dated July 25, 1896. Edited by Rafael Serra. Listed in Poyo, Gerald Eugene, *With All and for the Good of All,* p. 174. In Spanish. Complete holdings at the Biblioteca Nacional in Havana, Cuba.

El Domingo. Tucson, Ariz., 1891-1uuu.

Mentioned in *El Fronterizo,* abr. 10, 1891; cf. Somoza, *Literatura de la Revolución Mexicana...*, p. 229. No extant issues located.

Don Clarito. San Francisco, Calif., 1879-1uuu.

Listed in Miguélez, Armando, "Index of Spanish-Language Newspapers in the U. S. Southwest." Miguélez indicates the paper is mentioned in *Las Dos Republicas,* no place or dates are given for the source. No extant issues located.

Las Dos Américas. El Paso, Tex., 1898-1uuu.

Weekly.

In Spanish. In OCLC system.

Las Dos Américas: Revista Ilustrada, Recreativa. Nueva York: E. Ewer, 1906-19uu.

In LOCIS system.

Los Dos Laredos. Laredo, Tex., 1881-1uuu.

Mentioned in *El Fronterizo* (Tucson), mar. 27, 1881; cf. Somoza, *Literatura de la Revolución Mexicana...*, p. 250. No extant issues located.

Las Dos Naciones. St. Louis, Mo.: Ev. E. Carreras, 1894-1896.

Weekly.

T. 3, no. 118 dated marzo 30, 1896. In Spanish. In OCLC system.

Las Dos Repúblicas. Brownsville, Tex.: Romualdo Treviño, 18uu-1uuu.

Vol. 6, no. 643 dated abr. 24, 1895. In Spanish. In OCLC system.

Las Dos Repúblicas. Denver, Colorado: Cía. Publicista de "Las Dos Repúblicas", 1896-1uuu.

Weekly.

In Spanish. In OCLC system.

Las Dos Repúblicas. Los Angeles, Calif.: Antonio Cuyas, 1892-1898?

Weekly Mar. 15-June 7, 1892, semiweekly June 17, 1892-Apr. 23, 1893.

"*La Crónica...* established in 1872, bought by *The Two Republicas* on April 1, 1892," cf. May 31, 1892 issue, *Las Dos Repúblicas.* Absorbed *Crónica* (Los Angeles, California). Variant title: *The Two Republics.* In Spanish and English. Sept. 5, 1892. In OCLC system.

Las Dos Repúblicas. Tucson, Ariz., 1877-1879.

Weekly.

In Spanish. In OCLC system.

Las Dos Riberas. Rio Grande, Texas: Ignacio Gorena, 1915-1918.
> Weekly.
> Listed in Ríos-C., Herminio, "Toward a True Chicano Bibliography: Part II," p. 46. In Spanish. No extant issues located.

El Duende. Brownsville, Tex.: León A. Obregón, 1880-1uuu.
> Mentioned in Somoza, *Literatura de la Revolución Mexicana...*, p. 246. No extant issues located.

Eagle Pass Daily Guide (Eagle Pass, Texas). *See* **Daily Guide.**

Eagle Pass News-Guide (Eagle Pass, Texas). *See* **Daily Guide.**

East Las Vegas. Las Vegas, New Mexico, 1911-19uu.
> Listed in Ríos-C., Herminio, "Toward a True Chicano Bibliography: Part II," p. 44. No extant issues located.

Eastside Sun. Los Angeles, California: Dolores Sánchez, 1945-.
> Daily.
> Editor: John Sánchez. Listed in Ireland, Sandra L. Jones, *Ethnic Periodicals in Contemporary America*, p. 65. A Hispanic Asian publication. In Spanish and English. No extant issues located.

Ebenezer. Nueva York, N.Y., 194u-19uu.
> Monthly.
> Año 2, no. 3 dated marzo de 1945. "Organo de la Sociedad de Jóvenes". In English and Spanish. Repository: The Center for Puerto Rican Studies at Hunter College.

El Eccéntrico (San José, California). *See* **El Excéntrico.**

El Eco. Corpus Christi, Texas, 1912?-19uu.
> Listed in Historical Records Survey, Texas, *Texas Newspapers, 1813-1939*, p. 52. In Spanish. No extant issues located.

El Eco. Kingsville, Tex.: [s.n.], 19uu-19uu.
> Monthly.
> Núm. prog. 20, Época II dated ago. 1 de 1933. "Director: C.C. Acevedo". "Publicación mensual religiosa". Continues *Acción.* In Spanish. In OCLC system.

El Eco. San Antonio, Texas: J. G. Cavazos, 1938-19uu.
> Cited in Chabrán, Rafael and Richard Chabrán, "The Spanish-Language and Latino Press of the United States: Newspapers and Periodicals," p. 372. In Spanish. No extant issues located.

El Eco Antillano. Nueva York, N.Y., 1941-19uu.
> Vol. 1, no. 2 dated 19 de julio de 1941. Editor: Juan R. Emmanuelli. Repository: The Center for Puerto Rican Studies at Hunter College.

El Eco de Cuba. New York, N.Y., 1855-1uuu.
> Listed in Poyo, Gerald Eugene, *With All and for the Good of All,* p. 174. In Spanish. Repository: Archivo Nacional de Cuba, Havana.

Eco de Falfurrias. Falfurrias, Texas, 1909?-1919.
> Bi-weekly.
> Listed in "Más de cuatrocientos periódicos en español se han editado en Estados Unidos", with publication dates of 1913-1919. Also listed in Ríos-C., Herminio, "Toward a True Chicano Bibliography: Part II." This source indicates publication dates of 1909-1919. In Spanish. No extant issues located.

El Eco de Hidalgo. Hidalgo, Texas, 1897-1uuu.
> Weekly.
> Administrator: Ramón Garza; Redactor: J.A. Hernández. Listed in "Más de cuatrocientos periódicos en español se han editado en Estados Unidos". In Spanish. No extant issues located.

El Eco de la Exposición. New York, N.Y.: Felipe G. Cantón, 1892-1uuu.
> Monthly.
> Vol. 4, no. 3 dated Mar. 15, 1895. In Spanish. In OCLC system.

El Eco de la Frontera. Nogales, Ariz, 1887-1uuu.

Listed in Miguélez, Armando, "Index of Spanish-Language Newspapers in the U. S. Southwest." No extant issues located.

El Eco de la Patria. Los Angeles, Calif., 1878-1uuu.

Weekly.

Editor: Adalberto G. Gallardo (Feb. 14, 1878). In Spanish. In OCLC system.

El Eco de la Raza Latina. San Francisco, California: Dr. Ramón de Contador y Muñiz, 187u-1uuu.

Semi-weekly.

Año 1, no. 33 dated enero 9 de 1878. In Spanish. In OCLC system.

El Eco de Martí. Tampa, Fla., 1897-1uuu.

"Organo Oficial de la Orden Cubana y del Cuerpo del Consejo del P.R.C." Listed in Batista Villareal, Teresita, *Catálogo de Publicaciones periódicas cubanas. . .*, p. 142. This source indicates that the Biblioteca Nacional José Martí in Havana holds some issues of this title.

El Eco de México. Los Angeles, California, 1924?-19uu.

Daily.

Tom. 1, no. 60 dated Oct. 3, 1924. Editor: José S. Healy. "El diario de los mexicanos en Estados Unidos". In Spanish. In OCLC system.

El Eco de Mora. *See* **The Mora Echo.**

Eco de Socorro. Socorro, New Mexico, 1883?-1uuu.

Irregular.

Mentioned in Sheridan, *Los Tucsonenses,* p. 203. Also listed in "Más de cuatrocientos periódicos en español se han editado en Estados Unidos", with beginning publication date of 1887. In Spanish and English. No extant issues located.

El Eco de Sonora. Tucson, Arizona: F.T. Dávila, 1883?-1uuu.

Weekly.

Listed in *Rowell's American Newspaper Directory,* 1883, and Lutrell, Estelle, *Newspapers and Periodicals of Arizona, 1859-1911,* p. 60. In Spanish. No extant issues located.

El Eco del Comercio. El Paso, Tex., 1896-1908?

Mentioned in *El Fronterizo* (Tucson), mar. 7, 1908, p. 5; cf. Somoza, *Literatura de la Revolución Mexicana. . .*, 248. No extant issues located.

El Eco del Golfo. Corpus Christi, Tex., 1uuu-1uuu.

Mentioned in Lomas, *The Rebel,* p. xv.

El Eco del Norte. Mora, Nuevo México: Enrique Sosa, 1908-1922?

Weekly.

T. 1, num. 3 dated 14 de sept. de 1908. Ceased in 1922?, cf. Grove, Pearce S., *New Mexico Newspapers.* In Spanish. In OCLC system.

El Eco del Pacífico. San Francisco [Calif.]: [Derbec], 1856-18uu.

Daily (except Monday).

Año 5, no. 377 dated 9 de abr. de 1857. "Organo de la población española en California." Editor: J. Jofré. Previously published as p. 4 of *L'Echo du Pacifique,* cf. Gregory, Winifred, ed., *American Newspapers, 1821-1936.* In Spanish. In OCLC system.

Eco del Río Grande. Las Cruces, New Mexico: L. Lapoint, 187u-1878.

Weekly.

Vol. 2, no. 24 dated feb. 12, 1876. Variant title: *Rio Grande Eco.* In English and Spanish. In OCLC system.

Eco del Siglo. Las Cruces, Condado de Doña Ana, N. M.: M. Valdez y Arnold, 1882-18uu.

Weekly.

In Spanish. In OCLC system.

Eco del Socorro. Santa Fe, N. M., 1881-1uuu.

Mentioned in Somoza, *Literatura de la Revolución Mexicana...*, p. 242. No extant issues located.

El Eco del Valle. Las Cruces, Nuevo México: M. F. Lerma, 1905-19uu.
> Weekly.
> In Spanish. In OCLC system.

El Eco del Valle. Pomona, Calif.: Jake Proctor, 1927–19uu.
> In OCLC system.

El Eco Fronterizo. Brownsville, Texas: Agustín Gómez Robelo, 1921?-19uu.
> Weekly.
> Listed in Ríos-C., Herminio, "Toward a True Chicano Bibliography: Part II," p. 44 and "Más de cuatrocientos periódicos en español se han editado en Estados Unidos". Both sources indicate publication date of 1924. Also listed in *N. W. Ayer & Son's American Newspaper Annual and Directory,* 1924, with publication date of 1921. In Spanish. No extant issues located.

El Eco Fronterizo. El Paso, Tex.: [Franco y Ochoa], 1896-1uuu.
> Weekly.
> Vol. 1, no. 2 dated oct. 3, 1896. In Spanish. In OCLC system.

El Eco Fronterizo. Tucson, Ariz., 1916-19uu.
> Mentioned in Sheridan, *Los Tucsonenses,* p. 203. No extant issues located.

El Eco Liberal. Corpus Christi, Texas, 1889-1894.
> Weekly.
> Director: Francisco de P. González. Listed in "Más de cuatrocientos periódicos en español se han editado en Estados Unidos". In Spanish. No extant issues located.

El Eco Liberal. San Diego, Tex.: F. de P. González, 18uu-1uuu.
> Vol. [?], no. 28 dated July 20, 1889. Published in Floresville, Texas around 1895. In Spanish. In OCLC system.

El Eco Libra. Alice, Tex.: D. S. Booth, 18uu-1uuu.
> Weekly.
> Vol. 2, no. 44 dated Apr. 4, 1896. In OCLC system.

El Eco Mexicano. Los Angeles, Calif.: [s.n], 1885-1885.
> Daily (except Sunday).
> Vol. 1, no. 23 dated oct. 29 de 1885. Editor: José de La Vega, (oct. 29 de 1885). "El único diario que se publica en español en California". In OCLC system.

El Eco Mexicano. Tucson, Ariz., 1922-19uu.
> Listed in Miguélez, Armando, "Index of Spanish-Language Newspapers in the U. S. Southwest." Miguélez indicates paper is mentioned in *El Tucsonense,* 17-VI-1922. No extant issues located.

El Eco Parroquial: Revista Mensual. Colorado, N. M., 191u-19uu.
> Monthly.
> Vol. 2, no.13 dated enero 1914. In English and Spanish. In OCLC system.

Eco: Revista de la Prensa Española. Garden City, New Jersey: Doubleday, Doran & Co., Inc., 1904-1935?
> Semi-monthly; weekly.
> Editor: Arturo Torres. Listed in *N. W. Ayer & Son's Directory of Newspapers and Periodicals,* 1932, p. 632, and 1935, p. 602. In Spanish. In OCLC system.

El Economista Americano. Nueva York, 1885-1uuu.
> "Revista mercantil, industrial y política." Director: Charles H. Odemar. Colaborador: José Martí. Listed in Batista Villareal, Teresita, *Catálogo de Publicaciones periódicas cubanas...*, p. 143. This source indicates that the Biblioteca Nacional José Martí in Havana holds some issues of this title.

El Economista Internacional. New York, N.Y.: International Economist Pub., 1900-1907.
> Monthly.
> Editor: G. R. Perry. Listed in Rowell's *American Newspaper Directory*, 1907, p. 799. In

Spanish. No extant issues located.

Ecos de Fiesta en Tampa. Tampa, Florida: Rubén Fabelo, 195u-19uu.
Repository: University of South Florida, Tampa.

Ecos de la Catedral. San Antonio, Texas: Catedral de San Fernando, 19uu-19uu.
Weekly.
Vol. 4, no. 142 dated feb. 17, 1918. In English and Spanish. In OCLC system.

Ecos de Nueva York. New York: Echos Inc., 1946-1957?
Weekly.
Publisher: Enrique Ungría. Listed in Common Council for American Unity, *Foreign Language Publications in the United States: Newspaper Lists.* In Spanish. In OCLC system.

Ecos del Mundo. New York, N.Y.: Alex Pina, 1960?-19uu.
Weekly.
Año 1. no. 37 dated Aug. 6, 1960. Repository: The Center for Puerto Rican Studies at Hunter College, CUNY.

Ecos del Sanatorio. Tampa, Fl., 1941-19uu.
Biweekly.
Año 1, no. 4 dated agosto 1, 1941. "Organo acturiano de Tampa". Repository: University of South Florida, Tampa.

Ecuador. Key West, Florida, 1891-1uuu.
Weekly.
Listed in "Más de cuatrocientos periódicos en español se han editado en Estados Unidos". In Spanish. No extant issues located.

La Edad de Oro. New York, N.Y., 1889-1889.
Monthly.
"Publicación mensual de recreo e instrucción dedicada a los niños de América". In Spanish. In OCLC system.

La Educación. Washington, D. C.: Departamento de Asuntos Educativos, Secretaría General de la O. E.A., 1956-19uu.
Quarterly, semiannual.
In Spanish. In OCLC system.

Educación. Washington, D. C.: La Unión Panamericana, 1925-1929.
In Spanish. In OCLC system.

El Educador Popular. Nueva York, N.Y.: N. [i.e. Néstor] Ponce de León, 1873-1uuu.
Semimonthly.
"Periódico dedicado a la difusión de la instrucción primaria secundaria". In Spanish. In OCLC system.

The El Paso Times. El Paso, Tex.: Juan S. Hart and John E. Lord, 1886-1889.
Daily (twice on Wednesday).
Began with vol. 6, no. 128 dated May 30, 1886; ceased with v. 9, no. 275 dated Nov. 30, 1889. Later published by Times Pub. Co. Continues *El Paso Daily Times* (1883). Continued by *El Paso International Daily Times.* Variant title: *Daily Times.* In OCLC system.

E. L. A. Brooklyn-Belvedere Comet. Los Angeles, California: Dolores Sánchez, 1950-19uu.
Weekly.
Editor: Dolores Sánchez. Publisher: John Sánchez. Listed in *Gale Directory of Publications and Broadcast Media,* 1995, p. 106. In Spanish and English. No extant issues located.

Elaboraciones y Envases. Chicago, Illinois: The Canterbury Press, 19uu-19uu.
Bi-monthly.
Vol. 41, no. 1 dated agosto 1961. In Spanish. In OCLC system.

Electricidad en América. New York: Gage Internat. Pub. Corp., 19uu-19uu.
Monthly.

Text in Spanish with English section, 1919-1920. Text in Spanish, 1921-. In OCLC system.

Elegancia. New York, N.Y.: Elegancia Pub. Co., 1913-19uu.

Monthly.

Editor: María Surira. Listed in *N. W. Ayer & Son's American Newspaper Annual and Directory,* 1926, p. 728. In Spanish. No extant issues located.

El Embotellador. New York: Keller Publishing Co., 1946-19uu.

In Spanish. In OCLC system.

Empresa. Clayton, New Mexico: 1905-19uu.

Listed in "Más de cuatrocientos periódicos en español se han editado en Estados Unidos". In Spanish. No extant issues located.

La Empresa. Las Cruces, N. M.: Lorenzo Lapoint, 1896-1uuu.

Weekly.

In Spanish, Sept. 1896-Jan. 23, 1897; also in English, Feb. 27, 1897. In OCLC system.

El Ensayo. Phoenix, Ariz.: R.R. Valenzuela, 1916-19uu.

Weekly leaflet.

Mentioned in *El Tucsonense,* nov. 15, 1916, p. 4; cf. Somoza, *Literatura de la Revolución Mexicana...,* p. 226. No extant issues located.

La Enseñanza: Revista Americana de Instrucción y Recreo, Dedicada a la Juventud. New York; Mexico, 1870-1876.

Contains supplement: "El Album de los niños". In OCLC system.

Época. Folsom, N. M., 1907-19uu.

Mentioned in Somoza, *Literatura de la Revolución Mexicana...,* p. 240. No extant issues located.

La Época. Nogales, Ariz.: Brígido Caro, 1915-19uu.

Mentioned in Somoza, *Literatura de la Revolución Mexicana...,* p. 225. No extant issues located.

La Época. San Antonio, Tex., 1913?-1931.

Weekly.

Published 1916-1931, cf. Gregory, Winifred, ed., *American Newspapers, 1821-1936.* In Spanish. In OCLC system.

La Época. Terrero, New Mexico, 1909-19uu.

Listed in Ríos-C., Herminio, "Toward a True Chicano Bibliography: Part II," p. 44, and "Más de cuatrocientos periódicos en español se han editado en Estados Unidos". In Spanish and English. No extant issues located.

La Epoka de Nu York. New York, [N.Y.]: Alfred Mizrachi, 1919-1920?

Semiweekly.

Vol. 3, no. 214 dated Dec. 2, 1919-. Continues *Boz del pueblo* (New York, N. Y.). In Ladino and English. In OCLC system.

El Esclavo. Tampa, Fla., 1894-1uuu.

Año 1, no. 22 dated oct. 31, 1894. "Periódico obrero semanal." In Spanish. In OCLC system.

El Escritorio. New York: National Paper and Type Co., 1917-1922.

Monthly.

"Revista mensual ilustrada dedicada al negocio de papelería y comercio en general". Absorbed by *Arte Tipográfico y el Escritorio.* In Spanish. In OCLC system.

Escualdun Gazeta. Los Angeles, California: 1885-1uuu.

Irregular.

Editor: M.V. Biscailuz. "Basque," cf. Gregory, Winifred, ed., *American Newspapers, 1821-1936.* In OCLC system.

La Espada Republicana. Las Vegas, Nuevo México: Compañía Publicista de la Espada Republicana, 1908-19uu.

Weekly.

In OCLC system.

España Libre. Brooklyn, N.Y.: [Confederated Spanish Societies of the U. S.A., etc.],

1939-1977.
 Frequency varies.
 In English and Spanish, Jan. 17, 1958-Nov./Dec. 1976. Organ of Sociedades Hispanas Confederadas de los Estados Unidos de América (formerly Comité Antifascista Español de los Estados Unidos de Norte América). Continues *Frente Popular.* In OCLC system.
España Nueva. New York, 1923-1972.
 Listed in Chabrán, Rafael, "Spaniards."
España Republicana. New York, N.Y.: The Alianza Republicana Española, 1931-19uu.
 Monthly, Apr. 1931-Jan. 1932; semimonthly, Feb. 1, 1932-.
 Vol. 1, no. 5 has a separately paged supplement. "Organo de la Alianza Republicana Española de Nueva York." In OCLC system.
El Español. New Orleans, Louisiana, 1829-1830.
 Six times monthly (Apr. 6-August 26, 1829); eight times monthly (Dec. 11, 1829-March 31, 1830); eleven times monthly (April 1- August 8, 1930).
 Editor: Tiburcio Campe. Listed in Gregory, Winifred, ed., *American Newspapers, 1821-1936;* and MacCurdy, Raymond R. *A History and Bibliography of Spanish-Language Newspapers and Magazines in Louisiana, 1808-1949,* p. 35. In Spanish. No extant issues located.
El Español. San Antonio, Tex.: Pedro Serrano, 191u?-19uu.
 Mentioned in Sax, Antimaco, *Los mexicanos en el destierro,* p. 25. No extant issues located.
Española Valley Developer. Española, New Mexico: Henry López, 193u-19uu.
 Weekly.
 Editor: Vol. 4, no. 37 dated Oct 14, 1938. Editor: Carmen Yowell. Listed in *N. W. Ayer & Son's Directory of Newspapers and Periodicals,* 1944, p. 580. In English and Spanish. In OCLC system.
El Espectador. Berkeley, Calif.: Ignacio López, 1890-1uuu.
 Mentioned in *El Fronterizo* (Tucson), oct. 18, 1890, p. 3; cf. Somoza, *Literatura de la Revolución Mexicana...,* p. 231. No extant issues located.
El Espectador. Pomona, Ca.: Ignacio L. López, 1934?-19uu.
 Weekly.
 "An American publication written in Spanish." Vol. 3, no. 52 dated Feb. 5, 1937. In Spanish. In OCLC system.
El Espectador Mexicano. Austin, Texas, 1883-1uuu.
 Weekly.
 Director: Adolfo Duclós Salinas. Listed in "Más de cuatrocientos periódicos en español se han editado en Estados Unidos". In Spanish. No extant issues located.
El Espejo. Bernalillo, Nuevo Méjico: Chacón y Salazar, 187u-187u.
 Weekly.
 Vol. 1, no. 44 dated marzo 8, 1879. Variant title: *The Mirror.* In Spanish and English. In OCLC system.
El Espejo. Los Angeles, Calif., 1886-1887.
 Mentioned in *El Fronterizo* (Tucson), ene. 28, 1887, p. 3; cf. Somoza, *Literatura de la Revolución Mexicana...,* p. 232. No extant issues located.
Espejo. New York, [N.Y.]: Espejo Printing and Pub. Co., 1873-1893?
 Monthly.
 Editor: Narciso Villaverde, Nov. 1881-Oct. 1885. "Ciencias, artes, literatura, industria, instrucción, comercio". Continues *Espejo Masónico.* In Spanish and English. In OCLC system.
El Espejo del Valle de Taos. Bernalillo, New Mexico; Fernández de Taos, New Mexico: Urbano Chacón, 1878-1879.
 Weekly.
 Listed in Gregory, Winifred, ed., *American Newspapers, 1821-1936,* p. 434. Gregory

indicates this title was published in Bernalillo. Also listed in *Rowell's American Newspaper Directory,* 1878, page 485. Rowell indicates the periodical was published in Fernández de Taos. In Spanish and English. No extant issues located.

El Espejo Masónico. Nueva York: Andrés Cassard, 1866-18uu.
In Spanish. In OCLC system.

La Esperanza. Los Angeles, California: Claretian Fathers, 1929-19uu.
Weekly.
Editor: Rev. F. F. Zapatero. Listed in Common Council for American Unity, *Foreign Language Publications in the United States: Newspaper Lists.* Also listed in *N.W.Ayer & Son's Directory of Newspapers and Periodicals,* 1939, p. 85, and Ríos-C., Herminio, "Toward a True Chicano Bibliography: Part II," p. 40. In Spanish. No extant issues located.

La Estación. Tucson, Ariz.: Carlos Casanova e Ignacio González, 1890-1uuu.
Listed in Miguélez, Armando, "Index of Spanish-Language Newspapers in the U. S. Southwest." No extant issues located.

Estadística. Washington, D. C.: Inter-American Statistical Institute, Organization of American States, 1943-.
Quarterly.
"Journal of the Inter American Statistical Institute." Issues for 1943-46 published in México. In English and Spanish. In OCLC system.

Estado. Albuquerque, N. M., 1906-19uu.
Weekly.
Listed in Grove, Pearce S., *New Mexico Newspapers,* p. 39. In Spanish. No extant issues located.

The Estancia Herald. Estancia, New México: Allen Barrett, 909-1912.
Weekly.
Daily edition: *Daily Herald* (Estancia, N. M.), April 1 -Aug. 7, 1911. Ceased with Jan. 25, 1912, cf. Grove, Pearce S., *New Mexico Newspapers.* Variant title: *Heraldo de Estancia.* Merged with *Estancia News* to form *Estancia News-Herald.* In English and Spanish. In OCLC system.

The Estancia News. Estancia, Torrence County, N. M.: P.A. Speckmann, 1904?-1912.
Weekly.
Vol. 4, no. 5 dated nov. 15, 1907. Daily ed.: *Morning News* (Estancia, N. M.), Apr. 3, 1911-Mar. 30, 1912. Companion newspaper: *Las Nuevas de la Estancia* (1904-Mar. 28, 1908), which was absorbed by *The Estancia News* in April 1908, cf. Grove, Pearce S., *New Mexico Newspapers.* In English and Spanish. In OCLC system.

Estancia News-Herald. Estancia, Torrance County, New Mexico: J.A. Constant, 1912-1950.
Weekly.
Vol. 8, no. 13 dated Feb. 2, 1912. Formed by the merger of *Estancia News* and *The Estancia Herald.* In English and Spanish. In OCLC system.

Estancia Valley Citizen. Estancia, N. M.: G. C. Lawrence, 1960-1966.
Weekly.
Continued by *Torrence County Citizen.* In English and Spanish. In OCLC system.

El Estandarte de Springer. Springer, N. M.: G. E. Hosmer, 1889-1893.
Weekly.
Began publication with June 27, 1889; ceased June 15, 1893, cf. Groves, *New Mexico Newspapers.* Tomo 2 núm. 2 dated julio 10, 1890. A companion newspaper was published titled *Springer Banner.* In Spanish. In OCLC system.

Estrella (East Las Vegas, New Mexico). *See* **San Miguel County Star.**

La Estrella. Las Cruces, N. M.: La Estrella, 191u-1939.
Weekly.
Vol. 1, no. 10 dated 11 de feb. de 1911. In Spanish and English. In OCLC system.

La Estrella. Los Angeles, Calif., 1851-1879.
"Suplemento en español de *Los Angeles Weekly Star*". Repository: Bancroft Library

(University of California, Berkeley). Mentioned in Somoza, *Literatura de la Revolución Mexicana...*, p. 232.

La Estrella. Maldonado, N. M.: Sánchez y Medina, 189u-1uuu.

Vol. 1, no. 4 dated enero 30, 1897. In Spanish. In OCLC system.

La Estrella. San Antonio, TX, 1909-19uu.

Cited in Chabrán, Rafael and Richard Chabrán, "The Spanish-Language and Latino Press of the United States: Newspapers and Periodicals," p. 369. No extant issues located.

La Estrella de Cuba = Star of Cuba. Nueva York, N.Y., Hallet & Breen, 1870-1uuu.

Irregular.

Director: Juan Macías. In Spanish, Apr. 9-May 9, 1870; in Spanish and English, May 17, 1870-. In OCLC system.

La Estrella de Nuevo México. Albuquerque, N. M.: Jesús S. García, 1906-19uu.

Mentioned in Somoza, *Literatura de la Revolución Mexicana...*, p. 238. No extant issues located.

La Estrella de Nuevo México. Santa Fe, New Mexico: La Estrella de Nuevo México Publishing Co., 1895-1uuu.

Weekly.

Listed in *Rowell's American Newspaper Directory,* 1896, p. 643. In Spanish. No extant issues located.

La Estrella de Nuevo México. Socorro, Nuevo México: Pablo Trujillo y E. Sosa, 1896-189u.

Weekly.

Began with T. 2 no. 3 dated agosto 7, 1896-. Formerly published in Santa Fe. Absorbed in part by *Libertad* (San Marcial, N. M.). In Spanish. In OCLC system.

La Estrella de Occidente. Los Angeles, Calif.: Francisco P. Ramírez, 186u-1uuu.

Listed in Miguélez, Armando, "Index of Spanish-Language Newspapers in the U. S. Southwest." Miguélez indicates paper is mentioned in *El Hispanoamericano,* especial junio-julio, 1919. No extant issues located.

La Estrella de Panamá. New York, N.Y.: Panama: Star & Herald Co., 1853-.

Weekly.

Spanish edition of the *Star & Herald.* First appeared as Spanish section of the *Star & Herald* on Feb. 1, 1853. In Spanish. In OCLC system.

La Estrella del Norte. Nueva York [i.e. New York, N.Y.]: A. Vélez Alvarado, 1899-19uu.

Weekly.

In Spanish with parallel English translations. In OCLC system.

La Estrella del Socorro (New York, N.Y.). *See* **Socorro Star** (New York, N.Y.)

La Estrella del Socorro (Socorro, New Mexico). *See* **Socorro Star** (Socorro, New Mexico).

La Estrella Mejicana. Albuquerque, New Mexico: H.L. Ortiz, 1890-1890?

Weekly.

"Guía de la causa del pueblo". Ceased in Nov. 1890?, cf. Grove, Pearce S., *New Mexico Newspapers.* In OCLC system.

La Estrella Mejicana. Louisiana: A. Crebassol, 1836-18uu.

Weekly.

Listed in MacCurdy, Raymond R., *A History and Bibliography of Spanish-Language Newspapers and Magazines in Louisiana, 1808-1949,* p. 35. In Spanish. No extant issues located.

El Estudiante Latino-Americano. Ann Arbor, Mich.: [The Committee on Friendly Relations Among Foreign Students], 1918-.

Bimonthly.

Official organ of the Federación de Estudiantes Latino-Americanos. In OCLC system.

Evangelio Restaurado. El Paso, Texas: Misión Mexicana de la Iglesia de Jesucristo de los Santos de los Ultimos Días, 1927-19uu.

Monthly.

In Spanish. In OCLC system.

Evening Call. Key West, Florida, 1887-1uuu.
Daily.
Listed in "Más de cuatrocientos periódicos en español se han editado en Estados Unidos". In Spanish and English. No extant issues located.
Evolución. Laredo, Tex.: Publicista Idar, 1916?-19uu.
Daily (except Monday).
Tomo 1, no. 103 dated 1 de marzo de 1917. "Diario libre". In Spanish. In OCLC system.
Excélsior. Fresno, California: Catholic Press Society, Diocese of Monterey-Fresno, 1924-19uu.
Weekly.
Editor: Rev. Francis L. Markey. Listed in *N. W. Ayer & Son's American Newspaper Annual and Directory,* 1924, with inaugural date of 1949. Also listed in Ríos-C., Herminio, "Toward a True Chicano Bibliography: Part II," with beginning date of 1924. In Spanish. No extant issues located.
Excélsior. Phoenix, Ariz., 1950-1uuu.
Listed in Miguélez, Armando, "Index of Spanish-Language Newspapers in the U. S. Southwest." Miguélez indicates paper is mentioned in *El Tucsonense;* no dates are given for this source. No extant issues located.
El Excéntrico. [San José, Calif.]: El Excéntrico, 1949-19uu.
Monthly, 1949-1950; semimonthly, 1951-.
"Magazine social, fotográfico latino-americano". Some issues published under title: *El Eccéntrico.* Suspended Jan.-Sept. 1951. In Spanish and English. In OCLC system.
Exclusivo de Washington. . . A Puerto Rico. Washington, D. C.: Oficina del Estado Libre Asociado de Puerto Rico, 1958-19uu.
In Spanish. In OCLC system.
Éxito. New York, N. Y., 1957?-19uu.
In Spanish. Repository: The Center for Puerto Rican Studies at Hunter College.
El Éxito. San Antonio, Texas: El Exito Pub. Co., 1920-19uu.
Weekly.
Listed in *N. W. Ayer & Son's American Newspaper Annual and Directory,* 1924, p. 1031. In Spanish. No extant issues located.
El Expedicionario. Tampa, 1896-1897.
Weekly.
"Organo oficial del Club Discípulos de Martí." Listed in Batista Villareal, Teresita, *Catálogo de Publicaciones periódicas cubanas...,* p. 145. This source indicates that the Biblioteca Nacional José Martí in Havana holds some issues of this title.
El Explorador. Trinidad, Colo.: Urbano Chacón, 1876-1877.
Weekly.
Vol. 2, no. 74 dated jun. 29, 1876. Editors: U. Chacón, P. Chacón, 1876. English edition: *Colorado Pioneer,* 1876. In Spanish. In OCLC system.
Exportador Americano. New York, N.Y.: [J. C. Cochran Co.], 1uuu-1918.
Volumes 53-83 ran from Dec. 1903 thru July 1918. Absorbed *Correo Americano y Diario de Exportación.* In Spanish. In OCLC system.
El Expositor Bíblico. El Paso, Tex.,: Nashville, Tenn.: Casa Bautista de Publicaciones; Baptist Sunday School Board, 19uu-.
Quarterly.
Vol. 63 corresponds to year 1963. In Spanish. The library catalog of Casa Bautista de Publicaciones in El Paso indicates that from 1890 to 1916 this periodical was published in Mexico and since 1917 is published in El Paso. In OCLC system.
Fair Play. New York, N.Y.: The Fair Play for Cuba Committee, 1959-19uu.
Irregular.
Editor: Richard Gibson, cf. Peraza Sarausa, Fermín, *Directorio de Revistas y Periódicos de Cuba,* p. 31. No extant issues located.
El Fandango. San Antonio, Texas: P. Viola, 1927-19uu.

Weekly.

In Spanish. Repository: Bancroft Library (University of California, Berkeley).

El Farmacéutico. New York, N.Y., 1925-19uu.

V. 39, no. 6, dated June 1964. In OCLC system.

El Faro. Trinidad, Colorado, 1912?-1942.

Weekly.

Listed in Oehlerts, Donald E., *Guide to Colorado Newspapers, 1859-1963,* p. 97, with starting publication date of 1914. Also listed in "Más de cuatrocientos periódicos en español se han editado en Estados Unidos", and Gregory, Winifred, ed., *American Newspapers, 1821-1936,* p. 6. In Spanish. No extant issues located.

El Faro Bautista. Clendale, Ariz., 1932-19uu.

Mentioned in *El Tucsonense,* oct. 6, 1932, p. 2; cf. Somoza, *Literatura de la Revolución Mexicana...,* p. 225. No extant issues located.

El Faro del Río Grande. Bernalillo, Nuevo México: F.M. Chacón, 1914-1916?

Weekly.

Ceased in 1916?, cf. Grove, Pearce S., *New Mexico Newspapers.* In Spanish. In OCLC system.

El Faro Dominical. El Paso, Texas: Casa Bautista de Publicaciones, 1927-1972.

Quarterly.

Listed in Common Council for American Unity, *Foreign Language Publications in the United States: Newspaper Lists,* p. 8. Repository: Casa Bautista de Publicaciones, El Paso, Texas.

Faro Popular. Taos, N. M., 1892-1uuu.

Mentioned in Somoza, *Literatura de la Revolución Mexicana...,* p. 244. No extant issues located.

El Farol. Capitan, Condado de Lincoln, Nuevo México: La Compañía Publicista de El Farol, 1905-19uu.

Weekly.

In Spanish. In OCLC system.

El Farol. Pueblo, Col., 1948-19uu.

Listed in Miguélez, Armando, "Index of Spanish-Language Newspapers in the U. S. Southwest." No extant issues located.

La Fe Católica. San Antonio, Texas: Carlos Backmann, 1897?-19uu.

Weekly.

Tomo 1, no. 13 dated marzo 27, 1897. In Spanish. In OCLC system.

La Fe en la Democracia. Los Angeles, California, 1884?-1884.

Semiweekly.

Vol. 1, no. 4 dated 29 de oct. 1884. Editor: Juan de Toro (29 de oct. 1884). In OCLC system.

La Federación. Ibor City, Tampa, Fla: La Federación, 1899-19uu.

Weekly.

"Organo oficial de los Gremios de Torcedores, Rezagadores y Escogedores de Tampa". In Spanish. In OCLC system.

La Federación. Nueva York, 1873-18uu.

Bimonthly.

Director: Juana B. Martínez. Listed in Batista Villareal, Teresita, *Catálogo de Publicaciones periódicas cubanas...,* p. 146. This source indicates that the Biblioteca Nacional José Martí in La Havana holds some issues of this title.

El Federal. Tampa, Fla.: Centro Obrero, 1902-1903.

Weekly.

"Organo oficial de la Unión Federal del Estado de Florida, Asociación que se compone de los Gremios que se dedican a la Elaboración del Tabaco Habano". Continued by *Boletín Obrero.* In Spanish. In OCLC system.

Feminismo Internacional. New York City: [Elena Arizmendi & Co., etc.], 1922-1923.
Editor: Elena Arizmendi and others. "Revista mensual ilustrada, órgano de la Liga Internacional de Mujeres Ibéricas e Hispanoamericanas".Vol. 1, no. 1-2 have subtitle: "Revista mensual ilustrada, dedicada al mejoramiento moral, cultural y económico de la mujer". In OCLC system.

Fenicio. Phoenix, Ariz., 1uuu-1uuu.
Listed in Miguélez, Armando, "Index of Spanish-Language Newspapers in the U. S. Southwest." Miguélez indicates the paper is mentioned in *El Mensajero*, 28-III- 1936, p. 2. No extant issues located.

El Fénix. Clayton, New Mexico: Faustin Gallegos, 1899-19uu.
Weekly.
T. 4, no. 24 dated 3 enero 1903. Began in 1899, cf. Grove, Pearce S., *New Mexico Newspapers.* In Spanish and English. In OCLC system.

El Ferrocarril. San Antonio, Texas: Daniel Cruz, 1894-1906?
Weekly; bi-monthly?
Listed in *Rowell's American Newspaper Directory,* 1896, p. 946, with starting publication date of 1894 and a weekly frequency. Also listed in "Más de cuatrocientos periódicos en español se han editado en Estados Unidos", with publication dates of 1895-1906, and a bi-weekly frequency. In Spanish. No extant issues located.

El Ferrocarril. Tucson, Ariz., 1874?-18uu.
Monthly?
T. 1, no. 9 dated mayo 17 de 1875. Repository: Erasmo Vando Collection, Hunter College, CUNY.

El Fígaro. Corpus Christi, Texas, 1915-19uu.
Daily.
Editors: Lorenzo Yáñez, Jr. & Adrián Tapia. "Más de cuatrocientos periódicos en español se han editado en Estados Unidos". Also listed in Ríos-C., Herminio, "Toward a True Chicano Bibliography: Part II," p. 45. In Spanish. No extant issues located.

El Fígaro. Laredo, Texas: Luis d'Antin Zuloaga, 1892?-1uuu.
Weekly.
Tomo 1, no. 29 dated Dec. 18, 1892. "Semanario independiente, defensor de la verdad". In Spanish. In OCLC system.

Le Figaro. Nouvelles-Orleans, Louisiana: J. J. Regnard, 1838-18uu.
Daily.
In English, French and Spanish. In OCLC system.

El Filibustero. New York, N.Y., 1853-1855.
Edited by Juan and Francisco Bellido de Luna, cf. Poyo, Gerald Eugene, *With All and for the Good of All,* p. 7. In Spanish. No extant issues located.

The Filipino. Washington, D. C., 1906-1906.
"The proposed organ of the Filipino people in the United States." In English and Spanish. In OCLC system.

The Filipino People. [Washington, D. C.]: [M.L. Quezon], 1912-1916.
Monthly.
V. 1-4, no. 1 dated Sept. 1912-Aug. 1916. Variant title: *Pueblo Filipino.* In OCLC system.

The Filipino Student. Berkeley, California: [Filipino Students in America], 1912-1914.
Monthly.
Ceased with v. 2, no. 4 dated Jan. 1914, cf. *Union List of Serials.* In English. In OCLC system.

El Filopolista. Del Río, Texas: Clemente López, 1894-1895.
Weekly.
Editors: Amado Gutiérrez and Clemente López. Listed in "Más de cuatrocientos periódicos en español se han editado en Estados Unidos". Also listed in *Rowell's American Newspaper Directory,* 1896, p. 928. In Spanish. No extant issues located.

Finanzas, Industria, Comercio. Washington, D. C.: La Unión Panamericana, 1925-19uu. In Spanish. In OCLC system.

La Flecha. Wagon Mound, Nuevo México: W.T. Henderson & F. Nolan, 188u-18uu. Weekly.

> T. 2, no. 4 dated oct. 8, 1886. Merged with *Mora County Pioneer* (Watrous, N. M., 1887) to form *The Arrow-Pioneer.* In Spanish and English. In OCLC system.

Flecha-Explorador (Wagon Mound, New Mexico). *See* **The Arrow-Pioneer.**

La Flor del Valle. Las Cruces, Nuevo México: I. Armijo y M. Lerma, 1894-1uuu. Weekly.

> T. 1, núm. 3 dated feb. 3, 1894. In Spanish. In OCLC system.

Florida. Key West, Florida: José Castro & Juan Pérez Rolo, 1918-19uu. Weekly.

> Listed in *N.W. Ayer & Son's American Newspaper Annual and Directory,* 1918, p. 143. Also listed in "Más de cuatrocientos periódicos en español se han editado en Estados Unidos". In Spanish. No extant issues located.

Fort Brown Flag (Brownsville, Texas). *See* **La Bandera.**

The Forumeer. San Jose, Calif.: American G. I. Forum, 1948?-1980. Monthly.

> Place of publication varies: For Worth, Texas (1977-1978); El Paso, Texas (1979-1980). In OCLC system.

Frente Hispano. Nueva York, N.Y., 1934?-19uu

> "Luchador por libertad, paz y progreso". In Spanish. Repository: The Center for Puerto Rican Studies at Hunter College, CUNY.

Frente Popular. Brooklyn, New York, 1937-1939. Bimonthly.

> Vol. 3, no. 16 dated Jan. 1939. Organ of Comité Antifacista Español de los Estados Unidos de Norte América (later called Sociedades Hispanas Confederadas de los Estados Unidos de América). Continued by *España Libre.* In OCLC system.

Friend of the Home (Indiana Harbor, Indiana). *See* **El Amigo del Hogar.**

Friend's Mexican Mission Gazette. Brownsville, Tex. : Gulielma M. Purdie, 1874-1uuu Monthly.

> Vol. 1, no. 2 dated May, 1874. In OCLC system.

La Frontera. Calexico, California, 1924-1929. Weekly.

> Director: José G. Herrero. Colaboradores: Javier Sánchez Mejorada, Pablo Herrera y Miguel Bueno. Listed in "Más de cuatrocientos periódicos en español se han editado en Estados Unidos". Also listed in Ríos-C., Herminio, "Toward a True Chicano Bibliography: Part II," p. 40. In Spanish. No extant issues located.

El Fronterizo. Las Cruces, Nuevo Méjico: N.V. Bennett, 187u-18uu. Weekly.

> Vol. 1, no. 20 dated feb. 11 de 1875. In Spanish. In OCLC system.

El Fronterizo. Mission, Texas, 1914-1915. Weekly.

> Director: Samuel J. Treviño, Administrator: Agapito Cepeda. Listed in "Más de cuatrocientos periódicos en español se han editado en Estados Unidos". In Spanish. No extant issues located.

El Fronterizo. Nogales, Ariz.: Jesús Siqueiros y Espergencio Montijo, 1919-1920.

> Listed in Miguélez, Armando, "Index of Spanish-Language Newspapers in the U. S. Southwest." No extant issues located.

El Fronterizo. Phoenix, Arizona: Carlos Y. Velasco, 1922-1926? Weekly.

> "Follows *El Fronterizo*" (Tucson), cf. Gregory, Winifred, ed., *American Newspapers, 1821- 1936,* p. 20. In Spanish. No extant issues located.

El Fronterizo. Rio Grande City, Texas: Pedro Díaz, 1921?-19uu.
>Weekly.
>Época 1a., no. 139 dated enero 14 de 1922. Continued by *Rio Grande Herald.* In Spanish. In OCLC system.

El Fronterizo. Tucson, Arizona: C. I. Velasco, 1878-1914.
>Weekly.
>Began in Sept. 1878; ceased in 1914, cf. Lutrell, Estelle, *Newspapers and Periodicals of Arizona, 1859-191.* Vol. 2, no. 41 dated July 4, 1880. "Followed by *El Fronterizo* (Phoenix) 1922-1926?" cf. Gregory, Winifred, ed., *American Newspapers, 1821-1936.* In OCLC system.

El Fronterizo. Tucson, Ariz., 1926-1929.
>In OCLC system.

La Fuerza Consciente. 19uu-19uu.
>Monthly.
>Pubished during the Mexican Revolution, it was associated with the anarchist thought, cf. Chabrán, Rafael and Richard Chabrán, "The Spanish-Language and Latino Press of the United States: Newspapers and Periodicals," p. 368. In Spanish. No extant issues located.

The Future (New Orleans, Louisiana). *See* **L'Avenir du Peuple.**

La Gaceta. Albuquerque, New Mexico, 1926-19uu.
>Weekly.
>Listed in Ríos-C., Herminio, "Toward a True Chicano Bibliography: Part II," p. 42 and "Más de cuatrocientos periódicos en español se han editado en Estados Unidos". In Spanish. No extant issues located.

La Gaceta. Las Vegas, N. M., 1877-1878.
>Weekly.
>A companion paper for *Las Vegas Gazette.* Listed in Grove, Pearce S., *New Mexico Newspapers,* p. 401. In Spanish. No extant issues located.

La Gaceta. San Diego, Texas, 1918-19uu.
>Listed in Ríos-C., Herminio, "Toward a True Chicano Bibliography: Part II," p. 47, and "Más de cuatrocientos periódicos en español se han editado en Estados Unidos". In Spanish. No extant issues located.

La Gaceta. San Francisco, Calif.; Los Angeles, Calif., 1898-1900; 1900-1903.
>Weekly.
>Founded in San Francisco in 1898, then moved to Los Angeles in 1900, cf. "Más de cuatrocientos periódicos en español se han editado en Estados Unidos". In Spanish. No extant issues located.

La Gaceta. Santa Barbara, California: José Arzaga, 1879-1881?
>Weekly.
>In OCLC system.

Gaceta. Santa Fe, N. M., 1850?-1uuu.
>Weekly.
>Listed in Grove, Pearce S., *New Mexico Newspapers,* p. 446. In Spanish. No extant issues located.

La Gaceta. Tampa, Florida: La Gaceta Pub. Co., 1922-19uu.
>Weekly.
>Año 64, no. 27 dated jul. 4, 1986. In English, Italian and Spanish. In OCLC system.

La Gaceta de California. Hollywood, California: Miguel de Zárraga, 193u-.
>Semi-monthly.
>Año 1, no. 2 dated 1a. quincena de feb. de 1935. "Revista de la raza hispánica". In OCLC system.

La Gaceta de Estados Unidos. Tucson, Ariz., 1917-1018.
>Mentioned in *El Tucsonense,* jun. 17, 1922; cf. Somoza, *Literatura de la Revolución*

Mexicana..., p. 229. No extant issues located.

Gaceta de Las Vegas (Las Vegas, N. M.: Louis Hommel). *See* **Las Vegas Gazette** (Las Vegas, New Mexico: Louis Hommel, 187u).

La Gaceta de los Estados Unidos. Los Angeles, California: Eduardo Ruíz, 1918-192u.

Weekly, 1918-1919; bi-weekly, Apr. 30, 1920; three times a month, 1919 April 20, 1920.

Vol. 1, no. 25 dated 24 de agosto de 1918. Suspended with Nov. 10, 1918 issue; resumed with April 30, 1919 issue. In Spanish. In OCLC system. Thomas Sheridan lists a similar title around the same time published in Tucson, mentioned in *El Tucsonense* of Aug 13, 1921 as a periodical that has ceased publication by that year; cf. Sheridan, *Los Tucsonenses,* p. 203.

La Gaceta de Mora. Mora, Nuevo México: N. Segura, 1890-1891?

Weekly.

T. 1, no. 1 dated Mar. 27, 1890. Ceased in 1891?, cf. Grove, Pearce S., *New Mexico Newspapers.* In English and Spanish. In OCLC system.

Gaceta de Texas. Nacogdoches [Tex.: W. Shaler & J.A. de Toledo y Dubois], 1813-1813.

Probably only one issue appeared, cf. Wallace, J. M., *Gaceta to Gazette: A Checklist of Texas Newspapers, 1813-1846.* Continued by *Mexicano* (Natchitoches, La.: 1813). In Spanish. In OCLC system.

La Gaceta del Pueblo. New York, N.Y., 18uu-1uuu.

Mentioned in *El Americano* (New York, N.Y.), Ago., 1892, p. 2. No extant issues located.

Gaceta del Valle Imperial. Brawley, California: Brawley News, 1929-19uu.

Weekly.

Director: José Herrera. Listed in "Más de cuatrocientos periódicos en español se han editado en Estados Unidos". Also listed in *N.W. Ayer & Son's Directory of Newspapers and Periodicals,* 1939, p. 71, and Ríos-C., Herminio, "Toward a True Chicano Bibliography: Part II," p. 40. In Spanish. No extant issues located.

Gaceta Mexicana: Revista Quincenal. Houston, Texas: José Sarabia, 1928-19uu.

In Spanish. In OCLC system.

La Gaceta Popular. Las Cruces, Nuevo México: M. F. Lerma, 1918-192u.

Weekly.

In Spanish. In OCLC system.

Gaceta Semanaria de Santa Fe (Santa Fe, N. M.: W. W. H. Davis, 185u). *See* **Santa Fe Weekly Gazette.**

Gaceta Semanaria de Santa Fe (Santa Fe, N. M.: James L. Collins, 1854). *See* **Santa Fe Gazette** (Santa Fe, N. M.: James L. Collins, 1854).

Gaceta Semanaria de Santa Fe (Santa Fe, N. M.: Hezekiah S. Johnson, 1859). *See* **Santa Fe Gazette** (Santa Fe, N. M.: Hezekiah S. Johnson, 1859).

El Gallito. Chicago, Illinois, 1927-19uu.

Weekly.

Listed in Gregory, Winifred, ed., *American Newspapers, 1821-1936,* p. 9. In Spanish. Repository: Bancroft Library (University of California, Berkeley).

El Gallo. San Antonio, Tex., 1882-1uuu.

Mentioned in *El Fronterizo* (Tucson), Feb. 20, 1882, p. 3; cf. Somoza, *Literatura de la Revolución Mexicana...*, p. 251. No extant issues located.

The Gate City Sun. Raton, New Mexico: Hale Bicknell, 1930-1936.

Weekly.

Sections in Spanish: "La Victoria," May 8-23, 1930, and "Spanish Section," May 30-Aug. 22, 1930. Absorbed *Victoria* (Raton, N. M.), Continued by *Raton Reporter* (Raton, N. M., 1937). In English and Spanish. In OCLC system.

El Gato. Santa Fe, New Mexico: Enrique Sosa, 1894-1894.

Weekly.

Began in May 1894, ceased in August 1894, cf. Grove, Pearce S., *New Mexico*

Newspapers. In Spanish. In OCLC system.

The Gauntlet. Santa Fe, New Mexico, 1894-1894.

Weekly.

Began June 18, 1894, ceased June 25, 1894, cf. Grove, Pearce S., *New Mexico Newspapers.* In English and Spanish. Spanish section:"El Guante." In OCLC system.

Gazeta de Santa Fe (Santa Fe, N. M.: James L. Collins, 1854). *See* **Santa Fe Gazette** (Santa Fe, N. M.: James L. Collins, 1854).

Gazeta de Santa Fe (Santa Fe, N. M.: Hezekiah S. Johnson, 1859). *See* **Santa Fe Gazette** (Santa Fe, N. M.: Hezekiah S. Johnson, 1859).

Germinal. New York, N.Y., 1916-19uu.

Listed in Miguélez, Armando, "Index of Spanish-Language Newspapers in the U. S. Southwest." No extant issues located.

Gilmore Manual Azucarero de Cuba. *See* **Manual Azucarero de Cuba = Cuba Sugar Manual.**

La Golondrina. Socorro, New Mexico, 1898-1uuu.

Weekly.

In Spanish. In OCLC system.

Gráfica. Los Angeles, Calif.: Obre Publications, 1947-.

Bimonthly.

"For the Spanish-speaking family of the U. S. A." In OCLC system.

Gráfico. Los Angeles, California, 1928?-1933?

Weekly, biweekly.

Director: Ignacio F. Herrerías; editor in chief: Horacio Melgarejo Randolph; administrator: Luis Alvear V. Listed in Ríos-C., Hermonio, "Toward a True Chicano Bibliography: Part II," p. 41. Also listed in "Más de cuatrocientos periódicos en español se han editado en Estados Unidos". In Spanish. No extant issues located.

El Gráfico. New York, N.Y.: Columbus Publishing Company, 1916-1918.

Ceased publication with Vol. 2, no. 8 dated jun. 1918, cf. *Union List of Serials.* "Revista mensual ilustrada de literatura, arte, ciencias, política, viajes, modas, etc." In OCLC system.

Gráfico. New York, N.Y., 1927-19uu.

Irregular.

In Spanish. In OCLC system.

Gráfico. Nueva York, N.Y., 1953-19uu.

Vol. 1, no. 1 dated 5 de diciembre de 1953. Repository: Center for Puerto Rican Studies at Hunter College, CUNY.

Gráfico Internacional. San Francisco, California: Gráfico Internacional, Inc., 1933?-19uu.

Monthly.

Año 4, no. 21 dated feb. 1937. In Spanish. In OCLC system.

La Granja y el Hogar. East Las Vegas, New Mexico: Agente Agrícola del Condado de San Miguel, 1917-19uu.

Semimonthly.

Vol. 1, no. [?] dated jun. 15, 1917. In Spanish. In OCLC system.

El Gringo y Greaser. Manzano, N. M.: Kusz & Co., 1883-1884.

Semimonthly.

Began publication with vol. 1, no. 1 agosto 15, 1883; ceased with abril 7, 1884, cf. Groves, Pearce S., *New Mexico Newspapers.* A companion newspaper was published in English with same numbering but differing in content titled *Gringo & Greaser.* In Spanish. In OCLC system.

El Grito de la Verdad. Solomonvile,T. [Territorio] Arizona, Graham Co.: Benjamín Pizarro, 189u?-18uu.

Weekly.

In Spanish. In OCLC system.

El Grito del Pueblo. Beeville, Bee County, Texas, 1888-1uuu.
Established by P. P. González. Listed in Ezell, Camp. *Historical Story of Bee County, Texas*, p. 52. No extant issues located.

El Guadalhorce. 1839-1840.
In Spanish. In OCLC system.

La Guadalupana: Revista Mensual Católica. San Antonio, Tex.: Guadalupian Pub. Co., 192u-.
Monthly.
Año 2 núm. 3 dated enero de 1923. In Spanish. In OCLC system.

Guadalupe County Review. Santa Rosa, New Mexico: Independent Pub. Co., 1926-1931?
Weekly.
Editor: Mrs. J. T. Cole. Listed in *N. W. Ayer & Son's American Newspaper Annual and Directory*, 1928. Also listed in Grove, Pearce S., *New Mexico Newspapers*. In Spanish and English. No extant issues located.

Guaimaro. Brooklyn, 1895?-1uuu.
Editor: José Andreu. Repository: Archivo Nacional de Cuba, Havana.

El Guante (Santa Fe, New Mexico). *See* **The Gauntlet.**

El Guao: Publicación Venenosa. New York, 1853-1853.
Redactor: Ambrioso Valiente y Pedro Santacilia. Listed in Batista Villareal, Teresita, *Catálogo de Publicaciones periódicas cubanas...*, p. 150. This source indicates that the Biblioteca Nacional José Martí in Havana holds some issues of this title.

El Guarda del Bravo. Laredo, Texas: P. Aldama, 1904-1907?
Semi-weekly.
Editor: M. Muñoz. Listed in "Más de cuatrocientos periódicos en español se han editado en Estados Unidos" and *Rowell's American Newspaper Directory*, 1907, p. 1134. In Spanish. No extant issues located.

El Guía. New York, N.Y.: Manuel Jamardo González, 1uuu-1uuu.
Monthly.
Listed in Common Council for American Unity, *Foreign Language Publications in the United States: Newspaper Lists*, p. 6. No extant issues located.

Guía Comercial. New York, N.Y.: John H. Simmons, 1874-1uuu.
Monthly.
Listed in *Rowell's American Newspaper Directory*, 1875, p. 155. In Spanish. No extant issues located.

Guía de Importadores. New York, N.Y.: J.E. Sitterly and Sons, 1uuu-1uuu.
Monthly.
Listed in Common Council for American Unity, *Foreign Language Publications in the United States: Newspaper Lists*, p. 6. In Spanish. No extant issues located.

El Guía de Santa Fe. Santa Fe, New Mexico: Companía Aztec, 1886-1886.
Weekly.
In Spanish. In OCLC system.

La Guía del Comprador. Los Angeles, California, 1925-19uu.
Monthly.
Director: Ali Eguía Morán. Listed in Ríos-C., Herminio, "Toward a True Chicano Bibliography: Part II," 1972, p. 41, and "Más de cuatrocientos periódicos en español se han editado en Estados Unidos". In Spanish. No extant issues located.

Guía para Maestros de Niños. El Paso, Texas: Casa Bautista de Publicaciones, 195u-.
Quarterly.
T. 3, no. 1 dated enero-feb.-marzo 1957. "Designed for use with the International Sunday School Lessons." In OCLC system.

El Habanero: Papel Político, Científico y Literario. Philadelphia, Penn; New York, N.Y.: En la Impr. Gray y Bunce, 1824-1826.
Founded, edited and published by Félix Valera. Published in Philadelphia in 1824. Listed in Willging, Eugene Paul and Herta Hatzfeld, *Catholic Serials of the Nineteenth*

Century in the United States. Also cited in Poyo, Gerald Eugene, *With All and for the Good of All,* p. 2. In Spanish. In OCLC system.

El Hablador. Nueva-Orleans, [La.]: J.L. Sollée, 1845?-1846.
    Semiweekly.
    Vol. 1, no. 34 dated 1 de enero de 1846. Continued by *Patria* (New Orleans, La.: 1846). In Spanish. In OCLC system.

La Hacienda. Buffalo, N.Y.: La Hacienda Co.,1905-19uu.
    Monthly, 1905-; bimonthly Mar./Apr. 1979-. Imprint varies: North Miami, Fla. In OCLC system.

HAHR (Washington, D. C.). *See* **The Hispanic American Historical Review.**

Helados, Refrescos y Dulces. New York: Meyers Publications Inc., 1931-19uu.
    Monthly.
    In Spanish. In OCLC system.

Hemispherica. [New York, N.Y.], 1951-.
    Monthly (except June/July,Aug./Sept.)
    Bulletin of the Inter-American Association for Democracy and Freedom. In Spanish and English. In OCLC system.

Herald. Morenci,Arizona: J.M. Erickson, 1909-1912.
    Weekly.
    Listed in "Más de cuatrocientos periódicos en español se han editado en Estados Unidos". Spanish and English. No extant issues located.

Herald. Nogales, New Mexico, 1916-19uu.
    Listed in "Más de cuatrocientos periódicos en español se han editado en Estados Unidos". In Spanish. No extant issues located.

Herald. Rio Grande City,Texas: Romeo Pérez, 1919-1943?
    Weekly.
    Editor: Lino Pérez, Jr. Listed in *N. W. Ayer & Son's Directory of Newspapers and Periodicals,* 1943, p. 920. In Spanish and English. No extant issues located.

The Herald of Christian Science (Boston). *See* **El Heraldo de la Ciencia Cristiana.**

El Heraldo. Chicago, Illinois, 1927-19uu.
    Weekly.
    Listed in Gregory,Winifred, ed., *American Newspapers, 1821-1936,* p. 9. In Spanish. Repository: Bancroft Library (University of California, Berkeley).

El Heraldo. Nueva York [N.Y.]: El Heraldo Pub. Co., 1916-19uu.
    Weekly.
    Vol. 1, no. 2 dated 13 de mayo de 1916. In Spanish. In OCLC system.

El Heraldo. San Antonio,Tex.:A. C.Valdez, 1886?-18uu.
    Weekly.
    Vol. 8, no. 350 dated mar. 22, 1893. In Spanish and English. In OCLC system.

El Heraldo. San Bernardino, California: M. J. Ciriza, 1949-1959.
    Weekly.
    Listed in *N.W.Ayer & Son's Directory of Newspapers and Periodicals,* 1959, p. 118. In Spanish. No extant issues located.

El Heraldo. Socorro, Nuevo México: J.A.Torres, 1914?-1920?
    Weekly.
    Began with Nov. 2, 1914, ceased with Dec. 23, 1920?, cf. Grove, Pearce S., *New Mexico Newspapers.* Vol. 3, no. 131 dated 4 de mayo de 1917. In Spanish. In OCLC system.

El Heraldo. Taos, N. M., 1884-1889.
    Listed in Miguélez, Armando, "Index of Spanish-Language Newspapers in the U. S. Southwest." No extant issues located.

El Heraldo Americano. Nueva York, N.Y.: Spanish Pub. Co., 1910-19uu.
    Weekly; semimonthly, Jan. 1-Apr. 29, 1910.
    In Spanish. In OCLC system.

El Heraldo Cristiano. Eagle Pass, Tex., 19uu-19uu.
  Año 5 núm. 107 dated 1 febrero 1920. Repository: University of Texas, Pan American.
El Heraldo Cristiano. [Robstown, Tex.], 19uu-.
  Monthly (except August).
  Issues for oct. 1949-enero 1952 (no. 442-465) called also Época 2; feb. 1952-feb./marzo 1955 (no. 466-494) called also Época 3. "Organo oficial de la Conferencia de Río Grande en la Iglesia Metodista". In Spanish and English. In OCLC system.
El Heraldo de Arizona. Phoenix, Ariz.: Alberto Vizcarra, 1935-19uu.
  Mentioned in Somoza, *Literatura de la Revolución Mexicana...,* 226. No extant issues located.
El Heraldo de Brownsville. Brownsville, Texas: The Brownsville Herald, 1934-19uu.
  Daily (except Saturday).
  Issued with *Brownsville Herald* (Brownsville, Tex.: 1910). Publisher varies: Freedom Newspapers, abr. 14, 1987. In OCLC system.
Heraldo de Estancia (Estancia, New Mexico). *See* **The Estancia Herald.**
El Heraldo de la Ciencia Cristiana. [Boston: Christian Science Pub. Society], 1959-19uu.
  Title varies: 1959-60, *El Heraldo de la Christian Science, The Herald of Christian Science.* In Spanish and English. In OCLC system.
Heraldo de las Américas. Chicago, Illinois, 1924-19uu.
  Weekly.
  Listed in Gregory, Winifred, ed., *American Newspapers, 1821-1936,* p. 9. In Spanish. No extant issues located.
El Heraldo de México. Los Angeles, California: Caesar F. Marburgy Cía., 1915-1952.
    Daily (except Monday), Jan. 10, 1922-May 12, 1929; semi-weekly, April 2, 1916-Mar. 27, 1919; triweekly Mar. 29-June 1919; daily, July 1919-Jan. 8, 1922.
  "Defensor de los mexicanos en Estados Unidos". "Trisemanario independiente de información y comercio". In Spanish. In OCLC system.
El Heraldo de Santidad. Kansas City, Missouri: Publicaciones Internacionales, División de Comunicaciones de la Iglesia del Nazareno, 1945-1989.
  Monthly.
  In Spanish. In OCLC system.
El Heraldo de Taos. Taos, N. M.: Lorin W. Brown, 1885-1888.
  Weekly.
  Continues *El Heraldo del Condado de Taos.* Continued by *El Heraldo de Taoseño.* In Spanish. In OCLC system.
El Heraldo del Condado de Taos. Fernández de Taos, N. M.: J.M. Alvey, 1884-1885.
  Weekly.
  Continued by *El Heraldo de Taos.* In Spanish. In OCLC system.
El Heraldo del Valle. San Louis, Col., 1907-1949.
  Founder: J. R. Valdez. Repository: Costilla County Library, St. Louis, Colorado. Mentioned in Somoza, *Literatura de la Revolución Mexicana...,* p. 236.
Heraldo Dominical. Trinidad, Colorado, 1uuu-1uuu.
  Irregular.
  Listed in "Más de cuatrocientos periódicos en español se han editado en Estados Unidos". In Spanish. No extant issues located.
El Heraldo Dominical = Spanish Sunday Paper. Ybor City Fla., 1914-19uu.
  Weekly.
  Editor: Demetrie Rivera. In OCLC system.
Heraldo Evangélico. New York, 1951?-.
  In OCLC system.
El Heraldo Ganadero de Texas = The Texas Livestock Herald. San Antonio, Tex.: Texas Livestock Herald [1944?-1944?].
  In Spanish. In OCLC system.

El Heraldo Latino. Nueva York: Richards Dyspepsia Tablet Association, 1923?-19uu.
Irregular.
Año 3, T. 1 dated 1925. "Periódico Internacional de Noticias". In Spanish. In OCLC system.

El Heraldo Mexicano. Los Angeles, California, 1906-1913.
Weekly.
Director: Gral. Miguel Ruelas. Listed in "Más de cuatrocientos periódicos en español se han editado en Estados Unidos". No extant issues located.

El Heraldo Mexicano: Seminario Popular Independiente. San Antonio, Texas, 1927-19uu.
Weekly.
In Spanish. In OCLC system.

El Heraldo-Taoseño. [Taos, N. M.]: Lorin W. Brown, 1888-1889?
Weekly.
Began with t. 5, num. 14 dated 6 de oct. de 1888. Ceased in Apr. 1889, cf. Grove, Pearce S., *New Mexico Newspapers.* Continues *Heraldo de Taos.* In Spanish. In OCLC system.

Heraldos del Rey. El Paso, Texas, 1927-1972.
Quarterly.
Listed in Common Council for American Unity, *Foreign Language Publications in the United States: Newspaper Lists,* p. 9. In Spanish. Replaced by *Conquistadores.* Repository: Casa Bautista de Publicaciones Library in El Paso, Texas.

La Hermandad. Pueblo, Colo.: Alej. M. Darley, 1889-1907.
Monthly.
Vol. 2, no. 2 dated abr. 1890. In Spanish. In OCLC system.

Hijas de Cuba. New York, N.Y., 1895-1uuu.
Repository: Archivo Nacional de Cuba, Havana.

El Hijo del Fronterizo. Phoenix, Ariz.: Carlos I. Velasco, 1880-18uu.
Mentioned in *The Arizona Daily Star,* jun. 16, 1887, p. 4. Also mentioned in *El Fronterizo* (Tucson), ago. 15, 1889; cf. Somoza, *Literatura de la Revolución Mexicana...,* p. 226. No extant issues located.

El Hijo de El Fronterizo. Tucson, Arizona, 1912-19uu.
Continues *El Fronterizo.* In OCLC system.

Hispania. [University, Miss., etc.]: American Association of Teachers of Spanish and Portuguese, [etc.], 1918-.
Four nos. a year, 1918; 6 nos. a year, 1919-32; 4 nos. a year, 1933-47; 5 nos. a year, 1957-75; quarterly, May 1981-.
"A journal devoted to the interest of the teaching of Spanish and Portuguese." Published 1917-44 by the American Association of Teachers of Spanish; 1945- by the American Association of Teachers of Spanish and Portuguese. In OCLC system.

The Hispanic American Historical Review. Washington, D. C.: Board of Editors of the Hispanic American Review, 1918-.
Quarterly.
Managing editor: J. A. Robertson, 1918-. Suspended, 1923-25. Published Durham, N. C.: Duke University Press, Feb. 1978-. In English and Spanish. In OCLC system.

Hispanic Review. Philadelphia, Pa.: Dept. of Romance Languages of the University of Pennsylvania, 1933-.
"A quarterly journal devoted to research in the Hispanic languages & literatures." In English, Spanish, and Portuguese. In OCLC system.

Hispano América. San Francisco, Calif.: Hispano-América Pub. Co., 1917-1934.
Weekly, 1917-July 27, 1918; semiweekly, July 30, 1918-Mar. 4, 1919; weekly, Mar. 15, 1919-1934.
Directors: Joaquín Piña (1918), Julio G. Arce (1919), Néstor G. Arce (1934). Began with 3 a. época, año 4, no. 156 dated 15 de abr. de 1917. Published by La Crónica, Inc., June 10, 1917-1934. Continues *Crónica* (San Francisco, Calif.: 1914). Absorbed in part by

Mefistófeles (San Francisco, Calif.) July 27, 1918. Variant title: *Hispano-América,* July 27, 1918-1919. In Spanish. In OCLC system.

El Hispano-Americano. Belen, Nuevo México: P.A. Speckmann, 19uu-19uu.
Weekly.
T. 3, no. 44 dated Apr. 26, 1913. In Spanish. In OCLC system.

El Hispano-Americano. El Paso, Tex.: [Victor L. Ochoa], 189u-1uuu.
Daily (except Monday).
Año 6, no. 180 dated 7 de agosto de 1893. In Spanish. In OCLC system.

El Hispano-Americano. Las Vegas, N. M.: Victor Ochoa, 189u-1920.
Weekly.
Vol. IV, núm. 23 dated abril 21 de 1892. "Sucesor de *El Valle del Bravo, El Latino Americano* de El Paso, Texas, y *El Sol de Mayo,* de Las Vegas, N. M. Organo de la Orden de los Caballeros de Mutua Protección, de Nuevo México". In Spanish. In OCLC system.

El Hispano-Americano. Mora, N. M.: Compañía Publicista del Condado de Mora, 1908-19uu.
Weekly.
In Spanish and English. In OCLC system.

El Hispano Americano. [Roy, N. M.?]: Mora County Pub. Co., 1905-19uu.
Weekly.
Vol. 1 no. 4 dated Feb. 13, 1905. Title varies slighty. Other edition: *Weekly Hispano Americano.* In English and Spanish. In OCLC system.

El Hispano-Americano. San Diego, California: Spanish American Pub. Co., 1914-1937.
Daily, tri-weekly.
Founder: José García Cuadra. In Spanish and English. In OCLC system.

El Hispano-Americano. Socorro, N. M., 1891-1uuu.
Weekly.
Vol. 4, no. 2 dated nov. 10 de 1891. In Spanish. In OCLC system.

Hispanófila. Chapel Hill, N. C.: University of North Carolina, 1957-.
In English and Spanish. In OCLC system.

Historia Ilustrado de Nuevo México. Santa Fe, N. M., 1919-19uu.
Monthly.
Listed in Grove, Pearce S., *New Mexico Newspapers,* p. 448. In Spanish. No extant issues located.

Historias Infantiles. El Paso, Tex.: Casa Bautista de Publicaciones, 1957-1971.
Repository: Library of Casa Bautista de Publicaciones in El Paso, Texas.

El Hogar. Chama, N. M., 1uuu-1uuu.
Weekly.
Listed in Grove, Pearce S., *New Mexico Newspapers.* In Spanish. No extant issues located.

El Hogar. Floresville, Texas, 1914-1917?
Listed in Ríos-C., Herminio, "Toward a True Chicano Bibliography: Part II," p. 45, and "Más de cuatrocientos periódicos en español se han editado en Estados Unidos". In Spanish. No extant issues located.

El Hogar Cristiano. El Paso, Tex: Casa Bautista de Publicaciones, 1957-.
Quarterly.
In OCLC system.

Hoja Doctrinal: Frente Revolucionario Democrático (Cuba). Coral Gables, Florida: Comisión de Propaganda, Frente Revolucionario Democrático, 1960-.
In Spanish. In OCLC system.

Hoja Volante. Los Angeles, Calif.: Zamorano Club, 1934-.
Quarterly, May 1947; irregular, June 1934-Dec. 1938.
Suspended 1939-1946. In Spanish. In OCLC system.

La Hora de los Cuentos. El Paso, Texas: Casa Bautista de Publicaciones, 1947-1984.
Quarterly.

"Juvenile and religious." *Foreign Language Publications in the United States: Newspaper Lists,* p. 9. Continued by *Revista para Uniones de Párvulos y Principiantes* (1955-1984). Repository: Casa Bautista de Publicaciones, El Paso Texas.

El Horizonte. Corpus Christi, Tex.; San Diego; Tex.: José L. Montalbo & Bro., 1879-1uuu.
Semiweekly.
"Periódico independiente, literario, de variedades y anuncios". Tomo 1, no. 2 dated nov. 5, 1879. T.2 published in San Diego, Tex. In Spanish. In OCLC system.

El Horizonte. Nueva York, [N.Y.], 18uu-1uuu.
"Suplemento" dated 24 de set. de 1850. In Spanish. In OCLC system.

La Hormiga de Oro. Albuquerque: Enrique Sosa, 18uu-190u.
Weekly.
Continued by *Estrella de Nuevo México.* In Spanish. In OCLC system.

The Horse Fly. Taos, New Mexico, 1938-194u.
Weekly.
Editor: Spud Johnson. Ceased November 1941? "Smallest and most inadequate newspaper ever published." Later reappeared as a section of *El Crepúsculo* in May, 1950. Absorbed by *El Crepúsculo* (Taos, N. M.: 1948). In English. In OCLC system.

El Hospital. Cincinnati, Ohio [etc.]: Salud Publications International, Inc. [etc.], 1945-.
Bimonthly.
In OCLC system.

El Hospital. New York, N.Y.: Panamerican Club, 19uu-.
Monthly.
Vol. 3, no. 1 dated enero 1947. In Spanish. In OCLC system.

Huelga General. Los Angeles, California, 191u-19uu.
"Linked with the International Workers of the World activities," cf. Chabrán, Rafael and Richard Chabrán, "The Spanish-Language and Latino Press of the United States: Newspapers and Periodicals." In Spanish. No extant issues located.

Huérfano Independent. Walsenberg, Colo.: [T. O. Bigney], 1875-1uuu.
Weekly.
Vol. 1, no. 53 dated July 22, 1876. Published in La Veta, Colo., June 26, 1877. In English and Spanish. In OCLC system.

Humanidad. El Paso, Texas: Santiago R. De La Vega, 190u-19uu.
Cited in Lomas, Clara. "The Articulation of Gender in the Mexican Borderlands, 1900-1915," p. 296. Also mentioned in Carrasco Puente, Rafael. *La prensa en México...,* p. 243. Carrasco indicates the paper was published in San Antonio, Texas, in 1904. In Spanish. No extant issues located.

El Humo. San Antonio, Tex., 192u-19uu.
Listed in Miguélez, Armando, "Index of Spanish-Language Newspapers in the U. S. Southwest." Miguélez indicates paper is mentioned in *El Tucsonense,* no dates are given for this source. No extant issues located.

Ibérica. New York, N.Y., 1933-19uu.
In Spanish. In OCLC system.

Ibérica. New York, N.Y.: Agrupación de Combatientes y Exilados de la República Española, 1942-1952
Monthly.
In Spanish. In OCLC system.

Ibérica. New York, N.Y.: Ibérica Pub. Co., 1954?-1974.
Monthly.
In Spanish. Also issued in an English edition. In OCLC system.

El Ideal Católico Mexicano. Chicago, Illinois, 19uu-19uu.
Published by conservative Mexican Catholics "to counter the radical appeal of El Frente Popular Mexicano, a chapter of La Confederación de Trabajadores Mexicanos," cf. Chabrán, Rafael and Richard Chabrán, "The Spanish-Language and Latino Press of

the United States: Newspapers and Periodicals," p. 373. In Spanish. No extant issues located.

La Igualdad. Cayo Hueso, Fla., 187u-1uuu.
> Weekly, Dec. 9, 1876-Dec. 16, 1876; biweekly, Jan. 1, 1877-Jan. 14, 1877.
> Director: José Dolores Poyo. Año 1, no. 2 dated dic. 9 de 1876. "Periódico político cubano". In Spanish. In OCLC system.

Ilustración. Nueva York, N.Y., 1945-19uu.
> "Revista mensual para las personas que piensan y en particular para los obreros". Director: Edmundo Espínola. In Spanish. Repository: Center for Puerto Rican Studies at Hunter College.

La Ilustración Americana. New York, N.Y., 1866-1870.
> Weekly.
> Editor: Frank Leslie. Listed in "Más de cuatrocientos periódicos en español se han editado en Estados Unidos". In Spanish. No extant issues located.

La Ilustración Norte Americana. Chicago, Ill.: Hickox & Read Publishing Co., 1887-1uuu.
> Monthly.
> Editor: F. Martínez de Rivas. Listed in *Rowell's American Newspaper Directory,* 1896, p. 221. In Spanish. No extant issues located.

La Ilustración Norteamericana. New York, N.Y., 1890-1uuu.
> Monthly.
> Listed in "Más de cuatrocientos periódicos en español se han editado en Estados Unidos". In Spanish. No extant issues located.

El Imparcial. Albuquerque, Nuevo México: El Imparcial, 1903-19uu.
> Weekly.
> In Spanish. In OCLC system.

El Imparcial. Denver, Colo.: El Imparcial Pub. Co., 1932-19uu.
> Weekly.
> In OCLC system.

El Imparcial. New Orleans, Louisiana: Serapín Arredondo, 1862-1uuu.
> Weekly.
> Listed in *Rowell's American Newspaper Directory,* 1869, p. 40. In Spanish. No extant issues located.

El Imparcial. Phoenix, Ariz.: Carlos B. Bautista, 1937-1938.
> Listed in Miguélez, Armando, "Index of Spanish-Language Newspapers in the U. S. Southwest." No extant issues located.

El Imparcial. Phoenix, Ariz.: Arizona Sun Pub. 1956–19uu.
> In OCLC system.

El Imparcial. San Diego, California, 1927-19uu.
> Irregular.
> Listed in Ríos-C., Herminio, "Toward a True Chicano Bibliography: Part II," p. 41. In Spanish. No extant issues located

El Imparcial. San Francisco, Calif.: Victor P. Dextre, 1919?-19uu.
> Weekly.
> Vol. 12, no. 594 dated Nov. 20, 1931. Continued by *Semanario Imparcial.* In Spanish. In OCLC system.

El Imparcial. Tucson, Ariz; 1931-19uu.
> Listed in Miguélez, Armando. "Index of Spanish-Language Newspapers in the U. S. Southwest." Miguélez indicates the paper is mentioned in *El Tucsonense,* no dates for this source is given. No extant issues located.

El Imparcial. Walsenburg, Colo., 1911-1914.
> Mentioned in Somoza, *Literatura de la Revolución Mexicana. . .,* p. 237. No extant issues located.

El Imparcial de Chicago. Chicago, Illinois, 1957-19uu.

In Spanish. In OCLC system.

El Imparcial de Nueva York. Nueva York, N.Y.: El Imparcial Inc., 19uu-19uu.

Daily (except Sunday).

T. 8, no. 367 dated 7 de enero de 1959. "El Diario Ilustrado." Variant titles: *Diario de Nueva York, Imparcial el Diario Ilustrado de Nueva York.* In OCLC system.

El Imparcial de Texas. San Antonio, Tex.: El Imparcial de Texas, 1908-1924.

Weekly.

Published 1908-1924?, cf. Gregory, Winifred, ed., *American Newspapers, 1821-1936.* T. 8, no. 369 dated 13 de dic. de 1917. In Spanish. In OCLC system.

El Imparcial el Diario Ilustrado de Nueva York (New York, N.Y.). *See* **El Imparcial de Nueva York.**

Imprenta del Río Grande. Santa Fe, N. M., 1873-1uuu.

"Reportedly first Jesuit work in New Mexico; moved to Las Vegas, San Miguel County, and assumed the title *Revista Católica,* January 2, 1875," cf. Grove, Pearce S., *New Mexico Newspapers,* p. 448. In Spanish. No extant issues located.

La Independencia. Nueva York, [N.Y.]: Ignacio de Armas, 1873?-1880.

Weekly.

Subtitle: "Organo de Cuba libre e independiente". "Periódico politíco republicano". Directores: Ignacio de Armas (1873), Antonio Zambrana (1874), Juan Bellido de Luna (1874-80). In Spanish. In OCLC system. An inventory list from the Archivo Nacional de Cuba, Havana, deposited in the collection of the Recovering the U.S. Hispanic Literary Heritage project, shows that the Archivo owns one issue for September 15, 1867.

The Independent (New Orleans, Louisiana). *See* **El Independiente** (Nueva-Orleans).

Independent Democrat. Las Cruces, New Mexico: A. B. Fall, 1892-189u.

Weekly.

Continued by *Las Cruces Democrat.* In English and Spanish. In OCLC system.

The Independent. Walsenburg, Huérfano County, Colo.: The Independent Pub. Co., 1909-1915.

Weekly.

Continues *Independent y el Imparcial.* In English and Spanish (1910-1914). In OCLC system.

El Independent. New York, N.Y., 1898?-1uuu.

Director: Fidel G. Pierra. Repository: Archivo Nacional de Cuba, Havana.

The Independent y el Imparcial. Walsenburg, Colo.: Independent Pub. Co., 1915–1923.

In OCLC system.

The Independent (Las Vegas, New Mexico). *See* **El Independiente** (Las Vegas, N. M.).

El Independiente. Albuquerque, Nuevo Mexico: Independent Pub. Co.; 1933-1939.

Weekly.

Began with vol. 4, núm 5 dated sep. 22, 1933; ceased with v. 11, núm. 4 dated 22 dic. de1939. Other editions: *Bernalillo Times, Independent of Valencia County.* Continues *Independiente and the New Mexico Independent* (1933). Continued by *Independiente and the New Mexico Independent* (1939). In Spanish. In OCLC system.

El Independiente. Devine, Texas, 1911-19uu.

Irregular.

Director: Lorenzo Yáñez, Jr. Listed in "Más de cuatrocientos periódicos en español se han editado en Estados Unidos", and Ríos-C., Herminio, "Toward a True Chicano Bibliography: Part II," p. 45. In Spanish. No extant issues located.

El Independiente. El Paso, Tex.: Teresa Urrea [y] Lauro Aguirre, 189u-1uuu.

Weekly.

Año 4, no. 13 dated mayo 6 de 1896. Continued by *El Progresista.* In OCLC system.

El Independiente. Las Vegas, [N. M.]: La Cía. Publicista de "El Independiente", 1894-19uu.

Weekly.

Editor: Felipe Chacón (as of 1924). Manager: E. H. Salazar. In Spanish. Includes a companion paper called *The Independent* (1901-1928). In OCLC system.

El Independiente. Los Angeles, California: L. Larraquibel, 1895-1uuu.

Semi-weekly.

Listed in *Rowell's American Newspaper Directory,* 1896, p. 117. In Spanish. No extant issues located.

El Independiente. Mountainair, Condado de Torrance, Nuevo México: Mountainair Print. Co., 1917-19uu.

Weekly.

T. 1, no. 4 dated 26 de enero de 1918. In Spanish and English. In OCLC system.

El Independiente. Nogales, Arizona: Lauro Aguirre, 1893-1895?

Weekly; bi-weekly.

Listed in *Rowell's American Newspaper Directory,* 1896, p. 93, and "Más de cuatrocientos periódicos en español se han editado en Estados Unidos". In Spanish. No extant issues located.

El Independiente. New York, 1898-1998.

Weekly.

Listed in Batista Villareal, Teresita, *Catálogo de Publicaciones periódicas cubanas...*, p. 153. This source indicates that the Biblioteca Nacional José Martí in Havana holds a complete run (vol. 1-14, oct.-dic. 1998).

El Independiente. Nueva-Orleans [i.e. New Orleans, La.]: Cirilo Villaverde y Manuel Antonio Marino, 1853-1uuu.

Weekly.

"Organo de la democracia cubana". Published with an additional masthead in English: "The Independent." In Spanish and English. In OCLC system.

El Independiente. Nueva York, 1890-18uu.

Weekly.

"Semanario político, mercantil y de intereses generales". Continues *El Cubano.* Listed in Batista Villareal, Teresita, *Catálogo de Publicaciones periódicas cubanas...*, p. 153. This source indicates that the Biblioteca Nacional José Martí in La Havana holds some issues of this title.

El Independiente. Rio Grande City, Texas, 1924-1931.

Weekly.

"Director: José Salinas. Colaboradores: José Vizcayo, Jr., José Díaz, Conrado Espinoza, Juan José de la Garza, Angel Fernández." Listed in "Más de cuatrocientos periódicos en español se han editado en Estados Unidos". In Spanish. No extant issues located.

El Independiente. Solomonville, Ariz., 1895-1uuu.

Mentioned in *El Fronterizo* (Tucson) nov. 3, 1895, p. 3; cf. Somoza, *Literatura de la Revolución Mexicana...*, p. 227. No extant issues located.

El Independiente. Tampa, Florida, 1912-19uu.

Irregular.

Listed in "Más de cuatrocientos periódicos en español se han editado en Estados Unidos". In Spanish. No extant issues located.

El Independiente. Taos, N. M., 1918-19uu.

Mentioned in Somoza, *Literatura de la Revolución Mexicana...*, p. 244. No extant issues located.

El Independiente. Walsemburg, Colo.: José Escobar, 1896-1uuu.

Weekly.

In Spanish. In OCLC system.

El Independiente. Yuma, Ariz.: José Venegas, 1916-19uu.

Mentioned in *El Tucsonense,* jun. 17, 1916, p. 2; cf. Somoza, *Literatura de la Revolución Mexicana...*, p. 230. No extant issues located.

El Independiente and the New Mexico Independent. Albuquerque, Nuevo Mexico: El Independiente Print Co; 19uu-1933.

Weekly.

Vol. 3, núm. 30 dated marzo 17, 1933. Ceased with vol. 4, núm. 4 dated sept. 15, 1933= t. 43, núm. 12. In Spanish. Other editions: *Bernalillo Times.* Continues *New Mexico Independient (1930).* Continued by *El Independiente* (1933). In Spanish. In OCLC system.

El Independiente and the New Mexico Independent. Albuquerque, N. M.: Independent Pub. Co., 1939-1966.

Weekly.

Began with vol. 11, núm. 5 dated 29 de dic., 1939; ceased with vol. 25, núm. 41 dated 12 de agosto de 1966 (t. 49, núm. 27 to t. 75, núm. 11). Irregular numbering. In Spanish with some text in English: 1939-1957. In English with some text in Spanish: 1957-1966. Other editions: *Bernalillo Times, Independent of Valencia County.* Continues *El Independiente.* Continued by *Independiente of Bernalillo County.* In OCLC system.

El Independiente de Mora (Wagon Mound, New Mexico*). See* **Mora County Independent.**

El Independiente del Valle de la Mesilla. La Mesilla, N. M.: A. J. Fountain, J. S. Crouch, T. Casad [etc.], 1877-1879.

Weekly.

Companion newspaper published titled *Mesilla Valley Independent.* In Spanish. In OCLC system.

El Indicador. Nueva Orleans [i.e., New Orleans, La.]: L. Fischer & Cía., 1865-1869?

Weekly.

Began Jan. 29, 1865. Subtitle: Organo de la población española. In Spanish. In OCLC system.

El Indicador Industrial. New York, N. Y.: Latamer Publishers, Inc., 1944-19uu.

Año 6, no. 1 dated enero-marzo 1949. In Spanish. In OCLC system.

Indicador Mercantil. New York, N. Y.: El Indicador Mercantil, 19uu-19uu.

Bi-monthly.

Listed in Common Council for American Unity, *Foreign Language Publications in the United States: Newspaper Lists,* p. 6. No extant issues located.

El Indito. Old Albuquerque, N. M.: Armijo y Varela, 1900?-1905?

Weekly.

T. 1, no. 36 dated nov. 24 de 1900. In Spanish. In OCLC system.

La Industria. New York, N. Y., 1882-1uuu.

Monthly.

Listed in "Más de cuatrocientos periódicos en español se han editado en Estados Unidos". In Spanish. No extant issues located.

La Industrial. Douglas, Arizona: G. G. Televier, 1910-19uu.

Irregular.

Listed in Ríos-C., Herminio, "Toward a True Chicano Bibliography: Part II," p. 41, and "Más de cuatrocientos periódicos en español se han editado en Estados Unidos". No extant issues located.

Informaciones. Washington, D. C.: Interamerican Development Commission, 1944-19uu.

Monthly.

In Spanish. In OCLC system.

Informaciones Económicas. Washington, D. C.: Departamento de Asuntos Económicos y Sociales, Unión Panamericana, 1956-19uu.

In Spanish. In OCLC system.

El Informador. Sacramento, California: Informador del Norte, 1939-19uu.

Weekly.

Editor: José Herrera. Listed in *N. W. Ayer & Son's Directory of Newspapers and Periodicals,* 1943, p. 101. In Spanish. No extant issues located.

El Informador. Tucson, Ariz.: Francisco M. Robledo, 1935-19uu.

Mentioned in *La Alianza,* abr., 1955, p. 12; cf. Somoza, *Literatura de la Revolución*

Mexicana..., p. 229. No extant issues located.

Informativo Quincenal de la UNRRA. Washington, EE. UU: Administración de las Naciones Unidas para el Socorro y la Rehabilitación, 1945-1945.
> Biweekly.
> Continued by *Carta Quincenal de la UNRRA*. In Spanish. In OCLC system.

Ingeniería Internacional. New York: McGraw-Hill Co., 1919-1941.
> Monthly.
> [T. 5, no. 1] dated enero 1921. Split into *Ingeniería Internacional* (Edición de construcción), and *Ingeniería Internacional* (Edición de industria). In OCLC system.

Ingeniería Internacional. Edición de construcción. [Nueva York, E.U.A.]: [Business Publishers International Corp.], 1942-1942.
> Monthly.
> Continued in 1942 by *Ingeniería Internacional: Construcción.* Continues in part *Ingeniería Internacional.* In OCLC system.

Ingeniería Internacional. Edición de industria. Nueva York, E.U.A.: Business Publishers International Corp., 1942.
> Monthly.
> Continued in 1942 by *Ingeniería Internacional: Industria.* Continues in part *Ingeniería Internacional.* In OCLC system.

El Instructor. McAllen, Tex., 1954?-1958.
> Vol. 2, no. 8 dated agosto 15 de 1955. Editors: 1954-1955, Bill H. Reeves and Wayne Partain ; 1956-1958, Bill H. Reeves. Published in McAllen, Texas during 1954-1955, and in in Harlingen, Texas during 1956-1958. "Dedicado a la propagación del evangelio Novo-Testamentario." In OCLC system.

Ingeniería Internacional: Industria. Nueva York, E.U.A.: Business Publishers International Corp., 1942-1961?
> Monthly.
> Continues *Ingeniería Internacional* (Edición de industria). In OCLC system.

Inquietudes: Revista de Iniciación de Cultura Popular. Los Angeles, Calif.: Editorial Germinal, 1936-19uu.
> Monthly.
> In Spanish. In OCLC system.

Inter-América. Nueva York: Doubleday, Page, & Company, 1917-1926.
> Bimonthly.
> Spanish translations of articles in the United States press. Companion to *Inter-America* (New York, N.Y.: English), which consists of English translations of articles in the Spanish American press. "Se ha fundado a insinuación a la Dotación Carnegie para la Paz Internacional". Other edition: *Inter-America* (New York, N.Y.: English). In OCLC system.

El Internacional. Cincinnati, Ohio: Adolfo Duclós Salinas, 1894-1uuu.
> Weekly.
> Listed in *Rowell's American Newspaper Directory,* 1900, p. 807. In Spanish. No extant issues located.

El Internacional. Del Rio, Texas, 1923-1927.
> Weekly.
> Director: Amado Gutiérrez. Listed in "Más de cuatrocientos periódicos en español se han editado en Estados Unidos". Also listed in Ríos-C., Herminio, "Toward a True Chicano Bibliography: Part II," p. 45. In Spanish. No extant issues located.

El Internacional. El Paso, Texas, 1913-19uu.
> Daily.
> Founder: Enrique Aquirre; Director: W. Tovar y Bueno. Listed in "Más de cuatrocientos periódicos en español se han editado en Estados Unidos", and Ríos-C., Herminio, "Toward a True Chicano Bibliography: Part II." In Spanish. No extant issues located.

El Internacional. El Paso, Texas, 1925-19uu.
  Daily.
  Director: José E. Campos. Listed in "Más de cuatrocientos periódicos en español se han editado en Estados Unidos", and Ríos-C., Herminio, "Toward a True Chicano Bibliography: Part II," p. 45. In Spanish. No extant issues located.
Internacional. Los Angeles, California, 1930-19uu.
  Monthly.
  Listed in "Más de cuatrocientos periódicos en español se han editado en Estados Unidos". In Spanish. No extant issues located.
El Internacional. Miami, Florida, 1918-1925.
  Bi-weekly.
  Listed in Ríos-C., Herminio, "Toward a True Chicano Bibliography: Part II," p. 42. Ríos indicates it was published in Nogales, Arizona in 1926. Also cited in "Más de cuatrocientos periódicos en español se han editado en Estados Unidos". In Spanish. No extant issues located.
El Internacional. Nogales, Arizona, 1925-19uu.
  Weekly.
  Listed in *N. W. Ayer & Son's American Newspaper Annual and Directory,* 1926, p. 59. Also listed in Ríos-C., Herminio, "Toward a True Chicano Bibliography: Part II." Ríos indicates this paper was published in Miami from 1918-1925, and in 1926. In Spanish and English. No extant issues located.
Internacional. St. Louis, Missouri, 1889-1uuu.
  Monthly.
  Listed in "Más de cuatrocientos periódicos en español se han editado en Estados Unidos". In Spanish. No extant issues located.
El International. San Diego, Calif.: J. Isaac Aceves, 1933-19uu.
  Mentioned in *Hispano-América* (San Francisco), nov. 23, 1933; cf. Somoza, *Literatura de la Revolución Mexicana...,* p. 234. No extant issues located.
El Internacional. Tampa, Fla.: Centro Obrero, 1904-19uu.
  Continues *Boletín Obrero.* "Semanario dedicado a la propaganda sobre organización obrera". In Spanish and English. In OCLC system.
El Internacional. San Francisco, Calif.: Rubio Somoza & Co., 1924–19uu.
  In OCLC system.
El Internacional. Tampa, Fla., 1933-193u.
  Biweekly.
  During 1934 had a parallel title: *International.* "Organo local de las Uniones de la Internacional de Tabaqueros de América". Printer: Solís Print. In English and Spanish. In OCLC system.
El Internacional. Tampa, Fla.: Labor Temple, 1937-19uu.
  Año 2, num. 9 dated 6 junio 18, 1937. Editor: Pedro Ramírez Moya. "Official journal of the local Unions of Tampa, Cigarmakers International Union of America." In Spanish and English. In OCLC system.
El International. Tucson, Ariz.: Eugenio de la Peña, 1960-19uu.
  Mentioned in Somoza, *Literatura de la Revolución Mexicana...,* p. 229. No extant issues located.
The International. Presidio, Tex.: Juan Rivera, Sr., 1947-1960.
  Weekly.
  Continued by *The Presidio Voice* (Presidio, Tex.: 1961). In English and Spanish. In OCLC system.
International Council of Jewish Women: Newsletter. *See* **Newsletter** [Spanish edition]
The International News Guide. Eagle Pass, Texas: L. M. Hufman, 1939-1948.
  Weekly.
  Continues *Daily Guide.* Absorbed *La Voz Latina* (Eagle Pass, Tex.). Continued by

Eagle Pass News-Guide (Eagle Pass, Tex.: 1948). In English. In OCLC system.

El Intransigente. Key West, Fla., 1895?-1uuu.
Listed in Poyo, Gerald, Eugene, *With All, and for the Good of All*, p. 127. No extant issues located.

Intuición: Revista Mensual de Ideas, Sociología y Crítica Constructiva. New York, N.Y.: Intuición, 1929-1930.
In Spanish. In OCLC system.

El Iris. Tucson, A.T. [Ariz. Territory]: Francisco F. Velasco, 1886-1uuu.
In Spanish. In OCLC system.

El Iris de Paz. Nueva-Orleans [i.e. New Orleans, La.]: J. G. Negrete, 1841-18uu.
Semiweekly.
In Spanish. In OCLC system.

Israel y América Latina. Nueva York [i.e. New York, N.Y.], 1949-.
"Publicada por el Departamento Latinoamericano de la Agencia Judía para Palestina."
In Spanish. In OCLC system.

The Javelin. Carrizo Springs, Texas: J. L. McCaleb, 1889-1uuu.
Weekly.
Vol. 7, no. 6 dated Mar. 9, 1895. Dec. 23, 1980 issue has a separate Spanish edition. In OCLC system.

Jim Hogg County Enterprise. Hebbronville, Tex.: W. A. Dannelley and W. R. Quilliam, 1926-19uu.
Weekly.
In English and Spanish. In OCLC system.

Jornal del Pobre. Gallup, New Mexico, 1916-19uu.
Weekly.
Listed in Ríos-C., Herminio, "Toward a True Chicano Bibliography: Part II," and "Más de cuatrocientos periódicos en español se han editado en Estados Unidos". In Spanish. No extant issues located.

El Jornalero. Cleveland, N. M., 1894-1uuu.
Weekly.
Listed in Grove, Pearce S., *New Mexico Newspapers*, p. 293. Also mentioned in *El Independiente* (Las Vegas, N. M.), 9 jun., 1894, where the beginning publication year is confirmed. This source also indicates that the publisher was Don Diego A. Chacón. In Spanish. No extant issues located.

Journal. Key West, Florida: Morning Journal Pub. Co., 1908?-1920.
Semi-monthly?
Listed in *N. W. Ayer & Son's American Newspaper Annual and Directory*, 1918 as a weekly publication, and in "Más de cuatrocientos periódicos en español se han editado en Estados Unidos". In Spanish and English. No extant issues located.

The Journal of the American Medical Association. Chicago: American Medical Association, 1919-1928.
In Spanish. In OCLC system.

El Joven. Los Angeles, Calif., 1877-1878.
Weekly, 1877-; semiweekly, Apr. 12, 1878-.
Editors: J. F. Rodríguez (Sept. 18, 1877); A. Cuyás (Apr. 12, 1878). "The only Spanish independent news-paper published in Los Angeles." In OCLC system.

El Joven. Yuma, Arizona: Hodges and Meléndrez, 1882-1uuu.
Weekly.
Mentioned in *San Francisco Bulletin*, Feb. 6, 1882, cf. Lutrell, Estelle, *Newspapers and Periodicals of Arizona, 1859-1911*, p. 71. In Spanish. No extant issues located.

Juntos. Kingsville, Tex.: The Students, Presbyterian Pan American School, 1958-.
Annual.
In English. In OCLC system.

Justice. El Paso, Texas, 1906-1908.
>Weekly.

Listed in Ríos-C., Herminio, "Toward a True Chicano Bibliography: Part II," p. 45, and "Más de cuatrocientos periódicos en español se han editado en Estados Unidos". In Spanish and English. No extant issues located.

Justice. Phoenix, Arizona, P.G. de la Lama: 1916-1934.

Miguélez indicates the paper was published in Nogales in 1922. Also listed in "Más de cuatrocientos periódicos en español se han editado en Estados Unidos". In Spanish and English. No extant issues located.

La Justicia. El Paso, Tex.: Federico Ochoa, 1893-1uuu.
>Weekly.

"Semanario católico, de noticias y anuncios". In Spanish. In OCLC system.

La Justicia. El Paso, Texas, 1915-1916.
>Daily.

Director: José Luis Velasco. Listed in Ríos-C., Herminio, "Toward a True Chicano Bibliography: Part II," p. 45, and "Más de cuatrocientos periódicos en español se han editado en Estados Unidos". In Spanish and English. No extant issues located.

Justicia. Jersey City, N. J.: International Ladies Garment Worker's Union, 1934-19uu.
>Quarterly.

Spanish-language edition of *Justice*. In Spanish. In OCLC system.

La Justicia. Key West, Fla.: Federico Corbett, 188u-1uuu.

Listed in Poyo, Gerald Eugene, *With All, and for the Good of All*, p. 87. No extant issues located.

Justicia. Phoenix, Ariz.: Justicia Pub. Co., 19uu-19uu.
>Weekly.

Vol. 8, no. 56 dated oct. 13, 1928. "The only democratic Spanish paper in Arizona." In OCLC system.

Justicia. Sabinal, Texas, 1910?-19uu.
>Weekly.

Editor: Telésforo F. Torres. "Entered as second-class . . . July 9, 1909. . ." The only extant copy located is dated viernes mayo 10, 1910, and is in the possesion of editor's daughter. A microfilm copy is in the Recovering the U. S. Hispanic Literary Heritage project collection. In Spanish. Listed in Ríos-C., Herminio, "Toward a True Chicano Bibliography: Part II," and "Más de cuatrocientos periódicos en español se han editado en Estados Unidos" under the title *Justice*.

Juventud. Florence, Ariz., 1uuu-1uuu.

Listed in Miguélez, Armando, "Index of Spanish-Language Newspapers in the U. S. Southwest." Miguélez indicates the paper is mentioned in *El Tucsonense*, no date is given for this source. No extant issues located.

Juventud. Mesa, Ariz.: P. W. Guerrero y Dolores Murillo, 1944-19uu.

Listed in Miguélez, Armando, "Index of Spanish-Language Newspapers in the U. S. Southwest." Miguélez indicates the paper is mentioned in *Alianza*, no date is given for this source. No extant issues located.

La Juventud. New York, 1889?-1uuu.

Editor: Gonzalo de Quesada. Repository: Archivo Nacional de Cuba, Havana.

Juventud. Tucson, Ariz., 1893-1uuu.

Mentioned in *El Fronterizo* (Tucson), nov. 4, 1893; cf. Somoza, *Literatura de la Revolución Mexicana...*, p. 229. No extant issues located.

Juventud. Tucson, Ariz., 1937-19uu.

Listed in Miguélez, Armando, "Index of Spanish-Language Newspapers in the U. S. Southwest." No extant issues located.

La Juventud Laredense. Laredo, Tex., 1892-1uuu.

Mentioned in *El Fronterizo* (Tucson), jul. 23, 1892; cf. Somoza, *Literatura de la*

Revolución Mexicana..., p. 250. No extant issues located.

Kan-de-la. New York, N.Y., 1949-19uu.
>Weekly.
>
>Director:Armando Buya (pseudonym?). In Spanish. Repository:The Center for Puerto Rican Studies at Hunter College, CUNY.

El Labrador. Las Cruces, N. M.: Pino y Madrid, 1896-1914.
>Weekly.
>
>In Spanish."Semanario político de noticias, variedades y anuncios". In OCLC system.

Laredo Times. Laredo,Texas: J.S. Penn, 1881-188u.
>Weekly.
>
>Continued by *Laredo Weekly Times.* In OCLC system.

The Laredo Times. Laredo,Tex.:Times Pub. Co., 19uu-1982.
>Daily (except Saturday).
>
>48th year, no. 233 dated Mar. 15, 1929. Continues *Laredo Daily Times.* Continued by *Laredo Morning Times.* In English, with a section in Spanish entitled "El Tiempo de Laredo". In Spanish. In OCLC system.

The Las Vegan. Las Vegas, New Mexico: Las Vegan Publishing Co., 193u-1936.
>Twice a week.
>
>Variant title: *Morning Las Vegan.* In English and Spanish. In OCLC system.

The Las Vegas Acorn (Las Vegas, New Mexico). *See* **The Acorn.**

Las Vegas Advertiser. Las Vegas, New Mexico, 18uu-1uuu.
>Weekly.
>
>Listed in *Rowell's American Newspaper Directory,* 1874. In Spanish and English. No extant issues located.

Las Vegas Courier (East Las Vegas, New Mexico). *See* **Las Vegas Sunday Courier.**

Las Vegas Daily Gazette. [Las Vegas, N. M.]: J. H. Koogler, 1881-1886.
>Daily (except Monday).
>
>Began with Vol. 2, no. 305 dated June 28, 1881; ceased with v. 13, no. 257 (May 2, 1886). Continues *Las Vegas Morning Gazette.* Variant title: *Daily Gazette.* In English and Spanish, cf. Grove, Pearce S., *New Mexico Newspapers,* p. 406. In OCLC system.

Las Vegas Gazette. Las Vegas, New Mexico: Louis Hommel, 187u-18uu.
>Weekly.
>
>Vol. 1, no. 35 dated May 24, 1873.Variant titles: *Sunday Gazette, Gaceta de Las Vegas.* In English and Spanish. In OCLC system.

The Las Vegas Gazette. Las Vegas, [N. M.]: Pierce, Hardy,Warner, 1886-1886.
>Daily (except Sunday).
>
>Began with vol. 13, no. 258 dated May 3, 1886; ceased with v. 13, no. 288 dated June 6, 1886. Continues *Las Vegas Daily Gazette.* In English and Spanish, cf. Grove, Pearce S., *New Mexico Newspapers,* p. 411. In OCLC system.

Las Vegas Mail (Las Vegas, New Mexico). *See* **Las Vegas Weekly Mail.**

Las Vegas Morning Gazette. Las Vegas, N. M.: J.H. Kroogler, 1880-1881.
>Daily (except Monday).
>
>Began with Vol. 2, no. 46 dated Sept. 20, 1880; ceased with v. 2, no. 304 dated June 26, 1881. Continued by *Las Vegas Daily Gazette.* In English and Spanish, cf. Grove, Pearce S., *New Mexico Newspapers,* p. 414. In OCLC system.

Las Vegas Sunday Courier. East Las Vegas, N. M.: Geo.T. Gould, 1888-188u.
>Weekly.
>
>Ceased with Dec. 23, 1888?, cf. Grove, Pearce S., *New Mexico Newspapers.* Special campaign ed. of Oct. 29, 1888 titled *Las Vegas Courier.* In English and Spanish, cf. Grove, Pearce S., *New Mexico Newspapers.* In OCLC system.

Las Vegas Sunday Gazette. Las Vegas, N. M. 1872-1886.
>Weekly, September 27, 1872-October 1873; March 23, 1874-c.July 27, 1879; c. January 1883-March 1883; daily, July 28, 1879-June 1886.

Apparently suspended publication between October 1873 and March 22, 1874; preceded by *Las Vegas Mail;* included a companion paper: *La Gaceta,* March 15, 1877-December 1878, cf. Grove, Pearce S., *New Mexico Newspapers*, p. 418. Variant title: *Sunday Gazette.* In English and Spanish. No extant issues located.

Las Vegas Weekly Gazette. Las Vegas, N. Mex.: J. R. Koogler, 1872-18uu.
>   Weekly.
>   Began with Sept. 27, 1872 issue; ceased in March 1883; suspended in October 1873; resumed with Mar. 22, 1874 issue, cf. Grove, Pearce S., *New Mexico Newspapers.* In English and Spanish. In OCLC system.

Las Vegas Weekly Mail. Las Vegas, N. M., 1871-1872.
>   Weekly.
>   "Published by Simon H. Newman while in jail for political reasons. He and his co-editor, W. N. Bollinger, were forced to sell it in August or September of 1872. The buyer, May Hays, changed the name to the *Las Vegas Gazette,*" cf. Grove, Pearce S., *New Mexico Newspapers*, p. 419. Variant title: *Las Vegas Mail.* In English and Spanish. No extant issues located.

Las Vegas Weekly Optic. East Las Vegas, N. M.: R. A. Kistler [etc.], 1879-1898.
>   Weekly.
>   Vol. 9, no. 9 dated Jan. 3, 1889. Merged with *Stock Grower and Farmer* to form *Las Vegas Daily Optic and Stock Grower.* Other edition: *Las Vegas Daily Optic.* Includes a Spanish-language section. In OCLC system.

El Látigo. San Antonio, Tex.: Miguel Gonzales Dena, 18uu-1uuu.
>   Weekly.
>   Vol. 6, no. 263 dated mar. 4, 1898. In Spanish. In OCLC system.

Latin America. New Orleans, Louisiana, 1911-1916?
>   Semi-monthly.
>   Editor: Gen. E.A. Lever. A "periodical for the promotion and interchange of commerce between the United States and the Latin-American republics," cf. MacCurdy, Raymond R. *A History and Bibliography of Spanish-Language Newspapers and Magazines in Louisiana, 1808-1949,* p. 35. In Spanish and English. Repository: Louisiana Collection, Howard-Tilton Library at Tulane University, New Orleans, Louisiana.

The Latin-American Christian = El Christiano Latino-Americano. Brownsville, Texas: Church of Christ, 195u-.
>   Monthly (except July and August).
>   Vol. 2, no. 1 dated sept. 1958. Editor: John F. Wolfe (1958). In Spanish and English. In OCLC system.

Latin American News. Denver, Colo., 1938-19uu.
>   Weekly.
>   Vol. 2, no. 1 dated Feb. 9. 1939. "Colorado's only progressive Spanish-English newspaper." In OCLC system.

The Latin Times. East Chicago, Ind., 1956-.
>   Weekly.
>   Editor: Luis Verduzco. In English and Spanish. In OCLC system.

The Latin Voice (New Orleans, Louisiana*). See* **La Voz Latina.**

El Latino. San Diego, California: W. V. Johnston Pub. Co., 1938-19uu.
>   Weekly.
>   In Spanish. In OCLC system.

El Latino-Americano. Alice, Tex.: Amado Gutiérrez, 1913?-19uu.
>   Weekly.
>   Vol. 7, no. 10 dated Jan. 14, 1920. In Spanish. In OCLC system.

El Latino-Americano. El Paso, Tex.: [s.n]., 1891-1891.
>   Semiweekly.
>   Continues *El Valle del Bravo.* In Spanish. In OCLC system.

El Latino Americano. New Orleans, Louisiana, 1930-19uu.
  Monthly.
  Editor: Luis Buenrostro; co-editor John B. Palmer. Listed in "Más de cuatrocientos periódicos en español se han editado en Estados Unidos". This source indicates three numbers were published in 1930. In Spanish. No extant issues located.
Latinoamericano. Phoenix, Ariz., 1934-19uu.
  Listed in Miguélez, Armando, "Index of Spanish-Language Newspapers in the U. S. Southwest." Miguélez indicates the paper is mentioned in *El Mensajero,* 20-III-1934, p. 4. No place is given for this source. No extant issues located.
LEA: Librarians, Editors, Authors = Libros, Editores, Autores. Washington: Unión Panamericana, 1949-1950.
  In Spanish. In OCLC system.
Lecciones Bíblicas. El Paso, Tex.: Casa Bautista de Publicaciones, a Nashville, Tenn. Pub., Baptist Sunday School Board, 19uu-198u.
  Quarterly.
  Vol. 27 dated 1957. In Spanish. In OCLC system.
Lecciones Ilustradas. Edición para Maestros. El Paso, Tex: Casa Bautista de Publicaciones; Nashville, Tenn.: Baptist Sunday School Board, 19uu-198u.
  Quarterly.
  T. 63, no. 1 dated Jan.-Mar, 1982. "Para niños de 4 y 5 años". Continued by *Historias Bíblicas.* In Spanish. In OCLC system.
Lecciones Ilustradas: Alumnos. El Paso, Tex.: Casa Bautista de Publicaciones; Nashville, Tenn.: Baptist Sunday School Board, 19uu-198u.
  T. 63, no. 1 dated Jan.-Mar. 1982. "Para niños de 4 y 5 años". Continued by *Historias Bíblicas para Pre-escolares* (1986). In OCLC system.
La Liberación. [New York, N.Y.]: Comité Coordinador Pro-República Española, 1946-19uu.
  Weekly.
  Vol. 1, no. 7 dated 3 de mayo de 1946. Issued Mar. 22, 1946-Apr. 1949 by the Comité Coordinador Pro-República Española; May 7, 1949- by the Liberación Publishing Association. In Spanish. In OCLC system.
El Liberal. Brownsville, Texas, 1912-1917.
  Weekly.
  Listed in Ríos-C., Herminio, "Toward a True Chicano Bibliography: Part II," p. 44 and "Más de cuatrocientos periódicos en español se han editado en Estados Unidos". In Spanish. No extant issues located.
El Liberal. Floresville, Texas, 1898?-1uuu.
  Semi-monthly.
  Listed in "Más de cuatrocientos periódicos en español se han editado en Estados Unidos". In Spanish. No extant issues located.
El Liberal. Del Rio, Texas: Amado Gutiérrez, 1910?-1911.
  Weekly.
  Listed in Miguélez, Armando, "Index of Spanish-Language Newspaper in the U. S. Southwest." Miguélez indicates it is mentioned in *Regeneración,* 3-1x-1910, p.4. Also listed in Ríos-C., Herminio, "Toward a True Chicano Bibliography: Part II," p. 45, with publication dates of 1900-1911. Also listed in "Más de cuatrocientos periódicos en español se han editado en Estados Unidos", with publication dates of 1905-1911. In Spanish. No extant issues located.
Liberal. Las Cruces, N. M., 1891-1uuu.
  Weekly.
  Listed in Grove, Pearce S., *New Mexico Newspapers,* p. 155. In Spanish. No extant issues located.
El Liberal. Rio Grande, Texas, 1872-1875.
  Weekly.

Director: Antonio D. de León. Listed in "Más de cuatrocientos periódicos en español se han editado en Estados Unidos". In Spanish. No extant issues located.

La Libertad. Cayo Hueso, 1876-18uu.

"Periódico político". Director: Federico de Armas. Listed in Batista Villareal, Teresita, *Catálogo de publicaciones periódicas cubanas. . .*, p. 155. This source indicates that the Biblioteca Nacional José Martí in La Havana holds some issues of this title.

La Libertad. Dallas, Texas: José Velásquez, 1936-19uu.

Weekly.

Ríos-C., Herminio, "Toward a True Chicano Bibliography: Part II," p. 45. This source lists this paper twice, with identical information; it is assumed here to be a typographical error. Also listed in "Más de cuatrocientos periódicos en español se han editado en Estados Unidos". In Spanish. No extant issues located.

La Libertad. Key West, Florida, 1876-1uuu.

Listed in Poyo, Gerald Eugene, *With All and for the Good of All,* p. 175. In Spanish. No extant issues located.

La Libertad. Kingsville, Tex.: F. de P. González, 19uu-19uu.

Vol. 2a, no. 501 dated May 31, 1913. In Spanish. In OCLC system.

La Libertad. Miami, Fla; 1960-19uu.

Weekly.

Founded and for some years edited by Rolando Masferrer. In Spanish. In OCLC system.

La Libertad. New Orleans, Louisiana, 1869-1uuu.

Listed in Poyo, Gerald Eugene, *With All and for the Good of All,* p. 175. In Spanish. No extant issues located.

La Libertad. San Diego, Calif.; 1916-19uu.

Listed in Miguélez, Armando, "Index of Spanish-Language Newspapers in the U. S. Southwest." No extant issues located.

La Libertad. San Diego, Tex.: F. de P. González, 1908?-19uu.

Weekly.

"Semanario liberal." Epoca 2, núm. 384 dated abr. 2, 1910. In Spanish. In OCLC system.

La Libertad. San Diego, Texas: José Velásquez, 1939-1942.

Weekly.

Ser. 2, no. 3218 dated oct. 7, 1939; no. 3336, dated enero 24, 1942. In Spanish. In OCLC system.

La Libertad. Sn. Marcial, N. M.: C. T. Valdivia, 1896-1uuu.

Weekly.

Absorbed by *Estrella de Nuevo México.* "Semanario de política." In Spanish. In OCLC system.

La Libertad. Tampa, Fla; 1897?-1uuu.

Repository: Archivo Nacional de Cuba, Havana.

La Libertad. Tucson, Ariz., 1892-1uuu.

Mentioned in Sheridan, *Los Tucsonenses,* p. 203. No extant issues located.

Libertad y Trabajo. Los Angeles, 1908-19uu.

Weekly.

Official organ of Club "Tierra, Igualdad y Justicia." In OCLC system.

Liberté. New Orleans, Louisiana, 1869-1uuu.

Weekly.

"Organ of the interests of Cuba & Puerto Rico," cf. *Rowell's American Newspaper Directory, 1870,* p. 658. In Spanish and English. No extant issues located.

El Libre Pensador. Nueces County, Tex.: Catarino Garza, 1890-1uuu.

Mentioned in Gómez, *Sembradores. . .,* p. 291. Somoza lists this paper as been published in Eagle Pass, Texas by Garza with beginning publication date of 1887, cf. Somoza, *Literatura de la Revolución Mexicana. . .,* p. 247. No extant issues located.

El Libro Americano. Washington, D. C.: Unión Panamericana, Biblioteca Colón, 1938-1944.

Mimeographed. Began with t.1, no. 2 dated abr. 1938. In Spanish. In OCLC system.

Libros. New York, N.Y.: Libros Pub. Comp., 1940-19uu.

Monthly.

"Revista bibliográfica Americana." In OCLC system. In Spanish.

Líneas en Español. El Paso, Texas, 1913-1918.

Daily.

Listed in Ríos-C., Herminio, "Toward a True Chicano Bibliography: Part II," p. 46. In Spanish. No extant issues located.

Linoticias [Spanish edition]. Brooklyn, N.Y.: Mergenthaler Linotype Company, 19uu-.

Also issued in Portuguese. In Spanish. In OCLC system.

The Lion en Español. Oak Brook, Ill.: International Association of Lions Club, 19uu-.

T. xxxvii, no. 1 dated enero/feb./marzo 1980. In Spanish. In OCLC system.

El Loco-cuerdo. Key West, Fla.: 1910?–19uu. Supplement has date of dic. 18 de 1910.

In OCLC system.

La Llumanera de Nova York. Nueva York: Imprenta de El Cronista; Barcelona: Edición Anglo-Catalanés, 1874-1879.

Published together with the later title: *La Llumanera.* Originally published monthly (Nova York: Impr. de El Cronista). Continued by *La Llumanera.* In Catalan. In OCLC system.

Los Angeles Record. Edición en español. Los Angeles, Calif., 1927-19uu.

Mentioned in *El Tucsonense,* mar. 17, 1927.

Los Angeles Star. Los Angeles, California: Lewis & McElroy, 1851-1879.

Weekly.

Publisher: Lewis, McElroy & Rand, 1851; Lewis & Rand, 1852; James S. Waits, 1854; H. Hamilton, 1860. Editor: William A. Wallace, 1854. Suspended Oct. 1, 1864-May 16, 1868. Other editions: *Daily Los Angeles Star, Los Angeles Daily Star.* Continued by *Los Angeles Weekly Star.* Variant title: *Star.* In English and Spanish. In OCLC system.

Los Cerrillos Prospector. Carbonateville, N. M., 1879-1881?

Weekly.

"Moved to Los Cerrillos," cf. Grove, Pearce S., *New Mexico Newspapers,* p. 435. In English and Spanish. No extant issues located.

El Lucero. San Benito, Texas: El Lucero, 1942-19uu.

Weekly.

Listed in *N. W. Ayer & Son's Directory of Newspapers and Periodicals,* 1950, p. 967. No extant issues located.

Lucero Latino: Revista Mensual. Nueva Orleans, Louisiana: Latin-American Pub. Co., 1933-.

Monthly.

Fundador: Franklin Morales; Director: Lic. Marco Juan Figueroa. Editor: C. E. Morales. In Spanish. In OCLC system.

La Lucha. El Paso, Tex.: Teófilo Ocaña Caballero, 189u-1uuu.

Cited in Meléndez, A. Gabriel, *So All Is Not Lost ...* p. 64. No extant issues located.

La Lucha de Clases. San Antonio, Texas, 1915-19uu.

Cited in Chabrán, Rafael and Richard Chabrán, "The Spanish-Language and Latino Press of the United States: Newspapers and Periodicals." In Spanish. No extant issues located.

Lucha Obrera. San Francisco, Calif.: Partido Comunista E.U.A., 193u-1934.

Monthly.

Vol. 1, no. 8 dated enero 1934. Volume numbering irregular. Suspended jul.-agosto and nov.-dic. 1934. "Organo del oeste del Partido Comunista E.U.A." In OCLC system.

LULAC News. San Antonio, Texas: League of United Latin American Citizens, 1931-1979.

Monthly.

Place of publication varies frequently. Volume numbering irregular. Official organ of the League of United Latin American Citizens (LULAC). In Spanish and English. In

OCLC system.

La Luz. Angostura, Nuevo México: Compañía Impresora de Río Arriba, 1900-1908.

Weekly, Aug. 4, 1900-July 28, 1906; monthly, Aug. 1906-Apr. 1907, weekly, May 1907. Ceased with Oct. 24, 1908?, cf. Grove, Pearce S., *New Mexico Newspapers*. Listed in Ríos-C., Herminio, "Toward a True Chicano Bibliography: Part II," p. 42, with ending publication date of 1910. Published in Española, N. M., 1903-. In Spanish. In OCLC system.

La Luz. Dallas, Tex.: Banks Upshaw & Co., 19uu-19uu.

Semimonthly (October-May).

Año 14 no. 15 dated mayo 1-15, 1945. In Spanish. In OCLC system.

La Luz (Española, New Mexico: 1903*). See* **La Luz** (Angostura, Nuevo México).

La Luz. San Benito, Texas, 1913-19uu?

Irregular.

Listed in Ríos-C., Herminio, "Toward a True Chicano Bibliography: Part II," (1972), p. 47, and "Más de cuatrocientos periódicos en español se han editado en Estados Unidos". In Spanish. No extant issues located.

La Luz. Tucson, Ariz., 1896-1897.

Mentioned in Sheridan, *Los Tucsonenses,* p. 203. No extant issues located.

La Luz Apostólica. San Antonio, Texas: Latin American District Council, Assemblies of God, 19uu-19uu.

Monthly.

Listed in Common Council for American Unity, *Foreign Language Publications in the United States: Newspaper Lists.* In Spanish. No extant issues located.

Luz y Verdad. Laredo, Texas, 1921-1926.

Bi-weekly?, monthly?

Listed in Ríos-C., Herminio, "Toward a True Chicano Bibliography: Part II," p. 46, and "Más de cuatrocientos periódicos en español se han editado en Estados Unidos". In Spanish. No extant issues located.

Luz y Verdad (Río Grande, Texas*). See* **Luz y Verdad** (Weslaco, Texas).

Luz y Verdad. Weslaco, Texas; Rio Grande, Texas, 1931-1932.

Semi-monthly.

Founded by Apolonio Ramón; director: José Salinas. Listed in "Más de cuatrocientos periódicos en español se han editado en Estados Unidos". According to this source the paper began in Weslaco, then reapeared in Rio Grande until the end of 1932. No extant issues located.

El Luzero Sefardí. New York, N.Y.: The Sephardic Publishing Co., 1927–19uu.

Editors: Albert Levi and Moiz Solas. In OCLC system.

El Machete. Phoenix, Ariz., 19uu-19uu.

Listed in Miguélez, Armando, "Index of Spanish-Language Newspapers in the U. S. Southwest." Miguélez indicates the paper is mentioned in *El Mensajero,* 12-III- 1939, p.3. No extant issues located.

El Magazine de la Raza. New York, N.Y.: Transcontinental, 1918-19uu.

Bi-monthly.

Editor: Miguel Ordenio. In Spanish. In OCLC system.

Mail. Mora, N. M., 1874-1uuu.

Semimonthly.

Listed in Grove, Pearce S., *New Mexico Newspapers*, p. 296. In English and Spanish. No extant issues located.

El Malcriado. Los Angeles, California, 1923-1930.

Weekly.

Director: Daniel Venegas. Listed in "Más de cuatrocientos periódicos en español se han editado en Estados Unidos". Also listed in Ríos-C., Herminio, "Toward a True Chicano Bibliography: Part II" p. 41. In Spanish. Repository: Bancroft Library (University of California, Berkeley).

Bibliography

Manual Azucarero de Cuba = Cuba Sugar Manual. New Orleans, La.: Gilmore Pub., 1944-19uu.
   In Spanish. In OCLC system.
Mañana. McAllen, Texas, 1917-1919.
   Weekly.
   Editores: Lorenzo Yáñez, Jr. and Adrián Tapia. Listed in Ríos-C., Herminio, "Toward a True Chicano Bibliography: Part II," p. 46. Also listed in "Más de cuatrocientos periódicos en español se han editado en Estados Unidos". In Spanish. No extant issues located.
Medicina Clínica. Chicago, 1918-1922.
   In Spanish. In OCLC system.
Mefistófeles. San Francisco, Cal.: J. G. Arce, 191u-1918.
   Weekly.
   Vol. 2, no. 24 dated Mar. 9, 1918. Variant title: *Mefistófeles: Defensor de la Raza.* Absorbed by *Hispano América* (San Francisco, Calif.). In Spanish and English. In OCLC system.
Lo Mejor del Catholic Digest. St. Paul, Minnesota, 195u-19uu.
   Monthly.
   V. 3, no. 3 dated 1955. In 1955, Edward Larocque Tinker published *Pajitas al Viento: Ensayo Estudiantil de Acercamiento Interamericano* (St. Paul, Minn.: Catholic Digest International, 1955), detached from *Lo Mejor,* v. 3, no. 3, 1955. In Spanish and English. Listed in Common Council for American Unity, *Foreign Language Publications in the United States: Newspaper Lists,* p. 4. No extant issues located. In OCLC system.
El Mensagero Luisianés. Nueva Orleans [i.e. New Orleans], La.: Joaquín de Lisa, 1809-1811.
   Semi-weekly.
   Began in Sept. 1809, cf. Brigham, Clarence S. *History and Bibliography of American Newspapers: 1690-1820.* Ceased in 1811, cf. MacCurdy, Raymond R., *A History and Bibliography of Spanish-Language Newspapers and Magazines in Louisiana.* Subtitle: Periódico político de la Nueva Orleans. In Spanish and English. In OCLC system.
El Mensagero Semanal de Nueva York. New York, N.Y.: José Antonio Saco, 1828-1831.
   Weekly.
   "A periodical on the world situation published in New York City and Philadelphia for and by Cubans." Listed in Willging, Eugene Paul and Herta Hatzfeld, *Catholic Serials of the Nineteenth Century in the United States*; and Gregory, Winifred, ed., *American Newspapers, 1821-1936,* p. 472. Variant title: *Mensajero Semanal.* In Spanish. In OCLC system.
Mensaje. New York, N.Y., 195u-19uu.
   Año 2, no. 4 dated agosto, 1957.
   President: Eloy Vaquero. In Spanish and English. Repository: The Center for Puerto Rican Studies at Hunter College, CUNY.
Mensaje de Nueva York: Revista de Arte y Cultura en Estados Unidos. New York, N.Y., 1956-.
   In Spanish. In OCLC system.
Mensajeras del Maestro. El Paso, Tex.: Casa Bautista de Publicaciones, 1938-1942.
   Repository: Library of Casa Bautista de Publicaciones in El Paso, Texas.
El Mensajero. Albuquerque, N. M., 1911-19uu.
   Mentioned in Somoza, *Literatura de la Revolución Mexicana...,* p. 238. No extant issues located.
Mensajero. Del Rio, Texas, 1uuu-1906?
   Weekly.
El Mensajero. Del Rio, Tex., Crescencio Villarreal Márquez, 18uu, 1910?-1906?
   Mentioned in Somoza, *Literatura de la Revolución Mexicana...,* p. 247, and in *N. W. Ayer & Son's American Newspaper Annual,* 1906, p. 1118. No extant issues located.

El Mensajero. Mora, N. M.: Benedicto Sandoval, 1910-1912.
>   Weekly.
>   Began publication c. June 10, 1910, ceased publication 1912, cf. Grove, Pearce S., *New Mexico Newspapers*. T. 1, no. 39 dated 3 de marzo, 1911. In Spanish.
>   In OCLC system.

El Mensajero. New Orleans, Louisiana: El Mensajero Publishing Co. 1894-18uu.
>   Weekly.
>   "Semanario dedicado a los intereses comerciales de Nueva Orleans y de los países latino-americanos". Directors of publishing company: Miguel Barrera, Max Wessel, M. G. Zamora, Lamar C. Quintero, & Max Kruger; Barrera was editor, cf. MacCurdy, Raymond R., *A History and Bibliography of Spanish-Language Newspapers and Magazines in Louisiana, 1808-1949*, p. 36. No extant issues located.

El Mensajero. Phoenix, Arizona: J. M. Melendrey, 1900-1916.
>   Weekly.
>   "Published for short time semiweekly. Purchased... by A. S. Mills and Frank Loveitt and changed to the *Messenger* (English language)," cf. Lutrell, Estelle, *Newspapers and Periodicals of Arizona, 1859-1911*, p. 36. Listed in *Rowell's American Newspaper Directory*, 1907, p. 33 and "Más de cuatrocientos periódicos en español se han editado en Estados Unidos". In Spanish. No extant issues located.

El Mensajero. Phoenix, Arizona: Committee for Americanism and Inter-American Solidarity, 1925-19uu.
>   Monthly.
>   Editor: C. J. Carreón. Listed in *N. W. Ayer & Son's Directory of Newspapers and Periodicals*, 1945, p. 52, and Gregory, Winifred, ed., *American Newspapers, 1821-1936*, p. 20. In Spanish and English. No extant issues located.

El Mensajero Bautista. El Paso, Tex.: Casa Bautista de Publicaciones, 1917-1917.
>   Semi-monthly.
>   Continued by *Atalaya Bautista*. In Spanish. In OCLC system.

El Mensajero Cristiano. San Antonio, 1949-1950.
>   Editor: D. Orea Luna. "Organo en español de la Iglesia Luterana Americana". Continues *El Mensajero Luterano*. In Spanish. In OCLC system.

El Mensajero de Esperanza. Corpus Christi, Texas: Christian Triumph Company, 19uu-19uu.
>   Quarterly.
>   Listed in Common Council for American Unity, *Foreign Language Publications in the United States: Newspaper Lists,* p. 8. In Spanish. No extant issues located.

Mensajero Juvenil. El Paso, Tex.: Casa Bautista de Publicaciones, 1925-1927.
>   Repository: Library of Casa Bautista de Publicaciones in El Paso, Texas.

El Mensajero Luterano. San Antonio: [La Comisión de Misiones Mexicanas de la Iglesia Luterana Americana], 194u-1948.
>   "Organo en español de la Iglesia Luterana Americana". Continued by *Mensajero Cristiano*. In Spanish and English. In OCLC system.

El Mensajero Semanal (New York, N.Y.). *See* **El Mensagero Semanal de Nueva York.**

El Mentor Ilustrado: Revista Para los Niños. New York, 1881-1882?
>   Directors: Juan Bellido de Luna and son. Listed in Batista Villareal, Teresita, *Catálogo de Publicaciones periódicas cubanas...*, p. 41. This source indicates that the Biblioteca Nacional José Martí in Havana holds the issue corresponding to the index.

El Mercurio. Kansas City, Mo.: Alexander Robertson & Co., 1883-1884?
>   Monthly.
>   Covers "all the states and territories of the Union ... and through all Spanish-American countries." In Spanish and English. In OCLC system.

Mercurio. New Orleans, Louisiana: Mercurio Publishing Co. 1911-1927.
>   Monthly.
>   "Sucessive editors were Joseph Branyas, Enrique Dosolier Lareolla, José Llado de

Cosso, & F. Patrón," cf. MacCurdy, Raymond R. *A History and Bibliography of Spanish-Language Newspapers and Magazines in Louisiana, 1808-1949*, p. 36. In Spanish. In OCLC system.

El Mercurio. Phoenix, Arizona: F. T. Dávila, 1884-18uu.
> Weekly.
> Listed in Lutrell, Estelle, *Newspapers and Periodicals of Arizona, 1859-1911*, p. 37. In English and Spanish. No extant issues located.

El Mercurio. San Diego, California, 1898-1uuu.
> Irregular.
> Listed in "Más de cuatrocientos periódicos en español se han editado en Estados Unidos". In Spanish. No extant issues located.

Mercurio de Nueva York. New York, [N.Y.]: Lanuza, Mendia & Co., 1828-1831.
> Weekly.
> Began in 1828?; ceased in 1831, cf. Gregory, Winifred, ed., *American Newspapers, 1821-1936*. Año 1, no. 2 dated mayo 17 de 1828. In Spanish. In OCLC system.

The Mesilla Miner (Mesilla, Arizona*). See* **The Mesilla Times.**

The Mesilla News. Mesilla, New Mexico: L. Lapoint & Ira M. Bond, 1873-1885.
> Weekly.
> Began Nov. 2, 1873, ceased Feb. 1885, cf. Grove, Pearce S., *New Mexico Newspapers*. Continued by *News* (Albuquerque, N. M.). In Spanish and English. In OCLC system.

Mesilla News. Mesilla, New Mexico: Luis D. Valdez, 1938-19uu.
> Weekly.
> In English and Spanish. In OCLC system.

The Mesilla Times. Mesilla, Arizona [i.e. N. M.]: B.C. Murray & Co., 1860-1862.
> Weekly.
> Ceased in 1862?, cf. *Newspapers in Microform: United States, 1948-1983*. Suspended publication, Oct. 24- Dec. 12, 1861. "War size." Mesilla was the capital of the Confederate States Territory of Arizona, cf. Wyllys, Rufus Kay, *Arizona: the History of the Frontier State.* Preceded by a prospectus (one issue) titled *The Mesilla Miner,* June 9, 1860. Continues *The Mesilla Miner.* In English and Spanish. In OCLC system.

Mesilla Valley Bulletin. Las Cruces, N. M.: Bulletin Pub. Co. 1932?-1938?
> Weekly.
> Vol. 1, no. 24 dated Nov. 18, 1932. In English. In OCLC system.

Mesilla Valley Democrat. Las Cruces, N. M.: J. P. Booth, 1886-1890?
> Semiweekly, Sept. 28, 1886-; weekly Sept. 2, 1886-.
> Began with Aug. 20, 1886, ceased with Dec. 9, 1890?, cf. Grove, Pearce S., *New Mexico Newspapers.* In English and Spanish. In OCLC system.

Mesilla Valley Independent (La Mesilla, N. M.*). See* **El Independiente del Valle de la Mesilla.**

El Metodista. Socorro, N. M.: Thomas Harwood, 1886-1892.
> Monthly.
> Began with Año 2, núm. 3 dated dic. de 1886; ceased with Dec. 1892. Continues *Metodista Neo-Mexicano.* Continued by *El Abogado Cristiano Neo-Mexicano* (Socorro, N. M.: 1893). In Spanish and English. In OCLC system.

Metodista Neo-Mexicano. Socorro, N. M.: Chase & Harwood, 188u-1886.
> Monthly.
> Vol. 1, no. 9 dated May 1886; ceased with t. 2, núm. 2 dated nov. de 1886. Companion newspaper in English: *New Mexico Methodist.* Continued by *El Metodista.* In Spanish and English. In OCLC system.

Mexican Advocate. Nacogdoches, Texas: Milton Slocum, 1829?-18uu.
> Cited in Wallace, J. M. *Gaceta to Gazette: A Checklist of Texas Newspapers, 1813-1846,* p. 21-22. In Spanish and English. No extant issues located.

Mexican American Sun. Los Angeles, Calif.: Eastern Group Publications. 1945-.

Weekly.

Began in 1945.Vol. 38, no. 28 dated July 10, 1986. In English and Spanish. In OCLC system.

Mexican Citizen (Austin, Tex.). *See* **The Texas Gazette.**

The Mexican Review. Washington, D. C.: G. F. Weeks, etc. 1916-1922.

Monthly.

"The only periodical giving Mexican news in English." In English and Spanish. In OCLC system.

The Mexican Voice. Monrovia, Calif., 1938?-19uu.

Quarterly (1941-1944).

In English and Spanish. In OCLC system.

Mexican World. Fort Worth, Tex.: The World Co., Inc. 192u-.

Weekly.

Vol. 1, no. 28 dated May 13, 1924. In English. In OCLC system.

El Mexicano. Kansas City, Missouri., 1915-19uu.

Mentioned in Smith, "The Mexican Immigrant Press . . .," p. 83. No extant issues located.

El Mexicano. Los Angeles, Calif.: Manuel Carrilo, 1921-19uu.

In OCLC system.

El Mexicano. Na[t]chitoches [La], 1813-181u.

Weekly.

Vol. 1, no. 2 dated 19 de jun. de 1813-. Continues *Gaceta de Texas.* In Spanish and English. In OCLC system.

El Mexicano. Oxnard, California, 1918-19uu.

Bi-monthly.

Listed in Ríos-C., Herminio, "Toward a True Chicano Bibliography: Part II," p. 41 and "Más de cuatrocientos periódicos en español se han editado en Estados Unidos". No extant issues located.

El Mexicano de Texas. San Antonio, Texas: Marcial Padilla, 1868-1uuu.

Weekly.

Editor and proprietor, Calixto Munez, cf. *Rowell's American Newspaper Directory,* 1870, p. 747. Cited in Chabrán, Rafael and Richard Chabrán, "The Spanish-Language and Latino Press of the United States: Newspapers and Periodicals." In Spanish. No extant issues located.

El Mexicano Republicano. Phoenix, Arizona: R. Silva Aguilar, 1892-1uuu.

Weekly.

Listed in Lutrell, Estelle, *Newspapers and Periodicals of Arizona, 1859-1911,* p. 37, and *Rowell's American Newspaper Directory,* 1894. No extant issues located.

México. Chicago, Illinois: F. P. Miranda, 1925-1930.

Three times a week, 16 marzo 1929-20 nov. 1930; semiweekly, 6 abr. 1927-14 marzo 1929; weekly, 18 enero 1925-2 abr. 1927.

Continued by *Nacional* (Chicago, Ill.). In Spanish. In OCLC system.

México. Los Angeles, California, 1925-1929.

Weekly; monthly.

Listed in *N. W. Ayer & Son's American Newspaper Annual and Directory,* 1929. Also listed in Ríos-C., Herminio, "Toward a True Chicano Bibliography: Part II," p. 41, who lists it as a weekly publication. In Spanish. No extant issues located.

México. New York, N. Y.: R. Martínez Predomo, 1925-19uu.

Monthly.

Listed in *N. W. Ayer & Son's American Newspaper Annual and Directory,* 1926, p. 739, and "Más de cuatrocientos periódicos en español se han editado en Estados Unidos". In Spanish and English. No extant issues located.

México Internacional. San Antonio, Texas, 1909-1910.

Weekly.

Director: Rafael Téllez Girón. Listed in "Más de cuatrocientos periódicos en español se han editado en Estados Unidos", and Ríos-C., Herminio, "Toward a True Chicano Bibliography: Part II," p. 47. In Spanish. No extant issues located.

Mexico Journal. Alamo Heights, San Antonio, Tex.: F. N. Gallagher, 1945-19uu.

"A gazette of Mexican law, industry and trade." In OCLC system.

México-Libre. El Paso, Texas, 1915-19uu.

Weekly.

Listed in Ríos-C., Herminio, "Toward a True Chicano Bibliography: Part II," p. 45; and "Más de cuatrocientos periódicos en español se han editado en Estados Unidos". In Spanish. No extant issues located.

México Libre. Los Angeles, Calif.: Adolfo R. Carrillo; 1914-19uu.

Listed in Miguélez, Armando, "Index of Spanish Laguage Newspapers in the U. S. Southwest." No extant issues located.

México Libre. Nogales, Ariz.: Alberto B. Piña, 1918-1uuu.

Listed in Miguélez, Armando, "Index of Spanish-Language Newspapers in the U. S. Southwest." No extant issues located.

México Moderno (New York; Mexico City). See **Modern Mexico.**

El Mexico-Texano. Brownsville, Tex.: José María Rendón, 18uu-1uuu.

Vol. 1, no. 80 dated Nov. 15, 1889. In Spanish. In OCLC system.

Mexico Today and Border Bulletins. San Antonio, Tex., 1923-19uu.

In OCLC system.

1810. Del Rio, Tex.: Crecencio Villareal Márquez, 189u?-1uuu.

Mentioned in Gómez, *Sembradores...,* p. 29. No extant issues located.

Milicia. Kingsville, Tex.: Fernando Arredondo, 19uu-19uu.

Weekly.

Año 20, no. 15 dated Abr. 12, 1945. In Spanish. Continues *El Porvenir.* In OCLC system.

Mills' Mexico. Las Vegas, N. M.: T. B. Mills, 1884-1uuu.

Monthly.

Began publication with vol. 2, no. 2 dated Feb. 15, 1884. "Devoted to mining, manufacturing, stock raising and real estate." In English and Spanish, cf. Grove, Pearce S., *New Mexico Newspapers.* In OCLC system.

Minor. Albuquerque, Nuevo México, 1880-1uuu.

Listed in "Más de cuatrocientos periódicos en español se han editado en Estados Unidos". In English and Spanish. No extant issues located.

The Mirror (Bernalillo, New Mexico). See **El Espejo.**

Miscelánea Científica, Artística y Literaria (New York). See **Revista de la Crónica: Miscelánea Científica, Artística y Literaria.**

Miscelánea de la Crónica (New York). See **Revista de la Crónica: Miscelánea Científica, Artística y Literaria.**

El Misionero Bautista: Organo Oficial de la Convención Bautista Hispano-Americana de Nuevo México. Las Vegas, Nuevo México: La Convención, 1943-19uu.

Monthly, Mar. 1945; semimonthly, mar. 1948-Nov. 1949; monthly, Dec. 1949-.

T. 1, no. 4 dated agosto de 1943. Published in Albuquerque, N. M. in 1948-; in Roswell, N.M., July/Aug. 1951-. In Spanish. In OCLC system.

El Misisipí. New-Orleans, [La.]: Wm. H. Johnson & Co., 1808-1810.

Semiweekly.

Began in 1808; ceased in 1810, cf. Brigham, Clarence S., *History and Bibliography of American Newspapers: 1690-1820.* "Earliest Spanish-language periodical published in the United States." cf. Gutiérrez, Félix, "Spanish-Language Media in America," *Journalism History,* Vol. 4 no. 2, (Summer 1977), pp. 34-41. In Spanish and English. In OCLC system.

El Misisipí. N.-Orleans [i.e. New Orleans, La.]: Imprenta del Misisipi, 1834-1uuu.

Semiweekly.

"Periódico político, literario y mercantil". Vol. 2, núm. 21 dated 14 de marzo de 1835.

In Spanish. In OCLC system.
Modern Denistry. Brooklyn: Novocol Chemical Mfg., Co. Inc., 1945?-19uu.
Continued by *Odontología Moderna.* In Spanish. In OCLC system.
Modern Mexico. New York; Mexico City, 1uuu-1909.
Editor: Paul Hudson; Wm. C. Smith, manager. Also published in St. Louis, Missouri. Variant title: *México Moderno.* In Spanish and English. In OCLC system.
Modern Mexico. St. Louis: [Mo.], 1895-1909.
Monthly.
Editor: Paul Hudson, vol. 1-29, 1896-1909. Includes a few pages in Spanish, entitled, Feb. 1901: "Las dos naciones, periódico polítio, comercial, literario y de anuncios"; March 1902-. "México moderno y periódico político comercial, literario y de anuncios". Place of publication varies: St. Louis, New York, Mexico City. In English and Spanish. In OCLC system.
Monigotes. San Antonio, Tex., 1922-19uu.
Semanario de caricaturas, guasa y variedades, cf. Miguélez, Armando. "Index of Spanish-Language Newspapers in the U. S. Southwest." No extant issues located.
El Monitor. Albuquerque, N. M.: M. U. Vigil & R. S. Trejo, 1914-19uu.
Began with Apr. 3, 1914; ceased with oct. 23, 1914?, cf. Grove, Pearce S., *New Mexico Newspapers.* 1, no. 2 dated 10 de abril de 1914. In Spanish with an Italian language section. In OCLC system.
El Monitor. Calexico, California, 1918-1924.
Weekly; tri-weekly.
Director: Ricardo Covarrubias; colaboradores: Rogelio Escalona, José Cayetano Zepeda, Juan Ojeda M. y José Esperón. Listed in "Más de cuatrocientos periódicos en español se han editado en Estados Unidos". Also listed in Ríos-C., Herminio, "Toward a True Chicano Bibliography: Part II," 1972, p. 40. In Spanish. No extant issues located.
El Monitor. El Paso, Tex.: J. A. Escajeda, 189u-1uuu.
Weekly.
Vol. 2, no. 5 dated enero 30 de 1897. In Spanish. In OCLC system.
El Monitor. Los Angeles, Calif.: Monitor Pub. Co., 1898?-1898.
1a. época, no. 19 dated jul. 9 de 1898. "Semanario mexicano." Editor: I. Larranguibel (July 1898). Chiefly in Spanish. In OCLC system.
El Monitor. Nogales, Ariz.: Bernal y Aguirre, 1889?-1895?
Weekly.
Began in 1889?; ceased in 1895?, cf. Gregory, Winifred, ed., *American Newspapers, 1821-1936.* Año 5, no. 237 dated sept. 5 de 1890. Continues *El Monitor Fronterizo.* In Spanish. In OCLC system.
El Monitor. Riverside, Calif.: I. Hayden, 1933–1934.
In OCLC system.
El Monitor. San Antonio, Tex.: Compañía Publicadora del Monitor, 1888-1uuu.
Three times a week.
Vol. 1, no.14 dated 31 de mayo de 1888. In Spanish. In OCLC system.
El Monitor. Taos, New Mexico: J. M. Martínez, 189?-1uuu.
Irregular.
T. 1, núm. 22 dated 21 de set. de 1895. In Spanish and English. In OCLC system.
El Monitor. Tucson, Ariz.: J.C. Merino, 1909-1916.
Listed in Miguélez, Armando, "Index of Spanish-Language Newspapers in the U. S. Southwest." Miguélez indicates paper is mentioned in *Regeneración,* 3-IV-1910, p. 4. No extant issues located.
Monitor Democrático. San Antonio, Texas, 1910-1911.
Bi-weekly.
Director: Paulino Martínez. Listed in "Más de cuatrocientos periódicos en español se han editado en Estados Unidos". Also listed in Ríos-C., Herminio, "Toward a True

Chicano Bibliography: Part II" p. 47; and Chabrán, Rafael and Richard Chabrán, "The Spanish-Language and Latino Press of the United States: Newspapers and Periodicals," p. 369. In Spanish. No extant issues located.

El Monitor Fronterizo. Nogales, Arizona, E.U.A.: Roberto Bernal, 188u-1uuu.
Weekly.
Año 3, núm. 136 dated 14 de set. de 1888. In Spanish. "Semanario independiente, dedicado a la defensa de México y los intereses de los mexicanos en este país." Continued by *El Monitor* (Nogales, Ariz., 1889). In OCLC system.

El Monitor Mexicano. Los Angeles, Alta Calif.: T. C. Delgado, 18uu-19uu.
Weekly.
T. 2, no. 57 dated nov. 8 de 1890. T. 19, no. 44 dated 14 de dic. de 1907. In Spanish. In OCLC system.

El Monitor Republicano. Brownsville, Tex., 190u-19uu.
No. 27 dated nov. 25, 1909. "Responsable: R. Treviño." Repository: Special Collections, University of Texas, Brownsville, Texas.

El Monitor Tucsonenese. Tucson, Ariz., 1922-19uu.
Mentioned in Sheridan, *Los Tucsonenses,* p. 203. No extant issues located.

Mora Chronicle (Mora, New Mexico). *See* **La Crónica de Mora.**

Mora County Independent. Wagon Mound, N. M.: Mora County Independent, 1921-192u.
Weekly.
Began publication Oct. 15, 1921. Ceased publication Sept. 16, 1922?, cf. Grove, Pearce S., *New Mexico Newspapers,* Includes section in Spanish: *El Independiente de Mora.* In English and Spanish. In OCLC system.

Mora County News = Las Nuevas del Condado de Mora. Wagon Mound, New Mexico, 19uu-1932.
In English and Spanish. In OCLC system.

The Mora County Patriot. Mora, N. M.: Irvin Ogden, 1921-1927.
Weekly.
Ceased publication c. June 1, 1927, cf. New Mexico newspapers. Continues *Mora County Pantagraph.* Continued by *Mora County Star.* In English and Spanish, cf. Grove, Pearce S., *New Mexico Newspapers,* p. 297. In OCLC system.

Mora County Sentinel and El Combate (Wagon Mound, New Mexico). *See* **El Combate.**

Mora County Star. Mora, New Mexico: H. López, 1927-1949?
Weekly.
Editor: Frank L. López. Began in June 1927. Ceased in 1949?, cf. Grove, Pearce S., *New Mexico Newspapers.* [Vol. 1], no. 31 dated Jan. 5, 1928. Continues *Mora County Patriot.* In English and Spanish. Listed in "Más de cuatrocientos periódicos en español se han editado en Estados Unidos". This last source lists a periodical with same name published in Las Vegas, N. M. In OCLC system.

Mora Democrat (Mora, New Mexico). *See* **El Demócrata de Mora.**

The Mora Echo. Mora, N. M.: F. Nolan and R. Romero, 1890-189u.
Weekly.
T. 1, no. 1 dated 10 de jun. 1890; ceased in Dec. 1890?, cf. Grove, Pearce S., *New Mexico Newspapers.* In English with a Spanish-language section called "Eco de Mora". In OCLC system.

Morning Las Vegan (Las Vegas, New Mexico). *See* **The Las Vegan.**

El Moro de Paz. Nueva Orleans [i.e. New Orleans, La.]: J. A. Fernández de Trava, 1888?-1uuu.
Weekly.
Año 1, no. 18 dated 3 de feb. 1889. In OCLC system.

Mosaicos: Spanish-English Newspaper. San Antonio, Tex., 1955-19uu.
Repository: Houston Metropolitan Research Center, Houston Public Library, Houston, Texas.

El Mosquito. Key West, Florida, 1916-19uu.

Irregular.

Listed in "Más de cuatrocientos periódicos en español se han editado en Estados Unidos". In Spanish. No extant issues located.

El Mosquito. Long Beach, California: E. R. Hernández and L. Herrera, 1905-1907?

Weekly.

Listed in *Rowell's American Newspaper Directory,* 1907, p. 62. In Spanish. No extant issues located.

Mosquito. Mora, Nuevo México: Camilo Padilla, 1891-1892?

Weekly.

Began in Nov. 1891. Ceased with June 30, 1892?, cf. Grove, Pearce S., *New Mexico Newspapers.* In Spanish and English. In OCLC system.

El Mosquito. Tucson, Ariz., 1917-1925.

Mentioned in Sheridan, *Los Tucsonenses,* p. 203. Also mentioned in Somoza, *Literatura de la Revolución Mexicana. . .*, p. 229. Repository: University of Arizona Library.

El Mosquito. Ybor City, Florida, 1uuu-1uuu.

Weekly. Owner: E. Carbonnell, administrator: Rafael Hernández García. Repository: University of South Florida, Tampa.

La Mujer Moderna. San Antonio, Tex.?: Andrea Villareal González and Teresa Villareal 1915-1919. Mentioned in Lomas, *The Rebel,* p. xv.

El Mulato. [New York, N.Y.], 1854-1uuu.

Weekly.

"Periódico político, literario y de costumbres". Cited in Poyo, Gerald Eugene, *With All and for the Good of All,* p. 17. In Spanish. In OCLC system.

El Mundial. Los Angeles, California, 1927-19uu.

Irregular.

Listed in Ríos-C., Herminio, "Toward a True Chicano Bibliography: Part II," p. 41, and "Más de cuatrocientos periódicos en español se han editado en Estados Unidos". No extant issues located.

El Mundo. Brownsville, Tex.: Ignacio Martínez, 1886-1uuu.

In Spanish. In OCLC system.

El Mundo. Laredo, Texas: Ignacio Martínez, 1888-1891.

Weekly.

Listed in "Más de cuatrocientos periódicos en español se han editado en Estados Unidos". No extant issues located.

El Mundo. Miami Beach, Fla.: El Mundo, Inc., 1960-19uu.

Weekly.

"Cuban American." In Spanish. In OCLC system.

El Mundo. Wilmington, Del.: El Mundo, Inc., 1960-19uu.

Weekly.

"Edición Aérea semanal". "Editado en el exilio". In Spanish. In OCLC system.

El Mundo Americano. New York, N.Y., 1899-1uuu.

Monthly.

Listed in "Más de cuatrocientos periódicos en español se han editado en Estados Unidos". In Spanish. No extant issues located.

El Mundo Azucarero. [Nueva York], 1913-1956.

Bi-monthly, 1945; quarterly, 1944; monthly, 1938, 1946-56.

Many issues have also title in English. Merged with *Facts About Sugar* (later *Sugar*) Sept. 1933-Jan. 1934. Spanish ed. of *Louisiana Planter and Sugar Manufacturer* (later *Planter and Sugar Manufacturer*). Absorbed by *Sugar* (later *Sugar y Azúcar*). In Spanish. In OCLC system.

El Mundo de Hoy. Chicago, Illinois, 1910-19uu.

Monthly.

Listed in "Más de cuatrocientos periódicos en español se han editado en Estados Unidos". In Spanish. No extant issues located.

Mundo Latino: Revista Gráfica Semanal. New York, N.Y., 1948-19uu.

Weekly.

"Año 1, no. 1 dated mayo 15, 1948. Literatura, deportes, amenidades". Jefe de redacción: O. Sánchez Paláez. Editor: I. de la Vera. Repository: The Center for Puerto Rican Studies at Hunter College, CUNY.

El Mundo Nuevo. Nueva York: El Mundo Nuevo, América Ilustrada, 1871-1875.

Editors: May 1871-May 1874, Enrique Piñeyro (with J. M. Mestre, July 1872-May 1874); June 1874-Dec. 1875, J. C. Rodrigues. *El Mundo Nuevo* combined with *América Ilustrada* to form *El Mundo Nuevo-América Ilustrada,* and continued the volume numbering of *América Ilustrada.* In Spanish. In OCLC system.

Mundo Obrero. New York, N.Y.: Mundo Obrero Pub. Co., 1931-19uu.

Monthly.

In Spanish. In OCLC system.

El Mundo: Periódico Independiente, Político, Literario y Anunciador. Brownsville, Texas: Ignacio Martínez, 1886?-1uuu.

Semiweekly.

Began in 1886? T. 1, no. 7 dated mar. 7, 1886. In Spanish. In OCLC system.

Museo de las Familias. New York, 18uu-1uuu.

Mentioned in Trujillo, Enrique, *Album del Porvenir,* vol. 3, p. 108. No extant issues located.

El Mutualista. Laredo, Tex.: Juan Zardeneta, 1885?-1888.

Semiweekly.

Began in 1885? "Bisemanal político, comercial, noticioso y de anuncios". In Spanish. In OCLC system.

El Mutualista: Organo Mensual de la S. Mutualista Hispano-Azteca. Milwaukee: La Sociedad Mutualista Hispano-Azteca, 1947-1950.

Monthly.

This paper was reprinted with an introduction by the Spanish Speaking Outreach Institute, College of Letters and Science, University of Wisconsin-Milwaukee in 1983. In Spanish. In OCLC system.

La Nación Puertorriqueña. New York, N.Y., 1933-19uu.

Monthly.

"Organ of the Junta Nacional Puertorriqueña de Nueva York." In Spanish. In OCLC system.

El Nacional. Chicago, Ill.: El Nacional, 1930-19uu.

Semiweekly.

Began with vol. 6, no. 572 dated 6 dic. 1930. Continues *México* (Chicago, Ill.). In Spanish. In OCLC system.

El Nacional. El Paso, Texas, 1919-1920.

Weekly.

Director: J. Mena Castillo. Listed in "Más de cuatrocientos periódicos en español se han editado en Estados Unidos". In Spanish and English. No extant issues located.

El Nacional. New York, N.Y., 1898-1uuu.

Repository: Archivo Nacional de Cuba, Havana.

El Nacional. San Antonio, Texas, 1916-1924.

Daily.

Director: José Quiroga. Listed in "Más de cuatrocientos periódicos en español se han editado en Estados Unidos". In Spanish. No extant issues located.

Native. Bernalillo, New Mexico, 1880-1uuu.

Listed in "Más de cuatrocientos periódicos en español se han editado en Estados Unidos". In English and Spanish. No extant issues located.

Navidad. Rio Grande, Texas; Mercedes, Texas, 1926-1930.

Annual.

Editores: José Salinas & José Díaz. Listed in "Más de cuatrocientos periódicos en español se han editado en Estados Unidos". According to this source the serial was first published in Rio Grande City, and then in Mercedes, but specific dates are not given. In Spanish. No extant issues located.

New Duval. San Diego, Texas: Manuel Marroquín, 1956?-19uu.

Weekly.

Vol. 1, no. 10 dated Mar. 30, 1956. In English and Spanish. In OCLC system.

The New Mexican. Santa Fe, N. M.: Daniel L. Rood, 1849-1850.

Weekly.

Includes a Spanish section called "El Nuevo Mejicano." "Republished as supplement to *Santa Fe Daily New Mexican,*" January 10, 1921. In English and Spanish. In OCLC system.

New Mexican (Santa Fe, N. M.: Carlos Leib, 1863?-1868*). See* **El Nuevo Mejicano.**

New Mexican Advocate. Santa Fe, N. M., 1880-1uuu.

Monthly.

Listed in Grove, Pearce S., *New Mexico Newspapers,* p. 454. In English and Spanish. No extant issues located.

New Mexican Miner. East Las Vegas, N. M.: New Mexican Miner, 1880-18uu.

Monthly.

In English. In OCLC system.

New Mexican Review (Santa Fe, New Mexico*). See* **Santa Fe New Mexican Review.**

New Mexico Advertiser. Santa Fe, N. M., 1878-1880.

Weekly, daily.

Preceded by *New Mexico Advertiser Cooperator.* Listed in Grove, Pearce S., *New Mexico Newspapers,* p. 456. In English and Spanish. No extant issues located.

New Mexico Advertiser. Las Vegas, N. M., 1870-1878.

Weekly.

Listed in Grove, Pearce S., *New Mexico Newspapers,* p. 423. Preceded by *The Acorn.* In English and Spanish. No extant issues located.

New Mexico Catholic. Las Vegas, New Mexico, 1895-1uuu.

Semi-monthly.

Listed in "Más de cuatrocientos periódicos en español se han editado en Estados Unidos". In Spanish. No extant issues located.

New Mexico Christian Advocate (Albuquerque, New Mexico*). See* **El Abogado Cristiano Neo-Mexicano.**

New Mexico Cooperator. Santa Fe, N. M., 1876-1878.

Weekly.

Listed in Grove, Pearce S., *New Mexico Newspapers,* p. 456. Succeeded by *New Mexico Advertiser.* In English and Spanish. No extant issues located.

New Mexico Democrat. Santa Fe, N. M., 1871-1uuu.

Weekly.

Listed in Grove, Pearce S., *New Mexico Newspapers,* p. 456. In English and Spanish. No extant issues located.

New Mexico Herald. Las Vegas, New Mexico: Webb & Salazar, 1879-1uuu.

Weekly.

In English and Spanish. In OCLC system.

New Mexico Methodist (Socorro, New Mexico*). See* Metodista Neo-Mexicano.

New Mexico Patriot. Las Vegas, N. M., 1875-1uuu.

Weekly.

Listed in Grove, Pearce S., *New Mexico Newspapers,* p. 424. In English and Spanish. No extant issues located.

New Mexico Pot-pourri. Deming, N. M., 1892-1uuu.
Weekly.
Listed in Grove, Pearce S., *New Mexico Newspapers,* p. 275. In English and Spanish. No extant issues located.

The New Mexico Press. Albuquerque, N. M.: H. S. Johnson, 1864-1867?
Weekly.
Began publication with vol. 2, no. 27 dated July 19, 1864. In English and Spanish, cf. Grove, Pearce S., *New Mexico Newspapers.* In OCLC system.

New Mexico State Republican. Albuquerque, N. M.: J. G. Albright, 1919-1920.
Began publication with vol. 9, no. 31 dated July 4, 1919; ceased with Dec. 31, 1920, cf. Grove, Pearce S., *New Mexico Newspapers.* Continues *New Mexico State Independent.* In English and Spanish, cf. Grove. In OCLC system.

The New Mexico Sun and El Palito. Santa Fe, N. M., 1926-1927?
Weekly.
Merger of *El Palito* (Espanola, N. M.) and *New Mexico Sun* (Santa Fe, N. M., 1909). In English and Spanish, cf. Grove, Pearce S., *New Mexico Newspapers.* In OCLC system.

The New Mexico Union. Santa Fe, New Mexico: Association of Printers, 1872-1875.
Weekly.
Editor: Kirby Benedict. Ceased in 1875?, cf. Grove, Pearce S., *New Mexico Newspapers.* Spanish section called "La Unión del Nuevo Méjico." Variant title: *Santa Fe Union.* In English and Spanish. In OCLC system.

New Orleans Port Record. New Orleans, Louisiana: Public Information Dept. of the Board of Commissioners of the Port of New Orleans, 1942-1978.
Monthly.
In Spanish and English. In OCLC system.

New York Democrat. Nueva York, [N.Y.]: R. Lanza, 1870-1870.
Daily (except Sunday).
Published in an English edition called *Democrat.* Continued by *Demócrata de Nueva York.* In Spanish and English. In OCLC system.

New York Hispano. New York, N.Y.: New York Hispano Publishing Co., 1957-195u.
In Spanish and English. In OCLC system.

New York's Spanish Daily (Brooklyn, New York*). See* **El Diario de Nueva York.**

The News. Albuquerque, New Mexico: Ira M. Bond, 1885-1887.
Weekly.
Began in Feb. 1885, ceased in 1887, cf. Grove, Pearce S., *New Mexico Newspapers.* Continues *Mesilla News.* In English and Spanish. In OCLC system.

News. Lincoln, New Mexico, 1896-1uuu.
Listed in "Más de cuatrocientos periódicos en español se han editado en Estados Unidos". In Spanish and English. No extant issues located.

The News. Vaughn, New Mexico, 1926-1936?
Listed in Ríos-C., Herminio, "Toward a True Chicano Bibliography: Part II," p. 44, and "Más de cuatrocientos periódicos en español se han editado en Estados Unidos". In Spanish and English. No extant issues located.

The News-Bulletin. Belen, New Mexico: C. Waid & E. J. Lewis, 1947-1976.
Semi-weekly; three times a week.
Vol. 41, no. 87 dated Nov. 7, 1950. An English publication for Spanish Americans. Listed in Common Council for American Unity, *Foreign Language Publications in the United States: Newspaper Lists,* p. 10. Merged with *Valencia County News* to form *Valencia County News Bulletin.* Listed in Ríos-C., Herminio, "Toward a True Chicano Bibliography: Part II." Ríos indicates the paper is bilingual and that publication started on 1925. In Spanish and English. In OCLC system.

News Guide. Eagle Pass, Texas, 1917-1940.
　　Weekly; daily.
　　Listed in Ríos-C., Herminio, "Toward a True Chicano Bibliography: Part II," p. 45. In Spanish and English. No extant issues located.
Newsletter [Spanish edition]. New York, N.Y.: International Council of Jewish Women, 195u-19uu.
　　In Spanish. In OCLC system.
Nogales Morning Times. Nogales, Ariz., 1917-19uu.
　　Contains section in Spanish. Mentioned in *El Tucsonense,* mar. 17, 1917; cf. Somoza, *Literatura de la Revolución Mexicana...*, p. 226. No extant issues located.
Norte. New York, N.Y.: American International Publications, Inc., 1940-19uu.
　　Weekly.
　　Vol 6, no. 8 dated junio 1946. "Revista continental." Editor: J.A. Losada, cf. *N.W. Ayer & Son's Directory of Newspapers and Periodicals,* 1944, p. 640. In Spanish. In OCLC system.
Norte-América: Revista Mensual Ilustrada. [New York, N.Y.: Latin-American Publishing Company, 1928-1930].
　　Monthly.
　　In LOCIS system.
El Norte Americano. New York, N.Y., 1914-1921.
　　Monthly.
　　Listed in Keniston, Hayward, *Periodicals in American Libraries for the Study of the Hispanic Languages and Literatures,* and "Más de cuatrocientos periódicos en español se han editado en Estados Unidos". In Spanish. No extant issues located.
Nosotros. New York, N.Y., 1953-19uu.
　　Monthly.
　　Editor and director: William Rodríguez Santiago. In Spanish. Repository: Center for Puerto Rican Studies at Hunter College.
Notas de Kingsville. Kingsville, Tex.: D. Rodríguez, Jr., 1943-1961?
　　Biweekly, 1943-; weekly.
　　In Spanish and English. In OCLC system.
La Noticia Mundial. Chicago: Noticia Mundial Newspaper Co., 1927-19uu.
　　Weekly.
　　"El gran semanario hispano-americano de Chicago". In Spanish. In OCLC system.
El Noticiario. Clifton, Arizona, 1915-1uuu.
　　Irregular.
　　Listed in "Más de cuatrocientos periódicos en español se han editado en Estados Unidos". In Spanish. No extant issues located.
Noticias. Albuquerque, N. M., 1905-19uu.
　　Mentioned in Somoza, *Literatura de la Revolución Mexicana...*, p. 239. No extant issues located.
Las Noticias. Del Rio, Texas: D. P. Gonzales, 1927-19uu.
　　Weekly; irregular.
　　Editor: Lisandro Peña, cf. *N.W. Ayer & Son's Directory of Newspapers and Periodicals,* 1939, p. 881. Listed in Ríos-C., Herminio, "Toward a True Chicano Bibliography: Part II," p. 45, and "Más de cuatrocientos periódicos en español se han editado en Estados Unidos". In Spanish. No extant issues located.
Las Noticias. Del Río, Tex., 1950-19uu.
　　American G. I. Forum. Mentioned in Somoza, *Literatura de la Revolución Mexicana...*, p. 247. No extant issues located.
Las Noticias. El Paso, Tex.: E. Gutiérrez, 1899-1uuu.
　　Weekly.
　　In Spanish. In OCLC system.
Las Noticias. El Paso, Texas, 1923-19uu.

Daily.

Listed in Ríos-C., Herminio, "Toward a True Chicano Bibliography: Part II," p. 45 and "Más de cuatrocientos periódicos en español se han editado en Estados Unidos". This last source indicates paper was published for 6 months in 1923. In Spanish. No extant issues located.

Las Noticias. Laredo, Texas, 1929-19uu.

Weekly.

Listed in Ríos-C., Herminio, "Toward a True Chicano Bibliography: Part II" p. 46, and "Más de cuatrocientos periódicos en español se han editado en Estados Unidos". In Spanish. No extant issues located.

Las Noticias. Los Angeles, California, 1929-19uu.

Irregular.

Listed in Ríos-C., Herminio, "Toward a True Chicano Bibliography: Part II," p. 41, and "Más de cuatrocientos periódicos en español se han editado en Estados Unidos". No extant issues located.

Noticias de la Oficina de Información Obrera y Social. Washington, D. C.: Pan American Union, Division of Labor and Social Affairs, 1940-19uu.

In Spanish. In OCLC system.

Noticias del Hispano-Americano and the McKinley County Republican. Gallup, Nuevo México: Louis S. Freth, 1915-19uu.

Published with *Carbon City News* and *The McKinley County Republican.* In Spanish. In OCLC system.

Noticias del Pueblo (Albuquerque, New Mexico). *See* **People's News.**

Noticiero: Comisión Inter-Americana de Mujeres. Washington, D. C.: Unión Pan-americana, 1951-1980.

Irregular.

News bulletin of the Inter-American Commission of Women. Continued by *Inter-American Commission of Women: [newsletter].* (Spanish: *Comisión Interamericana de Mujeres: [noticias]*). Variant title: *Noticiero de la Comisión Interamericana de Mujeres.* In Spanish. In OCLC system.

El Noticiero del Norte. Sacramento, California: El Noticiero del Norte, 1958-19uu.

Repository: Stanford University Library. In Spanish.

El Noticiero del Sur-Oeste. Bayard, New Mexico: Dan Contreras, 1949?-19uu.

In Spanish. In OCLC system.

Noticiero Obrero Norteamericano. Washington: AFL-CIO, 1943-19uu.

In OCLC system.

El Noticioso. El Paso, Texas, 1895-1uuu.

Irregular.

Listed in "Más de cuatrocientos periódicos en español se han editado en Estados Unidos". In Spanish. No extant issues located.

El Noticioso. Phoenix, Ariz.: J. M. Meléndez, 1918-19uu.

Mentioned in *El Tucsonense,* mar. 6, 1918, p. 1; cf. Somoza, *Literatura de la Revolución Mexicana...,* p. 227. No extant issues located.

El Noticioso. San Antonio, Texas, 1907-1909.

Weekly.

Director: Adolfo Duclós Salinas. Listed in Ríos-C., Herminio, "Toward a True Chicano Bibliography: Part II," p. 47; and "Más de cuatrocientos periódicos en español se han editado en Estados Unidos". In Spanish. No extant issues located.

Noticioso de Ambos Mundos: Dedicado a las Artes Comercio, Agricultura, Política y Bellas Artes. New York, N.Y., 1836-1859?

Weekly.

In Spanish. In LOCIS system.

Las Novedades. Kingsville, Tex.: Amado Gutiérrez, 1935?-19uu.

Weekly.

Año 3, no. 9 dated nov. 19, 1937. In Spanish. In OCLC system.

Las Novedades. New York, N.Y., 1884-1uuu.

Mentioned in *El Cronista* (San Francisco), abr. 4, 1884, p. 3; cf. Somoza, *Literatura de la Revolución Mexicana...*, p. 246. No extant issues located.

Las Novedades: España y los Pueblos Hispano-Americanos. New York, N.Y.: J. G. García y Co., 1876-1918.

Weekly.

Año 1, num. 73 dated 29 de julio, 1876. Daily edition: *Diario de las Novedades.* In Spanish and English. In OCLC system.

La Novela Cine-Gráfica. [Los Angeles, Calif.]: ORBE, 1947-1964.

Semimonthly, Vol. 1, no. 1-v. 1, no. 4; monthly, Vol. 1, no. 5-June 1959; bimonthly, July-Aug. 1959-1964.

Continued by *Gráfica* (Hollywood, Los Angeles, Calif.). Variant title: *Cine-Gráfica.* In Spanish. In OCLC system.

Nuestro Boletín. Kingsville, Texas, 1942-19uu.

Vol. I, no. 6 dated junio de 1942. Religious publication. In Spanish.

Nuestros Niños. El Paso, Tex.: [Casa Bautista de Publicaciones], 1918-1985.

Monthly, 1936-; quarterly, 1957-.

T. 27, no. 1, pt. 1 dated enero 5 de 1936. Issued also in a teacher's edition. Continued by *Escolares A-Alumnos y Escolares A-Maestros (1985).* Calatog of the Library of Casa Bautista de Publicaciones in El Paso indicates that the periodical was published in Mexico from 1905 to 1914, and in El Paso from 1918 to 1984. *Nuestros Niños: Maestros.* In OCLC system.

La Nueva Centuria. Phoenix, Arizona: Quiñones Bros., 1906-19uu.

Weekly; irregular.

Listed in *Rowell's American Newspaper Directory,* 1907, p. 33, and "Más de cuatrocientos periódicos en español se han editado en Estados Unidos". In Spanish. No extant issues located.

La Nueva Democracia. [New York]: Committee on Cooperation in Latin America, 1920-1963.

Monthly; quarterly, oct. de 1962-.

Editors: Jan. 1920-, S. G. Inman; with Juan Ortis González, Jan. 1920-Mar. 1933. In Spanish. In OCLC system.

La Nueva Época. Alamogordo, Nuevo México: John E. Harrison, 1911-19uu.

Weekly.

In Spanish and English. In OCLC system.

La Nueva Era. Key West, Fla.: Morúa Delgado, 188u-1uuu.

Listed in Poyo, Gerald Eugene, *With All, and for the Good of All,* p. 87. No extant issues located.

La Nueva Era. Alamo Gordo, New Mexico: Miguel Chaparro, 1918-19uu.

Weekly; irregular.

Listed in *N. W. Ayer & Son's American Newspaper Annual and Directory,* 1918, p. 623, and "Más de cuatrocientos periódicos en español se han editado en Estados Unidos". In Spanish. No extant issues located.

La Nueva Era. Kingsville, Texas, 1927-19uu.

Irregular.

Listed in Ríos-C., Herminio, "Toward a True Chicano Bibliography: Part II," (1972), p. 46, and "Más de cuatrocientos periódicos en español se han editado en Estados Unidos". In Spanish. No extant issues located.

La Nueva Estrella. Santa Rosa, N. M.: Baca & Sena [etc.], 1910-1911.

Weekly.

Began publication with set. 16, 1910, ceased Dec. 8, 1911, cf. Grove Pearce S., *New*

Mexico Newspapers. Vol. no. 1, no 5 dated set. 16, 1910. In Spanish and English. In OCLC system.

La Nueva República. Tampa, 1897?-1uuu.
Repository:Archivo Nacional de Cuba, Havana.

Nueva Senda. [San Antonio?], 19uu-1969.
Vol. 36 dated 1961."Official publication of the council on Spanish-American Work." In English and Spanish. In OCLC system.

La Nueva Solidaridad: Publicación Semanal de Los Trabajadores Industriales del Mundo. Chicago, Ill.: Los Trabajadores, 1918-1919.
Biweekly.
Issued also in an English edition.: *New Solidarity.* Continued by *Solidaridad* (Chicago, Ill.) In OCLC system.

La Nueva Voz. Nueva York, N.Y.: Spanish Newspaper Co., 1939-1941.
Daily (except Sunday).
Año. 3, no. 704 dated Dec. 2, 1939. Ceased in 1941, cf. *N. W. Ayer & Son's Directory of Newspapers and Periodicals,* 1941."Diario democrático avanzado". Continues *La Voz* (New York, N.Y.: 1937). In Spanish. In OCLC system.

Nueva York al Día. New York: Nueva York al Día and Co., 19uu-19uu.
Año 7, No. 35 dated 18 sept. de 1943."Dedicated to the American hemisphere." "Latin American weekly newspaper." In OCLC system.

Las Nuevas. Santa Rosa, New Mexico: M.P. Martínez, 1924?-1926.
Weekly.
Began in 1924?. Vol. 1, no. 38 dated Jan. 9, 1925. Variant title: *Nuevas de Santa Rosa.* Absorbed in part by *The Santa Rosa News* (Santa Rosa, N. M.: 1926). In English and Spanish. In OCLC system.

Las Nuevas de la Estancia. Estancia, N. M.: P.A. Speckmann, 190u-1908.
Weekly.
T. 1, num. 46 dated 1 de set. 1905. Companion newspaper: *The Estancia News* (1904-1908). Absorbed by *The Estancia News* (Apr. 1908), cf. Grove, Pearce S., *New Mexico Newspapers.* In Spanish. In OCLC system.

Las Nuevas de la Liga Agrícola y Ganadera del Condado de Valencia. Los Lunas, N. M.: Valencia County Farm and Livestock Bureau, 1920-192u.
Monthly.
In Spanish. In OCLC system.

Las Nuevas de Mesilla. Mesilla, N. M., 1879-1uuu.
Listed in Miguélez, Armando, "Index of Spanish-Language Newspapers in the U. S. Southwest." No extant issues located.

Nuevas de Santa Rosa (Santa Rosa, N. M., 1926). *See* **The Santa Rosa News.**

Nuevas de Santa Rosa (Santa Rosa, N. M., 1924-1926). *See* **Las Nuevas.**

Nuevas Llegadas Desde Checoslovaquia Bajo la Dominación Nazi. Chicago, Ill.: Consejo Nacional Checoslovaco en América, 1940-1942.
2 nos. monthly, Jan.-May 1940; 4 nos. monthly, June 1940-Aug. 1942.
In Spanish. In OCLC system.

Nuevo Era. Denver, Colorado, 1934-1935.
Weekly.
Listed in Oehlerts, Donald E., *Guide to Colorado Newspapers, 1859-1963,* p. 49. In Spanish. No extant issues located.

El Nuevo Estado. Tierra Amarilla, N. M.: Eliseo M. Valdez, 1907-1925.
Weekly.
Issued in an English edition: *The New State,* Jan. 31, 1916-Jan. 22, 1917. Continues *New State Republicano* (Tierra Amarilla, N. M.). Continued by *Palito.* In Spanish and English. In OCLC system.

El Nuevo Mejicano. Santa Fe, N. M.: Carlos Leib, 1863?-1868.

Weekly.

Tomo 1, no. 17 dated abr. 25 de 1863. Section in English:"New Mexican." Daily edition: *Daily New Mexican* (Santa Fe, N.M 1868). Continued by *Weekly New Mexican.* In Spanish and English. In OCLC system.

El Nuevo Mejicano (Santa Fe, N. M.: Manderfield & Tucker, 1868-1883*).* *See* **Weekly New Mexican.**

Nuevo Mejicano Diario (Santa Fe, New Mexico*). See* **The Daily New Mexican.**

El Nuevo Mexicano. Española, N. M., 1937-19uu.

Mentioned in Somoza, *Literatura de la Revolución Mexicana. . .*, p. 240. No extant issues located.

El Nuevo Mexicano. Las Cruces, N. M., 1880-1uuu.

Mentioned in Somoza, *Literatura de la Revolución Mexicana. . .*, p. 240. No extant issues located.

El Nuevo Mexicano. Santa Fe, N. M.: Companía Publicista de Nuevo Mexicano, 1890-1958.

Weekly.

Companion newspaper to the English-language *Santa Fe New Mexican.* Absorbed by *New Mexican* (Santa Fe, N. M.: 1951). In Spanish. In OCLC system.

El Nuevo Mundo. Old Albuquerque, Nuevo México: El Nuevo Mundo, 1897-1901.

Weekly.

Absorbed by *La Bandera Americana,* cf. Grove, Pearce S., *New Mexico Newspapers.* In Spanish. In OCLC system.

El Nuevo Mundo. San Francisco, [Calif.]: José M. Vigil & Co., 1864-1868?

Triweekly, Nov. 4, 1864-Apr. 20, 1866; daily (except Monday), June 28, 1864-Nov. 2, 1864; semiweekly, 1867-.

Ceased with May 27, 1868 issue?, cf. *Newspapers in Microform: United States, 1948-1972.* Merged with *La Voz de Chile y de las Repúblicas Americanas* to form *La Voz de Chile y El Nuevo Mundo.* In OCLC system.

El Obrero. Brownsville, Texas: H. Borjas, 1893-1uuu.

Tri-weekly.

Listed in *Rowell's American Newspaper Directory,* 1896, p. 993. No extant issues located.

El Obrero. Laredo, Texas, 1916-1920.

Weekly.

Listed in Ríos-C., Herminio, "Toward a True Chicano Bibliography: Part II," p. 46, and "Más de cuatrocientos periódicos en español se han editado en Estados Unidos". In Spanish. No extant issues located.

El Obrero. New York City: Centro Obrero de Habla Español, 1931-1931.

Weekly.

Published in support of *Vida Obrera,* suppressed at that time. Official organ of the Centro Obrero de Habla Español. In Spanish. In OCLC system.

El Obrero de Morenci. Morenci, Arizona: Arizona Printing & Pub. Co., 1901-1904?

Weekly.

Listed in *Rowell's American Newspaper Directory, 1907,* p. 33, and "Más de cuatrocientos periódicos en español se han editado en Estados Unidos". In Spanish and English. No extant issues located.

Obrero Libre. Brooklyn, 1924-.

Monthly.

Official organ of the Unión Obrera Venezolana de los Estados Unidos. In OCLC system.

El Obrero Libre. Jerome, Ariz.: Cenobio Rivera Domínguez, 1917-19uu.

Cenobio Rivera Domínguez. Mentioned in *El Tucsonense,* nov. 13, 1916, p. 3. Also mentioned in *Jerome News,* Nov. 1, 1916; cf. Somoza, *Literatura de la Revolución Mexicana. . .,* p. 225. No extant issues located.

El Obrero Mexicano. Jerome, Ariz., 1908-19uu.

Mentioned in *El Fronterizo* (Tucson), mar. 21, 1908, p. 1; cf. Somoza, *Literatura de la Revolución Mexicana...*, p. 225. No extant issues located.

El Obrero: Periódico Independiente. San Antonio, Texas: Teresa & Andrea Villarreal, 1910?-19uu.

Mentioned in Lomas, Clara. "The Articulation of Gender in the Mexican Borderlands, 1900-1915," pp. 297-299. No extant issues located.

El Observador. Clifton, Arizona, 1914-1917.

Irregular.

Listed in Ríos-C., Herminio, "Toward a True Chicano Bibliography: Part II," p. 41, and "Más de cuatrocientos periódicos en español se han editado en Estados Unidos". No extant issues located.

El Observador. San Marcos, Texas, 195u-19uu.

Vol. IV, no. 4 dated julio y agosto de 1956. Director y administrador: Sr. C. C. Acevedo. "Publicación bimestral religiosa, informativa y literaria". In Spanish.

Observador. Las Vegas, N. M., 1898-1899.

Weekly.

Listed in Grove, Pearce S., *New Mexico Newspapers*, p. 424. In Spanish. No extant issues located.

El Observador Fronterizo. El Paso del Norte, Texas: Los Solterones, 1886-1uuu.

Weekly.

In Spanish. In OCLC system.

El Observador Fronterizo. Las Cruces, Nuevo Méjico: Observador Fronterizo, 1888-1888.

Weekly.

In Spanish. In OCLC system.

El Observador Ibero. New Orleans, Louisiana, 1888-1893?

Weekly; irregular.

Editors: Elías J. Díaz and José Pons. In OCLC system.

El Observador Mexicano. Phoenix, Ariz.: P. Bonillas y Salazar, 189u-1uuu.

Weekly.

Vol. 3, no. 76 dated feb. 2 de 1897. In Spanish. In OCLC system.

El Observador Militar Interamericano. [Washington, D. C.: Asociación Militar Interamericana], 194u-194u.

Bimonthly.

Año 2, no. 2 dated jul.-agosto 1946. In Spanish. In OCLC system.

El Observador = The Observer. Paterson, New Jersey: Ramón Carrión, 1960-19uu.

Weekly Jan. 6-Dec. 29, 1962; semi-weekly Jan. 8-June 11, 1966; semi-monthly Nov. 26-Dec. 24, 1966.

"The first Spanish Newspaper of New Jersey." In Spanish and English. In OCLC system.

The Observer (Paterson, New Jersey). *See* **El Observador = The Observer.**

El Ocasional. Phoenix, Arizona: J. M. Meléndez, 189u-1uuu.

Weekly, Oct. 30, 1897-Jul. 15, 1899; semimonthly, Nov. 21, 1897-Oct. 23, 1898. In Spanish. In OCLC system.

Odontología Moderna. Brooklyn: Novocol Chemical Mfg. Co., Inc., 19uu-19uu.

Vol. 10, no. 4 dated sept. 1954. Continues *Modern Denistry*. In OCLC system.

L'Omnibus. Nouvelle-Orléans [i.e. New Orleans, La.]: Societé de Jeunes Gens, 1840-1841.

Tri-weekly.

"Journal politique, litteraire et commercial." In French and Spanish. In OCLC system.

La Opinión. Los Angeles, Calif.: I.E. Lozano, 1926-.

Daily.

In Spanish. In OCLC system.

La Opinión. Tucson, Ariz., 1919-19uu.

Mentioned in Sheridan, *Los Tucsonenses*, p. 203. No extant issues located.

La Opinión de Río Arriba. Tierra Amarilla, Nuevo México: W. J. West, 1935-194u.
Weekly.
Vol. 1, no. 8 dated noviembre 28, 1935. Continued by *San Juan Valley Sun.* In English and Spanish. In OCLC system.

La Opinión: Eco de la Colonia Latinoamericana. Nueva York, 1886-18uu.
Weekly.
Director: José A. Rodríguez. Listed in Batista Villareal, Teresita, *Catálogo de Publicaciones periódicas cubanas...,* p. 160. This source indicates that the Biblioteca Nacional José Martí in Havana holds some issues of this title.

La Opinión: Periódico Político Independiente. Ybor City, Tampa, 1897-1uuu.
Weekly.
Director: Pedro N. Pequeño. Listed in Batista Villareal, Teresita, *Catálogo de Publicaciones periódicas cubanas...,* p. 160. This source indicates that the Biblioteca Nacional José Martí in La Havana holds some issues of this title.

La Opinión Pública. Albuquerque, N. M.: P. G. de La Lama, 1892-1896?
Weekly, June 1892-Aug. 6, 1892; semiweekly, Sept. 10, 1892-; weekly, Oct. 29, 1892-.
Began in June 1892, ceased in 1896?, cf. Grove, Pearce S., *New Mexico Newspapers.* Vol. 1, no. 3 dated jul. 2 de 1892. In Spanish. In OCLC system.

La Opinión Pública. Albuquerque, N. M.: La Compañía Publicista Sandoval, 1906-191u.
Weekly.
Began in 1906, ceased in 1915, cf. Grove, Pearce S., *New Mexico Newspapers.* Vol. 1, no. 14 dated 14 de jul. de 1906. In Spanish. In OCLC system.

La Opinión Pública. El Paso, Tex.: Pedro G. de la Lama, 189u-1uuu.
Weekly.
T. 1., no. 196 dated mayo 11 de 1895. In OCLC system.

La Opinión Pública. Solomonville, Ariz., 1895-1uuu.
Mentioned in *El Fronterizo,* nov. 16, 1895; c.f. Somoza, *Literatura de la Revolución Mexicana...,* p. 228. No extant issues located.

La Opinión Pública. Walsenburg, Colorado, 1904-1914.
Weekly; irregular.
Listed in Oehlerts, Donald E., *Guide to Colorado Newspapers, 1859-1963,* p. 79, and "Más de cuatrocientos periódicos en español se han editado en Estados Unidos". In Spanish. No extant issues located.

Oral Hygiene. Pittsburgh, Pa. 1930-.
In Spanish and English. In OCLC system.

Organo Oficial Asociación Interamericana de Igeniería Sanitaria. Washington, D. C., 1947-1950.
Superseded by *Ingeniería Sanitaria* in 1953. In Spanish, Portuguese and English. In OCLC system.

Orientación. McAllen, Texas, 1928-1929.
Semi-monthly.
Editor: Lorenzo Yáñez, Jr. Listed in "Más de cuatrocientos periódicos en español se han editado en Estados Unidos". In Spanish. No extant issues located.

Orientación. [New York]: Comité de Publicaciones en Español de la Iglesia Luterana Unida en América, 1952-.
In Spanish. In OCLC system.

Orientación: Boletín de las Comisiones Honoríficas y Sociedades Mexicanas en los Estados de Colorado y Wyoming. Denver, Colorado: Comisiones Honoríficas y Sociedades Mexicanas, 1938-19uu.
Monthly.
In Spanish. Repository: Stanford University Library.

El Oriente. Tampa, Florida, 1897-1uuu.
Cited in Poyo, Gerald Eugene, *With All and for the Good of All,* p. 130. In Spanish.

Repository: Archivo Nacional de Cuba, Havana.

Oye, Boricua. New York, 19uu-19uu.

A workers' newspaper. Mentioned in Colón, Jesús, *The Way It Was and Other Writings,* p. 67. No extant issues located.

El Padre. San José, Calif.: Rosicrucian Press, 1929-.

Santa Clara County Teachers' Association Official Publication. In Spanish. In OCLC system.

El Padre Padilla. El Paso, Tex., 19uu-19uu.

Mentioned in Carrasco Puente, Rafael. *La prensa en México...,* p. 243. No extant issues located.

El País. El Paso, Texas: Compañía Periodística de El Paso, 1926-1932?

Weekly.

Listed in *N. W. Ayer & Son's Directory of Newspapers and Periodicals,* 1932, p. 923. In Spanish. No extant issues located.

La Palabra. Nogales, Ariz., 19uu-19uu.

Mentioned in Richmond, Douglas W., *Venustiano Carranzas' Nationalist Struggle,* p. 310. No extant issues located.

El Palacio. [Santa Fe, N. M.]: [Museum of New Mexico], 1913-.

Frequency varies.

Editors: Apr. 1915-Nov.-Dec. 1956, P.A. F. Walter (with W. L. Mauzy), May 1944-Feb. 1946; H. R. Hobbs, 1946-June 1947; A. J. O. Anderson, July 1947-Nov./Dec. 1956); Feb. -Apr. 1958, B. T. Ellis. In OCLC system.

El Paladín. Brownsville, Tex.: Correo y González, 1916-19uu.

"Editor y administrador: José A. Correa." "Editor y proprietario: Romualdo Treviño." Repository: Special Collections, University of Texas, Brownsville, Texas.

El Paladín. Corpus Christi, Texas: E. H. Marín, 192u-194u.

Weekly; irregular.

Vol. 4, no. 46 dated oct. 25 de 1929. "Entered as a second class matter, April 8, 1926..." In OCLC system.

El Palito. Española, New Mexico: El Nuevo Estado Print Co., 1925-1926.

Weekly.

Began with año 16, no. 50 dated mayo 8 de 1925. Ceased in 1926, cf. Grove, Pearce S., *New Mexico Newspapers.* Continues *Nuevo Estado.* Merged with *The New Mexico Sun* (Santa Fe, N. M.: 1909), to form *New Mexico Sun and El Palito.* In Spanish. In OCLC system.

El Palito. Santa Fe, N. M., 1908-19uu.

Mentioned in Somoza, *Literatura de la Revolución Mexicana...,* p. 243. No extant issues located.

The Pan American. [New York: Famous Features Syndicate, Inc.], 1940-1950.

In OCLC system.

Pan American. San Antonio, Texas, 1944-19uu.

In English. In OCLC system.

Pan-American Labor Press = El Obrero Pan-Americano. San Antonio, Tex.: American Alliance for Labor and Democracy, 1918-19uu. In OCLC system.

Pan-American News. Denver, Colorado: Pan-American Pub. Co., 1945-19uu.

Monthly; bimonthly, 1949.

Vol. 2, no. 5 dated May 1, 1946. In English and Spanish. In OCLC system.

Pan-American Review. New Orleans, Louisiana: Dr. R. Guzmán, 1910-1916.

Semi-monthly; monthly.

In English and Spanish. In OCLC system.

Panamericana News. Taft, Texas, 1942-19uu.

Monthly.

Repository: University of California, Berkeley.

Panamérica Comercial. Washington, D. C.: Unión Panamericana, 1931-19uu.

Issued also in English with title: *Commercial PanAmerica,* and in Portuguese with title: *Comercial PanAmerica.* In Spanish. In OCLC system.

El Panamericano: Periódico Internacional de Noticias. Edicion de México. Norwalk, Conn.: El Panamericano Publishing Co., 194u?-19uu.
In Spanish. In OCLC system.

El Pan-Americano. Pomona, Calif.: Dr. Emilio Abitia, 1950–19uu. In OCLC system.

El Panorama. Chicago: Frank W. Parker School Press, 1919?-19uu.
Editor: Arthur G. Merril. "Lecturas fáciles para estudiantes de español." In Spanish. In OCLC system.

Panorama. Washington, D. C.: Departamento de Asuntos Culturales, Unión Panamericana, 1952-1955.
"Revista interamericana de cultura". In Spanish, French and Portuguese. In OCLC system.

La Pantalla. Los Angeles, California: New World Film Corp., 1926-1927?
Monthly.
Editor: Rafael Triyillo. Listed in *N. W. Ayer & Son's American Newspaper Annual and Directory,* 1927. Also listed in "Más de cuatrocientos periódicos en español se han editado en Estados Unidos". In Spanish. No extant issues located.

La Pantalla Mundial. Hollywood, California: La Pantalla Mundial, 1927-19uu.
Listed in *N. W. Ayer & Son's American Newspaper Annual and Directory,* 1928.
In Spanish. No extant issues located.

El Papagayo. New York, 1855?-1uuu.
Editor: Tello Rubio Montega; publisher: Miguel Teurbe Tolón. Repository: Archivo Nacional de Cuba, Havana.

Papel e Imprenta. Chicago: Davidson, Pub. Co., 1946-19uu.
Bimonthly.
"Al servicio de las industrias del papel y artes gráficas de la América Latina". In Spanish. In OCLC system.

Parnaso: La Revista Exclusiva del Poema y el Cuento en Español. Nueva York, N.Y., 1950- 19uu.
Monthly.
Año 1 no. II dated junio 1950. Director: M. Muñoz Rivera, assistant editor: Pedro Juan Soto, administrator: Poliano. Repository: Erasmo Vando Collection, Hunter College, CUNY.

El Parvenir. Albuquerque, N. M., 1922-19uu.
Weekly.
Listed in Grove, Pearce S., *New Mexico Newspapers,* p. 62. In Spanish. No extant issues located.

Pasatiempo. New York, N.Y.: Kelden Publishing Co., 1951-19uu.
Monthly.
Vol. 1, no. 10 dated marzo 1951. Director: Preston L. Golden. Repository: Center for Puerto Rican Studies at Hunter College.

The Pasco. Williamsburg, Va.: Pan American Student Chain, 1939-1941.
Quarterly.
"Official quarterly publication of the Pan American Student Chain." Variant title: *Pasco News.* In Spanish and English. In OCLC system.

Pasel Suelta. El Campo, Texas, 1924-19uu.
Monthly.
Listed in Historical Records Survey, *Texas Newspapers, 1813-1939.* In Spanish. No extant issues located.

El Paso del Norte. El Paso, Texas: [La Companía Internacional Publicista], 1904-1918?
Weekly; daily.
Año 1, no. 3 dated 12 de marzo de 1904. Listed in "Más de cuatrocientos periódicos en español se han editado en Estados Unidos". This source indicates it was published

weekly in 1906, and from 1910 to 1914 reappeared as daily. Director: F. Gamochipi, Administrator: T.F. Serrano. In Spanish. In OCLC system.

El Pastor Evangélico. El Paso, Tex.: Casa Bautista de Publicaciones, 1957-1972.
Quarterly.
In OCLC system.

La Patria. Denver, Colo.: A.F. Drago, 1891-1uuu. In Spanish. In OCLC system.

La Patria. El Paso, Tex., 1919-19uu.
Daily (except Sunday).
In Spanish. In OCLC system.

Patria. New York, N.Y.: J.A. Agramonte, 1892-190u?
Weekly, marzo 26, 1892-Sept. 14, 1895; semiweekly, Sept. 21, 1895-1898.
Founder: José Martí. In Spanish. In OCLC system. Also, the Archivo Nacional de Cuba holds some issues for the years 1895 to 1901.

La Patria. Nueva Orleans [i.e. New Orleans, La.]: J. L. Sollée, 1846-1850.
Daily (1847); semiweekly, Jan. 11-Dec. 31, 1846; triweekly Jan. 5, 1848-.
Continues *Hablador;* Continued by *Unión* (New Orleans, La.: 1851). In Spanish. In OCLC system.

La Patria. San Francisco, Calif,:Federico Biestar, 1886-1uuu. In OCLC system.

La Patria. Socorro N. M.: Antonio Anaya Sr., 1944-19uu.
Weekly.
In Spanish and English. In OCLC system.

Patria: El Periódico de Martí, sin Martí, pero con Martí. [s.l.: sn], 1959-.
Director: Armando García Sifredo, cf. Peraza Sarausa, Fermín, *Directorio de Revistas y Periódicos de Cuba,* p. 33. No extant issues located.

Patria Libre. Nogales, Arizona, 1917-19uu.
Bi-weekly.
Listed in Ríos-C., Herminio, "Toward a True Chicano Bibliography: Part II," p. 42. In Spanish. No extant issues located.

El Payo de Nuevo México. [Santa Fe, N. M.]: [Government of Mexico], 1845-18uu.
In Spanish. In OCLC system.

La Paz de Cuba. New York, N.Y., 1878-1uuu.
Weekly.
Manager: Don Nicolás María Serrano. Listed in *Rowell's American Newspaper Directory,* 1879, p. 243. In Spanish. No extant issues located.

La Paz y el Trabajo. New York, N.Y., 1910-19uu.
Monthly.
Cited in Kanellos, Nicolás, "A Socio-Historic Study of Hispanic Newspapers in the United States," p. 118. Subtitle: Revista mensual de comercio, literatura, ciencias, artes. No extant issues located.

Pecos Valley Eagle. Santa Rosa, N.M.: J.R.T. Herrera, 1932-19uu. In OCLC system.

El Pelayo. Nueva-Orleans [i.e. New Orleans, La.:]: [Eduardo San Just.], 1851-1uuu.
Three times a week, Nov. 2, 1851-Oct. 31, 1851; semi-weekly, Sept. 17, 1851-Oct. 31, 1851.
"Periódico político, literario y mercantil, órgano de la población española." In Spanish. In OCLC system.

El Pensamiento. San Francisco, California, 1896-1898?
Monthly.
Listed in Willging, Eugene Paul and Herta Hatzfeld, *Catholic Serials of the Nineteenth Century in the United States.* In Spanish. No extant issues located.

El Pensamiento Contemporáneo. Nueva York [New York]: Imprenta "El Polígloto", 1891-1892.
Monthly.
Director: Antonio de Llano, cf. "Más de cuatrocientos periódicos en español se han editado en Estados Unidos". "Ciencia, filosofía, historia, variedades." In Spanish. In OCLC

system.

Peñasqueros. Peñascos, N.M: Sahd's General Store, 1959–1uuu. In OCLC system.

People's News. Albuquerque, New Mexico: H. G. Rauert, 1935-19uu.
> Weekly.

Includes section in Spanish entitled "Noticias del pueblo." Variant title: *Weekly People's News*. In English and Spanish. In OCLC system.

El Pero Grullo. New Orleans, Louisiana, 1846-1uuu.
> "Published by a Literary Society," cf. MacCurdy, Raymond R. *A History and Bibliography of Spanish-Language Newspapers and Magazines in Louisiana, 1808-1949*, p. 38. No extant issues located.

Pesca y Marina. Los Angeles, California: Fernando Flores, Ltd., 1949-19uu.
> Bi-monthly.

Editors: J. Carner Ribalta, Juan Arias. Listed in *N. W. Ayer & Son's Directory of Newspapers and Periodicals*, 1959, as published in Los Angeles, California. There is another publication with the same title and publisher with dates 1948-1970, published in Tijuana, Baja California, México. In Spanish. No extant issues located.

Petróleo del Mundo. New York, N.Y.: World Petroleum, 1943-19uu.
> Monthly.

In Spanish. In OCLC system.

Phillippine Review. Berkeley, California: Philippine Review Pub. Co., 1905-1931?
> Bi-monthly; monthly, Nov. 1901-May 1902.

Listed in *N. W. Ayer & Son's American Newspaper Annual,* 1908, p. 54. Editors: April 1905, Ponciano Reyes; October 1906, Potenciano C. Guzón; March 1907, José de la Rama; May 1907, Pastor Gómez; July 1907, A. Magsaysay. In Spanish and English. Repository: Bancroft Library (University of California, Berkeley).

Phoenix. New Orleans, Louisiana, 18uu-1841.
> Editor: J. G. Negrete. Listed in MacCurdy, Raymond R. *A History and Bibliography of Spanish-Language Newspapers and Magazines in Louisiana, 1808-1949,* p. 39. No extant issues located.

El Picudo. Rio Grande City, Starr County, Texas 1906?-19uu.
> "Organo Defensor del Partido del Pueblo". Epoca 1, número 7 dated Agosto 18, 1906. Repository: University of Texas-Pan American.

Pierrot. Tucson, Ariz., c.1929-19uu.
> Mentioned in *El Tucsonense,* mar. 10, 1928; cf. Somoza, *Literatura de la Revolución Mexicana...*, p. 230. No extant issues located.

El Piloto. Corpus Christi, Tex., 191u-19uu.
> Mentioned in Sax, Antimaco, *Los mexicanos en el destierro,* p. 56. No extant issues located.

Pima County Record. Tucson, Arizona, 1880-1uuu.
> Irregular.

Listed in "Más de cuatrocientos periódicos en español se han editado en Estados Unidos". In Spanish. No extant issues located.

Pimienta. New York, N.Y.: W. Allan Sandler, 1958-19uu.
> Monthly.

Editor: Orestes Ramiro, cf. *N. W. Ayer & Son's Directory of Newspapers and Periodicals*, 1959, p. 728. No extant issues located.

PIP. [New York, N.Y.: Comité de Nueva York del Partido Independentista Puertorriqueño], 1953-19uu.
> Año 1, no. 6 dated agosto de 1953. Organo del Comité de Nueva York del Partido Independentista Pertorriqueño. In Spanish. In OCLC system.

Plain Talk. St. Johns, Arizona, 1906-19uu.
> Editor: George H. Crosby, Jr. Listed in Lutrell, Estelle, *Newspapers and Periodicals of Arizona, 1859-1911,* p. 49. In English and Spanish. No extant issues located.

Pluma Roja. Los Angeles, California, 1913-1915.

Director and editor: Blanca de Moncaleano. Cited in Lomas, Clara. "The Articulation of Gender in the Mexican Borderlands, 1900-1915," pp. 305-307. Linked to the Partido Liberal Mexicano (PLM) and an international anarchist movement. In Spanish. No extant issues located.

P.M.: Prensa Mexicana. Tucson, Ariz.; 1957-1962.

In OCLC system.

El Pobre Diablo. New Orleans, Louisiana, 1847-1uuu.

Listed in MacCurdy, Raymond R. *A History and Bibliography of Spanish-Language Newspapers and Magazines in Louisiana, 1808-1949,* p. 39. No extant issues located.

Poli-Oculos. San Antonio, Tex.: Alberto Buerón, 191u-19uu.

Mentioned in Sax, Antimaco, *Los mexicanos en el destierro,* p. 57. No extant issues located.

El Popular. Antonito, Colo., 1909-1910.

Mentioned in Somoza, *Literatura de la Revolución Mexicana. . .,* p. 235. No extant issues located.

El Popular. Kingsville, Texas: Eulalio Velázquez, 1913-1915?

Weekly.

Director: Eulalio Velázquez. Listed in Ríos-C., Herminio, "Toward a True Chicano Bibliography: Part II" p. 46, and "Más de cuatrocientos periódicos en español se han editado en Estados Unidos". In Spanish. No extant issues located.

El Portavoz. Nueva York, N.Y., 1927-19uu.

Monthly.

V.1 no. 2 dated diciembre de 1927. Repository: Erasmo Vando Collection, Hunter College, CUNY.

Porvenir del Pueblo (New Orleans, Louisiana). *See* **L' Avenir du Peuple.**

El Porvenir. Brownsville, Tex.: Paulino S. Preciado, 1890-1921.

Semi-weekly.

Listed in *Rowell's American Newspaper Directory,* 1902, p. 1300 and 1907, p. 1114; Ríos-C., Herminio, "Toward a True Chicano Bibliography: Part II" p. 44, and "Más de cuatrocientos periódicos en español se han editado en Estados Unidos". Also listed in Keniston, Hayward, *Periodicals in American Libraries for the Study of Hispanic Languages and Literature,* with publication dates 1917-1921. Repository: University of Illinois Library. Also, some holdings at Special Collections, University of Texas, Brownsville, Texas.

El Porvenir. Denver, Colo.: El Porvenir Pub. Co., 190u?-19uu.

Monthly.

In OCLC system.

El Porvenir. Kingsville, Texas: Petronilo M. Precido, 1923-19uu.

Weekly.

Listed in *N. W. Ayer & Son's American Newspaper Annual and Directory,* 1928, p. 1063. In Spanish. No extant issues located.

El Porvenir. Mission, Texas: El Porvenir Publishing Co., 1935-19uu.

Semi-monthly.

Listed in *N. W. Ayer & Son's Directory of Newspapers and Periodicals,* 1959, p. 1063, and Common Council for American Unity, *Foreign Language Publications in the United States: Newspaper Lists,* p. 10. In Spanish. No extant issues located.

El Porvenir. New York, N.Y., 189u-1uuu.

Weekly.

Vol. 7, no. 326 dated June 1, 1896. Editor: Enrique Trujillo, 1896-. In Spanish. In OCLC system. Also, the Archivo Nacional de Cuba holds some issues for years 1891 to 1897.

El Porvenir. Nueva-Orleans [i.e. New Orleans, La.], 1863-1uuu. Weekly.

"Organo de la población hispano-americana". In Spanish. In OCLC system.

El Porvenir. San Diego, Texas, 1927-19uu.
  Irregular.
  Listed in Ríos-C., Herminio, "Toward a True Chicano Bibliography: Part II," p. 47. In Spanish. No extant issues located.
El Porvenir. Tampa, Florida, 1891-1uuu.
  Irregular.
  Listed in "Más de cuatrocientos periódicos en español se han editado en Estados Unidos". In Spanish. No extant issues located.
El Porvenir. Weslaco, Texas: M. S. Domínguez, 1924-19uu.
  Weekly; irregular.
  Listed in "Más de cuatrocientos periódicos en español se han editado en Estados Unidos", and *N. W. Ayer & Son's American Newspaper Annual and Directory,* p. 1084. In Spanish. No extant issues located.
El Postillón. New York, 1892?-1uuu.
  Edited by Pachín Marín. The only known extant copy is deposited at the Archivo Nacional de Cuba, Havana.
El Precursor. Harlingen, Texas, 1915-1920.
  Weekly.
  Editor: Pedro Carrasco. Listed in "Más de cuatrocientos periódicos en español se han editado en Estados Unidos" and Ríos-C., Herminio, "Toward a True Chicano Bibliography: Part II." This last source indicates publication dates of 1918-1920. In Spanish. No extant issues located.
La Prensa. Los Angeles, Calif.: International Pub. Co., 1912?-1924?.
  Weekly, Dec. 8, 1917-Sept. 3, 1921; semiweekly, Sept. 10, 1921-Jan. 19, 1922.
  Published 1912-1924?, cf. Gregory, Winifred, ed., *American Newspapers, 1821-1936.* Vol. 6, no. 28 dated 8 de dic. de 1917. In Spanish. In OCLC system.
La Prensa. Mora, New Mexico; Wagon Mound, New Mexico; Las Vegas, New Mexico: Henry López, 1935?-19uu.
  Weekly.
  Vol. 1 no. 19 dated July 19, 1935. In English and Spanish. In OCLC system.
La Prensa. New York [N.Y.]: La Prensa Publ. Co., 1913-1963.
  Frequency varies.
  Año 4, no. 11 dated mar. 25, 1916. Merged with *Diario de Nueva York* to form *Diario de Nueva York—La Prensa.* In OCLC system.
La Prensa. San Antonio, Texas: La Prensa, 1913-1962.
  Daily; weekly.
  Publication suspended, Sept. 10-12, 1921. Issued also in a weekly edition. In Spanish. In OCLC system.
La Prensa. Tampa, Fla.: La Prensa Pub. Co., 1918–19uu. Director: Armando de Lamar. In OCLC system.
Prensa de Albuquerque (Albuquerque, New Mexico). *See* **The Albuquerque Press.**
La Prensa de Hoy. Los Angeles, California: Antonio Cárdenas?, 1940?-19uu.
  Weekly.
  In Spanish and English. Repository: Stanford University Library.
La Prensa del Valle. Harlingen, Texas, 1924-19uu.
  Irregular.
  Listed in Ríos-C., Herminio, "Toward a True Chicano Bibliography: Part II," p. 46, and "Más de cuatrocientos periódicos en español se han editado en Estados Unidos". In Spanish. No extant issues located.
La Prensa Mexicana. San Francisco, Ca.: F. Kunhardt, 1868-18uu.
  Triweekly.
  Vol. 1, no. 13 dated Aug. 1, 1868. "Organ of the Hispanic-American population of California." In Spanish. In OCLC system.

Prensa Libre. Chicago; Ill.: Janus Pub. Co., 1960-.
>In Spanish. In OCLC system.
La Prensa = The Press. Espanola, N. M.: Carmen Towell, 19uu-19uu.
>Weekly.
>Vol. 2, no. 12 dated Apr. 27, 1950. In Spanish and English. In OCLC system.
Prensa = The Press. Solomonville [i.e., Solomon], Arizona: Henry López, 19uu–19uu.
>Vol. 13, no. 21 dated Dec. 20, 1951. In OCLC system.
Presbyterian Panamericana. Kingsville, Tex.: Presbyterian Pan-American School, 1956-.
>Five numbers a year, Oct. 1972-. Ten numbers a year, 1956-June 1963. Seven numbers a year, Sept. 1963-June 1965. Ten numbers a year, Sept. 1965-June 1972.
>Formed by the union of *The Tex.-Mex Reflector,* and *Panamericana.* In English. In OCLC system.
El Presente. San Antonio, Texas, 1914-1915.
>Weekly.
>Editores: Arturo Elías, Luis Medina Barrón. Listed in Ríos-C., Herminio, "Toward a True Chicano Bibliography: Part II," p. 47, and "Más de cuatrocientos periódicos en español se han editado en Estados Unidos". In Spanish. No extant issues located.
Pro América. San Francisco, California, 1900-19uu.
>Monthly.
>Listed in "Más de cuatrocientos periódicos en español se han editado en Estados Unidos". In Spanish. No extant issues located.
Pro-Federación. Antonito, Colorado, 1916-1918.
>Weekly?; monthly?
>Listed in Oehlerts, Donald E., *Guide to Colorado Newspapers, 1859-1963,* as a weekly publication, while "Más de cuatrocientos periódicos en español se han editado en Estados Unidos" lists it as monthly. In Spanish. No extant issues located.
El Progresista. El Paso, Tex.: Lauro Aguirre, 18uu?-19uu.
>Weekly.
>Segunda época, año 7, no. 37 dated jun. 17 de 1901. Continues *Independiente* (El Paso, Tex.). In OCLC system.
El Progreso. El Paso, Tex., 1922-19uu.
>Repository: Bancroft Library (University of California, Berkeley). Mentioned in Somoza, *Literatura de la Revolución Mexicana...,* p. 248.
El Progreso. Encino, New Mexico, 1910-19uu.
>Listed in Ríos-C., Herminio, "Toward a True Chicano Bibliography: Part II," p. 42, and "Más de cuatrocientos periódicos en español se han editado en Estados Unidos". In Spanish. No extant issues located.
El Progreso. Floresville, Texas, 1915-19uu.
>Irregular.
>Listed in Ríos-C., Herminio, "Toward a True Chicano Bibliography: Part II," p. 45, and "Más de cuatrocientos periódicos en español se han editado en Estados Unidos". In Spanish. No extant issues located.
El Progreso. Laredo, Texas: Carlos Samper, 1913-1915.
>Weekly.
>Listed in Ríos-C., Herminio, "Toward a True Chicano Bibliography: Part II" p. 46, and "Más de cuatrocientos periódicos en español se han editado en Estados Unidos". Also listed in Villegas de Magnón, Leonor, *The Rebel,* p. 237. This source indicates paper was established in 1912. Founded by Leopoldo Villegas, edited by Santiago Paz and Osvaldo Sánchez. In Spanish. No extant issues located.
El Progreso. Mercedes, Tex.: Leo D. Walker, 191u-1916.
>Mentioned in Somoza, *Literatura de la Revolución Mexicana...,* p. 250. No extant issues located.
El Progreso. Mission, Texas, 1915-1921; 1924-19uu.

Weekly.

Listed in Ríos-C., Herminio, "Toward a True Chicano Bibliography: Part II" p. 46, and "Más de cuatrocientos periódicos en español se han editado en Estados Unidos". In Spanish. No extant issues located.

El Progreso. New York [N.Y.]: The Nessim Press, 1915-1915.

Weekly (irregular).

"Devoted to the interest of the Sephardim Jews in America." Continues *Boz del Pueblo* (New York, N.Y.). In Ladino and English. In OCLC system.

El Progreso. Parkview, New Mexico: J.G. Lucero, 1895-1uuu.

Weekly.

Editor: José L. Montoya. Listed in *Rowell's American Newspaper Directory,* 1896, p. 642. In Spanish. No extant issues located.

El Progreso. Philadelphia, Pennsylvania, 1887-1uuu.

Monthly.

Listed in "Más de cuatrocientos periódicos en español se han editado en Estados Unidos". In Spanish. No extant issues located.

El Progreso. Phoenix, Arizona: Pedro G. de la Lama, 1883-1901?

Daily; irregular.

Listed in *Rowell's American Newspaper Directory,* 1902, p. 31, and "Más de cuatrocientos periódicos en español se han editado en Estados Unidos". In Spanish. No extant issues located.

El Progreso. San Antonio, Texas, 1907-1908.

Cited in Chabrán, Rafael and Richard Chabrán, "The Spanish-Language and Latino Press of the United States: Newspapers and Periodicals," p. 369. In Spanish. No extant issues located.

El Progreso. San Francisco [California]: D. Alejandro Forbes, 1871-1uuu.

Semiweekly.

In Spanish and English. In OCLC system.

El Progreso. Socorro, New Mexico: Vincent & Fitch, 1887-1887.

Weekly.

In English and Spanish. In OCLC system.

El Progreso. Trinidad, Colo.: Salomón C. García, 1891?-1944?.

Weekly.

T. 1, num. [?] dated 11 de julio, 1891. In Spanish. In OCLC system.

El Progreso del Valle. Phoenix, Arizona, 1887-1uuu.

Weekly.

Listed in Gregory, Winifred, ed., *American Newspapers, 1821-1936,* p. 20. In Spanish. Repository: Bancroft Library (University of California, Berkeley).

Progreso Farmacéutico. New York, 19uu-19uu.

Tomo 6, 72 dated, 1943. Spanish edition of *Pharmaced Advance.* In OCLC system.

El Progresso Corpus Christi, Tex.: Rodolpho Mirabal, 193u-19uu.

Weekly.

Tomo. 2, no. 28 dated June 16, 1939. In Spanish. In OCLC system.

El Proletario. Brownsville, Tex., 1880-1uuu.

Mentioned in Leal, Luis, "The Spanish-Language Press: Function and Use," p. 161. No extant issues located.

El Promotor de Educación Cristiana [Nashville, Tenn.: Baptist Sunday School Board; El Paso, Tex.: Casa Bautista de Publicaciones, 1949-1994.

Quarterly.

In Spanish. The Library of Casa Bautista de Publicaciones in El Paso owns volumes from 1949 to 1994. In OCLC system.

El Promotor Escolar. Las Cruces, N. M.: Eusebio Reynoso, 1891-1892.

Weekly.

T. 1, no. 2 dated set. 12 de 1891. In Spanish. In OCLC system.

Propaganda. Key West, Florida, 1887-1uuu.

Irregular.

Listed in "Más de cuatrocientos periódicos en español se han editado en Estados Unidos". In Spanish. Repository: Archivo Nacional de Cuba, Havana.

Propaganda Ilustrada. New York: L. R. Guzmán, 1905-19uu.

Monthly.

In Spanish. In OCLC system.

El Propagandista. El Paso, Texas, 1941?-19uu.

Repository: Bancroft Library (University of California, Berkeley).

Protección. Tucson, Ariz., 1928-19uu.

Mentioned in *El Tucsonense*, mar. 10, 1928; cf. Somoza, *Literatura de la Revolución Mexicana...*, p. 230. No extant issues located.

La Publicidad. Los Angeles, Calif., 1947-19uu.

Weekly.

Mentioned in Somoza, *Literatura de la Revolución Mexicana...*, p. 233. No extant issues located.

El Pueblo. El Paso, Texas, 1926-19uu.

Irregular.

Listed in Ríos-C., Herminio, "Toward a True Chicano Bibliography: Part II," p. 45, and "Más de cuatrocientos periódicos en español se han editado en Estados Unidos". In Spanish. No extant issues located.

El Pueblo. Key West, Florida, 1887-1uuu.

Irregular.

Listed in "Más de cuatrocientos periódicos en español se han editado en Estados Unidos". In Spanish. No extant issues located.

El Pueblo. Los Angeles, Calif.: Ramón Fuente y José N. Orozco, 1924-19uu.

Listed in Miguélez, Armando, "Index of Spanish-Language Newspapers in the U. S. Southwest." No extant issues located.

El Pueblo. Los Angeles, Calif.: All-City Employees Association of Los Angeles, 19uu-19uu.

Monthly.

Vol. 28, no. 9 dated Sept. 1974. Issued by the Association under its later name, Oct. 1977-.: All City Employees Benefits Service Association. In English. In OCLC system.

El Pueblo. New York, N. Y., 1855-1uuu.

Cited in Poyo, Gerald Eugene, *With All and for the Good of All,* p. 15. Editor: Francisco Aguedo Estrada. In Spanish. Repository: Archivo Nacional de Cuba, Havana.

El Pueblo. Nueva York [N. Y.]: Ramón Ignacio Arnao, 187u-1uuu.

Año 1, no. 12 dated jul. 27 de 1876. In Spanish. In OCLC system. Also, an inventory list from the Archivo Nacional de Cuba, Havana, shows they hold two issues of similar title dated October 10, 1875 and December 7, 1875.

El Pueblo. Old Albuquerque, N. M.: Aerelio Zermeño, 1900-19uu.

Biweekly.

T. 1, no. 4 dated feb. 17 de 1900. In Spanish. In OCLC system.

Pueblo Filipino (Washington*). See* **The Filipino People.**

Pueblos Hispanos. New York, N. Y., 1943-1944.

"First editor": Juan Antonio Critiza, cf. Chabrán, Rafael and Richard Chabrán. "The Spanih Language and Latino Press of the United States: Newspapers and Periodicals," p. 369. This source indicates newspaper was begun by Spanish immigrants, but later was staffed by Puerto Ricans. In Spanish. Repository: University of Puerto Rico, Río Piedras Campus.

El Puerto. Brownsville, Tex.: Gilberto A. Cerda, 1954?-1954.

Weekly.

Vol. 1, no. 2 dated ene. [feb.] 6, 1954. "Semanario independiente de información general." Continued by *Puerto de Brownsville*. In Spanish. In OCLC system.

El Puerto. Houston, Texas: A. D. Salazar, 1935?-.

> Weekly.

> Año 1, no. 2 dated July 5, 1935. In Spanish. In OCLC system.

El Puerto de Brownsville. Brownsville, Tex.: Gilberto A. Cerda, 1954-.

> Weekly.

> Began with Año 1, no. 17 dated Mayo 22, 1954. Continues *El Puerto*. In Spanish and English. In OCLC system.

Puerto Rican Herald. New York, N.Y.: Luis Muñoz Rivera, 1901-19uu.

> Weekly.

> Listed in Chabrán, Rafael and Richard Chabrán, "The Spanish-Language and Latino Press of the United States: Newspapers and Periodicals," p. 371. In Spanish and English. No extant issues located.

Puerto Rico. El Paso, Texas, 1908-1909.

> Irregular.

> Director: Práxedis G. Guerrero. Listed in Ríos-C., Herminio, "Toward a True Chicano Bibliography: Part II" p. 45, and "Más de cuatrocientos periódicos en español se han editado en Estados Unidos". In Spanish. No extant issues located.

Puerto Rico en Marcha. Nueva York, N.Y., 1951-19uu.

> Director: J.A. Otero. In Spanish. In OCLC system.

Puerto Rico y Nueva York. New York, N.Y., 1954-19uu.

> "Magazine mensual ilustrado". Director: Salvador Medced. In Spanish. Repository: The Center for Puerto Rican Studies at Hunter College.

Punto Rojo. Edinburg, Tex., 1909-1910.

> Listed in Miguélez, Armando, "Index of Spanish-Language Newspapers in the U. S. Southwest." No extant issues located.

Punto Rojo. El Paso, Texas: Práxedis Guerrero, 1904?-19uu.

> Cited in Lomas, Clara. "The Articulation of Gender in the Mexican Borderlands, 1900-1915," p. 296. Linked to Partido Liberal Nacional groups. No extant issues located.

El Quimbo Habanero. New York, 1893-1uuu.

> Repository: Archivo Nacional de Cuba, Havana.

El Radical. Brooklyn, N.Y., 1893-18uu.

> Director: Pablo L. Rousseau. Listed in Batista Villareal, Teresita, *Catálogo de Publicaciones periódicas cubanas...*, p. 168. This source indicates that the Biblioteca Nacional José Martí in Havana holds some issues of this title.

Radio y Artículos Eléctricos. Chicago, Illinois: The Canterbury Press, 19uu-19uu.

> Monthly.

> Trade newspaper. Listed in Common Council for American Unity, *Foreign Language Publications in the United States: Newspaper Lists,* p. 3. No extant issues located.

Radiovisión. Old Greenwich, Conn.: Editora Technica, Ltd., 1951-19uu.

> Bi-monthly.

> Listed in *N. W. Ayer & Son's Directory of Newspapers and Periodicals*, 1959, p. 160. In Spanish. No extant issues located.

The Ranchero. Corpus Christi, Tex.: Henry A. Maltby, 1859-1863.

> Weekly.

> In OCLC system.

El Ranchero. Los Angeles, Calif.: Los Angeles County Farm Bureau, 19uu-1963.

> Monthly.

> Vol. 3, no. 1 dated July 1955. "Official publication, Los Angeles County Farm Bureau." In OCLC system.

El Ranchero. San Antonio, Tex.: J. A. Quintero, 1856-18uu.

> Weekly.

> In OCLC system.

El Ranchero Semanario. Brownsville, Texas: J. S. Mansur & Co. 1872-1uuu.
Weekly.
Listed in *Rowell's American Newspaper Directory,* 1872. In Spanish. No extant issues located.

Rayos de Luz. El Paso, Texas: P. Martínez, 1914?-19uu.
Weekly.
Tomo 1, no. 8 abril 13 de 1913. In Spanish. In OCLC system.

La Raza. Chicago, Illinois: J. M. Basco, 1928?-193u.
Weekly.
Editor: Francisco F. Betancourt. Listed in Gregory, Winifred, ed., *American Newspapers, 1821-1936; N. W. Ayer & Son's Directory of Newspapers and Periodicals,* 1932, p. 217; and "Más de cuatrocientos periódicos en español se han editado en Estados Unidos". In Spanish and English. No extant issues located.

La Raza. El Paso, Tex., 192u-19uu.
Mentioned in Somoza, *Literatura de la Revolución Mexicana...,* p. 249. No extant issues located.

La Raza. San Antonio, Texas, 1914-1915?
Daily.
Director: Guillermo Meade Fierro. Listed in Ríos-C., Herminio, "Toward a True Chicano Bibliography: Part II," p. 47, and "Más de cuatrocientos periódicos en español se han editado en Estados Unidos". In Spanish. No extant issues located.

La Raza. Tampa; Ybor City, Florida, 1uuu-1uuu.
Repository: Tony Pizzo Collection at University of South Florida, Tampa.

La Raza Latina. New York, N.Y.: Adolfo Llanos y Alcaraz, 1873?-1uuu.
Semi-weekly.
Listed in *Rowell's American Newspaper Directory,* 1880, p. 257. In Spanish. No extant issues located.

La Razón. Del Rio, Texas, 1927-19uu.
Director: A. Gutiérrez. Listed in Ríos-C., Herminio, "Toward a True Chicano Bibliography: Part II," p. 47, and "Más de cuatrocientos periódicos en español se han editado en Estados Unidos". In Spanish. No extant issues located.

El Rebelde. Los Angeles: Industrial Workers of the World, 1915-1917.
In Spanish. In OCLC system.

El Reconcentrado. Cayo Hueso [i.e. Key West], 1898?-1uuu.
Repository: Archivo Nacional de Cuba, Havana.

Red River Chronicle. San Hilario, N. M.: Dorsett Brothers, 1882-1884.
Weekly.
Began publication with Vol. 2, no. 46 dated Nov. 11, 1882. Ceased Sept. 26, 1884, cf. Groves, Pearce S., *New Mexico Newspapers.* A companion newspaper was published titled *Crónica del Río Colorado* (San Hilario, N. M.). Moved to Las Vegas, N. M. and began publishing as the *Las Vegas Daily Chronicle* on Oct. 3, 1884. In OCLC system.

Red River Chronicle. San Lorenzo, New Mexico: Dorsett Brothers, 1880-1882.
Weekly.
Began publication Aug. 21, 1880, cf. Grove, Pearce S., *New Mexico Newspapers.* Ceased with Vol. 2, no. 45 dated Nov. 4, 1882. Published in La Cinta, Calif. June 26, 1880-August 14, 1880, cf. Grove, Pearce S., *New Mexico Newspapers,* p. 393. In OCLC system.

El Redactor. Nueva York [i.e. New York]: Juan José de Lerena y Eugenio Bergonzio, 1826?-1831.
Three times a month, 1826-1830; weekly.
Año 2, no. 15 dated enero 21, de 1828. In Spanish. In OCLC system. Although the Library of Congress catalog shows ending publication date of 1831, an inventory list made in the Archivo Nacional de Cuba, in Havana, indicates they have an issue for 27-7-1833. This inventory list is deposited in the Recovering the U. S. Hispanic Literary

Heritage collection at the University of Houston.

La Reforma. Los Angeles, Calif.: E. F. de Celis, 1877-1878.

> Semiweekly.

> Began in 1877, ceased in 1878, cf. Gregory, Winifred, ed., *American Newspapers, 1821-1936.* Año 1, no. 43 dated mayo 16, 1878. Editor: E. F. de Celis, May 16, 1878. In OCLC system.

La Reforma. Tucson, Ariz.: R. R. Oriza, 1892-1uuu.

> Mentioned in *El Fronterizo* (Tucson), jul. 23, 1892; cf. Somoza, *Literatura de la Revolución Mexicana...*, p. 230. No extant issues located.

Reforma, Libertad y Justicia. Austin, Texas, 1908-19uu.

> Cited in Chabrán, Rafael and Richard Chabrán, "The Spanish-Language and Latino Press of the United States: Newspapers and Periodicals," p. 369. In Spanish. No extant issues located.

La Reforma Social. El Paso, Tex.: Lauro Aguirre, 1893-19uu.

> Daily (except Sunday).

> Epoca 4, año 2, num. 27 dated sept. 1, 1912. In Spanish. "Periódico libre-pensador". In OCLC system.

Regeneración. Los Angeles, Cal., 1904-1918.

> Weekly.

> "Semanal revolucionario". Editors: 1904, 1910-Mar. 1915, Ricardo Flores Inagón, Anselmo L. Figueroa; Oct. 1915-Oct. 6, 1917, Enrique Flores; Feb.-Mar. 1918, Ricardo Flores. In Spanish; later issues also have English section. Suspended Mar. 13-Sept. 1915, and Oct. 13, 1917-Jan. 1918. In OCLC system.

El Regidor. San Antonio, Tex.: Pablo Cruz, 1888-1916.

> Weekly.

> Año 10, no. 431 dated Sept. 30, 1897. Published 1888-1916, cf. Gregory, Winifred, ed., *American Newspapers, 1821-1936.* In Spanish. In OCLC system.

Register Tribune. Roswell, New Mexico, 1910-19uu.

> Listed in Ríos-C., Herminio, "Toward a True Chicano Bibliography: Part II" and "Más de cuatrocientos periódicos en español se han editado en Estados Unidos". In Spanish and English. No extant issues located.

Registro de Nuevo México. Santa Fe, Nuevo México: La Compañía State Pub. Co., 1916-1916.

> Weekly.

> Managing editor: Frank Staplin; editors: Isidoro Armijo, Frank Ortiz, Jr. Ceased with Nov. 7, 1916?, cf. Grove, Pearce S., *New Mexico Newspapers.* In Spanish. In OCLC system.

Registro de Roswell (Roswell, New Mexico). *See* **Roswell Record.**

El Reino de Dios. Denver, Colorado: Theatin Fathers, 19uu-19uu.

> Monthly.

> Religious newspaper. Listed in Common Council for American Unity, *Foreign Language Publications in the United States: Newspaper Lists,* p. 2. In Spanish. No extant issues located.

El Relámpago. Ratón, N. M.: Carlos M. Wood, 1904-1904.

> Weekly.

> In Spanish. In OCLC system.

Renacimiento. El Paso, Tex.: Rafael Ramírez, 1923-19uu.

> Weekly.

> "Semanario católico". In OCLC system.

El Repertorio Médico. New York, N.Y., 1883-1uuu.

> Monthly.

> Listed in "Más de cuatrocientos periódicos en español se han editado en Estados Unidos". In Spanish. No extant issues located.

El Reporter Latino-Americano. Boston: Shoe and Leather Reporter, 19uu-1934.

Monthly; bi-monthly.

Title varies slightly. Continued as a section in *Shoe and Leather Reporter (Edición latino-americana)*. In Spanish. In OCLC system.

La República. Brownsville, Texas: Sentinel Publishing Co. 1915-19uu.

Daily.

Manager: José García Vera. Printed in the offices of *The Daily Sentinel.* Repository: Special Collections, University of Texas, Brownsville, Texas.

La República. El Paso, Tex.: José Luis Velasco, 1918?-19uu.

Daily.

Año 2, tomo 2, no. 441, dated nov. 1, 1919. In Spanish. In OCLC system.

La República. New York, N.Y., 1884-1885.

Listed in Poyo, Gerald Eugene, *With All and for the Good of All,* p. 175. In Spanish. No extant issues located.

La República. New York, N.Y., 1887-1uuu.

Irregular.

Listed in "Más de cuatrocientos periódicos en español se han editado en Estados Unidos". In Spanish. No extant issues located.

La República. Nueva York: José María Céspedes y Arellano, 1871-187u.

Weekly.

Printer: M. M. Zarzamendi, 1871. Publishers: Céspedes y Comp., 1871; República Publishing Co., 1871. In Spanish and English. In OCLC system.

La República. San Antonio, Texas, 1913-19uu.

Weekly.

Director: Rafael Martínez. In Spanish. Listed in Ríos-C., Herminio, "Toward a True Chicano Bibliography: Part II," p. 47, and "Más de cuatrocientos periódicos en español se han editado en Estados Unidos". No extant issues located.

La República. San Francisco, Calif.: A. G. Packard, 1881-1uuu.

Weekly.

Began in 1881, cf. *Rowell's American Newspaper Directory,* 1887. T. 2, no. 77 dated 5 de agosto de 1882. Published by La República Pub. Co., Nov. 10, 1888. In Spanish and English. In OCLC system.

The Republican = El Republicano. Brownsville, Texas: Ambros y Segura, 1865-18uu.

Semi-weekly.

In English and Spanish. In OCLC system.

The Republican Review. Albuquerque, New Mexico: Republican Review, 1870-1876.

Weekly.

Beginning with Sep. 3, 1870, a companion newspaper, *La Revista Republicana,* published with same numbering Mar. 16-Aug. 27, 1870. Continues *Semi-Weekly Review* (Albuquerque, N. M.); Continued by *The Albuquerque Review* (1876). In English and Spanish. In OCLC system.

El Republicano (Brownsville, Texas*). See* **The Republican.**

El Republicano. Cayo Hueso [i.e. Key West, Florida]: s.n. 1868?-1uuu.

Weekly.

Año 2, no. 33 dated 15 de enero de 1870. Editor/fundador: José G. Raíces. In Spanish. In OCLC system. Also the Archivo Nacional de Cuba, Havana holds a few issues for the years 1868 to 1874.

El Republicano. Española, N. M., 1912-19uu.

Mentioned in Somoza, *Literatura de la Revolución Mexicana. . .*, p. 240. No extant issues located.

El Republicano. San Francisco [Calif.]: Aurelio Luis Gallardo, 1868-1uuu.

Semiweekly.

Vol. 1, no. 2 dated agosto 22 de 1868. In Spanish. In OCLC system.

El Republicano (Santa Fe, New Mexico: Edward T. Davis, 1847-18uu*). See* **Santa Fe**

Republican

El Republicano. Socorro, New Mexico: W. E. Martin, 1898?-19uu.

    Weekly.

    Began in 1898? T. 1, num. 18 dated agosto 27 de 1898. In English and Spanish. In OCLC system.

El Republicano. Tierra Amarilla, 1901-19uu.

    Somoza indicates the Museum of New Mexico Library holds copies of this periodical; cf. Somoza, *Literatura de la Revolución Mexicana...*, p. 244.

Republicano del Condado de San Miguel. Las Vegas, N. M., 1886-1uuu.

    Triweekly.

    English edition: *San Miguel County Republican.* In Spanish. In OCLC system.

Repúblicas. Denver, Colorado, 1895-1896.

    Weekly.

    Listed in Oehlerts, Donald E., *Guide to Colorado Newspapers, 1859-1963,* p. 40. In Spanish. No extant issues located.

Las Repúblicas. Trinidad, Colorado, 1895-1897.

    Weekly.

    Listed in Oehlerts, Donald E., *Guide to Colorado Newspapers, 1859-1963,* p. 96. In Spanish. No extant issues located.

Las Repúblicas Americanas. Chicago, Illinois, 1907-19uu.

    Monthly.

    Listed in "Más de cuatrocientos periódicos en español se han editado en Estados Unidos". In Spanish. No extant issues located.

Repúblicas Hispanas Unidas. Bronx, N.Y., 1943-19uu.

    Vol 1, no. 6 dated diciembre 18, [1943]. Editor: Nick Lugo. Repository: The Center for Puerto Rican Studies at Hunter College.

La Restauración. Brownsville, Tex., 1877-1878.

    Listed in Miguélez, Armando, "Index of Spanish-Language Newspapers in the U. S. Southwest." No extant issues located.

Resurrección: Revista Mensual Ilustrada de Literatura, Artes y Ciencias. San Francisco, California, 1908.

    Bi-weekly.

    Subtitle varies. In Spanish. In OCLC system.

Revista Aérea Latino Americana. New York: Strato Pub. Co. [etc.] 1937-.

    "Edición latino americano de Aero Digest" (Sept. 1937-March 1938). Editor: Eduardo Borda (1937-.) In Spanish. In OCLC system.

Revista Agrícola. Chicago, 1905-1906.

    Monthly.

    Editor: Hannibal H. Chandler, v. 1-2; Milton George, v. 3. In Spanish. In OCLC system.

Revista Agrícola Industrial. New York, N.Y.: R. de C. Palomino, Jr., & Dr. José J. Luis, 1877-1880?

    Monthly.

    Listed in *Rowell's American Newspaper Directory,* 1879, and "Más de cuatrocientos periódicos en español se han editado en Estados Unidos". In Spanish. No extant issues located.

La Revista Albuquerque (Albuquerque, New Mexico). *See* **The Albuquerque Review.**

Revista Americana de Derecho Internacional. Washington, D. C.: Sociedad Americana de Derecho Internacional, Imp. de B. S. Adams, 1912-1921.

    Quarterly.

    Edited by J. B. Scott. T. 6-15, enero 1912-oct. 1921. Superseded by *Revista de Derecho Internacional.* In Spanish and English. In OCLC system.

Revista Americana de Farmacia, Medicina y Hospitales. New York: A.R. Elliott Pub. Co., 1895-1921.

Monthly.

In Spanish. In OCLC system.

Revista Carmelita. Tucson, Ariz.: P. Carmelo Corbella and Estanislao Caralt, 1926-1958.

Mentioned in Somoza, *Literatura de la Revolución Mexicana. . .*, p. 230. No extant issues located.

Revista Católica. Las Vegas, N. M.: Imprensa del Río Grande, 1875-1962.

Weekly, Jan. 2, 1875-Dec. 28, 1952; semimonthly, Jan. 4, 1953-Sept. 16, 1962. "Semanario internacional hispano-americano." Published in El Paso, Tex. Jan. 6, 1918-1962. Absorbed by *Mensajero del corazón de Jesús.* In OCLC system.

La Revista Comercial. New Orleans, Louisiana: Henry Kershaw and Company, 1880-1uuu.

Listed in MacCurdy, Raymond R. *A History and Bibliography of Spanish-Language Newspapers and Magazines in Louisiana, 1808-1949,* p. 39. In Spanish. No extant issues located.

Revista Comercial Americana (Revista de las Américas): Decenario de Intereses Generales Pan-Americanos. New Orleans, Louisiana, 1906-1907?

Tri-monthly.

R. Echazarreta, proprietor; Angel Urgate, director and editor-in-chief; Adolfo Vivas, editor of the Spanish section; John S. Kendall, editor of the English section; Juan Argote, business manager. Cf. MacCurdy, Raymond R. *A History and Bibliography of Spanish-Language Newspapers and Magazines in Louisiana, 1808-1949* (1951). Listed in "Más de cuatrocientos periódicos en español se han editado en Estados Unidos". In Spanish and English. No extant issues located.

Revista Comercial Mexicana. New York, 1917-1917.

Monthly.

V. 1, no. 5 dated oct. 1917. In Spanish. In OCLC system.

La Revista de Albuquerque. Albuquerque, New Mexico: Goodwin, Bailhauche y Co., 1881-188u.

Weekly.

Vol. 1, no. 3 dated oct. 1 de 1881. In Spanish. In OCLC system.

Revista de Cayo Hueso. Cayo Hueso [i.e. Key West], 1897?-1uuu.

Irregular.

Director: Juan Vilaró. Listed in "Más de cuatrocientos periódicos en español se han editado en Estados Unidos". In Spanish. Repository: Biblioteca, Universidad de la Habana, Cuba.

Revista de Cuba Libre. Tampa, 1897-1uuu.

"Periódico fundado para arbitrar recursos a la causa de Cuba". Director: María Teresa Torriente. Listed in Batista Villareal, Teresita, *Catálogo de Publicaciones periódicas cubanas. . .*, p. 171. This source indicates that the Biblioteca Nacional José Martí in Havana holds some issues of this title.

Revista de Estudios Hispánicos. New York, Madrid: Instituto de las Españas en los Estados Unidos, 1928-1929.

"Organo del Departamento de Estudios Hispánicos de la Universidad de Puerto Rico del Instituto de las Españas en los Estados Unidos". "Con la colaboración del Centro de Estudios Históricos de Madrid, Columbia University de Nueva York y la Institución Cultural Española de Puerto Rico." In Spanish and English. In OCLC system.

Revista de la Crónica: Miscelánea Científica, Artística y Literaria. Nueva York: Impr. Española e Inglesa de W. G. Stewart, 1848-1848.

Variant titles: *Miscelánea Científica, Artística y Literaria, Miscelánea de la Crónica.* In Spanish. In OCLC system.

La Revista de la Florida. Tampa, Florida, 1887-1uuu.

Listed in Poyo, Gerald Eugene, *With All and for the Good of All,* p. 175. In Spanish. Repository: Archivo Nacional de Cuba, Havana.

Revista de Laredo. Laredo, Tex.: Nicasio Idar e Hijos, 191u-19uu.

Mentioned in Griswoold, p. 44. No extant issues located.

La Revista de Los Angeles. Los Angeles, Calif.: Fidel Padilla y Gabriel Navarro, 192u-19uu.
Listed in Miguélez, Armando, "Index of Spanish-Language Newspapers in the U. S. Southwest." Miguélez indicates the paper is mentioned in *La Alianza,* sept. 1950, p.11. No extant issues located.

Revista de los EE. UU. Tucson, Ariz.: Eduardo Ruíz, 1920-19uu.
Mentioned in *El Tucsonense,* abr. 1, 1920; cf. Somoza, *Literatura de la Revolución Mexicana...,* p. 230. No extant issues located.

Revista de Radiología y Fisioterapia. Chicago, Ill.: General Electric X-Ray Corp., 1943-1947.
Chiefly in Spanish with some articles in English. In OCLC system.

La Revista de Santo Domingo. New York, 1921-19uu.
Mentioned in Somoza, *Literatura de la Revolución Mexicana...,* p. 246. No extant issues located.

La Revista de Taos. Taos, Nuevo México: Antonio J. Baca, 1902-1902.
Weekly.
Merged with *Taos Cresset* to form *La Revista de Taos and The Taos Cresset* (Taos, N. M.: 1902). In Spanish. In OCLC system.

La Revista de Taos. Taos, Nuevo México: José Montaner, 1905-1922.
Weekly.
Began with año 4, no. 45 dated 11 de nov. de 1905, ended with año 21, no. 40 dated 6 de oct. de 1922. Continues *Revista de Taos and The Taos Cresset* (Taos, N. M.: 1905). Continued by *La Revista Popular de Nuevo México.* In Spanish and English. In OCLC system.

La Revista de Taos and The Taos Cresset. Taos, Nuevo México: Frank Staplin, 1902-190u.
Weekly.
T. 1, no. 17 dated 3 de jul. de 1902. Continues *La Revista de Taos* (1902). Continued by *La Revista de Taos* (1905-1922). Merged with *Taos Cresset* and *La Revista de Taos* (Taos, N. M.: 1902). In Spanish and English. In OCLC system.

La Revista de Taos and The Taos Cresset. Taos, Nuevo México: José Montaner, 1905-1905.
Weekly.
Began with año 4, no. 3 dated 21 de enero de 1905, ceased with año 4, no. 44 dated 4 de nov. de 1905. Continues *La Revista de Taos* and *The Taos Valley News.* Continued by *Revista de Taos* (Taos, N. M.: 1905). In English and Spanish. In OCLC system.

La Revista del Ateneo Hispano Americano. Washington, 1914-19uu.
"Organo Oficial del Ateneo Hispano Americano de Washington, E.E.U.U. de A." In Spanish and English. In OCLC system.

Revista del Mundo. New York, N.Y., 1921-19uu.
Monthly.
Listed in "Más de cuatrocientos periódicos en español se han editado en Estados Unidos". In Spanish. No extant issues located.

Revista del Pacífico. San Francisco, California: José L. Schlieden, 1895-1898?
Monthly.
Listed in *Rowell's American Newspaper Directory,* 1896, p. 131, and "Más de cuatrocientos periódicos en español se han editado en Estados Unidos". In Spanish. No extant issues located.

La Revista del Sábado. San Bernardino, Calif.: 1895-1uuu.
Mentioned in *El Fronterizo* (Tucson), oct. 26, 1895, p. 2; cf. Somoza, *Literatura de la Revolución Mexicana...,* p.233. No extant issues located.

Revista del Valle. Edinburg, Texas, 1915-19uu.
Irregular.
Listed in Ríos-C., Herminio, "Toward a True Chicano Bibliography: Part II," p. 45. In Spanish. No extant issues located.

La Revista Dental Americana. Filadelfia, Pa.: C. E. Edwards, 1893-1901.
Monthly.
T. 1, no. 3 dated nov. de 1893. In OCLC system.
La Revista Du Pont. Wilmington, Del.: E. I. du Pont de Nemours & Co., 1931-1961.
Quarterly 1931-1935, 1939-1944; bimonthly 1936-1938, 1945-1961.
Mostly in Spanish with some articles in Portuguese. In OCLC system.
Revista Escolar Panamericana = PanAmerican School Review. Atlanta, Ga., 1932-19uu.
"Revista mensual para fomentar y aumentar el mutuo interés entre los profesores alumnos y amigos de las universidades, colegios y escuelas secundarias de las Américas." In OCLC system.
Revista Evangélica. El Paso, Texas: Casa Bautista de Publicaciones, 1937-1956.
Monthly.
In OCLC system.
Revista Evangelista. Las Vegas, N. M., 1876-1uuu.
Somoza indicates the Huntington Library in San Marcos, California owns the issue of jul. 1877; cf. Somoza, *Literatura de la Revolución Mexicana...*, p. 245.
Revista Hispánica Moderna. [New York]: Casa de las Españas, Columbia University, 1934-.
Quarterly, Oct. 1934-1987.
Editor: Federico de Onís. "Boletín del Instituto de las Españas". Imprint varies. Includes "Sección escolar"; v. 2-3 with separate pagination. Includes songs with piano accompaniment. Includes section "Bibliografía hispano-americana". Continues in part *Boletín del Instituto de las Españas* (Hispanic Institute in the United States). Continued in part by *Revista Hispánica Moderna: Sección Escolar*. In Spanish and English. In OCLC system.
Revista Hispánica Moderna: Sección Escolar. New York, 1935-1937.
Quarterly.
"Organo de la Agrupación Nacional de Clubs de Estudiantes de Español." In Spanish. In OCLC system.
Revista Hispano-Americana (Los Angeles, Cal.). *See* **Spanish American Review =Revista Hispano-Americana.**
Revista Hispanoamericana. San Francisco, Calif.: Laura M. Cuenca, 1895-1uuu.
Mentioned in *El Fronterizo* (Tucson), ene. 19, 1895, p. 3; cf. Somoza, *Literatura de la Revolución Mexicana...*, p. 235. No extant issues located.
Revista Homilética. El Paso, Tex.: Casa Bautista de Publicaciones, 1923-1931.
Published in Spain by Dr. Eric Lund from 1914 to 1920. Repository: Library of Casa Bautista de Publicaciones in El Paso, Texas.
Revista Ibérica. Salt Lake City, Utah: University of Utah, 1953-.
"Boletín literario y lingüístico". In Spanish. In OCLC system.
Revista Ilustrada. El Paso, Tex., 1907-19uu.
Monthly.
Año 1, núm. 3 dated marzo 1907. In Spanish. In OCLC system.
Revista Ilustrada. Santa Fe, New Mexico: Camilo Padilla, 1917-1931?.
Weekly.
In English and Spanish. In OCLC system.
La Revista Ilustrada de Nueva York. Nueva York, [i.e. New York], 1882-1uuu.
Monthly.
Vol. 11, no. 1 dated enero 15 de 1890. Issued by: E. de Losada & Co., Feb. 1891-Jan. 1893; Power & Co., Feb. 1893-. Editor: 1890-. N. Bolet Peraza. Variant title: *Revista Ilustrada.* In Spanish. In OCLC system.
Revista Interamericana de Derecho Internacional. *See* **Revista Americana de Derecho Internacional.**
Revista Interamericana: Revista Dedicada al Estudio de la Cultura Iberoamericana.

Gainesville, Fla., 1939-.
Published in 1939 by the Institute of Inter-American Affairs, University of Florida, in cooperation with Los Pícaros de Quevedo. Reproduced from type-written copy. In English and Spanish. In OCLC system.

Revista Juvenil. El Paso, Tex.: Casa Bautista de Publicaciones, 1920-1925.
Repository: Library of Casa Bautista de Publicaciones in El Paso, Texas.

Revista Latino-Americana. Los Angeles, California: Manuel R. Sánchez, 1892-1893?
Weekly.
Listed in *Rowell's American Newspaper Directory,* 1896, p. 117, and Gregory, Winifred, ed, *American Newspapers, 1821-1936,* p. 39. In Spanish and English. No extant issues located.

Revista Latino-Americana. San Francisco, California: Beteta y Co., 1903-1904.
Listed in Keniston, Hayward, *Periodicals in American Libraries for the Study of Hispanic Languages and Literature.* Repository: Bancroft Library (University of California, Berkeley). In Spanish.

Revista Médica Panamericana. New York, 1926-.
"Organo de la Asociación Médica Panamericana". In OCLC system.

La Revista Médico-Quirúrgica Americana. Nueva York [i.e. New York, N.Y.], 1892-1895.
Monthly.
In Spanish. In OCLC system.

Revista Mensual. San Antonio, Texas, 1907-1909.
Monthly.
Director: Adolfo Duclós Salinas. Listed in Ríos-C., Herminio, "Toward a True Chicano Bibliography: Part II," p. 47, and "Más de cuatrocientos periódicos en español se han editado en Estados Unidos". In Spanish.

La Revista Mercantil: una revista auténtica de las condiciones existentes en el comercio de tejidos. New York, N.Y.: International Trade Papers, Inc., 19uu-1929.
Monthly.
Editor: F. S. Norman. Title varies: La Revista Mercantil de México, 1922-1928. In OCLC system.

La Revista Mercantil de Nueva Orleans: New Orleans, Louisiana: E.A. Brandao, 1uuu-1uuu.
Semi-monthly.
"Dedicada a los intereses mercantiles de Nueva Orleans e hispano americanos". Director: Manuel Aguero. Listed in MacCurdy, Raymond R. *A History and Bibliography of Spanish-Language Newspapers and Magazines in Louisiana, 1808-1949,* p. 39. No extant issues located.

La Revista Mexicana. St. Louis, Missouri, 1884-1uuu.
Mentioned in *El Cronista* (San Francisco), abr. 19, 1884; cf. Somoza, *Literatura de la Revolución Mexicana...*, p. 238. No extant issues located.

Revista Mexicana. San Antonio, 1915-1920.
"El mejor semanario de la América Latina". In Spanish. In OCLC system.

Revista Pan-Americana. New York, N.Y., 1906-1908.
Cited in Kanellos, Nicolás, "A Socio-Historic Study of Hispanic Newspapers in the United States," p. 118. No extant issues located.

Revista para Uniones de Adultos. El Paso, Tex.: Casa Bautista de Publicaciones, 1959-1972.
Continues *Revista para Uniones de Jóvenes y Adultos* (1955-1958). Repository: Library of Casa Bautista de Publicaciones in El Paso, Texas.

Revista para Uniones de Intermedios. El Paso, Tex.: Casa Bautista de Publicaciones, 1955-1972.
Continues *Revista Trimestral para Intermedios* (1942-1954). Continued by *Ahora* (1973-1984). Repository: Library of Casa Bautista de Publicaciones in El Paso, Texas.

Revista para Uniones de Jóvenes. El Paso, Tex.: Casa Bautista de Publicaciones, 1959-

1972.
Continues *Revista para Uniones de Jóvenes y Adultos* (1955-1958). Continued by
Adelante (1973-1984). Repository: Library of Casa Bautista de Publicaciones in El
Paso, Texas.

Revista para Uniones de Jóvenes y Adultos. El Paso, Tex.: Casa Bautista de
Publicaciones, 1955-1958.
Continues *Revista Trimestral para Jóvenes y Adultos* (1942-1954). Continued by
Revista para Uniones de Adultos (1959-1972) and *Revista para Uniones de Jóvenes*
(1959-1972).

Revista para Uniones de Párvulos y Principiantes. El Paso, Tex.: Casa Bautista de
Publicaciones, 1955-1984.
Name changed to *Revista para Párvulos y Principiantes* in 1962; cf. Casa Bautista de
Publicaciones Library Catalog (El Paso, Texas). Continues *La Hora de los Cuentos*
(1947-1954). Continued by *Jugar-Guía para líderes de niños que todavía no leen*
and *Aprender: Guía para líderes de niños en los primeros 3 años de escuela* (1985).

Revista para Uniones de Primarios. El Paso, Tex.: Casa Bautista de Publicaciones,
1955-1984.
Quarterly.
Continues *Revista trimestral para Primarios* (1942-1954). Continued by *Crecer-
Guía: Líderes de 9 a 11 años* (1985). In LOCIS system.

Revista Popular. Key West, Florida, 1889-1uuu.
Semi-monthly.
Listed in "Más de cuatrocientos periódicos en español se han editado en Estados
Unidos". In Spanish. No extant issues located.

Revista Popular. New York: R. Vélez, 1887-1uuu.
Monthly.
Año 3, núm. 32 dated mayo 25 de 1891. Director: Ramón y Antonio Vélez Alvarado, cf.
"Más de cuatrocientos periódicos en español se han editado en Estados Unidos".
J. Beniques, editor and publisher, cf. *Rowell's American Newspaper Directory,* 1896.
p. 707. In Spanish. In OCLC system.

Revista Popular (Taos, New Mexico). *See* **La Revista Popular de Nuevo México.**

La Revista Popular de Nuevo México. Taos, Nuevo México: Taos Print. & Pub. Co.,
1922-19uu.
Began with año 22, no. 1 dated 15 de oct. 1922. Continues *Revista de Taos* (Taos,
N. M.: 1905). Variant title: *Revista Popular.* In Spanish. In OCLC system.

Revista Popular de Santa Fe. Santa Fe, N. M., 1924-19uu.
Mentioned in Somoza, *Literatura de la Revolución Mexicana...*, p. 243. No extant
issues located.

Revista Récord. New York, N.Y., 1957-19uu.
Quarterly.
"Magazine pro-semanario de avanzada deportiva, cultural y social". Repository: The
Center for Puerto Rican Studies at Hunter College.

La Revista Republicana (Albuquerque, New Mexico). *See* **The Republican Review.**

Revista Rotaria. [Evanston, Ill.: Rotary International], 1933-1990.
Bimonthly.
In Spanish. In OCLC system.

Revista Teatral. New York, N.Y.: Victor Alonso, 19uu-19uu.
Weekly.
Listed in Common Council for American Unity, *Foreign Language Publications in the
United States: Newspaper Lists,* p. 7. In Spanish. No extant issues located.

Revista Trimestral de las Uniones Bautistas de Jóvenes. El Paso, Tex.: Casa Bautista
de Publicaciones, 1923-1924, 1936-1941.
Repository: Library of Casa Bautista de Publicaciones in El Paso, Texas.

Revista Trimestral para las Uniones de Jóvenes y Adultos. El Paso,Tex: Casa Bautista de Publicaciones, 1942-1954.
Continues *Revista Trimestral de Uniones de Jóvenes,* (1923-1924, 1936-1941). Repository: Library of Casa Bautista de Publicaciones in El Paso,Texas.
Revista Semanal. Laredo,Tex., 1930-19uu.
Mentioned in Somoza, *Literatura de la Revolución Mexicana. . .*, p. 250. No extant issues located.
Revista Trimestral para los Intermedios. El Paso,Tex.: Casa Bautista de Publicaciones, 1942-1954.
Repository: Library of Casa Bautista de Publicaciones in El Paso,Texas.
Revista Trimestral para Primarios. El Paso,Tex.: Casa Bautista de Publicaciones, 1942-1954.
Continued by *Revista para Uniones de Primarios* (1955-1984). Repository: Library of Casa Bautista de Publicaciones in El Paso,Texas.
La Revista Universal. El Paso,Tex., 188u-1uuu.
Mentioned in *El Fronterizo* (Tucson), may. 30, 1890; cf. Somoza, *Literatura de la Revolución Mexicana...*, p. 249. No extant issues located.
Revista Universal. New York, N.Y.: M. M. Zarzamendi, 1871-1uuu.
Monthly.
Listed in *Rowell's American Newspaper Directory,* 1872. Also listed in *N. W. Ayer & Son's American Newspaper Annual and Directory,* 1920, p. 682. In Spanish. No extant issues located.
Revista Universal: Magazine Hispano-Americana. New York: Los Andes Publishing Co., Inc. 19uu-1918?
Monthly.
Subtitle varies. Ceased in 1918? Editor: J. F. Urquidi, cf. *N. W. Ayer & Son's American Newspaper Annual and Directory,* 1920, p. 682. In Spanish. In OCLC system.
Revolución. Los Angeles, California: Anselmo Figueroa, 190u-19uu.
Weekly.
Listed in Ríos-C., Herminio, "Toward a True Chicano Bibliography: Part II" p. 41 and "Más de cuatrocientos periódicos en español se han editado en Estados Unidos". Also cited in Lomas, Clara. "The Articulation of Gender in the Mexican Borderlands, 1900-1915," p. 296. This source indicates paper was being published in 1907. Propaganda organ of the Partido Liberal Mexicano. In Spanish. Repository: University of California, Berkeley.
La Revolución. New York, N.Y., 1869-1876.
Weekly, three times a week, Oct. 16, 1869-; bi-weekly, Apr. 17-Oct. 13, 1869.
"Revolución; Cuba y Puerto Rico, Periódico Político", Apr. 17-Nov. 20, 1869. *La Revolución de Cuba,* Sept. 20, 1873. *Revolución,* Sept. 27, 1873-. Volume numbering irregular. In Spanish and English. In OCLC system.
La Revolución de Cuba. Nueva York [N.Y.: s.n.], 187u-1875?
Año 1, no. 51 dated 9 de nov. de 1872; octavo año, num 1 dated 23 de octubre de 1875. Continues *Revolución* (New York, N.Y.: 1869); Continued by *Revolución* (New York, N.Y.: 1873). In Spanish. In OCLC system.
The Rio Bravo. Brownsville,Texas: O. F. Johnson & F. J. Parker, 1851-18uu.
Weekly (every Wednesday).
Began in 1851, cf. Gregory, Winifred, ed., *American Newspapers, 1821-1936.* Vol. 1, no, 39 dated May 19, 1852. In English and Spanish. In OCLC system.
Rio Grande Eco (Las Cruces, New Mexico). *See* **Eco del Río Grande.**
Rio Grande Gazette. Las Cruces, N. M., 1868-1871.
Weekly.
Listed in Grove, Pearce S., *New Mexico Newspapers*, p. 159. Succeeded by *The Borderer* March 9, 1871. In English and Spanish. No extant issues located.

Rio Grande Herald. Rio Grande, Texas: Río Grande Herald Printing & Pub. Co., Inc., 19uu-19uu.
> Weekly.

Vol. 17, no. 820 dated Mar. 8, 1935. Continues *Fronterizo* (Río Grande City, Tex.). In English with section in Spanish. In OCLC system.

Rio Grande News =Las Nuevas del Río Grande. Eagle Pass, Tex., 1906-1909.
> Weekly.

Editor: Erwin W. Owen. In OCLC system.

Rio Grande Republican. Las Cruces, N. M.: C. Metcalfe, 1881-1uuu.
> Weekly.

Began publication May 21, 1881, cf. Grove, Pearce S., *New Mexico Newspapers*. In Spanish and English. In OCLC system.

La Risa. New Orleans, Lousiana: Alemán, Gómex y Cía; 1uuu-1uuu.
> Weekly.

Listed in MacCurdy, Raymond R., *A History and Bibliography of Spanish-Language Newspaper and Magazine in Louisiana, 1808-1949*, p. 39. In Spanish. No extant issues located.

La Riscossa. Tampa, Fla., 19uu-19uu.
> Monthly.

Seconda serie, anno 2, no. 3 dated 12 ott. 1940. "Organo di propaganda antifascista". In Italian, English and Spanish. In OCLC system.

Romances. Coral Gables, Fla., 1960-19uu.

Director: Ernesto Surís Busto, cf. Peraza Sarauza, Fermín, *Directorio de Revistas y Periódicos de Cuba*, p. 34.

Roswell Record. Roswell, N. M.: J. D. Lea, 1891-1913?
> Weekly, 1892-June 9, 1911; semiweekly, June 13, 1911-Oct. 21, 1913.

Ceased in 1913? Vol. 1, no. 45 dated Jan. 8, 1892. Spanish section: "El Registro de Roswell," June 13, 1911-Aug. 2, 1912. Daily edition: *Roswell Morning Record*, Mar. 2-Aug. 30, 1903; *Roswell Daily Record*, Sept. 1, 1903-1913. Absorbed *Roswell Journal*. In English and Spanish. In OCLC sytem.

Roy Record. Roy, N. M., 1905-1929?

Listed in Miguélez, Armando, "Index of Spanish-Languages Newspapers in the U. S. Southwest." No extant issues located.

La Roza. San Antonio, Texas, 1915-1916?
> Daily.

Listed in Gregory, Winifred, ed., *American Newspapers, 1821-1936*, p. 682. In Spanish. No extant issues located.

El Saber. Phoenix, Ariz., 19uu-1940.

Listed in Miguélez, Armando, "Index of Spanish-Language Newspapers in the U. S. Southwest." Miguélez indicates the paper is mentioned in *El Mensajero*, 16-VIII- 1940. No extant issues located.

El Sable. Corpus Christi, Texas, 1890-1uuu.
> Semi-monthly.

Director: M. Cavazos. Listed in "Más de cuatrocientos periódicos en español se han editado en Estados Unidos". In Spanish. No extant issues located.

El Sahuaro. Tucson, Ariz.: Federico Manzo, 1uuu-1925.

Listed in Miguélez, Armando, "Index of Spanish-Language Newspapers in the U. S. Southwest." No extant issues located.

St. Johns Herald (Saint Johns, Arizona). *See* **Snips and St. Johns Herald.**

Saludos: Revista de Buena Voluntad. New York [etc.], 1947-.
> Monthly (irregular).

"Organo oficial del Pan-American Good Neighbor Forum, Inc." In Spanish. In OCLC system.

San Miguel County Republican (Las Vegas, N. M.*). See* **Republicano del Condado de San Miguel**

San Miguel County Star. East Las Vegas, N. M.: Henry López, 1927-1948?
> Weekly.
> Ceased in Oct. 1948?, cf. Grove, Pearce S. *New Mexico Newspapers.*Vol. 1, no. 25 dated Jan. 19, 1928. Variant title: *Estrella.* In OCLC system.

Sancho Panza. El Paso, Tex.: Lorenzo B. Sáenz, 1891-1uuu.
> Weekly.
> Vol. 1, no. 11 dated nov. 8 de 1891. In Spanish and English. In OCLC system.

Sancho Panza. Santa Fe, New Mexico: Camilo Padilla, 1907-19uu.
> Monthly.
> Listed in *N.W.Ayer & Son's Directory of Newspapers and Periodicals*, 1935, with starting date of 1907. Also listed in "Más de cuatrocientos periódicos en español se han editado en Estados Unidos", and Ríos-C., Herminio, "Toward a True Chicano Bibliography: Part II," with starting date of 1935. In Spanish. No extant issues located.

Sangre Nueva: Revista Literaria Mensual. New York, 194u-19uu.
> Año III dated septiembre 1945. Director and editor: Alberto Vázquez B., chief executive: Santos Mercado, chief reporter: Augusto Avila Hoyos. Repository: Erasmo Vando Collection, Hunter College, CUNY.

Santa Fe Daily New Mexican (Santa Fe, New Mexico*). See* **Santa Fe New Mexican.**

The Santa Fe Daily Post. Santa Fe, New Mexico: A. P. Sullivan, 1870-1872.
> Daily (except Monday).
> Began in June 1870; ceased in March 1872, cf. Stratton, P.A., *The Territorial Press of New Mexico, 1834-1912.* Vol. 2 no. 193 dated Feb. 6, 1872. Spanish section called "Correo de Santa Fe". In English and Spanish. In OCLC system.

Santa Fe Gazette. Santa Fe, N. M.: James L. Collins, 1854-185u.
> Weekly.
> Vol. 4, no. 10 dated July 29, 1854. Spanish section has title "Gaceta semanaria de Santa Fe". Continued by *Santa Fe Weekly Gazette* (Santa Fe, N. M.: 185u). In English and Spanish. In OCLC system.

Santa Fe Gazette. Santa Fe, N. M.: Hezekiah S. Johnson, 1859-1864.
> Weekly.
> Title varies slightly. Issues for 1860-1864 have Spanish parallel title: *Gazeta Semanaria de Santa Fe.* Issue for May 28, 1864 has Spanish parallel title: *Gazeta de Santa Fe.* Vol. 2, no. 11 dated Mar. 19, 1859. Continues *Santa Fe Weekly Gazette* (Santa Fe, N. M.: 1855). Continued by *Santa Fe Weekly Gazette* (Santa Fe, N. M.: 1864). In English and Spanish. In OCLC system.

Santa Fe New Mexican Review. Santa Fe, N. M.: W. H. Bailhauche & Co., 1883-1885.
> Daily (except Monday).
> Began with Vol. 2, no. 85 dated June 6, 1883; ceased with v. 22, no. 108; dated June 26, 1885. Published as: *Santa Fe New Mexican Review,* June 8, 1883-1885. Weekly Edition: *Santa Fe New Mexican Review,* June 9-Aug. 2, 1883 and *Weekly New Mexican Review* (Santa Fe, N. M.: 1883), Aug. 9, 1883-Mar. 6, 1884; and; *Weekly New Mexican Review and Live Stock Journal,* Mar. 13, 1884-July 2, 1885. Variant title: *New Mexican Review.* In English and Spanish, cf. Grove, Pearce S., *New Mexico Newspapers,* p. 476. In OCLC system.

Santa Fe Republican. Santa Fe, New Mexico: Edward T. Davies, 1847-18uu.
> Weekly, Sept. 10, 1847-Apr. 2, 1848; weekly, Aug. 1-30, 1848; three times a month, May 3-July 24, 1848.
> Spanish section is called "El Republicano." In English and Spanish. In OCLC system.

Santa Fe Republican. Santa Fe, N. M.: Putnam O'Brien, 1862-1863.
> Weekly.
> Vol. 1, no. 2 dated June 21, 1862. Spanish section called *"El Republicano."* In OCLC system.

Santa Fe Union (Santa Fe, New Mexico). *See* **The New Mexico Union.**

Santa Fe Weekly Gazette. Santa Fe, New Mexico W. W. H. Davis, 185u-18uu.
Weekly.
Vol. 4, no. 39 dated Mar. 3, 1855. Spanish section has title "Gaceta semanaria de Santa Fe". Begins renumbering with v. 1, no. 1 on Nov. 5, 1857. Continues *Santa Fe Gazette* (Santa Fe, N. M.: 1854). Continued by *Santa Fe Gazette* (Santa Fe, N. M.: 1859). In Spanish and English. In OCLC system.

Santa Fe Weekly New Mexican (Santa Fe, N. M.: 1868). *See* **Weekly New Mexican** (N. M.: 1868).

Santa Fe Weekly Post. Santa Fe, New Mexico: A. P. Sullivan, 1869-1872?
Weekly.
Sections in Spanish: "Post semanaria de Santa Fe", Oct. 16, 1869; and "Correo de Santa Fe", Nov. 5, 1870-June 22, 1872. The official organ of New Mexico. In English and Spanish. In OCLC system.

The Santa Rosa News. Santa Rosa, New Mexico: M. P. Martínez, 1926-19uu.
Weekly.
Vol. 3, no. 31 dated Dec. 3, 1926. Continues *Las Nuevas.* Spanish section: "Las Nuevas." Continued by *News* (Santa Rosa, N. M. 1980). Variant titles: *Nuevas de Santa Rosa, De Baca County News.* In English and Spanish. In OCLC system.

Santa Rosa Sun. Santa Rosa, Guadalupe County, N. M.: F. D. Morse, 190u-19uu.
Weekly.
Vol. 6, no. 1 dated Nov. 8, 1907. In English and Spanish. Chiefly in Spanish, Feb. 2, 1917-Mar. 23, 1923. In OCLC system.

Scientific American (Export ed.). New York: Munn & Co., 1845-1908.
Monthly.
Variant titles: *América Científica e Industrial* (1895-Mar 1903), *América Científica, Industrial, Agrícola, y Ganadera* (Mar. 1903). In English and Spanish, 1895- Feb. 1903. No extant issues located.

Seguridad Industrial. Washington, D. C.: Organización de los Estados Americanos, Consejo Interamericano Económico y Social, Unión Panamericana, 1957-19uu. In Spanish. In OCLC system.

La Semana. Los Angeles, Calif.: Octavio Paz, 1919-19uu.
Weekly.
Edited by Octavio Paz and Ramón Puente. In OCLC system.

La Semana. Tucson, Ariz.: Francisco M. Robredo, 1933-19uu.
Mentioned in *La Alianza,* abr. 1955; cf. Somoza, *Literatura de la Revolución Mexicana...*, p. 230. No extant issues located.

La Semana de Nueva York. New York, N.Y.: E. Lorenzo, 1958-19uu.
Vol. 1, no. 5 dated abril 22, 1958. "Revista hispanoamericana de Nueva York." In Spanish. Repository: Center for Puerto Rican Studies at Hunter College.

La Semana = The Week. Nueva York, [N.Y.]: Week, Inc., 1906-19uu.
Weekly.
Began with Apr. 10, 1906 issue, cf. Gregory, Winifred, ed., *American Newspapers, 1821-1936.* Vol. 4, no. 4 dated 29 de abr., de 1908. In Spanish. In OCLC system.

El Semanario. Nueva York, N.Y.: N. Lawrence Sandler, 1955-19uu.
Vol. 1, no. 1 dated 10 de diciembre de 1955. Editor: Guillermo de la Fuente; managing editor: Antonio Dávila. In Spanish. Repository: The Center for Puerto Rican Studies at Hunter College.

Semanario de Santa Fe. Santa Fe, N. M., 1847-1uuu.
Mentioned in Somoza, *Literatura de la Revolución Mexicana...*, p. 243. No extant issues located.

Semanario Hispano. Nueva York: [Semanario Hispano], 1945?-19uu.
Weekly.

Año 1, no. 26 dated 9 marzo 1946. In Spanish. In OCLC system.

Semanario Imparcial. San Francisco, Calif.: A. Juan Campillo, 1938-19uu.
Weekly.
Continues *Imparcial* (San Francisco, Calif.). In Spanish. In OCLC system.

Semblanzas Literarias. Washington, D. C.: Unión Panamericana, 1951-1951.
In Spanish. In OCLC system.

El Sembrador. Lee's Summit, Missouri: Unity School of Christianity, 19uu-19uu.
Bi-monthly.
Listed in Common Council for American Unity, *Foreign Language Publications in the United States: Newspaper Lists,* p. 4. No extant issues located.

El Sendero Teosófico. Point Loma, California, 1911-19uu.
Monthly, quarterly.
Listed in Ríos-C., Herminio, "Toward a True Chicano Bibliography: Part II," p. 42 and "Más de cuatrocientos periódicos en español se han editado en Estados Unidos". No extant issues located.

El Separatista. New York, 1883?-1uuu.
Repository: Archivo Nacional de Cuba, Havana.

The Sephardic Bulletin. New York: Sephardic Community of New York, 1928–1930.
In OCLC system.

Septembrino. San Ignacio, Tex.: Nicanor Flores, 192u-19uu.
Mentioned in Somoza, *Literatura de la Revolución Mexicana. . .,* p. 252. No extant issues located.

Serie de Educación. Washington, D. C.: Unión Panamericana, 1936-1937.
In Spanish. In OCLC system

Serie Sobre Bibliotecas y Bibliografía. Washington, D. C.: La Unión Pan-Americana, 1930-19uu.
In Spanish. In OCLC system.

Servicio Cubano de Información. Coral Gables, Fla.: Carlos Todd, 1960-.
Weekly.
In Spanish. Issued also in English. In OCLC system.

7 días del Diario de la Marina en el Exilio. Miami Beach, Fla.: José L. Rivero, 1960-1961.
Weekly.
Año 129, núm. 116 dated 8 oct., 1960. In Spanish and English. In OCLC system.

El Siglo Veinte. Tucson, Arizona: José R. Vásquez, 1899-1uuu.
Weekly.
Listed in Lutrell, Estelle, *Newspapers and Periodicals of Arizona, 1859-1911,* p. 61. In Spanish. No extant issues located.

Simpatía. New Orleans, 1935-19uu.
In Spanish. In OCLC system.

The Sister Republic; A Commercial Magazine. Denver: Brady and Shiels, 1899-19uu.
Monthly, Mar. 1923-32; quarterly (irregular), Mar. 1916-Dec. 1922.
In English and Spanish. In OCLC system.

Snips and St. Johns Herald. St. Johns, Arizona: Lloyd C. Henning, 1903-1904.
Weekly.
Vol. 1, no. 33 dated Aug. 13, 1903. Vol. 1, no. 33 -v. 3, no. 1 also called *Snips and Herald.* "The official newspaper of Apache County." Published by Eli S. Perkins, Jan.-July 1903. Variant titles: *Snips St. Johns Herald, St. Johns Herald and Apache News.* Listed in Gregory, Winifred, ed., *American Newspapers, 1821-1936;* and "Más de cuatrocientos periódicos en español se han editado en Estados Unidos". Both sources indicate publication is bilingual. In OCLC system.

Soberanía. Nueva York, 1958?-19uu.
Año 1, num. 2 dated abril de 1958. "Organo del Partido Independentista Puertorriqueño en los Estados Unidos de Norte América." Administrator: José Roura.

Repository: Center for Puerto Rican Studies at Hunter College.

Social: Revista Semanal. Nueva York, 193u?-19uu.

Weekly, biweekly.

No. XIII dated enero 25, 1930. Chief reporter: José G. Menchaco. Repository: Erasmo Vando Collection, Hunter College, CUNY.

El Socialista. San Diego, California: Jesús M. de la Garza, 1898-1uuu.

Weekly.

Listed in *Rowell's American Newspaper Directory,* 1902, p. 954. In Spanish. No extant issues located.

La Sociedad. San Francisco [Calif.]: F. Epson, 1869-1895.

Semiweekly, weekly.

Began with Dec. 8, 1869 issue?; ceased in 1895?, cf. Gregory, Winifred, ed., *American Newspapers, 1821-1936.* Año 7, no. 685 dated 15 Julio, 1876. "Organ of the Mexican population of California," 1876. Editor: F. Epson, 1876. In Spanish; with some notices in English. In OCLC system.

Socorro Chieftain (Socorro, New Mexico). *See* **El Defensor Chieftain.**

Socorro Star. Nueva York [New York, N.Y.]: A. Vélez Alvarado, 1899-19uu.

Weekly.

Variant title: *La Estrella del Socorro.* In Spanish with parallel English translations. In OCLC system.

Socorro Star. Socorro, New Mexico: Socorro Pub. Co., 1884-1885?

Daily.

Ceased in Mar. 1885? cf. Grove, Pearce S., *New Mexico Newspapers.* Vol. 1, no. 39 dated Nov. 25, 1884. Has a section in Spanish called "La Estrella del Socorro". In OCLC system.

The Socorro Union. Socorro, New Mexico: T. A. Blake, 188u-18uu.

Weekly.

Vol. 1, no. 9 dated Feb. 24, 1887. Section in Spanish: "Unión de Socorro." In English and Spanish. In OCLC system.

El Sol. Alice, Texas: A.D. Smith, 1895-1910.

Weekly.

Listed in *Rowell's American Newspaper Directory,* 1907, p. 1109, with starting date of 1895. Also listed in Ríos-C., Herminio, "Toward a True Chicano Bibliography: Part II" p. 44, and "Más de cuatrocientos periódicos en español se han editado en Estados Unidos". These two last sources indicate starting date of 1904. In Spanish. No extant issues located.

El Sol. Denver, Colo.: El Sol Pub. Co., 1958-19uu.

Weekly.

In Spanish and English. In OCLC system.

El Sol. El Paso, Texas, 1926-19uu.

Weekly.

Listed in Ríos-C., Herminio, "Toward a True Chicano Bibliography: Part II," p. 46, and "Más de cuatrocientos periódicos en español se han editado en Estados Unidos". In Spanish. No extant issues located.

El Sol. Phoenix, Ariz: J.C. Franco, 1939-1981.

Weekly.

"Semanario popular independiente de información." "Spanish Pan-American Weekly Newspaper." Later published by Voz Hispana, Inc. In Spanish. In OCLC system.

El Sol. San Bernadino, Calif.: Eugenio Noqueras, 1950?–19uu. Vol. 18, no. 12 dated July 7, 1950. In OCLC system.

El Sol. San Marcos, Texas, 1956-1958.

In English. In OCLC system.

El Sol. Santa Rosa, N. M.: W. C. Burnett, 1911-1914.

Weekly.

Began publication with T. 1, no. 1 dated marzo 24, 1911; ceased Jan. 23, 1914, cf. Groves, Pearce S., *New Mexico Newspapers.* Companion newspaper to the *Santa Rosa Sun.* In Spanish and English. In OCLC system.

El Sol de Chicago. Chicago, Ill., 1959?-19uu.

Vol. 2, no. 90 dated 21 al 26 de marzo, 1960. Editor and general manager: J. Z. Rodríguez Beauchamp. In Spanish, some articles in English. Repository: The Center for Puerto Rican Studies at Hunter College, CUNY.

El Sol de Colorado. Denver, Colo.: Daniel T. Valdez, 1938-1938?

Mentioned in Somoza, *Literatura de la Revolución Mexicana. . .*, p. 236. No extant issues located.

El Sol de la Chesapeake. Baltimore, Maryland, 19uu-19uu.

Vol. 21, no. 8 dated Apr. 1926. In Spanish. Repository: Bancroft Library (University of California, Berkeley).

El Sol de Mayo. Las Vegas, N. M.: Romero y Baca, 1891-1892.

Weekly.

Absorbed by *Hispano-Americano* (Las Vegas, N. M.). In Spanish. In OCLC system.

El Sol de Mayo. Las Vegas, N. M.: Manuel Salazar y Otero, 1894-1894.

Weekly.

Separated from *Hispano-Americano* (Las Vegas, N. M.). Continued by *Sol de Mayo* (Las Vegas, N. M.: 1900). In Spanish. In OCLC system.

El Sol de Mayo. Las Vegas, N. M.: P. González, 1900-1902.

Weekly.

Originally published in Wagon Mound, N. M. Continued by *Combate* (Wagon Mound, N. M.). In Spanish. In OCLC system.

El Sol de San Bernardino. San Bernardino, California, 1926-1931?

Weekly; irregular.

Director: Roberto Isaías. Listed in Gregory, Winifred, ed., *American Newspapers, 1821-1936;* and "Más de cuatrocientos periódicos en español se han editado en Estados Unidos". This last source indicates publication dates of 1925-1930. In Spanish. No extant issues located.

La Solana. Laguna, N. M., 1878-1uuu.

Mentioned in Somoza, *Literatura de la Revolución Mexicana. . .*, p. 241. No extant issues located.

Solidaridad. Brooklyn, New York: Industrial Workers of the World, 1918-1930?

Weekly.

Listed in State Historical Society of Wisconsin Library, *Hispanic Americans in the United States,* p. 53. In Spanish. No extant issues located.

Solidaridad: Publicación de Los Trabajadores Industriales del Mundo. Chicago, Ill.: Los Trabajadores, 1920-193u.

Biweekly.

Tercera, no. 1 dated Dec. de 1920-23. Published in New York, N. Y., Aug. 1926-Apr. 16, 1927; Brooklyn, N. Y., Apr. 30, 1927-Jan. 11, 1930. Continues *Nueva Solidaridad.* In Spanish. In OCLC system.

La Sombra de Lincoln. Beeville, Texas: F. de P. González, 1898-1902.

Weekly.

Listed in *Rowell's American Newspaper Directory,* 1902, p. 928. In Spanish. No extant issues located.

La Sombra de Padilla (or El Padilla). New Orleans, Louisiana, 1845-19uu.

Editor: José Quintana Warnes. Listed in MacCurdy, Raymond R., *A History and Bibliography of Spanish-Language Newspapers and Magazines in Louisiana, 1808-1949,* p. 38. No extant issues located.

Sonora. Nogales, Arizona, 1921-19uu.

Monthly.

Listed in Ríos-C., Herminio, "Toward a True Chicano Bibliography: Part II" p. 42, and "Más de cuatrocientos periódicos en español se han editado en Estados Unidos". In Spanish. No extant issues located.

La Sonora. Tucson, Arizona: Charles H. Tully & Ignacio Bonillas, 1879-1uuu.
> Weekly.
> Listed in *Rowell's American Newspaper Directory,* 1880, p. 390, and Gregory, Winifred, ed., *American Newspapers, 1821-1936.* In Spanish. Repository: Bancroft Library (University of California, Berkeley).

Sonora Herald. Sonora, Calif.: J. White & J. G. Marvin, 1850-1856?
> Weekly.
> Also published a steamer edition. Publishers: White & Marvin, 1850. Publishers vary. Editors: John White, John G. Marvin, 1850. Suspended briefly in 1850, cf. Kemble, Edward Cleveland, *A History of California Newspapers, 1846-1858.* In English and Spanish. In OCLC system.

El Sordo. San Diego, Tex.: Francisco Maynez, 1889-1uuu.
> Weekly.
> Vol. 1, no. 2 dated July 10, 1889. In Spanish. In OCLC system.

The Southwest Miner = El Minero. Tucson, Arizona: International Union of Mine, Mill, and Smelter Workers, 1955-19uu. In OCLC system.

Southwestern Catholic. Santa Fe, N. M.: Catholic Pub. Co. of New Mexico, 1921-19uu.
> Weekly.
> Vol. 1, no. 2 dated Oct. 14, 1921. Variant title: *Católico del Sudoeste.* Somoza indicates that the writer Josefa Santana de López used to write in this newspaper, cf. Somoza, *Literatura de la Revolución Mexicana...,* 242. In OCLC system.

The Spanish American. Roy, Mora Co., N. M.: Roy Pub. Co., 1904?-1926?
> Monthly, Feb., 1905; weekly, Nov. 3, 1906-.
> Title in Spanish: *El Hispano Americano.* Vol. 1, no. 6 dated Feb., 1905. Continued by *Roy Record.* In English and Spanish. In OCLC system.

Spanish American Industrial Journal. San Antonio, Texas: 1894-19uu. "A monthly journal devoted to the interest of irrigation, mining, railroads, shipping, and manufacturing." Editor and manager: W.D. Hornaday. In English and Spanish. In OCLC system.

Spanish American Review = Revista Hispano-Americana. Los Angeles, California: Carlos Tully and Manuel R. Sánchez, 1889-1uuu.
> Weekly.
> Vol. 1, no. 5 dated Dec. 1, 1889. In English and Spanish. In OCLC system.

Spanish American Trade Journal. Saint Louis, Missouri: St. Louis Spanish Club Publishing Co., 1890-1uuu.
> Monthly.
> Listed in *Rowell's American Newspaper Directory,* 1906, p. 574. In English and Spanish. No extant issues located.

Spanish Echo. New York: American Publicity Committee on Spain, 1935-19uu. In OCLC system.

Spanish Labor Bulletin. New York: Spanish Labor Bureau Press, 1936-1939. In OCLC system.

Spanish Revolution. New York, N.Y.: United Libertarian Organization, 1957-19uu. In Spanish. In OCLC system.

Spanish Sunday Paper (Ybor City, Fla.). *See* **El Heraldo Dominical.**

El Sport. Tampa, Fla., 1897?-1uuu.
> Listed in Poyo, Gerald Eugene, *With All, and for the Good of All,* p. 130. No extant issues located.

Springer Banner (Springer, New Mexico). *See* **El Estandarte de Springer.**

Star (Los Angeles, California). *See* **Los Angeles Star.**

Star County Democrat. Grulla, Texas, 1934-19uu.

Appeared only during election time, cf. "Más de cuatrocientos periódicos en español se han editado en Estados Unidos". In Spanish and English. No extant issues located.

Sugar. [New York, etc.]: [Mona Palmer, etc], 1941-1956.
>Monthly.
>
>Includes: "Sugar Abstracts," published under the auspices of the international Society of Sugar Cane Technologists. Continues *Facts About Sugar.* Merged with *Mundo Azucarero* to form *Sugar y Azúcar.* In OCLC system.

Sugar y Azúcar. [Englewood Cliffs, N. J., etc.]: [Ruspam Communications, etc.], 1956-.
>Monthly; semimonthly.
>
>Published under the auspices of the International Society of Cane Sugar Technologists. Formed by the union of *Sugar* (New York, 1941), and *Mundo Azucarero.* In OCLC system.

Sun. Mora, N. M., 1940?-1944?
>Weekly.
>
>Listed in Grove, Pearce S., *New Mexico Newspapers*, p. 299. In English and Spanish. No extant issues located.

The Sun. San Diego, Tex.: W. L. Johnston, 1891?-1uuu.
>Weekly.
>
>Vol. 1, no. 18 dated Sept. 5, 1891. In Spanish. In OCLC system.

Sunday Gazette (Las Vegas, N. M: Louis Hommel*). See* **Las Vegas Gazette.**
>(Las Vegas, N. M.: 187u)

Sunday News (Tampa, Florida*). See* **Tampa Leader.**

El Sur-Americano. Nueva York [N.Y.]: Robert Wensio, 187u-1uuu.
>Semimonthly.
>
>Vol. 1, no. 8 dated 15 de enero de 1875. "A semi-monthly journal devoted to the interests of the South-American republics." In OCLC system.

The Swastika. Des Moines, New Mexico: H. H. Burris, 1913-.
>Weekly.
>
>Vol. 6, no. 52 dated July 25, 1913. Absorbed by *Greenville News.* In English and Spanish. In OCLC system.

Tampa Ilustrado. Tampa, Ybor City, Florida, 1912-19uu.
>Repository: Pizzo Collection at the University of South Florida, Tampa.

Tampa Latina. Tampa, Florida, 1879-1929.
>Repository: Pizzo Collection at the University of South Florida, Tampa.

Tampa Leader. Tampa, Fla.: Ramón Núñez, 19uu-19uu.
>Vol. 7, no. 14 dated Apr. 15, 1945. Variant title: *Sunday News.* In Spanish. In OCLC system.

The Taos Recorder and El Bien Público. Taos, New Mexico, 191u-19uu.
>Weekly.
>
>Vol. 1, no. [?] dated june 20, 1912. Continues *El Bien Público* (Taos, N. M.). In English and Spanish. In OCLC system.

The Taos Review. [Taos, N. M.]: The Review Pub. Co., 1936-1936.
>Weekly.
>
>Includes section in Spanish: "La Revista de Taos." Merged with *Taos Valley News* (Taos, N. M.: 1922); to form *Taos Review and The Taos Valley News.* In English and Spanish. In OCLC system.

The Taos Review and the Taos Valley News. Taos, New Mexico: The Review Pub. Co., 1936-1940.
>Weekly.
>
>Began with vol. 1, no. 15 dated Oct. 8, 1936; ceased with v. 5, no. 27 dated Dec. 26, 1940. Includes a section in Spanish: "Revista de Taos." Formed by the union of *Taos Review* (Taos, N. M.: 1936) and *Taos Valley News* (Taos, N. M.: 1922). Merged with *Taoseño* (Taos, N. M.: 1939) to form *Taoseño and The Taos Review.* In English and Spanish. In OCLC system.

Taos Star. Taos, New Mexico: Wells Publishing Corp., 1948-1950.
    Weekly.
    Spanish section has title: "La Estrella de Taos." Absorbed by *Crepúsculo.* In English and Spanish. In OCLC system.

The Taos Valley News. Taos, New Mexico: José Montaner, 190u-1917.
    Weekly.
    Began with v. 9, no. 1 dated Jan. 2, 1917. Ceased with vol. 2, no. 1 dated Jan. 1, 1910. Continued by *Taos Valley News and El Crepúsculo.* In English. In OCLC system.

Taos Valley News. Taos, New Mexico: Taos Print. & Pub. Co. 1922-1936.
    Weekly.
    Began with vol. 15, no. 29 dated July 18, 1922. Ceased with v. 25, no. 40 dated Oct. 1, 1936. Continues *Taos Valley News and El Crepúsculo.* Merged with *Taos Review* to form *The Taos Review and The Taos Valley News.* In English and Spanish. In OCLC system.

Taos Valley News and El Crepúsculo. Taos, New Mexico: Taos Print & Pub. Co., 1917-1922.
    Weekly.
    Began with vol. 9, no. 2 dated Jan. 9, 1917; ceased with v. 15, no. 28 dated July 11, 1922. Continues *Taos Valley News* (Taos, N. M.: 1910). Continued by *Taos Valley News* (Taos, N. M.: 1922). In Spanish and English. In OCLC system.

Taoseño. Taos, New Mexico: Placita Press, 1939-1940.
    Weekly.
    Began with vol. 1, no. 1 dated Nov. 1, 1939; ceased with v. 2, no. 9 dated Dec. 26, 1940. Merged with *Taos Review and The Taos Valley News to form Taoseño and The Taos Review.* Includes Spanish-language section titled "El Taoseño." In OCLC system.

The Taoseño. Taos, New Mexico: B. Petteys & D. McCarty, 1948-1948.
    Weekly.
    Began with vol. 13, no. 18 dated Feb. 19, 1948; ceased with v. 13, no. 41 dated July 29, 1948. Includes a Spanish-language section titled "Taoseño y la Revista de Taos". Continues *Taoseño and The Taos Review.* Continued by *Crepúsculo* (Taos, N. M.: 1948). In English and Spanish. In OCLC system.

The Taoseño and The Taos Review. Taos, New Mexico: Everett and Lucille Wheeler, 1941-1948.
    Weekly.
    Began with vol. 2, no. 10 dated Jan. 2, 1941; ceased with v. 13, no. 17 dated Feb. 12, 1948. Includes a Spanish-language section titled "El Taoseño y la revista de Taos". Formed by the union of *El Taoseño* and *Taos Review and The Taos Valley News.* Continued by *Taoseño* (Taos, N. M.: 1948). In English and Spanish. In OCLC system.

El Taquígrafo Gregg. New York: The Gregg Publishing Co, 19uu-19uu.
    Quarterly.
    Listed in Common Council for American Unity, *Foreign Language Publications in the United States: Newspaper Lists,* p. 7. In Spanish. No extant issues located.

El Tecolote. Houston, Tex.: R. Avila De La Vega, 19uu-19uu.
    Año. 7, num. 372 dated May 7, 1932. In Spanish and English. In OCLC system.

El Tecolote. San Francisco, Calif.: J. M. Pimentil, 1875?-1879?
    Daily (except Sunday).
    Began in Mar. 1875?, cf. *Newspapers in Microform.* Año 2, no. 409 dated mayo 4 de 1876. Ceased in 1879?, cf. Gregory, Winifred, ed., *American Newspapers, 1821-1936.* "Only Spanish daily newspaper published in California," 1876. In Spanish with some text in English. In OCLC system.

El Telégrafo. Nueva-Orleans [i.e. New Orleans, La.]: Manuel Ariza y F. Delaup, 1825?-1uuu.
    Semiweekly.
    Began with Nov. 1, 1825 issue? Vol. 1, no. 3 dated 8 de nov. de 1825. In Spanish. In

OCLC system.

El Telégrafo. New Orleans, Louisiana, 1849-1uuu.

Daily.

Editores: José Antonio Godoy/ J. O. Carreras, listed in MacCurdy, Raymond R., *A History and Bibliography of Spanish-Language Newspapers and Magazines in Louisiana, 1808-1949,* p. 40. No extant issues located.

El Telégrafo de las Floridas. Amelia Island, Florida, 1817-1uuu.

Weekly.

Listed in Brigham, Clarence S. *History and Bibliography of American Newspapers, 1690-1820.* In Spanish. No extant issues located.

Temas para las Uniones Bautistas de Jóvenes. El Paso, Texas: Casa Bautista de Publicaciones, 1929-1930.

Repository: Library of Casa Bautista de Publicaciones in El Paso, Texas.

Temas: Revista Ilustrada. New York, 1950-.

Monthly.

In English and Spanish. In OCLC system.

The Tex. Mex. Reflector. Kingsville, Tex.: Texas-Mexican Industrial Institute, 1921-1956.

Monthly, except July and Aug.

Ceased with v. 36, no. 10 dated June 1956? Merged with *Panamericana* to form *Presbyterian Panamericana.* Variant title: *Texas-Mexican Reflector.* In OCLC system.

The Texas Gazette. [San Felipe de] Austin, Tex.: Godwin Brown Cotten, 1829-1832.

Weekly.

Continued by *Texas Gazette and Brazoria Commercial Advertiser.* Sometimes published as *Mexican Citizen,* Mar. 17-May 26, 1831. Suspended Nov. 1829-Jan. 1830, and Dec. 1830. In OCLC system.

The Texas-Mexican Reflector (Kingsville, Texas). *See* **The Tex. Mex. Reflector.**

Textiles Panamericanos. [Atlanta, etc.: Billian Pub., etc.], 1941-19uu.

Bimonthly, May 1941-Sept.-Oct. 1943; monthly, May-Oct. 1946-; Quarterly, Marzo de 1985-.

In OCLC system.

Thurber-Whyland and Company's Spanish Review. New York: The Company, 187u-18uu.

Elías de Losada was in charge of the Spanish section, cf. Chamberlin, *La Revista Ilustrada de Nueva York* ... p. 10. No extant issues located.

El Tiempo. Las Cruces, N.M.: M. Valdez, 1882-1911.

Weekly.

Vol. 1, no. 6 dated nov. 9 de 1882. Absorbed by *Eco del Valle.* In Spanish. In OCLC system.

El Tiempo. Harlingen, Texas: M. Lara, 1935-19uu.

Weekly.

Listed in *N. W. Ayer & Son's Directory of Newspapers and Periodicals,* 1954, p. 965. In Spanish. No extant issues located.

El Tiempo. Houston, Tex.: El Tiempo Pub. Co., 1921-19uu.

Weekly.

Vol. 1, no. 16 dated Mar. 4, 1921. In Spanish. In OCLC system.

El Tiempo: Diario de Las Cruces, N. M. (Las Cruces, New Mexico). *See* **The Daily Times.**

El Tiempo. Raymondville, Texas: A. R. Rodríguez, 1937-1958.

Weekly.

Listed in Common Council for American Unity, *Foreign Language Publications in the United States: Newspaper Lists,* p.10, and "Más de cuatrocientos periódicos en español se han editado en Estados Unidos". In Spanish. No extant issues located.

El Tiempo. San Antonio, Texas: Pereida & Co., 1877-1uuu.

Weekly.

Editor: Ramón de Contador. In Spanish. In OCLC system.

El Tiempo. San Francisco, [Calif.]: F. Herrera, 186u-1uuu.
   Semi-weekly.
   Vol. 1, no. 51 dated feb. 9 de 1869. In Spanish. In OCLC system.
Tiempo de Laredo (Laredo, Texas: Times Pub. Co., 19uu-1982). *See* **The Laredo Times.**
La Tienda. New York, N.Y.: La Tienda Publishing Co., 1uuu-1uuu.
   Monthly.
   Listed in Common Council for American Unity, *Foreign Language Publications in the United States: Newspaper Lists,* p. 7. In Spanish. No extant issues located.
Tierra. Nueva York, N.Y.: Tierra, 1930-19uu.
   Three times a month.
   In Spanish and English. In OCLC system.
Times. Aguilar, Colorado: Jno. W. Sullivan, 1898-1uuu.
   Weekly.
   Listed in *Rowell's American Newspaper Directory,* 1902. In Spanish and English. No extant issues located.
El Times en Español. El Paso, Texas: El Paso Times Company, 1881-19uu.
   Daily.
   Director: W. Tovar y Bueno. Editor: E. C. Davis. Listed in "Más de cuatrocientos periódicos en español se han editado en Estados Unidos", and *N. W. Ayer & Son's American Newspaper Annual and Directory,* 1918, p. 958. In Spanish. No extant issues located.
The Times of Havana. Miami, Fla.: Havana Pub. Co., 1957-1965.
   Monthly, June 1964-Oct. 1, 1965; weekly, Apr. 20, 1961-May 14/21, 1964.
   Ceased in 1965? Published in Havana, Cuba, 1957-1960. Sometimes published as "Caribbean edition" or "American ed." Continued by *Times of the Americas.* In Spanish and English. In OCLC system.
La Tinaja. Maxwell, New Mexico: Journalism Class of Maxwell Public School, 1937-19uu.
   Bi-monthly.
   In OCLC system.
Tipográfica. Raton, N. M., 1902-19uu.
   Weekly.
   Listed in Grove, Pearce S., *New Mexico Newspapers,* p. 116. In Spanish. No extant issues located.
Todos. New York, N.Y.: Todos Magazine, Inc. 1958-19uu.
   Vol. 1, no. 27 dated oct. 12, 1958. Editor-Publisher: Oscar Ríos. Repository: The Center for Puerto Rican Studies at Hunter College. In Spanish.
The Topic. Albuquerque, New Mexico: Topic Pub. Co., 1934-19uu.
   Weekly.
   Vol. 1, no. 23 dated Jan. 4, 1935. In English and Spanish. In OCLC system.
Tópicos de Tolleson. Tolleson, Ariz., 1938-19uu.
   Listed in Miguélez, Armando, "Index of Spanish-Language Newspapers in the U. S. Southwest." Miguélez indicates the paper is mentioned in *El Mensajero,* 15-V- 1938. No extant issues located.
El Toro. El Paso, Tex., 1921-19uu.
   Repository: Bancroft Library (University of California, Berkeley). Mentioned in Somoza, *Literatura de la Revolución Mexicana...,* p. 249.
Toros. [Chula Vista, Calif.], 1957–1963? In OCLC system.
Toros y Tauromaquia: Bull Fight Review. Chula Vista, Calif.: 1957–19uu.
   In OCLC system.
El Trabajo. San Antonio, Texas, 1919-19uu.
   Weekly.
   Director: José J. Rebollar. Listed in "Más de cuatrocientos periódicos en español se han editado en Estados Unidos", and Ríos-C., Herminio, "Toward a True Chicano Bibliography: Part II," p. 47. In Spanish. No extant issues located.

El Trabajo: Periódico Semanario. Davenport, Iowa: [El Trabajo Publishing Co.], 1925-19uu.
   Irregular.
   Editor: R. Torres Delgado. In Spanish. Repository: Bancroft Library (University of California, Berkeley)
Trabajos Manuales. El Paso: Casa Bautista de Publicaciones, 1953-1960.
   Repository: Library of Casa Bautista de Publicaciones in El Paso, Texas.
Traducción-Prensa. Tampa, Fla.: Traducción-Prensa Pub. Co., 19uu-19uu.
   Daily.
   Año 39, no. 86 dated 18 Abr. 1946. In Spanish. In OCLC system.
Las Tres Américas. Nueva York, 1893-1uuu.
   Monthly.
   Editor: N. Bolet Peraza, 1893-. In Spanish. In OCLC system.
Tri-Mex Tripod. Taft, Tex. : Presbyterian School for Mexican Girls, Tripod Club, 19uu-19uu.
   Vol. 8, no. 1 dated Oct. 5, 1940. In OCLC system.
La Tribuna. Houston, Tex.: Alonso Capetillo & Adolfo Jiménez, 1924?-19uu.
   Año. 1, num. 5 dated July 4, 1924. In Spanish. In OCLC system.
Tribuna. Los Angeles, Calif., 1928-1uuu.
   Listed in Miguélez, Armando, "Index of Spanish-Language Newspapers in the U. S. Southwest." No extant issues located.
La Tribuna. New York, N. Y.: Miguel de Zárraga, 1921-1922.
   Mentioned in Somoza, *Literatura de la Revolución Mexicana. . .*, p. 246. No extant issues located.
La Tribuna. Santa Fe: N. M., 1881-1uuu.
   Listed in Miguélez, Armando, "Index of Spanish-Language Newspapers in the U. S. Southwest." No extant issues located.
Tribuna del Pueblo. Tampa, Florida, 19uu-19uu.
   Associated with La Sociedad de Torcedores de Tampa, the important cigarworkers union (also called La Resistencia), cf. Chabrán, Rafael and Richard Chabrán, "The Spanish-Language and Latino Press of the United States: Newspapers and Periodicals." In Spanish. No extant issues located.
La Tribuna del Trabajo. Key West, Fla.: Carlos Baliño, 188u-18uu.
   Listed in Poyo, *With All, and for the Good of All,* p. 87. No extant issues located.
Tribuna Hispana. New York, 1926-1928.
   Monthly (May 1927-July 1928); weekly (Nov. 7, 1926-Jan. 2, 1927).
   In Spanish. In OCLC system.
El Tribuno Cubano. Nueva York [N. Y.]: C. [Cirilo] Villaverde, 18uu-1uuu.
   Weekly.
   Vol. 2, no. 10 dated agosto 23 de 1876. Editor: R. Rubiera de Armas, Aug. 23-Oct. 21, 1876. Subtitle varies: "Revista política, literaria y anuncios", Aug. 23, 1876; "Periódico politíco", Sept. 15-Oct. 21, 1876. In Spanish. In OCLC system.
Trinchera. Miami, 1960?-.
   Irregular.
   "Organo oficial del Directorio Revolucionario Estudiantil de Cuba". In OCLC system.
Trinidad Weekly Advertiser = El Anunciador de Trinidad. Trinidad, Colo.: M. Beshoar, 1882-1uuu.
   Weekly.
   Began in 1882, cf. *Rowell's American Newspaper Directory,* 1884. Vol. 1, no. 22 dated May 21, 1883. Published by The Advertiser Pub. Co. June 9, 1884-. Published as *Weekly Advertiser,* Feb. 4, 1884. Variant title: *Anunciador de Trinidad.* In English and Spanish. In OCLC system.
Trinidad Weekly Times. Trinidad, Las Animas County, Colo.: E. S. Lenfestey, 1881-1uuu.
   Weekly.
   Vol. 1, no. 51 dated Dec. 31, 1881. Continues *Trinidad Times.* In English and Spanish.

In OCLC system.

El Triunfo. Antoñito, Colo., 1uuu-1uuu.
Listed in Miguélez, Armando, "Index of Spanish-Language Newspapers in the U. S. Southwest." No extant issues located.

Triunfo. Tampa, Florida: Howard Press, 1937-19uu.
Weekly.
Listed in Gregory, Winifred, ed., *American Newspapers, 1821-1936.* Also listed in *N.W. Ayer & Son's Directory of Newspapers and Periodicals,* 1941, p. 166. In Spanish and English. No extant issues located.

La Trompeta. Corpus Christi, Texas, 1912-19uu.
Monthly.
Listed in Ríos-C., Herminio, "Toward a True Chicano Bibliography: Part II," p. 45. In Spanish. No extant issues located.

La Trompeta Evangélica de la Iglesia de Dios. San Antonio, Tex., 1948-19uu.
In Spanish. In OCLC system.

El Trueno. Tucson, Arizona, 1895-1uuu.
Weekly.
Listed in Gregory, Winifred, ed., *American Newspapers, 1821-1936.* In Spanish. No extant issues located.

The Truth (Corpus Christi, Texas: Santos de La Paz). *See* **La Verdad.**

The Truth. Miami, Fla., 1957-.
Frequency varies.
Ed. by Saviur Cancio Peña. Consists of anti-dictatorship propaganda. Variant title: *La Verdad.* In English and Spanish. In OCLC system.

The Truth (New York, N.Y.). *See* **La Verdad** (Nueva York: Cora Montgomery, 1848-185u.)

Tucson Cultural. Tucson, Ariz., 1943-1944.
Mentioned in Somoza, *Literatura de la Revolución Mexicana...*, p. 230. No extant issues located.

El Tucsonense. Tucson, Ariz., 1915-1957.
In Spanish. In OCLC system.

La Tuerca. Albuquerque, Nuevo México: Gaceta Pub. Co., 192u-192u.
Vol. 1, no. 29 dated jul. 8, 1826. In Spanish. In OCLC system.

Two Laredos. Laredo, Texas: Norwood & Paschal, 1879?-1880?
Weekly.
Listed in *Rowell's American Newspaper Directory,* 1880, and "Más de cuatrocientos periódicos en español se han editado en Estados Unidos". In Spanish and English. No extant issues located.

The Two Republics. Boston, Mass, 1881-1uuu.
Listed in Miguélez, Armando, "Index of Spanish-Language Newspapers in the U. S. Southwest." No extant issues located.

The Two Republics (Los Angeles, California). *See* **Las Dos Repúblicas.**

La Unión. Brownsville, Texas: H. Borjas (as of 1905), 1901-19uu.
Bi-weekly.
Listed in "Más de cuatrocientos periódicos en español se han editado en Estados Unidos". In Spanish. No extant issues located.

La Unión. Hidalgo, Texas, 1897-1898.
Bi-weekly.
Director: Ignacio G. Salas. Listed in "Más de cuatrocientos periódicos en español se han editado en Estados Unidos". No extant issues located.

La Unión. Los Angeles, Alta Calif.: E. Olivas, 1895-1912?
Weekly.
Began in 1895; ceased in 1912, cf. Gregory, Winifred, ed., *American Newspapers, 1821-1936.* T. 25 [i.e. 8], no. 43 dated nov. 21 de 1896. Continues *El Monitor Mexicano*

(18uu-189u). In Spanish. In OCLC system.

La Unión. Nogales, Ariz.: Alianza Hispano Americana, Logia 6, 1918-19uu.
Listed in Miguélez, Armando. "Index of Spanish-Language Newspapers in the U. S. Southwest." No extant issues located.

La Unión. Nueva Orleans [i.e. New Orleans, La.: s.n.], 1851-1851?
Triweekly.
Subtitle: Periódico político, literario, científico y comercial. "Organo de los pueblos hispano-americanos". Continues *Patria* (New Orleans, La.: 1846). In Spanish and English. In OCLC system.

La Unión. New Orleans, Louisiana: Rafael Lanza, 1873-1uuu.
Weekly.
Listed in *Rowell's American Newspaper Directory,* 1873, p. 93. In Spanish. No extant issues located.

Unión. Phoenix, Arizona, 1884-1uuu.
Weekly.
Editors: Aguirre & Cellio. Listed in Lutrell, Estelle, *Newspapers and Periodicals of Arizona, 1859-1911,* p. 41. In English and Spanish. No extant issues located.

La Unión. Ratón, Nuevo México: Antonio Cajal y Severiano Sánchez, 189u-1uuu.
Weekly.
T. 1, no. 9 dated 26 de feb. de 1898. In Spanish. In OCLC system.

Unión. San Francisco, California: Espejo & Rodríguez, 1873-1uuu.
Weekly.
Listed in *Rowell's American Newspaper Directory,* 1873. In Spanish. No extant issues located.

Unión. Santa Ana, Calif.: Ricardo Plasencia, 1931?–19uu. Año 2, no. 63 dated mayo 2, 1935. In OCLC system.

La Unión. Tucson, Ariz., 1892-1uuu.
Mentioned in Sheridan, *Los Tucsonenses,* p. 203. No extant issues located.

The Union County Leader. Clayton, New Mexico: Union County Leader, Inc., 1929-.
Weekly, Mar. 1929; semiweekly, Apr. 1, 1929-1931; weekly, 1931-.
Absorbed *Clayton News.* In English. In OCLC system.

La Unión de Albuquerque. Old Albuquerque, Nuevo México: La Unión de Albuquerque, 1892?-189u.
Weekly.
Began with Aug. 12, 1892?; ceased in 1894?, cf. Grove, Pearce S., *New Mexico Newspapers.* T. 1, no. 24 dated enero 20 de 1893. In Spanish. In OCLC system.

La Unión de América. St. Louis, Mo.: Pedro León, 1886-1uuu.
Monthly.
"Periódico literario, mercantil y de intereses generales." In Spanish and English. In OCLC system.

La Unión del Nuevo Méjico (Santa Fe, New Mexico). *See* **The New Mexico Union.**

La Unión del Pueblo. Clayton, N. M.: E. D. Armijo, 1913-19uu.
Weekly.
Companion newspaper to *Clayton Citizen.* In Spanish and English. In OCLC system.

Union Democrat. Clayton, New Mexico, 1889-1uuu.
Listed in Grove, Pearce S., *New Mexico Newspapers,* p. 571. Also listed in "Más de cuatrocientos periódicos en español se han editado en Estados Unidos". In English and Spanish. No extant issues located.

La Unión Industrial. Phoenix, Ariz.: Asunción Sánchez y G. Meléndrez, 1910-19uu.
Mentioned in *Regeneración,* sept. 3, 1910, p. 4; cf. Somoza, *Literatura de la Revolución Mexicana...,* p. 227. No extant issues located.

Unión: Revista Boliviana. Nueva York, 1945?-19uu.
"Organo del Capítulo Neoyorquino de la Liga Internacional de Acción Boliviana."

Editor: Juan Ramón López Suie. Repository: Erasmo Vando Collection, Hunter College, CUNY.

El Unionista. San Antonio, Tex.: El Unionista, 1919-192u.
University of California, Berkeley holds some issues from 1919 to 1922.

El Universal. Corpus Christi, Tex.: Rudy Mirabel, 19uu-19uu.
Vol. [?], no. 30 dated Apr. 13, 1956. In Spanish. In OCLC system.

El Universal. New York, N.Y., 1898-1uuu.
Listed in "Más de cuatrocientos periódicos en español se han editado en Estados Unidos". In Spanish. No extant issues located.

Universal Commerce. New York, N.Y.: D'Aquila Publications Inc., 19uu-19uu.
Monthly: six Spanish and six English issues per year.
Listed in Common Council for American Unity, *Foreign Language Publications in the United States: Newspaper Lists*. In English and Spanish. No extant issues located.

El Universitario. Austin, Tex., 1930-19uu.
Organo oficial del Club Latinoamericano de Estudiantes en la Universidad de Texas de Austin, cf. Miguélez, Armando. "Index of Spanish-Language Newspapers in the U. S. Southwest." No extant issues located.

El Vacilón. San Antonio, Tex.: P. Viola, 1924-19uu.
Tomo. 3, no. 46 dated Nov. 13, 1926. In Spanish. In OCLC system.

Valencia County Vindicator. Los Lunas, N. M.: [s.n], 1883-18uu.
Weekly.
In English and Spanish. In OCLC system.

El Valle del Bravo. El Paso, Tex.: Victor L. Ochoa, 1889-18uu.
Weekly.
Continued by *El Hispano-Americano* (El Paso, Texas). In Spanish. In OCLC system.

The Valley Herald and El Heraldo del Valle. San Luis, Colorado: [s.n.], 19uu-19uu.
Weekly.
Vol. 38, no. 30 dated Aug. 10, 1944. Merged with *San Luis Valley News* to form *San Luis Valley News and The Valley Herald*. In English and Spanish. In OCLC system.

La Vanguardia: Periódico de Opinión Pública Mexicana. Austin, Tex.: La Vanguardia
Pub. Co., 1920-192u.
Weekly.
In Spanish. In OCLC system.

La Vara. New York, N.Y.: Sephardic Pub. Co., 1922-1948.
Weekly.
Vol. 11, no. 536 dated Dec. 2, 1932. In Ladino and English. In OCLC system.

Los Vecinos. Los Angeles, Calif.: Asociación Internacional de California, 1914-19uu.
Monthly.
In Spanish. In OCLC system.

Venezuela Futura. New York, N.Y., 1931-19uu.
Monthly.
In Spanish. In OCLC system.

La Verdad. Anderson, Ind.: Spanish Literature Co., 19uu-19uu.
Quarterly.
Tomo 12, número 3 dated Julio-Septiembre 1932. In Spanish. In OCLC system.

La Verdad. Corpus Christi, Texas: Santos de la Paz, 1942-19uu.
Weekly.
Began in 1942? Vol. 7, no. 18 dated June 10, 1949. Variant title: *The Truth*. In Spanish and English. In OCLC system.

La Verdad. Corpus Christi, Texas, 1950-1975.
In Spanish and English. In OCLC system.

La Verdad. Del Rio, Tex., 1951-19uu.

American G.I Forum. Mentioned in Somoza, *Literatura de la Revolución Mexicana...*, p. 247. No extant issues located.

Verdad. Denver, Col., 1937-1941.

Mentioned in Somoza, *Literatura de la Revolución Mexicana...*, p. 236. No extant issues located.

La Verdad. Falfurrias, Tex.: Sabas Alaniz, 19uu-19uu.

Weekly.

Año 6, núm. 12 dated June 23, 1939. In Spanish and English. In OCLC system.

Verdad. Las Cruces, N. M.: Pinito Pino, 1890-189u.

Weekly.

In Spanish. In OCLC system.

Verdad. Las Cruces, Nuevo México: La Compañía Publicista de la Verdad, 1898-1uuu.

Weekly.

In Spanish. In OCLC system.

La Verdad (Miami, Florida). *See* **The Truth.**

La Verdad. New York, 1876?-1uuu.

Directors: Diego V. Tejera (1877), L. Quintero (1878). Repository: Biblioteca, Universidad de la Habana, Cuba.

La Verdad. Nueva Orleans, 1845-18uu.

Redactor: F. de P. Serrano. Listed in Batista Villareal, Teresita, *Catálogo de Publicaciones periódicas cubanas...*, p. 177. This source indicates that the Biblioteca Nacional José Martí in Havana holds some issues of this title.

La Verdad. Nueva York: Cora Montgomery, 1848-185u.

Three times a month; semimonthly, Jan.-May 1848.

Supported freedom for Cuba, cf. Fox, Louis Hewitt, *New York City Newspapers, 1820-1850.* Variant title: *The Truth.* In Spanish and English. In OCLC system. Also, the Archivo Nacional de Cuba, Havana, holds some issues.

La Verdad. Phoenix, Arizona: G. Meléndrez, 1888-1890?

Irregular.

Listed in Lutrell, Estelle, *Newspapers and Periodicals of Arizona, 1859-1911,* p. 41. Also listed in "Más de cuatrocientos periódicos en español se han editado en Estados Unidos". In Spanish. No extant issues located.

La Verdad. Roma, Texas, 1897-1uuu.

Weekly.

Director: José de J. Sánchez. Listed in "Más de cuatrocientos periódicos en español se han editado en Estados Unidos". In Spanish. No extant issues located.

La Verdad. [Santa Fe: N. M.], 1844-1845.

Weekly.

Began in Feb. 1844; ceased about June 14, 1845, cf. Grove, Pearce S., *New Mexico Newspapers,* T. 1, no. 32 dated 12 de set. de 1844. "Periódico del Nuevo-Méjico". Official newspaper of the Department of New Mexico under the Government of Mexico, cf. Grove. In Spanish. In OCLC system.

Verdad. Santa Fe, N. M., 1908-19uu.

Mentioned in Somoza, *Literatura de la Revolución Mexicana...*, p. 243. No extant issues located.

La Verdad: Periódico Política Cubana. Nueva York, [N.Y.]: D.V. Tejera, 1876-1uuu.

Weekly.

In Spanish. In OCLC system.

Vésper. Laredo, Texas, 19uu-19uu.

Cited in Lomas, Clara. "The Articulation of Gender in the Mexican Borderlands, 1900-1915," p. 296, and Chabrán, Rafael and Richard Chabrán, "The Spanish-Language and Latino Press of the United States: Newspapers and Periodicals," p. 368. In Spanish. No extant issues located.

Vía Libre. New York, N.Y.: Vía Libre, 1939-1940.
Monthly, Dec. 1939-July 1940; irregular, Mar.-Oct. 1939.
"Organo de la Federación Libertaria". In Spanish. In OCLC system.
Victoria. Española, N. M., 1937-19uu.
Mentioned in Somoza, *Literatura de la Revolución Mexicana. . .*, p. 240. No extant issues located.
La Victoria. Ratón, Nuevo México: Luis Martínez, 19uu-1929.
Weekly.
Año 3, núm. 102 dated 13 de enero, 1927. Absorbed by *Gate City Sun.* In Spanish and English. In OCLC system.
Victory. Spanish edition. New York, N.Y.: Crowell-Collier Pub. Co., 1943-1945.
Bimonthly.
In Spanish. In OCLC system.
Vida Alegre. New York, N.Y., 19uu-19uu.
Año 2, num 17 dated junio 7 de 1931. "Semanario joco-serio, satírico y literario". Director and administrator: Conrado Rosario. In Spanish. Repository: Center for Puerto Rican Studies at Hunter College, CUNY.
Vida Hispana. Bronx, N.Y., 1952-1955.
Monthly (irregular).
In Spanish. In OCLC system.
Vida Hispana de Nueva York. New York, N.Y.: Puerto Rican Advertising Agency, 1955-19uu.
Año 1, num. 1 dated febrero 1955. Editor y gerente: A. Valentín Bello. In Spanish. Repository: Center for Puerto Rican Studies at Hunter College, CUNY.
Vida Obrera. New York, N.Y.: Vida Obrera Pub. Co., 1929-19uu.
Weekly.
Began in 1929, cf. *Union List of Serials,* 2nd ed. Vol. 3, no. 1 dated Sept. 1, 1930. Vol. 3, no. 23 (Feb. 2, 1931) misdated 1930. Suspended publication between v. 3, no. 43 (July 6, 1931) and v. 3, no. 44 (Oct. 17, 1931) Variant title: *Workers' Life.* "Vocero de los obreros de habla española. Organo del Partido Comunista de los Estados Unidos". In Spanish. In OCLC system.
La Vigía. Key West, Florida, 1897-1uuu.
Cited in Poyo, Gerald Eugene, *With All and for the Good of All,* p. 128. In Spanish. No extant issues located.
Visión: Revista Latinoamericana. New York, N.Y.: Casa Visión, 1950-19uu.
Biweekly.
In Spanish. In OCLC system.
Vita Nuova. Chicago, Illinois: Pasquale Ricciardi De Carlo, 1uuu-1uuu.
Monthly.
Listed in *N.W. Ayer & Son's Directory of Newspapers and Periodicals*, 1937, p. 215, and "Más de cuatrocientos periódicos en español se han editado en Estados Unidos". In Spanish, English and Italian. No extant issues located.
El Vocero de la unión Internacional de Tabaqueros. Tampa, Fla., 1941-19uu.
In Spanish. In OCLC system.
The Voice: Combined with La Voz Latina. Phoenix, Arizona: Latin-American Club of Arizona, 1936-19uu.
Merger of *Voice* and *Voz Latina de Arizona.* In OCLC system.
The Voice: La Voz de la Raza. Phoenix, Arizona: W. G. Matley, 193u-19uu.
Repository: Arizona Department of Library, Archives and Public Records, Phoenix.
Voluntad. New York, N.Y., 1916-19uu.
Editado por el grupo Rebelión, cf. Miguélez, Armando, "Index of Spanish-Language Newspapers in the U. S. Southwest." No extant issues located.
El Voluntario. Rio Grande City, Tex.: Casimiro Pérez Alvarez, 1892?-1uuu.
Irregular.

Began in 1892? "Periódico independiente, órgano del elemento México-Texano sin distinción de color político". Epoca 1a. no. 12 dated oct. 16 de 1892. In Spanish. In OCLC system.

Vosotros. New York, N.Y., 1954-19uu.
Monthly.
Año 1, no. 1 dated sept. 1, 1954. Editor and director: José E. Sotomayor. Repository: Center for Puerto Rican Studies at Hunter College, CUNY.

Vox Populi. Brownsville, Tex., 1910-19uu.
Tomo 1 dated dic. 19, 1910. "Semanario humorístico y de política". Administrator: Eleno Ayala, editor: Romualdo Treviño. Redactor: J.A. Hernández. Repository: University of Texas, Brownsville, Texas.

La Voz. Nueva York, N.Y.: Spanish Newspaper Co., 1937-1939.
Daily (except Sunday).
"Diario democrático avanzado". Continued by *Nueva Voz* (New York, N.Y.: 1939). In Spanish. In OCLC system.

La Voz. San Antonio, Tex.: Estrella Printing Co., 1935?-19uu.
Weekly.
Año 3, no. 122 dated Oct. 11, 1937. "Periódico de acción católica y justicia social". "Official Spanish organ of the Archdiocese of San Antonio." In Spanish and English. In OCLC system.

La Voz. San Diego, Texas, 1935-1936.
Director: Servando Cárdenas; colaboradores: Manuel Castañeda, J. Vizcaya, y José Díaz, cf. "Más de cuatrocientos periódicos en español se han editado en Estados Unidos". In English. In OCLC system.

La Voz. Tucson, Ariz.: Fernando Rubio, 1954-1964.
Mentioned in Somoza, *Literatura de la Revolución Mexicana...*, p. 230. No extant issues located.

La Voz: A Bilingual Publication for Students and Teachers of Spanish. New York: Las Américas Publishing Co, 1956-.
Monthly.
In Spanish and English. In OCLC system.

La Voz Católica. Denver, Col., 1929-19uu.
An article from this periodical was reproduced in *El Tucsonense,* sep. 7, 1929; cf. Somoza, *Literatura de la Revolución Mexicana...*, p. 236. No extant issues located.

La Voz de California. Los Angeles, Calif., 1893-1uuu.
Mentioned in *El Fronterizo* (Tucson), ago. 5, 1893; cf. Somoza, *Literatura de la Revolución Mexicana...*, p. 233. No extant issues located.

La Voz de Chile y de las Repúblicas Americanas. San Francisco, [Calif.]: Felipe Fierro, 186u-1868.
Weekly (1867); semiweekly (1868).
In Spanish. In OCLC system.

La Voz de Chile y El Nuevo Mundo. San Francisco [Calif.]: Felipe Fierro & Co. 1868-1870.
Semiweekly.
Began with May 28, 1868 issue. Ceased in 1870?, cf. Gregory, Winifred, ed., *American Newspapers, 1821-1936.* Vol. 11, no. 592 dated mayo 29, 1868. Formed by the union of *El Nuevo Mundo* (San Francisco, Calif.) and *La Voz de Chile y de las Repúblicas Americanas.* Continued by *Voz del Nuevo Mundo.* In Spanish. In OCLC system.

La Voz de Clifton. Clifton, Arizona: Benjamin Pizarro, 1897-1900?
Weekly.
Listed in Lutrell, Estelle, *Newspapers and Periodicals of Arizona, 1859-1911,* p. 18. In Spanish. No extant issues located.

La Voz de Cuba. New York: La Voz Pub. Co., 195u-.
Biweekly.

In Spanish. In OCLC system.

La Voz de Juárez. Laredo, Texas; San Antonio, Texas, 1908-1919.
Weekly.
Listed in "Más de cuatrocientos periódicos en español se han editado en Estados Unidos". This source indicates paper was published in San Antonio and Laredo in 1908, 1910 and part of 1911. Also listed in Ríos-C., Herminio, "Toward a True Chicano Bibliography: Part II," p. 47. In Spanish. No extant issues located.

La Voz de la América. Nueva York [New York, N.Y.], 1865-1867?
Irregular.
No. 2 dated dic. 30 de 1865. Title varies slightly: *Voz de América,* Jan. 10, 1867. "Organo político de las repúblicas hispano-americanas y de las Antillas españolas". In Spanish. In OCLC system.

Voz de la Colonia. Fillmore, California; Santa Paula, California: Jesús N. Jiménez, 1924-1932.
Weekly; Irregular.
Listed in Gregory, Winifred, ed., *American Newspapers, 1821-1936;* and Ríos-C., Herminio, "Toward a True Chicano Bibliography: Part II," p. 40. Also listed in "Más de cuatrocientos periódicos en español se han editado en Estados Unidos". This last source indicates paper was moved from Fillmore to Santa Paula in 1928. In Spanish. No extant issues located.

La Voz de la Justicia. Los Angeles, Calif., 1876-18uu.
Weekly.
In Spanish. In OCLC system.

La Voz de la Mujer. El Paso, Texas: Isidra T. de Cárdenas, 1907-19uu.
In her essay "The Articulation of Gender in the Mexican Borderlands, 1900-1915," Lomas examines this newspaper. In Spanish. Repository: Bancroft Library (University of California, Berkeley).

La Voz de la Oposición. Tucson, Ariz., 18uu-1887.
Listed in Miguélez, Armando, "Index of Spanish-Language Newspapers in the U. S. Southwest." No extant issues located.

La Voz de la Parroquia. San Antonio, Texas: Publicidad Estrella, 1935-19uu.
Weekly.
In Spanish and English. In OCLC system.

La Voz de la Patria. Nueva York [N.Y.]: J.J. Govantes, 1876-1uuu.
Weekly.
"Periódico cubano". Published a supplement on Oct. 10, 1876, on the anniversary of the start of Cuba's Revolution. In Spanish. In OCLC system.

La Voz de la 500. Tampa, Fl., 1941-.
"Official publication of Cigarmakers' Local 500." In Spanish. In OCLC system.

La Voz de la Raza. Denver, Colo.: Paco Sánchez, 1956-1958.
Mentioned in Somoza, *Literatura de la Revolución Mexicana...*, p. 236. No extant issues located.

La Voz de Hatuey. Cayo Hueso [Key West], Fla.: Manuel P. Delgado, 1884-1uuu.
Listed in Batista Villareal, Teresita, *Catálogo de Publicaciones periódicas cubanas...*, p. 179. This source indicates that the Biblioteca Nacional José Martí in Havana holds some issues of this title.

La Voz de Marfa. Marfa, Tex.: Juan Rivera, 1928-19uu.
Weekly.
Vol. 1 no. 2 dated sept. 16, 1928. In Spanish. In OCLC system.

La Voz de Méjico. San Francisco, California: E. Payot, 1862-1866.
Triweekly (every Tuesday, Friday and Sunday).
Ceased in 1866, cf. *Newspapers in Microform,* 1973. "Periódico de política, noticias, comercio, literatura, etc." In Spanish. In OCLC system.

La Voz de México. Chicago, Illinois: La Voz de México Publishing Co., 1948-19uu.

Daily.

Editor: Mario Lasso. Listed in *N. W. Ayer & Son's Directory of Newspapers and Periodicals*, 1952, p. 248. In Spanish and English. No extant issues located.

La Voz de México. Kansas City, Missouri., 1915-19uu.

Mentioned in Smith, "The Mexican Immigrant Press . . .," p. 83. No extant issues located.

La Voz de México. San Antonio, Tex.: B. Cuéllar, 1924-19uu.

Órgano de la Liga Nacionalista Mexicana, cf. Miguélez, Armando, "Index of Spanish-Language Newspapers in the U. S. Southwest." No extant issues located.

La Voz de México. Tucson, Ariz., 1920-19uu.

Listed in Miguélez, Armando, "Index of Spanish-Language Newspapers in the U. S. Southwest." Miguélez indicates the paper is mentioned in *El Tucsonense*, 17-VI- 1922. No extant issues located.

La Voz de Nuevo México. Albuquerque, Nuevo México: Baca & Escobar, 1894-1uuu.

Weekly.

In Spanish. In OCLC system.

La Voz de Phoenix. Phoenix, Ariz; 1950-19uu.

Listed in Miguélez, Armando, "Index of Spanish-Language Newspapers in the U. S. Southwest." No extant issues located.

La Voz de Puerto Rico. Nueva York, N.Y. 1950-19uu.

Monthly.

Año 2, núm. 1 dated febrero, 1950. " Es la voz de los más destacados escritores puertorriqueños e hispanos". Director: Teófilo Maldonado. Repository: Center for Puerto Rican Studies at Hunter College, CUNY.

La Voz de Puerto Rico en USA. Brooklyn, N.Y.: Raymond González, 1956-19uu.

Monthly.

Vol. 1, no. 1 dated abril 1956. Repository: Center for Puerto Rican Studies at Hunter College.

La Voz de Puerto Rico en U. S. A. New York, N.Y., 1874-1uuu.

"One of the first papers specifically oriented to a Puerto Rican audience in the United States," cf. Chabrán, Rafael and Richard Chabrán, "The Spanish-Language and Latino Press of the United States: Newspapers and Periodicals," p. 371. No extant issues located.

La Voz de Tucson. Tucson, Ariz., 1895-1896.

Mentioned in Sheridan, *Los Tucsonenses*, p. 203. No extant issues located.

La Voz de Tucson Tucson, Ariz., 1920-19uu.

Listed in Miguélez, Armando, "Index of Spanish-Language Newspaper in the U. S. Southwest." Miguélez indicates that the Arizona Pioneer Historical Society owns one copy of the paper.

La Voz del Artista. New York, N.Y.: Spanish-American Artist Association, 1960?-19uu.

Bimonthly.

Director: Roy Migueli. "Official bulletin of the Spanish American Artist Association of New York, Inc." In Spanish. Repository: Recovering the U. S. Hispanic Literary Heritage.

La Voz del Esclavo. Tampa, Fla.: [P. Calcagno], 1900-19uu.

"Published by Spanish immigrants, Italians and Cubans." "Saldrá cuando pueda." In English and Spanish. In OCLC system.

La Voz del Mundo. Calexico, California: B.W. Curry, 1934-19uu.

Daily (except Sunday).

Listed in Common Council for American Unity, *Foreign Language Publications in the United States: Newspaper Lists*, p. [1], *N.W. Ayer & Son's Directory of Newspapers and Periodicals*, 1939, p. 72, and Ríos-C., Herminio, "Toward a True Chicano Bibliography: Part II," p. 40. Ayer lists title as *Voz-Mundo* and indicate Ramón Castro is the editor. In Spanish. No extant issues located.

La Voz del Nuevo Mundo. San Francisco, [Calif.]: Felipe Fierro, 18uu-1uuu.

Semi-weekly.

Bibliography

Vol. 23, no. 1,146 dated set. 26 de 1873. Continues *Voz de Chile y El Nuevo Mundo*. In Spanish. Rowell indicates editor is Felipe Fierro and J. J. Madero & Co. is the publisher. In OCLC system.

La Voz del Pueblo (Las Vegas, 1890). *See* **La Voz del Pueblo** (Santa Fe, 1889-1924).

La Voz del Pueblo. Nueva York, 1878-18uu.

"Periódico político, económico y de intereses generales". Director: Pablo Bottle, Reporter: J. G. Listed in Batista Villareal, Teresita, *Catálogo de Publicaciones periódicas cubanas...*, p. 180. This source indicates that the Biblioteca Nacional José Martí in Havana holds some issues of this title.

La Voz del Pueblo. Phoenix, Arizona, 1950?-19uu.

Año 1, vol. 1, no. 7 dated Sept. 1950. Jefe de redacción: José Rosell. Anuncios: Ernesto P. Mendivil. In Spanish. Repository: Arizona Department of Library, Archives and Public Records, Phoenix.

La Voz del Pueblo. Runge, Texas, 1918?-19uu.

Irregular.

Listed in Ríos-C., Herminio, "Toward a True Chicano Bibliography: Part II" and "Más de cuatrocientos periódicos en español se han editado en Estados Unidos". In Spanish. No extant issues located.

La Voz del Pueblo. Santa Fe, Nuevo México: La Asociación Impresora de "La Voz del Pueblo", 1888-1888.

Weekly.

T. 1, no. 11 dated oct. 20, 1888. Began Aug. 11, 1888, cf. Grove, Pearce S., *New Mexico Newspapers*. In Spanish. In OCLC system.

La Voz del Pueblo. Santa Fe, Nuevo Méjico: L. H. Salazar y N. Montoya, Cía. Pub "La Voz del Pueblo", 1889-1924.

Weekly.

Administrator: Felix Martínez. Published in Las Vegas, N. M., June 14, 1890. In Spanish. In OCLC system.

La Voz del Pueblo de Santa Fe, Nuevo México. Santa Fe, Nuevo México: Santa Fe Publishers, 1940-19uu.

In Spanish and English. In OCLC system.

La Voz del Río Grande. Española, N. M.: El Nuevo Estado Print. Co., 1926-19uu.

Weekly.

Año 1, núm. 8 dated set. 10 de 1926. In Spanish. In OCLC system.

La Voz del Valle. Antonito, Colo.: M. P. Smith, 1898-19uu.

Weekly.

Vol. 3 [2], no. 7 [8] dated Oct. 12, 1899. Editors: Charles G. Smith, Oct.-Nov. 1899; J. D. Frazey, Feb. 1900-. In Spanish. In OCLC system.

La Voz Latina. Eagle Pass, Texas: L. M. Hufman, 1939-1948.

Weekly.

Vol. 23, no. 2 dated Feb. 17, 1939. In Spanish. Absorbed by *International News-Guide*. Listed in Historical Records Survey Texas, *Texas Newspapers 1813-1939*, p. 69. No extant issues located.

La Voz Latina. Nueva Orleans [i.e. New Orleans, La.]: Courier Print. & Pub. Co., 1935-19uu.

Biweekly, 1935-Jan. 28, 1944; monthly, Feb. 1944-.

Published with an additional masthead in English: "The Latin Voice," Sept. 13, 1935-July 24, 1936. In Spanish and English. In OCLC system.

La Voz Latina de Arizona. Phoenix, Ariz.: Club Latina Americana de Arizona, 1936-1936.

Merged with *Voice* to form *Voice Combined with La Voz Latina*. In Spanish. In OCLC system.

Voz-Mundo (Calexico, California). *See* **La Voz del Mundo.**

La Voz Pública. Santa Fe, N. M., 1932-1942.

Listed in Miguélez, Armando, "Index of Spanish-Language Newspapers in the U. S.

Southwest." No extant issues located.

La Voz Pública. Santa Rosa, New Mexico: Plácido Baca y Baca, 1898-1912.
Weekly.
T. 10, no. 5 dated enero 2, 1903. Published May 20, 1911- in Vaughn, N. M. In Spanish and English. In OCLC system.

La Voz Pública. Santa Rosa, Nuevo México: La Voz Pública Pub. Co., 191u-192u.
Weekly.
Vol. 2, no. 42 dated enero 5, 1917. Issued also in an English language edition: *The Public Voice.* In Spanish and English. In OCLC system.

La Voz Trabajadora. Albuquerque, New Mexico, 1905-19uu.
Irregular.
Listed in "Más de cuatrocientos periódicos en español se han editado en Estados Unidos". In Spanish. No extant issues located.

Wagon Mound Pantagraph. Wagon Mound, New Mexico: M. M. Padgett, 1909-1921.
Weekly.
Began with June 21, 1909, cf. Grove, Pearce S., *New Mexico Newspapers.*Vol. 3, no. 44 dated Apr. 19, 1912. Absorbed *Combate* (Wagon Mound). Continued by *Mora County Pantagraph.* Variant title: *Wagon Mound Pantagraph & El Combate* (Nov. 16, 1918-May 17, 1919). In Spanish. In OCLC system.

Wagon Mound Pantagraph & El Combate (Wagon Mound, New Mexico). *See* Wagon Mound Pantagraph.

Wagon Mound Sentinel. Wagon Mound, New Mexico: Sentinel Pub. Co., 1918-1921.
Weekly.
Ceased in 1921?, cf. Grove, Pearce S., *New Mexico Newspapers.* Includes Spanish-language section called "El Centinela." Continues *Mora County Sentinel.* Text in English and Spanish: Mar. 13, 1918-Dec. 13, 1919; In Spanish only, dec. 20, 1919- in Spanish only. In OCLC system.

The Walsenburg World. Walsenburg, Colo.: G.M. Magill, 1989–1993. Some issues include text in Spanish. In OCLC system.

Week (New York, N.Y.). *See* **La Semana.**

Weekly Advertiser (Trinidad, Colorado). *See* **Trinidad Weekly Advertiser = El Anunciador de Trinidad.**

Weekly Hispano Americano. Roy, N. M.: Mora County Pub. Co., 1905-1905.
Weekly.
In OCLC system.

Weekly New Mexican. Santa Fe, New Mexico: Mandfield & Tuck, 1868-1883.
Weekly.
Section in Spanish: El Nuevo Mejicano, 1868-Sept. 24, 1881. "Preceded by *Santa Fe Republican;* merged with *Albuquerque Evening Review* to form *Santa Fe New Mexican Review,* June 6, 1883, and *Weekly New Mexican Review,* June 9, 1883; reassumed the title *Santa Fe Daily New Mexican,* July 7, 1885; reassumed the title *Santa Fe Weekly New Mexican,* January 19, 1888; reportedly absorbed *The Santa Fe New Mexican Capitol Examiner,* September 1, 1940," cf. Grove, Pearce S., *New Mexico Newspapers.* Daily editions: *Daily New Mexican* (Santa Fe, N. M.: 1868) 1868-Mar.24, 1881, and *Santa Fe Daily New Mexican* (Santa Fe, N. M.: 1881), Mar. 25 1881-1883, Continues *El Nuevo Mexicano.* In English and Spanish. In OCLC system.

Weekly People's News (Albuquerque, New Mexico). *See* **People's News.**

West Denver Herald. Denver, Colorado, 1900-1906.
Weekly.
Listed in Oehlerts, Donald E., *Guide to Colorado Newspapers, 1859-1963,* p. 43. In Spanish. No extant issues located.

West Tampa Leader. West Tampa, Florida: West Tampa Leader Publishing Co., 1940-19uu.
Editor: Ramón Guzmán. Año 1, núm. 3 dated diciembre 8, 1940. In English and Spanish.

Repository: University of South Florida, Tampa.

Workers' Life (New York, N.Y.). *See* **Vida Obrera.**

Wyvernwood Chronicle. Los Angeles, California: Dolores Sánchez, 1950-1991.

Weekly.

Editor: Rose Soto. Listed in *Gale Directory of Publications and Broadcast Media,* 1995. In Spanish and English. No extant issues located.

El Yara. Key West, Fla.: [J. D. P. Estenoz], 1878-19uu.

Daily (except Monday).

Vol. 11, no. 47 dated May 26, 1889. "Cuban Independent." In OCLC system. Also, the Archivo Nacional de Cuba, Havana, holds some issues.

Ybor City Sunday News. Tampa, Florida: Ramón Núñez, 19uu-.

Weekly.

Listed in Common Council for American Unity, *Foreign Language Publications in the United States: Newspaper Lists,* p. 3. Ramón Núñez also published *Tampa Leader* in the 1940s, and *The Tampa Record.* In Spanish and English. In OCLC system.

El Yunque. New York, N.Y., 1952-19uu.

Monthly.

"Publicación de información y orientación sobre problemas de Puerto Rico y demás países hispanos". Director: J. Dávila Semprit. Repository: Center for Puerto Rican Studies at Hunter College, CUNY.

Zapata County News. Laredo, Texas: T. L. Green, 19uu-19uu.

Weekly.

Vol. 8, no. 49A dated nov. 8, 1945. In Spanish and English. In OCLC system

El Zaragoza. Brownsville [Tex.]: Emilio Velasco, 1865-186u.

Semiweekly.

In Spanish. In OCLC system.

Zig-Zag: Semanario humorístico. Miami, 1938-19uu.

Director: José Roseñada, cf. Peraza Sarauza, Fermín, *Directorio de Revistas y Periódicos de Cuba.*

El Zumbón. Phoenix, Ariz., 1940-19uu.

Listed in Miguélez, Armando, "Index of Spanish-Language Newspapers in the U. S. Southwest." Miguélez indicates the paper is mentioned in *El Mensajero,* 25-X- 1940. No extant issues located.

El Zurriago. El Paso, Texas: Lorenzo B. Sáenz, 1892-1uuu.

In Spanish. In OCLC system.

Geographic Index

ARIZONA

Clifton

El Noticiario * (191519uu)
El Observador * (19141917)
La Voz de Clifton * (18971900)

Douglas

El Centenario * (190619uu)
El Correo * (190619uu)
El Correo Mexicano * (191619uu)
Demócrata * (1uuu1uuu)
El Democrático * (190619uu)
La Industrial * (191019uu)

Florence

Juventud * (1uuu1uuu)

Glendale

El Faro Bautista * (1932-19uu)

Holbrook

The Argus (1895-1900)

Jerome

El Clarín Disperso * (1916-19uu)
El Obrero Libre * (1917-19uu)
El Obrero Mexicano * (1908-19uu)

Mesa

Juventud * (1944-19uu)

Mesilla

The Mesilla Times (1860-1862)

Miami

Alma Latina (1932-19uu)

Morenci

Herald * (1909-1912)
El Obrero de Morenci * (1901-1904)

Nogales

El Átomo * (1892-1uuu)
El Cronista * (18941uuu)
El Día * (19151920)
El Eco de la Frontera * (18871uuu)
El Fronterizo * (19191920)
Herald (Nogales) * (191619uu)
El Independiente * (18931895)
El Internacional * (192519uu)
México Libre * (19181uuu)
El Monitor (18891995)
El Monitor Fronterizo (18881uuu)
Nogales Morning Times * (1917-19uu)
La Palabra * (19uu-19uu)
Patria Libre * (191719uu)
Sonora * (192119uu)
La Unión * (191819uu)

Phoenix

Alianza * (1909-19uu)
El Demócrata (1898-19uu)
El Ensayo * (1916-19uu)
Excelsior * (1950-1uuu)
Fenicio * (1uuu-1uuu)
El Fronterizo * (1922-1926)
El Heraldo de Arizona (1935-19uu)
El Hijo del Fronterizo *(1880-18uu)
El Imparcial * (1956-19uu)
El Imparcial * (1937-1938)
Justice * (1916-1934)
Justicia (19uu-19uu)
Latinoamericano * (1934-19uu)
El Machete * (19uu-19uu)
El Mensajero * (1900-1916)
El Mensajero (1925-19uu)
El Mercurio * (1884-18uu)
El Mexicano Republicano * (18921uuu)
El Noticioso * (1918-19uu)
La Nueva Centuria * (190619uu)
El Observador Mexicano (189u1uuu)
La Ocasional (1897-1899)
El Progreso * (1883-1901)
El Progreso del Valle * (1887-1uuu)
El Saber * (19uu-1940)
El Sol (19391981)
Unión * (18841uuu)
La Unión Industrial * (1910-19uu)
La Verdad * (1888-1890)
The Voice: Combined with La Voz Latina (1936-19uu)
The Voice: la Voz de la Raza (193u-19uu)
La Voz de Phoenix * (1950-19uu)
La Voz del Pueblo (1950-19uu)
La Voz Latina de Arizona (1936-1936)
El Zumbón * (1940-19uu)

Solomonville

El Grito de la Verdad (189u1-8uu)
El Independiente * (1895-1uuu)
La Opinión Pública (1895-1uuu)
Prensa = The Press (19uu-19uu)

St. Johns

Apachito * (1905-1907)
Plain Talk * (1906-19uu)
Snips and St. Johns Herald (1903-1904)

Tolleson

Tópicos de Tolleson * (1938-19uu)

Tucson

Al Día * (1920-19uu)
El Alacrán * (1879-1uuu)
La Alianza (1899-19uu)
Alianza * (1907-19uu)
El Amigo del Pueblo * (1882-1uuu)
El Angel del Hogar * (1uuu1uuu)
La Antorcha * (1876-1uuu)
Arizona * (1943-1950)
El Azteca * (1925-19uu)
Blanco y Negro (1921-19uu)
Boletín de la Semana Devota * (1922-1923)
The Border (1907-19uu)
El Campeón * (1918-19uu)
Chantecler (1928-19uu)
La Chispa * (1uuu-1uuu)
El Chismoso * (1931-19uu)
La Colonia Mexicana * (1883-1884)
El Combate * (1916-19uu)
El Correo * (1922-19uu)
El Correo de América * (1918-19uu)
El Correo de Tucson * (1921-19uu)
La Cucaracha * (1925-19uu)
Daily Reporter * (1950-19uu)
El Defensor * (1uuu-1uuu)
El Defensor del Pueblo * (1904-19uu)
El Dios Momo * (1918-19uu)
El Domingo * (1891-1uuu)
Las Dos Repúblicas (1877-1879)
El Eco de Sonora * (1883-1uuu)
El Eco Mexicano * (1922-19uu)
La Estación * (1890-1uuu)
El Fronterizo (1878-1914)
El Fronterizo (1926-1929)

El Hijo del Fronterizo (191219uu)
El Informador * (1935-19uu)
El Imparcial * (19311-9uu)
El Internacional * (1960-19uu)
El Iris (1886-1uuu)
Juventud * (1893-1uuu)
Juventud * (1937-19uu)
La Luz * (1896-1897)
El Monitor * (1909-1916)
El Monitor Tucsonense * (1922-19uu)
El Mosquito * (1917-1925)
La Opinión * (1919-19uu)
Pierrot * (1929-19uu)
Pima County Record * (1880-1uuu)
P.M.: Prensa Mexicana * (1957-1962)
Protección * (1928-19uu)
La Reforma * (1892-1uuu)
Revista de los EE.UU. * (1920-19uu)
Revista Carmelita * (1926-1958)
El Sahuaro * (19uu-1925)
La Semana (1933-19uu)
El Siglo Veinte * (1899-1uuu)
La Sonora (1879-1uuu)
The Southwest Miner = El Minero
   (1955-19uu)
El Trueno * (1895-1uuu)
Tucson Cultural * (1943-1944)
El Tucsonense (1915-1957)
La Unión (1892-1uuu)
La Voz * (1954-1964)
La Voz de la Oposición * (18uu-1887)
La Voz de México * (1920-19uu)
La Voz de Tucson (1920-19uu)
La Voz de Tucson * (1920-19uu)

Yuma

El Independiente * (1916-19uu)
El Joven * (1882-1uuu)

CALIFORNIA

Azusa

The Azusa News (188u-1890)
Azusa Valley News (1885-1894)

Bakersfield

Ahora (1957.)
El Boletín (1958-19uu)
El Correo Mexicano * (1913-19uu)
La Crónica Mexicana * (1895-1uuu)

Berkeley

Boletín de Sigma Delta Pi (1934-1934)
El Espectador * (1890-1uu)
The Filipino Student (1912-1914)
Philipine Review (1905-1931)

Brawley

Gaceta del Valle Imperial * (1929-19uu)

Calexico

La Crónica * (1924-1934)
La Frontera * (1924-1929)
El Monitor * (1918-1924)
La Voz del Mundo * (1934-19uu)

Chula Vista

Toros y Tauromaquia: Bull Fight Review
   (1957-19uu)

Fillmore

Voz de la Colonia * (1924-1932)

Fresno

Excelsior * (1924-19uu)

* No extant issues located

* No extant issues located

El Pueblo * (1924-19uu)
El Ranchero (19uu-1963)
El Rebelde (1915-1917)
La Reforma (1877-1878)
Regeneración (1910-1918)
La Revista de Los Angeles * (192u-19uu)
Revista Latino-Americana * (1892-1893)
Revolución (190u-19uu)
La Semana (1919-19uu)
Spanish American Review = Revista
   Hispano-Americana (1889-1uuu)
Tribuna * (1928-1uuu)
La Unión (1895-1912)
Los Vecinos (1914-19uu)
La Voz de California * (1893-1uuu)
La Voz de la Justicia (1876-18uu)
Wyvernwood Chronicle * (1950-1991)

Merced

El Cronista Mexicano * (1894-1uuu)

Monrovia

The Mexican Voice (1938-19uu)

Oxnard

El Mexicano * (1918-19uu)

Point Loma

El Sendero Teosófico * (1911–19uu)

Pomona

El Eco del Valle (1927-19uu)
El Espectador (1934-19uu)

Redlands

El Amigo del Hogar (1906-19uu)

Riverside

El Monitor (1933-1934)

Sacramento

El Informador * (1939-19uu)
El Noticiero del Norte (1958-19uu)

San Bernardino

La Actualidad * (1895-1902)
El Heraldo * (1949-1959)
El Sol (1950-19uu)
El Sol de San Bernardino * (1926-1931)

San Diego

Baja California (1918-19uu)
El Hispano Americano (1914-1937)
El Imparcial * 1927-19uu)
El Internacional * (1933-19uu)
El Latino * (1938-19uu)
La Libertad * (1916-19uu)
El Mercurio * (1898-1uuu)
El Socialista * (1898-1uuu)

San Francisco

Alba Roja * (1uuu-1uuu)
Alta California *(1878-1880)
Las Américas (1914-19uu)
Anglo Spanish Merchant (1880-1883)
El Anunciador del Pacífico * (1896-1uuu)
Apretavis * (1915-19uu)
La Aurora: Breve y sin Presunción
   (1940-19uu)
Azucena * (1907-1916)
La Bandera Mexicana (1863-1uuu)
California Moderna * (1905-19uu)
The California Star (1847-1848)

Californian (1846-1848)
Centro América (1921-19uu)

* No extant issues located

El Comercio * (1uuu-1uuu)
El Comercio Ilustrado * (1894-1906)
El Correo de Ultramar * (18uu-1uuu)
La Correspondencia (1885-1887)
El Crepúsculo * (1873-1874)
La Crónica (185u-1uuu)
La Crónica (1914-1917)
El Cronista (1884-1uuu)
El Demócrata (19uu-1952)
Don Clarito * (1879-1uuu)
El Eco de la Raza Latina (187u-1uuu)
El Eco del Pacífico (1856-18uu)
La Gaceta * (1898-1900)
Gráfico Internacional (1933-19uu)
Hispano América (1917-1934)
El Imparcial (1931-1938)
Lucha Obrera (193u-1934)
Mefistófeles (191u-1918)
El Nuevo Mundo (1864-1868)
El Pensamiento * (1896-1898)
La Patria (1886-1uuu)
La Prensa Mexicana (1868-18uu)
Pro América * (1900-19uu)
El Progreso (1871-1uuu)
La República (1881-1uuu)
El Republicano (1868-1uuu)
Resurección: Revista Mensual...
   (1908-19uu)
Revista del Pacífico * (1895-1898)
Revista Hispanoamericana *
   (1895-1uuu)
Revista Latino Americana (1903-1904)
Semanario Imparcial (1938-19uu)
La Sociedad (1869-1895)
El Tecolote (1875-1879)
El Tiempo (186u-1uuu)
Unión * (1873-1uuu)
La Voz de Chile y de Las Repúblicas
   Americanas (186u-1868)
La Voz de Chile y El Nuevo Mundo
   (1868-1870)
La Voz de Méjico (1862-1866)
La Voz del Nuevo Mundo (1873-1uuu)

San Jose

El Excéntrico (194919uu)

The Forumeer (1948-1980)
El Padre (1929-.)

Santa Ana

Unión (1931-1935)

Santa Barbara

El Barbareno (1895-1uuu)
El Boletín * (1892-1uuu)
La Gaceta (1879-1881)

Santa Paula

Voz de la Colonia * (1924-1932)

Sonora

American Flag (1861-1864)
Sonora Herald (1850-1856)

COLORADO

Aguilar

Times * (1898-1uuu)

Antonito

La Aurora * (1911-1924)
El Popular * (1919-1910)
Pro Federación * (1916-1918)
El Triunfo * (1uuu-1uuu)
La Voz del Valle (1898-1uuu)
Denver

Antena: Spanish News (1947-19uu)
Challenge (194619uu)

The Colorado Clarion (1953-19uu)
El Defensor Popular * (1924-1925)
Las Dos Repúblicas (1896-1uuu)
El Imparcial (19321-9uu)
Latin American News (1938-19uu)
Nuevo Era * (1934-1935)
Orientación: Boletín de las Comisiones...
  (1938-19uu)
Pan-American News (1945-19uu)
La Patria (1891-1uu)
El Porvenir (190u-19uu)
El Reino de Dios * (19uu-19uu)
Repúblicas * (1895-1896)
The Sister Republic: a Commercial...
  (1899-19uu)
El Sol (1958-19uu)
El Sol de Colorado * (1938-1938)
Verdad * (1937-1941)
La Voz Católica * (1929-19uu)
La Voz de la Raza * (1956-1958)
West Denver Herald * (1900-1906)

Pueblo

El Coloradeño (19uu-19uu)
El Farol * (1948-19uu)
La Hermandad (1889-1907)

San Luis

Abeja * (1901-19uu)
Costilla County Free Press (1948.)
El Defensor del Pueblo * (1909-1914)
El Demócrata del Condado de Costilla
  (1923-1939)
The Valley Herald and El Heraldo del Valle
  (19uu-19uu)

Trinidad

El Anciano (1882-1uuu)
El Anunciador (1904-19uu)
The Colorado Pioneer (1875-1878)
El Explorador (1876-1877)
El Faro * (1912-1942)
Heraldo Dominical * (1uuu-1uuu)
El Progreso (1891-1944)
Las Repúblicas * (1895-1897)
Trinidad Weekly Advertiser = El
  Anunciador de Trinidad (1882-1uuu)
Trinidad Weekly Times (1881-1uuu)

Walsenburg

El Clarín Americano * (1919-1920)
The Clarion (19uu-19uu)
Huérfano Independent (1875-1uuu)
El Imparcial * (1911-1914)
The Independent (1909-1915)
El Independiente (1896-1uuu)
La Opinión Pública * (1904-1914)
The Walsenburg World (1989-1993)

CONNECTICUT

Norwalk

El Panamericano (194u-19uu)

Old Greenwich

Radiovisión * (1951-19uu)

DELAWARE

Wilmington

Boletín del Agricultor (19uu-1954)
El Mundo. Edición aérea semanal
  (1960-19uu)
La Revista de Dupont (1931-1961)

FLORIDA

Amelia Island

El Telégrafo de las Floridas * (1817)

Coral Gables

Boletín Semanal Informativo... * (1960-.)
Hoja Doctrinal (1960-.)
Romances * (1960-19uu)
Servicio Cubano de Información (1960.)

Gainsville

Revista Interamericana: Revista Dedicada...
  (1939-.)

Key West

Centinela * (1907-1915)
El Cubano * (1890-1892)
Ecuador * (1891-1uuu)
Evening Call * (1887-1uuu)
Florida * (1918-19uu)
La Igualdad (187u-1uuu)
El Intransigente * (1895-1uuu)
Journal * (1908-1920)
La Libertad (18761uuu)
El Mosquito * (1916-19uu)
Propaganda (1887-1uuu)
El Pueblo * (1887-1uuu)
El Reconcentrado (1898-1uuu)
El Republicano (1869-1uuu)
Revista de Cayo Hueso (1897-1898)
Revista Popular * (1889-1uuu)
La Tribuna del Trabajo * (188u-18uu)
La Vigía * (1897-1uuu)
La Voz de Hatuey (1884-1uuu)
El Yara (1878-19uu)

Miami

Astro * (1960-19uu)

El Avance Criollo (1960-1962)
Cuba Libre * (1959-19uu)
Cuban News (1935-1935)
Diario de las Américas (1953-.)
El Internacional * (1918-1925)
La Libertad (1960-19uu)
The Times of Havana (1957-1965)
Trinchera (1960-.)
The Truth (1957-.)
Zigzag: Semanario Humorístico *
  (1938-19uu)

Miami Beach

El Mundo (1960-19uu)
7 Días del Diario de la Marina en el
  Exilio (1960-1961)

Tampa

La Alegría (1901-19uu)
El Astur (1926-19uu)
El Bien Público * (1920-19uu)
Boletín (1941-19uu)
Boletín de El Internacional (1936-1937)
Boletín del Comité de Defensa (1938-19uu)
Boletín Obrero (1903-190u)
El Comercio (1941-19uu)
La Contienda * (19uu-19uu)
Cuba (1893-1899)
Cuban Herald * (1902-19uu)
El Cubano (191u-19uu)
La Defensa (19uu-19uu)
El Diario de Tampa (1908-19uu)
El Eco de Martí (1897-1uuu)
Ecos de Fiesta en Tampa (195u-19uu)
Ecos del Sanatorio (1941-19uu)
El Esclavo (1894-1uuu)
El Expedicionario (1896-1897)
El Federal (1902-1903)
La Federación (1899-19uu)
La Gaceta (1922-19uu)
El Heraldo Dominical = Spanish Sunday
  Paper (1914-19uu)

El Independiente * (1912-19uu)
El Internacional (1904-19uu)
El Internacional (1933-193u)
El Internacional (1937-19uu)
La Libertad (1897-1uuu)
El Mosquito (1uuu-1uuu)
La Nueva República (1897-1uuu)
La Opinión * (1897-1uuu)
El Oriente (1897-1uuu)
El Porvenir * (1891-1uuu)
La Prensa (19uu-19uu)
La Raza (1uuu-1uuu)
Revista de Cuba Libre * (1897-1uuu)
La Revista de la Florida (1887-1uuu)
La Riscossa (19uu-19uu)
El Sport * (1879-1uuu)
Tampa Ilustrado (1912-19uu)
Tampa Latina (1879-1929)
Tampa Leader (19uu-19uu)
Traducción Prensa (194619uu)
Tribuna del Pueblo * (19uu-19uu)
Triunfo * (1957-19uu)
Vocero de la Unión de Tabaqueros
   (1941-19uu)
Voz de la 500 (1941-.)
La Voz del Esclavo (1900-19uu)
West Tampa Leader (1940-19uu)
Ybor City Sunday News (19uu-19uu)

GEORGIA

Atlanta

Revista Escolar Panamericana (1932-19uu)
Textiles Panamericanos (1941-19uu)

ILLINOIS

Chicago

ABC (19uu-19uu)
Adelanto Bienestar Cultura * (1936-1950)
El Centinela (1959-.)
La Chispa * (1931-19uu)

El Correo de México * (1922-19uu)
Correo Mexicano: el Diario de la Raza
   (1926-19uu)
Le Courier * (1895-1uuu)
La Defensa * (1933-19uu)
La Defensa del Ideal Católico Mexicano *
   (1uuu-1uuu)
Defensa Obrera (1918-19uu)
Elaboraciones y Envases (19uu-19uu)
El Gallito (1927-19uu)
El Heraldo (1927-19uu)
Heraldo de las Américas * (1924-19uu)
El Ideal Católico Mexicano * (19uu-19uu)
La Ilustración Norte Americana *
   (1887-1uuu)
El Imparcial de Chicago (1957-19uu)
The Journal of the American Medical
   Association (1919-1928)
Medicina Clínica (1918-1922)
México (1925-1930)
El Mundo de Hoy * (1910-19uu)
El Nacional (1930-19uu)
La Noticia Mundial (1927-19uu)
La Nueva Solidaridad... (1918-1919)
Nuevas Legadas desde Checoslovaquia...
   (1940-1942)
El Panorama (1919-19uu)
Papel e Imprenta (1946-19uu)
Prensa Libre (1960-.)
Radio y Artículos Eléctricos * (19uu-19uu)
La Raza * (1928-1932)
Las Repúblicas Americanas * (1907-19uu)
Revista Agrícola (1905-1906)
Revista de Radiología y Fisioterapia
   (1943-1947)
El Sol de Chicago (1959-19uu)
Solidaridad: Publicación de los
   Trabajadores... (1920-193u)
Vita Nuova * (1uuu-1uuu)
La Voz de México * (1948-19uu)

Evanston

Revista Rotaria (1933-1990)

L'Omnibus (1840-1841)
Pan-American Review (1910-1916)
La Patria (1846-1850)
El Pelayo (1851-1uuu)
El Pero Grullo * (1846-1uuu)
Phoenix * (18uu-1841)
El Pobre Diablo * (1847-1uuu)
El Porvenir (1863-1uuu)
La Revista Comercial * (1880-1uuu)
Revista Comercial Americana * (1906-1907)
La Revista Mercantil de Nueva Orleans *
  (1uuu-1uuu)
La Risa * (1uuu-1uuu)
Simpatía (1935-19uu)
La Sombra de Padilla * (1845-19uu)
El Telégrafo (1849-1uuu)
El Telégrafo * (1825-1uuu)
La Unión * (1873-1uuu)
La Unión (1851-1851)
La Verdad (1845-18uu)
La Voz Latina (1935-19uu)

City Unknown

La Estrella Mejicana * (1836-18uu)

MARYLAND

Baltimore

El Sol de la Chesapeake (19uu-19uu)

MASSACHUSETTS

Boston

La Aurora (1845-18uu)
El Heraldo de la Ciencia Cristiana
  (1959-19uu)
El Reporter LatinoAmericano (19uu-1934)
The Two Republics * (1881-1uuu)

MICHIGAN

Ann Arbor

El Estudiante Latino-Americano (1918-.)

Springfield

El Compañero * (19uu-19uu)

MINNESOTA

St. Paul

Lo Mejor del Catholic Digest * (195u-19uu)

MISSOURI

Kansas City

Conquista Juvenil (1955-.)
El Cosmopolita (1914-1919)
El Heraldo de Santidad (1945-1989)
El Mercurio (1883-1884)

Lee's Summit

El Sembrador * (19uu-19uu)

St. Louis

El Comercio del Valle (1876-1890)
El Correo del Valle * (1880-1886)
Las Dos Naciones (1894-1896)
El Internacional * (1933-19uu)
Internacional * (1889-1uuu)
Modern Mexico (1895-1909)
La Revista Mexicana * (1884-1uuu)
Spanish American Trade Journal *
  (1890-1uuu)
La Unión de América (1886-1uuu)

University City

Hispania (1918-.)

NEW JERSEY

Englewood Cliffs

Sugar y Azúcar (1956-.)

Garden City

El Eco: Revista de la Prensa Española
(1904-1935)

Jersey City

Justicia (1934-19uu)

New Brunswick

Charlatán * (1951-19uu)

Paterson

El Observador = The Observer (1960-19uu)

Rutherford

Actualidades Médicas (1929-1932)

City Unknown

El Despertar (1891-1902)

NEW MEXICO

Alamo Gordo

La Nueva ...poca (1911-19uu)
La Nueva Era * (1918-19uu)

Albuquerque

El Abogado Cristiano (1uuu-1903)
El Abogado Cristiano Fronterizo *
(1880-1uuu)
El Abogado Cristiano Hispano-Americano
(1907-1908)
El Abogado Cristiano Neo-Mexicano
(1904-1907)
Albuquerque Mirror * (1879-1uuu)
The Albuquerque Press (1867-1867)
The Albuquerque Review (1876-1880)
La Aurora * (1928-19uu)
La Bandera Americana (1895-1938)
Bandera de la Unión * (1863-1uuu)
Bernalillo Condado Demócrata (18uu1uuu)
El Combate (18921919)
El Defensor del Pueblo * (1891-1uuu)
El Demócrata (1878-18uu)
El Demócrata * (193119uu)
Demócrata and La Aurora * (191119uu)
Estado *(190619uu)
La Estrella de Nuevo México * (1906-19uu)
La Estrella Mejicana (1890-1890)
La Gaceta * (1926-19uu)
La Hormiga de Oro (18uu-190u)
El Imparcial (1903-19uu)
El Independiente (1933-1939)
El Independiente and the New Mexico...
(1939-1966)
El Independiente and the New Mexico...
(19uu-1933)
El Indito (1900-1905)
Minor * (1880-1uuu)
El Monitor (1914-19uu)
El Mensajero * (1911-19uu)
The New Mexico Press (1864-1867)
New Mexico State Republican (1919-1920)
The News (1885-1887)
Noticias * (1905-19uu)
El Nuevo Mundo (1897-1901)
La Opinión Pública (1892-1896)
La Opinión Pública (1906-191u)
El Parvenir * (1922-19uu)

People's News (1935-19uu)
El Pueblo (1900-19uu)
The Republican Review (1870-1876)
La Revista de Albuquerque (1881-188u)
The Topic (1934-19uu)
La Tuerca * (1uuu-1uuu)
La Unión de Albuquerque (1892-189u)
La Voz de Nuevo México (1894-1uuu)
La Voz Trabajadora * (1905-19uu)

Angostura

La Luz (1900-1908)

Bayard

El Noticiero del Sur-Oeste (1949-.)

Belen

Belen News (19uu-1947)
El Hispano-Americano (19uu-19uu)
The News-Bulletin (1947-1976)

Bernalillo

El Agricultor Moderno (19uu-19uu)
Bernalillo Mirror * (1878-1879)
Bernalillo Native (18uu-1uuu)
Bernalillo News * (1880-1882)
The Bernalillo Times (1929-1971)
El Espejo (187u-187u)
El Espejo del Valle de Taos * (1878-1879)
El Faro del Río Grande (1914-1916)
Native * (1880-1uuu)

Capitan

El Capitán (1900-1900)
El Farol (1905-19uu)

Carbonateville

Los Cerrillos Prospector * (1879-1881)

Chama

El Hogar * (1uuu-1uuu)

Clayton

El Cosmopolita (191u-19uu)
El Defensor del Pueblo * (1902-19uu)
Empresa * (1905-19uu)
El Fénix (1899-19uu)
The Union County Leader (1929-.)
La Unión del Pueblo (1913-19uu)
Union Democrat * (1889-1uuu)

Cleveland

El Jornalero * (1uuu-1uuu)

Colorado

El Eco Parroquial (191u-19uu)

Deming

New Mexico Potpourri * (1892-1uuu)

Des Moines

The Swastika (1913-19uu)

East Las Vegas

Atrevido * (1887-1uuu)
La Aurora (19uu-19uu)
Boletín Agrícola y Ganadero... (1918-191u)
La Granja y el Hogar (1917-19uu)
New Mexican Miner (1880-18uu)

Encino

El Progreso * (1910-19uu)

Espanola

Española Valley Developer (193u-19uu)

* No extant issues located

El Nuevo Mexicano * (1937-19uu)
El Palito (1925-1926)
Prensa (19uu-19uu)
El Republicano * (1912-19uu)
Victoria * (1937-19uu)
La Voz del Río Grande (1926-19uu)

Estancia

The Estancia Herald (1909-1912)
The Estancia News (1904-1912)
Estancia News-Herald (1912-1950)
Estancia Valley Citizen (1960-1966)
Las Nuevas de la Estancia (19uu-1908)

Folson

La Cometa (19uu-19uu)
...poca * (1907-19uu)

Gallup

Jornal del Pobre * (1916-19uu)
Noticias del Hispano-Americano...
   (1915-19uu)

La Luz

Angostura (1900-1902)

La Mesilla

El Defensor del Pueblo (1890-1892)
El Demócrata (187u-18uu)
El Independiente del Valle de la Mesilla
   (1877-1879)
Mesilla News (1938-19uu)
The Mesilla News (1873-1885)
The Mesilla Times (1860-1862)
Las Nuevas de Mesilla * (1879-1uuu)

Laguna

La Solana * (1878-1uuu)

Las Cruces

The Borderer (1871-1875)
Catholic Banner * (1912-1914)
El Cobrador * (1899-1uuu)
La Crónica de Valencia * (1890-1895)
Las Cruces Citizen (1902-1968)
Las Cruces Daily News (1889-1889)
Las Cruces Daily Times (1889-1uuu)
The Daily Times (1893-1uuu)
El Demócrata (1894-1894)
El Demócrata Independiente (1897-1902)
Eco del Río Grande (187u-1878)
Eco del Siglo (1882-18uu)
El Eco del Valle (1905-19uu)
La Empresa (1896-1uuu)
La Estrella (191u-1939)
La Flor del Valle (1894-1uuu)
El Fronterizo (187u-18uu)
La Gaceta Popular (1918-192u)
Independent Democrat (1892-189u)
El Labrador (1896-1914)
Liberal * (1891-1uuu)
Mesilla Valley Bulletin (1932-1938)
Mesilla Valley Democrat (1886-1890)
El Nuevo Mexicano * (1880-1uuu)
El Observador Fronterizo (1888-1888)
El Promotor Escolar (1891-1892)
Rio Grande Gazette * (1868-1871)
Rio Grande Republican (1881-1uuu)
El Tiempo (1882-1911)
Verdad (1890-189u)
Verdad (1898-1uuu)

Las Vegas

The Acorn (1873-1875)
Albuquerque * (1913-19uu)
El Anciano * (1889-1890; 1898-1899)
Anunciador de N. Méjico (1871-1878)
Aurora * (1900-19uu)
Boletín de Anuncios (1877-1uuu)
La Cachiporra (1888-18uu)

La Cachiporrita (1890-189u)

Campaign Bulletin (1880-18uu)

Católico de Nuevo México * (18uu-1uuu)

The Chronicle (1886-1886)

The Chronicle (18uu-1uuu)

El Clarín Mexicano (189u-1uuu)

The Daily Chronicle Las Vegas (1884-18uu)

El Demócrata * (1895-1uuu)

East Las Vegas * (1911-19uu)

La Espada Republicana (190819uu)

La Gaceta * (1877-1878)

El Hispano-Americano (189u-1920)

El Independiente (1894-19uu)

The Las Vegan (193u-1936)

Las Vegas (1879-1uuu)

Las Vegas Advertiser * (18uu-1uuu)

Las Vegas Daily Gazette (1881-1886)

Las Vegas Gazette (187u-18uu)

The Las Vegas Gazette (1886-1886)

Las Vegas Morning Gazette (1880-1881)

Las Vegas Sunday Courier (1888-188u)

Las Vegas Sunday Gazette (1872-1886)

Las Vegas Weekly Gazette (1872-18uu)

Las Vegas Weekly Mail (1871-1872)

Las Vegas Weekly Optic (1879-1898)

Mills' Mexico (1884-1uuu)

El Misionero Bautista (1943-19uu)

New Mexico Advertiser * (1870-1878)

New Mexico Catholic * (1895-1uuu)

New Mexico Herald (1879-1uuu)

New Mexico Patriot * (1875-1uuu)

Observador * (1898-1899)

La Prensa (1935-19uu)

Revista Católica (1875-1962)

Revista Evangélica * (1876-1uuu)

Republicano del Condado de San Miguel (1886-1uuu)

San Miguel County Star (19271948)

El Sol de Mayo (1891-1892)

El Sol de Mayo (1894-1894)

El Sol de Mayo (1900-1902)

Lincoln

News * (1896-1uuu)

Logan

La Crónica * (1907-19uu)

Los Lunas

Las Nuevas de la Liga Agrícola y Ganadera... (1920-192u)

Valencia County Vindicator (1883-18uu)

Maldonado

La Estrella (1897-1uuu)

Manzano

El Gringo y Greaser (1883-1884)

Maxwell

La Tinaja (1937-19uu)

Mora

La Crónica * (1889-1uuu)

La Crónica de Mora (1889-1890)

El Demócrata de Mora (1888-1889)

El Eco del Norte (1908-1922)

La Gaceta de Mora (1890-1891)

El Hispano Americano (1908-19uu)

Mail * (1874-1uuu)

El Mensajero (1910-1012)

The Mora County Patriot (1921-1927)

Mora County Star (1927-1949)

The Mora Echo (1890-189u)

Mosquito (1891-1892)

La Prensa (1935-19uu)

Sun * (1940-1944)

Mountainair

El Independiente (1917-19uu)

* No extant issues located

Parkview

El Progreso *(189519uu)

Penasco

Peñasqueros (1959-19uu)

Raton

El Amigo del Pueblo * (189u-1uuu)
Colfax County Reporter (18uu-19uu)
El Cometa * (1910-19uu)
The Gate City Sun (1930-1936)
El Relámpago (1904-1904)
Tipográfica * (1902-19uu)
La Unión (1898-1uuu)
La Victoria (19uu-1929)

Roswell

Register Tribune *
  1910-19uu
Roswell Record
  1891-1913

Roy

El Hispano Americano (1905-19uu)
Roy Record * (1905-1929)
The Spanish American (1904-1926)
Weekly Hispano Americano (1905-1905)

San Acacia

El Comercio (1901-19uu)

San Hilario

La Crónica del Río Colorado (1882-1884)
Red River Chronicle (1882-1884)

San Lorenzo

La Crónica del Río Colorado (1880-1882)
Red River Chronicle (1880-1882)

San Marcial

La Libertad (1896-1uuu)

Santa Fe

El Abogado del Estado de Nuevo México *
  (1889-1uuu)
Adelante (19uu-19uu)
El Amigo del País (185u-1uuu)
The Ancon * (1844-1845)
La Aurora (1884-1884)
El Boletín (19uu-19uu)
El Boletín Popular (1885-1908)
City News * (1874-1876)
El Clarín Mejicano (1873-18uu)
El Correo de Santa Fe * (1869-1uuu)
El Crepúsculo de la Libertad * (1834-183u)
The Daily New Mexican (1868-1881)
El Demócrata = The Democrat (1857-18uu)
La Estrella de Nuevo México * (1895-1uuu)
Gaceta * (1850-1uuu)
El Gato (1894-1894)
The Gauntlet (1894-1894)
El Guía de Santa Fe (1886-1886)
Historia Ilustrado de Nuevo México *
  (1919-19uu)
Imprenta del Río Grande * (1873-1uuu)
The New Mexican (1849-1850)
New Mexican Advocate * (1880-1uuu)
New Mexico Advertiser * (1878-1880)
New Mexico Cooperator * (1876-1878)
New Mexico Democrat * (1871-1uuu)
The New Mexico Sun and El Palito
  (1926-1927)
The New Mexico Union (1872-1875)
El Nuevo Mejicano (1863-1868)
El Nuevo Mexicano (1890-1958)
El Palacio (1913-.)

El Palito * (1908-19uu)
El Payo de Nuevo México (1845-18uu)
Registro de Nuevo México (1916-1916)
Revista Ilustrada (1907-1931)
Revista Popular de Santa Fe * (1924-19uu)
Sancho Panza * (1907-19uu)
The Santa Fe Daily Post (1870-1872)
Santa Fe Gazette (1854-185u)
Santa Fe Gazette (1859-1864)
Santa Fe New Mexican Review
   (1883-1885)
Santa Fe Republican (1847-18uu)
Santa Fe Republican (1862-1863)
Santa Fe Weekly Gazette (185u-18uu)
Santa Fe Weekly Post (1869-1872)
Semanario de Santa Fe * (1847-1uuu)
Southwestern Catholic (1921-19uu)
La Tribuna * (1881-1uuu)
La Verdad (1844-1845)
La Verdad * (1908-19uu)
La Voz del Pueblo (1888-1888)
La Voz del Pueblo (1889-1924)
La Voz del Pueblo de Santa Fe (1940-19uu)
La Voz Pública * (1932-1942)
Weekly New Mexican (1868-1883)

Santa Rosa

Guadalupe County Review * (1926-1931)
La Nueva Estrella (1910-1911)
Las Nuevas (1924-1926)
Pecos Valley Eagle (1932-19uu)
The Santa Rosa News (1926-19uu)
Santa Rosa Sun (190u-19uu)
El Sol (1911-1914)
La Voz Pública (1898-1912)
La Voz Pública (191u-192u)

Socorro

El Abogado Cristiano Neo-Mexicano
   (1893-1uuu)
El Combate (18uu-18uu)
El Defensor (1950-1959)

El Defensor Chieftain (1959-.)
El Defensor del Pueblo (1904-1950)
Eco de Socorro * (1883-1uuu)
Eco del Socorro (1887-1uuu)
La Estrella de Nuevo México (1896-189u)
La Golondrina (1898-1uuu)
El Heraldo (1914-1920)
El Hispano Americano (1891-1uuu)
El Metodista (1886-1892)
Metodista NeoMexicano (188u-1886)
La Patria (1944-19uu)
El Progreso (1887-1887)
El Republicano (1898-19uu)
Socorro Star (1884-1885)
The Socorro Union (188u-18uu)

Springer

El Estandarte de Springer (1889-1893)

Springs

Banner * (1890-1uuu)

Taos

El Bien Público (1910-1912)
El Boletín Popular (1919-19uu)
El Crepúsculo * (1835-1uuu)
El Crepúsculo (1948-1955)
El Crepúsculo de la Libertad (1955-1960)
El Espejo del Valle de Taos * (1878-1879)
Faro Polular * (1892-1uuu)
El Heraldo * (1884-1889)
El Heraldo de Taos (1885-1888)
El Heraldo del Condado de Taos
   (1884-1885)
El Heraldo-Taoseño (1888-1889)
The Horse Fly (1938-194u)
El Monitor (189u-1uuu)
La Revista de Taos (1902-1902)
La Revista de Taos (1905-1922)
La Revista de Taos and the Taos Cresset
   (1902-190u)

La Revista de Taos and the Taos Cresset
(1905-1905)
La Revista Popular de Nuevo México
(1922-19uu)
The Taos Recorder and El Bien Público
(191u-19uu)
The Taos Review (1936-1936)
The Taos Review and the Taos Valley News
(1936-1940)
Taos Star (1948-1950)
Taos Valley News (190u-1917)
Taos Valley News (19221936)
Taos Valley News and El Crepúsculo
(1917-1922)
The Taoseño (1948-1948)
Taoseño (1939-1940)
The Taoseño and the Taos Review
(1941-1948)

Terrero

La Época * (1909-19uu)

Tierra Amarilla

El Nuevo Estado (1907-1925)
La Opinión de Río Arriba (1935-194u)
El Republicano * (1901-19uu)

Vaughn

The News * (1926-1936)

Wagon Mound

The Arrow-Pioneer (188u-1888)
El Combate (1902-1918)
El Cometa * (1895-1uuu)
La Flecha (188u-18uu)
Mora County News = Las Nuevas del
Condado... (19uu-1932)
La Prensa (1935-19uu)
Wagon Mound Pantagraph (1909-1921)
Wagon Mound Sentinel (1918-1921)

NEW YORK

Bronx

Repúblicas Hispanas Unidas (1943-19uu)
Vida Hispana (1952-1955)

Brooklyn

El Atalaya * (19uu-19uu)
Boletín Linotypico * (19uu-19uu)
Brooklyn Colonia Latina (1938-19uu)
El Caribe (1923-19uu)
El Curioso (1934-19uu)
Despertad * (19uu-19uu)
El Diario de Nueva York (1948-1963)
España Libre (1939-.)
Frente Popular (1937-1939)
Guaimaro (1895-1uuu)
Linoticias (19uu-.)
Modern Dentistry (1945-19uu)
Obrero Libre (1924-19uu)
Odontología Moderna (1954-19uu)
El Radical (1893-18uu)
Solidaridad * (1918-1930)
La Voz de Puerto Rico en USA (1956-19uu)

Buffalo

La Hacienda (1905-19uu)

New York City

Acción Cívica (1928-19uu)
Ahora (19uu-19uu)
Aki Nueva York (1955-19uu)
Alba de Nueva York (1954-19uu)
Alhambra (1929-1930)
Alma Boricua (1934-1935)
Alma Latina (1916-.)
Ambas Américas (1867-1868)
América (1908-1922)
La América: Periódico Quincenal...
(1871-1uuu)

* No extant issues located

La América Científica, Industrial, Agrícola y
   Ganadera (1890-1909)
América Clínica (1941-1964)
América Continental (1956-19uu)
La América Futura * (1917-1921)
América Ilustrada (187u-1uuu)
Americana (1947-19uu)
El Americano (1892-1uuu)
Las Américas (1940-1944)
Las Américas: Órgano Oficial de la All
   Americas... (1914-.)
El Amigo de los Niños (18uu-18uu)
El Anunciador (193u-19uu)
El Anunciador * (1885-1911)
El Anunciador Hispano-Americano *
   (1879-1880)
El Arte Tipográfico (1904-1922)
El Arte Tipográfico y el Escritorio
   (1922-1927)
Artes y Letras (1933-1939)
Artistas Hispanos (1948-19uu)
El Ateneo: Repertorio Ilustrado...
   (1874-1877)
Ateneo: Revista Cultural (1934-19uu)
Aurora (1922-19uu)
El Automóvil Americano (19uu-19uu)
El Avisador Cubano (1885-1888)
El Avisador Hispano Americano
   (1888-1889)
Las Avispas (1896-1uuu)
Bibliografía Hispanoamericana (1934-1937)
Biblioteca Hispánica (1900-1921)
Boletín (1931-1934)
Boletín Católico Checoslovaco (1941-1946)
Boletín Checoslovaco (19uu-.)
El Boletín Comercial (1871-1uuu)
Boletín de Información (1938-19uu)
El Boletín de la Liga Puertorriqueña e
   Hispana (1928-1933)
El Boletín de la Revolución (1868-1869)
Boletín de las Naciones Unidas
   (1948-1953)
Boletín de Noticias y Precios Corrientes
   (1862-1862)
Boletín en Español (1943-.)

Boletín Latino Americano del CIO *
   (19uu-19uu)
Boletín Oficial New History (1934-19uu)
Boletín Oficial: Club Cubano... (194u-19uu)
El Boricua (194u-19uu)
Borinquen (1898-1uuu)
La Boz del Pueblo (1915-1919)
Brazo y Cerebro * (1912-1914)
El Cable (18uu-1878)
El Cafetal (1903-19uu)
El Campo Internacional (1920-19uu)
Cara al Sol (1938-194u)
Carta Informativa Americana (1941-1943)
Carteles de América * (1960-.)
Cascabeles (1934-19uu)
Catholic Expositor (1844-1844)
Cine Mundial * (1918-19uu)
Cine Variedades (1953-19uu)
Circular del Joyero * (1874-1uuu)
El Comercio (187u-1uuu)
El Cometa (1855-1uuu)
Compendio Médico (19uu.)
El Comprador Hispano-Americano *
   (1888-1902)
Concarajícara (1897-1uuu)
El Continental (1862-186u)
El Continental * (191u-19uu)
Correo Americano de Medicina y Cirugía
   (1923-1924)
El Correo Americano y Diario Exportación
   (18uu-1897)
El Correo de América (1897-1uuu)
El Correo de Nueva York (18uu-1uuu)
El Correo Hispano-Americano *
   (1868-1uuu)
Cosas (1931-19uu)
El Crisol (1945-19uu)
La Crónica (1848-1867)
La Crónica (1949-19uu)
El Cronista (1867-1877)
Cuba (189u-19uu)
Cuba (1932-1uuu)
Cuba Libre (1895-1uuu)
Cuba y América (18971-898)
Cuba y Puerto Rico (1897-18uu)

   * No extant issues located

construcción (1942-1942)

Ingeniería Internacional. Edición de
  Industria (1942-1942)

Ingeniería Internacional: Industria
  (1942-1961)

Inter América (1917-1926)

Intuición ... (1929-1930)

Israel y América Latina (1949-.)

La Juventud (1889-1uuu)

Kandela (1949-19uu)

La Liberación (1946-19uu)

Libros (1940-19uu)

La Llumanera de Nova York (1874-1879)

El Lucero Zefardí * (1927-19uu)

El Machete Criollo (1927-19uu)

El Magazine de la Raza (1918-19uu)

El Mensagero Semanal de Nueva York
  (1828-1831)

Mensaje (195u-19uu)

Mensaje de Nueva York: Revista... (1956-.)

El Mentor Ilustrado * (1881-1882)

Mercurio de Nueva York (1828-1831)

México * (1925-19uu)

Modern Mexico (1uuu-1909)

El Mulato (1854-1uuu)

El Mundo Americano * (1899-1uuu)

El Mundo Azucarero (1913-1956)

Mundo Latino: Revista Gráfica Semanal
  (1948-19uu)

El Mundo Nuevo (1871-1875)

Mundo Obrero (1931-19uu)

Museo de las Familias * (18uu-1uuu)

Nación Puertorriqueña (1933-19uu)

El Nacional (1898-1uuu)

New York Democrat (1870-1870)

New York Hispano (1957-195u)

Newsletter (195u-19uu)

Norte (1940-19uu)

El Norte Americano * (1914-1921)

NorteAmérica (1928-1930)

Nosotros (1953-19uu)

Noticioso de Ambos Mundos (1836-1859)

Novedades * (1915-19uu)

Las Novedades: España y los Pueblos
  Hispano-Americanos (1876-1918)

La Nueva Democracia (1920-1963)

La Nueva Voz (1939-1941)

Nueva York al Día (19uu-19uu)

El Obrero (1931-1931)

La Opinión (1886-18uu)

Orientación (1952-.)

Oye Boricua * (19uu-19uu)

The Pan American (1940-1950)

El Papagayo (1855-1uuu)

Parnaso * (1950-19uu)

Pasatiempo (1951-19uu)

Patria (1892-190u)

La Paz de Cuba * (1878-1uuu)

La Paz y el Trabajo * (1910-19uu)

El Pensamiento Contemporáneo
  (1891-1892)

Petróleo del Mundo (1943-19uu)

Pimienta * (1958-19uu)

PIP (1953-19uu)

El Portavoz (1927-19uu)

El Porvenir (1896-1uuu)

El Postillón (1892-1uuu)

La Prensa (1913-1963)

El Progreso (1915-1915)

Progreso Farmacéutico (19uu-19uu)

Propaganda Ilustrada (19051-9uu)

El Pueblo (1855-1uuu)

El Pueblo (187u-1uuu)

Pueblos Hispanos (1943-1944)

Puerto Rican Herald * (1901-19uu)

Puerto Rico en Marcha (1951-19uu)

Puerto Rico y Nueva York (1954-19uu)

El Quimbo Habanero (1893-1uuu)

La Raza Latina * (1873-1uuu)

El Redactor (1826-1831)

El Repertorio Médico * (1883-1uuu)

La República * (1884-1885)

La República (1887-1uuu) *

La República (1871-187u)

Revista Aérea Latino Americana (1937-.)

Revista Agrícola Industrial * (1877-1880)

Revista Americana de Farmacia...
  (1895-1921)

Revista Comercial Mexicana (1917-1917)

Revista de Estudios Hispánicos (1928-1929)

* No extant issues located

Revista de la Crónica: Miscelánea...
  (1848-1848)
Revista del Mundo * (1921-19uu)
Revista Hispánica Moderna (1934-.)
Revista Hispánica Moderna: Sección
  Escolar (1935-1937)
La Revista Ilustrada de Nueva York
  (1882-1uuu)
Revista Médica Panamericana (1926-.)
La Revista Médico Quirúrgica... (1892-1895)
La Revista Mercantil * (19uu-1929)
Revista PanAmericana * (1906-1908)
Revista Popular * (1888-1905)
Revista Récord (1957-19uu)
Revista Teatral * (19uu-19uu)
Revista Universal * (1871-1uuu)
Revista Universal: Magazine
  Hispano-Americano (19uu-1918)
La Revolución (1869-1876)
La Revolución de Cuba (187u-1875)
Saludos: Revista de Buena Voluntad (1947-.)
Sangre Nueva (194u-19uu)
Scientific American. Export edition *
  (1845-1908)
La Semana = The Week (1906-19uu)
La Semana de Nueva York (1954-19uu)
El Semanario (1955-19uu)
Semanario Hispano (1945-19uu)
El Separatista (1883-1uuu)
Sephardic Bulletin (1928-1930)
Soberanía (1958-19uu)
Social: Revista Semanal (193u-19uu)
Socorro Star (1899-1uuu)
Spanish Echo (1935-19uu)
Spanish Labor Bulletin (1936-1939)
Spanish Revolution (1957-19uu)
Sugar (1941-1956)
El SurAmericano (187u-1uuu)
El Taquígrafo Gregg * (19uu-19uu)
Temas: Revista Ilustrada (1950-.)
Thurber-Whyland and Company's
  Spanish Review * (1879-18uu)
La Tienda * (1uuu-1uuu)
Tierra (1930-19uu)

Todos (1958-19uu)
Las Tres Américas (1893-1uuu)
La Tribuna * (1921-1922)
Tribuna Hispana (1926-1928)
El Tribuno Cubano (18uu-1uuu)
Unión: Revista Boloviana (1945-19uu)
El Universal * (1898-1uuu)
Universal Commerce *(19uu-19uu)
La Vara (1922-1948)
Venezuela Futura (1931-19uu)
La Verdad (1876-1uuu)
La Verdad (1848-185u)
La Verdad: Periódico Política
  Cubana (1876-1uuu)
Vía Libre (1939-1940)
Victory (1943-1945)
Vida Alegre (19uu-19uu)
Vida Hispana de Nueva York (1955-19uu)
Vida Obrera (1929-19uu)
Visión: la Revista Latinoamericana (1950-.)
Voluntad * (1916-19uu)
Vosotros (1954-19uu)
La Voz (1937-1939)
La Voz: a Bilingual Publication... (1956-.)
La Voz de Cuba (195u-.)
La Voz de la América (1865-1867)
La Voz de la Patria (1876-1uuu)
La Voz de Puerto Rico (1950-19uu)
La Voz de Puerto Rico en U.S.A. *
  (1874-1uuu)
La Voz del Artista (1960-19uu)
La Voz del Pueblo (1870-1uuu)
El Yunque (1952-19uu)

NORTH CAROLINA

Chapel Hill

Hispanófila (1957-.)

OHIO

Cincinnati

El Hospital (1945-.)
El Internacional * (1894-1uuu)

PENNSYLVANIA

Philadelphia

América Comercial * (19uu-19uu)
El Arte Tipográfico (1927-197u)
El Habanero (1824-1826)
Hispanic Review (1933-.)
El Progreso * (1887-1uuu)
La Revista Dental Americana (1893-1901)

Pittsburgh

Oral Hygiene (1930-.)

TENNESSEE

Nashville

Ahora (19uu-1uu)
Conquistadores. Ed. de Maestros (19uu-.)
El Promotor de Educación Cristiana
   (1949-1994)

TEXAS

Alice

El Cosmopolita (19uu-19uu)
El Demófilo * (19uu-19uu)
El Eco Libra (18uu-1uuu)
El Latino-Americano (1913-19uu)
El Sol * (1895-1910)

Austin

El Demócrata (1944-19uu)
El Espectador Mexicano * (1833-1uuu)
Reforma, Libertad y Justicia * (1908-19uu)

The Texas Gazette (1829-1832)
El Universitario * (1930-19uu)
La Vanguardia (1920-192u)

Bee County

Amigo de los Hombres * (189u-1uuu)

Beeville

El Grito del Pueblo * (1888-1uuu)
La Sombra de Lincoln * (1898-1902)

Brownsville

El Adelante (1908-1913)
La Bandera (1848-1863)
El Bien Público * (1879-1uuu)
Boletín Estraordinario (1865-18uu)
La Calavera (19uu-19uu)
El Cazador * (1896-1uuu)
El Centinela (1849-1uuu)
Centinela del Río Grande (1850-18uu)
El Comercio (1901-19uu)
El Correo del Río Grande (1866-1uuu)
El Cronista del Valle (1917-19uu)
The Daily Ranchero and Republican
   (1859-1879)
The Democrat = El Demócrata
   (1875-18uu)
The Democrat and Ranchero (1879-1880)
El Demócrata (1875-18uu)
El Diario de la Frontera (1912-1913;
   1915-19uu)
Las Dos Repúblicas (18uu-1uuu)
El Duende * (1880-1uuu)
El Eco Fronterizo * (1921-19uu)
Friendís Mexican Mission Gazette
   (1874-1uuu)
El Heraldo de Brownsville (1934-19uu)
The Latin American Christian =
   El Cristiano... (195u-.)
El Liberal * (1912-1917)
El México-Texano (1889-1uuu)
El Monitor Republicano (190u-19uu)

* No extant issues located

El Paso

Actualidad (1936-19uu)
El Azteca * (1922-19uu)
El Agente Comercial (1900-1900)
Ahora (19uu-.)
Albores Seráficos * (1930-19uu)
El Atalaya (19uu-1925)
El Atalaya Bautista (1926-.)
El Atalaya Bautista: Semanario
 Evangélico (191u-19uu)
El Azote (192u-19uu)
La Bandera Roja * (190u-19uu)
La Buena Noticia * (19uu-19uu)
La Buena Prensa (1923-19uu)
El Centinela * (1887-1uuu)
El Ciudadano (1892-1uuu)
El Clarín del Norte (19uu-19uu)
El Combate * (1915-19uu)
Conquistadores. Ed. de Alumnos (19uu-.)
Conquistadores. Ed. de Maestros (19uu-.)
El Continental (1926-19uu)
La Constitución * (191u-19uu)
El Correo del Bravo (191u-19uu)
El Defensor (1894-1uuu)
El Defensor del Pueblo * (1906-19uu)
La Democracia (190u-19uu)
El Día (191u-19uu)
El Diario * (1905-19uu)
Diario de El Paso * (1924-1928)
Las Dos Américas (1898-1uuu)
El Eco del Comercio * (1869-1908)
El Eco Fronterizo (1896-1uuu)
The El Paso Times (1886-1889)
Evangelio Restaurado (1927-19uu)
El Expositor Bíblico (1900-1900)
El Faro Dominical (1927-1972)
Guía para Maestros de Niños (195u-.)
Heraldos del Rey (1927-1972)
El HispanoAmericano (1891-1uuu)
Historias Infantiles (1957-1971)
El Hogar Cristiano (1957-.)
La Hora de los Cuentos (1947-1984)
Humanidad * (190u-19uu)
El Independiente (189u-1uuu)

El Internacional * (1913-19uu)
El Internacional * (1925-19uu)
Justice * (1906-1908)
La Justicia (1915-1916)
La Justicia * (1893-1uuu)
El LatinoAmericano (1891-189u)
Lecciones Bíblicas (19uu-198u)
Lecciones Ilustradas: Alumnos (19uu-198u)
Lecciones Ilustradas. Edición para maestros
 (19uu-198u)
Líneas en Español * (1913-1918)
Mensajeras del Maestro (1938-1942)
El Mensajero Bautista (1917-1917)
Mensajero Juvenil (1925-1927)
México Libre * (1915-19uu)
El Monitor (189u-1uuu)
El Nacional * (1919-1920)
Las Noticias (1923-19uu)
Las Noticias * (1899-1uuu)
El Noticioso * (1895-1uuu)
Nuestros Niños (1918-1985)
El Observador Fronterizo (1886-1uuu)
La Opinión Pública (189u-1uuu)
El Padre Padilla * (19uu-19uu)
El País * (1926-1932)
El Paso del Norte (1904-1918)
El Pastor Evangélico (1957-1972)
La Patria (1919-19uu)
El Progreso (1922-19uu)
El Progresista (18uu-19uu)
El Promotor de Educación Cristiana
 (1949-1994)
El Propagandista (1941-19uu)
El Pueblo * (1926-19uu)
Puerto Rico * (1908-1909)
Punto Rojo * (1904-19uu)
Rayos de Luz (1914-19uu)
La Raza * (192u-19uu)
La Reforma Social (1893-19uu)
Renacimiento (1923-19uu)
La República (1918-19uu)
Revista Católica (1918-1962)
Revista Evangélica (1876-1879)
Revista Evangélica (1937-1957)
Revista Homilética (1923-1931)

* No extant issues located

Revista Ilustrada (1917-19uu)
La Revista Juvenil (1920-1925)
Revista para Uniones de Adultos
  (1959-1972)
Revista para Uniones de Intermedios
  (1955-1972)
Revista para Uniones de Jóvenes
  (1959-1972)
Revista para Uniones de Jóvenes y Adultos
  (1955-1958)
Revista para Uniones de Párvulos y...
  (1955-1984)
Revista para Uniones de Primarios
  (1955-1984)
Revista Trimestral de las Uniones de
  Jóvenes (1923-1924; 1936-1941)
Revista Trimestral para las Uniones de
  Jóvenes y Adultos (1942-1954)
Revista Trimestral para los Intermedios
  (1942-1954)
Revista Trimestral para Primarios
  (1942-1954)
La Revista Universal * (188u-1uuu)
Sancho Panza * (1891-1uuu)
El Sol * (1926-19uu)
Temas: Revista Ilustrada (1950-.)
Temas para las Uniones Bautistas de
  Jóvenes (1929-1930)
El Times en Español * (1881-19uu)
El Toro * (1921-19uu)
Trabajos Manuales (1953-1960)
El Valle del Bravo (1889-18uu)
La Voz de la Mujer (1907-19uu)
El Zurriago (1892-1uuu)

Falfurrias

Eco de Falfurrias * (1909-1919)
La Verdad (19uu-19uu)

Floresville

Eco Liberal (1895-1uuu)
El Hogar * (1914-1917)

El Liberal * (1898-1uuu)
El Progreso * (1915-19uu)

Fort Worth

Mexican World (192u-19uu)

Grulla

Star County Democrat * (1934-19uu)

Harlingen

El Precursor * (1915-1920)
La Prensa del valle * (1924-19uu)
El Tiempo * (1935-19uu)

Hebbronville

Jim Hogg County Enterprise (1926-19uu)

Hidalgo

El Centinela * (1899-1901)
El Eco de Hidalgo * (1897-1uuu)
La Unión * (1897-1898)

Houston

Gaceta Mexicana: Revista... (1928-19uu)
El Puerto (1935-.)
El Tecolote (19uu-19uu)
El Tiempo (1921-19uu)
La Tribuna (1924-19uu)

Kingsville

Acción (1931-193u)
Alfa (19uu-1958)
Alfa y Omega (1958-.)
El Eco (19uu-19uu)
Juntos (1958-.)
La Libertad (19uu-19uu)
Milicia (1945-19uu)

Notas de Kingsville (1943-1961)
Las Novedades (1935-19uu)
Nuestro Boletín * (1942-19uu)
La Nueva Era * (1927-19uu)
El Popular * (1913-1915)
El Porvenir * (1923-19uu)
Presbyterian Panamericana (1956-.)
The Tex. Mex. Reflector (1921-1956

Laredo

El Abogado Cristiano Fronterizo
  (1880-1uuu)
Alfa (19uu-19uu)
Aurora * (190u-19uu)
El Boletín Fronterizo Comercial *
  (1930-19uu)
El Chinaco * (1890-1892)
El Coadjutor * (1890-1uuu)
La Colonia Mexicana (1885-1uuu)
La Corregidora * (190u-19uu)
El Correo de Laredo (1891-1uuu)
La Crónica (1909-19uu)
El Defensor del Obrero (1906-19uu)
El Defensor del Pueblo * (19uu-19uu)
El Demócrata * (1900-1918)
El Demócrata Fronterizo (1896-1920)
El Diputado (1882-1uuu)
Los Dos Laredos * (1881-1uuu)
Evolución (1916-19uu)
El Fígaro (1892-1uuu)
El Guarda del Bravo * (1904-1907)
La Juventud Laredense * (1892-1uuu)
Laredo Times (1881-188u)
The Laredo Times (1929-1982)
Luz y Verdad * (1921-1926)
El Mundo * (1888-1891)
El Mutualista (1885-1888)
Las Noticias * (1929-19uu)
El Obrero * (1916-1920)
El Progreso * (1913-1915)
La Revista Semanal * (188u-1uuu)
Two Laredos * (1879-1880)
Vésper * (19uu-19uu)
La Voz de Juárez * (1908-1919)

Zapata County News (19uu-19uu)

Marfa

La Voz de Marfa (1928-19uu)

McAllen

Calaveras * (1917-19uu)
El Consejero (1958-19uu)
Diógenes * (1921-1933)
El Instructor (1954-1958)
Mañana * (1917-1919)
Orientación * (1928-1929)

Mcqueenley

Alba Roja * (1912-19uu)

Mercedes

Alma Azul * (1927-19uu)
Centro de Valle * (1927-1929)
Navidad * (1926-1930)
El Progreso * (191u-1916)

Mission

El Fronterizo * (1914-1915)
El Porvenir * (1935-19uu)
El Progreso * (1915-1921; 1924-19uu)

Nacogdoches

La Gaceta de Texas (1813-1813)
Mexican Advocate * (1892-1uuu)

Nueces County

El Libre Pensador * (1890-1uuu)

Presidio

The International (1947-1960)

* No extant issues located

Raymondville

El Tiempo * (1937-1958)

Rio Grande City

Actualidades (1914-1930)
El Bien Público * (1892-1900)
El Cromo * (1891-1uuu)
Las Dos Riberas * (1915-1918)
El Fronterizo (1921-19uu)
Herald * (1919-1943)
El Independiente (1924-1931)
El Liberal (1872-1875)
Navidad * (1926-1930)
El Picudo (1906-19uu)
Rio Grande Herald (1935-19uu)
El Voluntario (1892-1uuu)

Robstown

El Heraldo Cristiano (19uu-)

Roma

La Verdad * (1897-1uuu)

Runge

La Voz del Pueblo * (1918-19uu)

Sabinal

Justicia (1910-19uu)

San Antonio

Adelante (1916-1920)
El Agricultor Mexicano * (1918-1919)
Alma Latina (1932-19uu)
Amigo del Pueblo * (1908-1917)
El Badajo * (191u-19uu)
El Bautista Mexicano (193u-19uu)
El Bejareño (1855-18uu)

Boletín Mexicano * (1926-19uu)
Chiltipiquín * (1914-1915)
Claridades * (1915-19uu)
El Correo (1858-18uu)
El Correo Mexicano (1890-1914)
El Cronista Mexicano * (1891-1901)
La Defensa * (1917-1921)
El Eco * (1838-19uu)
Ecos de la Catedral (19uu–19uu)
La Época (1913-1931)
El Español (191u-19uu)
La Estrella * (1909-19uu)
El Éxito * (1920-19uu)
El Fandango (1927-19uu)
La Fe Católica (1897-19uu)
El Ferrocarril * (1894-1906)
El Gallo * (1882-1uuu)
La Guadalupana: Revista… (192u-.)
El Heraldo (1886-18uu)
El Heraldo Ganadero de Texas (1944-1944)
El Heraldo Mexicano: Seminario…
    (1927-19uu)
El Humo * (192u-19uu)
El Imparcial de Texas (1908-1924)
El Látigo (18uu-1uuu)
Lucha de Clases * (1915-19uu)
LULAC News (1931-1979)
La Luz Apostólica * (19uu-19uu)
El Mensajero Cristiano (1949-1950)
El Mensajero Luterano (194u-1948)
El Mexicano de Texas * (1868-1uuu)
México Internacional * (1909-1910)
Mexico Journal (1945-19uu)
Monigotes * (1922-19uu)
El Monitor (1888-1uuu)
Monitor Democrático * (1910-1911)
Mosaicos: Spanish-English… (1955-19uu)
El Nacional (1916-1924)
El Noticioso (1907-1909)
Nueva Senda (19uu-1969)
El Obrero: Periódico Independiente *
    (1910-19uu)
Pan American (1944-19uu)
Poli-Oculos * (191u-19uu)

La Prensa (1913-1962)
El Presente * (1914-1915)
El Progreso (1907-1908)
El Ranchero (1856-18uu)
La Raza (1914-1915)
El Regidor (1888-1916)
La República * (1913-19uu)
Revista Mensual (1907-1909)
Revista Mexicana (1915-1920)
La Roza (1915-1916)
Spanish American Industrial Journal
  (1894-19uu)
El Tiempo (1877-1uuu)
El Trabajo * (1919-19uu)
La Trompeta Evangélica de la Iglesia de
  Dios (1948-19uu)
El Unionista (1919-192u)
El Vacilón (1924-19uu)
La Voz (1935-19uu)
La Voz de Juárez * (1908-1919)
La Voz de la Parroquia (1935-19uu)
La Voz de México * (1924-19uu)

San Benito

Alfa y Omega (1958-.)
El Lucero * (1942-19uu)
La Luz * (1913-19uu)

San Diego

Alma * (1938-1941)
El Demócrata (19uu-.)
El Eco Liberal (18uu-1uuu)
La Gaceta * (1918-19uu)
El Horizonte (1879-1uuu)
La Libertad (1908-19uu)
La Libertad (1939-1942)
New Duval (1956-19uu)
El Porvenir (1927-19uu)
El Sordo (1899-1uuu)
The Sun (1891-1uuu)
La Voz (1935-1936)

San Juan

El Correo de la Virgen (195u-.)

San Marcos

El Observador (195u-19uu)
El Sol (1956-1958)

San Ignacio

El Demócrata (1915-19uu)
Septembrino * (192u-19uu)

Santa Margarita

The Corpus Christi Ranchero (1863-1864)

Taft

Pan Americana News (1942-19uu)
Tri-Mex Tripod (19uu-19uu)

Uribeño

El Aldeano (1906-19uu)

Victoria

Cunbres * (1939-1941)

Weslaco

Luz y Verdad (1931-1932)
El Porvenir (1924-19uu)

UTAH

Salt Lake City

Revista Ibérica (1953-.)

* No extant issues located

VIRGINIA

Williamsburg

The Pasco (1939-1941)

WASHINGTON DC

American Junior Red Cross.
  Spanish edition * (19uu-19uu)
The Americas (1944-.)
Américas. Edición en español (1949-.)
Anales de la Organización de los Estados
  Americanos (1949-1958)
Arqueología Americana (1926-.)
Asociación Interamericana de Ingeniería
  (1947-1950)
Boletín (1922-.)
Boletín (1946-1946)
Boletín (1949-19uu)
Boletín de Artes Visuales (1957-1969)
Boletín de Ciencias y Tecnología
  (1950-1950)
Boletín de Educación Social del Trabajador
  (1954-.)
Boletín de Información Vial (1928-19uu)
Boletín de la Oficina Internacional de
  las... (1908-1910)
Boletín de la Oficina Sanitaria
  Panamericana (1923-.)
Boletín de la Unión Panamericana
  (1910-1911)
Boletín de la Unión Panamericana (1911-.)
Boletín de Música y Artes Visuales
  (1952-1956)
Boletín Interamericano de Música
  (1957-1973)
Boletín: Puerto Rico Agricultural
  Experiment Station (1902-19uu)
Bulletin of the Pan American Union
  (1910-1948)
Carta Quincenal de la UNRRA (1945-1945)
Chilean Gazette (1942-19uu)
Ciencia Interamericana (1960-19uu)

Ciencia y Tecnología (1960-19uu)
Ciencias Sociales (1950-1956)
Comercio Interamericana (1946-1953)
Cuba Libre (1898-1uuu)
Educación (1925-1929)
Educación (1956-19uu)
Estadística (1943-.)
Exclusivo de Washington * (1958-19uu)
The Filipino (1906-1906)
The Filipino People (1912-1916)
Finanzas, Industria, Comercio (1925-19uu)
The Hispanic American Historical Review
  (1918-.)
Informaciones (1944-19uuu)
Informaciones Económicas (1956-19uu)
Informativo Quincenal de la UNRRA
  (1945-1945)
LEA: Librarians, Editors, Authors...
  (1949-1950)
El Libro Americano (1938-1944)
The Mexican Review (1916-1922)
Noticias de la Oficina de Información
  Obrera y Social (1940-19uu)
Noticiero: Comisión... (1951-1980)
Noticiero Obrero Norteamericano
  (1943-19uu)
El Observador Militar Interamericano
  (194u-194u)
Organo Oficial Asociación Interamericana
  de Ingeniería Sanitaria (1947-1950)
Panamérica Comercial (1932-19uu)
Panorama (1952-1955)
Revista Americana de Derecho...
  (1912-1921)
La Revista del Ateneo Hispano Americano
  (1914-19uu)
Serie sobre Bibliotecas y Bibliografía
  (1930-19uu)
Seguridad Industrial (1957-19uu)
Semblanzas Literarias (1951-1951)
Serie de Educaión (1936-1937)

WISCONSIN

Milwaukee

El Mutualista: Organo Mensual de la...
  (1947-1950)

Stevens Point

Cultura * (1925-19uu)

PLACE UNKNOWN

County Independent ((1921-192u)
La Fuerza Consciente * (19uu-19uu)
El Guadalhorce (1839-1840)
Patria: El Periódico de Martí... (1959-.)

Chronological Index

The entries are arranged according to beginning publication dates. When an initial date of publication was unknown, the date of a known volume/number or the ending publishing date was used to place the record within a more specific period. A "u" in the dates of publication reflects an unknown digit. Unknown digits in main heading categories reflecting single years, decades and centuries are found at the end of the corresponding category.

1808
1808-1810   El Misisipí

1809
1809-1811   El Mensagero Luisianés

1813
1813-1813   La Gaceta de Texas
1813-181u   El Mexicano (Na[t]chitoches)

1817
1817-1uuu   El Telégrafo de las Floridas

1824
1824-1826   El Habanero...

1825
1825-1uuu   El Telégrafo (New Orleans)

1826
1826-1831   El Redactor

1827
1827-1830   L'Abeille

1828
1828-1831   El Mensagero Semanal de
            Nueva York
1828-1831   Mercurio de Nueva York

1829
1829-1830   El Español
1829-1832   The Texas Gazette
1829-1uuu   Mexican Advocate

1834
1834-1uuu   El Misisipí

1835
1835-1uuu   El Crepúsculo

1836
1836-1836   El Correo Atlántico
1836-1859   Noticioso de Ambos Mundos
1836-18uu   La Estrella Mejicana (Louisiana)

1838
1838-18uu   Le Figaro (NouvellesOrleans)

1839
1839-1840   El Guadalhorce

1840
1840-1841   L'Avenir du Peuple
1840-1841   L'Omnibus

1841
1841-18uu   El Iris de Paz

1843

1843-18uu Avispa de Nueva Orleans

1844

1844-1845 The Ancon

1844-1845 La Verdad (Santa Fe)

1845

1845-1846 El Hablador

1845-18uu La Aurora (Boston)

1845-18uu El Payo de Nuevo México

1845-18uu La Verdad (New Orleans)

1845-1908 Scientific American. Export
edition

1845-19uu La Sombra de Padilla

1846

1846-1848 Californian

1846-1850 La Patria (Nueva Orleans)

1846-1uuu El Pero Grullo

1847

1847-1848 The California Star

1847-18uu Santa Fe Republican

1847-1uuu El Pobre Diablo

1847-1uuu Semanario de Santa Fe

1848

1848-1848 Revista de la Crónica:
Miscelánea...

1848-185u La Verdad (Nueva York)

1848-1863 La Bandera

1848-1867 La Crónica (New York)

1848-1uuu The Corpus Christi Star

1849

1849-1850 The New Mexican

1849-1uuu El Centinela (Brownsville)

1849-1uuu El Telégrafo (New Orleans)

1850

1850-1856 Sonora Herald

1850-18uu Centinela del Río Grande

1850-1uuu Gaceta (Santa Fe)

18uu-1uuu El Horizonte (Nueva York)

1851

1851-1851 La Unión (Nueva Orleans)

1851-1879 Los Angeles Star

1851-18uu The Rio Bravo

1851-1uuu El Pelayo

1852

1852-1854 El Cubano

1853

1853-1853 El Guao...

1853-1855 El Filibustero

1853-1uuu El Independiente
(Nueva-Orleans)

1853-. La Estrella de Panamá

1854

1854-185u Santa Fe Gazette

1854-1uuu El Mulato

185u-1uuu El Amigo del País

185u-1uuu La Crónica (San Francisco)

1855

1855-1859 El Clamor P´blico

1855-18uu El Bejareño

1855-1uuu El Cometa (Nueva York)

1855-1uuu El Eco de Cuba

1855-1uuu El Papagayo

1855-1uuu El Pueblo (New York)

185u-18uu Santa Fe Weekly Gazette

1856

1856-18uu El Eco del Pacífico

1856-18uu El Ranchero (San Antonio)

1870-1870 El Demócrata de Nueva York
1870-1870 New York Democrat
1870-1872 The Santa Fe Daily Post
1870-1876 La Enseñanza: Revista
           Americana...
18701-876 The Republican Review
1870-1878 New Mexico Advertiser
           (Las Vegas)
1870-1uuu Diario Cubano
1870-1uuu La Estrella de Cuba = Star of
           Cuba
1870-1uuu La Voz del Pueblo (New York)

1871

187-11872 Las Vegas Weekly Mail
1871-1875 The Borderer
1871-1875 El Mundo Nuevo
1871-1878 Anunciador de N. Méjico
1871-187u La República (Nueva York)
1871-1uuu La América: Periódico
           Quincenal...
1871-1uuu El Boletín Comercial
1871-1uuu New Mexico Democrat
1871-1uuu El Progreso (San Francisco)
1871-1uuu Revista Universal

1872

1872-1875 El Liberal (Rio Grande)
1872-1875 The New Mexico Union
1872-1886 Las Vegas Sunday Gazette
1872-1892 La Crónica (Los Angeles)
1872-18uu Las Vegas Weekly Gazette
1872-1uuu El Ranchero Semanario
187u-1875 La Revolución de Cuba

1873

1873-1875 The Acorn
1873-1880 La Independencia
1873-1885 The Mesilla News
1873-1893 Espejo (New York)
1873-18uu El Clarín Mejicano (Santa Fe)
1873-18uu La Federación
1873-1uuu El Educador Popular
1873-1uuu La Federación

1873-1uuu Imprenta del Río Grande
1873-1uuu La Raza Latina
1873-1uuu La Unión (New Orleans)
1873-1uuu Unión (San Francisco)
187u-18uu Las Vegas Gazette
18uu-1uuu La Voz del Nuevo Mundo
           (San Francisco)

1874

1874-1876 City News
1874-1877 El Ateneo: Repertorio
           Ilustrado...
1874-1879 La Llumanera de Nova York
1874-18uu El Ferrocarril
1874-1uuu Circular del Joyero
1874-1uuu Friend's Mexican
           Mission Gazette
1874-1uuu Guía Comercial
1874-1uuu Mail
1874-1uuu La Voz de Puerto Rico en
           U.S.A.
18uu-1uuu El Correo de Nueva York

1875

1875-1878 The Colorado Pioneer
1875-1879 El Tecolote (San Francisco)
1875-18uu The Democrat = El Demócrata
1875-18uu El Demócrata (Brownsville)
1875-1962 Revista Católica (Las Vegas)
1875-1uuu Huérfano Independent
1875-1uuu New Mexico Patriot
187u-18uu El Fronterizo (Las Cruces)
187u-1uuu El Comercio (Nueva York)
187u-1uuu El Sur-Americano

1876

1876-1877 El Explorador
1876-1878 New Mexico Cooperator
1876-1879 Revista Evangélica (Las Vegas)
1876-1880 The Albuquerque Review
1876-1890 El Comercio del Valle
1876-18uu La Libertad (Cayo Hueso)
1876-18uu La Voz de la Justicia

1881

1881-1882	El Mentor Ilustrado
1881-1886	Las Vegas Daily Gazette
1881-188u	Laredo Times
1881-188u	La Revista de Albuquerque
1881-19uu	El Times en Español
1881-1uuu	El Correo Universal
1881-1uuu	La República (San Francisco)
1881-1uuu	Rio Grande Republican
1881-1uuu	La Tribuna (Santa Fe)
1881-1uuu	Trinidad Weekly Times
1881-1uuu	The Two Republics

1882

1882-1882	El Demócrata (Los Angeles)
1882-1884	La Crónica del Río Colorado (San Hilario)
1882-18uu	Eco del Siglo
1882-1911	El Tiempo (Las Cruces)
1882-1uuu	El Anciano (Trinidad)
1882-1uuu	El Diputado
1882-1uuu	La Industria
1882-1uuu	El Joven (Yuma)
1882-1uuu	La Revista Ilustrada de Nueva York
1882-1uuu	Trinidad Weekly Advertiser = El Anunciador de Trinidad

1883

1883-1884	La Colonia Mexicana (Tucson)
1883-1884	El Gringo y Greaser
1883-1884	El Mercurio (Kansas City)
1883-1885	Santa Fe New Mexican Review
1883-18uu	Valencia County Vindicator
1883-1901	El Progreso (Phoenix)
1883-1uuu	El Eco de Sonora
1883-1uuu	El Espectador Mexicano
1883-1uuu	El Repertorio Médico
1883-1uuu	El Separatista

1884

1884-1884	La Aurora (Santa Fe)
1884-1884	La Fe en la Democracia
1884-1885	El Heraldo del Condado de Taos
1884-1885	La República (New York)
1884-1885	Socorro Star (Socorro)
1884-1889	El Heraldo (Taos)
1884-18uu	The Daily Chronicle
1884-18uu	El Mercurio (Phoenix)
1884-1uuu	El Cronista (San Francisco)
1884-1uuu	Mills' Mexico
1884-1uuu	Las Novedades
1884-1uuu	La Revista Mexicana
1884 1uuu	Unión (Phoenix)
1884-1uuu	La Voz del Hatuey
18uu-1uuu	The Chronicle (Las Vegas)

1885

1885-1885	El Eco Mexicano (Los Angeles)
1885-1887	La Correspondencia
1885-1887	The News (Albuquerque)
1885-1888	El Avisador Cubano
1885-1888	El Heraldo de Taos
1885-1888	El Mutualista
1885-1894	Azusa Valley News
1885-1908	El Boletín Popular
1885-1911	El Anunciador (New York)
1885-1uuu	La Colonia Mexicana (Laredo)
1885-1uuu	El Economista Americano
1885-1uuu	Escualdum Gazeta

1886

1886-1886	The Chronicle (Las Vegas)
18861-886	El Guía de Santa Fe
1886-1886	The Las Vegas Gazette
1886-1889	The El Paso Times
1886-1890	Mesilla Valley Democrat
1886-1892	El Metodista
1886-18uu	El Heraldo (San Antonio)
1886-18uu	La Opinión: Eco de la Colonia…
1886-1uuu	El Comercio Mexicano
1886-1uuu	El Iris
1886-1uuu	El Mundo (Brownsville)
1886-1uuu	El Mundo: Periódico Independiente…

1890-1891 La Gaceta de Mora
1890-1892 El Chinaco
1890-1892 El Cubano (Key West)
1890-1892 El Defensor del Pueblo
(La Mesilla)
1890-1895 La Crónica de Valencia
1890-189u La Cachiporrita
1890-189u The Mora Echo
1890-189u Verdad (Las Cruces)
1890-18uu El Independiente (Nueva York)
1890-1909 La América Científica,
Industrial, Agrícola y Ganadera
1890-1914 El Correo Mexicano
(San Antonio)
1890-1921 El Porvenir (Brownsville)
1890-1958 El Nuevo Mexicano (Santa Fe)
1890-1uuu Banner
1890-1uuu El Coadjutor
1890-1uuu La Estación
1890-1uuu La Ilustración Norteamericana
(New York)
1890-1uuu El Libre Pensador
1890-1uuu El Sable
1890-1uuu Spanish American Trade
Journal
18uu-19uu El Monitor Mexicano
(Los Angeles)

1891
1891-1891 El LatinoAmericano (El Paso)
1891-1892 Mosquito (Mora)
1891-1892 El Pensamiento
Contemporáneo
1891-1892 El Promotor Escolar
1891-1892 El Sol de Mayo
1891-1901 El Cronista Mexicano
1891-1902 El Despertar
1891-1913 Roswell Record
1891-1944 El Progreso (Trinidad)
1891-1uuu El Correo de Laredo
1891-1uuu El Cromo
1891-1uuu Ecuador
1891-1uuu El Hispano-Americano
(El Paso)

1891-1uuu El Hispano-Americano
(Socorro)
1891-1uuu Liberal (Las Cruces)
1891-1uuu La Patria (Denver)
1891-1uuu El Porvenir (Tampa)
1891-1uuu Sancho Panza (El Paso)
1891-1uuu The Sun (San Diego)

1892
1892-1893 Revista Latino-Americana
(Los Angeles)
1892-1895 La Revista MédicoQuirúrgica...
1892-1896 La Opinión Pública
(Albuquerque)
1892-1898 Las Dos Repúblicas
(Los Angeles)
1892-189u La Unión de Albuquerque
1892-189u Independent Democrat
1892-1900 El Bien Público (Rio Grande)
1892-190u Patria (New York)
1892-1919 El Combate (Albuquerque)
1892-1uuu El Americano (Nueva York)
1892-1uuu El Ciudadano
1892-1uuu El Eco de la Exposición
1892-1uuu El Fígaro (Laredo)
1892-1uuu La Juventud Laredense
1892-1uuu La Libertad (Tucson)
1892-1uuu El Mexicano Republicano
1892-1uuu New Mexico Potpourri
1892-1uuu El Postillón
1892-1uuu La Reforma
1892-1uuu La Unión (Tucson)
1892-1uuu El Voluntario
1892-1uuu El Zurriago
189u-1920 El Hispano-Americano
(Las Vegas)

1893
1893-1895 El Independiente (Nogales)
1893-1899 Cuba (Tampa)
1893-18uu El Radical
1893-1901 La Revista Dental Americana
1893-19uu La Reforma Social

1896-1uuu El Porvenir (New York)
189u-1uuu El Amigo del Pueblo (Raton)
189u-1uuu El Independiente (El Paso)
18uu-1897 El Correo Americano y Diario
           Exportación
18uu-1uuu El Eco Libra

1897

1897-1898 La Contienda: Radical Cubano
1897-1898 Cuba y América (New York)
1897-1898 La Unión (Hidalgo)
1897-1900 La Voz de Clifton
1897-1901 El Nuevo Mundo
           (Old Albuquerque)
1897-1902 El Demócrata Independiente
1897-18uu Cuba y Puerto Rico
1897-19uu La Fe Católica
1897-1uuu La Opinión: Periódico
           Político…
1897-1uuu El Comerciante y Agricultor
1897-1uuu Concarajícara
1897-1uuu El Correo de América
           (New York)
1897-1uuu El Eco de Hidalgo
1897-1uuu El Eco de Martí
1897-1uuu La Estrella (Maldonado)
1897-1uuu La Libertad (Tampa)
1897-1uuu La Nueva República
1897-1uuu El Oriente
1897-1uuu La Opinión: Periódico Político
18971uuu   Revista de Cayo Hueso
1897-1uuu Revista de Cuba Libre
1897-1uuu El Sport
1897-1uuu La Verdad (Roma)
1897-1uuu La Vigía
189u-1uuu El Monitor (El Paso)
189u-1uuu El Observador Mexicano

1898

1898-1898 El Independiente (New York)
1898-1898 El Monitor (Los Angeles)
1898-1899 Observador (Las Vegas)
1898-1900 La Gaceta (San Francisco
           and Los Angeles)

1898-1902 La Sombra de Lincoln
1898-1912 La Voz Pública (Santa Rosa)
1898-19uu Borinquen: "rgano de la
           Sección…
1898-19uu El Demócrata (Phoenix)
1898-19uu El Republicano (Socorro)
1898-1uuu El Correo de Cuba
1898-1uuu Cuba Libre
1898-1uuu Cuba Libre
1898-1uuu Las Dos Américas (El Paso)
1898-1uuu La Golondrina
1898-1uuu El Independent (New York)
1898-1uuu El Liberal (Floresville)
1898-1uuu El Mercurio (San Diego)
1898-1uuu El Nacional (New York)
1898-1uuu El Reconcentrado
1898-1uuu El Socialista
1898-1uuu Times
1898-1uuu La Unión (Raton)
1898-1uuu El Universal (New York)
1898-1uuu La Voz del Valle
1898-1uuu Verdad (Las Cruces)
189u-19uu Cuba (New York)
18uu-18uu El Combate (Socorro)
18uu-1uuu El Látigo

1899

1899-1901 El Centinela (Hidalgo)
1899-19uu La Alianza (Tucson)
1899-19uu La Estrella del Norte
1899-19uu La Federación
1899-19uu El Fénix
1899-19uu Las Noticias
1899-19uu The Sister Republic: a
           Commercial…
1899-1uuu El Cobrador
1899-1uuu El Mundo Americano
18991uuu   Las Noticias (El Paso)
1899-1uuu El Siglo Veinte
1899-1uuu Socorro Star (Nueva York)

189u

189u-18uu El Grito de la Verdad
189u-1uuu Amigo de los Hombres

1904-1950 El Defensor del Pueblo (Socorro)
1904-19uu El Anunciador (Trinidad)
1904-19uu El Defensor del Pueblo (Tucson)
1904-19uu La Humanidad
1904-19uu El Internacional (Tampa)
1904-19uu Punto Rojo (El Paso)
1904-1918 Regenerácion

1905

1905-1905 La Revista de Taos and The Taos Cresset
1905-1905 Weekly Hispano Americano
1905-1906 Revista Agrícola
1905-1907 Apachito
1905-1907 El Mosquito (Long Beach)
1905-1922 La Revista de Taos
1905-1929 Roy Record
1905-1931 Philipine Review
1905-19uu California Moderna
1905-19uu El Diario
1905-19uu El Eco del Valle
1905-19uu Empresa (Clayton)
1905-19uu El Farol (Capitan)
1905-19uu La Hacienda
1905-19uu El Hispano Americano (Roy)
1905-19uu Noticias (Albuquerque)
1905-19uu Propaganda Ilustrada
1905-19uu La Voz Trabajadora
19uu-1908 Las Nuevas de la Estancia
19uu-19uu El Clarín del Norte
1uuu-1905 El Americano (New Orleans)
1uuu-1uuu Alba Roja (San Francisco)

1906

1906-1906 The Filipino
1906-1907 Revista Comercial Americana
1906-1908 Justice (El Paso)
1906-1908 Revista PanAmericana
1906-19uu Las Dos Américas: Revista Ilustrada...
1906-1909 Rio Grande News = Las Nuevas de Río Grande

1906-1913 El Heraldo Mexicano
1906-191u La Opinión Pública (Albuquerque)
1906-19uu El Aldeano
1906-19uu El Amigo del Hogar (Redlands)
1906-19uu El Centenario
1906-19uu El Correo (Douglas)
1906-19uu El Cronista (Los Angeles)
1906-19uu El Defensor del Obrero
1906-19uu El Democrático
1906-19uu Estado
1906-19uu La Nueva Centuria
1906-19uu El Picudo
1906-19uu Plain Talk
1906-19uu La Semana = The Week
190u-19uu La Democracia
19uu-1906 Mensajero (Del Rio)

1907

1907-1908 El Abogado Cristiano Hispano-Americano
1907-1908 El Progreso (San Antonio)
1907-1909 El Noticioso (San Antonio)
1907-1909 Revista Mensual
1907-1915 Centinela (Key West)
1907-1916 Azucena
1907-1925 El Nuevo Estado
1907-1931 Revista Ilustrada (Santa Fe)
1907-19uu Alianza (Tucson)
1907-19uu El Correo Mexicano (Los Angeles)
1907-19uu La Crónica (Logan)
1907-19uu Las Repúblicas Americanas
1907-19uu Revista Ilustrada (El Paso)
1907-19uu Sancho Panza (Santa Fe)
1907-19uu La Voz de la Mujer
190u-19uu Revolución (Los Angeles)
190u-19uu Santa Rosa Sun

1908

1908-1909 Puerto Rico (El Paso)
1908-1910 Boletín de la Oficina Internacional de las...
1908-1913 El Adelante

1912

1912-1913; 1915-19uu El Diario de la
    Frontera
1912-1914 The Filipino Student
1912-1914 Brazo y Cerebro
1912-1914 Catholic Banner
1912-1916 The Filipino People
1912-1917 El Liberal (Brownsville)
1912-1921 Revista Americana de
    Derecho…
1912-1924 La Prensa (Los Angeles)
1912-1942 El Faro
1912-1950 Estancia NewsHerald
1912-19uu Alba Roja (Mcqueenley)
1912–19uu El Eco (Corpus Christi)
1912-19uu El Hijo de El Fronterizo
1912-19uu El Independiente (Tampa)
1912-19uu El Republicano (Española)
1912-19uu Tampa Ilustrado
1912-19uu La Trompeta (Corpus Cristi)
191u-19uu The Taos Recorder and
    El Bien Público
19uu-19uu La Cometa (Folsom)
19uu-19uu El Cosmopolita (Alice)

1913

1913-1915 El Popular
1913-1915 El Progreso (Laredo)
1913-1915 Pluma Roja
1913-1918 Líneas en Español
1913-1931 La Época (San Antonio)
1913-1956 El Mundo Azucarero
1913-1962 La Prensa (San Antonio)
1913-1963 La Prensa (New York)
1913-19uu Albuquerque
1913-19uu El Correo Mexicano
    (Bakersfield)
1913-19uu Elegancia
1913-19uu El Internacional (El Paso)
1913-19uu El LatinoAmericano (Alice)
1913-19uu La Luz (San Benito)
1913-19uu La República (San Antonio)
1913-19uu The Swástika

191319uu La Unión del Pueblo
1913-. El Palacio
191u-19uu El Correo del Bravo
19uu-19uu El HispanoAmericano (Belen)
19uu-19uu La Libertad (Kingsville)

1914

1914-1915 Chiltipiquín
1914-1915 El Fronterizo (Mission)
1914-1915 El Presente
1914-1915 La Raza (San Antonio)
1914-1916 El Faro del Río Grande
1914-1917 La Crónica (San Francisco)
1914-1917 El Hogar (Floresville)
1914-1917 El Observador (Clifton)
1914-1919 El Cosmopolita (Kansas City)
1914-1920 El Heraldo (Socorro)
1914-1921 El Norte Americano
1914-1930 Actualidades
1914-1937 El Hispano-Americano
    (San Diego)
1914-19uu Las Américas (San Francisco)
1914-19uu El Heraldo Dominical =
    Spanish Sunday Paper
1914-19uu México Libre (Los Angeles)
1914-19uu El Monitor (Albuquerque)
1914-19uu Rayos de Luz
1914-19uu La Revista del Ateneo
    Hispano-Americano
1914-19u Los Vecinos
1914-. Las Américas (New York)
191u-19uu El Eco Parroquial

1915

1915-1915 El Progreso (New York)
1915-1916 La Justicia (El Paso)
1915-1916 La Roza
1915-1917 El Rebelde (Los Angeles)
1915-1918 Las Dos Riberas
1915-1919 La Boz del Pueblo
1915-1919 La Mujer Moderna
1915-1920 El Día (Nogales)
1915-1920 El Precursor
1915-1920 Revista Mexicana

1918-19uu   El Campeón
1918-19uu   Cine Mundial
1918-19uu   El Correo de América (Tucson)
1918-19uu   Defensa Obrera
1918-19uu   Florida
1918-19uu   La Gaceta (San Diego)
1918-19uu   La Gaceta de los
            Estados Unidos
1918-19uu   El Independiente (Taos, N.M.)
1918-19uu   El Magazine de la Raza
1918-19uu   El Mexicano (Oxnard)
1918-1uuu   México Libre (Nogales)
1918-19uu   El Noticioso
1918-19uu   La Nueva Era (Alamo Gordo)
1918-19uu   Pan-American Labor Press
1918-19uu   La Prensa (Tampa)
1918-19uu   La República (El Paso)
1918-19uu   La Unión (Nogales)
1918-19uu   La Voz del Pueblo (Runge)
1918-.   El Estudiante LatinoAmericano
1918-.   The Hispanic American
            Historical Review
1918-.   Hispania
191u-1918   Mefistófeles
19uu-1918   Revista Universal: Magazine
            Hispano-Americano
19uu-19uu   Cultura Obrera
19uu-19uu   Ecos de la Catedral

1919

191u-19uu   El Atalaya Bautista: Semanario
            Evangélico… (El Paso)
191u-19uu   El Cosmopolita (Clayton)
191u-19uu   El Día (El Paso)
1919-1920   El Clarín Americano
1919-1920   La Epoka de Nu York
1919-1920   El Fronterizo (Nogales)
1919-1920   El Nacional (El Paso)
1919-1920   New Mexico State Republican
1919-1928   The Journal of the American
            Medical Association
1919-1941   Ingeniería Internacional
1919-1943   Herald (Rio Grande)
1919-192u   El Unionista

1919-19uu   El Boletín Popular
1919-19uu   El Panorama
1919-19uu   La Patria (El Paso)
1919-19uu   La Semana
1919-19uu   El Trabajo
1919-19uu   Electricidad en América
1919-19uu   Historia Ilustrado de Nuevo
            México
1919-19uu   La Opinión

191u

191u-1916   El Progreso (Mercedes, Tex.)
191u-19uu   El Badajo
191u-19uu   El Continental (New York)
191u-19uu   La Constitución
191u-19uu   El Español
191u-19uu   Huelga General
191u-19uu   El Piloto
191u-19uu   Poli-Óculos
191u-19uu   Revista de Laredo

1920

1920-1925   Revista Juvenil
1920-1927   Corriere del Popolo
1920-192u   Las Nuevas de la Liga
            Agrícola y Ganadera…
1920-192u   La Vanguardia
1920-193u   Solidaridad: Publicación de los
            Trabajadores…
1920-1963   La Nueva Democracia
1920-19uu   El Bien Público (Tampa)
1920-19uu   El Campo Internacional
1920-19uu   El Éxito (San Antonio)
1920-19uu   Revista de los EE. UU.
1920-19uu   La Voz de México (Tucson)
1920-19uu   La Voz de Tucson
19uu-19uu   El Coloradeño
19uu-19uu   El Herado Cristiano

1921

1921-1922   La Tribuna
1921-1926   Luz y Verdad (Laredo)
1921-1927   The Mora County Patriot
1921-192u   Mora County Independent

1925

1925-1926	El Palito
1925-1927	Mensajero Juvenil
1925-1929	Educación
1925-1929	México (Los Angeles)
1925-1930	México (Chicago)
1925-193u	El Amigo del Hogar (Indiana Harbor)
1925-19uu	El Azteca
1925-19uu	Cultura
1925-19uu	La Cucaracha
1925-19uu	El Farmacéutico
1925-19uu	Finanzas, Industria, Comercio
1925-19uu	La Guía del Comprador
1925-19uu	El Internacional (El Paso)
1925-19uu	El Internacional (Nogales)
1925-19uu	El Mensajero (Phoenix)
1925-19uu	México (New York)
1925-19uu	El Nacional
1925-19uu	El Trabajo: Periódico Semanario…
19uu-1925	El Atalaya (El Paso)

1926

1926-1927	The New Mexico Sun and El Palito
1926-1927	La Pantalla
1926-1928	Tribuna Hispana
1926-1929	El Fronterizo (Tucson)
1926-1930	Navidad
1926-1931	Guadalupe County Review
1926-1931	El Sol de San Bernardino
1926-1932	El País
1926-1936	The News (Vaughn)
1926-1958	Revista Carmelita
1926-19uu	La Alianza (Los Angeles)
1926-19uu	El Astur
1926-19uu	Boletín Mexicano
1926-19uu	El Continental (El Paso)
1926-19uu	Correo Mexicano: El Diario de la Raza
1926-19uu	Cultura Hispánica (New York)
1926-19uu	La Gaceta (Albuquerque)
1926-19uu	Jim Hogg County Enterprise

1926-19uu	El Pueblo (El Paso)
1926-19uu	The Santa Rosa News
1926-19uu	El Sol (El Paso)
1926-19uu	La Voz del Río Grande
1926-.	Arqueología Americana
1926-.	El Atalaya Bautista (El Paso)
1926-.	Cinelandia
1926-.	La Opinión
1926-.	Revista Médica Panamericana
192u-194u	El Paladín (Corpus Cristi)
19uu-19uu	El Sol de Chesapeake

1927

1927-1929	Centro de Valle
1927-1948	San Miguel County Star
1927-1949	Mora County Star
1927-1953	Cultura Proletaria
1927-1972	El Faro Dominical
1927-1972	Heraldos del Rey
1927-197u	El Arte Tipográfico (Philadelphia)
1927-19uu	El Eco del Valle
1927-19uu	El Fandango
1927-19uu	El Gallito
1927-19uu	El Heraldo (Chicago)
1927-19uu	El Heraldo Mexicano: Semanario…
1927-19uu	El Imparcial (San Diego)
1927-19uu	Los Angeles Record
1927-19uu	Evangelio Restaurado
1927-19uu	Gráfico (New York)
1927-19uu	El Luzero Sefardí
1927-19uu	El Machete Criollo
1927-19uu	El Mundial
1927-19uu	La Noticia Mundial
1927-19uu	Las Noticias (Del Rio)
1927-19uu	La Nueva Era (Kingsville)
192719uu	La Pantalla Mundial
1927-19uu	El Portavoz
1927-19uu	El Porvenir (San Diego)
1927-19uu	La Razón
19uu-1929	La Victoria

1932-19uu Pecos Valley Eagle
1932-19uu Revista Escolar Panamericana
19uu-1958 Alfa (Kingsville)
19uu-19uu El Tecolote (Houston)
19uu-19uu La Verdad (Anderson)

1933
1933-1934 El Monitor
1933-1939 El Independiente
           (Albuquerque)
1933-1939 Artes y Letras
1933-193u El Internacional (Tampa)
1933-1990 Revista Rotaria
1933-19uu La Defensa (Chicago)
1933-19uu Gráfico Internacional
1933-19uu El Internacional
1933-19uu La Nación Puertorriqueña
1933-19uu La Semana (Tucson, Ariz.)
1933-.   Hispanic Review
1933-.   Lucero Latino: Revista…
19uu-1933 El Independiente and the New
           Mexico…
19uu-19uu El Eco (Kingsville)

1934
1934-1934 Boletín de Sigma Delta Pi
1934-1935 Alma Boricua
1934-1935 Nuevo [sic] Era
1934-1937 Bibliografía Hispanoamericana
1934-19uu Ateneo: Revista Cultural
1934-19uu Boletín New History
1934-19uu Cascabeles
1934-19uu El Curioso
1934-19uu El Espectador
1934-19uu El Heraldo de Brownsville
1934-19uu The Topic
1934-19uu La Voz del Mundo
193419uu   Frente Hispano
193419uu   Justicia (Jersey City)
193419uu   Latinoamericano
1934-19uu Star County Democrat
1934-.   Hoja Volante
1934-.   Revista Hispánica Moderna

193u-1934 Lucha Obrera

1935
1935-1935 Cuban News
1935-1936 La Voz (San Diego)
1935-1937 Revista Hispánica Moderna:
           Sección Escolar
1935-194u La Opinión de Río Arriba
1935-19uu Cinema
1935-19uu Cuban
1935-19uu El Informador
1935-19uu Las Novedades (Kingsville)
1935-19uu People's News
1935-19uu El Porvenir (Mission)
1935-19uu La Prensa (Wagon Mound)
1935-19uu Rio Grande Herald
1935-19uu Simpatía
1935-19uu Spanish Echo
1935-19uu El Tiempo (Harlingen)
1935-19uu La Voz de la Parroquia
1935-19uu La Voz Latina (Nueva Orleans)
1935-19uu La Voz (San Antonio)
1935-.   El Puerto (Houston)
193u-.   La Gaceta de California

1936
1936-1936 The Taos Review
1936-1936 The Voice: Combined with
           La Voz Latina
1936-1936 La Voz Latina de Arizona
1936-1937 Boletín de El Internacional
1936-1937 Serie de Educación
1936-1939 Spanish Labor Bulletin
1936-1940 The Taos Review and the Taos
           Valley News
1936-1950 Adelanto Bienestar Cultura
1936-19uu Actualidad (El Paso)
1936-19uu Inquietudes …
1936-19uu La Libertad (Dallas)
1936-.   El Bautista Mexicano (Dallas)
19uu-19uu La Prensa (Tampa)

1937

1937-1938 El Imparcial (Phoenix)
1937-1939 Frente Popular
1937-1939 La Voz (Nueva York)
1937-1941 Verdad (Denver, Col.)
1937-1956 Revista Evangélica (El Paso)
1937-1958 El Tiempo (Raymondville)
1937-19uu Delta
1937-19uu El Internacional (Tampa)
1937-19uu Juventud (Tucson)
1937-19uu El Nuevo Mexicano
(Espanola, N.M.)
1937-19uu La Tinaja
1937-19uu Triunfo (Tampa)
1937-19uu Victoria
1937-. Revista Aérea Latino Americana

1938

1938-1938 El Sol de Colorado
1938-1942 Mensajeras del Maestro
1938-1944 El Libro Americano
1938-194u Cara al Sol
1938-194u The Horse Fly
1938-19uu Boletín de Información
1938-19uu Boletín del Comité de Defensa
1938-19uu Brooklyn Colonia Latina
1938-19uu El Eco (San Antonio)
1938-19uu Latin American News
1938-19uu El Latino
1938-19uu Mesilla News
1938-19uu The Mexican Voice
1938-19uu Orientación: Boletín de las
Comisiones...
1938-19uu Semanario Imparcial
1938-19uu Tópicos de Tolleson
1938-19uu Zigzag: Semanario Humorístico
193u-1943 El Antifacista
193u-19uu El Anunciador (New York)
193u-19uu Española Valley Developer

1939

1939-1940 Taoseño
1939-1940 Vía Libre
1939-1941 The Pasco
1939-1941 La Nueva Voz

1939-1942 La Libertad (San Diego)
1939-1948 The International News Guide
1939-1948 La Voz Latina (Eagle Pass)
1939-1966 El Independiente and the New
Mexico...
1939-1981 El Sol (Phoenix)
1939-19uu Ariel ...
1939-19uu El Informador
1939-19uu Social: Revista Semanal
1939-19uu La Voz Latina
1939-. España Libre
1939-. Revista Interamericana: Revista
Dedicada...
193u-19uu El Progresso (Corpus Cristi)
19uu-19uu La Verdad (Falfurrias)

193u

193u-1936 The Las Vegan
193u-19uu El Bautista Mexicano
193u-19uu The Voice: la Voz de la Raza

1940

1940-1942 Nuevas Llegadas desde
Checoslovaquia...
1940-1944 Las Américas (New York)
1940-1944 Sun (Mora)
1940-1950 The Pan American (New York)
1940-19uu La Aurora: Breve y sin
Presunción
1940-19uu Brújula
1940-19uu Norte
1940-19uu Noticias de la Oficina de
Información Obrera ..
1940-19uu La Prensa de Hoy
1940-19uu Libros
1940-19uu La Voz del Pueblo de Santa Fe
1940-19uu El Zumbón
1940-19uu West Tampa Leader
19uu-19uu La Riscossa

1941

1941-1943 Carta Informativa Americana
1941-1946 Boletín Católico Checoslovaco
1941-1948 The Taoseño and the
Taos Review

1941-1956	Sugar
1941-1964	América Clínica
1941-19uu	Boletín (Tampa)
1941-19uu	El Comercio (Tampa)
1941-19uu	La Defensa
1941-19uu	El Eco Antillano
1941-19uu	El Propagandista
1941-19uu	Ecos del Sanatorio
1941-19uu	Textiles Panamericanos
1941-19uu	Vocero de la Unión Internacional de Tabaqueros
1941-.	Voz de la 500
19uu-19uu	Adelante
19uu-.	El Demócrata (San Diego)

1942

1942-1942	Ingeniería Internacional. Edición de construcción
1942-1942	Ingeniería Internacional. Edición de Industria
1942-1952	Ibérica
1942-1954	Revista Trimestral para las Uniones de Jóvenes y Adultos
1942-1954	Revista Trimestral para los Intermedios
1942-1954	Revista Trimestral para Primarios
1942-1961	Ingeniería Internacional: Industria
1942-1978	New Orleans Port Record
1942-19uu	Chilean Gazette
1942-19uu	El Lucero (San Benito)
1942-19uu	Pana-mericana News
1942-19uu	La Verdad (Corpus Christi)
19uu-.	Boletín Checoslovaco

1943

1943-1944	Pueblos Hispanos
1943-1944	Tucson Cultural
1943-1945	Victory
1943-1947	Revista de Radiología y Fisioterapia
1943-1961	Notas de Kingsville
1943-19uu	América Unida

1943-19uu	El Misionero Bautista
194319uu	Noticiero Obrero Norteamericano
1943-19uu	Petróleo del Mundo
194319uu	Repúblicas Hispanas Unidas
1943-.	Boletín en Español
1943-.	Estadística
19uu-19uu	Nueva York al Día
19uu-19uu	Progreso Farmacéutico

1944

1944-1944	El Heraldo Ganadero de Texas
1944-19uu	El Demócrata (Austin)
1944-19uu	El Indicador Industrial
1944-19uu	Informaciones
1944-19uu	Juventud (Mesa)
1944-19uu	Manual Azucarero de Cuba = Cuba Sugar Manual
1944-19uu	Pan American (San Antonio)
19uu-19uu	The Valley Herald and El Heraldo del Valle
1944-19uu	La Patria (Socorro)
1944-.	The Americas (Washington)

1945

1945-1945	Carta Quincenal de la UNRRA
1945-1945	Informativo Quincenal de la UNRRA
1945-1989	El Heraldo de Santidad
1945-19uu	El Crisol
1945-19uu	Ilustración
1945-19uu	Mexico Journal
1945-19uu	Milicia
1945-19uu	Modern Dentistry
1945-19uu	PanAmerican News
1945-19uu	Semanario Hispano
1945-19uu	Unión: Revista Boliviana
1945-.	El Hospital (Cincinnati)
1945-.	Eastside Sun
1945-.	Mexican American Sun
194u-19uu	Ebenezer
19uu-194u	Aristo
19uu-19uu	El Boletín (Santa Fe)
19uu-19uu	The Clarion

1950-1uuu	Excélsior (Phoenix)
1950-19uu	Las Noticias (Del Rio, Tex.)
1950-19uu	Parnaso
1950-19uu	El Pan-Americano
1950-19uu	El Sol (San Bernardino)
1950-19uu	La Voz de Phoenix
1950-19uu	La Voz de Puerto Rico
1950-19uu	La Voz del Pueblo (Phoenix)
1950-.	Temas: Revista Ilustrada
1950-.	Visión: la Revista Latinoamericana
19uu-19uu	Ahora (Nueva York)
19uu-19uu	La Prensa = The Press

1951

1951-1951	Semblanzas Literarias
1951-1980	Noticiero
1951-19uu	Charlatán
1951-19uu	Pasatiempo
1951-19uu	Puerto Rico en Marcha
1951-19uu	Radiovisión
1951-19uu	La Verdad (Del Rio, Tex.)
1951-.	Hemispherica…
1951-.	Heraldo Evangélico
19uu-19uu	Prensa (Solomon, Ariz.)

1952

1952-1955	Panorama
19521955	Vida Hispana
1952-1956	Boletín de Música y Artes Visuales
1952-19uu	Cancionero Fílmico
1952-19uu	El Yunque
1952-.	Agricultura de las Américas
1952-.	Orientación (New York)

1953

1953-1960	Trabajos Manuales
1953-19uu	Cine Variedades
1953-19uu	Gráfico (Nueva York)
1953-19uu	Nosotros
195319uu	PIP
1953-.	Diario Las Américas
1953-.	Revista Ibérica

1954

1954-1954	El Puerto (Brownsville)
1954-1958	El Instructor
1954-1964	La Voz (Tucson, Ariz.)
1954-1974	Ibérica
1954-19uu	Alba de Nueva York
1954-19uu	Odontología Moderna
1954-19uu	Puerto Rico y Nueva York
1954-19uu	Vosotros
1954-.	El Puerto de Brownsville
1954-.	Bulletin: InterAmerican Tropical Tuna Commission…
195u.	El Correo de la Virgen
19uu-1954	Boletín del Agricultor

1955

1955-1958	Revista para Uniones de Jóvenes y Adultos
1955-1960	El Crepúsculo de la Libertad
1955-1972	Revista para Uniones de Intermedios
1955-1984	Revista para Uniones de Párvulos y…
1955-1984	Revista para Uniones de Primarios
1955-19uu	Aki Nueva York
1955-19uu	Mosaicos: SpanishEnglish…
1955-19uu	El Semanario
1955-19uu	The Southwest Miner = El Minero
1955-19uu	Vida Hispana de Nueva York
1955-.	Conquista Juvenil
195u-19uu	Lo Mejor del Catholic Digest
19uu-1963	El Ranchero (Los Angeles)

1956

1956-1958	El Sol (San Marcos)
1956-1958	La Voz de la Raza
1956-19uu	La Voz de Puerto Rico en USA
1956-19uu	América Continental
1956-19uu	La Educación
1956-19uu	Informaciones Económicas
1956-19uu	El Imparcial
1956-19uu	Latin Times

1960-.	Carteles de América
1960-.	Frente Revolucionario-Democrático (Cuba)
1960-.	Hoja Doctrinal
1960-.	Hoja Doctrinal: Frente…
1960-.	Prensa Libre
1960-.	Servicio Cubano de Información
1960-.	Trinchera

19uu

19uu-1932	Mora Conty News = Las Nuevas del Condado…
19uu-1934	El Reporter LatinoAmericano
19uu-1940	El Saber
19uu-1947	Belen news
19uu-1969	Nueva Senda
19uu-198u	Lecciones Ilustradas: Alumnos
19uu-198u	Lecciones Ilustradas. Edición para maestros
19uu-19uu	Acción (Fullerton)
19uu-19uu	América Comercial
19uu-19uu	American Junior Red Cross. Spanish edition.
19uu-19uu	La Atalaya (Brooklyn)
19uu-19uu	El Automóvil Americano
19uu-19uu	Boletín Latino Americano del CIO
19uu-19uu	Boletín Linotypico
19uu-19uu	La Buena Noticia
19uu-19uu	La Calavera
19uu-19uu	El Comercio (Los Angeles)
19uu-19uu	El Compañero
19uu19uu	El Defensor del Pueblo (Laredo)
19uu-19uu	El Demófilo
19uu-19uu	Despertad (Brooklyn)
19uu-19uu	Elaboraciones y Envases
19uu-19uu	La Fuerza Consciente
19uu-19uu	El Ideal Católico Mexicano
19uu-19uu	El Indicador Mercantil
19uu-19uu	La Luz Apostólica
19uu-19uu	El Machete
19uu-19uu	El Mensajero de Esperanza

19uu-19uu	Oye Boricua
19uu-19uu	El Padre Padilla
19uu-19uu	El Pueblo (Los Angeles)
19uu-19uu	El Reino de Dios
19uu-19uu	El Sembrador
19uu-19uu	El Taquígrafo Gregg
19uu-19uu	La Palabra
19uu-19uu	Radio y Artículos Eléctricos
19uu-19uu	Revista Teatral
19uu-19uu	Tribuna del Pueblo
19uu-19uu	Universal Commerce
19uu-19uu	Vésper
19uu-.	Ahora (El Paso)
19uu-.	El Amigo de los Niños
19uu-.	Compendio Médico
19uu-.	Conquistadores. Ed. de alumnos. (El Paso)
19uu-.	Conquistadores. Ed. de maestros. (Nashville)
19uu-.	Linoticias
19uu-.	The Lion en Español
19uu-.	Ybor City Sunday News

1uuu

1uuu-1925	El Sahuaro
1uuu-1uuu	El Angel del Hogar
1uuu-1uuu	La Chispa (Tucson)
1uuu-1uuu	El Comercio (San Francisco)
1uuu-1uuu	La Contienda
1uuu1uuu	La Defensa del Ideal Católico Mexicano
1uuu-1uuu	El Defensor (Tucson)
1uuu-1uuu	Fenicio
1uuu-1uuu	El Guía
1uuu-1uuu	Guía de Importadores
1uuu-1uuu	Heraldo Dominical
1uuu-1uuu	El Hogar (Chama)
1uuu-1uuu	El Jornalero
1uuu-1uuu	Juventud (Florence)
1uuu-1uuu	El Mosquito (Ybor City)
1uuu-1uuu	La Raza (Tampa)
1uuu-1uuu	La Revista Mercantil de Nueva Orleans

Subject Index

Bernal y Aguirre, 222
Beshoar, M., 266
Betances, Ramón Emeterio, 19
Betancourt, Francisco F., 245
Beteta y Co., 252
Bicknell, Hale, 195
biculturation, 93
Biestar, Federico, 236
Bigney, T. O., 202
bilingual education, 92
bilingual newspapers in Texas, 76
bilingualism in newspapers, 77
Billian Pub., 264
Biscailuz, M. V., 186
Blake, T. A., 259
Blasini, Juan J., 176
Board of Commissioners of the
  Port of New Orleans, 227
Boehmer, Jas. O., 175
Bolet Peraza, Nicanor, 70, 251, 266
El Boletín Comercial (New York), 74
Boletín de la Unión Panamericana, 74
*Boletín de Noticias y Precios
  Corrientes*, 74
Boletín Obrero, 63
*Boletín Oficial de la Liga Puertorriqueña
  e Hispana*, 108-109
Bolívar, Simón, 85
Bollinger, W. N., 212
Bond, Ira M., 219, 227
Bonillas, Ignacio, 260
Bonillas y Salazar, P., 233
Booth, D. S., 184
Booth, J. P., 219
Borda, Eduardo, 248
El Boricua Publishing Corp., 160
Borinquen, 20
Borjas, H., 232, 266
Borjas, Hilario, 144
Botell, Arnulfo, 71
Bottle, Pablo, 275
Brady and Shiels, 258
Brandao, E. A., 252
Branyas, Joseph, 218
Brawley News, 195
Brown, Lorin W., 199, 200
Bueno, Miguel, 193
Buenrostro, Luis, 213
Buerón, Alberto, 239
Bulletin (Bureau of the American

Republics), 74
Bureau of the American Republics, 74
Burgos, Julia de, 111
Burnett, W. C., 259
Burris, H. H., 262
Business Publishers International Corp.,
  153, 162, 207
Buya, Armando, 211

C
Caballería, John, 144
Caballero, Pedro, 70
Cabot, Edward C., 171
Cadilla, Carmen Alicia, 70
Caesar F. Marburgy Cía., 198
El Cafetal Journal Co., 161
Cahill, John F., 167
Cajal, Antonio, 268
Calcagno, P., 274
California Native American press, 87-96
The Californian, 77
Cámara Agrícola y de Ganadería, 157
Campe, Tiburcio, 187
Campillo, A. Juan, 257
Campos, J. C., 180
Campos, José E., 208
Campos, T., 170
Campurí, José, 58
Cancio Peña, Saviur, 267
Cano, Octavio, 164
The Canterbury Press, 185, 244
Cantón, Felipe G., 182
Capetillo, Alonso, 266
Capitán Printing Co., 161
Capítulo Neoyorquino de la Liga
  Internacional de Acción Boliviana, 268
Caracol, 106
Caralt, Estanislao, 249
Carbonell, E., 224
Carbonell, Eligio, 168
Carbonell, Néstor, 174
Carbonell Leonello, Néstor, 168
Cárdenas, Antonio, 240
Cárdenas, Isidra T., 24, 273
Cárdenas, J., 179
Cárdenas, Justo, 165, 170
Cárdenas, Servando, 147, 175, 272
Cardona, Francisco, 58
Carner, Ribalta, Ltd., 238
Caro, Brígido, 180, 186

Carrasco, Pedro, 240
Carreón, C.J., 218
Carreras, Ev. E., 181
Carreras, J.O., 264
Carrillo, Adolfo R., 21, 221
Carrilo, Manuel, 220
Carrión, Ramón, 233
Casa Bautista de Publicaciones, 145, 152,
   168, 190, 191, 197, 200, 201, 202, 213,
   217, 218, 230, 236, 242, 251, 252, 253,
   254, 264, 266
Casa de las Españas, Columbia University,
   156, 251
Casa Editorial Lozano, 43
Casa Visión, 271
Casad, T., 206
Casanova, Carlos, 188
Casasús, Horacio, 168
Cassard, Andrés, 188
Castañeda, Manuel, 272
Castelán, José, 163, 181
Castillo, José S., 172
Castillo Pub. Co., 147
Castro, J. C., 47, 172
Castro, José, 193
Castro, Ramón, 274
Catedral de San Fernando, 185
Catholic Church, 80
Catholic Digest International, 217
Catholic press, 80
Catholic Press Society, Diocese of
   Monterey-Fresno, 190
Catholic Pub. Co., 260
Cavazos, J.G., 182
Cavazos, M., 255
Cecilia Valdés (Villaverde, Cirilo), 12
Celis, E. F. de, 245-246
El Centinela Publishing Co., 162
Central American civil wars, 27-28
Centro Asturiano, 146, 152
Centro de Cultura (Santa Fe), 86
Centro de Estudios Históricos de
   Madrid, 249
Centro Obrero de Habla Española, 232
Centro Obrero (Tampa), 159, 191, 208
Cepeda, Agapito, 144, 193
Cerda, Gilberto A., 243, 244
Cerro, Angel del, 159
Céspedes y Arellano, José María, 247
Céspedes y Comp., 247

Cestero, Ferdinand, 70
Chacón, Diego A., 166
Chacón, Eusebio, 86
Chacón, Felipe M., 191, 205
Chacón, P., 190
Chacón & Perea, 155
Chacón, Urbano, 153, 166, 187, 190
Chacón y Salazar, 187
Chalk, O. Roy, 60
Chalmers Pub. Co., 164
Chamizo, Carlos G., 147
Chandler, Hannibal H., 248
Chapa, Fernando A., 101-102
Chaparro, Miguel, 230
Charles B. Richardson y Cía., 158, 168
Chase & Harwood, 219
Chaves, I.L., 153
Chicano Movement, 95
Chicano Movement publications, 105-106
Chicote (pseud.), 45
Chilean Embassy, 163
El Chinaco, 21
Chocano, José Santos, 70
Christian Science Pub. Society, 198
Christian Triumph Company, 218
chronicle. *See crónica*
Chronicle Pub. Co., 164
Cía. Publicista de El Boletín Popular, 159
Cía. Publicista de El Imparcial, 204
Cía. Publicista de Las Dos Repúblicas, 181
cigar manufacturing industry, 61
cigar workers, 61-62, 62-63
Cigarmakers International Union of
   America, 208
Cigarmakers' Local 500, 273
Cintrón, José, 176
CIO Committee on Latin American
   Affairs, 159
Circular del Joyero, 74
Círculo de Obreros Católicos de
   San José, 27, 149
Ciriza, M. J., 198
El Clamor Público, 77, 88-89, 90, 91, 93, 99
Claretian Fathers, 188
Clemente Zenea, Juan, 13
Club Azteca, 154
Club Borinquen, 20
Club Cubano Interamericano, 159
Club Discípulos de Martí, 190
Club Latina Americana de Arizona, 275

About the Authors

Nicolás Kanellos is an award-winning author of numerous reference and historical works on Hispanic culture in the United States. His books include *The Hispanic-American Almanac, Hispanic Firsts, A History of Hispanic Theater in the United States,* and *Thirty Million Strong: Reclaiming Our Hispanic Legacy.* Dr. Kanellos, who received his Ph.D. from the University of Texas, is Brown Foundation Professor of Hispanic Literature in the Department of Modern and Classical Languages at the University of Houston. He is also the Director of the Recovering the U. S. Hispanic Literary Heritage Program. In 1988 President Ronald Reagan honored Dr. Kanellos with the White House Hispanic Heritage Award for Literature; and in 1994, President Bill Clinton appointed him to the National Council on the Humanities.

Helvetia Martell, a respected indexer and bibliographer, was formerly Periodical Project Research Coordinator for Recovering the U. S. Hispanic Literary Heritage. She is now with the Inter-American Defense College Library in Washington, D. C.

The authors thankfully acknowledge the assistance of many people in undertaking this massive project. Ana Carranza, Liz Hernández, Jo Ann Pospisil, John Michael Rivera, Cristina Rivera-Garza, Ana Pérez, Eddie Selden, and Juan Sánchez made significant contributions as research assistants. This book also benefited from the aid of Elsie Herdman-Dodge, former coordinator of Recovering the U. S. Hispanic Literary Heritage; Alejandra Balestra, the current coordinator; Debbie Long, Recovery Office Manager; Linda Thompson, Dean of Bibliographic Services at the University of Houston's M. D. Anderson Library; and from data-entry work by Lormeides Polén and Zandra Treviño. Keitha Ramsey, formerly librarian at the University of Houston, merits special mention for her help—among the innumerable librarians, at institutions across the country, who graciously lent a hand.

About
Recovering the U. S. Hispanic Literary Heritage

Recovering the U. S. Hispanic Literary Heritage is a nationwide scholarly program to locate, compile, preserve, and disseminate literary and historical contributions made by U. S. Hispanics from the colonial era through 1960 in what today comprises the fifty states of the Union. The project's scope includes novels, poetry, short fiction, literary prose, folklore, speeches, and historical documents by U. S.-born Hispanics as well as immigrants and exiles of Cuban, Puerto Rican, Mexican, Spanish, and South American descent. Its board of editorial advisors includes twenty-five internationally renowned scholars from across the United States, Puerto Rico, and Mexico and its work includes not only print but Internet and CD-ROM media, scholarly conferences, and curriculum enrichment. Through the project, these recovered works will become accessible to scholars, students, and the world at large, broadening and enriching our understanding of U. S. history and literature.